Supplementary Despatches and Memoranda of Field Marshal Arthur, Duke of Wellington, K.G.

Arthur Wellesley Wellington

SUPPLEMENTARY

DESPATCHES AND MEMORANDA

OF

FIELD MARSHAL

ARTHUR DUKE OF WELLINGTON, K.G.

Wellesley 1st.

INDIA.

1797—1805.

EDITED BY HIS SON,

THE DUKE OF WELLINGTON.

VOLUME THE THIRD.

[Dec. 14, 1801—Feb. 14, 1803.]

LONDON:

JOHN MURRAY, ALBEMARLE STREET.

MDCCCLIX.

SUPPLEMENTARY DESPATCHES.

To Lieutenant-Colonel Close. [1004.]

MY DEAR COLONEL, Seringapatam, 14th Dec., 1801.

A letter which Piele received from you this morning has reminded me that I have not written to you since you went away. I have, however, been on a little tour to the Nundydroog district, which I should have made longer, only that I was obliged to return here to make the preparations for our expedition into Bullum. In consequence of the termination of hostilities to the southward, the Commander-in-Chief has ordered to this country the 77th regiment, two strong battalions of sepoys, and the corps of pioneers. This force, with a strong battalion or a battalion and a half from the garrison, with ten pieces of cannon and four small mortars, are destined for this service, and I hope that we shall march from hence in the beginning of the next month.

Besides this force I had given orders to collect a small detachment in Canara in order to co-operate on that side ; but the 75th regiment, which was to have been the foundation of it, has been ordered to Bombay, and the battalion of sepoys which was to have formed part must go to Goa. Our footing there has been on the decline for some time past. In the month of June last I made arrangements for reinforcing Sir William Clarke, and at last orders have been received from the Governor-General to hold in readiness a battalion for this service, which General Stuart requires shall be 1200 strong, and which will therefore take two Bombay battalions to complete it. So that by the whole of this arrangement I get in a regiment and two battalions at one door, and I send out the same number at the other.

As the service in Bullum will probably be brought to a conclusion by a brisk attack upon Arrekeery, I don't much regret the want of the force in Canara for that part of the business. But Kistnapah Naig has lately shown some inclination to give himself up to Mr. Ravenshaw, which I have requested the latter to encourage as much as possible, and the good effects of which might be in some degree accelerated by his perceiving that a large force was collected on all sides of him. I shall bring down the cavalry from Santa Bednore towards the army, which will move from hence in order to make as much noise as possible.

You will probably have heard from Webbe that he is appointed Resident here. This is a good arrangement for the public as well as for Webbe. It gives him the facility to remain in this country with credit to himself until the late orders can be reconsidered. I acknowledge that I did not like to see him in the situation of private secretary.

By this time I conclude that you have commenced the duties of your new situation.* I hope that you like it, and that the climate agrees with your health.

Allow me to recommend to your good offices my friends upon the frontier, the Bhow's family and young Goklah. They are all *my* friends, although they are setting to fighting as fast as possible. I shall keep up a civil communication with all of them, and have preserved my influence over them so far as to prevent their plundering the country of the Company or of the Rajah.

I also wish to recommend to you the Nabob of Savanore. He is a gentleman by birth as well as in his manners and appearance, and is sadly reduced. Old Goklah plundered him about a year previous to his death, and lately young Goklah has followed the example of his father, and has even gone farther, for he has driven him out of Savanore, and the poor man has lately written to me for protection at Polliam, a small village in Soonda, near Budnaghur. I mention these people to you only in case you should find it practicable to be of use to them. It is not improbable that there may be a jealousy at Poonah of our interfering at all in their favour; and if that be the case, it is better that nothing should be said about them.

Piele will inform you how matters are going on in this country. Everything appeared to prosper on my road to the Nundydroog district, and through it: I saw and admired your favourite places, the two Balapores, which are flourishing indeed. I have written to Bombay for a large cargo of potatoes, which I propose to present to Purneah for seed for

* Political Resident at Poonah.

that district. We only want plenty of that to make potatoes as flourishing in Mysore as they are in Ireland.

Believe me, &c.,

ARTHUR WELLESLEY.

To Lieutenant-Colonel Spry.   [1005.]

SIR,   Seringapatam, 14th Dec., 1801.

The Commander-in-Chief has informed me that the 77th regiment, under your command, are on their march from Trichinopoly to the Mysore country, by the Gudjelhatty pass. I was much concerned to learn at the same time that this corps suffers much from the series of active and fatiguing services on which it has been employed since the commencement of the year 1799. I have still hopes, however, that the expectations of the Commander-in-Chief in sending the 77th regiment to the Mysore country will be fulfilled, and that I shall have the advantage of the assistance of part of them in the proposed service in the Bullum country. At all events I have every disposition to place that part of the corps which has suffered most from its fatigues in quarters in which it can refresh, and I shall hope for your assistance in the field in the command of that part of the corps which you may think most capable of service, with such other Europeans as I may be able to add to it.

As it will be necessary that I should make the arrangements, without loss of time, for taking part of the regiment de Meuron to the field, and as that part will be great in proportion to the number of the 77th which you will propose to put in garrison, I shall be glad to hear from you upon this subject as soon as possible; and I shall be obliged to you to let me know what number you think can take the field.

I send a duplicate of this letter by a hircarrah to the Gudjelhatty pass. He will be furnished with orders to the aumildars, &c. &c., of the country to furnish the regiment under your command with all the necessary supplies on their march through the territories of the Rajah of Mysore to this place. A tappall also will be posted on the road from hence to the Gudjelhatty pass ; and I beg to receive from you a statement of all that you may want.

I have, &c.,

ARTHUR WELLESLEY.

Since writing the above it has occurred to me that the 77th regiment may be with two battalions of Native infantry also on the march from Trichinopoly, and that you may not be the commanding officer of the detachment. If that should be the case, I request you to be so kind as to communicate the latter part of this letter to the officer who may command the detachment.

[1006.]   *To the Deputy-Adjutant-General.*

SIR,   Seringapatam, 14th Dec., 1801.

I have to inform you that Colonel John Conrad Sartorius, of the Bombay Engineers, died at Cannanore on the 10th instant.

I have, &c.,

ARTHUR WELLESLEY.

[1007.]   *To Colonel Stevenson.*

MY DEAR COLONEL,   Seringapatam, 15th Dec., 1801.

I have received your letter of the 11th instant. I highly approve of your arrangements for occupying the stations which will become vacant when you will send away the Travancore troops, and will discharge the sebundies and militia, measures which, however anxious I may be to enter into the views of the Court of Directors to curtail the military expenses, I should be very desirous to avoid till the new government has had more time to settle. However, upon this point the government will alone be responsible. All I can say is, that I see on all sides fresh want of troops; and it appears, therefore, to be very desirable that we should not part with any, of however inferior a description, until matters become more settled.

I conclude that you will give orders for the movements which will be necessary for the relief of the battalions in Wynaad.

I shall be glad to hear further from you upon the subject of your proposed arsenal at Cannanore.

The appointment of Major Gray to be Brigade-Major will be done away with of course, as the detachment will no longer take the field. I had, however, particular orders from the Commander-in-Chief not to allow of any extraordinary staff whatever upon the proposed service. If this appointment has not been done away already, it ought as soon as possible.

I have written to the Commander-in-Chief respecting the appointment of Lieutenant-Colonel Bland. Medical appointments and removals in some degree come under Bombay by the orders of the government of Madras under which we act. I will, however, turn over the whole subject in my mind, and will communicate to you my thoughts upon it.

I sent yesterday a basket of cabbage plants and a basket of celery plants to Mrs. Stevenson, and one of each to Mrs. Lewis. The rains have been so heavy that those are the first I have been able to rear. Remember me kindly to the two ladies and all your family.

> Believe me, &c.,
>
> ARTHUR WELLESLEY.

To Major Robertson.   [1008.]

SIR,   Seringapatam, 16th Dec., 1801.

I have the honour to inform you that I expect to take the field shortly, and I request that you will make the following arrangements for the supply of the troops, and for their equipment.

You will be so kind as to prepare to victual as paymaster a body of Europeans amounting to 600 men, exclusive of the 19th dragoons at present in the field. As salt provision and biscuit for these Europeans may be essentially necessary on the service on which they will be employed, you will prepare a quantity of each of those articles to last that number of men ten days. It may likewise be very convenient, and even necessary, to be able to move their arrack upon bullocks, or men's heads; you will accordingly prepare small kegs of the usual size to carry arrack for that number of men for ten days. You will also prepare to send to the field rice for 3500 Natives for five days at full allowance.   This rice is to be beaten from the best of the paddy captured at Seringapatam.   You will be so kind as to make the necessary arrangements for hiring 1000 carriage bullocks for the service upon this occasion.

I expect that the troops will arrive here at the end of this month, and I am desirous of marching from hence as early in the next month as possible.

I have, &c.,

ARTHUR WELLESLEY.

[1009.]   *To Lieut.-General Stuart.*

SIR,   Seringapatam, 16th Dec., 1801.

I have the honour to enclose a memorandum which contains all the details of the information which I have collected on the subject upon which you wrote to me on the 6th instant.

I cannot find out that there is any timber ready cut in the jungles near Cancancotta.   There is another jungle at a greater distance, where there are some withered trees which would be dry timber and fit for immediate use, if cut.

In case you should wish to adopt the proposed arrangement immediately, there is now in Seringapatam a quantity of seasoned captured timber, which probably would not be worked up before the period when the timber for which contracts might now be made would be fit for use.   At all events, this timber might be made into timber-carriages.

I have, &c.,

ARTHUR WELLESLEY.

MEMORANDUM ON GUN CARRIAGES.

16th Dec., 1801.

The first point upon which information is required is whether timber for the construction of gun carriages can be procured in the neighbourhood of Seringapatam, and from what parts of the country it is brought.

Timber can be got at Seringapatam in any quantities; it is now sold in the bazaar at the rate of $1\frac{1}{2}$ sultauny fanam per maund of 30 pounds, and 1 maund $16\frac{3}{4}$ seers weight of dry timber measures about 1 foot cube.   One foot cube of half dry timber will weigh about 1 maund and 48¾ seers, and 1 foot cube of green timber will weigh 2¼ maunds.

A beam of 30 feet in length, by 1 square, will weigh, if green, 77 maunds 20 seers, and costs 8,7,20; if half dry, 58 maunds 30 seers; if dry, 40 maunds; and as they all sell by weight, the green timber will cost most money.

This timber is cut in the woods on the borders of Wynaad, in the neighbourhood of Cancancotta.   These woods are about 60 miles distant from Seringapatam.   The timber is cut either by the people of the neighbouring villages, or by persons sent out on purpose from Seringapatam, and it is brought in on hired country carts.   It does not appear that those who cut the timber pay any duty or rent to the Sircar for permission to cut it; the natural price of the timber at Seringapatam is consequently made up of the expense of felling it, and that of bringing it to Seringapatam on carts.

Of these the former is very small indeed, as will appear by a statement of the latter.   A bandy, with two buffaloes, will draw in from the jungles to Seringapatam a beam weighing 30 maunds, which will sell in the bazaar for 3 star pagodas 1½ sultauny fanam.   The bandy is generally 24 days on the road, and its hire cannot be estimated at less than 2½ star pagodas. The remaining half pagoda, 1½ sultauny fanam, may then be deemed to be that part of the price of the timber which pays the expense of felling, and gives a profit to the timber merchant. Accordingly it appears by the best accounts which have been procured that a beam such as has been above described may be cut and pared at the jungle for less than a rupee, and that the remainder of the half pagoda, 1½ sultauny fanam, or about 3 sultauny fanams, are the profit of the merchant.   In proportion as beams increase in size, additional yokes of buffaloes are required to draw them in; and those which, on account of their size, cannot be weighed, are sold according to the number of yokes which have been employed in that manner, calculating each yoke at 3 star pagodas 1½ sultauny fanam, and to draw 30 maunds of timber.

It does not appear that it would be possible to adopt any mode of avoiding the expense of felling the timber.   If persons already in the Company's pay are to be employed upon this work, that for which they are entertained must be at a stand, or others must be hired to perform it; and, in all probability, such persons would not cut the timber so quickly or so well as those whose particular business it is. The same observations apply to the employment of persons upon the work who are in the service of the Rajah, only with this difference, that if they should be taken from the Rajah's service to be employed upon the Company's work, they must be paid by the Company.

In regard to the second article of expense which makes the price of the timber, the carriage from the jungles to Seringapatam, there is no doubt whatever but that it may be much lessened, if not entirely avoided, by the employment upon this work of the Company's draught cattle. These draught cattle are kept at all events, and to work them in this manner could do them no harm, and would cost nothing. The expense of this mode of bringing in the timber would be only the construction and wear and tear of the timber carriages.

The state of the prices at Seringapatam of the different kinds of timber throws great light upon this subject, and shows the present state of the timber trade. It appears that whatever may be the kind of timber which is brought to be sold, it is sold by weight: consequently that the best timber, the driest, that which is most fit for use, as it will weigh the least, is the cheapest.

This fact proves two others which are very material in the consideration of this subject. First, it proves that there is a total want of capital among those who cut down the timber, and who manage the trade, and that they cannot afford to allow it to remain on the ground where it is felled till it seasons; secondly, it proves that the greater part of the price of the timber is created by the expense of transporting it from the jungles to Seringapatam. Green timber weighs nearly double what dry does, and requires double the number of cattle, and of course double the expense, to draw it in. Although there is no purchaser of timber, even among the Natives, who does not know the advantage of having a dry beam rather than a green one, yet they are obliged to buy the green or to get none; and as they buy it by weight, they pay for it the full expense which its greater weight occasions in bringing it in.

If a timber merchant procure in the jungles a dry beam, by having found and cut down a newly withered tree, he brings it in at half the expense that he would bring in a green beam, as it only weighs half what the latter does, and consequently he can afford to sell it at half the price. I have gone thus at length into the consideration of this part of the subject, as it will have much influence in deciding what will follow hereafter.

The next point of inquiry is, whether iron and steel of a good quality can be procured at or in the neighbourhood of Seringapatam. There is now in the stores of Seringapatam a quantity of iron which could not be used up in less than three years, if the proposed manufactory of gun carriages should be established on the most extensive scale. Besides this iron, that article and steel of an excellent quality can be procured at no less than thirteen different places, from 5 to 60 miles distant from Seringapatam, in any quantities; the best kind of common iron at 6 canterai or sultauny fanams per maund; bar iron, 1 star pagoda per maund; and steel, 1 star pagoda 15 fanams per maund. These articles, if brought in by the Company's cattle, would of course be cheaper.

There is, in the fort of Seringapatam, a large enclosure, where the Mysore palace was formerly situated, which would answer well for a timber store and for a work yard, and the necessary sheds might be erected at small expense with the old timber which was taken from the palace. Until all the grain is disposed of, there are no buildings which could be appropriated immediately to these purposes. When the grain is sold, as the Company will never want in Seringapatam such a store of grain as would require all the granaries, some of those buildings may be used as timber storehouses, and they are contiguous to the yard above proposed to be made a work yard.

So many artificers of different kinds have been sent from Seringapatam to the Ceded Districts, the coasts of Malabar and Canara, &c. &c., and there has been so little employment for them at Seringapatam in proportion to their numbers, that there are at present but few at that place not attached to some of the corps or departments. If, however, the proposed arrangement should take place, there will be no difficulty in collecting at Seringapatam any number of artificers that can be required.

Upon the whole I conclude that no arrangement can promise more fairly to succeed than that now under consideration.

The Company's draught cattle being stationed in the Mysore country might be used to transport the carriages when constructed to the different parts where they might be wanted, and no additional expense would be incurred on this account any more than on the account of bringing in the materials for their construction.

Having thus answered the queries put, and detailed the information which I have been able to collect upon each, I proceed to the consideration of the subject in another point of view, and I shall take the liberty of stating my opinion regarding the mode of carrying the arrangement into execution.

It is obvious from what I have above detailed that the great expense of procuring the principal material which is used in the construction of carriages might be almost entirely avoided by the use of the Company's draught cattle in bringing it into Seringapatam. These might be made use of on this service without disadvantage, or even inconvenience.

The question is, whether the Company can take advantage of this establishment as proposed, and at the same time procure their carriages, as they do now, through the commissary of supply. This officer now furnishes carriages made of materials also furnished by him upon indents and estimates, the latter of which are made out by other persons. These estimates, and the bills founded upon them, are made out according to the bazaar price of the materials which are used in the construction of the articles estimated for, and it is obvious that in this material (timber) the Company must pay the expense of its carriage from the jungle to Seringapatam, which I have above shown is the greatest part of the expense, and which they otherwise would avoid.

There is no possibility of taking advantage of the establishment of cattle under that system. The cattle cannot be lent to the commissary of supply; nor can the expense of the timber required in the construction of a carriage be estimated upon the data of its expense at the jungle, which, in fact, with this establishment of cattle, is what alone it ought to cost the Company; nor can the Company become timber merchants to their own commissary of supply, which would be the case if the Company were to cut the trees and were to carry them into Seringapatam and deliver them to that officer at certain rates, which he should again charge for them when used in the construction of carriages. The result then is, that if the establishment of cattle is to be used in this manner, the existing regulations regarding the commissary of supply must be departed from.

The next consideration is, whether an agency for the construction of these carriages would answer.

Agencies have been tried in many parts of India, and have not answered. In this business, however, many of the objections against the employment of the commissary of supply, who is in fact no more than an agent, are equally forcible against the employment of an agent, and there are many other objections to the employment of a person of that description which are peculiar to his character.

In my opinion the mode of carrying this plan into execution, and which would enable government to form an accurate notion of its expense, would be,

1st. To order that a contract should be entered into with some native at Seringapatam to furnish certain quantities of timber felled in the jungles in the neighbourhood of Cancancotta. This timber to be paid for according to its dimensions, and to be received by the guard stationed at Cancancotta as it is cut,

2nd. That this timber should be drawn into Seringapatam by the Company's bullocks on timber carriages to be constructed, and there lodged in store, under charge of the commissary of stores, in the same manner as any other article furnished by contract.

3rd. That when received it should be surveyed, measured, and marked with the year and date of its being surveyed; then registered, and reported to the Military Board as every other article of store.

4th. That the gun carriages should be constructed in the arsenal under the inspection of the commissary of stores.

5th. That an addition of artificers should be made to his establishment in proportion to the number of carriages which it is supposed would be required from him in every month, and that according to the number of artificers allowed to him he should be required to furnish carriages.

ARTHUR WELLESLEY.

[1010.]   *To Sir William Clarke.*

MY DEAR SIR,   Seringapatam, 19th Dec., 1801.

In consequence of orders which I have received from government to be prepared to reinforce and assist you as much as possible, and of a letter from the Commander-in-Chief, by which I learn that intelligence has reached Madras of the arrival at Colombo of a Portuguese frigate having on board 300 European soldiers for Goa, I have ordered the 1st battalion 3rd Bombay regiment from Cundapoor to Seedasheeghur without delay. I herewith enclose an order to the commanding officer of that corps to consider himself under your command; and that, as well as the grenadier battalion, is at your disposal. You must make your own arrangements with Captain Stewart for bringing your troops up to Goa from Seedasheeghur.

I shall be ready to march to your assistance in high style and force as soon as the troops arrive from the southern division of the army, which will be, I hope, by the end of this month. I communicated to General Stuart my letter to you of the 11th instant, and he approves of it highly.

The 75th are ordered to Bombay by the Governor-General, a disposition which I cannot alter, otherwise they should form part of the Governor of Goa's camp upon his island.

Believe me, &c.,

ARTHUR WELLESLEY.

[1011.]   *To Josiah Webbe, Esq.*

MY DEAR WEBBE,   Seringapatam, 19th Dec., 1801.

I sincerely congratulate you upon your appointment to be Resident in Mysore, and I rejoice much that the manner in which it has been offered to you has given you satisfaction. I am convinced that Lord Wellesley is very sensible of the services which you have rendered to his government, and that he has done, and will still do, everything in his power to occasion the recal of the offensive orders regarding you; but my last letter will have shown you that I doubt his success, at least before he returns to Europe. Your appointment to be Resident in

Mysore, however, enables you to stay in the country without doing yourself an injury, till you see the event of Lord Wellesley's letters consequent on the last letters from Europe.

I am much obliged to you for your letter of the 11th. I conclude that General Stuart will have communicated to you all the letters which I have written to him lately, and the papers which I have sent him regarding Goa. Sir William Clarke will have at Seedasheeghur two battalions of Native infantry, which together will amount to above 1200 men. Till the troops arrive from the southern division I have nothing else that I can send him. When they arrive I shall march immediately to the Bullum country, equipped in such a manner as that I shall be prepared either to go to the assistance of Sir William Clarke, or to take up my old ground in the Mahratta territory, should the intelligence which you have given turn out to be such as to render that measure necessary. If that measure should be necessary, it will not be difficult to receive the reinforcements which I shall require from the Ceded Districts. In the mean time I have got the brinjarries and everything in hand as heretofore, and such a foundation for supplies laid, that I believe I shall be better off than I was before.

I have written to the General this day to tell him that, notwithstanding the call for troops for Goa, I had not thought it proper to alter the disposition of the 75th, which he had arranged for Bombay. If he should think proper, however, to order this regiment to Goa, his orders will arrive before it will be collected at Mangalore preparatory to its embarkation.

Believe me, &c.,

ARTHUR WELLESLEY.

To Captain Mackay. [1012.]

SIR, Seringapatam, 21st Dec., 1801.

I have received your letter of the 20th instant.

I believe you are aware that the regular mode of reference to the Military Auditor-General is through the Paymaster; but as I conceive that you think my opinion will be of service to you, I proceed to give it. The elephants and cattle under your charge are generally stationed at some place at a distance from any large town or military garrison or cantonment, in order that they may procure forage for nothing without inconvenience or prejudice to the inhabitants; and it is necessary that they should be moved from one place to another, as no one or even ten districts could furnish the forage for them.

I do not conceive that you would do your duty if you were not to be constantly with the cattle; and as they are at such a distance from this and every other military station, I do not conceive that you can do it by remaining in this or any other garrison. It is also absolutely necessary that when the cattle move, you should move with them.

Under these circumstances I should imagine that the Military Auditor-General will be of opinion that you ought to be allowed tents (for without them no man can remain long in the field in this country), and lascars, and carriage for the poles, and the batta which is given to officers to defray the expenses incident to their line of service requiring that they should be constantly moving.

In regard to the artificers, I have already given my opinion upon them. It is absolutely necessary that the cattle should graze during a great part of the year near the Western Ghauts; and if they are not in some degree covered (and if you have not the assistance of some artificers, I don't conceive in what manner they are to be covered) they will suffer considerably.

I have, &c.,

ARTHUR WELLESLEY.

[1013.]   *To Major Macaulay.*

MY DEAR MACAULAY,   Seringapatam, 22nd Dec., 1801.

I am ashamed of having been so long without writing to you, but I have no excuse excepting forgetfulness. Since I wrote to you last, and received your last letter, I have been over to the Nundydroog district to inspect the corps which had been raised there by Cuppage, and to see that part of the country, into which I had never before had an opportunity of going. I found the corps a very fine one, and in good order, and the country, which was always a favourite part of Mysore with Close, in the most flourishing state. Bangalore also is getting on fast. Purneah has begun to rebuild the fort, and, in my opinion, he will make it as good as it ever was in no great length of time, and at a small expense.

I expect shortly to go into the field with a detachment against the Bullum Polygar, who is still unsubdued. I shall be strong enough, I hope; but I wish that I had a few more English troops, and fewer Natives. I don't imagine that the latter are very active in a jungle.

The southern disturbances have been brought to a most fortunate conclusion, on which I congratulate you. I hope that tranquillity there will be permanent.

An unfortunate event has occurred in the Ceded Districts. Major Strachan made an attack upon a fort, the name of which I don't know, and was repulsed with the loss of about 60 men killed and wounded, the greatest number of them belonging to the 25th dragoons; he was wounded himself, as were Captain Crane and Captain Dair, and Captain Maitland was killed. I believe that other officers have likewise been wounded. Major Strachan had not with him any European infantry.

You will have heard of Webbe's appointment to the Residency of Mysore: it is a good arrangement for him, as it enables him to remain in the country with credit to himself till the effect of Lord Wellesley's representation upon the late orders to the government of Fort St. George can be known. I acknowledge that I did not like to see him in the office of private secretary. Lord Clive could have had the benefit of his assistance without placing him in it, and Webbe's acceptance of it, if he should have retained it for any length of time, would have drawn upon him a fresh mark of the displeasure of the Court of Directors. It was evident that he was dismissed from his former office in order that other people might influence and conduct the measures of the government, and it would therefore have been as well if he had not accepted an office which still ostensibly enabled him to do both, without giving him any more authority than he would have had if he had remained out of office entirely.

I agree with you in not thinking much of the new ministry. There is too much moderation and candour for these bad times: besides, they have not agreed among themselves upon all occasions, and I see that they have submitted to abuse from the opposition, and instead of retorting it according to the good old custom, they have deprecated it, and have held a tone of moderation and submission which will soon drive them out. I see all this in the journals which I receive sometimes from Manesty.

Remember me kindly to Colonel Agnew, if he should be with you.

Believe me, &c.,

ARTHUR WELLESLEY.

[1014.]

To Major-General Campbell.

SIR, Seringapatam, 26th Dec., 1801.

I received last night your letter of the 20th instant, and I regret exceedingly the circumstances which you have detailed to me.

I have this morning sent from hence to Bellary, stores of which the enclosed paper contains a list; and when the draught bullocks come in from their grazing ground (which I hope will be to-morrow, as I sent for them last night on the receipt of your letter), I will send to you two iron 18-pounders complete, with all their equipments, and 400 rounds of ammunition.

I hope that the stores of which the enclosed is a list will reach Bellary on the 10th of January, and that the guns will reach the same place on the 12th or 13th.

I have sent one of my own hircarrahs, a man on whom I can depend, in charge of the former, with a guard of 1 havildar and 12 men, and 10 store lascars; and I shall be obliged to you if you will give orders that these people may be sent back from Bellary. An European will go in charge of the guns and their stores, with a similar guard. I conclude that if it should be necessary, you will give orders that these guards may be reinforced at Rydroog, by which place they will pass.

I should send a larger proportion of stores with the heavy guns, only that it would take more time to procure bullocks to carry them; and, as I understand from Captain Freese that you have 18-pound shot at Gooty, I hope that the proportion to be sent at present will be sufficient to lay open the fort before which you are. If, however, more bullocks should be ready before the ·guns go, more powder shall be sent, and cartridge bags; and, at all events, as bullocks can be procured, powder and cartridge bags shall be sent to you. I hope to hear from you by return of post if you should want shot.

I should have sent you this equipment and these stores from Chittledroog, according to your desire, only that I am not certain that every thing at that place is in the state of readiness in which it is here.

At all events, I know from experience that it is impossible to procure at Chittledroog bullocks, or any thing that is necessary to move ordnance or stores, and these must have been sent from hence. Chittledroog lies about 40 miles out of the direct road from Seringapatam to Bellary, which distance the bullocks would have had to go in addition to that which they will go under the present arrangement. Supposing the equipment to have been ready on their arrival, there would still have been some delay in sending it off; and, upon the whole, I conceive that I shall have saved you five or six days by sending every thing from hence.

I am sorry that I cannot send you any 6-pounder carriages: I have only the number required for the service on which the troops in this country are likely to be employed immediately.

Wishing you every success, and hoping soon to hear of it,

I have, &c.,

ARTHUR WELLESLEY.

To Lieutenant-Colonel Williamson.　　　　　　　　　　[1015.]

SIR,　　　　　　　　　　　　Seringapatam, 27th Dec., 1801.

I have received and have attentively perused the proceedings of the general court martial of which you are president; and as I am so unfortunate as to differ in opinion from its members both in regard to their decision on the guilt of Lieutenant —— of the crime stated in the second charge, and in regard to the punishment sentenced, I think myself obliged to request that the decision of the general court martial on these points may be revised. In a common case, considering the inconvenience which the service has suffered, and may still suffer, from the employment of the time of so many officers upon such a business, I should have thought it proper to confirm the sentence of the court martial, rather than that it should sit longer ; but in a case like this, which is likely to become a subject of future discussion by our superiors, and by those who employ us, and in which the credit of the whole army and the character of every officer belonging to it are in some degree involved, I should not act as I ought by those who employ me, by the army, or by the general court martial of which you are president, if I did not represent to you my reasons for thinking that the decisions of the court martial in the instances alluded to ought to be reconsidered and altered.

The court martial have acquitted Lieutenant —— of the crime stated in the second charge on account of the prevarication of the evidence, and for want of sufficient evidence.

On a perusal of the evidence I observe that all the witnesses have sworn positively to one fact, viz., that in order to force from them certain sums of money, they were made to stand in the sun in the bazaar at Seedasheeghur with stores on their heads. They differ regarding the hour of the day, and Lieutenant ——'s being present, and the number of times this punishment was inflicted upon them.   But considering the nature of Native witnesses in general, and the extraordinary agreement of these in their account of the fact, there remains on my mind no doubt whatever of it.   Is it to be supposed possible that nine men would come forward to swear publicly at Seedasheeghur that they had been forced to stand with stores on their heads in the bazaar in the middle of the day, if the fact had not been true?   Would it not have occurred to them, as it must to every body, that hundreds might have come forward to contradict them?

If then the court martial believe that this fact took place, (and there does not appear to me any reason for disbelieving it), as in that instance Lieutenant —— certainly did oppress the inhabitants, he must be supposed guilty of the crime stated in the second charge.

The general court martial have found Lieutenant —— guilty of flogging Banar, of whom it appears that he died subsequent to the flogging, and that Lieutenant —— made som' of the inhabitants sign a paper, stating that he had died consequence of being poisoned ; of interfering with the aumilc of Ankola, and making use of the sepoys under his command to force the aumildar to deliver to him rice; of withholding payment from the grain dealers who supplied the troops under his command with rice, on which charge it appears that he obliged the dealers to deliver the rice according to his own measurement, and at his own price; and of beating Chenburvay Chitty in two instances.

In the course of this trial the evidence has been proved of a system of oppression and exaction at Seedasheeghur during the command of Lieutenant ——, such as it is to be hoped does not disgrace the army in any other place; and yet the general court martial have marked their sense of the crimes of which they have found Lieutenant —— guilty, and of his general conduct, as it appears on their proceedings, in no other manner than by a suspension from rank and pay for six months, and by a reprimand.

I entreat them to compare the crimes of which they have found him guilty with those of others, to reconsider this sentence, and to reflect on the disgrace which will be attached to the character of the whole profession if it be supposed that a person found guilty of such crimes can be suffered to remain among them.

I have, &c.,

ARTHUR WELLESLEY.

To the Right Hon. Lord Clive.   [1016.]

MY LORD,   Seringapatam, 28th Dec., 1801.

There is a report in circulation that orders have been received from Europe to remodel the medical establishment of this government, under the operation of which another member is to be added to the Medical Board, who is to be taken from the head surgeons by selection. As there is a chance that this report may be well founded, I take the liberty of recommending to your Lordship Mr. Anderson, the head surgeon in Mysore. I have seen him in all situations, in the field and in garrison, and I may safely say that in his line he has no equal in this army. I draw your Lordship's attention to him from a sincere conviction that he is the ablest man in his profession in this country. As the officer in the command of the troops in the Mysore country, I shall regret the promotion which will deprive me of his assistance and advice upon all occasions.

I hope I may be permitted to take this opportunity of expressing my concern at the events which have been the occasion of your Lordship's expected departure. I should have requested the permission of your Lordship and the Commander-in-Chief to go to Madras, in order to pay my respects to you previous to your departure, and to thank you in person for the many favours and kindnesses I have received from you, only that I am about to take the field with the troops. I beg, however, that your Lordship will believe that I shall ever retain a lively recollection of, and be grateful for them.

I have, &c.,

ARTHUR WELLESLEY.

[1017.]   *To Colonel Stevenson.*

MY DEAR COLONEL,   Seringapatam, 30th Dec., 1801.

I have received your letters of the 24th and 26th. Barclay writes to you this day to beg that the 22nd may be drawn from Wynaad into Malabar, and you will arrange your troops in Malabar in such manner as you may think proper. If, however, you are decidedly of opinion that a battalion can be spared from Malabar without incurring risk, I think it advisable that the province of Canara should be reinforced. Before this time Sir William Clarke will have called away all the troops, and that province will have been left with the 1st of the 8th only. This is a new battalion, and not a very good one, I believe.

I have no very great confidence in the operation of a jungle war in which Europeans are not employed, and therefore I don't propose to employ any troops in the field in Canara for the want of that species. The reinforcement to that province, therefore, which I recommend, is only desirable in case Malabar should be sufficiently provided for. Security in the former at the expense of the latter would be but bad policy.

In regard to the guns in Wynaad, I recommend that they

should be left there. I should think that till the Rajah is caught or driven out of the country, it will be desirable to keep your posts at Peria Ghaut and Lakerycotta, however weak, and a gun at each, as I understand is the case at present. The other two guns may be kept at the head-quarters of the battalion, wherever they may be fixed. We don't want the guns here at present, and, in my opinion, it will be better to leave in Wynaad those pieces of ordnance which cost nothing, and may be wanted, than to bring them here prematurely.

My letter will have shown you the fate of your application to the Commander-in-Chief in favour of Mr. Henderson. I wait till I hear further respecting your plan for an arsenal before I say anything upon the subject. I expect to march on the 4th or 5th.

Believe me, &c.,

ARTHUR WELLESLEY.

To Lieut.-Colonel Macalister.   [1018.]

Sir,   Seringapatam, 31st Dec., 1801.

I have received your letter of the 27th and its enclosures from Major Paterson.

I enclose you an extract of the order given out by Lieutenant-General Harris regulating bazaars, which order is nearly a copy of that issued by Lord Cornwallis, and is that according to which I have regulated the bazaars of the different bodies of troops which have been under my command.

According to this order, of which, of course, I approve, Major Paterson would have the power of adjusting any matter that might arise interiorly in the bazaar attached to the regiment under his command, and of course would have the power of giving orders that slight punishments should be inflicted on those whom he should think deserving of them.

I observed, however, in a former letter, that although I approved of this system and should always adhere to it, and although it has the sanction of such high authority, it is by no means a standing regulation of the army. Government, for wise reasons, has left the commanding officers of different bodies of troops the power of regulating the bazaars attached to them in the manner they may think proper, and has held them responsible that the troops are well supplied with good and cheap provisions; and as long as that is the case, there has been no interference in the particular regulations of any bazaar. According to this principle I consider that you, as commanding officer of the detachment of cavalry in the field, a part of which are the 19th dragoons, have the power of regulating the bazaars attached to that detachment as you may think proper, under the general restriction above mentioned; and you have a right to prevent the punishment of any bazaar man by any person excepting those to whom you will delegate such authority. Not only you have this right, but according to the principle adopted by Lord Cornwallis, and at one time by General Harris, the former of whom prevented European regiments of infantry from having bazaars at all, you might withdraw the bazaar entirely from the 19th dragoons, provided you could make it clear that such a regulation would tend to make provisions and other supplies more plentiful, regular and cheap. I don't mean to recommend such a regulation or such an exercise of the right alluded to; I mention it only to show how far the power of the commanding officer of a detachment extends over its bazaars, and how far it has already been exercised by the great and high authorities above mentioned.

Under these circumstances, although I cannot say I approve of the system adopted in your detachment, I cannot request you to recall the order of which a complaint has been made. If what I have above said be not satisfactory, I must beg again that this matter may be referred to the Commander-in-Chief. I recommend, however, in preference to any further discussion or reference, that the whole matter may be forgotten, and that a spirit and system of conciliation may be introduced in future into all discussions of this nature. I beg that you will communicate this letter to Major Paterson.

I have, &c.,

ARTHUR WELLESLEY.

To the Secretary of the Military Board.   [1019.]

SIR,   'Seringapatam, 4th Jan., 1802.

I enclose a certificate of the prices of grain at Seringapatam and in the neighbourhood, and I will take care that a similar one shall be sent in future on the 1st of every month.

I have, &c.,

.ARTHUR WELLESLEY.

To Lieut.-Colonel de Meuron.   [1020.]

SIR,   Seringapatam, 5th Jan., 1802.

I am about to quit Seringapatam in command of the troops in the field, and during my absence the command of this place will devolve upon you. I expect that Colonel Carlisle, of the 1st battalion of artillery, will shortly join his corps, at which time, as being the senior officer, you will deliver over the command to him.

I beg to refer you to the instructions which I left you on going to Nundydroog on the 13th November last, for a general statement of my wishes regarding the duties of the garrison, the police of the place, &c. &c. I shall never be at any great distance from you; and you will always find me ready to assist you with my advice on any point which you may think it necessary to refer to me.

I beg, however, particularly to request your assistance and support of Captain Symons in the conduct of the arduous duties imposed upon him, as well by the regulation of government in the establishment of the courts of Cutchery and Foujdarry and in the execution of his office of collector, as in the department of police, which I heretofore informed you I had placed under his management as an arrangement of public expediency.

Upon this point I am exceedingly anxious, as Captain Symons has conducted the police much to my satisfaction and to the general advantage, and any interruption to the execution of his duties, however momentary, would be attended with much public inconvenience.

I have, &c.,

ARTHUR WELLESLEY.

[1021.]   *To J. G. Ravenshaw, Esq.*

Sir,   Camp at Kikerry, 7th Jan., 1802.

I had yesterday the honour of receiving your letter of the 30th of December.

I think it possible that the Bullum Polygar may have been induced to refrain from holding any further communication with you, from an idea that I should have been obliged to march into the Ceded Districts to the assistance of Major-General Campbell, with whose misfortune you will probably have been made acquainted. I received an account last night, however, of General Campbell's complete success against the fort which he before had failed in taking. This intelligence, which is now public in this camp, and that of my having marched from Seringapatam on the 5th instant towards the Bullum country with a force fully sufficient for the object in view, will probably induce the Polygar to renew his communications with you. I sincerely hope he will, and that with a desire to bring matters to an amicable conclusion.

At all events I shall continue the military operations in the same manner as if he were holding no communication with you, unless I should hear that he has actually given himself up. In that case I shall do everything in my power to preserve the country from injury, and I shall exert myself to induce this government to make such a provision for him as will be at the same time honourable to him and consistent with the peace and security of the country.

I will keep you informed of everything that will occur.

I have, &c.,

Arthur Wellesley.

[1022.]   *To Sir William Clarke.*

Sir,   Camp at Kikerry, 7th Jan., 1802.

I have received your letters of the 24th, 29th, and 31st December, and I beg to congratulate you upon your success and present state of security.

I mean that you should have at Goa the whole of the grenadier battalion, and of the 1st of the 3rd ; and as soon as you will have been joined by these troops, you may as well discharge from the service the *Active*, which you inform me that you have hired. I conclude that you will have given your own orders to the officers commanding the different detachments of the Native battalions above mentioned to join you at Goa. If you have not done so, I request that you will give them the necessary orders without loss of time.

That part of the 4th, which you have ordered from Hullihall to Seedasheeghur, may remain at the latter for the present. It is my intention to relieve that corps from the province of Soonda above the Ghauts as soon as circumstances will permit, and in the mean time, as I have a body of troops in the field, half of it will be sufficient for the duty at Hullihall and the security of the Company's territory.

I beg that you will send the 75th regiment on to Bombay as soon as you think that you can spare that corps from Goa with safety to your position. I conclude that, according to the instructions which I sent him, Major Gray has taken care to give orders that the transports which were intended to convey the 75th regiment from Mangalore to Bombay should follow him to Goa. If he should have omitted to leave those orders at Mangalore, I request you to desire him to send them there without loss of time.

As you have been joined by a body of troops which places you in a state of security, I beg you to send to join their corps the convalescent men belonging to the 2nd of the 2nd and 1st of the 4th: they may go to Cannanore.

I have, &c.,

ARTHUR WELLESLEY.

To Lieutenant-Colonel Macalister.   [1023.]

SIR,   Camp at Kikerry, 7th Jan., 1802.

I have received your letter of the 6th instant, with an enclosure from Major ————.

You will be so kind as to desire Major ———— to specify particularly the grounds of complaint which he has against you, in order that I may lay them before the Commander-in-Chief. In stating his complaint, however, I don't see any necessity for his noticing the *contempt* which he supposes to have been shown to my recommendation, as, if that exist anywhere, I can notice it myself. I also have to observe that, if the complaints which Major ———— has to make of you are not better founded, or of a nature less futile and frivolous than those which he has written to me in his letter of the 6th instant, he will do well to forego his intention of making them. It is certainly impossible for time to be thrown away with less advantage to the public than mine would be in reading, forwarding, and commenting upon such complaints, and than that, still more valuable, of the Commander-in-Chief would be in considering them; and it is more than probable that his Excellency would pronounce an opinion upon them which would not be very agreeable to Major ————. You will be so kind as to communicate this letter to Major ————.

I have, &c.,

ARTHUR WELLESLEY.

[1024.]   *To Lieutenant-Colonel Spry.*

SIR,   14th Jan., 1802.

The detachment which has been placed under your command by this day's orders is intended to attack the forest of Arrekeery on one side, at the same time that it will be attacked on another by the detachment placed under the orders of Lieutenant-Colonel Cuppage, and on a third by the remainder of the troops under my command from the side of Munserabad. It is my wish that the attack should commence on all sides at ten o'clock in the morning of the 16th instant; and I request you to commence your march from camp in such time as to be at the point of attack at that hour.

I enclose an account of the road by which it is intended that you should advance towards Arrekeery, and the person will accompany this letter who will point it out to you.

It is not impossible, however, but that you may meet with obstacles on this road not mentioned in the enclosed paper, and not known to your guide; but I hope that you will not meet with any of a very serious nature. When you will have gained the village of Sodleghee your object will be to attack the Arrekeery ditch. You will be the best judge at Sodleghee how far this may be practicable ; particularly if you should not be able to bring your guns to Sodleghee to bear upon the ditch.

If you should be so fortunate as to carry the ditch, you will move on to the village of Arrekeery, which you will secure ; and afterwards you will employ such part of your detachment as you may not think it necessary to employ on that service to attack the rear of those who will defend Arrekeery against the detachment which will attack that place on the side of Munserabad. In moving to the attack of the ditch of Arrekeery, the guns will, of course, be left at Sodleghee ; or if it should not be possible to bring them through the jungle on this side of Sodleghee, it will be necessary to leave them at the pagoda : a reserve should be in charge of them wherever you may find it necessary to leave them ; and, at all events, it is desirable that the village of Sodleghee should be secured.

A detachment of the Rajah's troops, consisting of 200 infantry and 100 bildars and pioneers, will be sent to place themselves under your command. You will find them useful in securing Sodleghee, or in other services that may occur.

I recommend it to you to give orders that the European troops under your command should cook one day's salt provisions on the 15th for the next day.

The Rajah's cavalry will occupy all the open ground in the neighbourhood of the forest of Arrekeery ; but I recommend that you should order your camp equipage and baggage into one of the villages in the neighbourhood of your camp, and that you should leave any sick or convalescent men that you may have to guard them.

I have, &c.,

ARTHUR WELLESLEY.

[ENCLOSURE.] *

The Koodringee Road.

First, after passing the river, there are dry paddy-fields ; then a rising ground, open. On the top of this rising ground is a ditch and bank. On the left hand is another rising ground, higher than that on which the ditch is.

---

* The draft from which the above enclosure has been printed was written by Colonel Wellesley in pencil on the back of an old letter.—ED.

After passing the ditch, on the left side, is a small pagoda. Beyond is a close jungle, and then paddy-fields. Then the ditch and bamboo-hedge of Sodleghee.

The paddy-fields beyond Sodleghee reach to Arrekeery ditch. The village of Sodleghee is on higher ground than the ditch.

If it should be necessary to bring the guns beyond the pagoda, the jungle must be opened for them; and if it should be necessary to bring them into the village of Sodleghee, the bamboo-hedge, &c., must be opened for the purpose.

To go to Setteegall from hence no difficulty.

Beyond Setteegall a paddy-field with a nullah in it; beyond the nullah a hill; then a valley with small jungle in it, and in the jungle there is a tett or stockade; beyond the stockade a plain, and on the plain a ditch and bank. Beyond the ditch and bank is the village of Hoonagall, on the left hand side.

The village of Hoonagall must be carried. It is surrounded by bamboos and a ditch. Close to Hoonagall is a high hill which commands the ditch of Arrekeery. Beyond Hoonagall is a bank of a tank which must be passed to the ditch of Arrekeery. Paddy-fields on one side, the water on the other.

The paddy-fields are all dry.

———————————— - -

[1025.]   *To Lieutenant-Colonel Cuppage.*

SIR,   15th Jan., 1802.

From the intelligence which I have received since my arrival here, and from the general view which I have had of the forest of Arrekeery, I have reason to believe that the village of that name is an object of comparatively trifling importance; that it lies in low ground, and is commanded by the heights, which, if our operations are confined to the possession of the village, will remain in the hands of the Polygars.

Under these circumstances, I have to request that if you should be able to enter the village of Arrekeery, and if you should find its situation to be such as I have above described, you will endeavour to communicate with me on the Beemanara hill, and attack the jungly hill which is above the village of Arrekeery. The highest part of that hill is apparently that on which the tree in the form of an umbrella stands, which, I am informed, is immediately above the village and pagoda of Arrekeery. Your guides will point it out to you. The detachment which will attack the forest from this side will move towards the same point.

I have, &c.,

ARTHUR WELLESLEY.

To the Deputy Adjutant-General.

[1026.]

SIR,   Camp at Munserabad, 17th Jan., 1802.

The troops intended for the service in the field having arrived at Seringapatam on the 31st of December and the 2nd of January, and all the equipments being prepared, I marched from Seringapatam towards Bullum on the 5th of January, and was joined at Chinroypatam by the brigade of cavalry under the orders of Lieutenant-Colonel Macalister on the 8th.

I took opportunities of examining the forest of Arrekeery, in which the Bullum Rajah had his principal and strongest holds and all his force, on the 13th, 14th, and 15th, from the ground on which the troops halted on those days; and I determined to divide the infantry under my command into three bodies, and to attack the forest, which was everywhere fortified, on three sides, while the infantry of the Rajah of Mysore should cut off the retreat to the Ghauts, of which the Bullum Rajah had possession, and his Highness's cavalry and that under Lieutenant-Colonel Macalister should occupy all the open ground in the neighbourhood of the forest. Accordingly I divided the infantry into three divisions, the first commanded by Lieutenant-Colonel A. Cuppage, the second by Major English, and the third, which was destined to attack the principal posts which Lieutenant-Colonel Montresor had carried heretofore, by Lieutenant-Colonel Spry. I was with this last division. The three attacks made by these divisions commenced at ten o'clock yesterday, and, notwithstanding the obstacles which each had to encounter, all of them succeeded. The divisions under the orders of Lieutenant-Colonel Spry and Major English entered Arrekeery from opposite sides of the forest at the same moment, and that under Lieutenant-Colonel Cuppage was at no great distance. The troops of the Rajah of Mysore and the cavalry at the same time performed the service allotted to them.

Our troops are in possession of all the principal posts in the forest.

In the performance of this service I have had every reason to be satisfied with the zeal, alacrity, and good conduct of all. My acknowledgments are, however, particularly due to Lieutenant-Colonel Spry, Lieutenant-Colonel Cuppage, and Major English, who commanded the three divisions which made the attacks; to Captain Blair, who commanded the artillery; to Captain Heitland and his pioneers; and to Captain Colebrooke of the Guides, and Captain Weston of the 77th, who had been employed in this country under Lieutenant-Colonel Montresor, and from whom I derived much information and assistance. Lieutenant-Colonel Cuppage has reported in very favourable terms the assistance which he received from Lieutenant Hofman, who commanded the detachment of the 77th, which formed part of his division.

I enclose returns of the killed and wounded on this service.

I have to mention that the troops of the Rajah of Mysore conducted themselves well, and after having carried the post which it was intended they should attack, were of essential service in covering the right flank of the division commanded by Lieutenant-Colonel Spry.

It is my intention now to lay open the forest of Arrekeery as far as may be in my power. I shall then proceed towards the Ghauts, and open the communication with the province of Canara by Bissolee and the Soobramany Pagoda; and in the mean time if I should receive any intelligence of the motions of the Bullum Rajah, I shall not fail to pursue him. A detachment of the troops of the Rajah of Mysore are now out in pursuit of him.

In the course of a few days I shall send off the cavalry under Lieutenant-Colonel Macalister to meet the remount horses on their road from Mangalore.

I have, &c.,

ARTHUR WELLESLEY.

[1027.]   *To J. G. Ravenshaw, Esq.*

SIR,   Camp at Munserabad, 18th Jan., 1802.

I have the pleasure to inform you that on the 16th instant I attacked and carried all the Bullum Rajah's posts in the forest of Arrekeery, with but small loss on our side. Our troops are now in possession of the forest. The Bullum Rajah has made his escape towards the Ghauts ; but as I follow him to-morrow, I have hopes that before long we shall be able to settle everything in this country.

It is not improbable but that some of his adherents may communicate with you again, and I therefore make you acquainted with the terms upon which I have recommended to the Dewan to give them cowle :

1st. That they should cut down the bamboo fence which surrounds their villages.

2nd. That they should fill up the ditches which surround them.

3rd. That they should deliver up their arms.

4th. That they should pay the annual revenue.

I have recommended him to apprise them that if they do not commence carrying into execution the two first conditions on the day after the cowle will have been given to them, it shall be declared void, and that he will proceed against them with the greatest rigour.

I have also recommended to him to publish a proclamation, holding forth cowle to the whole country upon these terms.

Whether he attends to my recommendation or not, or whether the cowle is accepted generally or not, it is my intention to proceed forthwith towards the Ghauts, and, as far as may be in my power, to carry into execution the two first proposals in every village that I may meet with.   The causes of the rebellion in this country are its extraordinary strength, and the means which the heads of villages have to combine and resist the officers of the government in the works which they have round them. If these are destroyed, they must either quit the country or submit, and I imagine that they will prefer the latter.

I shall certainly go to the Bissolee Ghaut, and I propose to open it, and hereafter to have the communication between Seringapatam and the province of Canara by that road.

If it be convenient to you, I should be glad to meet you at the Bissolee Ghaut ; and as to open this communication is an object of the greatest public importance, I shall be obliged to you if you will be so kind as to have in readiness all the assistance that you may be able to procure of working people, &c. &c., in order that no time may be lost in finishing the work. They might be assembled at the Soobramany Pagoda.

I have received intimation from the Commander-in-Chief that

it is probable that he may want transports to convey to Bombay about 350 Europeans and their officers from Mangalore in a short time. I shall be obliged to you if you will let me know whether the port of Mangalore will afford the means of transporting these troops, and if you will be so kind as to make arrangements for procuring them as soon as I may receive the orders of the Commander-in-Chief upon the subject. I believe that I am not quite regular in troubling you with this matter; but I am not aware that there is any officer under the government of Fort St. George, in the province of Canara, who is particularly charged with the marine department.

I have, &c.,

ARTHUR WELLESLEY.

[1028.]   *To Major English.*

SIR,   Camp at Munserabad, 18th Jan., 1802.

I am about to move towards the Ghauts with the troops, and I leave you in command of the posts in the forest of Arrekeery, with the detachment detailed in the orders of this day, which I request you to encamp on the high ground near the stockade, inside of the outer ditch. I have given a memorandum to Captain Heitland of the works which I wish should be carried on during my absence.

Many of the stores of the detachment will be left at Munserabad, and I shall be obliged to you if you will send over there a small guard to take care of them. A party of the Rajah's infantry and 100 bildars will be left at Arrekeery, under your orders. I have desired that a tappall may be posted between Arrekeery and me, and you will be so kind as to let me hear from you occasionally, particularly if the enemy should show himself again in your neighbourhood. You will keep up a constant communication with the person in charge of the Rajah's fort at Munserabad.

It is desirable that as soon as convenient you should establish a post on the high ground up to which the new road from Munserabad runs, and that you should make a short communication between that post and the ground on which you are encamped. It is also desirable that you should have a road opened between Arrekeery and the outer lines or barriers towards

Ooscotta and Careeoonshee by the way by which the troops under your command advanced on the 16th instant.

I have, &c.,

ARTHUR WELLESLEY.

To Lieut.-Colonel Close.   [1029.]

MY DEAR COLONEL,   Camp at Munserabad, 18th Jan., 1802.

You will be glad to learn that I attacked and carried all the Bullum Rajah's posts in Arrekeery on the 16th instant. Our troops are now in possession, we have a good post just above Arrekeery, and roads of communication between that and others which give us the entire possession of the jungle. The Rajah is gone to the Ghauts, and I follow him to-morrow, leaving a force in Arrekeery which will keep it against him should he be inclined to try to regain possession of it.

I marched from Seringapatam on the 5th with four battalions of sepoys, the 77th reduced to 300 men, and about 240 of the regiment de Meuron, ten guns, the four small mortars that we had in Wynaad, and 500 pioneers. I was joined at Chinroy-patam by the 19th dragoons and the 5th regiment of cavalry, with their guns.

I arrived at Polliam on the 12th, and reconnoitred the forest on all sides on the 13th, 14th, and 15th, and I determined to make three great attacks upon it with the Company's troops, while the Rajah's troops should attack a passage which the Bullum Rajah had to the jungles near the Ghauts by a ruined fort, called Saduckabad, from their Munserabad and Ooscotta camps at the same moment.

I encamped on the 15th at Munserabad, and on the 16th, in the morning, made the attacks as soon as the fog had cleared away. Two of the divisions which attacked from entirely opposite sides of the forest arrived in the village of Arrekeery at the same moment, and the third, commanded by Colonel A. Cuppage, was at no great distance. The Rajah's troops, after having carried Saduckabad and got possession of the passage to the Ghauts and opened the communication between Munserabad and Ooscotta by the road which we went before, attacked the forest likewise near the great attack made by our troops, and were of essential service in covering our right flank. The cavalry (Company's and Rajah's) occupied all the open ground to cut off the fugitives.

The forest was everywhere strongly fortified in the Polygar style, but particularly at the place which I attacked, being the same which Tolfrey and Montresor attacked before. However, we have lost but few men, no officer touched ; one European of de Meuron is killed, and but few wounded, and that slightly.

The General has given me notice that he shall take away from me the 77th immediately, and under those circumstances I conceive that I have no time to lose.

Although I have not done all to Arrekeery forest which I could wish, having secured our post, I think it better to take advantage of the service of the 77th during the time that I shall have them, and to proceed immediately to destroy everything else like strength in the country, than to risk all by waiting here so long as that, when I move, I shall want their assistance. The beating, however, which the Rajah got the other day must have made some impression, and I do not think it probable that I shall have any more trouble.

My intention is to lay open all the strong villages, which are, in fact, the causes of the rebellion, and wherever the Rajah has anything like a post of strength, to take possession and destroy it. I have recommended to Purneah to require from the ryots to whom he may think it proper to give cowle, that they should cut down their bamboo hedges and level their ditches, and that he should inform them that he shall consider the cowle as void if he does not find that they take some steps towards carrying those articles of it into execution on the very day after it is given to them. If we can succeed in reducing the strength of the villages to such a state as that the aumildar's peons can enter them when he pleases, I don't think that in this open country we have anything else to wish for. Either the patels must submit, or quit the country.

We have lately distressed this country much by stopping its intercourse with Canara as well as with Mysore. In short, the rebels cannot go on without Arrekeery, which they have lost ; but unless we prevent them from making a new Arrekeery, they will be as bad in another year as they were before.

I received your letter from Purneah, and I am glad to find that you have a prospect of success in your negotiations. Your anxiety regarding this country will have been relieved when you will have heard that Webbe succeeds you. I'll write to you when anything occurs worthy of your attention.

Believe me, &c.,

ARTHUR WELLESLEY.

To Sir William Clarke. [1030.]

MY DEAR SIR, Camp at Ooscotta, 19th Jan., 1802.

In my letter of yesterday I omitted to congratulate you upon the success of your negotiations. It is great indeed, and places us at Goa upon the best footing.

I have this instant received your letter of the 12th, by which I learn that you have not called in the remainder of the grenadier battalion and of the 1st of the 3rd. I conclude that you will have done so upon the receipt of my letter of the 7th.

Your requisition for more troops appears founded upon the Governor-General's letter to you of the 11th December, an extract of which you have sent me. It does not appear that you have any additional reason to fear an attack from the French, or the conduct which the viceroy may adopt in case of their appearance, since the 5th instant, when you reported that you had sent to Bombay four companies of the 75th; besides, in your calculation of your means of defence against every possible attack, you have entirely omitted the Portuguese European troops in our pay, their native troops, and the naval force cruising off Goa. Under these circumstances, and, as I don't imagine that it is the intention of the Governor-General that the security of Goa should be provided for, under every possible contingency however remote, at the expense of the security and tranquillity of the other territories under the government and protection of the Company, I must take upon me to decline to send the European troops which you have required until I shall have received the orders of the Commander-in-Chief, subsequent to his knowledge of your wants.

Believe me, &c.,

ARTHUR WELLESLEY.

[1031.]   *To Lieut.-General Stuart.*

SIR,   Camp near Ooscotta, 19th Jan., 1802.

I enclose copies of papers which I have received from Sir William Clarke.

I before desired him to take the whole of the grenadier battalion and of the 1st of the 3rd, and on the 5th instant he informed me that he had sent four companies of the 75th to Bombay, I conclude because he thought his post was then in security with the force which he had. He does not mention any alteration that has taken place since the 5th instant which may have induced him to make this new requisition, and it is therefore to be attributed solely to the extract of the letter from the Governor-General, which he has enclosed.

In this requisition Sir William has stated the utmost force which he would require, even if it were certain that he was to be attacked immediately, and he has desired that the troops may be sent to him; but as his being attacked so suddenly is very improbable, and as I can't conceive that the Governor-General means that Sir William should be provided with troops against every possible event, however remote, at the expense of the security and tranquillity of every other part of the country, I don't propose to send him more troops till I shall receive your further orders. In the calculation of the means of defence now at Goa, and of those wanting, Sir William Clarke has entirely omitted the Portuguese European troops in our pay, their native troops, and the naval force cruising off the harbour.

I have, &c.,

ARTHUR WELLESLEY.

[1032.]   *To the Chief Secretary of Government.*

SIR,   Camp at Woochinga, 20th Jan., 1802.

I have had the honour of receiving your letter of the 11th November, 1801, with its enclosures, being extracts of a letter from the Court of Directors of the 10th of June.* I am highly sensible of the mark which the Honourable Court have been pleased

* The Chief Secretary had informed Colonel Wellesley in the letter referred to that the Court of Directors had ordered a reduction of the table money hitherto allowed him as commanding the forces above the Ghauts, from

to give of their approbation of the services of their troops which I had the honour to command.

In addition to the force serving within the territories of the Rajah of Mysore, the troops in the provinces of Malabar, Canara, and Soonda, and those at Goa, have been placed under my command by orders from government; and in other respects my duties are more extensive than those intrusted to the commanding officer of the subsidiary force at Hyderabad. I have been so fortunate as to have performed them to the satisfaction of the governments of Fort St. George and to that of the government of Bombay, while the troops in Malabar and Canara, and at Goa, were under that Presidency, and that of the three Commanders-in-Chief under whose orders I have served. The Honourable Court have, however, been pleased to determine that my situation shall be placed on the same footing in point of

600 to 400 pagodas per month; and at the same time had transmitted the annexed—

Extract of a General Letter from the Honourable Court of Directors in the Political Department, dated 10th June, 1801.

" Para. 2. In the early part of the operations against the rebel Dhoondiah, we noticed with particular satisfaction the judicious and spirited conduct displayed by Colonel Stevenson and Lieutenant-Colonel Dalrymple. From subsequent advices, particularly a letter from Governor Duncan of the 15th September last, which speaks of the decided and brilliant advantage gained by the Honourable Colonel Wellesley on the 30th July over a division of Dhoondiah's army, we entertained a well founded expectation of a speedy termination to the present contest, more especially as it was stated that on the 31st August the Colonel was within two days' march of the enemy. Your despatches by the *Triton* have announced the important intelligence of the total defeat and destruction of the rebel and his army on the 10th of September last. Strongly impressed with a sense of the political advantages which must be the consequence of the complete overthrow of Dhoondiah and his forces, we desire that our thanks may be conveyed to the Honourable Colonel Wellesley for his distinguished services in the late campaign, and to the officers and troops under his command for their zealous and successful co-operation.

" 16. We approve of the compensation advised in these paragraphs of (250) two hundred and fifty pagodas a month to the secretary, and (100) one hundred pagodas a month to the assistants to the Mysore Commissioners; and as we entertain a very high sense of the merits of the Commissioners themselves in the execution of the important trust reposed in them, we have agreed to authorise you to present the sum of (10,000) ten thousand pagodas to each of the following gentlemen for their services upon that occasion :

The Honourable Colonel Wellesley,
The Honourable Henry Wellesley, and
Lieutenant-Colonels Kirkpatrick and Close.

" For this amount we direct that you draw bills upon the Court of Directors at 8s. per pagoda, payable at 365 days after sight."

salary with that of the commanding officer of the subsidiary force at Hyderabad.

I am by no means desirous that the Right Honourable the Governor in Council should take this subject into his consideration with a view to his granting an addition to the allowance ordered for me by the Honourable Court of Directors; but I beg to draw his attention to it in justice to myself and my situation, and I shall be obliged to his Lordship if he will transmit this letter to be laid before them, with such remarks as he may think proper, in order that they may have a true knowledge of the extent of the trust reposed in, and of the nature of the duties performed by, the commanding officer in Mysore.

In order to throw more light upon this subject, I enclose a statement of the number of troops which were under my command on the 1st of January, and the number of stations in which they were distributed.

I have, &c.,

ARTHUR WELLESLEY.

[1033.]   *To Josiah Webbe, Esq.*

MY DEAR WEBBE,   Camp at Woochinga, 20th Jan., 1802.

I understand that Piele wrote to you on the 16th, after our success against Arrekeery. I intended to have stayed there for a few days in order to lay open the jungle and all the villages in the forest, so as to deprive the Polygar of all hopes of establishing himself there again, and to show the people of the country that we were determined to keep possession; but on the 18th I received a letter from General Stuart, in which he informed me that if Sir William Clarke found it necessary to retain the 75th regiment at Goa, the 77th regiment must go to Bombay. At this time I had secured the strongest posts in Arrekeery; and in the course of that day I made communications between them, strengthened them still more, and laid open a great road through the forest to the Rajah's fort of Munserabad. Then I thought it best to defer doing more to the jungle till a later period, and to proceed immediately while I might expect to have the benefit of the assistance of the 77th to destroy the other holds which the Bullum Rajah is supposed to have in the neighbourhood of the Ghauts. Accordingly I left a battalion of sepoys,

four guns, and one company of de Meuron's regiment at Arrekeery, and I am now on my way towards the Ghauts.

We have destroyed this day all the barriers about this place,
and I shall be to-morrow at the top of the Bissolee Ghaut.

I understand that the Bullum Rajah is at present in a place
called Cagenkeerah, which is on the top of the Sampighee Ghaut.
This is about thirty miles to the northward of Bissolee. If I
find this intelligence to be correct, I shall send a detachment
down the Bissolee Ghaut to march through Canara and up the
Sampighee Ghaut, while I attack him at Cagenkeerah from this
side. I hardly hope that he will wait for us ; but at all events
I shall go to Cagenkeerah to destroy the stronghold which he
has there.

I have recommended Purneah to hold out cowle to the
inhabitants of the country upon the terms of cutting down the
hedges and levelling the ditches which surround their villages,
giving up their arms, and paying the usual revenue, at the same
time informing them that if they did not immediately commence carrying into execution the two first articles, he should
consider the cowle as void. He has adopted this plan, excepting
from the cowle the Polygar and twenty of the principal gours
or patels, who have been the cause of the rebellion, and its
chief supporters. It has already had very good effects. The
inhabitants of many villages have taken the cowle, and a commencement has been made to lay open the villages. If this be
entirely effected, the rebellion must be at an end, as the country is in general so open that cavalry can act in it. This
is by far the most beautiful part of Mysore, and I believe
as rich as any other. The country is full of inhabitants, and
every valley is cultivated. There appears no thick jungle as far
even as the Ghauts, and I have great hopes that we shall soon
bring this warfare to a close.

I will let you know from time to time how we get on.

> Believe me, &c.,
>
> ARTHUR WELLESLEY.

To Josiah Webbe, Esq.   [1034.]

MY DEAR WEBBE,   Camp at Bashielly, 21st Jan., 1802.

After I had written to you yesterday, I learned that almost all
the Bullum Rajah's followers had quitted him, and that he was

wandering in the jungles near Cagenkeerah almost alone. I have not, therefore, thought it necessary to send a detachment into Canara; and I was glad to be able to avoid doing so, as from the uncertainty in which we are of the state of the Ghauts, I am afraid that I should not have been able to arrange a co-operation in an attack from above and below at the same time.

The Dewan of the Bullum Rajah was either caught by, or came in to, one of the parties of the Rajah's troops this morning; and he is now with another party in pursuit of the Rajah in the jungles, in a quarter to which he says he has fled.

The cowle, the terms of which I stated to you in my letter of yesterday, is asked for by the inhabitants of the country in all quarters, and I have myself witnessed their compliance with the principal terms. In short, matters here appear settling fast. I shall still, however, open the road to the Sampighee Ghaut, and afterwards to the Bissolee Ghaut. The country has become closer and more difficult as we have approached the Ghauts. I went forward about ten miles from hence this morning, and found the country very close indeed, and very rough.

Believe me, &c.,

ARTHUR WELLESLEY.

[1035.]   *To Colonel Stevenson.*

MY DEAR COLONEL,   Camp at Hutty Hilly, 23rd Jan., 1802.

Since I wrote to you last we have pressed the Bullum Rajah so hard that he has been left entirely alone; we have taken his Dewan (a Brahmin), and his brother-in-law called Conetty Naig. The Rajah is in some danger of being taken also, I hope. While all this is going on, we are opening a road to the Ghauts through the centre of the rebel country. The inhabitants are in their villages, everything is quiet, and they are destroying their bamboo hedges and ditches in consequence of their cowle. So much for Bullum. In answer to your letter of the 13th I have to observe that it is absolutely necessary that there should be in Wynaad artillerymen for one brigade of guns, and these may remain at Captain Dickenson's head-quarters, excepting the non-commissioned officers and the gun-Lascars, at the posts at the head of the Tambercherry and

Peria Ghauts. This detachment of artillerymen in Wynaad may be relieved from the head-quarters at Cannanore as often as you please ; and you may take from Wynaad to Cannanore all the artillery above the number here stated. The pioneers are well employed ; their work does not appear of any great consequence at present, but hereafter its value may be incalculable.

Till I received your letter of the 18th of January I had not heard of any intention of having a breeze with the Rajah of Cochin. If such an intention exists, and is to be carried into execution, certainly all the disposable force in Malabar must have a part in it ; at the same time we must take care that we don't expose those districts to a renewal of disturbance in which you have lately established tranquillity. Your disposition of the troops, as far as I am able to judge of it at present, provides for both objects, if there should be any breeze with the Rajah of Cochin ; but, as I hope and trust this will be delayed as long as possible, if the Rajah of Cochin will allow us to delay it, it will be well to postpone taking any steps for carrying this disposition into effect till you hear further, and something more decided, upon the subject.

I am glad to find that General Stuart agrees in opinion with me upon so many points. Troops are wanted everywhere, and that is one reason for delaying to dismiss or reduce any even of the worst kind ; but there is another reason for not doing so in Malabar, which is applicable peculiarly to the state of that country. We are now trying a new system of government there, which we are resolved to force upon the people whether they like it or not. We have also determined to prevent the practice of carrying arms, which has been common there hitherto, and to which we have been informed that the people are particularly partial. The people of Malabar are not to be coaxed into submission to government, or to give up their arms : terror, however, will induce them to either or both. But they are sufficiently sagacious to see that when we reduce a large number of our troops, and make detachments into other parts where their services may be required, they have no reason to fear ; and when they don't fear the government, they will not submit to it, and will not deliver in their arms. A contrary mode of reasoning will lead to all the conclusions drawn by the Commissioners, which ended in their dismissal from office, and the overthrow of their system of government.

In my opinion Malabar can never be reckoned upon excepting as a country ripe for insurrection, a state in which it has probably ever been till you entered it; and whenever I hear that the force stationed in it is to be diminished, I consider that insomuch is the chance of the permanence of its tranquillity diminished likewise.

The General's reasons for continuing the Europeans at Cochin are unanswerable. I thought, however, that it was your intention to inquire into the state of the fort, and the number of European inhabitants at Cochin, before you should make any further proposition for removing the Europeans from Cochin to Cannanore.

The principle of General Stuart's opinion regarding the removal of the guns and artillerymen from Canara to Cannanore is the same as mine is regarding the removal of the artillerymen from Wynaad. Whenever we find it necessary for the security of the troops, or to render them more efficient, to leave guns with them, we ought to give them the means of using them, or, in other words, to leave artillery likewise. Accordingly my opinion is decided that there ought to be artillery for a brigade in Canara. The remainder may go to Cannanore; the artillery in Canara may be relieved as often as you please.

I was in hopes to have heard further from you respecting the establishment of your depôt at Cannanore, particularly that you would have stated the extent of it, the species of stores which you would have kept there, their quantities, &c. &c. The settlement of the Bullum country has materially altered the question of establishing the depôt for Canara at Cannanore. However, when I know what you think upon this subject, you shall have my sentiments upon it at large.

I have this instant heard of the peace at home. As far as we can judge of its terms they are favourable to us; but we are to admit the French and the Dutch to their settlements in India, particularly to those on the Malabar coast. Our situation in Malabar, therefore, becomes still more critical than it was, and all our measures in that country must be still more decided, though cautious, than they have been even lately.

Believe me, &c.,

ARTHUR WELLESLEY.

To J. G. Ravenshaw, Esq.   [1086.]

SIR,   Camp at Hutty Hilly, 23rd Jan., 1802.

I am now opening a road to Cagenkeerah, a jungly tract
on the top of the Sampighee Ghaut, which I propose likewise to
lay open.   This road runs through the centre of the rebel country.
As the Rajah has been, and will still be, so hard pressed by
our troops in this country, it is possible that he may take
refuge in Canara.   I shall therefore be much obliged to you if
you will give orders to your peons who guard the frontiers to
keep a good look out on the roads leading to all the Ghauts.

There are seven of them from Bullum into Canara, viz.:
1st. Bissolee, or Soobramany Ghaut; 2nd. Sampighee Ghaut,
practicable for cattle; 3rd. Damaun Ghaut, practicable for
men; 4th. Seisul Ghaut, practicable for cattle; 5th. Wombat
Morry Ghaut, practicable for cattle; 6th. Hubby Naly Ghaut,
practicable for men; 7th. Nodaykull Ghaut, practicable for men.
I shall be much obliged to you if you will desire the postmaster
in Canara to post runners on the road between Mangalore and
the Soobramany Pagoda.   The Sampighee Ghaut may, however, be the first opened, and I am informed it is the shortest
road to Mangalore; but I request that the tappall runners may
be laid upon the Soobramany road, because I believe it is best
known, and because at all events that Ghaut will be opened
before they are ready to carry the tappall.   The Mysore postmaster will run the tappall to the Soobramany Pagoda.

I hope to hear from you respecting the shipping upon which
I troubled you on the 18th instant.   I am almost certain that
it will be wanted, though not so much so as to induce me to
request that you would give orders that it be hired forthwith.

I have, &c.,

ARTHUR WELLESLEY.

To Lieutenant-General Stuart.   [1087.]

SIR,   Camp at Hutty Hilly, 24th Jan., 1802.

As it is probable that the presence of the Company's troops
will not be required in this district for a much greater length
of time, and that you will then be desirous that they should be
distributed in quarters, I proceed, in obedience to your former

orders, to state my opinion, first, regarding the force which ought to be in Mysore, including Soonda and Wynaad; secondly, regarding the places at which the troops ought to be stationed.

There ought to be in Mysore one regiment of dragoons, one of Native cavalry, three companies of artillery, two regiments of European infantry, if possible, and eight battalions of Native infantry.

The stations which it is necessary to occupy are, Hullihall, in the province of Soonda, with one battalion; Nuggur with one battalion; Chittledroog with one battalion; Nundydroog and its dependencies and Paughur with one battalion; Wynaad one battalion; Seringapatam one regiment of Europeans and three battalions.

The dragoons ought to be cantoned at Sera, the Native cavalry at Santa Bednore, and the other regiment of European infantry might be at Bangalore. The largest body of them ought to be collected at Seringapatam for the sake of practice, and there ought to be detachments from this body, one at Chittledroog, and another for a brigade of guns at Hullihall in Soonda. These ought to be relieved frequently. The surplus two battalions of the infantry ought likewise to be at Seringapatam.

The principles upon which I have made this calculation and distribution are as follows:

There are certain points in Mysore and places upon the frontier which it is absolutely necessary to occupy with troops. These are, 1st, Hullihall in Soonda, where there must always be a battalion on account of its vicinity to the Mahratta frontier, its distance from, and its local situation relative to other posts.

2nd, Nuggur: to which place some of the reasons apply which apply to Hullihall, and this additional one, viz. that it is a place of great riches, which would certainly be plundered by some of the marauders upon the frontier if it were not held by the Company's troops. A smaller garrison, however, than a battalion has held it, particularly when troops have been in the field on the northern frontier; and, if this distribution should be adopted, I propose that for this year the battalion at Nuggur should furnish a detachment for the Bullum country.

3rd, Chittledroog: this place is important both in regard to its local situation and its great strength. A much larger garrison than one battalion would be required for it; but it has been found so unfavourable to the health of Natives as well as Europeans, its means of supply are so barren, and its inhabitants so unwilling to afford the assistance which would be required in case of the necessity of moving troops from thence, that I have preferred to place the disposable force in another situation.

4th, Nundydroog: this fort is in the centre of a Polygar country. One battalion stationed here keeps the Polygars in order from the frontiers of the Carnatic to Sera.

5th. Wynaad: a battalion in this district will be for some. time absolutely necessary. It lies on the back of the most disaffected districts in Malabar; and our troops stationed there not only give us an opportunity of curbing the disaffected in that province, but if we don't occupy it in strength they will fly into it. An equipment and a body of troops must then be fitted out to drive them from thence.

6th. Seringapatam: till Seringapatam is repaired and its works reformed it is necessary that the guards should be very numerous, and consequently the place requires a large garrison. Besides, this garrison furnishes a detachment for the Rajah at Mysore, a guard at Cancancotta, a company for the Resident, guards for the public elephants and cattle, and constant detachments with treasure and stores to all parts. It is, however, very evident that about 400 European infantry, one company of artillery, and one complete battalion, will do the duty of Seringapatam; and those troops would be sufficient for its security if a body of troops were in the field in the Mysore country or in any of the neighbouring provinces.

In all these newly-conquered territories, where there are necessarily a number of weak garrisons, particularly in Mysore, which country is bordered by the Mahrattas, is full of Polygars, and is surrounded by provinces in which there are numbers of the same description, it is impossible to be certain of tranquillity unless there is a force which is disposable, and can be put into the field at a short notice without inconvenience or danger to the garrisons which are to be occupied permanently.

The disposable force in Mysore would be:

One regiment of dragoons; one of Native cavalry; two companies of artillery; one of European infantry, if a second regiment of European infantry can be spared; two battalions of Native infantry; and the detachments of Native infantry which might be drawn from other posts without endangering them, as there would be in that case a body of troops in the field.

I shall now state the principles upon which I have proposed the distribution of this disposable force when its services would not be required in the field.

I have proposed Sera for the dragoons, and Santa Bednore for the Native cavalry. It would be better if both could be brought nearer the frontier and both could be stationed in one place; but the neighbourhood of Chittledroog has been found unhealthy; it is not certain that water can be procured at all seasons in those districts, excepting upon the Toombuddra, and there the western rains prevail, and are very heavy. I have thought it best to divide the two regiments, because it is probable that the dragoons will soon be augmented; and in any event they will require barracks immediately, for the building of which materials must be collected. The Native cavalry will likewise require some barracks, the officers will want houses, &c., &c. If both corps are placed in one situation, it is impossible to expect to be able to provide the materials for building for both in any reasonable space of time; and I doubt whether Sera would afford water, or either of the places would afford wood and forage, for both regiments during the entire year. I have therefore thought it best that they should be separated; and I have fixed upon these situations as being the most advanced towards the frontier which have the advantages of water, forage, wood, gram, meat, and materials for building.

If the whole of the family of the late Sultaun were removed to Vellore, I should propose that the disposable European regiment should be placed at Seringapatam, as being in every respect the best situation in the Mysore country for troops, and that from which alone it has hitherto been found practicable to equip them for the field; but as until the family of Tippoo Sultaun are removed there will be a want of buildings for a second European regiment, if both are complete, it will be best to station it at Bangalore. At this place it is imagined that buildings for such a body of men can be repaired.

The whole of the artillery ought to be decidedly at Seringapatam, where the arsenal and stores are; and the two battalions of Native infantry ought to be there likewise. When their services will not be wanted in the field they will give such strength to the garrison as to make its duty easy, and the discipline of the troops can be carried on. On the other hand, if they are to take the field, they will be at the spot from whence they and all the troops must be equipped with everything.

There are now in Mysore, including Soonda and Wynaad, one regiment of dragoons, one of Native cavalry, three companies of artillery, one regiment of European infantry, and nine battalions of Native infantry, of which two belong to the Bombay establishment. One battalion, therefore, might be immediately spared for service in other parts.

I shall be obliged to you if you will let me know as soon as may be convenient whether you approve of this arrangement. My reason for wishing to have your decision soon, particularly regarding the cavalry, is, that I think I should be able to cover in the dragoons at Sera before the heavy rains, with the assistance of the Dewan in procuring materials, if I were certain that you would have a cavalry station at that place. In regard to the other parts of the disposition, they don't press so much. As, however, the service on which the troops are now employed will soon be brought to a conclusion, it is desirable, for the sake of economy, that they should not be kept in the field longer than is necessary, and I·cannot put them in garrison till I shall have your orders after receiving this letter.

I have, &c.,

ARTHUR WELLESLEY.

To the Secretary of Government, Judicial Department.   [1038.]

SIR,   25th Jan., 1802.

I enclose the Judicial Report for 1801.

This report, by which it appears that so many causes have been heard and decided, affords an ample proof of the diligence of the gentleman who has performed this laborious duty. He has already given so many proofs of his ability, his patience, and perseverance, particularly in the conduct of inquiries into affairs in which Natives are concerned, that what I can say upon those points can add but little to the impression which his Lordship must already have received of his character. It is but justice, however, to Captain Symons to take this opportunity of stating that since he has been at Seringapatam he has particularly displayed those qualities, that the confidence of all descriptions of persons in the justice and propriety of his decisions is unbounded, and that I have every reason to be satisfied with his conduct.

.   I have, &c.,

ARTHUR WELLESLEY.

[1039.]   *To Lieut.-General Stuart.*

SIR,   25th Jan., 1802.

Colonel Stevenson has transmitted to me a copy of your letter to him of the 7th instant, in which you have referred to my opinion upon many points relating to the province of Malabar.

I beg to enclose you extracts of different letters which I have written to Colonel Stevenson upon these points, which will best explain the opinions which I have already given to him.

I have never given Colonel Stevenson any decided opinion regarding his plan of having a depôt of ordnance and stores at Cannanore, because I have never received from him any positive communication of his own notions upon the subject.

Cannanore is certainly the best place to put the stores in which it may be necessary to keep in the provinces of Canara and Malabar; but as Cannanore is nearly entirely unprovided with buildings, and is not secure either on the sea or on the land side, I think that it would not be prudent to lodge a large quantity of stores in that place.

I have, &c.,

ARTHUR WELLESLEY.

[1040.]   *To Lieut.-Colonel Spry.*

DEAR SIR,   Camp at Oomatoor, 28th Jan., 1802.

I have just received a letter from Sir William Clarke, dated the 21st instant, in which he informs me that he had sent to Bombay the remainder of the 75th regiment. I therefore think it certain that the 77th regiment will not go there.

As, however, in these times it is necessary to be prepared for every event, I think that the best thing you can do is to halt where you are, till I receive the Commander-in-Chief's positive and final orders, fixing the destination of the 77th regiment. It is almost certain that that destination will not now be Bombay, and therefore there is no occasion for your being in a hurry to go down the Ghauts. On the other hand, as troops may now be expected from Egypt to the western coast, the Commander-in-Chief might wish that the 77th should remain on this side of the Ghauts. I therefore request you to halt where this will find you till you hear farther from me.

I will take care that you shall be supplied with provisions and all you can want.

Believe me, &c.,

ARTHUR WELLESLEY.

To Lieut.-General Stuart. [1041.]

SIR, Camp at Oomatoor, 28th Jan., 1802.

The 77th regiment will be in Canara to-morrow, and at Mangalore about the 2nd or 3rd of the month. Vessels can be got for them at that place to take them to Bombay, if you should think proper to order them there; but I have not desired that the vessels may be taken up, or that any expense should be incurred in preparations for the embarkation of the 77th, till I receive your further orders. It was a laborious work to open the road into Canara, which is the cause of the delay of the march of the 77th.

I am going to the northern parts of this district. The Bullum Rajah is concealed in some of the jungles in that quarter, with but few, if any followers. I leave the pioneers, &c., and a corps at work upon the Bissolee Ghaut.

I enclose you a letter which I have received from Colonel Stevenson. This officer must be well known to you, and I have no doubt that if the arrangement which he proposes should be a proper one, you will recommend it to government without the necessity of my urging it in any manner.

I am, &c.,

ARTHUR WELLESLEY.

P. S. Since writing the above I have received a letter, of

which the enclosed is an extract, from Sir William Clarke. The reason for your wishing to send the 77th regiment to Bombay does not exist at present. I conclude, therefore, that you will not be desirous to send them there. I have accordingly written to Colonel Spry to desire that they will halt at the top of the Ghaut till I receive your answer to my letter of the 18th instant. If you should desire in that letter that they should go to Bombay, I shall be certain that their services will not be required on this side of the Ghauts, and I shall send them into Canara forthwith.

[1042.]   *To J. G. Ravenshaw, Esq.*

SIR,   .   Camp at Hebsalle, 30th Jan., 1802.

I have received repeated information that the aumildar of Murdahal, by name Nunjee Riah, has given assistance to the rebel Rajah of Bullum, particularly that he had supplied him with arms and ammunition; but as this information was unsupported by any proof, I did not think it necessary to give it any further attention, or to trouble you upon it. However, it has at last appeared that he is in correspondence with the Bullum Rajah; that he has promised to afford him the means of escaping through the district under his management; and of these facts there is proof. Under these circumstances I have written to the tahsildar of Soobramany, Mudhoo Rao, to request that upon the receipt of my letter he will arrest the person of Nunjee Riah, the aumildar of Murdahal, and place the power of the district in hands more worthy of the trust until he should receive your further instructions.

I have, &c.,

ARTHUR WELLESLEY.

[1043.]   *To Sir William Clarke.*

SIR,   Camp at Aneybaloo, 31st Jan., 1802.

I have had the honour of receiving your letter of the 22nd instant, enclosing one from Captain Fisher, relative to tent lascars. I understand that an establishment of lascars has been fixed for Goa, which I conclude is intended for the care of tents as well as of every other species of military stores in the same manner as in other military stations.   If the number of lascars allotted to Goa be not sufficient for the care of the number of tents which have lately been sent there, it will be necessary to support the application for an additional number of lascars by a statement of the number of tents which they have to take care of.   When a call is made upon a commissary of stores for a larger number of tent lascars to attend tents in camp than his establishment can afford, it is usual to make application for permission to hire a certain number of additional tent lascars in order to be enabled to answer this extraordinary call; but this application must also be supported by a statement of particulars.

I have also received your letter of the 23rd instant, enclosing one from Major Gray of the 75th regiment, in which he desires that that regiment may receive field allowances on the same footing as the Bengal artillery from the 29th December; and you recommend that this application should be complied with, and that this benefit should be extended to the 84th regiment, and to the Native battalions which landed at Goa at the same time with the 75th regiment.   I shall forward these letters to be laid before the Commander-in-Chief.

An application for field allowances would have been understood; but an application for field allowances on the footing of the Bengal artillery, without stating what those allowances are, cannot be attended to.   I understand that government some time ago took into consideration the state of the troops at Goa, and the dearness of the necessaries of life, &c., at that place; but determined that those troops should receive only the same allowances with others in garrisons in other parts of the country.   The claim then of Major Gray to field allowances stands upon the ground of the orders given to him by me to prepare for field service, which orders were afterwards countermanded.

I have always been particularly desirous to avoid putting officers and soldiers to unnecessary expenses in preparations for the field; and I certainly should have avoided giving this notice to the 75th regiment, as I was aware, and I informed Lieut.-Colonel Williamson, that they would not take the field till the first week in January; only that I knew the difficulty which the public departments would find in procuring for the troops in the province of Canara the necessary equipments. However, the case of the 75th regiment is by no means a new one; it happens constantly to corps to be ordered to prepare for field service, and to have those orders recalled at the moment probably when they expected to take the field; and I know no instance of an allowance having been made by government as a compensation for the expenses incurred in the preparations.

Under these circumstances I don't think that there is any prospect whatever that the application of Major Gray will be complied with.

That which you have made for one of the Native battalions stands on the same ground with that which has been made by Major Gray for the 75th regiment.

In regard to that made for the 84th regiment and the grenadier battalion, I have only to observe that I do not conceive that government will alter the resolution to which they have already come regarding the troops at Goa, and that they will now increase their allowances.

I have, &c.,

ARTHUR WELLESLEY.

[1044.] *To J. G. Ravenshaw, Esq.*

SIR, Camp at Heeremundy, 1st Feb., 1802.

I have to acknowledge the receipt of your letter of the 28th of January.

The prisoners you mention are not yet arrived. I have not yet seen the person who gave the information regarding the aumildar of Murdahal; as soon as I shall have seen him I will send you an account of what he says. I have sent the 77th regiment to Mangalore. The transports respecting which I wrote to you will not be wanted; but I am much obliged to you for the trouble which you have taken respecting them.

The 77th regiment went down the Sampighee Ghaut, and will proceed by Murdahal, Oopermyny, and Buntwell, to Mangalore. I am at present encamped at about seven miles from the Seisu Ghaut, and at an equal distance from the Hubby Naly Ghaut.

The Bullum Rajah is supposed to be between the two, in a jungle which is surrounded by the troops of the Rajah of Mysore.   He has hitherto been able to avoid them, although they have once pushed him so hard as to have taken a Brahmin who had engaged to guide him out of the jungle, and who was with him. I go there to-morrow to see what farther steps can be taken in order to secure his person.   There are several reports in circulation of his intention to endeavour to escape disguised as a religious beggar.   It would be well if orders were given to the peons on the frontiers to stop all persons of that description, or indeed all persons entering the province of Canara from this district who should not be able to give a good account of themselves.

I have found the roads in the neighbourhood of the Ghauts and through the Ghauts to be in general paved.   As roads of this description stand the weather best, I have desired Captain Heitland, of the pioneers, not to break up the pavement, but to repair it ; to remove the large and uneven stones, and to replace them with others of a small size.   I recommend the same system to you when you will repair the roads in Canara, if they also should be already paved.

I have, &c.,

ARTHUR WELLESLEY.

To Lieutenant-Colonel Whitelocke, 77th regiment.   [1045.]

DEAR SIR,   Camp at Heeremundy, 1st Feb., 1802.

I have received a letter from the Commander-in-Chief, in which he desires me to send the 77th regiment to Goa to relieve the 75th.   However, as I think it probable that Sir William Clarke will not want the 77th, and as I deem it most necessary for them that they should have rest, I have ordered them to march to Mangalore, there to remain unless Sir William Clarke should require their services, in which case they will go to Goa.

The Commander-in-Chief has been pleased to allow me to decide the question which I referred to him regarding yourself. I certainly think that the most proper place for the Lieutenant-Colonel of a regiment is with his regiment, and if you had not before been removed from it, I should not have thought of removing you from it at present. However, as the Commander-in-Chief does not object to your being absent from your regiment, as your being in the command of Chittledroog appears agreeable to you, and as it is not inconvenient to the service, I don't propose to order that you should join your regiment.

Believe me, &c.,

ARTHUR WELLESLEY.

I have issued an order directing you to resume the command at Chittledroog.

[1046.]   *To Sir William Clarke.*

MY DEAR SIR,   Camp at Hoeremundy, 1st Feb., 1802.

I have received the orders of the Commander-in-Chief to send you the 77th regiment, which corps will be at Mangalore by the time that you will receive this letter.

It appears to me probable, however, that you will not require the services of this corps; and if that should be the case, as in the event of a general peace in Europe it is likely that all the British troops will withdraw from Goa immediately, and that the 77th will then have to return to Mangalore, it is better that they should now remain there. They went into the field in the beginning of the year 1799, and I may safely say that they have been in camp ever since, and have been more harassed than any other regiment in the service. Under these circumstances, rest is absolutely necessary to them; and of this they have no chance if they are to go to Goa now, with a probability amounting almost to a certainty of returning into Canara again before the monsoon sets in. I am, therefore, exceedingly desirous that they should remain at Mangalore.

If, however, you should think their services necessary at Goa, rest is out of the question; and you will be so kind as to write to Lieutenant-Colonel Spry, their commanding officer, stating that you want them, and he has my orders to embark immediately for Goa on transports which will have been sent from Bombay to bring them there, under the notion that you could not spare the 75th regiment.

I must inform you that the 77th regiment have not more than 350 men for duty.

Believe me, &c.,

ARTHUR WELLESLEY.

To Lieutenant-Colonel Spry.   [1047.]

DEAR SIR,   Camp at Heeremundy, 1st Feb., 1802.

I have received a letter from General Stuart, in which he desires that the 77th may go to Mangalore and there embark for Goa, on ships which he expects would be sent for them from Bombay.   He also desires that the six companies of the 75th, which he thought were still at Goa, should embark on the same ships after the 77th should have left them, and should proceed from Goa to Bombay.

When the General wrote this letter, he was aware of the peace in Europe.   However, as it is most probable that Sir William Clarke will not now want the services of another European regiment, and as to send the 77th regiment to Goa, from whence it may be necessary that they should return in a short time, will entirely defeat the object in view in sending them into quarters at all, I prefer to retain you at Mangalore for the present, and to write to Sir William Clarke to give him the option of calling for you if he should find it necessary.

You will accordingly, as soon as convenient after you will receive this letter, commence your march to Mangalore, and upon your arrival there you will occupy the cantonments which the 75th have left.   Orders will go to you this day respecting the disposal of your camp equipage, &c. &c., upon your arrival at Mangalore.

If you should receive from Sir William Clarke a letter desiring the 77th regiment may go to Goa, you will be so kind as to embark the regiment in vessels which will have been sent from Bombay for its use, and you will proceed to Goa.   If you should not receive such a requisition from Sir William Clarke, you will remain at Mangalore till I send you the Commander-in-Chief's orders subsequent to a letter which I write to him this day ; and you will detain the transports and have the regiment in readiness to embark till you receive these orders.

In my opinion, Sir William Clarke will not want your services, and the Commander-in-Chief will allow the regiment to remain at Mangalore; but it is as well to be prepared for every event. I expect that I shall be able to send you the Commander-in-Chief's final orders before you will have been many days at Mangalore.

Believe me, &c.,

ARTHUR WELLESLEY.

[1048.]   *To Lieutenant-General Stuart.*

SIR,   Camp at Heeremundy, 1st Feb., 1802.

I have had the honour of receiving your letter of the 26th January. Lieutenant-Colonel Spry had got down the Ghaut before he received my orders to halt at the top of it. I shall not want the 77th regiment in the Bullum country, and upon the receipt of your letter of the 26th January I have ordered them to proceed immediately to Mangalore, to be prepared to embark for Goa as soon as Sir William Clarke will send a requisition for them. It is more than probable that Sir William Clarke will not require their services, and indeed that their arrival at Goa at this moment, when the intelligence of a general peace may be expected, may embarrass him. However, upon this point he is the best judge, and I have apprised him that the corps is ready at Mangalore to proceed to Goa if he should want it.

The 77th have been so much harassed, and quarters of refreshment are so necessary to them, that I shall deem it fortunate for them if Sir William Clarke should not want them. If he should call for them, it is probable that in a few weeks he will have to send them and all the troops back again; and the rest and refreshment which are so necessary to them will be so far delayed. Mangalore appears in every respect the best situation for this corps for some time, and if Sir William Clarke does not want them, and you approve of it, they shall remain there.

I am infinitely sensible of the confidence you are pleased to

place in me, which it shall be my constant endeavour to deserve.
I certainly think that a Lieutenant-Colonel of a regiment is in
his proper place at the head of his regiment; but as you inform
me that it is probable that Colonel Stevenson will be removed to
the command of the subsidiary force at Hyderabad, I rather
believe it will be more convenient to the public service that
Lieutenant-Colonel Whitelocke should remain at Chittledroog
than that he should go into Canara, and accordingly I shall
leave him there.

The province of Malabar will become exceedingly interesting
upon the conclusion of the peace and the readmission of the
French and Dutch to their settlements upon the coast.

I will pay the greatest attention not only to the distribution
of the troops in that province and in Canara, and to placing
the command in proper hands, but to everything which relates
to it.

I have, &c.,

ARTHUR WELLESLEY.

To Lieutenant-General Stuart.   [1049.]

SIR,   Camp, 2nd Feb., 1802.

I have had the honour of receiving your letters of the 27th
January. I am glad to find that the arrangement which I
have made for the 77th regiment, and which I communicated
to you in my letter of yesterday, has met with your approbation.

I have perused the paper to which you allude regarding
Seringapatam, and which has been laid before the Governor-
General. At that time I made a memorandum of my sentiments upon the subject, for which I have sent to Seringapatam,
and which I expect to-morrow or next day, and I will then
give you my sentiments upon this subject in detail. In the
mean time I beg to assure you that I agree entirely in the
sentiments which you have communicated to me in your letter
of the 27th January; and I am convinced that a nearer view
and better knowledge of the advantages and resources of Seringapatam would alter the opinion of the person who wrote the
paper in question.

There is no doubt whatever but that the greater experience which we now have of the climate, and the improvements which have consequently been made in the buildings occupied by the officers and troops, but particularly in those occupied by the latter, have made Seringapatam a more healthy place than it was, and probably as healthy a place for European troops as any other on the coast. It has not been possible hitherto to accommodate the Native troops so well as the Europeans. Indeed, knowing the respect which is paid to the opinion of Mr. Webbe, and which it so well deserves, I have been cautious in proposing any improvements but what might appear absolutely necessary. Accordingly the Native troops are far more unhealthy than the Europeans.

In regard to the fortifications of Seringapatam I must observe that time and the weather have been very destructive to them. The British army laid open a great part of the place, and the effects of its fire were felt in almost all parts of it. No repairs have been given to the works; the rain, consequently, has penetrated into the ramparts and has done them considerable injury. I believe, however, that Seringapatam can still be put in a complete state at an expense two-thirds less than that estimated by General Ross. But, if it be necessary (which it appears to me to be), or even desirable, to keep up Seringapatam, I can't imagine that the finances of the India Company are in such a state as that the expenditure of one lac of pagodas more or less ought to induce the government to forego the execution of so useful a project, and to prefer another only because it may be cheaper. In this reasoning I don't mean to insinuate that the repair of Seringapatam will cost more than the repair of Bangalore, and the construction of the buildings at the latter which the former has already. On the contrary, I am convinced it will cost less; but I urge this reasoning merely to show the propriety of putting the consideration of the expense for a moment out of the question, when it is so important to consider in what situation the depôt of stores, &c. &c., for the western provinces, Mysore, and the northern frontier, is to be placed?

I have, &c.,

ARTHUR WELLESLEY.

To Lieutenant-Colonel Monypenny.   [1050.]

MY DEAR COLONEL,   Camp at Heeremundy, 2nd Feb., 1802.

I yesterday received your letter of the 25th January. Between ourselves it is perfectly true that the 77th regiment were to have gone to Bombay, and in that case I had determined that the command at Chittledroog should be vacant. Sir William Clarke, however, found that he could spare the 75th regiment to the Presidency of Bombay without risking his charge, and the consequence is that I have sent the 77th regiment to Mangalore.

General Stuart was pleased to allow me to decide whether Lieutenant-Colonel Whitelocke should remain with his regiment or should return to Chittledroog. Between ourselves again I am about to state to you the reason for which I ordered yesterday, before I received your letter, that he should resume his command.

The General, in a letter which I received from him yesterday, informed me of the probability that Colonel Stevenson would be removed from the command in Malabar and Canara to Hyderabad, and he desired me to be prepared accordingly. I conceived that I could not be worse prepared for this event than by having the commanding officer of Chittledroog the senior officer in those provinces, and I therefore sent him back to his old station.

Having thus pointed out to you the circumstances which at present prevent my making the arrangement which you wish for, I must inform you that had the command been vacant I should have found it difficult to remove your regiment to Chittledroog. I have lately written to General Stuart to recommend a permanent distribution of the troops in Mysore, and I strongly urged the propriety of not putting a regiment at the Droog. My reasons are numerous; but the principal of them are its entire want of accommodations for a regiment, its want of supplies, means, &c. &c. I know that the 73rd would be healthy anywhere, and I rather believe that good buildings would bring good health with them. But I should have found it a difficult task to propose now to the General that a regiment of Europeans should be placed at Chittledroog when about a week ago I wrote to him to object to it.

I have asked the General for another regiment of Europeans, and I have proposed to him that they should be at Bangalore. The situation is in every respect an eligible one, and I need not assure you that I should be happy to see you in the command of it.

I rather wish that what I have above written to you should be between ourselves. You will be able, however, to find out from your friends at Madras whether the General will give me another regiment; I will let you know whether he adopts the proposal of placing it at Bangalore; and if he do, I think we can contrive to have the choice fixed upon the 73rd.

Believe me, &c.,

ARTHUR WELLESLEY.

[1051.]   *To Josiah Webbe, Esq.*

MY DEAR WEBBE,   Camp, 2nd Feb., 1802.

Since I wrote to you last the pursuit of the Bullum Rajah has been continued till he has been driven quite into the Ghauts, with about half a dozen followers. The Rajah's troops are in possession of all the villages in the neighbourhood of the jungles in which the Bullum Rajah is supposed to be, so that unless he is favoured and assisted by the Canara aumildars he must starve. We have caught many of his principal people and relations, some of whom must, I imagine, be executed; and Purneah has collected in this camp the patels of the different villages to the number, he says, of 250.

The Sampighee Ghaut is opened, and the Company's pioneers and a Native corps and some of the Rajah's bildars are employed upon the Bissolee or Soobramany Ghaut. I am now in the neighbourhood of two other Ghauts, the Hubby Nala and the Seisul Ghaut, which I propose also to open.

The country is settling fast; the inhabitants are in their villages, and have made some progress in dismantling them. They have likewise delivered in some of their arms and ammunition. Purneah has assembled the gours here in order to complete the settlement, that they may witness the execution of some of the Bullum Rajah's adherents who have been caught, and that he may secure the persons of some who, it might be expected, would renew the rebellion if the force in the country should be weakened.   He talks with confidence of getting from them the revenue of the two last years.

Although we still continue the pursuit of the Rajah, I am not very sanguine in my expectations of success.   The whole of the western face of the Ghauts, from Soopah to Palghaut-cherry, is covered with a thick short jungle, which appears impenetrable, and we have no intelligence to what quarter he is gone.   All the villages in the country, particularly those in the neighbourhood of the Ghauts, are held by the Rajah's troops, who are at the same time kept in motion both in the upper country and in Canara; but it is very evident to me that if he can get food he will remain in those jungles to all eternity, notwithstanding our efforts to catch him, or drive him out, unless some of his few people should quit him and give us intelligence of the exact spot in which we may find him.

These efforts, however, shall be continued, and everything shall be done which I can devise to bring the business to that best of all conclusions.   In the mean time, I have strongly urged Purneah to insist upon the performance of all the terms of the cowle as a certain mode of keeping the country quiet, whether the Rajah is caught or not.   I don't think that I ever saw a country naturally so strong as this is, and to the strength of which so many additions have been made by the natives themselves. Every village is a strong fortification, of which it would require good troops to get possession; and in some cases ten or a dozen of these villages are connected by natural or made defences of great strength.   Within these defences the inhabitants have all that they want; and here they would hold out for ever against the troops which the aumildars might bring to force them to pay the revenue.   The only mode, therefore, of settling the country permanently, even supposing the Rajah should be caught, is to destroy its strength and to force the inhabitants to give up their arms.

I shall be glad to hear the result of Malcolm's mission.   I think Lord Clive will stay.

Believe me, &c.,

ARTHUR WELLESLEY.

[1052.]   *To J. G. Ravenshaw, Esq.*

SIR,   **Camp, 3rd Feb., 1802.**

I have the honour to enclose a statement of the facts which
are the result of the examination of the persons against Nunjee
Riah, the late aumildar of Murdahal. In my opinion the best
thing to do with him is to send him to the army, where I will
try him by military process as a rebel, under the authority which
I hold from government for that purpose.

Chinna Gour and Soman Gour, the two persons mentioned
in the enclosed paper, are the principal causes of the rebellion,
and are men of considerable weight in this country. They are
both in Canara at this moment.

I have, &c.,

ARTHUR WELLESLEY.

[ENCLOSURE IN THE HAND-WRITING OF COLONEL WELLESLEY.]

Facts against Nunjee Riah, Aumildar of Murdahal.

Two of the gours of the Bullum district, by name Chinna
Gour and Soman Gour, who have fled with the Rajah, and
are particularly attached to the rebel cause, desired Soobiah,
a Brahmin who was in their company at Hubby Nala, to write a
letter to Nunjee Riah, the aumildar of Murdahal. Soobiah did
write this letter, and desired Nookinjee Daira to take and
deliver it to Ninnanah at Seravy, and to desire Ninnanah to
carry and deliver it to Nunjee Riah at Murdahal.

Nookinjee Daira took the letter and gave it to Ninnanah,
who delivered it to Nunjee Riah, as desired. Nunjee Riah
gave no written answer, but desired Ninnanah to allow a
Brahmin by name Soobiah to pass if he should come into his
district.

Ninnanah says that, after delivering the letter, he saw
Soobiah at a village called Nairunhy, in the Murdahal talook ;
that he told Soobiah of the orders he had received to allow
him to pass, and that Soobiah consequently went on to Murdahal.

To Josiah Webbe, Esq.   [1053.]

MY DEAR WEBBE,   Camp, 3rd Feb., 1802.

I have this instant received your letter of the 29th January.

It is much better that you should delay to meet the Dewan for some time than that you should at the present moment draw him away from this country. Everything depends upon his completing the settlement himself, and if he goes away the whole will be at a stand.

I hope this letter will reach you before you will have written to Piele to propose the meeting at Bangalore.

If, however, you should write to Piele upon the subject, I will request him to defer making the proposition to Purneah until I shall have received your answer to this letter. I think Purneah will be at liberty to meet you at Bangalore towards the end of March.

Believe me, &c.,

ARTHUR WELLESLEY.

To Lieutenant-General Stuart.   [1054.]

SIR,   Camp, 5th Feb., 1802.

I have the honour to enclose a memorandum upon the subject treated of in your letter of the 27th of January.

This memorandum was written in the month of July last, and I never intended to communicate it to anybody in its present form. I thought it probable that before the Governor-General should order the destruction of the fort of Seringapatam, he would require from me my sentiments upon Mr. Webbe's memorandum, and I wrote them at the time of perusing it, intending to put them in the form of a letter when I should be called upon for them. However, I think it better to send you this paper, with this explanation, than to delay it in order to make any alteration whatever.

I beg to observe that the more I consider the subject, the more convinced I am of the utility of Seringapatam.

Upon a subject of this kind, in my opinion, we ought to take into consideration every event at all within the verge of probability. We have seen the French navies contend with those of

Great Britain; and an opinion has frequently been advanced by those who are in the habit of considering these questions, that during this war the navy of France would have been as formidable as her army if it had not been for the Continental contest, which rendered the land service more necessary to her. It is not then absolutely impossible for France and her allies or dependents to have a formidable navy.

If she should in a future war have a navy in this country equal to contend with that of Great Britain, upon what will the power of the Company in the Peninsula depend? Not upon Fort St. George, or any place upon the coast, because those places will follow the fate of the fleet, whatever that is; but upon the stability of the power and resources of the Company in the inland country.

As I have pointed out in the enclosed memorandum, there is no place which gives such power or has such resources as Seringapatam, and which, in case of such an event as that which I have in contemplation, would be so capable of keeping in awe the Native powers, or of affording a foundation on which the edifice of the Company's power in the Peninsula might be raised again, and their affairs retrieved.

In addition to the 27th paragraph of the enclosed memorandum, I have to observe that, considering the manner in which the troops in general are necessarily posted in India in times of peace, to place the great depôt of stores at Chittledroog, or in any very advanced situation, might be either unsafe, or that depôt might be useless to the troops.

When hostilities should become necessary on the northern frontier, a length of time must elapse before a body of troops could be collected; and till they were collected, unless there were a large garrison in Chittledroog (a much larger garrison than Seringapatam would require under any circumstances whatever), the depôt of stores would be in danger.

The enemy would be at all times nearer to this depôt than the great body of our army, and before a body could be collected to be opposed to him, he would place himself between us and our stores. Our army consequently, which would be intended for operations on the northern frontier, and for the use of which this depôt at Chittledroog would have been formed, would have to be equipped from some other place, which would of course be Madras. Thus the depôt at Chittledroog would be rendered entirely useless, and the operations of the army would be stopped for months.

I have, &c.,

ARTHUR WELLESLEY.

To Lieutenant-Colonel Maxwell.   [1055.]

MY DEAR COLONEL,   Camp, 7th Feb., 1802.

West has communicated to me your letter of the 6th instant. The day on which I refused Major ———— leave to be absent from the 19th dragoons longer than till the 1st of February, (because, in the first place, I did not think the service on which the troops were employed so far advanced as to permit me to allow any officer to go away, and, in the next place, because the sanction of the Commander-in-Chief was necessary for the absence of an officer beyond the returns), was the 23rd of January, and not the 24th the day on which Major ———— wrote to Lieutenant-Colonel Robertson to ask for the leave of the Commander-in-Chief, after he had received my refusal. Nay, Major ———— went further; he said that neither Lieutenant-Colonel Macalister nor I had any objection to his being absent, although he knew that, on the day before he wrote, I had expressed my disapprobation of such applications, and my objection to complying with them till I should see more clearly the end of the service on which we were employed.

These circumstances give occasion to my making to you a remark which has frequently occurred to me regarding Major ————. It is, that he has no scruple whatever of doing himself those things which, if they were done by officers under his command, would most justly excite his utmost indignation, and would occasion his making a complaint of their conduct to their superiors. I ought consequently to do that which Major ———— would do under similar circumstances to an officer under his command, viz. to refuse him leave of absence, and to lay his conduct before the Commander-in-Chief. But as he and I will most probably not be much longer together, and as he has a wife and a family (who in my eyes cover a multitude of sins, &c.), whom I should not wish to distress by keeping him away from them one moment longer than the service really requires it, I beg that you will inform him that he shall quit the 19th dragoons as soon as I shall receive from him the regular application for leave of absence, with which application I shall recommend a compliance at head-quarters.

I authorise you to communicate this letter to Major ———.

Believe me, &c.,

ARTHUR WELLESLEY.

I shall write to you to-morrow upon another subject.

[1056.]   *To Josiah Webbe, Esq.*

MY DEAR WEBBE,   Camp, 7th Feb., 1802.

One of the principal gours of this country, a man who has been a great cause of the rebellion, was brought in last night; there is still another who has not been brought in yet, whom we expect to get to-morrow, and we hope to have from him such intelligence of the Rajah's motions as will enable us to take him. In the mean time the cutting of the jungles and the opening of the villages go on. We have opened the Seisul Ghaut into Canara.

I think that I shall break up in a few days. My intention is to leave in this country a small light detachment with the pioneers and bildars. They shall move about from place to place, and assist the inhabitants in dismantling their fortifications. A small detachment with two guns shall encamp in the neighbourhood of Bailoor, in order to give countenance to Purneah's operations in that district, and I shall leave a party with guns upon the heights above Arrekeery.

The Europeans, &c., shall go back to Seringapatam.

In the course of a short time the whole may be drawn off excepting the light detachment, which I think ought to remain in the district till the rains. Indeed, if we can get cover for them, I think that they ought to remain in this neighbourhood during the rains.

Purneah has ordered that the plan which I recommended to him in this district should be carried into execution in the neighbouring districts of Bailoor, Oostara, and Maharaj Droog, in which the fortifications are as strong and as numerous, and the people as well inclined to make use of them against the government, as in this country. The destruction of them has, however, been commenced, and the detachment which I propose to have at Bailoor will accelerate the work, at the same time that it will be able to move to the assistance of the light detachment in Bullum if that should be necessary, which I am convinced it will not. Purneah proposes to remain in the country for another month after the troops will have quitted it.

Believe me, &c.,
ARTHUR WELLESLEY.

To Major Munro.   [1057.]

MY DEAR MUNRO,   Camp at Ongahully, 8th Feb., 1802.

You will have heard that I have been for this last month employed in the Bullum country. Matters here have gone on much to my satisfaction, and I think that in a few days I shall be able to break up the army.

I have not caught the Rajah, and I have just heard that he has left the country, and has fled with an intention of going through the Rydroog district, across the Toombuddra, into the Solapoor country.

I know that his family is with the Solapoor Polygar, and though I am not quite certain that he has left Bullum, it is so probable that he will endeavour to reach his family, that I am induced to request that you will give orders to your aumildars in the Rydroog and Bellary districts, and those bordering upon Sondoor, to be very particular in their examination of all strangers passing to the northward. I am informed that the Rajah had only a handkerchief on his head and short drawers on his *breech*, and he had with him when he went away three people, viz. Kistnaig (the brother of his wife in Solapoor), Timnirah, and Nairnah, two Brahmins. I have sent for a particular description of the Rajah, and of the three people who went with him : if it comes before the post goes out, you shall have it with this letter ; if not, I'll send it to you to-morrow.

Believe me, &c.,
ARTHUR WELLESLEY.

To Lieutenant-General Stuart.   [1058.]

SIR,   Camp, 8th Feb., 1802.

In obedience to your orders I proceed to state my opinion of the force required for the provinces of Malabar and Canara, and of the distribution of that force.

F 2

There ought to be in Canara one European regiment and three battalions of Native infantry, if the British troops should be withdrawn from Goa; if they should remain at Goa, one regiment and two battalions will be sufficient for the service in Canara. One regiment and one battalion ought to be stationed at Mangalore to furnish the detachments in the southern part of the province; one battalion at Cundapoor. If the British troops are withdrawn from Goa, there ought to be a battalion at Seedasheeghur.

The province of Malabar, exclusive of Wynaad, for which provision has been made in the distribution for Mysore, ought to have one regiment of Europeans, five battalions of Native infantry, and three companies of artillery, from which detachments might be furnished to Canara; five companies of Europeans and one battalion of Natives at Cochin, till the Dutch shall occupy that place; one battalion of Natives at Angarypur; one battalion at Calicut; one battalion at Montana; five companies of Europeans, and one battalion of Native infantry, and three companies of artillery at Cannanore. When the Dutch will occupy Cochin and the French Mahé, the whole European regiments should be collected at Cannanore. The battalion at Cochin ought likewise to be removed thither; and a strong detachment from that place ought to occupy Tellicherry.

Till the Pyche Rajah is taken, or till the new system of civil administration has had time to settle, it will be proper, in my opinion, to retain in the service the battalions of Nair, Tier, and Moplah sebundies, and they might remain in their present stations, viz. the Nair sebundies in the southward low districts, the Tier sebundies at Cotaparamba, the Moplah sebundies at Pyche. Many detachments are required from the corps stationed in Malabar, but it will be easy to furnish them all, and to have a small force disposable at Cannanore.

Having thus detailed the distribution of the troops which in my opinion ought to be made in the provinces of Canara and Malabar, I have to observe that there are troops sufficient for it even if the British troops remain at Goa. If they should be withdrawn from Goa, there will be one Native battalion and two companies of artillery (one of Bombay, the other of Bengal artillery) above the number required. The European regiments, the 77th or the 84th, may then be moved into

Mysore, and will make the number of that description of troops required in this country.

I have, &c.,

ARTHUR WELLESLEY.

To Lieutenant-Colonel Maxwell.   [1059.]

MY DEAR COLONEL,   Camp at Ongahully, 9th Feb., 1802.

I should have written to you yesterday, according to the intention which I announced to you in my letter of the day before, only that we marched, and we were prevented from quitting our old ground till so late in the morning on account of the thickest fog I have ever seen, that we did not reach this place till it was late.

I have received an answer from the Commander-in-Chief relative to my proposition to canton the 19th dragoons at Sera ; and he has consented to that arrangement. I propose therefore to order you to march to that place as soon as I shall have seen the regiment. This I expect will be in the course of very few days. I do not believe, however, that the regiment will remain at Sera for any great length of time. The general distribution of the army which will be made at the conclusion of the peace will alter present arrangements in a great degree, and the consequent introduction of the French into the Peninsula may render it necessary to move the 19th dragoons from the Mysore country entirely. However, as long as you remain in this country, and as it is possible to keep the regiment in cantonments, you will be at Sera.

I shall make arrangements immediately for building barracks for your men ; and when I order you to Sera, I propose to appoint you to the command of that station.

Yours most faithfully,

ARTHUR WELLESLEY.

To W. H. Gordon, Esq.   [1060.]

DEAR GORDON,   Camp at Ongahully, 9th Feb., 1802.

I am induced to believe, from the tenor of the letters which I have received lately from Madras, that Seringapatam will at last be made as useful to the service as I have long wished to see it, and to the degree of which I know it is capable. I am sorry to find, however, that under present arrangements its resources, so far from being equal to answer the increased demands which will be made upon the stores of that place from all parts, have not been able to supply the limited demand of the last year, and that some articles in particular, of which I know there is no want, have not been supplied, although the indents for them have been made and passed nearly a year ago.

It is not my wish to interfere in the office of any gentleman; but you will not be surprised at my declaring my determination that the service shall go on. Accordingly if I find that under existing arrangements the supplies of the articles which will be required from Seringapatam are not equal to the demand or to the capabilities of the place, I shall be under the necessity of recommending the adoption of some other mode of furnishing them, either that of holding out the articles for contract, or some other mode.

You will readily believe that I shall be sorry to interfere in your office to your disadvantage, and I hope that you will be able to make arrangements to supply the articles which are required from you with more celerity, which will preclude the necessity of all interference; but if that be not done, we must try some mode which will procure readily, and at a cheap rate, the resources of the Mysore country for the service.

I hope to be at Seringapatam in a few days.

Believe me, &c.,

ARTHUR WELLESLEY.

[1061.]   *To Lieutenant-General Stuart.*

SIR,   Camp, 9th Feb., 1802.

I send you this day the proposed distribution of the troops in Malabar and Canara. As the 77th regiment had marched to Mangalore before I received your letter of the 1st instant, and as the Mysore country is in complete tranquillity, I have thought it better to leave that corps in Canara, where an European regiment is wanted. Hereafter if the British troops evacuate Goa, either the 84th or the 77th may come to the Mysore country.

I have informed you that I had desired Lieutenant-Colonel ————— to resume the command at Chittledroog. I observe that in his letter to you of the 26th January he says that he had learned from me that the 77th regiment was to proceed to Bombay. When I had referred for your consideration a proposition to retain the 77th regiment in Canara on the 18th January, and had not received your answer to it, it would have been improper to inform any person that you intended to send the 77th regiment to Bombay, and accordingly I did not mention it to anybody. Lieutenant-Colonel ————— informed me that he had received a letter from a person at Madras stating that the regiment was to go to Bombay, and I then told him that you had expressed such an intention, but that you would probably alter it upon receiving farther information. I mention this lest you should imagine that I had been the occasion of your being troubled with an application from Lieutenant-Colonel —————.

The person in whose hands I should wish to see the command in Malabar is Lieutenant-Colonel Montresor, of whose abilities, discretion, and activity I have a high opinion. He is, however, in Egypt, and some time will probably elapse before he will return. I therefore request more time to consider this subject. The officer on whom the command will devolve when Colonel Stevenson quits Malabar is Lieutenant-Colonel Boles, who, I have no doubt, will conduct matters well till some person can be permanently appointed.

I should recommend that the province of Malabar may be an entirely separate command; it is fully enough to occupy the attention of any one man, and will be more interesting when the French and Dutch return to their settlements. No additional expense would be incurred by this arrangement, as the troops in Canara might report directly to the commanding officer in Mysore. Indeed, the communication between Seringapatam and all parts of Canara is so much shorter than between Cannanore and the same places, that this arrangement would be a more convenient one in every respect. Notwithstanding that Colonel Stevenson commanded in both provinces, I was under the necessity, in all the late arrangements for reinforcing Goa, of communicating directly with the commanding officers of corps in Canara.

I will have the honour of submitting to you a proposition for the depôt at Cannanore according to the plan stated in your letter of the 2nd instant, which I think will answer perfectly. I propose to meet Colonel Stevenson at Seringapatam to converse with him upon this and other subjects relative to Malabar, as I shall be able to break up from this country in the course of a few days.

I have written orders to stop the recruiting of the sebundies in Malabar. I am in constant communication with the collector, Major Macleod; and as soon as I receive from him such intelligence as to induce me to believe that his settlement is secure, I will submit to you a proposition to disband the troops.

I have already had a conversation with the Dewan respecting the buildings which will be required at Sera for the 19th dragoons, and I find that temporary buildings can be erected there for them at a small expense.

When I shall break up this detachment, I shall have the honour of submitting to you the detail of the distribution for this country of which you have approved.

I have, &c.,

ARTHUR WELLESLEY.

[1062.]   *To Lieutenant-Colonel ————.*

DEAR SIR,   Camp, 9th Feb., 1802.

The Commander-in-Chief has been pleased to send me your letter to him of the 26th January, in which I observe the following paragraph: "I have learnt, Sir, with concern, from Colonel Wellesley, that the 77th regiment is to proceed, immediately after this service is over, to Bombay."

I beg to recall to your recollection that in the conversation which I had with you upon this subject on the 25th or 26th of January, you informed me that you had received the intelligence above mentioned from "a person at the elbow of the Commander-in-Chief," and that I then informed you that the Commander-in-Chief had had such an intention regarding the 77th regiment, but that I thought it probable he would alter it when he should receive further information.

It would have been extremely improper if I had made known the intentions of the Commander-in-Chief, which I thought it probable he would alter upon receiving further information; and accordingly you will recollect my observation that I had received those his orders on the 18th of January, but that, in consequence of the reference which I had made to him upon them, I had not made them public.

In my own justification I have apprised the Commander-in-Chief of these circumstances.

Yours faithfully,

ARTHUR WELLESLEY.

* * *

To Colonel Stevenson.   [1063.]

MY DEAR COLONEL,   Camp, 9th Feb., 1802.

I desired Barclay, about a week ago, to inform you that you were to be appointed to command at Hyderabad ; he forgot it, however, and I conclude that before you will have received this letter you will have heard that you are appointed. I congratulate you upon this appointment most sincerely ; and I approve entirely of the sentiments regarding your situation which you have expressed in your letter of the 3rd, which I have just received. I conclude that you will soon begin your journey to your new situation. Affairs in this country are in such a state that I propose to break up almost immediately, and I mean to meet you at Seringapatam. I defer till then to deliver any opinion upon your proposed depôt at Cannanore and Tellicherry : I shall take that opportunity of talking to you upon that subject and others relative to Malabar.

I agree in opinion with you regarding the proscribed prisoners mentioned in your letter of the 3rd. They ought certainly to suffer if they have failed to perform the conditions on which they asked to have their pardon.

Malabar will become very interesting indeed now. Lieutenant-Colonel Boles, being the officer next to you in rank, should be called to Cannanore as soon as possible ; and I shall be obliged to you if you will make known to him your plans and intentions on all points.

Before you go away, I wish that you would have a conference with Mr. Williams respecting a communication between Tellicherry and Calicut without passing through the French territory. It is not probable that the French and we may be upon such bad terms as that they will refuse us a passage; but it is as well to be prepared for every event. Accordingly I shall be obliged to you if you will desire Mr. Williams to make this road, and tell him to recollect that it may be necessary to use it during the monsoon.

In a letter which I have received from General Stuart he desires me to remove our own English ordnance and stores from Cochin. This ought to be done directly; and I beg that you will give orders that they may be removed to Cannanore without loss of time.

Let me hear from you when you start, and whether you will want any assistance on the road.

Believe me, &c.,

ARTHUR WELLESLEY.

[1064.]   *To Josiah Webbe, Esq.*

MY DEAR WEBBE,   Camp at Ongahully, 9th Feb., 1802.

I have the pleasure to inform you that we have taken the Rajah of Bullum. A near relation of his gave himself up the night before last, and informed us that the Rajah had gone off towards Rydroog and the Solapoor country about five days ago. We immediately sent off descriptions of him and his four followers to Munro, and all the aumildars in the Mysore country, and continued our measures still in this country. I imagine that this relation was sent in either to induce us to stop our search here, or to make us believe that the Rajah was gone so far that the pursuit of him was hopeless, and that, with the hope that this plan had succeeded, he was going off. He was taken by a party of the Rajah of Mysore's horse on the borders of the jungle.

Believe me, &c.,

ARTHUR WELLESLEY.

[1065.]   *To Purneah.*

10th Feb., 1802.

1. I am about to withdraw from this country with some of the troops, and I proceed now to give you an account of the troops which I shall leave in this country for the present, and to make you acquainted with the orders which I have given them.

2. The officer who will command the troops in the Bullum district is Captain M'Farlane. He will remain with a detachment and the body of pioneers and bildars now at work at the Seisul Ghaut, till the post there is completed.

3. He will then proceed with these pioneers and bildars to lay open the villages the names of which are in the margin,* and in the course of his performance of this service he will join himself with the other pioneers and bildars now at work on the Bissolee Ghaut.

4. I have directed him, in case of the appearance of disturbance or of opposition to your aumildars in any part of the country, to proceed to such part immediately with all his troops, and to adopt the most prompt and the most vigorous measures to punish those who may be guilty of it.

5. The party of troops, of pioneers, and of bildars, now at work upon the Bissolee Ghaut, have orders to construct a post there, and to finish that post which has been commenced at the top of the Sampighee Ghaut.

6. These posts, and that at the top of the Seisul Ghaut, will be given over to your troops as soon as they are finished.

When these posts at Bissolee and upon the top of the Sampighee Ghaut are finished, the great body of the pioneers and bildars will join Captain M'Farlane's detachment and the pioneers and bildars now employed on the Seisul Ghaut, and the whole will proceed together to perform the work above mentioned of opening the villages and levelling the ditches which surround them.

* *West of Munserabad.*

| Higgiddy. | Koommariny. | Karminny. |

North of Munserabad.

Treepoor.	Haanbaar.
Bannacull.	Bemblie.
Moorgirrah.	Ongahully.
Kissa-Kollaloo.	Hebsalle.

South of Munserabad.

Arrekeery.	Camun Hully.
Koodringee.	Niddle Hully.
Ibberee.	Ey Goor.
Coormatoor.	Troommatoor.
Sodleghee.	Kerroorie.
Turrikerra.	Mangle.
Bakir Hully.	Hirsegall.

7. I recommend that you should leave with the pioneers the bildars who have been with them hitherto, viz. 450 with the party employed at Bissolee, and 200 with the party employed at the Seisul Ghaut. I have given orders that all the doolies which are not essentially necessary for carrying away the sick and wounded from Arrekeery should be sent into Munserabad, and given in charge to the killadar there, and that the dooly boys of those doolies should likewise be given over to his charge. I have left all the tools with Captain M'Farlane, and I recommend that you should add these dooly boys to the number of workmen now employed under that officer.

As soon as the work in this country will be finished, they can take the Company's doolies from Munserabad to Seringapatam, which I beg you to order.

8. In addition to the troops above mentioned, I leave a detachment and two guns upon Beemanara Hill. I have desired, however, that, after a certain time, if matters should be quiet in this country, this detachment should withdraw; and I beg that you will be so kind as to give orders that a body of the Rajah's infantry should be in readiness to take up this post as soon as they will withdraw from it.

Our troops will not quit it till yours are in it.

9. As you have given orders that certain arrangements should be made in the districts of Oostara, Bailoor, and Maharaj Droog, which will tend eventually to the establishment and preservation of the peace in those districts and in Bullum, I have given orders that a detachment of the Company's troops and two guns should encamp at Bailoor. My object in this is that they should be prepared to enforce obedience to your orders in those districts if any person should presume to doubt respecting carrying them into execution; and at the same time that this detachment should be in readiness to move to the assistance of Captain M'Farlane in case that should be necessary, which I imagine it will not.

I have to request that you will desire the aumildars and the officers of the Rajah's service in charge of his troops to communicate constantly with Captain M'Farlane, with the officer who will command the camp at Bailoor, and with all the officers of the British troops in charge of posts or detachments. Desire the aumildars not to fail to give the most speedy intelligence of

everything that occurs to Captain M'Farlane, particularly of
any expected disturbance.

Having now detailed to you the arrangements which I have
made of the Company's troops, and the orders which I have
given them, I proceed to point out what I think you had best
do with the Rajah's troops in this country.

In my opinion it will be proper that for some time some of
the Rajah's troops should remain in every village, at least until
the inhabitants shall have cut the hedges and levelled the
ditches which surround them.   Afterwards they may by degrees
be withdrawn from the smaller villages; but there ought to
be detachments in those whose names are in the margin during
the rains.* Besides this, there ought to be a post on Beemanara Hill, and one at the top of the Bissolee, the Sampighee,
and the Seisul Ghauts.

In order to support and give strength and confidence to these
small, dispersed parties, there ought to be a party of 500 of
your best infantry collected in one body under an active sirdar.
He should keep in motion from place to place, in communication with, but at a distance from, Captain M'Farlane's party;
and as soon as he should hear of any disturbance anywhere, he
ought to fly to that place.

The remainder of the troops might withdraw.

In sundry conversations and by letter I have pointed out to
you frequently the mode which in my opinion ought to be
adopted to bring this country to a regular state of subjection
to your government.   The fortifications of the villages must be
destroyed, or an army will be required to collect the revenue,
and you must make the people give up their arms.   Orders are
given to the Company's officers and pioneers to destroy the
fortifications of the villages effectually.   The next business will
be to prevent the people from constructing them again.

For this you have nothing to depend upon but the vigilance
and the activity of the person whom you leave here as aumildar.
He ought to be particularly instructed upon this subject.   In
those villages in which your troops will be stationed he cannot
fail to obtain a knowledge of it, in case any designs should be
entertained which may be injurious to your authority; but he

* Ongahully.   Hutty Hilly.
  Bannacull.   Hongraloo.
  Ey Goor.

should endeavour to establish a channel of intelligence from every part of the country. As soon as he hears of any design of that kind he should proceed immediately to the place himself with the utmost celerity, and punish the guilty with the rigour which they will deserve. On these occasions everything will depend upon his activity, and he cannot be too quick.

When the rains will be over, it may be expected that some of the trees which we shall have cut down will have grown again. The aumildar, or some person immediately under him, ought to force the inhabitants to cut them again, and he ought not to withdraw his troops from the village till the roads to it are laid open, and in the state in which we shall now leave them. I need not point out to you the necessity that there is that the person to whom you will give charge of this district should be one of sound discretion, in whom you can place the utmost confidence. It is absolutely necessary that he should possess your confidence and have your full support in all he does, and that he should understand clearly that he is certain of remaining in his situation as long as he conducts himself well.

In case, notwithstanding all our exertions and precautions, there should be disturbance in this country again, and the communication should be cut off between the Mysore country and the posts upon the Bissolee, the Sampighee, and the Seisul Ghauts, I write to the Company's officers in Canara to desire that they will take care to keep them supplied with provisions and everything they can want. Those posts, therefore, must be kept at all events.

I have, &c.,

ARTHUR WELLESLEY.

[1066.]   INSTRUCTIONS FOR CAPTAIN HEITLAND.

10th Feb., 1802.

As soon as he will have finished the work on the Bissolee Ghaut according to former instructions, he is to construct a small post on the top of it. He is then to proceed to the Sampighee Ghaut, and finish the post of which he made a commencement at the top of it.

Afterwards he will proceed to level the ditches at the villages mentioned in the margin, and to cut broadways into them through the jungle. The roots of the trees on the roads which he will open into these villages must be taken up.

Captain M'Farlane is left in command of the troops in the Bullum country, to whom instructions have been given to communicate with, and to join himself and the pioneers and bildars under Lieutenant Davis to Captain Heitland, and to proceed all together upon this last work.

ARTHUR WELLESLEY.

To J. G. Ravenshaw, Esq. [1067.]

SIR, Camp at Ongahully, 10th Feb., 1802.

I have the pleasure to inform you that the Rajah of Bullum was taken and brought into my camp yesterday. This event, and the forward state of the other arrangements for settling this country, have enabled me to break up the detachment which has been in it hitherto under my command, and I set out on my return to Seringapatam to-morrow.

Captain M'Farlane will remain in this country in command of the troops, which will consist principally of a light detachment, and of the pioneers and bildars. They are now employed in finishing the work upon the Soobramany and Seisul Ghauts. I have taken the liberty of desiring Captain M'Farlane to inform you if he should require your assistance in any manner, and to correspond with your aumildars upon the service if he should find it necessary. I shall be obliged to you if you will inform them that he commands in these districts, and if you will desire them to afford him the same assistance which they would to me if I were to remain here.

There will be posts on the top of each of the Soobramany, the Sampighee, and the Seisul Ghauts, occupied by the troops of the Rajah of Mysore. In case of the renewal of disturbances in this district, of which I have no apprehension whatever, I shall be obliged to you if you will desire your aumildars to consider these troops as friends, and to afford them all the assistance of provisions, &c. &c., which it may be in their power to give.

'I have, &c.,

ARTHUR WELLESLEY.

[1068.]   MEMORANDUM.—INSTRUCTIONS FOR CAPTAIN M'FARLANE.

10th Feb., 1802.

Captain M'Farlane is to be left with five companies of the 5th regiment in the Bullum district, and in command of all the troops which will remain in it.

There are three companies of the 10th and two guns at Arrekeery, the 1st battalion 1st regiment, and the pioneers.

Captain M'Farlane will remain with his five companies, with the pioneers and bildars under Lieutenant Davis, until the Seisul Ghaut and the post directed to be constructed at the top of it are completed. He will then move in such direction as he may think proper in order to carry into execution the following plan :—

It has been proposed to dismantle the fortifications, and to cut the jungle and level the ditches which surround the villages in this country ; and the inhabitants have been ordered to carry into execution these works. In some cases they have made some progress, in others but very little : it is therefore desirable that Captain M'Farlane should proceed with the bildars and pioneers to the places mentioned in the enclosed paper, and lay them open in such a manner as that the villages will be accessible to any, the worst species of troops that the aumildars can employ, and that it will not be possible for the inhabitants to fortify them again without the knowledge of the aumildars, and without giving them time to put a stop to their work before they can have made any considerable progress in it.

It will probably be impossible to lay open any village entirely, but it will be possible to level the ditches which surround them, and to cut through the jungle one or two broad ways into each, from which the roots of the trees ought to be taken.

In the execution of this plan Captain M'Farlane will join himself as soon as may be convenient with Captain Heitland, and the great body of the pioneers and bildars, and afterwards proceed with him in the execution of it. Enclosed is a copy of the instructions given to Captain Heitland, by which Captain M'Farlane will perceive the work which that officer has to perform in the first instance ; and he will observe that there will be no occasion for joining himself with Captain Heitland till that work is finished.

As soon as Captain M'Farlane will have joined Captain

Heitland, the 1st of the 1st are to be ordered to commence their march to Seringapatam. They are to be joined when they pass Arrekeery by the two guns and artillery stationed there.

The three companies of the 10th may at the same time give over the post at Arrekeery to the Rajah's troops, who will be ordered to be in readiness to take possession of it; and those three companies are to join their corps encamped at Bailoor.

Captain M'Farlane is, however, to understand that there will be no occasion for sending away these troops if he should have any substantial reason to believe that there will be any disturbance in the Bullum district, or any opposition to the execution of the plan which he is ordered to enforce.

If there should be any such disturbance or opposition, or if Captain M'Farlane should receive notice from the aumildar or principal person employed in the district on the part of the Sircar (who will receive directions to communicate with him constantly) that there is an appearance of disturbance in any part, he will move thither directly, and will take the most prompt and efficacious measures to put an end to such disturbance, and to punish those who may have ventured to oppose the authority of government. Five companies of the 5th regiment and seven companies of the 10th regiment will be encamped at Bailoor. In case of such disturbance as is above supposed, Captain M'Farlane will give immediate notice thereof to the commanding officer of these troops, who has orders to move in the most expeditious manner into the Bullum district to such place as Captain M'Farlane may point out.

The posts ordered to be constructed at the head of the Bissolee, the Sampighee, and the Seisul Ghauts, are to be given over to the Rajah's troops as soon as they are completed.

The great object in leaving Captain M'Farlane in this district is that he may see the plan above mentioned carried into execution, and that the inhabitants may not lose the impression which they have received of the actiyity and vigour of the operations of a body of British troops. The first object is, as he will perceive, to lay open the country so that the aumildar's peons and troops may at all times go to all parts of it; the next is, that in case of opposition, or the slightest appearance of disturbance, he should collect with the greatest celerity, and appear in force at the spot where such opposition may have

existed or disturbance may have been threatened, and that
should then act with the utmost vigour and despatch.

It is unnecessary to recommend to Captain M‘Farlan
constant communication with and a conciliating conduct tow:
the natives and the servants of the Rajah's government. All
intelligence of the country will depend in a great measure u
it, and he will succeed in nothing excepting he adopts suc
line of conduct.

Musket ammunition and intrenching tools have been orde
to be sent from this camp to Captain M‘Farlane. He will
so kind as to order such working parties from the troops un
his command as he may think proper, and he will send a ret
to the Deputy Adjutant-General at Seringapatam weekly, s
ing the number of men which he has ordered for work each (
which order will be confirmed.

The tools will be useful in case the Rajah's servants she
be able to supply Captain M‘Farlane with an additi
number of bildars. There are besides some tools and a quantit
musket ammunition at Arrekeery, for which carriage will be :
Mr. Mills, the conductor in charge of the stores, will app
Captain M‘Farlane of the quantity of musket ammunition tl
is at Arrekeery.

Mr. Ravenshaw, the Company's collector in Canara
apprised that Captain M‘Farlane is appointed to comm
the troops in this district, and Captain M‘Farlane is reques
to correspond with him and his aumildars upon the object
the service if he should find it necessary.

ARTHUR WELLESLE*

[1069.]   INSTRUCTIONS FOR MAJOR ENGLISH.

10th Feb., 18(

The camp upon Arrekeery, under the orders of Major Engl
is to break up.

The company of de Meuron's regiment, all the sick of
1st of the 1st and of the 1st of the 2nd, those of the 5th an
the 10th regiment which require further medical assistance.
carriage, are to join the regiment de Meuron and the 1st batta
2nd regiment as they will pass Arrekeery under the comm
of Lieutenant-Colonel Mackay.

Major English, with seven companies of the 10th, will march as soon as convenient with the sick of that corps who don't require carriage or an hospital, and of the 5th of the same description, to Ongahully on the Hemavutty, where he will join five companies of the 5th. Major English will take with him two 6-pounder field pieces, and their tumbrils and artillerymen. When Major English will have been joined at Ongahully by the five companies of the 5th above mentioned, he will march to Bailoor, where he will remain encamped. He will leave at Arrekeery three companies of the 10th, and two guns and tumbrils and their artillerymen. The post at Arrekeery is to be under the orders of Captain M'Farlane, the commanding officer in Bullum.

The object in assembling a detachment at Bailoor, under the orders of Major English, is to give countenance and support to certain arrangements which the Dewan has given orders should be carried into execution in the districts of Bailoor, Oostara, and Maharaj Droog. These arrangements are of the same nature with those ordered in Bullum, viz., to lay open the hedges and level the ditches which surround the villages, and to collect the arms from the inhabitants.

The persons employed in those districts on the part of the Sircar have been desired to communicate with Major English, and to give him the earliest intelligence of the probability of any disturbance or opposition to the orders of government ; and Major English is requested, in case he should receive intimation of any such, to take the most speedy and effectual measures to support the authority of the Dewan, and to enforce obedience to his orders. Another object in collecting the detachment at Bailoor is that assistance may be speedily given to Captain M'Farlane in Bullum, if it should be necessary. Accordingly orders have been given that Major English may be apprised of everything that passes in that district, and he is requested to afford the most prompt assistance to Captain M'Farlane.

ARTHUR WELLESLEY.

INSTRUCTIONS FOR LIEUTENANT-COLONEL MACKAY.   [1070.]

Camp at Ongahully, 10th Feb., 1802.

Lieutenant-Colonel Mackay is to march in the morning, with the troops which have been placed under his command by this day's orders, towards Munserabad.   On his arrival in the neighbourhood of that fort, he will be joined by the artillery and ordnance, and stores and provision departments which are stationed there, the heads of which have been instructed to place themselves under the orders of Lieutenant-Colonel Mackay.

He is then to proceed to the neighbourhood of Arrekeery, where he is to be joined by one company of de Meuron's regiment stationed there, and by certain sick and wounded belonging to different corps of the detachment, which Mr. Wise, who is now in charge of them, has received orders to hand over to the charge of Mr. Assistant-Surgeon Francke.

Doolies have been ordered from the 19th dragoons to assist in carrying these sick from Arrekeery.   Lieutenant-Colonel Mackay will wait till these doolies arrive.   It is very desirable that as many of the bearers (commonly called Mysore bearers) as can be spared should be left in the country, as they are usually employed as bildars.   Lieutenant-Colonel Mackay will, therefore, be so kind as to send to the killadar of Munserabad as many doolies as may not be absolutely required for the removal of the hospital from Arrekeery, and for the service of the artillery and the detachment of de Meuron's regiment, and he will take care that the bearers of these doolies are Mysore bearers.

Before Lieutenant-Colonel Mackay moves from Arrekeery, it is probable that certain doolies and bearers, which have been in the 77th regiment, will return from Mangalore.   If they should arrive, they are to be used in the removal of the hospital from Arrekeery; and this will give Lieutenant-Colonel Mackay an opportunity of leaving a larger number of doolies and of Mysore bearers at Munserabad.

After having been joined by the hospital, &c., from Arrekeery, Lieutenant-Colonel Mackay is to proceed by easy marches by Ooscotta and Chinroypatam to Seringapatam.

ARTHUR WELLESLEY.

[1071.]   *To Josiah Webbe, Esq.*

MY DEAR WEBBE,   Camp, 10th Feb., 1802.

I find that the Rajah of Bullum was taken nearly in the manner which I told you yesterday.   It does not appear that he was about to go off, but he had sent into a village for provisions. Some of the Rajah of Mysore's horse were posted there according to the plan of which I before gave you information, and the village people discovered his retreat in the jungles to the horsemen, on condition that these would give up their families whom they had seized.

I break up the detachment to-morrow, and I will give you a detailed account of the measures taken to arrange everything here permanently.

The Rajah and six others have been executed this day.

Believe me, &c.,

ARTHUR WELLESLEY.

INSTRUCTIONS FOR THE COMMANDING OFFICER OF THE 1ST BATTALION 5TH REGIMENT.   [1072.]

Camp at Ongahully, 10th Feb., 1802.

The five companies of this battalion, under the orders of Captain M'Farlane, are forthwith to be completed to their numbers, and they are to remain for some time under the orders of that officer in the Bullum district.

The other five companies are to remain encamped on this ground till they will be joined by a detachment of the 2nd of the 10th regiment and two guns, when the whole will proceed according to orders which the senior officer of that detachment will have received.

The thirty bullock loads of ammunition and the intrenching tools, which are to be left with the 5th regiment, are to be sent to join Captain M'Farlane at the Seisul Ghaut.

ARTHUR WELLESLEY.

G. O.   Camp at Ongahully, Wednesday, 10th Feb., 1802.   [1073.]

Upon breaking up the detachment, Colonel Wellesley has to make his acknowledgment of the regularity, good order, and discipline of the troops, which he will not fail to report to the Commander in Chief.

The Colonel is obliged upon this occasion to notice a material defect in the equipments of all the Native corps, viz. an almost entire want of carriage for their sick. He is aware of the diffi-

culty of procuring carriage of the best kind for the sick; but
that difficulty, like others, can be surmounted; and Colonel
Wellesley takes this opportunity of making public his determination, in case he should have occasion again to take the field
with the troops, to report to the Commander in Chief the name
of every commanding officer of a Native corps who shall not
have for his battalion such carriage for his sick as Colonel
Wellesley can approve of.

ARTHUR WELLESLEY.

[1074.]   *To the Deputy Adjutant-General.*

SIR,   Camp at Hassen, 13th Feb., 1802.

In pursuance of the intention of which I apprised you in my
letter of the 17th January, I opened a road from the forest of
Arrekeery towards the Ghauts, which was carried in the first
instance to the head of the Sampighee Ghaut, which is some
distance from that which leads into Canara by the Soobramany
Pagoda. I preferred this line, as I understood that the Bullum
Rajah had at Cagenkeerah, on the top of this Ghaut, a stronghold, which it was necessary to destroy. After the road into
Canara was completed by this Ghaut, I commenced upon that
by Bissolee and the Soobramany Pagoda, to finish which I left
the great body of the pioneers and the 1st battalion 1st regiment, and I marched with the remainder of the detachment to
the northward of Munserabad, where I laid open another road
through the Bullum country, and into Canara, by the Seisul
Ghaut.

In the mean time the Bullum Rajah had been pushed so
hard that he had been abandoned by nearly all his followers.
Many of his relations and principal people had fallen into our
hands, and he had taken refuge in the extensive jungles which
cover the western face of the Ghauts. To pursue him in these
jungles would have been useless unless we had had accurate
intelligence of the spot in which he had concealed himself; and
I therefore thought it best to disperse the troops of the Rajah
of Mysore in all the villages on the borders of, as well as in, the
jungles, in which provisions could be got, in hopes that we
should in this manner either find out where he was concealed,
or force him to fly to another part of the country, in which we

might have a better chance of procuring intelligence of his
motions. On the 9th instant the Bullum Rajah sent for provisions to a village which was occupied by some horsemen in
the service of the Rajah of Mysore, who in consequence received
intelligence of the spot where he was concealed, and went into
the jungles dismounted, and took him and the people who
were with him. He was executed on the 10th with six others,
some of whom were with him at the time he was taken, and
others had afforded him assistance since they had been pardoned
by the Dewan.

While these operations were going on, other measures were
adopted to prevent the possibility of the renewal of the rebellion even if those taken to secure the person of the Bullum Rajah
had failed. All the villages in the Bullum country are surrounded by a strong jungle and ditches. In some instances
several of these villages are connected within what may be called
one line of defence, the inhabitants having inside all that they
want, and by means of which they had secured a communication with the Western Ghauts and the sea. The country,
naturally strong, was so much strengthened by these defences
that none but the best troops could penetrate it; and consequently, whatever might be the fate of the Bullum Rajah, it was
to be expected that as soon as the season should oblige the
Company's troops to withdraw, the rebellion would be renewed.
I therefore prevailed upon the Dewan to take advantage of the
impression which had been made by the success at Arrekeery, and to offer cowle to the inhabitants upon the terms of
their destroying the fortifications which surround their villages,
delivering up their arms and ammunition, and paying the
arrears of the revenue. These terms have been accepted, and
a commencement has been made to carry them into execution
in all parts of the country. Besides this, the principal people
of the country, to the number of 300, were assembled in my camp
with their families, and the Dewan had determined to detain
as hostages those who had been principally concerned in the
late rebellion, and to suffer none to depart till they shall have
delivered in all their arms, and should have paid the arrears of
the revenue.

Matters being thus far settled in the Bullum country, I determined to break up the detachment which had been there
under my command. I had ordered the 77th regiment to march

to Mangalore, in Canara, according to the former orders of the
Commander-in-Chief, on the 28th of January, as soon as I
found that I should have no further occasion for their assistance,
and as the Sampighee Ghaut was opened.   I have ordered the
detachment of de Meuron's regiment, the 1st battalion 2nd
regiment, the guns and stores and artillery to Seringapatam,
excepting four guns with artillery which remain, two upon
Arrekeery, and two with a detachment encamped at Bailoor.

Captain M'Farlane remains in the Bullum country with five
companies of the 1st of the 5th.   As soon as he will have joined
himself with the great body of pioneers, the 1st of the 1st and the
guns upon Arrekeery will also withdraw, and proceed to Seringapatam.   It is my intention that this detachment of Captain
M'Farlane's should remain in the Bullum country with the
pioneers for some time longer.   The assistance of the pioneers
is required to complete the destruction of the fortifications
round many of the villages; and the presence of a small detachment of the Company's troops will serve to keep up the
impression which they have already made upon the inhabitants,
and will give confidence to the Rajah's servants.

As soon as the 1st of the 1st will withdraw, the post upon
Arrekeery will be given over to the Rajah of Mysore's troops.

I have ordered that five companies of the 1st of the 5th,
and the 2nd of the 10th, excepting a small detachment of
that corps which is still at Arrekeery, and two guns, should
encamp at Bailoor.   The district of this name borders upon
Bullum; the country is exactly of the same kind in this district,
Oostara, and Maharaj Droog; the villages are fortified in the
same manner; and the inhabitants, if they have not been in
actual rebellion, have been in constant communication with,
and have afforded assistance to, the rebels in Bullum.   I therefore recommended to the Dewan to adopt the same measures
to prevent them from resisting the officers of his government
which he had adopted in Bullum; and I have encamped this
detachment at Bailoor as a centrical situation, in order to give
countenance and support to his authority.   Having passed
through these districts, I have seen that a commencement has
been made to lay open the country in all parts of it, and the
Dewan has informed me that the inhabitants have begun to
give in their arms.   Before the end of this month I expect that I
shall be able to order this detachment to break up from Bailoor.

I shall hereafter have the ·honour of enclosing copies of the orders which I have issued during the service of which I have above given you an account, which may require the confirmation of the Commander-in-Chief or of government.

I have, &c.,

ARTHUR WELLESLEY.

To Lieutenant-Colonel Close. [1075.]

MY DEAR COLONEL, Camp at Hassen, 13th Feb., 1802.

It will have given you pleasure to hear from Piele of our complete success in the Bullum country. We took the Rajah on the 9th, and hanged him and six others on the 10th, and matters are brought to such a settlement that I have broke up the detachment, and am on my return to Seringapatam.

I have opened three roads into Canara, one by Bissolee and the Soobramany Pagoda, another by the Sampighee Ghaut, a third to the northward by the Seisul Ghaut. I have built a redoubt on the top of each of these for the Rajah's troops, and one on the heights of Arrekeery. The fortifications round all the villages in the country are destroyed, and the Company's pioneers remain to complete this work, with a small light detachment under Captain M'Farlane, to keep alive the terror which we have inspired, and to give confidence to the Rajah's servants.

Purneah's troops have been indefatigable. They ran the Bullum Rajah into the jungles on the western side of the Ghauts, into which it would have been useless to follow him if we could not have got intelligence of the place in which he was concealed. I therefore placed them in small parties in every village in the country in which it was possible for the Rajah to procure provisions. I sent some of them into Canara, and I kept Mr. Ravenshaw's peons and aumildars upon the look-out. My intention was to force the Rajah out of the jungles to a part of the country in which I might have a better chance of intelligence of his motions, or if he remained in them, to find out where he was concealed.

On the 9th he sent into one of the villages for provisions. The families of the principal inhabitants had been seized, and they promised to show where he was concealed if their families were given back to them. The horsemen went into the jungle dismounted, and caught the Rajah and all his people.

Purneah contrived to collect in my camp 300 of the patels. You must recollect enough of the politics of Bullum to know that they are the leaders of all the mischief. They witnessed *the suspension* of the Rajah and their brethren.

Purneah proposes to detain some of them, and the families of others entirely; to suffer none to depart till they shall have delivered in all the arms, ammunition, and property of which we got an account from the Rajah before he was hanged, and shall have paid the revenue of two years and a half, which he has demanded from them. Purneah's abilities have astonished me; he is so different from another man of the same kind whom I before dealt with, I mean Ball Kishen Bhow. He has done everything that I could wish him to do.

I recommended that the same orders should be issued in the districts of Maharaj Droog, Bailoor, and Oostara which we had given in Bullum; that the villages should be laid open, and the arms given in to the Sircar. I have the pleasure to inform you that many arms have been given in, and all the villages that I passed on the road have been laid open. I have sent a small detachment and guns to Bailoor in order to give countenance and support to Purneah's authority upon this occasion; but I believe I shall be able to break up this detachment before the end of the month.

I enclose you the description of an officer of the Bombay army who has absconded from Seedasheeghur, and who, I apprehend, is gone into the Mahratta territory on the coast. He had been lately tried by a general court-martial, which, having found him guilty of murder and a number of other shocking crimes, sentenced him to be suspended for a few months. Strange to tell, I prevailed upon this general court-martial to alter their sentence on a revision, and they have broke him, and the sentence is now before the Commander-in-Chief. I imagine that he must have been informed of the sentence, and of the intention of government to have him tried before the civil tribunals for the murder. I don't know whether you can claim him, supposing him to have gone into the Mahratta territory; but if you can, I send you the description of him.

You will have heard of the last change at Madras; it keeps Webbe from us; but we-have his support at the fountain-head, and I have no doubt but that our little man here will keep all matters going on as well as if Webbe were at his elbow. The Bullum country is the finest, I think, in Mysore. Purneah is delighted with it.

Believe me, &c.,

ARTHUR WELLESLEY.

To J. H. Piele, Esq. [1076.]

MY DEAR PIELE, Seringapatam, 16th Feb., 1802.

I have received your letter of the 13th. When Govind Rao and Balajee Rao first went out with Purneah's troops, I recommended that the lower order of the ryots should have cowle ; and I believe that in expectation of the same mercy many of the superior patels came in. Chinna Gour may have come in on this expectation, or, which is still more probable, he may have come in in consequence of a message which was sent to him by Purneah. In regard to him, therefore, the question will be, what was the nature of the message which Purneah sent him? If Purneah held out any promises or hopes to him, they ought to be fulfilled; if he did not, the punishment which you propose for him is the best he can have, as he will thereby be a lasting example of the evil consequences of rebellion.

I am glad to hear that matters are going on so well. I have an exact account from Heitland of the Bissolee Ghaut. He says that the descent is so gradual that it can scarcely be perceived, and that the pass will be an excellent one for wheel carriages. As it is paved, it will be durable.

Believe me, &c.,

ARTHUR WELLESLEY.

To J. G. Ravenshaw, Esq. [1077.]

SIR, Seringapatam, 16th Feb., 1802.

I have had the honour of receiving your letters of the 2nd, 8th, and 11th instant nearly at the same moment, as they have followed me from camp. It appears by the first that you had employed Nunjee Riah to carry on a correspondence with the

Rajah of Bullum and some of his adherents, for the purposes of which you had apprised me heretofore, and it is certainly reasonable to suppose that he carried on no correspondence not authorized by you.

As, however, the servants of the government of the Rajah of Mysore knew only that he carried on this correspondence, and as they could not know that you or I had authorized that any correspondence should be carried on with the rebels, they must have considered the conduct of Nunjee Riah to be criminal, and in that case they acted right in giving information of it.

It is unfortunate that in all cases of rebellion, particularly in that now under my consideration, there was no time for delay. If there had been, I should certainly have referred it to you ; but as it was, and as it appeared to me at the time, that which was most pressing was to arrest the person of Nunjee Riah and to prevent him from putting in execution his plans in favour of the rebels.

In my opinion, the guilt or innocence of Nunjee Riah will depend entirely upon the nature of his correspondence with Soobiah, and upon the identity of the person of Soobiah with that of the person of the same name who heretofore had a conference with you. It is impossible to form a judgment upon these points without a farther investigation ; and even after that, unless the letter received from Soobiah and Soobiah himself are produced, it will be difficult to decide correctly. From what you have said in your letters of the 2nd and 8th, I am strongly inclined to believe that Nunjee Riah is not guilty, and I am convinced that the event of his trial would be an acquittal.

Under these circumstances, I recommend that he should be set at large, and even restored to his office, unless you should have reason to believe that he has concealed from you the nature of this correspondence with Soobiah.

To bring to trial or to punish those who have informed against Nunjee Riah, I am afraid would not answer. Their plea would naturally be that they knew nothing of the permission he had from you to correspond with the rebels; that all they knew was that he was ostensibly a person under the Company's government; that he did correspond with them ; and that they thought it their duty to give intelligence of this circumstance. This plea would save them.

It may be said that it is hard upon Nunjee Riah that he should have been disgraced, and that he should have no redress. To this remark I have to answer, that every secret negotiator incurs the risk of suffering, as he has for a moment, when his negotiations are discovered, and before it can be known that he was properly authorized.

I wrote to the man who had in his custody the prisoners Narseya Arsoo and his family, to beg that he would deliver them over to Purneah's peons. In regard to the other three, as belonging to Canara, I beg you will do with them as you may think proper. The tahsildar sent to camp the prisoners who were in his custody.

I have desired to have a particular account of the places to which Chinna Gour and Soman Gour went in the province of Canara, and as soon as I receive it I will send it to you.

If you are desirous of it, I'll order that Suncana may be tried by military process for the crime of rebellion, of which he has been guilty. I wish, however, that you would send me a particular account of his crimes, and a list of the persons who will appear to prove them. The officers who will try him shall assemble in Canara.

In regard to the persons mentioned in your letter of the 11th as having held communication with the Bullum country, and in particular supplied its inhabitants with salt, I think that it would be best to bring them before the civil tribunals. Their disobedience of your orders, however improper and however criminal in this instance, does not appear to be a crime of such magnitude as government had in contemplation when they gave me powers to try individuals by military process.

I have, &c.,

ARTHUR WELLESLEY.

To Colonel Sir William Clarke. [1078.]

MY DEAR SIR,   Seringapatam, 16th Feb., 1802.

I received last night your letter of the 8th. I reported to the Commander-in-Chief that I had ordered the 77th to Mangalore, to be in readiness for your call, and that I had written to you to represent how desirable it was that this corps should have some rest, if their services were not absolutely necessary at Goa. The enclosed extract of a letter of the 8th instant, in answer to this report, will point out to you what General Stuart thinks upon this subject.

The General's orders to me to send the 77th regiment to Goa were dated the 26th January, the day on which the first news of the peace arrived at Madras; and I enclosed you an extract of a letter which I received from him, dated the 27th January. From this last, as well as from that of the 8th instant, it is very clear that General Stuart had no private reason to believe that you ought to be reinforced; on the contrary, that he thinks it desirable that you should not take the 77th regiment.

I judge by your letter of the 8th instant that you want the 77th regiment, only because you imagine that General Stuart has received information of the views of the enemy which, in his opinion, renders it desirable that you should be reinforced. The enclosed papers will entirely undeceive you upon that point, and I therefore hope that you will not call for the 77th regiment. At all events, I don't think it necessary that I should order it to join you. .

Everything is concluded in Bullum as I could wish.

Believe me, &c.,

ARTHUR WELLESLEY.

[1079.]   *To the Secretary of the Commander-in-Chief.*

SIR,   19th Feb., 1802.

. I enclose a letter from the officer commanding the 1st battalion 1st regiment, relative to working money for the men under his command, and I have received representations of a similar nature from the officers commanding the other corps which have been in the field.

According to the orders of government there is a difference between working money allowed in time of war and in time of peace; and the Military Auditor-General has considered all working parties as in time of peace, excepting those employed at a siege, and has retrenched from the officers who have drawn it the difference of the working money.

In the campaign of 1800, in the Mahratta territory, the troops constructed a redoubt upon the river Werdah; and during the time they were at work they were covered by another body of troops, and the enemy's cavalry were at all times in sight of them, but the Military Auditor-General considered that work as performed in time of peace.

The roads cut and the redoubts and posts constructed in Wynaad and Cotiote were works performed by the troops, generally under the fire of the enemy, and always covered by another body ; but these works were considered as having been done in time of peace, although men were killed and others wounded in the performance of some of them. Everybody knows that many of the works which troops are liable to perform during a siege are attended with less danger than those which I have above mentioned.

Although I have been so fortunate as not to have had any of the working parties which I have lately ordered fired upon, I should think myself inexcusable if I had not taken care to cover them, a precaution which I should not think necessary in a time of peace. Yet if working money for the troops be drawn according to the orders of government as for a time of war, which these precautions denote, the Military Auditor-General will retrench it. Under these circumstances it is desirable that the orders of government upon this subject should be more fully explained, and that it should be clearly understood what is to be considered as time of war and what of peace, in relation to work performed by the troops. Upon this point I beg to observe that it cannot be the wish of an officer in command of a body of troops to employ any of them at work unnecessarily. Before he determines to employ them he must be convinced that he is gaining time for his own operations, which is most valuable both to him and the public in this country, where the season for military operations is so short.

It is scarcely necessary to point out that the troops will not work with such good will or so well for one silver fanam *per diem* as they will for three, and that in fact the government lose in time more than they save in money by this construction placed upon their orders. Indeed the fanam *per diem* scarcely pays for the wear and tear of the sepoys' clothes while they are employed upon these works, to which they are so unaccustomed.

I beg that you will lay this matter before the Commander-in-Chief, and that you will urge him to recommend to government that when troops are employed in working parties in the field, they should be considered as working parties in time of war.

I have, &c.,

ARTHUR WELLESLEY.

To the Secretary of the Military Board.

SIR,   Seringapatam, 20th Feb., 1802.

In the course of the last westerly monsoon the river Cauvery rose to such a height that one of the uprights of the bridge was carried away, and one or two others were shaken; but it does not appear that any of them were immediately material to its safety at that time, although the want of them may injure the bridge hereafter. Having consulted with the Native engineer belonging to this government who built the bridge, he is of opinion that the damage ought to be repaired; and as the river is at this moment at the lowest, I have desired the engineer to employ his department upon the work without loss of time.

Besides this bridge over one of the great branches of the Cauvery, there is another over another branch of that river (commonly called the Mysore Nullah), which is the Company's boundary. This bridge received much damage during the siege of Seringapatam, and has been repaired only in a temporary manner. It is exceedingly useful, indeed necessary, to the island of Seringapatam, as, if it were not there, the other bridge over the great river would be useless, and the communication with the southern and western countries would be entirely stopped during six months in the year.

I have had a conversation with the Native engineers upon the subject of this bridge likewise, and they are clearly of opinion that it ought to be repaired before the river rises again, otherwise that when it does rise the bridge will fall. They say that, if the work be commenced immediately, there is time for it; and upon a rough calculation they estimate the expense at one thousand rupees, provided they are allowed to take from the fort the stones of a pagoda which was blown up during the siege of Seringapatam. I anxiously recommend that this work should be undertaken without delay, and that these Native engineers should be employed upon it. I have already desired them to make out a detailed and precise estimate of the expense, supposing that they should be allowed to take the stones they want, which I will transmit to be laid before the Military Board as soon as I shall have received it.

I have also had a conversation with the Rajah's servants upon this subject, and I imagine that, as the river over which this bridge goes is the boundary between the Company and his Highness, his government will not be found disinclined to pay half the expense of the repair of the bridge over it.

I have, &c.,

ARTHUR WELLESLEY.

To J. H. Piele, Esq.   [1081.]

MY DEAR PIELE,   Seringapatam, 24th Feb., 1802.

I have received your letter of the 21st. You are quite in the right to prevent any encroachment on the part of the officers of the army in the civil affairs of the country, at the same time I approve highly of Purneah's intention to make officers in command of stations an allowance in lieu of what they would receive if they were in garrisons in other parts of the country. In regard to Sera, it is very desirable that the business of the arrack should be regulated. Not only the discipline of the army and the health of the troops are materially concerned in a restraint on the free use and sale of it, but the peace of the place will be much disturbed if the dragoons can get at it.

Under these circumstances I would recommend it to Purneah to give the commanding officer at Sera no allowance, but to desire the aumildar to manage the arrack as he likes, and to give him the profit of it. It may be depended upon that in whatever way it may be managed there will be perpetual disputes and complaints between the aumildar and the commanding officer unless there should be such an arrangement as I have above proposed. However, you know best whether this will suit Purneah's arrangements; and if it does not, of course I have no wish for it.

I have appointed Colonel Maxwell to command at Sera, and Colonel Cuppage at Nuggur. I shall be obliged to you if you will recommend them both to Purneah. I have urged both to adhere to a conciliating line of conduct towards the Rajah's officers, and particularly to the latter. I have recommended an imitation of Disney's conduct, which met with the approbation of Lieutenant-Colonel Close.

I think that the ryots cannot be better employed than in ploughing the ground, particularly as this is the season for that operation. The pioneers and bildars will go to every village I mentioned in the letter to Purneah as soon as they will have finished with the Ghauts and the posts on the top of them, lest the villagers should have left anything undone.

Believe me, &c.,

ARTHUR WELLESLEY.

[1082.]   *To Major Macleod.*

MY DEAR MACLEOD,   Seringapatam, 25th Feb., 1802.

The departure of Colonel Stevenson from Malabar at this time is very unlucky, although the officer who will succeed to him is a respectable man. I shall, however, give much of my attention to all that passes in that quarter, and I shall be obliged to you if you will favour me with such intelligence as you may receive which you may think interesting to me or to the public cause.

I am very anxious to learn from you the nature of the situation of the Rajah of Cochin under the Company's government.

You know that Cochin will be given to the Dutch, and I wish to learn whether all the Rajah's connection with the Company will then cease, or whether part of his country is not dependent upon the Company as sovereigns of Malabar exclusive of their present holding at Cochin. If it should be true that the Rajah of Cochin will be dependent both upon the Company and upon the Dutch, which will be the case if the last question should be answered in the affirmative, his situation will be a delicate one, and we must be prepared to act in regard to him in the most prompt and vigorous manner whenever it may appear necessary.

Believe me, &c.,

ARTHUR WELLESLEY.

To J. H. Piele, Esq.   [1083.]

MY DEAR PIELE,   Seringapatam, 25th Feb., 1802.

I have just received your letter of the 22nd.   Purneah must
be the best judge of the necessity of his remaining longer in
Bullum.   If he has completed the settlement with the inhabitants, and has made the arrangements for preserving the peace
of the country which I recommended to him, I don't see any
reason why he should remain in Bullum one moment longer.
Before he goes I wish he would acquaint Captain M'Farlane
with the name of the aumildar, and if the command of the
flying column is in the hands of a different person with his
name.

I have ordered the five companies of the 5th from Bailoor to
Nuggur, but I shall leave the 10th at Bailoor for some time
longer.

If Webbe comes to Bangalore, I'll go there to meet him.

Believe me, &c.,

ARTHUR WELLESLEY.

To Lieutenant Bell.   [1084.]

SIR,   Seringapatam, 26th Feb., 1802.

On your arrival at Sera, you are, in concert with Lieutenant-
Colonel Maxwell, to fix upon a spot of ground on which you
can erect a temporary barrack for his Majesty's 19th dragoons,
being in number 500 men, with a guard-room, cook-room, and
necessary.

I propose that the walls of this building should be of mud,
that it should have cocoa-nut or palmyra uprights in the centre
in order to support the roof, and save the expense of beams,
and that it should be thatched according to the mode practised
in that part of the country with date leaves and straw or grass.
It will be necessary that it should have good doors and windows,
which you will do well to order at Seringapatam, and that it
should have a verandah all round.

I have desired that the aumildar at Sera may prepare the
materials which you will require for the construction of this
building, and a commencement has been made to procure them.

On your arrival there you will ascertain from him the prices of each article of materials which you will require, and you will immediately make an estimate of the expense which will be incurred in the construction, which you will transmit to me.

I write by this occasion to Lieutenant-Colonel Maxwell to desire that he will give you every assistance in lascars, &c., &c., to enable you to complete the building as soon as possible.

I have, &c.,

ARTHUR WELLESLEY.

[1035.]   *To Captain Mackay.*

MY DEAR MACKAY,   Seringapatam, 26th Feb., 1802.

I have taken into consideration, and have had some conversation with Bajee Rao upon the subject of, your last proposition regarding gram for the gun bullocks, which I understood to have been, firstly, that all gram should be allowed to pass duty free to the Karkhana; secondly, that you should once a month settle with the Rajah's officers the account of the duties on the gram which you would have consumed.

Several inconveniences will attend the adoption of either of these propositions. When the Sircar remits the duties on any particular article in favour of any person, the loss is not in proportion to the amount of the duty which would have been paid. A door is open to fraud both on the part of the dealers in general, and on that of the collectors of the revenue, by which the Sircar is always a loser. It is, therefore, very improbable that they will consent to a plan of this kind, unless the advantage to the Company is as plain, at least, as their own loss.

The advantage to the Company in this instance is very problematical, and at all events, supposing it to be certain, I don't think it necessary that the Company should have it. If you are to pay the whole duty to the Sircar, the Company gain nothing in point of expense; but you say that the expense is not occasioned by the amount of the duty, but by the wages of those whom the contractor must have in his service to pay it.

In answer I have to observe, in the first instance, that I don't see any reason why the person who is intrusted by the contractor to purchase a quantity of gram in the country should not be trusted to pay the duty on it as it passes along the road. In the next place I have to observe, that a regiment of cavalry uses as much gram as your bullocks, and the gram-agent may be considered, for the sake of argument, in the light of a contractor. He finds no difficulty in paying his duties on the roads, and I don't see any reason why your contractor should.

I may, therefore, safely conclude that the advantage of this proposition to the Company would be nothing, and if you should pay the whole duty, it would be nothing to the contractor; and it is probably brought forward only to throw additional obstacles in the way of the execution of a contract into which he has probably unwarily entered. Not only would the adoption of your propositions be injurious to the Rajah's Sircar, and of no advantage to the Company and the contractor, but it would be highly troublesome to you and to me. At the end of every month there would be a discussion between you and the government regarding the quantity of gram which your bullocks would have consumed, which would go through me. On the other hand, the Sircar would find out that sometimes the contractor would have brought the gram from a greater distance and through more chokeys than they expected when they made the bargain, and this would bring on another discussion upon the subject between me and the Resident.

I have had a discussion upon the subject of this gram now for three years, and I don't wish for a renewal of it upon new grounds; I shall, therefore, set my face against the adoption of this arrangement.

Believe me, &c.,

ARTHUR WELLESLEY.

To Josiah Webbe, Esq.   [1086.]

MY DEAR WEBBE,   Seringapatam, 26th Feb., 1802.

I should have written to you, according to the intention which I announced in my letter of the 10th, in order to give you the details of all that I had done to insure the settlement of Bullum. only that I found that I should have done no more than repeat what I had written you before, unless I entered into details which no man could understand who had not been in the country, I therefore thought it best to forego that intention.

The accounts from Bullum since I quitted the country are very satisfactory. It is in a state of perfect tranquillity, and cultivation going on. Purneah is coming away immediately. Our pioneers, however, and five companies of Native infantry will remain in the country till they will have completely destroyed the fortifications round some of the principal villages. I imagine that this operation will take to the end of March.

Purneah's first intention was to have gone to Bangalore to meet you. He has heard, however, that you have deferred your journey to this country for some time, and he now proposes to come here. He can meet you at Bangalore, whenever you please, without inconvenience.

Believe me, &c.,

ARTHUR WELLESLEY.

[1087.]   *To Josiah Webbe, Esq.*

MY DEAR WEBBE,   Seringapatam, 27th Feb., 1802.

Purneah can meet you at Bangalore whenever you please after the first week in March. He is now coming away from Bullum, and I expect him at Seringapatam in the course of a few days.

I hope that you will not resign the Residency. Of course I shall look after the French and Dutch when they return to Malabar, and will keep you informed of everything that passes.

It is impossible for a man to be more ignorant of European politics than Purneah is; indeed, he does not appear to me to have had any knowledge of the late orders from Europe, and the proposed changes of men and measures at Madras, which were so likely to affect his own situation. I attribute his salutary ignorance upon these points to his not having any communication with Madras dubashes, who know everything.

I will meet you at Bangalore when you come there.

Believe me, &c.,

ARTHUR WELLESLEY.

[1088.]   *To Lieutenant-General Stuart.*

SIR,   Seringapatam, 4th March, 1802.

I have received two or three representations from Lieutenant-Colonel Spry, who commands at present at Mangalore, in which

he has stated the want of a fort adjutant, or some person of
that description, to conduct the details of the garrison. Mangalore is the principal place in the province, and I imagine that
a fort adjutant is necessary there: knowing, however, your
desire that no new staff appointments should be made, I am
unwilling to recommend this one officially until I receive your
approbation of it.

I have, &c.,

ARTHUR WELLESLEY.

To Lieutenant-Colonel Spry.   [1089.]

DEAR SIR,   Seringapatam, 4th March, 1802.

I have received your letter of the 27th February.

As the staff of the army has lately been the subject of much
inquiry, and as a great number of staff appointments have in
consequence been struck off, I am unwilling to make a new
appointment, however necessary I think it, until I receive
General Stuart's sanction. I have written to him, however, to
recommend it; and if he should consent, I will give the appointment to Lieutenant Bruttou of the 75th regiment.

Believe me, &c.,

ARTHUR WELLESLEY.

To the Secretary of the Military Board.   [1090.]

SIR,   Seringapatam, 4th March, 1802.

There are on the returns of the arsenal of Seringapatam, on
the 1st of February, 934 lascars, 601 of whom are on command; and of this number there are nearly 500 who will
never return to the garrison. They have either gone away
with corps which have been sent into other garrisons, and
it is probable the lascars with them, or they have deserted
the service, or have died when detached from the arsenal; and
of this disposition of them, or of these casualties, no official
communication has been received. Under these circumstances
I am desirous to have permission to have the return corrected.

I have the honour to enclose a list of the lascars returned
on command on the 1st of February, who will never return

to the arsenal, and whom I should wish to strike off the strength entirely. I have noted opposite each detachment in what manner I have reason to believe that they have been disposed of.

I likewise enclose a list of lascars returned on command on the 1st of February, but who I have reason to believe will return to the arsenal. I should wish still to keep them on the strength; and they and the number present would make up the establishment.

I have, &c.,

ARTHUR WELLESLEY.

[1091.]   *To Lieutenant-Colonel Maxwell.*

MY DEAR COLONEL,   Seringapatam, 5th March, 1802.

I have received your letter of the 3rd instant, and I am very glad to find that Lieutenant Bell is likely to give you satisfaction. You will find him zealous and diligent, and that he gets on with the work which he has in hand.

As you have fixed upon the ground, it does not signify much; but in general I think that we make our buildings in these upper countries too near the water, and that the health of the officers and troops has suffered from such a position of their dwellings as much as from any other cause. Allow them to build where they please. It is probable that tent allowance will be given soon, and that that will be the only allowance which they will have to cover themselves from the weather; but let them bear in mind what I told you when I informed you that the regiment was to go to Sera, viz., that it is not impossible but that upon the conclusion of the peace, and the introduction of the French into Pondicherry, it may be necessary to reinforce the centre division of the Carnatic, and that in that case the 19th would probably go to that part of the country. It is desirable for them, therefore, that they should avoid expense.

I have desired that letters may be written to the aumildar of Sera to request that materials may be furnished for the officers upon your requisition, as well as those which I have already ordered for the soldiers' barracks. I am convinced that they will do everything in their power to conciliate the natives, and that they will not pitch upon any spot for their houses which could interfere with any person.

I am obliged to you for the assistance which you propose that Serjeant Brennan shall give to Mr. Bell. I am sorry to hear that he is likely to be disappointed in his expectations of a quartermaster's warrant, but he is so useful a man that he must get on, if not at present, at no very distant time.

Pray present my best compliments to all friends in the 19th.

Believe me, &c.,

ARTHUR WELLESLEY.

To Lieutenant-Colonel Boles.   [1092.]

SIR,   Seringapatam, 6th March, 1802.

I have had the honour of receiving your letter of the 2nd instant, enclosing one from Major Macleod to you, and two from government to Colonel Stevenson. I return the latter.

Upon perusing the resolutions of government, I have no doubt but that the powers given to the officer commanding in Malabar devolve upon you. In the first place, I observe that, although the letter of the 25th September which conveys those powers is addressed to Colonel Stevenson, it communicates certain resolutions of government which pointedly state that the powers granted to *the commanding officer* to try rebels by military process shall extend to all cases of a criminal nature. In the next place, I observe that the system of government for Malabar, communicated in that letter of the 25th September, is, that the criminal tribunal shall be abolished, and that all persons guilty of crimes shall be tried by military process. Government could not have intended that one commanding officer only should have the power of trying criminals; and if they had had such an intention, they would have taken care to provide for the criminal jurisdiction of the province at the time that they gave the orders for his removal to another station. Upon the whole, therefore, I am convinced, as well from the terms in which the resolutions of government are conveyed, as from the principle of the late reform in the criminal jurisdiction in Malabar, that government intend that the powers given to

Colonel Stevenson shall be exercised by his successors ; and I request that you will be so kind as to take measures for the immediate trial of the criminals in confinement at Calicut.

The powers to try rebels by military process were originally given to me ; but I have no power to try persons in that manner who may be guilty of other crimes, otherwise I should give orders for the trial of those now in confinement, as there appear doubts on your mind of the propriety of your giving them. I shall, however, this day communicate to government your doubts respecting the exercise of the powers given to the officer commanding in Malabar, and the opinion which I have given you.

I have, &c.,

ARTHUR WELLESLEY.

[1098.]   *To Major Macleod.*

MY DEAR MACLEOD,   Seringapatam, 7th March, 1802.

I have had the pleasure of receiving your letter of the 1st. The line from the Tambercherry Pass through Wynaad by Edatera to Seringapatam · is the great one made by Hyder, and used by Tippoo, and is certainly, as you say, the most important for us. Lieutenant-Colonel Close travelled by that road from Lakerycottah last year, and by his account it appears that the road is in general as good and as fine now as it ever can have been ; in fact, that the only bad places on it are in the cultivated lands, in which of course the roads will always be indifferent. ·

I intend to adopt your plan of having the head-quarters of Wynaad at Pancoorta Cottah.

At present a plan is under discussion for giving tent allowance to the army, in which is included one for making commanding officers of Native corps find cantonments for their troops. Till this plan is decided on, government are unwilling to consent to incur any expense on account of barracks or cantonments for the Native troops, and of course will be unwilling to consent to the removal of the head-quarters in Wynaad, when that removal is to be attended by the incurring of a fresh expense to build a cantonment. As soon, however, as the plan is decided upon, it will be easy to remove the troops. If it be adopted, the expense will fall upon the commanding officer, to which government will have no objection; if it be not adopted, a new cantonment must be built at all events, if not where you propose, at Manundwaddy or Poollingal, and in that case it will be the same thing to government where it is built.

It will be a good thing to arrange some system of *espionage* at Mahé and Cochin before the French and Dutch get admittance into those places; afterwards it may not be easy. It is most desirable that we should have accurate and minute intelligence of all that passes there, particularly that we should know the nature and extent of their communications with your Rajahs.

Believe me, &c.,

ARTHUR WELLESLEY.

To Major Macleod. [1094.]

MY DEAR MACLEOD, Seringapatam, 11th March, 1802.

I have received a letter from General Stuart, in which he informs me that orders have been received to discharge from the service all the Nair, Tier, and Moplah sebundies in Malabar, and all local and volunteer corps in other parts, and to reduce the numbers of the regular battalions to the peace establishment of 1796, that is to say, to 900 each battalion. The number of battalions is not to be altered at present.

In consequence of this information, I write this day to Colonel Boles to desire that he will make the necessary arrangements for disbanding the three corps of sebundies.

The General has desired that I would suggest to you the propriety of taking into the service, as revenue or police peons, as many of these discharged sebundies as you may be willing to entertain in those capacities, rather than to let loose upon Malabar at once so large a body of men accustomed to arms. You will be the best judge how far you can attend to this suggestion. If you can take into the service any number of these people, I think the peace of the country will be benefited.

The General says that he intends to propose to government that waste land may be given to the discharged sebundies and sepoys in the different parts of the country; but I don't think that will answer any purpose. The land will still remain waste, and they will be idle vagabonds.

Believe me, &c.,

ARTHUR WELLESLEY.

[1095.]   *To Lieutenant-Colonel Spry.*

DEAR SIR,   Seringapatam, 14th March, 1802.

I enclose an extract of a letter which I have received from the Commander-in-Chief, in answer to one which I wrote to him, in which I requested that a staff officer might be appointed at Mangalore, and I am concerned that he will not attend to our request. In order, however, to save you trouble, I have settled with Captain Barclay that from this day he is to send copies of all general orders to the two stations of Cundapoor and Seedasheeghur. I conclude that you get them at Mangalore from the Presidency.

I have received your letter this morning regarding the state of the barracks at Mangalore, and I write this day to the Military Board to remind them of your letter to them upon that subject. You will do well, however, to send me a statement of the repairs required to the barracks, lest the Board should delay to order them so long as to render it probable that they would not be finished before the rains set in. Let me know also what length of time you think will be required to execute them.

Believe me, &c.,

ARTHUR WELLESLEY.

[1096.]   *To Colonel Stevenson.*

MY DEAR COLONEL,   Seringapatam, 14th March, 1802.

I have received your letters of the 11th and 12th. The second was not necessary. I assure you that I am always glad to receive your opinions on every subject, and I do you no more than justice in believing that they are dictated by the best motives and the most correct views of the public interests.

I think I understand the cause of General Stuart's opinion regarding the police. He knows well the jealousy at home and

among some in this country of military power and military expenses, and he knows also that the former is necessary for a
government which exists only by the sword, and that the greater
part of the latter is occasioned by that necessity and by the
constant support given to the civil by the military power.
Latterly the complaints of the growth of the military expenses
have been more frequent than usual ; and inasmuch as they have
been likely to occasion a very great diminution of the numbers
and strength of the army, it is probable that they will do much
mischief. General Stuart, therefore, is glad to avail himself
of anything which does not create a military expense (that is,
an expense paid by the military paymaster), which will perform
some of the service required from the military, and will give
some support to the civil government. The police in Malabar
is of this description, and that is the reason why the General
wishes that it should be maintained. What you say, however, regarding the operations of this police is very true. These ought
to be submitted to the commanding officer, particularly if they
are of any consequence, before they are attempted, otherwise he
may be unexpectedly involved in hostilities of the most extensive and serious nature. I will give a hint to Macleod upon
the subject, which I am convinced will be sufficient.

Your ideas and mine regarding the powers of the military in
the common affairs of police agree entirely.

I am glad to find that you get on so well. Our weather has
been cooler latterly, and I hope has extended to you. Remember me kindly to Mrs. Stevenson and Lewis, and kiss my
godson for me. Robertson leaves us to-morrow.

Believe me, &c.,

ARTHUR WELLESLEY.

To Lieutenant-General Stuart. [1097.]

SIR,   Seringapatam, 15th March, 1802.

The arrangement which I intended to propose to you for the
arsenal at Cannanore has been delayed on account of the want
of the returns from the different arsenals in Malabar and
Canara. However, they are now arrived, and I shall have the
pleasure of sending it to you in the course of a few days.

The expense attending the 19th dragoons, alluded to in your

letter of the 11th March, ceased from the day on which that corps went into Sera, and with that all its field establishment. I have this day ordered that the half of the bullocks attached to the 5th regiment of cavalry may be discharged, leaving only one bullock for two horses ; and as soon as I hear what is to be done regarding the tent allowance and the proposed mode of building cantonments for the Native troops, I will order the 5th regiment over to Santa Bednore, where I proposed that they should be cantoned. The remount horses will all have come up the Ghauts by the end of this month, and there is, therefore, no reason why the 5th regiment should remain longer in its present situation, excepting that government should not have decided in what manner a cantonment for it is to be provided. When this corps goes to Santa Bednore, all its field expenses will cease forthwith.

From the amount of the sum stated in your letter of the 11th, I imagine that the expenses of the bullocks attached to the gram department of the regiment of cavalry in the Ceded Districts are included in it. The expense of the bullocks attached to the two regiments in Mysore, supposing both to be complete, would not exceed 1500 pagodas *per mensem*.

I am infinitely sensible of your favour to me in allowing me to retain Major Ogg, if I should find his services essential in the situation of Persian interpreter. During the absence of the Resident, and indeed I may say at all times, I am in constant communication with this government and with the Mahratta chiefs on the frontier, and the Rajahs and Polygars throughout the country. These communications are occasionally held in each of the Persian, Mahratta, Canarese, Malabar, and Moorish languages, all of which Major Ogg understands in some degree, and I acknowledge that I should be much embarrassed if I should lose his assistance. He is in a very bad state of health, and I am afraid would be of little use with any corps which he might join : I have the less scruple, therefore, in presuming upon your favour so far as to request that he may be allowed to remain with me.

Since I have been in this country I have done everything in my power to conciliate the Rajah of Koorg, and I have the pleasure to say that I have succeeded in pleasing him. I am glad that this has met with your approbation. I have just received from the Rajah a box for you, and two for the Governor-General, containing khelauts upon the occasion of the marriage of his daughter. I will take the earliest opportunity of transmitting them to Madras.

I have, &c.,

ARTHUR WELLESLEY.

To the Secretary of the Military Board.   [1098.]

SIR,   Seringapatam, 15th March, 1802.

I have the honour to enclose an extract of a letter which I received from the late Commander-in-Chief, General Harris, dated the 4th July, 1799, and an extract of one from the Secretary of Government, dated the 22nd November, 1799, which contain the only directions that I have received regarding the captured stores in Seringapatam, or those belonging to the Rajah of Mysore at Chittledroog. In order to throw more light upon this subject, I likewise enclose a copy of a letter from Lieutenant-Colonel Agnew to Major-General Popham, the President of the Committee of Prize, which is referred to in the enclosed extract of a letter from General Harris.

In consequence of the orders contained in the letter from General Harris, the returns of the captured stores at Seringapatam have been kept separate. They have been valued, and the valuation of them has been transmitted to the Deputy Adjutant-General, to be laid before the Commander-in-Chief.

If it should be determined that the value of these stores shall belong to the captors of Seringapatam, and if the government should take them at the valuation which has been fixed on them, there will be no difficulty in settling the account of the stores which have been already issued for the public service. If government should pay for the quantities as they stood on the day the valuation was made, and the issues should have been made since, of course nothing will be due for them. If the issues should have been made previous to the valuation, the value of the stores issued will be due to the captors, supposing that the stores are their property. If it should be determined that the stores are not to be given to the captors, the property must be that of the Company; and in that case there will be nothing due on account of the issues which have been made.

In consequence of the orders contained in the enclosed extract of a letter from the Secretary of Government, I gave directions that the stores in the forts in the Mysore country should be in charge of the Company's officers, and that the returns of them should be kept separate. As instructions upon the subject were sent to the Resident, I did not interfere any farther.

There will be no difficulty, however, in settling this account. If the valuation of these stores at Seringapatam should be approved of, it will answer for that of all the other stores in the country, and credit may be given to the Rajah for the quantities received by the Company's officers at that rate. No stores were issued till the Company's officers took charge of them, and of course there can be no demand upon the Company for any issue previous to the period at which the quantities and quality were ascertained.

I have, &c.,

ARTHUR WELLESLEY.

[1099.]   *To Major Macleod.*

MY DEAR MACLEOD,   Seringapatam, 15th March, 1802.

I have received from Colonel Boles a very interesting report by Lieutenant Williams upon the subject of the road which I desired some time ago might be made round Mahé.

I cannot send it to you, but I wish that you would see it as well as the plan, and the letter which I wrote to Colonel Boles upon the subject this day.

It appears by that report that the French have claims to certain districts on the northern as well as on the southern side of the Mahé river, the justice of which is not acknowledged by the natives. Lieutenant Williams proposed to carry the road outside the boundary of the districts to which the French have this disputable claim, because he thought that was my wish ; but he was well aware of the advantage which would be taken in a future discussion on these claims of our adopting this line of road, and he has, therefore, indirectly proposed two others. One of them leads directly across the districts the right to the possession of which may be disputed ; the other leads to a distance from the boundary of those districts, and joins the high road from Cotaparamba to Moondaal.

I have desired him to make the former to be used as the road round Mahé when the French get possession; at the same time, in case they should lay claim to the possession of the district through which it will pass, and should object to our using it, that he should have the other ready to keep up the communication between our northern and southern districts.

This subject is well deserving your attention. The great efforts of the French against us hereafter will be in India, and they will be eager to seize any the slightest cause of dispute. It is desirable, therefore, that the grounds of their claim to these districts near Mahé should be clearly ascertained; that they may be given to them if they are theirs, and that if not, we should be prepared with all the arguments to dispute the possession, and to defend our rights.

Believe me, &c.,

ARTHUR WELLESLEY.

To F. Reeves, Esq.   [1100.]

SIR,   Seringapatam, 16th March, 1802.

Captain Barclay has communicated to me your letter to him of the 10th instant, and its enclosures.

As it appears by the orders of government to the Military Board that it is the intention that rice for three months shall be laid in store for all the troops in Canara, of course it is necessary that you should make provision for the 77th regiment at Mangalore, as well as for the other corps.

The garrisons at Jemalabad and Behul, being detachments from Mangalore, are to be supplied at those stations with three months' grain; but it will be proper that you should subtract from the quantity to be laid in at Mangalore the quantities which you will lay in at Jemalabad and Behul.

You will observe by the General Orders of the 27th February that there will be at Cundapoor a battalion from which two companies will be detached to Seedasheeghur. I do not imagine that during the next monsoon the garrison of Seedasheeghur will consist of more troops than are detailed in those orders. However, if the British garrison should be withdrawn from Goa, one battalion will be thrown into Seedasheeghur; and in that case the supply of grain in store will be absolutely necessary at that station, as I understand that unless provision be previously made, it is particularly difficult to procure grain in that part of the country.

I mention this circumstance at present lest you should think it unnecessary to lay in grain at Seedasheeghur in consequence of the orders of the 27th February last.

I have, &c.,

ARTHUR WELLESLEY.

[1101.]   *To J. H. Piele, Esq.*

MY DEAR PIELE,   Seringapatam, 19th March, 1802.

In consequence of our placing the 19th dragoons at Sera, it is necessary that Grant should provide barrack-cots at that place for their accommodation. His cots are now at Chittledroog and at Nuggur; and under his contract with the government he is obliged to move them wherever they may be required at his own expense; it is impossible to hire coolies at either of those places, and he is therefore desirous that Purneah should give him some assistance, and should have the cots forwarded from village to village, for which Grant will pay the expense. The number which he wishes to move from Chittledroog to Sera is 300; the number from Nuggur to Sera is 150. I am aware that it will be impossible to move all these at one time, but I have arranged to send a sepoy or two with each detachment, so that if Purneah can give Grant the assistance required, the cots will come without much difficulty and without being broke. Let me hear from you upon this subject.

Believe me, &c.,

ARTHUR WELLESLEY.

I shall be at Bangalore on the 1st or 2nd of April, if I find that Webbe really comes.

[1102.]   *To A. Read, Esq.*

SIR,   Seringapatam, 19th March, 1802.

I have received your letter of the 15th, and I have this day sent orders to Nuggur for a detachment of one European officer and 50 men to be sent to Bonawassi as soon as possible.

This place is nearer to Bonawassi than Hullihall, and men can be spared from it with more convenience.

I shall be obliged to you if you will send back the detachment which will come from Hullihall as soon as you will be joined by that which will march from Nuggur.

I have lately heard frequently of the disturbances in the Mahratta territory occasioned by the contest between Goklah and Baba Saheb, in which the former has hitherto had rather the advantage.

Some of the straggling parties of horse belonging to Baba Saheb's army have entered the territories of the Rajah of Mysore, and have plundered some villages. I have in consequence desired that a party of horse may be collected on the frontier, and that they should have as little scruple in pursuing the plunderers within their own frontier as these have in entering ours. I have also written to Baba Saheb to desire that he will exert himself to oblige his troops to respect the territory of the Company and of the Rajah of Mysore, and to inform him of the arrangements which I had made for their protection.

You are quite right in calling for a detachment to Bonawassi, particularly as you have money there. The Mahratta chiefs in general are very unable, supposing them to be willing, to restrain their plundering troops, and a large sum of money weakly guarded is a temptation which few even of the best of them can withstand. Besides, Soonda itself is not free from thieves, who are not unlikely to attempt to get possession of it, and to pass themselves off as the plunderers attached to the Mahratta camp.

I shall be obliged to you if you will make arrangements for quartering the troops which will go to Bonawassi in one of the choultries or other buildings about the place.

I have, &c.,

ARTHUR WELLESLEY.

To the Deputy Adjutant-General. [1103.]

SIR, Seringapatam, 19th March, 1802.

I have had the honour to receive Brigadier-Major Winslow's letter of the 16th March.

I should be happy to comply with the desire of Lieutenant

Colonel Shee to withdraw his resignation of his commission in the 33rd regiment, but as the officers have been recommended for the succession, and lodged their money for the purchase at some inconvenience to themselves, and as I understand from a letter which I have received from Mr. Cochrane this day that Lieutenant Colonel Shee is by no means in a state of health to afford a well-grounded hope of his recovery, I think it proper to decline to give my consent as Lieutenant Colonel of the 33rd regiment to the resignation of this commission being withdrawn.

I have also to observe that Lieutenant Colonel Shee's family experienced some indulgence at the time that he was permitted to resign his commission; and that I recollect instances in the 33rd regiment of officers whose resignations have not been received because they were given in when they were in a state of health similar to that in which it appears that Lieutenant Colonel Shee was when he sent in his. A departure from the rule then adopted by the late Commander-in-Chief in those instances might appear hard upon the regiment, particularly if adopted with the consent of the Lieutenant Colonel.

Upon the whole therefore, considering the subject in reference to the benefit of the regiment, of the officers who serve in it, of Lieutenant Colonel Shee's family, and to precedent upon other occasions, I am induced to decline giving my consent to the withdrawal of Lieutenant Colonel Shee's resignation.

I have, &c.,

ARTHUR WELLESLEY.

[1104.]   *To the Chief Secretary of Government.*

SIR,   Seringapatam, 10th March, 1802.

In consequence of the orders received to send the 19th regiment of dragoons to Sera, and to provide at that place for their temporary accommodation, I desired Lieutenant Bell, who has acted hitherto as engineer at Seringapatam, and who in that capacity has given me much satisfaction, to go to Sera on his way to join his corps, and to superintend the erection of a temporary barrack for the 19th dragoons.

Enclosed I have the honour to send a copy of the orders which I gave to Lieutenant Bell, a copy of a letter which I have received from him, dated the 8th instant, the prices of materials at Sera, and his estimate of the expense of the work.

I have ordered a verandah all round the building because the rains are so heavy during the western monsoon that the mud walls would come down if not protected from their effects in that manner; and good doors and windows, because I am aware from experience that to have the power of shutting out the wind and rain is the only mode of preserving the health of the troops.

I hope that the Right Hon. the Governor in Council will approve of the orders which I have given upon this occasion. The estimate of the expense appears moderate. The expensive parts of the work are the doors and windows, which I have above observed are necessary for the preservation of the health of the troops in this country, and will answer for any other place to which it might hereafter be thought proper to move the cantonment.

During my absence from Seringapatam a part of the barrack of the 1st battalion 2nd regiment was burnt down by accident, and I have the honour to enclose an estimate of the expense of the repair of it.

I have, &c.,

ARTHUR WELLESLEY.

To Lieutenant-General Stuart. [1105.]

SIR,   Seringapatam, 20th March, 1802.

I have the honour to enclose a list of stores which I should propose to have at Cannanore and at Mangalore. It contains for the former those stores which are daily required by the troops, and which it is desirable should be supplied to them as near as possible to their quarters, and those which are necessary for ten field pieces which ought to be in the province of Malabar. It contains for the latter only the stores which are necessary for four field pieces which ought to be in Canara, and some musket ammunition. I hope that the troops in Canara may be supplied from the magazine at Cannanore or Seringapatam with the articles for which there is a daily demand.

On the day after to-morrow I will transmit you a statement of the stores which are now in the provinces of Malabar and

Canara which are surplus to this proposed establishment. It will also show those of which there are deficiencies.

The British stores and ordnance are already removed from Cochin to Cannanore, according to your former orders. I propose immediately to give orders that the stores shall likewise be moved from Mangalore to Cannanore which may be surplus to the proposed establishment at the former. I shall then be glad to receive your orders regarding the surplus which will be at Cannanore, and I shall take the liberty of submitting to you my ideas upon the subject when I send you the statement above mentioned.

I should propose to leave the ordnance establishment at Cannanore as it is now, and as directed by the government orders of the 21st October, 1801 ; to reduce that at Cochin to one conductor, one syrang, and twelve lascars, merely to take care of the foreign stores till the Dutch take possession of the place ; to abolish those at Calicut and Tellicherry entirely ; and to reduce that at Mangalore to one conductor, one syrang, twenty lascars, and a proportion of artificers for four field pieces. The department at Paulgautcherry may remain as it is.

In sending you this paper I take the opportunity of mentioning the assistance which I have received from Captain Freese in making it out, as well as upon other occasions, particularly in fitting out the late equipment for field service, and in sending the ordnance stores to the assistance of Major-General Campbell in the Ceded Districts. He is now only acting as commissary, and the officer who is commissary (Captain Scott) is a most respectable man, to whom I am under many obligations for the services he rendered me during the campaign in the Mahratta territory. His object is to be commissary at the arsenal at Madras, for which situation he is particularly qualified, and in which there is some probability of a vacancy in consequence of late promotions. If that should be the case, I shall be infinitely obliged to you if you will be so kind as to recommend that Captain Freese may be permanently appointed commissary at Seringapatam, and I am particularly anxious that this arrangement should be made.

I have, &c.,

ARTHUR WELLESLEY.

To Josiah Webbe, Esq.   [1106.]

MY DEAR WEBBE,   Seringapatam, 22nd March, 1802.

I am very glad to find that the King's ministers are likely again to take the power over this country into their own hands, and make use of the control which they have over the gentry in Leadenhall-street. I do not know exactly the points upon which Lord Wellesley is at issue with them, but I judge from Malcolm's account of the letters which he has received from England, that whatever they may be, he will be supported by the Board of Control, particularly as he appears disposed to make every reduction in the military expenses which is at all practicable.

I agree with you entirely about the peace. It establishes the French power over Europe, and when we shall have disarmed we shall have no security excepting in our own abjectness. There is a report that the finances were in a very embarrassed state, which I am afraid is true, as there could have been no other inducement to make such a peace.

I look upon the question of reduction in this country to stand upon grounds entirely independent of peace or war in Europe. We have carried on no offensive operations in this quarter, and we have long ceased to fear an attack from the French. The size of our army is to be attributed to the demands for its services existing in India, and is by no means occasioned by the war in Europe. The question is, whether those demands are likely to be lessened or to cease upon the conclusion of the peace. I rather believe that as that event will be accompanied by the return of the French and Dutch to their settlements in India, it might be concluded with more truth that the army ought to be increased rather than diminished.

The people of England, however, will not willingly hear of the existence of our large military establishments in India in time of profound peace in Europe. They will not easily believe that there is a necessity for them in India in the most peaceable times, and some reduction is therefore absolutely necessary. On this ground only does the peace influence the question of reduction. But it is very clear that the army ought to be reduced as little as possible, particularly that its effective strength ought to be kept entire.

If there is to be any reduction of numbers below what they will be after the supernumeraries are struck off, I think the best mode will undoubtedly be to decrease the number of men in each battalion, rather than to disband any of the regiments. By this mode it will be more easy at all times to increase the army to its present numbers; and as by either mode the officers must still be in the service, on the establishment, and in the receipt of their pay and batta, it will be equally economical for the present. Hereafter, however, when the number of officers will have decreased, to disband some of the regiments will be the more economical mode; but it will be attended with the disadvantage of great difficulty in increasing the numbers of the army again.

I am glad to hear that your commission goes on so well. It would certainly have been impossible to make the arrangements for the perpetual settlement by means of a board of revenue composed of such discordant materials as that at Madras is at present.

I return Malcolm's letter.

Let me know on what day you propose to leave Madras, and on what day you will be at Bangalore, in order that I may have my palanquin boys posted in time.

Believe me, &c.,
ARTHUR WELLESLEY.

[1107.]   *To Lieutenant-General Stuart.*

SIR,   Seringapatam, 23rd March, 1802.

I have the honour to enclose a statement of the stores at Cochin, Cannanore, and Mangalore, and an account of those wanting to complete the estimate which I sent you on the 20th, and of those which will be surplus to that estimate. The stores at Cochin are already removed to Cannanore and Tellicherry, and I mean to give orders that those at Mangalore surplus to the proposed establishment for that place should likewise be removed thither as soon as I shall receive your sentiments upon that arrangement.

Upon looking over the enclosed paper I observe 5000 muskets put down as an establishment for Cannanore. This is a mistake; it is not my intention that there should be any muskets at that place. I propose that the troops in Malabar and Canara should be supplied with arms from hence. Such of the surplus stores mentioned in the enclosed paper as are worth moving, I should propose to move to Seringapatam by means of the Company's cattle early in the next season. It is now too late to begin such an arrangement. Before it could be considered by you, and means taken here to carry it into execution, the rainy season would be so near as to take away any chance we might have of effecting it. All the stores, therefore, must remain at Cannanore and Tellicherry during the next rains, and those not wanted there can be brought here when the season becomes fair and the roads good.

I have, &c.,

ARTHUR WELLESLEY.

To the Chief Secretary of Government.

[1108.]

SIR,   Seringapatam, 25th March, 1802.

I received last night your letter of the 16th instant, and I shall accordingly proceed forthwith to make the arrangements for the conveyance from Seringapatam to Vellore of the families of Hyder Ali and Tippoo Sultaun, in obedience to the orders of the Right Hon. the Governor in Council.

Upon inquiry I find that 250 doolies will be required for the removal of one of these families, for which 1500 bearers will be wanted. I shall be obliged to you if you will lay my request before the Right Hon. the Governor in Council that he will give orders that these bearers may be hired at Madras and sent here as soon as may be convenient.

It will be possible to procure some dooly bearers in this country, but by no means the number which will be required to carry 250 doolies; and as the season for cultivation is now coming in, and the people who carry the doolies are the cultivators, I am very desirous to avoid making any requisition upon this government for assistance upon this occasion. It appears to me to be very desirable, for many reasons referable to their comfort and happiness, that the whole of each of these families should be removed at one time, which is the occasion of the demand for this large number of doolies; but if each family be not removed at one time, so much time will elapse before

the dooly boys will have returned from Vellore after making
the different trips, that the river Cauvery will have filled before
the last of the families will have quitted this place, and then
their removal will become much more inconvenient to themselves, and difficult to those who are to carry it into execution.
I am therefore very anxious that the whole number of dooly
boys above required should be supplied as soon as possible.

I have, &c.,

ARTHUR WELLESLEY.

[1109.]   *To Lieutenant-Colonel Dallas.*

MY DEAR COLONEL,   Seringapatam, 25th March, 1802.

I have received a letter from government in which I am
ordered to make arrangements in concert with you for the
removal successively of the families of Hyder and Tippoo. I
look upon this order as conveying authority not only to suggest
arrangements, but to carry them into execution, and I shall act
accordingly.

Upon inquiry from Marriott I find that to remove either of
these families will require 250 doolies and 100 carts, besides
tents, &c. &c., in abundance. I write this day to government
to desire that 1500 dooly boys may be hired and sent to
Seringapatam as soon as possible. I beg to know from you
what number of doolies the stores at Vellore can furnish, as I
will desire that the boys may be ordered to stop there to bring
them up, and I must give orders that those may be made immediately which will be above the number which your stores
and mine can supply.

I shall also be glad to know how many platform carts your
stores can supply, and I will send down bullocks for them forthwith. I have as many tents and kanauts as will answer. Let
me know how soon the buildings will be prepared which are
intended for the accommodation of the family which is to leave
this place last. It will save much expense and trouble if they
can be ready at an early period, as the same equipment will
then answer for the removal of both families. If government
are quick in sending up the boys, and we have tolerable luck,
we shall have the second family off before the river fills, which
will be about the 15th June.

We ended our previous correspondence upon this subject by your sending me a set of billiard balls. I wish you would begin this one by a present of a similar kind, only let them be rather smaller than the last. Elliott sent me a copy of the order you gave out on the review of my regiment. I rejoice that you are pleased with them. I have commanded them now for nearly ten years, during nine of which I have scarcely been away from them, and I have always found them to be the quietest and best behaved body of men in the army.

Believe me, &c.,

ARTHUR WELLESLEY.

To A. Read, Esq.   [1110.]

SIR,   Seringapatam, 25th March, 1802.

I have the honour to enclose the translation of a letter which I have received from Chintomeny Rao, one of the Mahratta chiefs upon the frontier, who, during the late campaign in the Mahratta territory, served with the army under my command. He is of the family of the late Pursheram Bhow.

I am very desirous that his wishes should be complied with, and I shall be much obliged to you if you will let me know whether you think that to comply with them will be attended with any inconvenience. I do not conceive that it will be proper to allow him to send his own people into the jungles to cut the timber, but the aumildar might have it cut for him, and he might send and pay for it.

I shall delay to answer the letter, of which the enclosed is a translation, till I hear from you in answer to this; and if you should think that it will not be inconvenient to comply with the request of Chintomeny Rao, and that the arrangement which I have proposed for cutting the timber is the best, I shall be obliged to you if you will point out the place to which he is to send for it.

I have, &c.,

ARTHUR WELLESLEY.

[ENCLOSURE.]

(Translation of Mahratta letter.)

To the Hon. Colonel Wellesley, from Chintomeny Rao, Pundoo Rung.

(After compliments.)   20th Sherwal.

I am in want of teak wood for building, which is not to be procured in this country. I wish to cut some in the Kittoor and Hullihall jungles, and will be obliged to you if you will write to the officer in command at Hullihall on the subject.

[1111.]

To J. H. Piele, Esq.

My dear Piele,　　　　　　　　　Seringapatam, 25th March, 1802.

The family of the rebel rajah are arrived at Chittledroog, and I write orders to the old baldhead to hand them over to the aumildar.

I have told Grant what you say respecting his cots, and if they arrive at Sera in the time you mention, it will answer his expectations. He has desired that I would request you to settle the price which he is to pay for the carriage of his cots, as there was some difference of opinion between him and Purneah when the last were carried for him.

He is perfectly willing, however, to pay the sum which it was at last settled he should pay upon that occasion, viz., a seer of rice and a pice for each cooly for each stage or day's journey. I have given orders that a small party of sepoys shall accompany each detachment of cots, so that there will be no breakage as there was heretofore.

Believe me, &c.,

Arthur Wellesley.

[1112.]

To the Secretary of the Military Board.

Sir,　　　　　　　　　Seringapatam, 26th March, 1802.

I wrote to you on the 14th instant to request that you would draw the attention of the Military Board to the report which had been forwarded to be laid before them in December last, upon the state of the barracks occupied by the European soldiers at Mangalore; and on the 17th I took the liberty of adverting to the state of the barracks at Cannanore. The storms which usually precede the rains on the western coast have already commenced, and I beg leave again to request that the subject above alluded to may be brought before the Military Board.

The troops at those places must before now have suffered some inconvenience from the state of their barracks; but this will be greatly increased as the rainy season approaches. The repair of the barracks also will become more difficult; and if they should come down entirely, which, from a letter which I have received this morning from Lieutenant-Colonel Spry, there is reason to fear, it will be scarcely possible to move the soldiers out of the province of Canara.

I have, &c.,
ARTHUR WELLESLEY.

To J. H. Piele, Esq.   [1113.]

MY DEAR PIELE,   Seringapatam, 26th March, 1802.

When I sent to government the estimate of the expense of the repairs required to the fort at Nuggur, and to the buildings occupied by the troops and their stores, I recommended that the repairs should be intrusted to the aumildar, that half the expense attending the repair of the fort should be defrayed by the Company according to the treaty, and that the whole of that attending the repair of the public buildings should be paid by them likewise. Government complied with this recommendation, and I understand that the repairs have been going on ever since.

I am acquainted with Ram Rao, the man who has charge of these works at Nuggur, and I have a very good opinion of him; but as the Company are to pay half the expense of the repairs of the fort, and the whole of the expense of the repairs of the public buildings, and besides are to pay half of a certain expense to be incurred annually for tatties, drain-making, &c., &c., to prevent the works and buildings from receiving injury from the rains, would it not be proper to give orders to the commanding officer there to make some report upon the works?

I am very unwilling to allow the commanding officer to interfere at all in the works which are going on, but I should propose, if Purneah has no objection to it, to send him a copy of the estimate, and to desire him to report at a certain period whether the works, for the expenses of which an estimate has been made, have been completed according to that estimate or not.

Let me have your opinion upon this subject. If you think that such an order will not be attended with inconvenient interference on the part of the commanding officer, I will give it, and I will communicate to you the draft of it before I send it.

Believe me, &c.,
ARTHUR WELLESLEY.

[1114.]   *To Lieutenant-Colonel Dallas.*

MY DEAR COLONEL,   Seringapatam, 26th March, 1802.

Your letter of the 23rd gives a full answer to mine which I wrote to you yesterday. You will observe that I conceive that it is intended that all commissaries are to attend to our orders, and I therefore propose to write to you a public letter stating what I shall require from your arsenal, and to request that you will give orders that the articles which I shall require may be put in a serviceable state.

Marriott is mistaken respecting my wish that Tippoo's family should go first; I wished that Hyder's should, as I want the palace which they now occupy to make an hospital for the garrison. I have accordingly desired Marriott to make his arrangements to send off Hyder's women first. I have also desired him to take into consideration your suggestion that some of the inferior tribe should travel in covered carts. If this can be done, it will reduce our demand upon Madras for dooly boys, and thus obviate delay. I shall have plenty of carts, but shall send for the four which you have in store at Vellore.

Although the buildings for Tippoo's women will not be prepared for their reception till August, I shall push on our arrangements so as to get them off by the middle of June, in order to avoid the difficulty of getting them over the river when it fills. If the palace at Vellore be not prepared when they will arrive there, it will not be very inconvenient for them to remain in their tents in the neighbourhood till the palace will be ready for their reception.

                    Believe me, &c.,

                          ARTHUR WELLESLEY.

[1115.]   *To Captain Colebrooke.*

DEAR COLEBROOKE,   Seringapatam, 28th March, 1802.

Barclay has shown me your letter to him of the 24th. It is certainly very desirable that we should make our road into Canara as short as possible, and I shall therefore be obliged to you if you will make inquiries regarding the shortest road from the Bissolee Ghaut to this place. It is not impossible but that there may be a road from Amblimichapatnam or Woochingee through Koorg, and by Periapatam, which would be the shortest, as it is the straightest line ; but the country through which such a road must pass is very rough and jungly, and it is probable that the road would be very bad.   It is worth while, however, to inquire whether there is such a road, and if there be, what is its state, length, &c., &c.

It is more probable that there is a road direct from Ooscotta or Maharaj Droog to Seringapatam ; this would certainly be longer than the other to Woochingee, which I have supposed may exist, but it would be better.   It would also pass at some distance from Periapatam.   Whether there is a road direct from Woochingee through Koorg or not, it is worth while to ascertain whether there is one direct from Ooscotta or Maharaj Droog.

I write this day to the Rajah of Koorg to inform him that I have desired you to ascertain these points, and to request that he will facilitate your operations.   I will desire him to send one of his people to meet you at Maharaj Droog.   If you don't go there, send one of your people to meet the man whom the Rajah of Koorg will send there.

Believe me, &c.,

ARTHUR WELLESLEY.

To Captain Symons.   [1116.]

MY DEAR SYMONS,   Seringapatam, 29th March, 1802.

I have received a letter from General Stuart, in which he encloses a minute upon the subject of the memorandum regarding gun-carriages, which I transmitted to him in the month of December last.   In that memorandum I proposed and recommended that the timber which would be required for the proposed manufactory should be cut by contract ; that some of the most intelligent of the natives of Seringapatam should have the contract for it ; and that the bargain with them should particularly specify that the timber should be paid for according to its dimensions, instead of according to its weight, which is the mode at present in use of deciding on its price.   These propositions of mine have been adopted, and I must now request your assistance in carrying them into execution.

The person with whom I should prefer to contract would be

Naik Shamiah; however, upon this point you must be the best judge, and I shall certainly interfere in no manner whatever in arranging this contract. The timber is to be taken off the hands of the contractor at the jungles, and he is to be paid for it as soon as he will have placed and delivered it into the hands of the person who is to be employed there on the part of the Company to receive it; and the price, as I have above mentioned, is to be in proportion to the dimensions of the beams, not to their weight.

In the memorandum which I wrote upon this subject, which was made out almost entirely from information which I received from you, I stated that the price of cutting a beam of the weight of 30 maunds is about one rupee, and that the profit on the cutting of that beam, and on bringing it in to Seringapatam, is about three sultauny fanams. As the expense of bringing the timber to Seringapatam will not fall upon the contractor, and will, in fact, not exist at all, as it is intended that the Company's bullocks and carts shall bring in the timber, it is not necessary in making this contract to provide for that part of the profit, and therefore we may fairly strike off from the whole expense of felling and paring a tree of that weight at least two sultauny fanams. The whole expense then of felling and paring a beam of that weight would be rather less than half a pagoda. What I have above stated will give you some idea of my notions regarding the price at which the contract ought to be made.

In all our former calculations upon this subject we considered the weight of the timber only. I recommended, however (and the General has adopted the idea), that the contract should be made for cutting and paring the trees, and that they should be paid for according to their dimensions: it will be necessary, therefore, that we should enter into some calculations in order to show the relation between weight and dimensions, and to enable us to make our bargain definitively with the contractor. According to my calculations, a beam weighing 30 maunds, when cut and pared, will be 11 feet long and 1 foot cube. Supposing that half a pagoda would be the expense of cutting and paring that beam, we might go on by doubling its dimensions. Thus the contract might run, that for every beam 11 feet long and 1 cube the contractor should have half a pagoda; for every one above those dimensions, till they come to 22 feet long and 1 cube, he should have a pagoda; for every one above those dimensions till they come to 33 feet long, one pagoda and a half; and so on, the increase of cubical inches in the thickness being calculated in the same manner as feet in the length.

I beg that you will take this subject into consideration, and let me know the result. I send you with this letter one which I have received from General Stuart, his minute upon the subject, and my memorandum and the papers which I have received from you. The perusal of these will give you some lights, will at least show you more clearly what we mean, and will enable us to understand one another more perfectly when we talk about it.

You will observe that this arrangement strikes a little at the profits made by the commissary of supply here, and I am therefore desirous that it should not be talked of unnecessarily until we are prepared with our contractor to commence operations; otherwise dubash influence might prevent any person offering for the contract.

Believe me, &c.,

ARTHUR WELLESLEY.

To Lieutenant-Colonel Close. [1117.]

MY DEAR COLONEL,   Seringapatam, 30th March, 1802.

I have received your letters, for which I am much obliged to you. Matters in Bullum remain in the greatest tranquillity. Captain M'Farlane is there with five companies of Native infantry and the pioneers, and he is continuing to lay open the country in the manner that I told you I had ordered. I shall draw off everybody from that country as soon as the rains are commencing in the hills.

I hope that there will not be much longer delay in the course of your negotiations at Poonah. It is very desirable that they should be brought nearly to a close before the Republicans come to India.

I don't understand exactly the nature of the present dispute between Baba Saheb and Goklah, but they are fighting daily; hitherto their skirmishes have tended to the advantage of the latter. You know that the claim of the Bhow's family to the Savanore and Darwar countries is grounded upon their charges

for the expenses of Lord Cornwallis's Mysore war. It appears
that those countries were given over by the Peshwah to Hurry
Punt to pay the expenses of his and the Bhow's army; Hurry
Punt could come to no settlement with the Bhow, and at last
gave him over the countries in liquidation of his claim.

In these countries thus given by the Sircar in jaghire, or in
payment of debts due by the state, it is usual, I believe, for the
Sircar to hold the strong places, and to keep the revenues of
certain districts to pay the troops which may be employed in
the countries ceded. Goklah's troops are immediately in the
employment of the Sircar, and he depends for their payment
on the revenues of the districts thus held by the Sircar. The
Savanore and Darwar countries have been so frequently overrun
by armies that it stands to reason they cannot be so productive,
although certainly in a high state of cultivation, as they have
been heretofore. It is probable, therefore, that Goklah finds
that the districts belonging immediately to the Sircar, which
have been given to him for the payment of his troops, are not
sufficient for that purpose, and that he is desirous of encroach-
ing upon the other, who stands in the light of a public creditor.
I suppose he uses the old argument: the public force must be
paid first, and next the public debts. This I imagine to be the
groundwork of the present dispute, and I dare say that it is
kept alive by the intrigues at Poonah.

After a consideration of the arguments for and against
Seringapatam, it has been determined to keep it, and repair it.
Some time ago I received from General Stuart a letter, in
which he desired to have some information, and my ideas regarding the teak wood of this country, and the establishment
at Seringapatam of a manufactory of gun-carriages. I went
into a long inquiry on the subject, and the result was very
favourable to the plan. In the course of the inquiry it appeared that nearly six parts out of seven of the price of every
beam of timber were occasioned by the expense of transporting
it from the jungles to Seringapatam. This fact is the groundwork of the plan which I proposed for the establishment and
carrying on of the manufactory.

I proposed, 1stly, that the timber should be cut and pared
by contract; 2ndly, that it should be delivered at the jungles
to a person to be employed there to receive it on the part of
the Company, should be measured and marked, and be paid

for to the contractor according to its dimensions, not according to its weight, which is the common mode of settling the price of timber in this country; 3rdly, that it should be brought in to Seringapatam on the Company's carriages drawn by their cattle; 4thly, that the manufactory should be carried on at the Company's expense, under the superintendence of an agent with a salary.

The Company's bullocks are kept at all events; this work will do them no harm, and will cost no money. It was impossible, under the circumstances of cutting the timber by contract, and bringing it in for nothing excepting the wear and tear of the carriages, to arrange matters so as to throw the business into the hands of the commissary of supply. Either we must have submitted to paying a larger price for the timber than we knew it was worth, or we must have made ourselves timber merchants to the commissary of supply; and even then the arrangement would have been a complicated one, and the business would not have been carried on to so much advantage as under the superintendence of a good agent. This plan has been adopted, and is to be carried into execution as soon as we can cut the timber.

I am going to Bangalore in a few days. Let me hear from you occasionally.

Believe me, &c.,

ARTHUR WELLESLEY.

To W. H. Gordon, Esq.   [1118.]

SIR,   Seringapatam, April, 1802.

Government having in contemplation certain arrangements at Seringapatam, in order to carry which into execution they will require a large quantity of timber, and understanding from report that you have some, they have desired me to inquire whether you will sell it, and at what rate?

In case you should be inclined to dispose of your timber, I shall be obliged to you if you will send me an account of it, stating the following particulars, in order that government may have the whole subject before them when they will take it into their consideration :—

Firstly, the number and dimensions of each beam.

Secondly, the length of time which has elapsed since each has been cut, or has been in your possession.

As it is probable that you will be inclined to settle the price of this timber with government on the most liberal terms, I should wish that the account should also state,

Thirdly, the sum of money which each beam cost you.

When you will transmit this account, I request you to make me acquainted with the terms on which you will dispose of your timber.

I have, &c.,

ARTHUR WELLESLEY.

[1119.]

To A. Read, Esq.

SIR,   Seringapatam, 1st April, 1802.

An order goes this day to Captain Greenly to remain at Bonawassi till joined by the remainder of the corps to which he belongs on its march to Cundapoor.

You will have learned that, by the sentence of the general court martial which tried the late Lieutenant ——— at Seedasheeghur, the grain-dealers who were defrauded of part of the price of the grain which they furnished to a detachment of the Company's troops under his command are to be paid the money of which they have been defrauded. By order of the Commander-in-Chief I wrote to the commanding officer of the battalion to which Lieutenant ——— belonged to desire that any money due to him by the Company might be secured to answer these demands. In consequence of this letter, which was laid before the government of Bombay, certain sums of money belonging to Mr. ———, in the hands of Mr. Adamson of Bombay, have been officially attached by order of the Governor in Council of Bombay, to answer any public demands which may appear against him.

A formal requisition will be made for its payment as soon as any specific claim is made on behalf of the grain-dealers in Canara.

There are two modes in which it will be possible for you to obtain this money from the government of Bombay: one is to send me the specific claims of the grain-dealers, and I will forward them to the government of Bombay; the other is, that

you should forward them to the Board of Revenue at Fort
St. George, through whose means and those of government
they might likewise reach the government of Bombay. I recommend, however, the former, as the most likely to obtain the
money for the grain-dealers speedily.

I have, &c.,

ARTHUR WELLESLEY.

To Lieutenant-Colonel Cuppage.   [1120.]

SIR,   Seringapatam, 1st April, 1802.

I some time ago made a proposition to government to repair
the fort of Nuggur.   Under the treaty with the Rajah of
Mysore it is settled that those forts in his Highness's territories,
which the Company's government should think proper, should
be put and kept in a state of repair, and that the expense of
such repairs should be defrayed, half by the Company and half
by the Rajah.   Under these circumstances, and as it was not
convenient to send an engineer to Nuggur to give to the fort
the repairs which it required, I desired and settled that the
work should be performed under the superintendence of the
aumildar, upon estimates of which the enclosed papers are
translations.   One of them is an estimate of the expense which
must now be incurred to put the fort, and the buildings which
it contains, in a state of repair; the other is an estimate or
memorandum of the expenses which must be incurred annually,
in order to prevent the damage which the fort would otherwise
suffer from the rains.

In the first is included an expense of 783 pagds. 7¼ fs. for the
repairs of the buildings.   This falls entirely upon the Company,
as the treaty does not provide that the Rajah shall pay half
of the expense of the buildings required for the Company's
troops, their stores and provisions.

I beg that, as soon after the receipt of this letter as possible,
you will communicate with the aumildar upon this subject, and
learn from him what quantity of the work of which he estimated
the expense, as in the enclosed paper, has been completed.   If
any part of it be completed, or as soon as any part will be
completed, I request you to assemble a committee of officers, of

which you are to be one, to survey such work, and report to me its state, &c. &c.

I also request to have from you, as soon as you are enabled to form it, your opinion of the general progress of the works ordered, and of the manner in which they are performed.

You will observe, that the "Memorandum of the Annual Expense" to be incurred contains little more than a list of people to be employed on the works, and an account of the expense of tatties, &c., for the protection of the fort and the buildings during the rains. These people and the tatties are absolutely necessary; and if you should observe that the work required from them, as described in the enclosed memorandum, is not performed, or that the tatties are not furnished, I beg to hear from you.

I have, &c.,

ARTHUR WELLESLEY.

[1121.]   *To Lieutenant-Colonel Boles.*

SIR,   Seringapatam, 3rd April, 1802.

I beg that you will give orders to the garrison-storekeeper at Cochin to dispose, by public auction, of all the provisions in store at Cochin, excepting the arrack and those other provisions of which a description will follow hereafter.

The arrack must be embarked and sent to Cannanore, excepting the quantity which it may be necessary to leave at Cochin for the use of the European garrison, which it will be proper to keep there till the Dutch will take possession of the place. It is probable now that the Dutch will not be able to take possession till after the monsoon; and it will be necessary, therefore, to leave at Cochin a quantity of arrack which will last the European troops till that period. You will be the best judge whether it is probable that, during that period, the garrison which will be left at Cochin will want any of the provisions which are in store there. If you should be of opinion that they will want any of them, you will give orders that such of them as you think they will want may not be sold. If you should be of opinion that the garrison will not require the provisions, the whole of them are to be sold.

I approve of your proposal to relieve the 1st battalion 4th regiment in Wynaad, and of the arrangement according to which you propose to carry that measure into effect. The 1st of the 4th is, however, equal to the duties in Wynaad; and you will observe that you will lose by the proposed arrangement in the southern division of Malabar, where men are most wanted, the difference between the strength of Major Howden's corps and that of the 1st of the 4th regiment. Unless, therefore, you are of opinion that the latter corps will derive great benefit from the change, I believe it would be as well to leave matters as they are till after the monsoon.

I have no objection to the change of the head-quarters in Wynaad to Poollingal. The reason for which the situation recommended by Colonel Stevenson has not been adopted is, that an arrangement for procuring quarters for the Native troops is under the consideration of government, and till a decision has been made upon that subject it has not been thought proper to give orders that any expense may be incurred on account of new cantonments for the Native troops. It is my intention, however, that eventually they should be cantoned at Panamburcottah.

. I have written twice lately regarding the state of the cantonments for the European troops at Cannanore and Mangalore, and I expect every day to receive orders upon the subject.

I have, &c.,

ARTHUR WELLESLEY.

I beg to hear from you the particulars of the arrangement which you will make for the removal of the arrack and provisions from Cochin.

To Lieutenant Cobb. [1122.]

DEAR SIR, Seringapatam, 3rd April, 1802.

The reason for which I was desirous that you should repay by monthly payments the sum of money which I had lent you was, that I thought it would be the most convenient mode to you; and I was unwilling to send your bills to England for acceptance and payment until you received positive assurances from your friends, on whom they are drawn, that they would pay them. It has happened to me before now to advance money to gentlemen for bills on their relations, which bills have afterwards been protested, and have been returned to me with the costs of the protests, which have amounted to two-thirds of the sum originally lent. I have, therefore, determined never to send a bill home for payment until I am certain that it will be paid; and I have, accordingly, kept in my hands your bills until you hear from your friends upon the subject.

It appears that it will now be inconvenient to you to pay the sum monthly which you have paid hitherto. I shall be sorry to put you to any inconvenience, and I beg that you will discontinue to pay it. If, after having discharged the sum for your horse, you can recommence the payment of it without inconvenience to yourself, I conclude that you will do so; if not, I beg that you will defer it till it will be perfectly convenient to you.

As the commanding officer and the paymaster of your regiment had a knowledge of this arrangement between you and me, I beg that you will communicate this letter to those gentlemen.

Believe me, &c.,

ARTHUR WELLESLEY.

[1123.] *To Lieutenant-General Stuart.*

SIR, Seringapatam, 4th April, 1802.

I enclose some despatches received in the night from Sir William Clarke. They convey intelligence of a disagreeable nature; but, as by the expected return of Major-General Baird from Egypt with a large body of troops the government of Bombay will have a commanding force at their disposal, it is to be hoped that this disaster will not have any very bad effects.

The whole corps of pioneers are still in the Bullum country, completing the destruction of the fortified villages. I have ordered two companies of that corps to march forthwith from thence into the Ceded Districts, under the directions of Captain Colebrooke. I have, likewise, ordered another company from thence to Seringapatam, in order to commence the proposed works here. The remainder shall follow as soon as they will have completed their business in Bullum, which I consider to be essential to the future peace of that district.

In the mean time I have made all the arrangements for carrying on the works here on the principles on which they were carried on in the last year, and which were approved of by government. The labours of Captain Heitland in Bullum have made him sick; but I hope that he will be sufficiently recovered to take charge of the work by the time that the first detachment of pioneers will come in.

I have not yet concluded the contract for cutting the timber. It is difficult to make the natives understand the advantages which they, as well as the public, will derive from making the price of the timber depend upon the size of the beams, and not upon their weight. However, I hope that we shall overcome this difficulty. I hear of a large number of newly-withered trees, which are to be first cut, and will answer for immediate use.

I have had a conversation with Mr. Gordon upon the subject of the timber in his possession. He appears disposed to let the public have it upon reasonable terms. He will give me an account of the number and size of the beams, the sums of money which they have cost him, and the length of time which has elapsed since he got them. He desires what appears to me fair enough, that the Company should pay him what the timber cost him, and should make him some reasonable allowance in addition thereto, as compensation for the loss of the interest of the money vested in this timber for such a length of time. If he were to sell the timber to any other person, he would have this profit at least upon it, and probably more.

I have written to him officially upon the subject, and as soon as I receive his answer I will transmit it to you.

I have no doubt but that the yard will answer well. At present it is much hampered with rubbish, mud, &c., taken from the old palace when it was pulled down. These will assist in filling the ditch of the fort; and I therefore delay doing anything to the yard till I begin that work. I shall begin it, however, in a fortnight, and then a few days will clear the yard.

We are miserably off here for want of an engineer: we certainly have now the worst in the service. Lieutenant Bell, who preceded him, was diligent, and not unwilling to take advice; but I can get this gentleman to do nothing.

You will have seen before the Council the contents of the requisition which I have been obliged to make for dooly-

bearers to carry away the families of the late Hyder Ali
and Tippoo Sultaun.   Since I wrote last upon the subject I have
had a letter from Lieutenant-Colonel Dallas, in which he states
that he had a communication with Futteh Hyder regarding the
number of doolies and bearers which these women had required,
who had declared that, although the women would certainly
prefer to be carried in doolies, there was no objection to their
going in covered platform-carts, and he recommended that we
should adopt that mode of conveyance for a large number of
them.   I should wish, therefore, to give orders that an additional number of platform-carts may be made : they will always
be useful, and the present expense of them will fall upon the
family fund.

If you should adopt this measure, I shall be obliged to you
if, to save time, you will intimate that 700 dooly-bearers,
instead of 1200, the number for which I last made a requisition, will be sufficient.

I have, &c.,
ARTHUR WELLESLEY.

[1124.]   *To the Secretary of the Military Board.*

SIR,   Seringapatam, 6th April, 1802.

I have had the honour of receiving your letter of the
1st April.

All the carts which the arsenal at Seringapatam can supply
will be required in a short time for the removal of the families
of Hyder Ali and Tippoo Sultaun to Vellore.   If, therefore, the
Military Board are desirous that the stores of which you have
enclosed the lists should be moved from Seringapatam and
Ryacottah respectively to Nundydroog immediately, it will be
necessary to hire carts for that service.   But, as I do not see
any immediate necessity for sending the stores to Nundydroog,
I shall omit to order that the carts may be hired till I receive
the directions of the Military Board ; and I beg leave to recommend that the stores may not be sent to Nundydroog till the
Company's carts may be unemployed, and can be used on that
service.

I have, &c.,
ARTHUR WELLESLEY.

To Lieutenant-General Stuart. [1125.]

SIR, Seringapatam, 7th April, 1802.

I have the honour to enclose a contract which I have arranged with a native of this place, by name Shamiah, for cutting timber in the jungles bordering on Wynaad. If it should meet with your approbation, I hope to be favoured with your orders to sign it. You will observe that the price stated in this contract is higher than that taken as a datum in the calculation in the minute of which you enclosed me a copy in your letter of the 24th of March. In the memorandum which I had the honour of submitting to you upon this subject, I stated that the actual cost of cutting and paring a tree which would make a beam weighing 30 maunds would be less than a rupee, and this beam would be about eleven feet long and one cube. Upon this calculation, the expense would be about one Madras silver fanam per cubic foot. To this expense, however, which I have estimated as the actual cost of cutting and paring the tree, must be added, according to the estimate in my memorandum, the profit of the merchant or contractor. This profit would be one-twelfth upon the whole expense, or a Madras fanam, and would increase the price of each foot of timber about 7 cash.

I mention this circumstance to point out that the estimate which I originally made was not erroneous, and is not inconsistent with the price stated in the contract. Indeed, the price stated in the memorandum is high, as will appear by what follows hereafter.

You will observe that one of the operations to be performed by the contractor is to pile the timber. Although he may have as many piles as he may think proper, it stands to reason that it will be necessary that he should move some of the beams, and to move them even one hundred yards from the place on which they are felled will cost some money.

Accordingly, in making this contract I have found that to pile the timber is the most expensive operation required from the contractor.

He offered repeatedly to cut, pare, and mark a tree of the dimensions above stated for about eight Madras fanams, or three Sultany pice, or 60 cash per cubic foot. The additional price stated in the contract is to be attributed entirely to the necessity of collecting the timber in piles.

I have taken the subject into consideration with a view to performing that part of the work by means already in the Company's service, by which that part of the expense would be saved; but I do not find that any mode within my power would answer.

The trees will be cut in extensive jungles, through which the Company's wheel-carriages cannot penetrate. These jungles are exceedingly unwholesome, and it is probable that the people whom we might send into them for the purpose of performing this part of the work would suffer considerably in their health.

Supposing that these difficulties in the execution of this part of the work by the Company's means did not exist, I am afraid that we should find it difficult to arrange the mode according to which the timber should be delivered, when felled and pared, to the conductor by the contractor, without going more into detail than is ever desirable with this kind of people.

Upon the whole, therefore, I have thought it best to insist upon the contractor's piling the timber; and I am happy to observe that, notwithstanding that the expense occasioned by this operation more than doubles the price of the timber, it will add to your estimate of the cost of a carriage for a 24-pounder only 3p. 13f. 40c.

In the memorandum which I had heretofore the honour of submitting to you upon this subject, I stated some of the objections which occurred to me to the employment of persons in the service of the Company and of the Rajah of Mysore in cutting the timber. A farther inquiry and consideration of the subject have strengthened those objections. It is certain that persons who have not been employed in this kind of work will not perform it well or with advantage to the public; and such is the reputed unwholesomeness of the jungles, that I fear none of the people whom we might send into them would live, or, at least, would be able to perform any service for any great length of time. The contractor will employ the people of the country, who are accustomed to the work and to the jungles; and I believe that we shall find that he will furnish as large a quantity of timber as can be worked up.

I will take care that the Mysore government shall give no molestation to the contractor.

In case your Excellency should approve of the terms of this

contract, I expect to procure immediately a large quantity of withered timber, which can be worked up forthwith.

There is besides at present in the Company's possession a quantity of seasoned timber, which was found at Scringapatam when the fort was taken, and I expect in a few days to be able to submit to your Excellency a proposition from Mr. Gordon for the sale of the timber in his possession. The manufactory, therefore, might now be established with advantage to the public.

As, however, we must wait at least a year before the green timber which will now be cut will be fit for use, it will be proper to establish the manufactory at first upon a limited scale, and to form its establishment only of such an extent as will manufacture the materials in the Company's possession, or within their reach, in the space of time which will elapse before the green timber will be fit for use.

By the end of this month I hope that the yard of the Mysore palace will be cleared of its rubbish, and that I shall have it in my power to submit to you the plans of the buildings and other improvements which will be necessary for the manufactory.

I have, &c.,

ARTHUR WELLESLEY.

To Captain Heitland.   [1126.]

SIR,   Seringapatam, 9th April, 1802.

Government have sent me orders to recommence the work on the inner ditch of the fort of Seringapatam, which was discontinued by their orders in the month of July last. I propose to employ upon it the pioneers and such assistance as I can procure for them, and that you should superintend the work as heretofore.

I have ordered into Seringapatam, in order to commence the work as soon as possible, Captain-Lieutenant Davies and 100 pioneers; and I have desired Naik Shamiah to have in readiness 2000 commatties on the 20th instant. As it appears that he can procure as many of that description of people as we shall want, I have not made a requisition for any assistance from the Rajah's government.

I beg to refer you to my letter to you of the 9th of June,

1801, for a description of the work to be performed, for the establishment of writers and conicopolies which you will be allowed in order to keep the accounts of the people employed, and for that of artificers to keep the tools of the work-people in repair; to that of the 28th of June, 1801, from the Deputy-Adjutant-General, for the rate of hire which will be allowed to Shamiah's commatties; and to that of the 17th of June from the Deputy-Adjutant-General for the allowance to be given to Shamiah himself, and for the rate of hire which will be allowed to basket coolies. I also refer you to a letter from the Deputy-Adjutant-General of the 28th of June, 1801, for the mode of settling the accounts of the people to be employed under your superintendence.

I have, &c.,

ARTHUR WELLESLEY.

[1127.]   *To Lieutenant-Colonel Boles.*

SIR,   Bangalore, 12th April, 1802.

I have received the orders of the Commander-in-Chief to desire that the corps on the Bombay establishment, serving under the government of Fort St. George, may not be reduced according to the orders of the government of Bombay. These orders have been suspended by the government of Fort St. George.

The Commander-in-Chief has not confirmed your order appointing Corporal Clayton a conductor; and he desires that the conductor at Calicut may be removed to Cannanore, in order to fill the vacancy in the store department at the latter place.

I expect every day to receive the orders of government establishing tent-allowance for the troops, which I understand from the Military Board provides a mode of repairing and building barracks for the Native troops. This allowance is to take place from the 1st of May next, and it stands to reason that government will not at present incur any expense for the repair of buildings for which provision is made by the order in question.

The time passes, however, for the repair of the buildings occupied by the Native troops in Malabar and Canara, and it is probable that, if they are not repaired forthwith, the monsoon will set in before they can be repaired. I therefore suggest to you the propriety of stating in your General Orders the circumstance which I have above-mentioned, and of your urging officers commanding corps of Native troops to commence forthwith the repairs of the buildings which are to be occupied by the troops under their command during the monsoon, so that they may be preserved from its pernicious effects.

I enclose a memorandum of the repairs required to certain buildings at certain stations in the provinces under your command, of which you will order the immediate execution.

I have, &c.,

ARTHUR WELLESLEY.

The following repairs to the buildings hereafter stated :—

Cotaparamba.—A place of arms and storehouse, for the number of men to be cantoned there during the monsoon, to be cadjanned.

Paulghautcherry.—The small repairs required to the place of arms and storehouses of provisions and ordnance stores to be given, and the tiles on those buildings to be turned.

Mangalore.—Temporary repairs to be given to the storehouse and to the place of arms for the Native corps.

Calicut.—The storehouse for the battalion and the place of arms to be cadjanned.

Seedasheeghur.—The storehouse and place of arms to be cadjanned.

Cochin.—Temporary repairs to be given to the buildings required to cover the European troops, the stores, and the arms of the Native troops.

Angarypur.—A storeroom to be built, established expense 52 pagodas.

The barrack of arms to be cadjanned.

ARTHUR WELLESLEY.

I returned from Bangalore yesterday evening.

To Lieutenant-Colonel Maxwell. [1128.]

MY DEAR COLONEL, Seringapatam, 16th April, 1802.

I hope that your barracks are getting on, as the weather looks very threatening, and I fear that the monsoon will be earlier than usual. You must have a committee upon the barracks, and they must not be passed if the thatch be not put on in the manner described in my letter to Lieutenant Bell upon that subject.

Dr. Anderson tells me that your hospital suits you very well. If it suit in point of situation, as connected with your barracks, I beg that you will ask the aumildar whether you can have it permanently. If you can have it permanently, desire Mr. Bell to break out windows, and to wall it up with windows and doors, and organize it for an hospital, as I have organized similar buildings at this place; also to build a temporary necessary and cook-room for it, to estimate the expense of the whole, and to forward the estimate to me.

I expect shortly to receive 18 horses, which Mr. Manesty has sent from Bussora to this place to be sold. If you or any of the gentlemen of the 19th want Arabs, you may as well employ some of your friends here to buy for you.

Believe me, &c.,
ARTHUR WELLESLEY.

[1129.]   *To Lieutenant-General Stuart.*

SIR,   Seringapatam, 17th April, 1802.

In my letter of the 23rd of March upon the subject of the removal of the stores from Cochin to Tellicherry and Cannanore, I informed you that it appeared to me to be then too late to commence removing the stores from those places which should be surplus to the proposed establishment at Cannanore, and I proposed that this measure should be postponed till the commencement of the next fair season. These stores, those from Mangalore, and those from Calicut are now divided between Tellicherry and Cannanore. It has been impossible to collect the whole at the latter place, as some of the buildings which might be used to hold them are occupied by the European troops, the cantonments being in ruins; and even if those buildings could be applied to that purpose, they would not be sufficient to hold all the stores now collected at the two places. It becomes, therefore, absolutely necessary to leave a part at Tellicherry till, by the change of the season, we may be able to remove the surplus to the establishment at Seringapatam.

I observe, however, by the government orders, that the store establishment at Tellicherry has been struck off, agreeably to the recommendation which I took the liberty of making to you when I imagined that there would be no stores at that station; but as I have above pointed out that it will be necessary to keep some of them at Tellicherry for a time, I beg leave now to recommend that the establishment originally fixed for that place may be continued till it may be possible to remove from thence all the stores.

By the letters which I have lately received from Egypt, I have reason to believe that the army under Major-General Baird will shortly return to India. I beg leave to recall to your recollection the recommendation which I heretofore took the liberty of making of Lieutenant-Colonel Montresor to be appointed to the command in Malabar. If you should approve of this arrangement, it would be desirable that the 80th regiment should relieve the Bombay regiment at Cannanore, and I imagine that this relief will not be more advantageous to the public service than it will be agreeable to the government of Bombay.

I have, &c.,

ARTHUR WELLESLEY.

To Josiah Webbe, Esq. [1130.]

MY DEAR WEBBE, Seringapatam, 17th April, 1802.

Many thanks for the extract of the letter from Colonel Close.

I suspect that matters are rather worse than they are represented to be in the despatches which Colonel Close received. It appears that Mr. Duncan commenced a negotiation with Mulhar Rao, having determined to have recourse to arms in case it should fail. It has failed, and he has had recourse to arms, and without success. This appears not only upon the face of the story, but by the acts of Mr. Duncan and Major Walker and of the temporary government of Bombay. Major Walker took post, and called for reinforcements; Mr. Duncan sends for troops to all quarters, and the temporary government despatch them with all celerity. This would not be necessary if the event of the battle had been at all successful, or even if Major Walker were able to recommence it.

But I perceive that these events did not take place in the neighbourhood of Brodera, as we imagined, but in the Ahmedabad district. As far as I can judge by the map, Ahmedabad is at a great distance from the sea, and, of course, the difficulty in reinforcing Major Walker must be greater than we imagined. However, the force sent from Bombay is very large, and if they can join it with that under Colonel Anderson from Surat, and equip it tolerably, matters may still go well.

I will take care that the old lady at Chinnapatam shall not receive any farther payments on account of her pension.

I hear from Dr. Anderson that Mr. Dick intends to bring before the Council the subject of the garden at Bangalore. I think it not improbable.

Believe me, &c.,

ARTHUR WELLESLEY.

[1131.] *To Lieutenant-Colonel Montresor.*

MY DEAR COLONEL, Seringapatam, 17th April, 1802.

As this letter will be delivered to you upon your arrival at Bombay, I shall not enter into the subject of your different letters from Egypt any more than to thank you for them, nor shall I give you any Indian news, which you will hear to better advantage from your friends at Bombay. Indeed the attention of all of us is now directed to Major Walker's recent failure in Guzerat, and we are all desirous of hearing from that quarter, rather than of writing news thither.

You will have heard that Colonel Stevenson has been removed from the command in the provinces of Malabar and Canara to that of the subsidiary force at Hyderabad, and the command of those provinces is now in the hands of Lieutenant-Colonel Boles till an officer can be found to hold it. When Colonel Stevenson was removed, General Stuart desired me to recommend an officer to be appointed to this command, and I recommended yourself, and that this temporary arrangement should be made till you could return with your corps from Egypt. The General gave no answer to the recommendation of yourself, but he consented to the arrangement proposed as far as it regarded Lieutenant-Colonel Boles, and, as far as I can learn his private opinion, it is that some other person ought to be appointed to that important station.

I write to the General this day again to recommend that you may be called down to Malabar and Canara, and, preparatory to that arrangement and in order to facilitate it, to propose that he should desire General Lake to place the 80th regiment at Cannanore.   As the General has allowed me to do nearly what I please in these provinces, I think that he will grant my request in this instance, and I hope that what I have done will be agreeable to you.

The situation which you will hold, if I should succeed, will be one of the most important in India, and in my opinion the most desirable which an officer of your rank can have, excepting probably my own : to which, indeed, I have also to observe that that which you will have is the high road ; and, as you will have the rank of Colonel, and those provinces are to remain under Mysore, there is every reason to believe that it will be permanent.   You will command at Cannanore, where I have proposed that a regiment of Europeans, the artillery of the provinces, and two battalions of sepoys should be cantoned, and you will besides have the table allowance of Brigadier.

I shall apprise you of General Stuart's answer to my letter ; in the mean time I beg that you will keep to yourself what I have written to you, and that you will arrange matters with your friends at Bombay in such a manner as that if the 80th regiment be ordered to Malabar, it may not be so situated as to render it quite impossible to bring it down there.

Believe me, &c.,

ARTHUR WELLESLEY.

To Lieutenant-Colonel Cuppage.   [1132.]

SIR,   Seringapatam, 18th April, 1802.

I have received your letter of the 14th instant and its enclosure.   I observe that the magazine is not repaired as it ought to be, and that the conductor in charge of the stores at Nuggur reports that the roof still admits the rain.

I beg you to notice this circumstance to the aumildar, and

L 2

point out to him the absolute necessity of making this building waterproof.

I have, &c.,

ARTHUR WELLESLEY.

[1133.]   *To the Chief Secretary of Government.*

SIR,   Seringapatam, 19th April, 1802.

I enclose an account of the expense of the erection of a court-house and of a gaol at Seringapatam, and a letter which I have received from Captain Symons upon that subject.

It appears that the expense incurred upon this occasion exceeds the estimate, but the cause of this circumstance is sufficiently explained in the letter from Captain Symons, to which I request you to draw the attention of the Right Hon. the Governor in Council.

The experience which we have had of the nature of the climate of Mysore has demonstrated the bad effects of living in buildings from which the weather cannot be excluded; and therefore I beg leave to state my opinion that Captain Symons acted judiciously in altering the plan of the building when by a farther acquaintance with the climate he found that it would not answer. The same experience has shown us that mud walls will not stand under the torrents of rain which fall in this country.

I have examined both buildings, which are well constructed for the purpose for which they were built, and I therefore beg leave to recommend that the whole expense incurred in building them may be paid.

I have, &c.,

ARTHUR WELLESLEY.

[1134.]   *To Josiah Webbe, Esq.*

MY DEAR WEBBE,   Seringapatam, 19th April, 1802.

I don't think that we shall experience any inconvenience in the employment of Purneah's runners to carry our tappalls. Purneah has never failed yet in anything that he has undertaken for us, and I don't think that he will fail in this arrangement.

I recollect having had a conversation with Close upon this subject, and he objected strongly to the principle of loading Purneah with any of the Company's concerns. He said, what is true, that he has enough to do to realise the revenue of this country, and that it would not answer to make him or the officers of his government responsible for the execution of any of the arrangements usually carried on by the inferior departments. I think this objection well founded in general, and the question is, whether it is better to spend a little money upon this occasion, or to load Purneah with this concern. I believe, upon the whole, it would be best to incur a little expense, particularly as we must interfere, in some degree, with his tappall in order to render its operations as regular as we should require them to be.

In the first place, we must have our own conicopolies at all the principal stations to receive our letters, and make up and open the packets. They must be delivered by the conicopoly here to the person employed by Purneah to despatch the runners. The tappall must be despatched from each station at stated hours, and it must arrive regularly, as at present.

Secondly, there is a certain revenue collected upon the carriage of letters. It would not be quite reasonable that we should interfere with Purneah's tappall so far as to fix the time at which it shall depart and arrive, and that we should make his runners carry our letters without paying part of the expense out of the revenue collected. To act thus would be unjust. If, then, we pay part of the revenue, or a stipulated sum for the carriage of our letters, one of our inferior departments, that of the Postmaster-General, or that of the Deputy Postmaster in this country, must interfere directly in one of the arrangements of this government.

I think, upon the whole, that, although we should experience no inconvenience in the arrangement, it would be better to avoid it, and to spend even the 20,000 pagodas *per annum*. If, however, it should be adopted at all, I am so convinced that it will be executed as we could wish, that I see no reason why the Madras tappall, as well as the others, should not be included in it.

Believe me, &c.,

ARTHUR WELLESLEY.

[1135.]

To Major Malcolm.

MY DEAR MALCOLM,   Seringapatam, 20th April, 1802.

I have received your letter of the 27th March, for which I am much obliged to you.

The arrangements made by you at Madras must have been very satisfactory to Lord Wellesley. They have secured the accomplishment of an important measure, the permanent settlement of the revenue in the territories under the government of Fort St. George, and the cordiality and co-operation of that government with the Supreme government at the present crisis.

If the permanent settlement of the revenue had been left to the present Board of Revenue, that measure would never have been effected ; and if Lord Clive had gone to England, the government which would have succeeded to him would have quarrelled with the Supreme government, and, under the spurious names of reform of military expenditure and increase of investment, would have been guilty of every enormity that has lately met with the approbation and patronage of the Court of Directors.

The merit of the arrangements which have prevented these evils depends upon the characters of the individuals affected by them ; and the degree of approbation which will be given to them at home will be in proportion to the knowledge which people have of the characters of the leading men in India, particularly of those of the favourites of the Court of Directors. I hope, therefore, that Lord Wellesley has taken care in his despatches to bring a few facts to the knowledge of his friends in England.

I rejoice to hear that he intends to go home, if justice be not done to him by the Court of Directors ; and if the ministers do not give him security that he shall not be again liable to the corrupt and vulgar interference of Leadenhall Street in the operations of his government. Their appointment to all the principal offices at Fort St. George, and the encouragement which I understand they have given to their councils to oppose the acts of their governors, are inconsistent with the spirit of, if not directly contrary to, the law ; and their sending out to India all those who have been sent home for misbehaviour must, if not prevented in future, end in the annihilation of all British power in India.

All these measures are aimed directly at Lord Wellesley, and he cannot remain in the government, and no *gentleman* can succeed to him, if means are not taken to prevent them in future.

It is reported that * * * *'s conduct at —— has at last come to Lord Wellesley's ears. I rejoice at this most sincerely, and I hope that he will be treated as he deserves. His conduct for a length of time has really been a disgrace to the British name and nation; and I was certain that Lord Wellesley could not know all.

Believe me, &c.,

ARTHUR WELLESLEY.

To Lieutenant-General Stuart.　　　　　　　　　[1136.]

SIR,　　　　　　　　　　　Seringapatam, 21st April, 1802.

I had yesterday the honour of receiving your letter of the 16th, and it gives me great pleasure to be able to take this early opportunity of giving you the additional information which is required regarding the proposed gun-carriage manufactory. I am well pleased that the subject should be inquired into; and I am convinced that the more it is inquired into, the more likely is it that the plan will be adopted, provided that the object of those who make the inquiries is really to gain useful knowledge, and not to throw impediments in the way of the execution of a plan intended for the public advantage.

The contractor understands that he is to pile the timber in such places as the conductor will point out, as is expressed in the contract, viz., that he is to pile the timber under the superintendence and inspection of the conductor. He is willing that it should be inserted in the contract that the piles shall be placed in situations accessible to the Company's wheel-carriages.

The timber will be taken from these piles and placed upon the carriages by the lascars and the drivers of the bullocks.

According to the plan first proposed, and to the minute written by you, it was intended that the timber should be allowed to remain a certain time in the jungle, because it would season equally well there, and because, as it would lose half its weight when dry, it would be less difficult to transport it to Seringapatam. If it were possible to procure carts which would give employment to all the Company's cattle, they would bring in as much timber in one trip, which, at the utmost, would take only twenty days, as the manufactory could work up in a year, unless it be established upon a very extended scale. But, as we cannot look for more than 150 to 200 carriages, it will probably require two or three trips, which will take about two months of time to bring in this timber. The question is, whether, in this season next year, there is a probability that the Company's cattle will be so far employed as that 800 of them cannot be spared for this service. I don't see any reason to believe that there will be such extensive employment for the cattle either in this season next year, or, in all probability, for many years to come. If, however, there should be such employment for them, it must be considered as a casual circumstance, and not as an ordinary event, which must be taken into the calculation in considering a subject of this kind; and, at all events, there can be no doubt but that, if the timber be ready-cut in the jungles, it will be possible, at some time or other, to spare the Company's cattle to bring it in.

But if the Company's cattle, from circumstances which cannot now be foreseen or expected, cannot be employed on this service, buffalo-carts can be hired for it: their price is about two-and-a-half star pagodas for the trip to the jungles and back again; and each cart with two buffaloes will bring about 28 or 30 maunds of timber. The beams which will have this weight will vary in their size in proportion to their dryness; and when they come to a very large size, additional yokes of buffaloes must be employed, and the same price must be paid for each yoke.

In calculating the price of timber at Seringapatam, the carriage costs about seven times the price of the cutting at the jungle, including the profit to the merchant. Thus, a beam of 11 feet in length, the actual cost of cutting and paring which, without piling, will be about one rupee at the jungle, besides the profit, will cost about 8 or 8½ rupees to remove it to Seringapatam.

The expense of cutting, paring, and piling 11 cubic feet at the jungle, according to the contract, will be about 19 f. 40 c., or the sixth of the expense of the carriage of such a beam to Seringapatam. The use of hired cattle and carts on this service will add six times the expense to the timber, or, in other words, the timber to be used in constructing a 24-pounder will cost 44 p. 41 f. 20 c., instead of 6 p. 18 f. 60 c., according to my calculation, founded upon the contract, or 3 p. 5 f. 20 c., according to that in your minute.

I should propose to employ at Cancancotta, on this service, one conductor, one moochie man (to mark the timber with English characters or figures), one second tindal, and twenty lascars; and one havildar, one naik, and twelve sepoys.

The establishment of the garrison of Seringapatam cannot, at present, afford a conductor; but I imagine there are some supernumerary conductors, one of whom can be employed on this service. The other persons required will belong to the establishments already in the garrison of Seringapatam. As it will be necessary to relieve them very frequently, and as they will be constantly out on duty, I propose that they should all have batta, and I enclose a paper which states the monthly expense to be incurred on their account.

The employment of the public cattle on this service will cause no additional expense, either on their account or on that of their servants.

The woodcutters can distinguish a tree which is so far withered as that its timber will be unserviceable, and will not cut it; but the contractor clearly understands, and it may be inserted in the contract, that trees which may be unserviceable when tendered shall be rejected. This insertion, however, will apply only to the present moment, as hereafter, when the timber which he will tender will not be dried or withered, it is to be supposed that the whole of it will be serviceable.

I hope that the explanation which I have above given will be satisfactory to you; and I beg to assure you that I shall never deem it a trouble to be employed by you in anything in which I can be serviceable to the public. I am convinced that this plan will answer: all our inquiries and calculations prove it, which ought to be sufficient for our satisfaction. But there is another circumstance, which will prove it, probably, more clearly than our calculations to the satisfaction of others. I am informed that Mr. Gordon has made an offer to make all kinds of carriages at Seringapatam at an expense 40 per cent. less than that incurred by the employment of a contractor. Mr. Gordon, however, must have hired the cattle and carriages to bring in the timber and the iron, must have bought the iron, and must have incurred various expenses to which the Company will be liable, and it is probable that in an offer of this kind he took care to secure a profit for himself which would cover all risks. I observe that the calculation of expense made by you brings it near 70 per cent. less than that incurred by the employment of the contractor. The Company will get the timber and iron at one-sixth of the expense which would be incurred by Mr. Gordon, and no allowance is made for profit. I have, above, pointed out the difference of expense of the timber for a 24-pounder by the employment of hired cattle and carts to bring it to Seringapatam; and, upon the whole, I conclude that, if Mr. Gordon's calculation, upon which he founded his offer to make carriages at an expense 40 per cent. less than that occasioned by the contractor, was a just one, that calculation in your minute, which brings the expense of carriages at the manufactory to near 70 per cent. less than that incurred by the employment of the contractor, is not erroneous.

The price to be added to each carriage by the salary of the superintendent, and by the batta to the conductor, &c., at the jungle, will be trifling; and the more extended the scale of the manufactory, the less expense will be to be added to that of each carriage on this account. But this is not the ground on which the employment of an agent to superintend the work on account of the Company is preferable to every other plan: the superior benefits to be derived from it are incalculable, besides that it has to recommend it greater economy.

I have, &c.,

ARTHUR WELLESLEY.

[1137.]   *To the Secretary of the Military Board.*

SIR,   Seringapatam, 22nd April, 1802.

In consequence of the orders received from the Military Board, I have desired the commanding officers at Cannanore and Mangalore to give orders that repairs might be given to the barracks occupied by the European troops at those stations with temporary materials, without loss of time. I have, also, desired that orders might be given by the commanding officer in Malabar and Canara that repairs might be given to the buildings at the different stations in those provinces as detailed in the enclosed paper.

Since the receipt of these orders he has represented to me that the sheds required for the public elephants and bullocks at Cannanore, and the store-room and place of arms of a Native corps stationed there, are likewise in want of repair.   As, upon a reference to the letter from the Board and the report from the senior engineer, it appeared to me that it was intended that those buildings should be repaired, I have given directions that the necessary repairs should be given to them with temporary materials.

The commanding officer in Malabar has, likewise, represented that the store-room and place of arms for the corps stationed at Montana are in want of repairs.   The buildings at this station are not noticed in the report from the senior engineer; but as the rainy season approaches, and it is obvious that the repairs required must be given to these buildings, I have given orders accordingly to the commanding officer in Malabar, of which I hope that the Military Board will approve.

Several officers have applied to me for permission to purchase tents from the stores; and I beg to know whether I may be allowed to authorise their being sold to them under the provisions stated in the general orders by the Commander-in-Chief.

I have, &c.,

ARTHUR WELLESLEY.

The Deputy Adjutant-General to Lieutenant-Colonel Mackay, 1st battalion [1138.]
2nd Regiment Native Infantry.

Seringapatam, 28th April, 1802.

The Honourable Colonel Wellesley, commanding in Mysore, has perused your letter of this date, and the answers given by Lieutenants C—— and P—— to the complaint preferred against them; and he directs me to acquaint you, for the information of those officers, that as it appears from their own statements that they committed acts of violence in the bazaar, which might cause the losses to the inhabitants which are stated in their complaint, and of which, from the nature of the acts, and the manner of committing them, the officers cannot be supposed capable of forming a correct judgment, he desires they will wait upon the master of the police, and settle the amount of the loss sustained by the inhabitants through their acts, as reported by Major Symons.

Colonel Wellesley desires me to acquaint you, further, that he has had reports of various acts of violence, of a nature similar to those above alluded to, committed by officers in the garrison of Seringapatam, which he has reason to believe must have come to your knowledge: that it is with no less concern than surprise that he finds officers setting so bad an example to the troops in the garrison; and that, in case of the repetition of such acts, he will be under the necessity of bringing the conduct of the persons who may be guilty of them to a public discussion, of which Colonel Wellesley requests that you will apprise the two officers above named in particular.

[1139.] *To J. H. Piele, Esq.*

MY DEAR PIELE,　　　　　　　　Seringapatam, 29th April, 1802.

I have received your letter of the 27th. I shall inquire from Marriott whether your inhabiting that part of the palace called mine will give uneasiness to any of the family at Vellore; and if it should not be probable that it will, you shall have it forthwith. If it should be likely to give them uneasiness, it would be best that you should delay going into it till the ladies go to Vellore, which will be in the middle of June.

You are become too numerous in family for me to be able to accommodate you in the Dowlut Baug at present; but I am going to make some alterations which will give me the command of another room, and will otherwise render the house more convenient. I will write to you as soon as I shall have consulted Marriott.

Webbe spoke to me upon the subject of the Laal Baug; but I did not hear from him that anything was decided. I approved much of the plan which he had in contemplation.

I enclose you an extract of a letter which I have received from Colonel Cuppage upon the subject of the magazine at Nuggur. I shall be obliged to you if you will tell Purneah that I recommended that the magazine should be constructed as therein proposed by Colonel Cuppage, and that it is absolutely necessary for its safety that the doors should be hung on copper hinges, and that the nails in it, bolts, &c., should be of the same metal.

That matter upon which you spoke to me regarding Nuggur is settled to your satisfaction.

I think of going to Sera in a few days, to see how matters are going on there.

> I am, &c.,
> ARTHUR WELLESLEY.

To the Officer Commanding Five Companies, 2nd Battalion 3rd Regiment. [1140.]

SIR,   Seringapatam, 30th April, 1802.

The object in sending the detachment from the 2nd battalion 3rd regiment under your command is to furnish an escort to certain ladies belonging to the zenana of the late Hyder Ali, who are going to Vellore under charge of Captain Marriott.

By my desire he has already arranged with the Dewan of the Rajah of Mysore the marches which these people will make, and the places at which they will halt, in order that no inconvenience may be felt for want of supplies on the road; and you will be so kind as to make your marches according to this arrangement, which Captain Marriott will communicate to you.

You will furnish Captain Marriott with such guards and escorts as he will require.

You will be so kind as to take care to prevent all interference with the women by the officers and soldiers under your command.

Your knowledge of the customs and prejudices of the country must point out to you how very unwilling they are to be looked at; an attempt to see them can scarcely succeed, and will only serve to gratify a vain curiosity if it should; and I, therefore, hope that it will be prevented if possible.

> I have, &c.,
> ARTHUR WELLESLEY.

The detachment is to return to Seringapatam without loss of time when the ladies will have arrived at Vellore.

[1141.]   *To D. Manesty, Esq.*

SIR,   Seringapatam, 1st May, 1802.

I wrote to you some days ago, and informed you that your
horses were not arrived, and that I had not heard of them.
Since I wrote that letter they have come here from Mahé
with your servant Ahmed, in number thirteen.

I was rather embarrassed respecting the price which I should
ask for the horses. I intended to purchase some of them myself, and I am not a very good judge of horses or of their
value. I therefore thought that the best and fairest mode for
all parties would be to desire two gentlemen at this place to
examine the horses, to have them described, and to furnish me
with their opinion respecting the price which I should ask for
them. Captain Cunningham, the Deputy-Quartermaster-
General, and Captain Steele performed this office; and I
enclose a paper (No. 1)* which I received from them. As it
appeared to me probable that I might dispose of the horses at
a larger price than they thought them worth by setting them
up to auction, I determined to adopt that mode of disposing

* No. 1.

DESCRIPTION ROLL of THIRTEEN ARAB HORSES sent from Bussora by
SAMUEL MANESTY, Esq., to Seringapatam.

                                  Seringapatam, 28th April, 1802.

No.	Colour.	Age.		Size.		Price of Horses.	Remarks.
		Years.	Months.	Hands.	Inches.	Pag.	
1	Grey	6	6	14	1½	250	
2	Ditto	6	6	13	3	170	
3	Ditto	7	..	14	..	200	
4	Ditto	6	..	14	1½	230	
5	Ditto	6	..	14	½	170	
6	Iron grey ..	8	..	14	1	175	{Lame in the near fore leg.
7	Nutting grey	8	..	14	1½	150	
8	Bay	7	..	14	2	200	{A little lame in near fore leg.
9	Ditto	7	..	14	2	250	
10	Ditto	8	..	14	2½	250	
11	Ditto	8	..	14	..	175	
12	Ditto	8	6	14	1½	200	
13	Ditto	4	..	14	2½	225	

(Signed)   WM. CUNNINGHAM, Captain.
(Signed)   G. STEELE, Captain Lieut., Artillery.

of them. I enclose an account of the sale of 10 of them this day (No. 2).*

The money shall be remitted to your agents at Madras, excepting 10 pagodas, which I propose to give to the person who held the auction.

The three horses unsold shall go towards Madras to-morrow morning.

I hope that you will think that I have done the best to dispose of your horses to advantage. It is in general supposed that they have sold high, as they are much out of condition.

I repeat the request that if you should send any horses to Seringapatam in future, you will fix the lowest price which you will take for them. They shall be sold, as these have been, by public auction, and you will have all the advantage of the market ; but I feel much distressed at being obliged to fix a price upon the property of any gentleman, and I should wish to decline doing so in future.

I have, &c.,

ARTHUR WELLESLEY.

To Lieutenant-Colonel Dallas.   [1142.]

MY DEAR COLONEL,   Seringapatam, 1st May, 1802.

I have the pleasure to inform you that the first detachment of ladies, being those devoted heretofore to the amusement of

* No. 2.

A LIST of HORSES sold by Public Auction in Seringapatam, 1st May, 1802.

No.	Colour.	Age.	Purchasers' Names.	Amount.
				Pagodas.
1	Grey	6 years old ..	Captain West ..	365
2	Ditto	ditto ..	Captain Quin ..	245
3	Ditto	7 years old ..	Colonel Orrock ..	204
4	Ditto	6 ditto ..	Captain West ..	285
5	Ditto	6 ditto ..	Captain Marriott..	175
6	Iron grey ..	3 ditto ..	Major Ogg	235
7	Nutting grey ..	3 ditto.	.. ..	..
8	Bay	7 ditto.	.. ..	..
9	Ditto	7 ditto ..	Captain West ..	310
10	Ditto	6 ditto.	.. ..	..
11	Ditto	3 ditto ..	Captain West ..	260
12	Ditto	3 ditto ..	Ditto ..	201
13	Ditto	4 ditto ..	Ditto ..	240
			Total pagodas	2470

old Hyder, march to-morrow morning for Vellore.   I have
desired Marriott to lose no time in getting there, nor in
bringing back that part of the equipment which is to be used
in the removal of the second and last detachment, particularly the
tents, kanauts, and doolies, and I hope that he will arrive
here so early in the next month as that the ladies may cross the
Cauvery before it will fill.   He will discharge the hired carts at
Vellore; as we shall have the Company's platform-carts in sufficient number for the removal of the persons and baggage of the
second detachment.

I shall be obliged to you if you will give Marriott every
assistance in returning as soon as possible, and that you will
urge his speedy departure from Vellore as soon as he will have
lodged there in safety the present charge on his hands.

It is necessary that I should take the earliest opportunity of
drawing your attention to a circumstance regarding these
zenanas which may hereafter be of infinite consequence.   Although several women have died, others have been removed
with the Princes, and others have been sent to their relations,
the number of women now in the zenanas is nearly as large as
it was when Seringapatam fell into the hands of the Company.

The cause of this is, first that the slaves and other attendants
of the women who have died have not been discharged, which
is probably reasonable enough; secondly, that the women have
contrived to introduce fresh slaves and attendants into the
zenana.   I have desired Marriott to have a list made of the
names of all those who have been introduced since the death of
Tippoo, and I find that they amount to 200.

I acknowledge that if I had found out this circumstance at
an earlier period, I should have desired that every one of them
might be turned out immediately; but as the women were on
the eve of their departure from Vellore, and might feel inconvenience, and, at all events, would pretend they felt inconvenience, from the want of their attendants, I have omitted to
desire that they may be discharged, and they will go to
Vellore.

It is proper, however, that you should decide immediately
what is to become of them.   In my opinion, they ought to be
turned out and sent back to their friends, if they have any, as
soon as possible.   It is not reasonable that the expense of these
zenanas upon the Company should be. made perpetual, which

will be the consequence of suffering the women to take in fresh slaves and attendants; or that its duration should be so much increased as it must be by the addition of the 200 women who have been introduced since the death of Tippoo.

On the other hand, if these 200 women are suffered to remain in the zenana and kept in the service for any length of time, they will have nearly the same claim for a provision that those have who were found in the zenana when Tippoo died. At all events, we cannot suffer them to starve, which will be more probable some years hence, when their relations will have forgotten them, than it is at this moment; and therefore I conclude that you must determine either to turn them away at an early period after the arrival of the women at Vellore, or to pass the subject over in silence and to allow them to remain on the establishment in the same manner as the other women till they die.

You have now the subject before you, and will decide it as you think proper.

I certainly should discharge the women immediately.

Believe me, &c.,

ARTHUR WELLESLEY.

To Lieutenant-General Stuart. [1143.]

SIR, Seringapatam, 1st May, 1802.

In consequence of the receipt of your letter of the 24th of April, I have desired Lieutenant-Colonel Boles to make arrangements for sending a conductor and some lascars to Tellicherry from Cannanore, and I have desired him to recommend such temporary addition to the store establishment at Cannanore as may be found necessary under present circumstances.

I have desired that the timber contract may be made out again, and that the additions may be made to it which are stated in my letter of the 21st of April. The cutting of the trees has been already commenced, and the contractor has no doubt but that in a short time he will have the trees cut which you have ordered.

I now enclose Mr. Gordon's account of his timber, and a letter from him, in which he explains the manner in which he has made it out. I recommend that this timber should be taken.

I likewise enclose a letter from Mr. Gordon upon the subject of pitch and tar which he has at Seringapatam.

To do Mr. Gordon justice, he has never failed in furnishing the supplies called for, and he deserves any encouragement which can be given to him with justice to the public.

The sled, of which you have enclosed me a plan, will not answer in this country without wheels, for we have not 500 yards of level ground in any part of it, particularly towards the Ghauts. When I shall receive the more perfect plan which you propose to send me, I will have one made, however; as although it will not answer as a sled in the form of a wheel-carriage, it may be the best transporting carriage for the heavy timber.

I shall immediately send out the conductor and lascars to the jungle, and I will send you a copy of the instructions which I propose to give him.

There is a man here by the name of James Adams, who belonged to the Bombay army, and was serjeant-major of the late provincial corps of Tiers. He is by trade a carpenter, and he was for some time employed in making gun-carriages at Bombay. He appears a sober, well-behaved man, and I am very desirous that he should be employed in the manufactory at this place. In the mean time, till it could be commenced, he would be very useful at Cancancotta, particularly at first, as his knowledge of timber would preclude the chance of any being taken from the contractor which should be too dry for use. Upon the whole, therefore, I beg leave to recommend that he may be appointed a conductor, and attached to this station.

I have, &c.,

ARTHUR WELLESLEY.

[1144.]   *To Lieutenant-Colonel Spry.*

MY DEAR SIR,   Seringapatam, 2nd May, 1802.

I have received your letter, in which you have enclosed one from Mr. Brutton. I think that gentleman's case an exceedingly hard one, and nothing would give me greater pleasure than to be able to do anything for his advantage.

Although Brigade-Major Spens is appointed aide-de-camp to the Acting-Governor of Bombay, the appointment, from its nature, can be considered only as temporary, and he may reasonably expect that his appointment in Malabar will not be filled, at least till it shall be seen whether he will be appointed Deputy-Quartermaster-General, which he expects. Accordingly he has asked for leave of absence till the 15th of September; and as arrangements are made for carrying on the duties of his office during his absence, I rather believe that the leave for which he has asked will be granted.

If his office in Malabar should be considered as vacant at present, or if it should be vacated hereafter, it appears that it is the wish of the Commander-in-Chief that Captain Watson should obtain it: a wish which must be considered as a law, if Captain Watson should be willing to accept the office. But if Captain Watson should not be desirous to have the situation, I rather believe that it will be necessary to consult the wishes of the commanding-officer in Malabar and Canara regarding the person to be appointed his Brigade-Major when the vacancy will happen. I have always made it a rule, in the recommenda-tion of persons to fill staff situations, to consult the wishes of those who are most interested in their being properly filled; and in this instance I should think it proper to be certain at least that Lieutenant Brutton would not be disagreeable to the officer to whom he would be the staff-officer. Under these circumstances, I cannot promise that Lieutenant Brutton shall be the Brigade-Major in Malabar if Major Spens should resign; but if Captain Watson should not be willing to accept the appointment, I will certainly recommend Lieutenant Brutton to whoever may be commanding-officer in Malabar, and will state my opinion of his claims for it.

The horses, respecting which I wrote to you, arrived here two or three days ago from Mahé.

Believe me, &c.,

ARTHUR WELLESLEY.

To Lieutenant-General Stuart.   [1145.]

SIR,   Seringapatam, 4th May, 1802.

I adopt this mode of drawing your attention to the effects which the late orders of government regarding the Paymasters of stations drawing bills of exchange on the Paymaster-General will have in this country.

M 2

The sums of money which we have been in the habit of receiving hitherto are the Rajah's kist, after paying the expenses of the Residency; small sums occasionally from the collectors in Canara and Soonda, after they have provided for the expenses of the establishments in those provinces and at Goa; and the sums which the Paymaster is able to procure for his bills on the Paymaster-General. Of these, the first and last were the only certain sources of supply, and now, in consequence of the late orders of government, the first only remains.

The amount of the kist applicable to military purposes may be nearly 50,000 pagodas monthly; the expenses, including the garrison of Seringapatam and the province of Soonda, may be about 80,000 pagodas; the difference, therefore, is to be made up by the other resources. They have not been found adequate to furnishing the sum required hitherto, and the produce of bills upon the Paymaster-General has provided for the deficiency.

The money which has found its way into the pay-office in this manner, and has been applicable to the payment of the troops in this country, is that which comes into the hands of suttlers for supplies; that which the officers of the army are inclined to pay to their tradesmen at Madras; and the sums which some of them may have after paying their monthly expenses.

It is very obvious that none of these sums can be lent to the Company, and equally so that they must find their way to Madras, if not through the Company's pay-office, by other means; and, as there is no trade in this country with the eastern coast, the money must be sent down by coolies in such manner as may be most safe and convenient. The deficiency, however, which the want of these sums will leave at the pay-office will be very large, and must be made up by remittances of cash from Madras. Thus the Mysore country, which can but ill afford it, will be constantly drained of its specie, and, in return, Madras will be drained of its specie likewise to supply the wants of the Mysore country. There is no trade in this country which might bring money into it, and therefore the only possible mode of providing for a deficiency of funds for the payment of the troops is by a remittance from the Presidency in cash.

This, it will be acknowledged, is not the least expensive and most convenient mode to the public of providing for our wants; but at the same time it is likely to be very inconvenient to the troops. As a great proportion of the money which will be required for their monthly payment will come from a distance, and as, from the nature of the seasons in this country and the impediments which they occasion upon the roads, the time of travelling this distance is very uncertain, it cannot be expected that the troops will be paid regularly unless large sums of money are sent to the pay-office, and there suffered to lie for some time till they are wanted.

If these large sums of money are sent, the expense and inconvenience to the public will be still greater than it would be if they were sent only monthly as the disbursements require them.

Thus the troops will suffer for want of their regular pay, and this country, which at this moment goes on principally by the regular monthly expenditure within it of so large a sum of money, will suffer still more. In fact, our situation is entirely different from that of the British troops and establishments in other provinces under the government of Fort St. George, and regulations applicable to them would be ruinous to us. We are at a great distance from the sea; we have but little intercourse with either coast which is to bring resources of money into the country, and the only chance we have is to keep in regular circulation what we have got.

I can easily conceive, however, that it must be highly inconvenient at the Treasury to provide for the bills which are drawn upon the Paymaster-General by the provincial Paymasters, and I conclude that the late orders of government are occasioned by the desire of remedying this inconvenience. There is a great difference between the abuse and the use of a custom for the public convenience and benefit; and, in reference to this country, I think that the matter might be so regulated as that the troops would have all the advantage and the public would suffer no inconvenience, particularly as I have above endeavoured to show that the money wanted for the troops must eventually come from Madras. On this ground I take the liberty of suggesting to you that the Paymaster in Mysore might still be allowed to draw bills on the Paymaster-General under the following restrictions; that after ascertaining the amount of the probable demands upon him at any particular time, he should ascertain the amount which he is likely to receive from the collectors in Soonda and Canara, and that he should be permitted to draw only for the balance required to make his payment after the receipt from those collectors and of the kist from the Rajah ; that he should be required to make a detailed statement of the demands upon him, of his resources, and of the sums for which it will be required to draw bills, to the Paymaster-General before he draws one, and that he should on no account draw for more than is absolutely required to make his payment.

I hope that you will excuse the liberty which I have taken in drawing your attention to this subject, and that you will attribute my motive for so doing to my desire that the troops should suffer no inconvenience, and that the prosperity of this country should continue to increase.

I have, &c.,

ARTHUR WELLESLEY.

[1146.]   *To the Adjutant-General.*

SIR,   Seringapatam, 4th May, 1802.

Lieutenant-Colonel Boles informs me that, in consequence of the requisition of the collector, founded on certain disturbances in the district of Ernaad, in the southern division of Malabar, he had given orders for the assembly of a field detachment at Angarypur, under the command of Major Howden, of which orders I enclose a copy. I beg leave to recommend that they may be confirmed.

Those disturbances were promoted by Goorcul, Any Moota, and Mahomed Cutty, three notorious freebooters, who have long disturbed the peace of the country and despised the authority of government. By a letter, however, which I have received from the collector in Malabar this day, dated the 1st instant, I learn that Any Moota, the principal of the three, was killed in an affair with the armed police, under Captain Watson, on the 29th of April, and the collector was in hopes that he should be enabled to catch Goorcul in a short time.

I have, &c.,

ARTHUR WELLESLEY.

MEMORANDUM FOR CAPTAIN HEITLAND.   [1147.]

5th May, 1802.

During my absence at Sera, I should wish the work to go on at the ditch, and I recommend the following objects to Captain Heitland's attention.

1st. To continue to fill the ditch from the western angle, as far as *   on the south side, and as far as Captain Grant's house on the north side.

As soon as all the earth which composed the old unformed rampart will have been thrown into the ditch on the north side, I should wish Captain Heitland to employ some commatties to level the yard of the Mysore Palace, and to heap together in one part of it the materials for building. This yard must be brought to the general level of the fort, by which I mean the level of the parade as it will be hereafter; and the earth which is removed from it to be thrown into the northern ditch, in the place where it appears that earth will be most wanted, viz. behind the range of houses on the parade.

If the earth taken from this yard should not be sufficient to fill the ditch, Captain Heitland will employ the commatties upon the parade to take off as many feet as will be sufficient.

2ndly. I have given Captain Symons a memorandum respecting a piece of ground which I should wish to have cleared of the mud houses and walls upon it, which extends from Mr. Clarke's houses, in the rear of Captain Heitland's and the granaries, as far as the south ramparts.

Captain Symons will communicate with Captain Heitland on this subject, and I should wish that this piece of ground were cleared of its old walls as soon as may be practicable, and the earth must be thrown into the south ditch.

Before this work can be commenced upon, however, it will be necessary that the unformed rampart on the south side of the fort should be thrown into the ditch; and accordingly, I wish that as soon as such progress will be made on the north side as that it will be necessary to commence carrying the earth from a distance, a proportion of the commatties who will not be required on the north side should be employed on the south side; and that afterwards the ground above mentioned should

* Blank in manuscript.

be cleared of its walls, and the earth disposed of to fill up what the rampart, &c., cannot.

3rdly. Major Symons will point out to Captain Heitland two spots of ground on each side of the flag-cavalier, which are intended for sites on which the sepoys are to hut.

Captain Heitland will form an opinion whether the earth to be taken from the old walls on these pieces of ground will be so useful to the work of filling up the ditch as to make it worth while to wait to clear them till the whole of the unfinished rampart, &c., will have been thrown into the ditch on the southern side; and if he should be of this opinion he will wait. But if he should be of opinion that this earth will be of no great consequence, particularly as the earth of the cavalier (called the Butchers) can be used for this purpose, I should wish that some of the commatties should be employed in clearing these pieces of ground as soon as Major Symons will inform Captain Heitland that the inhabitants have moved out of their houses and have taken away their materials.

4thly. The wall of the palace in front of Captain Grant's house to be pulled down and thrown into the north ditch. The useful materials to be saved.

Before this work is commenced, however, it will be necessary that Captain Heitland should determine whether to fill the ditch below the place where the great watercourse is to be built which is to carry off the surplus water of the aqueducts will not be attended with inconvenience, and even dangerous, if the fall of rain should be heavy.

If he should be of opinion that this will be dangerous, he will delay pulling down this wall till the watercourse will be finished, and the water will have a free passage across the present inner ditch and through the outer rampart.

I cannot sufficiently recommend to Captain Heitland the greatest attention to all the drains which are to carry off the rain-water, &c., from the fort through the outer rampart. Their old course ought to be ascertained from the high grounds in the fort and the spots at which they go through the rampart. The whole of it might be cleared and paved, particularly where it approaches the new work.

ARTHUR WELLESLEY.

To the Chief Secretary of Government.   [1148.]

SIR,   Seringapatam, 6th May, 1802.

I have the honour to enclose the copy of a report which I have received from Mr. Anderson regarding the possibility of rendering useful as an hospital the building hitherto occupied by the ladies of the .zenana of Hyder Ali. I beg to recommend that the plan proposed by Mr. Anderson may be put in execution. An hospital is much wanted at Seringapatam; the alterations proposed for this building will render. it fit for this purpose, and the public will thereby save nearly 20,000 pagodas, the amount of the expense which it has been estimated that the hospital will cost, of which a plan has been sent to the Military Board.

I have, &c.,

ARTHUR WELLESLEY.

To A. Read, Esq.   [1149.]

SIR,   Seringapatam, 7th May, 1802.

I have the honour to inform you that the Dewan of the Rajah of Mysore has communicated to me intelligence which he has received of the resort of a large gang of thieves upon the frontier of Mysore and Coimbatoor, who are in the habit of plundering both countries occasionally, and taking refuge in the other.

The intelligence appears so correct and minute, that I think it probable that the result of an attempt to seize this gang will be successful; and in concert with Mr. Piele I have recommended to the Dewan to lose no time in making his arrangements to surround their place of refuge near Beleekull with his troops, and to endeavour to seize as many of them as he can.

In the course of the execution of this service, either previous to the attack upon Beleekull or in the pursuit of the thieves, it may be necessary that the Rajah's troops should enter the Company's territories under your management, and I shall be obliged to you if you will give orders that they may be received and treated as friends. If the thieves should escape from Beleekull, they may run towards Gudjelhatty, or towards Setteegall.

I have, &c.,

ARTHUR WELLESLEY.

[1150.]   *To the Adjutant-General.*

SIR,   Seringapatam, 7th May, 1802.

I have the honour to enclose an extract of a letter from
Lieutenant-Colonel Boles, by which it appears that Major
Fridge, of the 1st battalion 8th Bombay regiment, carried into
execution the orders of the government of Bombay to reduce
the establishment of the regiments of Bombay Native infantry
without waiting for directions from his immediate superiors
acting under the government of Fort St. George. The consequence is that the 1st of the 4th and 2nd of the 2nd have not
received the number of drafts allotted to them by the Commander-in-Chief, and the 1st of the 8th Bombay Native infantry is weaker by above 200 men than it ought to be. As
these mistakes have occurred more than once, it would be very
desirable either to arrange with the government of Bombay
that the orders from that Presidency should be issued only
through the commanding officer in Mysore, or that it should be
understood by the officers commanding corps upon the Bombay
establishment, that although they may receive the orders direct
from Bombay, obedience to them is to be delayed till their
commanding officer, acting under the authority of the government of Fort St. George, can make them acquainted with the
wishes of the Commander-in-Chief upon the subject.

I propose to go to Sera to-morrow to inspect the cantonments
lately erected at that place for the use of the 19th dragoons, and
I hope to be at Seringapatam again in the course of a fortnight.

I have, &c.,

ARTHUR WELLESLEY.

[1151.]   *To the Secretary of the Commander-in-Chief.*

SIR,   Chinna, 9th May, 1802.

I have had the honour of receiving your letter of the 5th
instant with its enclosures. There can be no doubt but that the
larger the space of the clear ground round any fort, the greater
will be the advantage with a view to defence. But in regard to
the fort of Hullihall, I have to observe that nothing can render it
strong against an European attack; and the object therefore to
be looked for in the defences to be given to it is, that those who

are to defend it should have all the advantages which the situation of the place can afford to enable them to oppose the attack of a Native enemy. Upon this ground I have no hesitation in saying that an esplanade of 250 yards is as large as will be necessary.

I have, &c.,

ARTHUR WELLESLEY.

To the Secretary of the Military Board.   [1152.]

SIR,   Chinna, 9th May, 1802.

I have had the honour of receiving your letter of the 4th instant with its enclosures, relative to assistance to labourers required by Captain Johnson at Hullihall. A part of the pioneers are at present employed at Seringapatam upon a work ordered by government, and a part are still in the Bullum district employed in works which have received the approbation of the Commander-in-Chief and of government. The season, however, will shortly oblige the latter to quit Bullum, and the pioneers are ordered to Seringapatam to assist in the government works. If the Board should be desirous that 100 of them should go to Hullihall, they shall be sent forthwith; but I have to observe that it does not appear, even by Captain Johnson's letter of the 23rd April, that their assistance is absolutely necessary to enable him to carry on the work upon which he is employed. He states that Soonda does not produce commatties or bricklayers, but that artificers of that description can be procured from Malabar, Canara, and Goa, provided they are not obliged to bring with them common labourers. He does not state that common labourers cannot be procured from Soonda, and I have no doubt but that if Mr. Read the collector be applied to, Captain Johnson will be relieved from the necessity either of insisting that the artificers procured in Malabar, Canara, and Goa should bring with them labourers, or of calling upon the Military Board for the assistance of pioneers or other persons at present in the pay and employment of the Company. If that should be the case, I beg to observe that the Military Board are already in possession of my sentiments regarding the propriety of placing establishments of this description under the orders of an engineer to assist him in performing works of which he has estimated the expense; and if the Board should have done me the honour to agree in opinion with me upon that subject, they will think that if common labourers can be procured in Soonda, it is better that they should be hired there than that the pioneers should be sent.

I have, &c.,

ARTHUR WELLESLEY.

[1153.]   *To the Brigade-Major, King's Troops.*

SIR,   Nagmunglum, 10th May, 1802.

I enclose some papers which I have received from Lieutenant-Colonel Maxwell upon the subject of a murder supposed to have been committed at Sera by Collins, a trumpeter in the 19th dragoons. As I have very little doubt that he is guilty of the crime of which he is accused, and as I think it probable that the Commander-in-Chief will be desirous that he should be tried by the civil tribunal, I should order him to Fort St. George immediately, only that it will not be possible for him to arrive there in time to be tried at the sessions of oyer and terminer which commence on the 24th instant. Accordingly I delay giving any further orders regarding him till I receive the directions of the Commander-in-Chief.

I have, &c.,

ARTHUR WELLESLEY.

[1154.]   *To Lieutenant-Colonel Boles.*

SIR,   Nagmunglum, 10th May, 1802.

I have had the honour of receiving your letter of the 6th instant with its enclosures, being letters from Captain Bentley upon the subject of the repairs ordered to the stores at Cannanore, and from Lieutenant Williams upon the subject of houses for the corps of pioneers. It appears by the former that Captain Bentley is desirous that the repairs required to the store-houses at Cannanore should not be given to them, because some time will elapse before the persons who are to give the repairs can be collected, and it is possible that rain will fall, and that the stores will then be damaged, during the time that they will be occupied in repairing the roofs of the store-houses. The question is whether it is probable that the stores will suffer from the fall of rain during the monsoon. If the roofs of the houses are not repaired, and if that should be the case, or, in other words, if it be true that the store-houses really required the repairs which it has been reported they did, it would be better to incur some risk that the stores would receive some damage during a short period of time, than to make it certain that they would be rendered entirely useless by being exposed to the rain of the whole monsoon. Accordingly, if it should be necessary to uncover the buildings entirely in order to turn the tiles upon them, of which I doubt, I should have preferred that to the delay of a work which must be necessary for the preservation of the stores. If, therefore, it be not now too late to have this work performed, I should wish that it were commenced without delay, particularly if, in the performance of it, it should not be necessary to uncover the building entirely.

In the general orders upon the subject of tent allowance, I observe that it is proposed to publish some further regulations which will go into details probably regarding every description of persons not provided for in the general orders which have been published. These regulations will doubtless include the corps of pioneers, and I should wish to defer making any reference upon the subject at least till they are published. However, I must observe, that pioneers are, in general, very capable of building their own houses with the assistance of workmen, which the officer commanding the corps has it in his power to give them; and I shall be very unwilling to recommend, and must see very clearly a necessity for it before I do recommend, that any allowance shall be given for building houses for them.

I have, &c.,

ARTHUR WELLESLEY.

To Colonel Carlisle.   [1155.]

MY DEAR COLONEL,   Nagmunglum, 10th May, 1802.

I received orders from General Stuart some time ago to learn from Mr. Gordon whether he would sell his timber to the public; and if he would, its quantity, the dimensions of the beams, the time which had elapsed since they had been cut, and the price of each. The enclosed paper, which has been in General Stuart's possession, was the result of my inquiries upon this subject. The General, however, is desirous that a committee should be ordered to survey this timber, and I shall be obliged to you if you will give orders accordingly. They must report the number and dimensions of the beams, their state, whether fit for service or not, and as nearly as they can learn it, the length of time which has elapsed since they were cut in the jungle. It is not necessary that they should make any report on their prices. I have written to Mr. Gordon to request that he will allow the timber to be shown to the committee whom you will order to survey it. Before I quitted Seringapatam I omitted to request that you would order a committee to survey some timber which I had desired the engineer to take down from an unfinished building in the rear of the palace, occupied by Mr. Piele. This committee must mark the beams with the letter P, in order to distinguish that from other timber. They must number them, and ascertain their dimensions, which must be entered in their report according to the form already used in surveying the timber taken from the Mysore Palace. As soon as this timber will be surveyed, it must be given in charge to the commissary of stores. Although Quin does not belong to the garrison, he will be able to give you some useful assistance in both these committees.

Believe me, &c.,

ARTHUR WELLESLEY.

[1156.]   *To W. H. Gordon, Esq.*

DEAR GORDON,   Nagmunglum, 10th May, 1802.

I have received a letter from General Stuart in which he has desired that I will order a committee to survey the timber in your possession of which you gave me an account, and to report that its quantity and dimensions are correct, that it has been cut during the time stated, and that it is fit for service. I write to Colonel Carlisle upon the subject this day, and shall be obliged to you if you will allow the timber to be shown to the committees which he will order to survey it. Regarding the pitch the General says, " Mr. Gordon's letter on the subject of pitch and tar I shall lay before the Military Board, but I am very doubtful of their taking it off his hands at his price, which appears high.   Mr. Gordon, no doubt, has great merit in so punctually furnishing the supplies called for, and therefore deserves encouragement; at the same time I understand his prices are sometimes far from being moderate."

Believe me, &c.,
ARTHUR WELLESLEY.

To Josiah Webbe, Esq. [1157.]

MY DEAR WEBBE,   Belloor, 11th May, 1802.

I return the letters which you have sent for my perusal, and am much obliged to you for them.   It is unfortunate that Lord Clive had not an opportunity of writing upon the subject of sending the delinquents back to India at the same time that he wrote upon the interference in the internal arrangements of his government, as the whole subject would then have appeared in its true colours at one view.   However, I conclude that he will not have omitted to remark upon a practice so injurious to the public interest, and that it will still come before the public. But people are so lazy that it would have been better if they had but one letter to read instead of many, to learn all this enormity.

In the distribution which I proposed for the Mysore country, and which has been adopted by General Stuart, I did not propose to place any corps at Bangalore, unless the General should prefer that station to Seringapatam for a regiment of Europeans.   The General, however, has desired to have all the Europeans at Seringapatam, and we are to have nothing at Bangalore excepting a small guard to take care of the Company's arrack and money which are there occasionally, and an officer to keep up the communication, and to take care that articles coming from the Carnatic shall go either to the westward or northward according to their destination.   I cannot recommend on any public grounds that a corps should be stationed at Bangalore under the command of Capper, although I don't think that it will be at all inconvenient to place one at that station.   There are three corps at Seringapatam, one of which might easily be spared for this purpose, but I repeat that

I don't think it necessary, and cannot recommend it on any public grounds.

Malcolm has written to me respecting what you say about Lord Wellesley and Lord Hobart, and I rejoice at it most sincerely. Till I had received his letter, however, I was not aware that any thing had passed, or of more than that they had not corresponded for some time.

I am going to Sera to see how matters are going on there. I expect to be back at Seringapatam in about ten days.

Believe me, &c.,

ARTHUR WELLESLEY.

[1158.]   *To Lieutenant William Henry.*

SIR,   Ball Hully, 12th May, 1802.

I have the pleasure to inform you that I have this day received a letter from the Adjutant-General, in which he tells me that when the Adjutancy of the 1st of the 16th becomes vacant by the promotion of the officer who now holds the situation, he will remind the Commander-in-Chief of my application in your favour. As, however, you are not very high in the regiment, your chance will depend much upon the qualifications of the officers senior to you now in that battalion, and upon the recommendation of the commanding officer. But upon this point I have to observe that there have been symptoms of insubordination and disunion in that corps lately which may induce the Commander-in-Chief to be desirous of choosing an Adjutant in the second battalion.

I have, &c.,

ARTHUR WELLESLEY.

[1159.]   *To Lieutenant-Colonel Agnew.*

MY DEAR COLONEL,   Nettoor, 13th May, 1802.

I am much obliged to you for your letter of the 8th, and for your recollection of my application to General Stuart in favour of the serjeant-major of Tiers.

A man by the name of Mitchell was sent from Madras to be

at the head of the laboratory at Seringapatam as a serjeant; in the mean time he was made a conductor, but he is still at the head of the laboratory, and there is no laboratory serjeant. Adams might either be made a conductor, and be attached to the garrison, on the ground of Mitchell's superintending the laboratory, or he might be made laboratory serjeant. Considering that the store establishment at Seringapatam is deficient one deputy commissary, it might probably be possible to appoint him conductor: however, I am perfectly satisfied with whatever General Stuart may decide upon this point.

Believe me, &c.,

ARTHUR WELLESLEY.

To — Harington, Esq.   [1160.]

MY DEAR SIR,   Kittoor, 13th May, 1802.

Mr. Manesty lately sent thirteen horses to Seringapatam to be sold, and to be sent on to Madras in case it should not be possible to sell them at Seringapatam, and he desired that the produce of the horses should be remitted to your house on his account.

The horses were sold at Seringapatam for 3070 star pagodas, of which sum bills have been given to Mr. Gordon, the paymaster at Seringapatam, for 920 star pagodas on your house, and the remainder of the money is in his hands, part in Porto Novo pagodas and part in Company's rupees. Owing to the order lately given out by government, which forbids the provincial paymaster to draw bills upon the Paymaster-General, I have not yet been able to make any arrangement for sending the remainder of this money to Madras, and unless you can suggest some other mode, I am afraid that I shall be obliged to send it up to you by coolies.

I shall be glad to hear from you upon this subject. I rather believe that I could get a bill for the money upon Bombay, if that would suit Mr. Manesty equally well. You will be able to form a judgment upon this point by a reference to the directions which he will have sent to your house regarding the disposal of the probable produce of these horses, and I shall be obliged to you for your opinion upon it.

Yours faithfully,

ARTHUR WELLESLEY.

[1161.]   *To Lieutenant-General Stuart.*

SIR,   Angeysamoodra, 14th May, 1802.

I have the honour to enclose a draft of the instructions which I propose to give to the person who will be employed in the jungles on the part of the Company in superintending the cutting of the timber by the contractor, and in other duties connected therewith. I don't propose to send any person to Cancancotta on this business till I shall receive your farther orders regarding Serjeant-Major Adams.

I have, &c.,

ARTHUR WELLESLEY.

DRAFT OF INSTRUCTIONS.

1. Orders having been given to make a contract with persons at Seringapatam for cutting timber in the forests bordering on Wynaad, in the neighbourhood of Cancancotta, Maggrecardie, and Anagoor, a contract has been entered into with Shamiah for this purpose.

2. The terms of the contract are, that for a certain price stated therein to be paid him for each foot of timber, he is to cut, square, mark, number, and collect into piles the timber intended for the Company. The piles of timber are to be placed in situations in the jungle accessible to the Company's wheel-carriages, under the superintendence and direction of a person to be employed there on the part of the Company, and the timber must be serviceable.

3. By order of the Commander-in-Chief, I have fixed upon you to perform this service, and others which will be detailed in these instructions. You are to reside at Cancancotta, and Maggrecardie, and Anagoor. You are to be assisted by one moochy man, one tindal, and twenty lascars from the garrison of Seringapatam, and to have one havildar and twelve sepoys under your directions.

4. You are to see that the contractor performs his contract in the following instances: firstly, that he cuts timber of the dimensions ordered by the Military Board; secondly, that he squares, marks, and numbers it; thirdly, that he collects it in piles in

situations accessible to the Company's wheel-carriages ; fourthly, that the timber is serviceable.

5. You are to view the timber before it is collected in piles, and are to measure each beam, and mark each with English characters as follows :

1802.

No. 1.

L.	..	..	..	..	..	.. 20
B.	..	..	..	..	..	.. 1
T.	..	..	..	..	..	.. 1

The year must be that in which the beam is cut. The numbers on the beams must commence with No. 1 in every year, the measurement must be in English feet, and the letter L. is for length, B. for breadth, and T. for thickness. You are to enter into a register, to be kept for that purpose, according to form A, the mark, the number, and dimensions of each beam.

6. You are then to direct that the timber which you will have viewed, measured, and registered, may be collected into a pile or piles, and you will take an account of the number of beams and marks on them in each pile.

7. As soon as the timber will thus have been collected in piles in situations accessible to the Company's wheel-carriages, you are to take charge of it, and are to give the contractor a receipt for it, specifying the marks, numbers, and dimensions of each beam, according to the form B.

8. On the first day in every month you are to send to the commanding officer of Seringapatam two copies of the register of the preceding month which you are required to make of the timber, in the 5th paragraph.

9. Orders have been given to the contractor to cut down 5000 trees of the largest dimensions. You will report occasionally the progress which he makes in cutting this timber.

10. Orders have likewise been given to him to cut down for immediate use certain trees, which it is reported have withered, and the timber of which is supposed to be fit for immediate service. You will take particular care that this timber is not too dry to be used in the construction of carriages.

ARTHUR WELLESLEY.

N 2

Form A.—Register of Teak Timber, cut in the forests by the contractor, Shamiah, for the use of the Honourable Company; taken in the month of May, 1802.

Cancancotta, 1st June, 1802.

Number.	Year.	Length.	Breadth.	Thickness.	Month cut down.	Remarks.
1	1802	20	1	1	April.	In the forest of Cancancotta.

Form B.—Received from Shamiah, contractor for supplying the Honourable Company with Teak Timber,   Beams, of which the following is the description :—

Cancancotta, May, 1802.

Number.	Year.	Length.	Breadth.	Thickness.	
1	1802	20	1	1	

[1162.]   *To Colonel Carlisle.*

MY DEAR COLONEL,   Angeysamoodra, 14th May, 1802.

In consequence of the intelligence received from you of the bad state of health of Captain Heitland, which has been confirmed by other accounts received from Seringapatam, I am in some degree of apprehension that he will not be able to carry on the works which I have intrusted to his superintendence. The instructions regarding the mode of carrying on these works have been given to him at different times; some in the last year, and some lately, and many of them verbally. If Captain Heitland should be so sick as we have reason to believe he is, not only he will be unable to carry on the works himself, but he will be incapable of communicating to any other officer the instructions under which he was to have acted. The only person, excepting myself, thoroughly acquainted with my intentions is Captain Barclay. I have frequently conversed with him on the subject; he has seen, and indeed has copies of, all the instructions. In consequence of Captain Heitland's sickness, and lest it should be so violent as to prevent him either from carrying on the work himself or communicating to any other person the instructions under which he was to have acted, I have deter-

mined to send Captain Barclay to Seringapatam.   He will be
able to make known my intentions to the officer who will have
charge of the works during Captain Heitland's sickness.   I
hope that thus it will occasion neither inconvenience nor delay.

Believe me, &c.,

ARTHUR WELLESLEY.

To Josiah Webbe, Esq.   [1163.]

MY DEAR WEBBE,   Sera, 15th May, 1802.

I have received a letter from Piele, by which I learn that
Captain Mackay has been furnished with a dustuck, by which
all the gram purchased for the Company is exempted from payment of duties.   I think it probable that this arrangement was
made without your knowledge, or at all events without your
adverting to the consequences, and therefore I write to apprise
you of what has ·passed heretofore upon this subject, particularly regarding the exception of the gram purchased by Captain
Mackay from the payment of duties.   For some time Purneah
furnished gram for the Company's draught bullocks, which was
the occasion of a perpetual contest between him and Captain
Mackay, which was carried on through the Resident and me.
At length Captain Mackay found out that there was a man in
Seringapatam who was willing to contract to furnish gram for
the cattle at the rate of seven seers for a rupee more than
Purneah gave ; that is to say, Purneah gave eighty-four seers
for a rupee, which was the rate of the Sheher gram, and the
new contractor offered to give the gram seven seers for a rupee
cheaper than Sheher Ganjam.   As this gram concern was one
that weighed most upon Purneah, as it was a constant subject
of altercation, and one which was exceedingly unpleasant to
him, I eagerly seized the opportunity of freeing him from it,
and gave authority to Captain Mackay to conclude the bargain
with the contractor.   Under the treaty with the Rajah all
articles come to Seringapatam duty free, and it stands to
reason that gram in Sheher Ganjam must be nearly as cheap as
it can be all the year through in any other particular part of the
country.   The contractor very soon found this out, and declared
that he could not perform his contract unless he was excused
from the payment of the duties upon the gram, which he said

he always had in contemplation when he made the bargain with Captain Mackay.   To this proposition I gave a direct negative, and desired Captain Mackay to break the contract rather than bring it forward.   My reasons for giving this negative were, that I did not think it fair or honourable to make a proposition to the Rajah's government, the object of which was to save a sum of money to the Company in the expense of feeding their cattle, which sum of money was to come directly out of the pocket of the Rajah of Mysore.   Secondly, I was aware that (supposing the first objection was not well founded) all exemptions from duties were exceedingly inconvenient and hurtful to the government.   They open the door to fraud on the part of the dealers and on the part of the aumildars in the country, and the government never fails to lose a large sum in addition to that which they would receive as duty on the article consumed by those in whose favour alone it is intended to grant the exemption.

After I had given a negative to this proposition, and the contract was in consequence broken, and a new one entered into, another proposition was made to me by Captain Mackay, which was, that gram should be allowed to pass through the country duty free, and that the duties should be paid monthly to the government by the contractor.   I happen to have by me a copy of the letter which I wrote to Captain Mackay in answer to this proposition, and as it shows what my sentiments were upon the whole subject, and that Captain Mackay was not unacquainted with them, I enclose it to you.

After this you may easily conceive how much surprised I was to learn that he had got a dustuck which exempted him from the payment of duties on the gram purchased for the Company, which dustuck I conclude was given to him by government.   In my opinion government have no right to give such a dustuck.   The country is that of the Rajah of Mysore, and the duties collected in it form part of his revenue; and they have just as good a right to grant Captain Mackay a tuncaw or a sunnud to collect a sum of money on any particular district, as they have to give him a dustuck to exempt him from paying a particular duty.   No right to grant this dustuck is given to them, because their cattle consume the gram which is the object of it.   If it be, why was it particularly stipulated in the treaty that duties should be collected on articles going to

Seringapatam ?   The Company's troops and establishments are situated there, and they must be equally the objects on which this natural right should be exercised with the Company's cattle, and the article of the treaty must be unnecessary.   If this right exist, why are not dustucks granted to exempt from duties all articles of provision passing to this place, and to every other occupied by the Company's troops and establishments within the Mysore country?   The fact is, that it does not exist.

Upon the whole, therefore, I conclude that this dustuck o ught not to have been given by government, whatever may be the state of the case regarding its being given by the Rajah of Mysore.   But I have already stated my reasons for thinking that such a thing ought not to be proposed to him, and for which I should always object to it.

Believe me, &c.,

ARTHUR WELLESLEY.

To Lieutenant-Colonel Cuppage.   [1164.]

SIR,   Sera, 15th May, 1802.

I beg that upon the receipt of this letter you will detach one European officer and thirty men from the troops under your command to Bonawassi, in Soonda, at which place the officer will receive charge of treasure which he is to escort to Seringapatam.   He will proceed from Nuggur by Chandergooty to Bonawassi, and will return by Chandergooty, Shikarpoor, Hooly Honore, Bankipoor, Turrikerra, Chinroypatam, to Seringapatam.   Mr. Read, the collector, will deliver the treasure to him.   As it is probable that you will not have had an opportunity of making your arrangements for supplying this detachment of the corps under your command with tents, according to the orders fixing the tent allowance for the troops, and that the officer will likewise be unprovided with a tent on the march through a country in which the western monsoon prevails to a great degree, I beg that you will make use of the Honourable Company's tents in store at Nuggur for this occasion, which will be taken from the stores in the usual manner by indent. The carriage and attendance upon the tents, however, must be paid for by you and the officer who will be detached respectively, according to the provisions of the order above alluded to.

I have, &c.,

ARTHUR WELLESLEY.

[1165.]   *To Major Elliott, H.M.'s 33rd Regt.*

MY DEAR ELLIOTT,   Sera, 15th May, 1802.

I enclose a letter which I have received from Mr. Goodlad, of which I request your consideration, as well as of the circumstances which follow hereafter.

When I returned from Bombay in May last I found Goodlad in arrest, by order of Colonel Shee, for taking Utley out shooting with him contrary to orders, and the Colonel was exceedingly angry with him. After some negotiations I prevailed upon the Colonel to allow Goodlad to make an apology, which he accepted; he released him from arrest, and I believe replaced him in the grenadier company.

Shortly after this the Colonel and Goodlad had a fresh dispute, or a renewal of the old one, which had been settled by my interference, at a dinner which was given to me by the garrison mess at Seringapatam. In the course of this dispute something passed which neither party was ever willing to explain; but Colonel Shee declared that in consequence of it he must insist upon Goodlad's engaging to exchange from the regiment, and upon his taking leave of absence till he could effect the exchange. I did not understand that Goodlad entered into the engagement to make the exchange, but he took the leave of absence in hopes that before the term of it should have expired, he should be promoted into another regiment, or that something would happen which would enable him to remain in his regiment.

Upon this transaction I have to observe that Goodlad never had the option of standing a court martial; something occurred between him and Colonel Shee, I may safely say, when both parties were drunk, which neither would explain; and it is probable that the inquiry into it by a court martial would have been as fatal to one as the other.

I acknowledge that I for one applaud the delicacy of officers regarding those with whom they are to associate and do duty, but I believe that this principle may be carried too far, and that in its effects it may be injurious rather than beneficial to the reputation of the corps in general. In this instance an officer gets into a dispute with his commanding officer, and something passes which cannot be explained to the credit or advantage of either party. The officer from circumstances is obliged to go away upon leave of absence. These drunken quarrels are certainly very bad, but give me leave to ask, are they worse in a subaltern than in a commanding officer? If they are not, I beg to know on what grounds the officers refuse to associate and do duty with Lieutenant Goodlad; having associated and done duty with Lieutenant-Colonel Shee for so many months subsequent to the transaction alluded to? Surely if it be proper to take such strong notice of the conduct of Lieutenant Goodlad at present, the same sense of propriety ought to have induced them long ago to take notice of that of Lieutenant-Colonel Shee.

But I agree that in the course of this drunken quarrel something may have occurred which gives ground for censuring the conduct of Lieutenant Goodlad. A drunken quarrel is very bad, and is always to be lamented, but probably the less it is inquired into the better. If it be inquired into, however, the inquiry must be carried into all the circumstances, and the conduct of both parties must be the subject of it; and applying this rule to the case under my consideration, I beg to put the question, whether the officers of the regiment never heard of a part of Colonel Shee's conduct in this very quarrel which would deservedly meet their censure and that of the world in general; and if they did, I beg to know for what reason they have not brought forward this part of his conduct, and have not refused to associate with him unless it could be explained to their satisfaction? In fact, my dear Elliott, their present severity towards Goodlad cannot be reconciled with their former lenity towards Colonel Shee, and, if persisted in, will cast upon the corps the imputation of inconsistency.

As for my part, I conceive that a regiment has no right to call upon an officer to quit his corps unless they can prove before a court martial that he has been guilty of something which will induce the court martial to dismiss him from the service. They then give him his option on solid grounds, and he makes it. But in this case can the officers of the 33rd regiment prove anything against Lieutenant Goodlad? They cannot, unless they can bring forward Lieutenant-Colonel Shee, who, for his own sake, will tell nothing. They ought, therefore, to beware how they call on Lieutenant Goodlad to quit the regiment. Supposing he was to say he would not, and was to appeal to the Commander-in-Chief?

The altercation would, I acknowledge, be an unpleasant one, but not more unpleasant for Lieutenant Goodlad than for the officers of the 33rd, and it would infallibly end in their being obliged to receive him and to do duty with him.

Recollect that his case is far different from that of Mr. Irwine, who has been received again. He never had the option of a court martial, and never promised to quit rather than stand his trial. He never in this manner tacitly acknowledged his own guilt, and his case must stand upon its own merits.

Upon the whole, considering it in every point of view, I am of opinion that Lieutenant Goodlad's conduct in the instance under discussion cannot be considered more liable to censure than that of Lieutenant-Colonel Shee; that the regiment having passed over that of Lieutenant-Colonel Shee, they must likewise pass over that of Goodlad; and that at all events the officers cannot reasonably or fairly require him to quit his regiment, unless, if he should refuse to do so, they can produce before a court martial such evidence as will break him.

I wish you to lay the enclosed letter and the circumstances which I have above stated before the heads of the corps as my real opinion of this whole transaction.

There may be other matters in Goodlad's conduct deserving of censure, but I have taken no notice of these, as they have not been brought forward by the corps in any shape.

Believe me, &c.,

ARTHUR WELLESLEY.

[1166.]   *To J. G. Ravenshaw, Esq.*

SIR,   Chinna, 23rd May, 1802.

I am very much obliged to you for your account of the roads in Canara, contained in your letter of the 12th instant.

The improvements which you propose to make to the high road from Mangalore to Seringapatam are very desirable, and will render it very convenient to those who are obliged to travel on it. I have lately discovered a shorter line from the road of the Bissolee Pass to Seringapatam, than that now used, by nearly sixty miles. It passes through part of the territories of the Rajah of Koorg, and in that part it wants repair. But after the present monsoon I intend to propose to the Rajah to repair this road, and to make certain arrangements regarding the duties collected within his country, which will render the passage through this part of it more convenient to travellers and traders. We shall thus bring ourselves as near your part of the coast as we can well be. I believe the best mode of settling the amount of the money disbursed by you for works performed in the Bissolee Ghaut would be, that I should sanction it in a contingent bill, and I propose to adopt this mode. As the coolies were employed in general within the territories of the Company, it would not answer to charge the expense of their hire to the government of the Rajah of Mysore.

I am glad that you have restored Nunjee Riah to his situation. I have no intention at present of employing the pioneers on the Balroy Droog Ghaut, or again at all in that part of the country. I will, however, draw the attention of the Dewan to the state of the Ghaut; I will urge him strongly to repair that part of it belonging to Mysore early in the next season, and I have no doubt but that he will attend to my suggestions upon this subject.

I have, &c.,

ARTHUR WELLESLEY.

To Lieutenant-General Stuart.   [1167.]

SIR,   Seringapatam, 28th May, 1802,

I have had the honour to receive your letter of the 23rd instant, with your minute upon the works of Seringapatam, and the plan of the reform proposed by Lieutenant-Colonel Trapaud and Lieutenant Frazer. You did not send me the note written and the estimate prepared by those officers; but I can form an opinion from the plan of their intentions, and I agree with them entirely.

I have already had occasion to communicate to the Military Board and to Major-General Ross my opinion upon the reform of the works of Seringapatam, and I particularly objected to the plan proposed by Captain Norris to withdraw the line of defence from the banks of the river to the high ground. In my opinion the great strength of Seringapatam consists in its position on the river Cauvery; if placed anywhere else, it would be of little, if of any consequence; and although it is very true that a good engineer might be able to construct works of greater regularity and apparent strength on the proposed new line, I doubt whether the removal from the river would not deprive the place of that alone which renders it really formidable to those who are to attack it.

I believe that Major-General Ross was never thoroughly convinced by my arguments, but government determined that the defences should not be removed from the river, and instructed him to frame his plan accordingly.

In my opinion all that Seringapatam wants is the stone glacis to be completed, and the power of giving a flanking fire on the points of attack near the western angle. These wants are provided in the new plan; and if that be well carried into execution, the place will be as strong as it is necessary to make it.

I beg to observe that it will be absolutely necessary to send an engineer to Seringapatam to carry into execution the proposed works: the gentleman belonging to that corps, who is here at present, does not appear to me to be capable of executing them.

I transmitted to the Adjutant-General Mr. Anderson's report on the sickness by which the 19th dragoons had been afflicted, and it appears by that paper that it does not exist at present to any great degree, but that it will be necessary that some of the men should be moved. I have accordingly desired Lieutenant-Colonel Maxwell to make arrangements for moving to this place (by the advice of Mr. Anderson) such men as Mr. Anderson and Mr. Murray will point out. The barracks built for the 19th at Sera are excellent, and their accommodations in other respects very good; they are also well situated at Sera for the general purposes of the service. But I acknowledge that I shall be sorry to see them remain there, if the sickness does not cease entirely upon the removal of those cases for whom Mr. Anderson thinks it necessary.

Sera has always been the most healthy spot in the Mysore country, and there is no doubt that the sickness which has prevailed there lately is casual, and will probably never occur again; but I should be sorry to see the experiment tried how long it would last in such a corps as the 19th dragoons.

I have, &c.,

ARTHUR WELLESLEY.

To Lieutenant-Colonel Maxwell.   [1168.]

MY DEAR COLONEL,   Seringapatam, 31st May, 1802.

I had the pleasure of receiving your letter of the 28th last night.

In my opinion the best thing to do with the 19th dragoons is to move forthwith every man who can move to Cheyloor, and to leave in the hospital those who cannot move at present, but who may be able to move in doolies as soon as those go up for which you have indented on this place. If it be found that the climate of Cheyloor answers, and if the men recover their health, the majority of them may return to Sera in the course of a fortnight or three weeks, provided that you shall find that the climate of that place has regained its accustomed salubrity. Those men who will at that time require a greater change of climate, or whose health will still be in a weakly state, may be sent on to Seringapatam in the doolies which I now send you.

I write orders to Mr. Gordon to supply you at Sera with bamboo coolies forthwith, and to take measures for victualling your men at Cheyloor; also to supply any carriage that may be wanted for the privates' tents, if the Company's camels which you have still with you are not sufficient for that service. You will accordingly make your demands upon his servant at Sera for all that you want, which is to be supplied by the paymaster's office, and send your indents here. The officers must have batta of course.

I give notice to the Sircar that you will want gram at Cheyloor for a fortnight or three weeks.

Make your own arrangements for the care of your hospital at Sera, and of your sick in camp at Cheyloor; but I hope that there will be very few of the former in a short time after the thirty-six doolies will have reached you. Some of them will, I trust, go off to-morrow.

Desire Mr. Bell to go on with the works ordered in the same manner as if you were on the spot.

I am exceedingly anxious for the perfect recovery of your corps; an anxiety which is participated by the Commander-in-Chief, and I hope that this removal will have the desired effect.

Believe me, &c.,

ARTHUR WELLESLEY.

I find upon inquiry that you have camels enough to carry all your privates' tents.

[1169.]   *To Lieutenant-Colonel Spry.*

MY DEAR SIR,   Seringapatam, 1st June, 1802.

You will perceive by my public letter of this date that I have given you a good deal of trouble.

It is not astonishing that the Military Board should be surprised at the size of Captain Atkins's estimate, as you will perceive when you learn that I have lately built a barrack at Sera, where all kinds of materials are nearly twice as dear as in Canara, for 1300 pagodas, including cook-rooms, &c. This barrack is 1000 feet long, has a verandah five feet broad on all sides, the walls of unburnt bricks, with teak-wood doors and windows: in short, the barrack at Sera will last for years without requiring any but trifling repairs; and, in all probability, that which now costs 2000 pagodas this year in Canara will require the same or a larger expense in the next season.

Believe me, &c.,

ARTHUR WELLESLEY.

[1170.]   *To Jonathan Duncan, Esq.*

MY DEAR SIR,   Seringapatam, 4th June, 1802.

I have had the pleasure of receiving your letter of the 7th May, and I sincerely congratulate you upon the successful termination of all your troubles in Guzerat. I was aware of your being without instructions from the Governor-General, and I felt for your situation at the moment of the failure of the attack proposed by Major Walker. However, everything has at last turned out so well that I don't think you have to regret even that check.

Since I wrote to you on the 28th of January matters have been so quiet in this country that I have had no intelligence to give you worthy of your attention. In a few days after I wrote to you I succeeded in obtaining possession of the person of the Bullum Rajah. He was executed; and that event, and the measures which I have adopted in Bullum to render the country more accessible to troops and to settle it, have kept it in perfect tranquillity. We have, consequently, had nothing to do since, and I hope that our tranquillity will be permanent.

I believe that, in general, the territories under the government of Fort St. George were never in a more peaceable state than they are at present. I don't know of any detachment of troops in the field excepting three battalions belonging to the corps stationed at Hyderabad, employed against the Solapoor Polygar. I understand also that the Nizam's government have settled their differences with this Polygar, and that their troops are likely to return to Hyderabad immediately.

We hear nothing yet of a successor to Lord Clive. His Lordship certainly informed the Court of Directors that he would not hold the government longer than January, 1803; and not even so long, unless certain points were explained to his satisfaction. The points on which he and the Court are at issue are the interference of the Court in the appointments to offices under this government, the sending back to India persons sent home for their crimes, and the encouragement given by the Court of Directors to a spirit of controversy and opposition in the Councils. The Court of Directors have appointed persons to the office of Chief Secretary of Government, to situations in the Boards of Revenue and Trade, and to the principal commercial residencies under this government. The selections for these offices have not only been made without the consent or recommendation of Lord Clive, but have been from persons of whose conduct his Lordship has disapproved publicly, and from others whom he or his predecessors have sent home for their misdemeanors.

They have sent back to India with appointments to offices,

or with strong recommendations, many persons who have been
sent home; among others, one young gentleman who was con-
victed, and did not even deny that he had taken a bribe to
make a judicial decision.

They have in a manner ordered their councillors to oppose
their Governors; and the consequence is, that the greatest part
of the time of the Governor is now employed in answering the
opposition of the members of his Council.   In my opinion, the
interference of the government at home in the disposal of the
patronage of the governments abroad, and the encouragement
given to controversy and opposition in the Councils, are directly
contrary to the spirit, if not to the letter, of the Act of Parliament.   At all events, these acts are in direct contradiction to
the principles upon which we are taught to believe the Act of
Parliament was framed, and it is very obvious that a continuance of them will soon settle all questions of British power
in India.

We are well aware of the manner in which persons sent home
for their crimes obtain the consent of the Court of Directors to
come out again, and others obtain their orders to the governments abroad to appoint them to offices for which they may
have been deemed entirely unfit.   These modes of obtaining
the favour and recommendation of the government at home may
be highly profitable to those who are concerned in them; but
they won't answer for a foreign and distant government, particularly not for the British government in India.   Upon the
whole, I cannot but applaud Lord Clive's determination to
bring these subjects before the public if such an explanation be
not given of them as will enable him or any person of character
to hold the government hereafter.

Believe me, &c.,

ARTHUR WELLESLEY.

[1171.]   *To the Adjutant-General.*

SIR,   Seringapatam, 5th June, 1802.

I have the honour to enclose a copy of the orders issued by
me from the 18th April to 31st May, which require the confirmation of the Commander-in-Chief.

As it was not possible that Lieutenant-Colonel Macalister or the officers under his command could be prepared with tents or houses at Santa Bednore, I thought it proper to allow the 5th regiment of cavalry to occupy the tents which had been in use with that corps. A similar want of tents in the 2nd battalion 3rd regiment was the cause of the order issued on the 27th April regarding that corps. I beg leave to request that these orders may be confirmed, and to recommend that the commanding officer and officers of the 2nd of the 3rd may be required to pay the expense of batta incurred for the lascars who have done duty with the tents which have been lent to them respectively.

The orders of the 26th May regarding the Committee at Paughur were issued in consequence of the communication by Captain Baynes of a correspondence between him and the Military Board upon the subject of the stores at Paughur, Mudgherry, and Mergasie; in the course of which it appeared that Captain Baynes was very doubtful regarding the quantity of stores those forts contained, and that Mr. Conductor Evatt had never received regular charge of the stores at any place excepting Paughur.

After I had issued the order of the 26th May regarding the removal of the sick and convalescent men of the 19th dragoons from Sera to Seringapatam, according to the opinion given by Mr. Anderson, he recommended that they should be moved only to Cheyloor, and that the removal should be of the whole regiment for a fortnight or three weeks, as the most certain mode of completely eradicating the disorder, with which nearly every man had been afflicted. Accordingly I issued the order of the 31st of May.

I have the honour to enclose a report of working parties employed in Bullum from the 30th March to the 13th May, of which I request the confirmation of the Commander-in-Chief.

I have, &c.,

ARTHUR WELLESLEY.

To Lieutenant-Colonel Spry.

[1172.]

MY DEAR SIR,   Seringapatam, 5th June, 1802.

I have had the pleasure of receiving your letter of the 30th May, and have taken into consideration the subject to which it relates.

My opinion is, that, when the commanding officer in Canara pointed out a piece of ground for a cantonment for the 75th regiment, he intended that it should be the spot for a cantonment for the corps which should relieve the 75th; and it stands to reason that the ground allotted to the officers was not excepted from the general rule. Accordingly, I conclude that the officers of the 75th regiment have no grant of the ground on which they built their houses, and that their right to it must have depended upon their being officers belonging to the corps which occupied the cantonment. If this be true, they can have no possible right to sell any more of their houses than the materials; indeed, a purchaser of more would throw away his money, as it would be in the power of the commanding officer in the cantonment allotted by government to his regiment to prevent any person, excepting one belonging to the regiment, from residing within his lines.

I am very far from being of opinion that an officer who succeeds to another in a cantonment ought to insist upon his selling his house for the value of the materials. In many cases the house must be worth a larger sum, and it would be for the convenience and benefit of the supposed purchaser that the materials should be allowed to stand in the shape of a house, for which benefit it is but fair that the purchaser should pay something; but, although the purchaser ought to pay some advance on the value of the materials, I am far from thinking the seller entitled to the whole sum which he would get for the house from any man in the bazaar. In short, this question, like most others, depends much upon the disposition of both parties to accommodate each other. On the one hand, the purchaser ought to give a fair price for the house, being rather more than the value of the materials, to which alone the seller can have any right; and on the other, the seller ought not to attempt to ask for it the full sum which he would get for it if he should have the power of selling it in the bazaar.

This is my private opinion upon the question which you have put to me. I observe, however, that it is one of general importance, the decision upon which may affect more corps than the 75th and 77th regiments, and I am rather desirous that it should be decided by the Commander-in-Chief. I beg, therefore, that you will write me a public letter upon the subject, which I can refer to him.

Believe me, &c.,

ARTHUR WELLESLEY.

To Lieutenant-Colonel Boles.   [1173.]

SIR,   Seringapatam, 6th June, 1802.

I have the honour to enclose you the translation of a letter which I have received from the Rajah of Koorg upon the subject of a person who has been taken up in his country, supposed to belong to the Pyche Rajah. I have written to the Rajah of Koorg, in answer to this letter, to request that he will send the person in question to Cannanore to be delivered over to you with all the evidence that there may be against him. If he should turn out to be one of the proscribed persons, it will be necessary that he should be executed; if not, it will be necessary that he should be tried as soon as possible by the court martial now sitting at Calicut, or in such other manner as you may think proper.

I have told the Rajah of Koorg that you will send a guard to escort the prisoner, if you should learn from him that it will be necessary, and I beg that you will act accordingly.

I have, &c.,

ARTHUR WELLESLEY.

To Major Malcolm.   [1174.]

MY DEAR MALCOLM,   Seringapatam, 7th June, 1802.

I enclose a letter for the Governor-General from the Rajah of Koorg, which was opened by my Persian interpreter by mistake. I likewise enclose the translation of a letter which I have received from the Rajah of Koorg by the same occasion, and I shall be obliged to you if you will urge the Governor-General to comply with the Rajah's requests. The Board of Revenue at Fort St. George have already approved of the little attentions which were paid to the Rajah of Soonda, on his passage through Canara, by the collectors, at my request.

Believe me, &c.,

ARTHUR WELLESLEY.

[1175.]   *To the Chief Secretary of Government.*

SIR,   Seringapatam, 9th June, 1802.

In obedience to the passport regulations I have the honour to enclose a list and descriptions of the Europeans residing at Seringapatam who are not in the service of His Majesty and of the Honourable Company.

Excepting the person last mentioned in this list, they are all more or less engaged in trade with the natives, and, consequently, there are occasional disputes between them and the latter in which questions of property are involved. These disputes cannot be settled by the Court of Cutchery or that of the magistrate at Seringapatam in cases where the Europeans are defendants, because they are not liable to the jurisdiction, and yet they have the full benefit of an appeal to the courts in cases in which they are plaintiffs. In recommending that certificates should be granted to all these Europeans, I beg leave to suggest that they may be required to bind themselves to abide by the decisions of the Cutchery and the Magistrates' Court in cases in which natives may be plaintiffs, as a condition on which the certificate will be granted to them. I have to observe that this condition is common in the provinces under the government of Fort William, where these courts exist, and that the persons whose names I now enclose have expressed their willingness to bind themselves to abide by the decision of the country courts in every case.

I have, &c.,

ARTHUR WELLESLEY.

[1176.]   *To the Secretary of the Military Board.*

SIR,   Seringapatam, 9th June, 1802.

I have the honour to enclose the copy of a letter which I have received from Lieutenant-Colonel Macalister upon the subject of gram for the 5th regiment of cavalry, in answer to one which I wrote to him in consequence of information which I had received from the residency stating that the quarter-master of the 5th regiment of cavalry had refused to take the gram which the Rajah's officers had supplied for that regiment at the desire of the Resident, upon the requisition of the gram-agent general.

It appears by the letter from Lieutenant-Colonel Macalister that the Military Board have given orders that the gram in store at Chittledroog shall be consumed by the regiments of cavalry stationed at Sera and Santa Bednore; of which orders the Rajah's government, who have supplied gram at those stations, or the Resident, have received no intimation, and, consequently, the government will sustain some loss. But I beg leave to observe that the Company will sustain some loss as well as the Rajah's government by this arrangement. The distance of Sera from Chittledroog is about fifty miles, that of Santa Bednore about thirty-six. A bullock which will carry seventy seers of gram, and whose hire will be one-and-a-half pagoda for one month, will go thrice to the former in that space of time and four times to the latter. The gram, consequently, which will be delivered at Sera will cost one-and-a-half pagoda for 210 seers, or about one rupee for 40 seers, and that which will be delivered at Santa Bednore will cost one-and-a-half pagoda for 280 seers, or about one rupee for 52 seers. To this expense, occasioned by the removal of the gram from Chittledroog, is to be added that of gunny bags to hold it.

The price of the gram furnished by the Sircar to the regiment at Santa Bednore is one rupee for 63 seers, and the price of that delivered at Sera is one rupee for 70 seers. Thus it appears that the Sircar for one rupee furnish at Santa Bednore 11 seers more, and at Sera 30 seers more, than the Company can carry for the same sum to those places respectively, of gram which is their own property.

The gram at Chittledroog is old, and will injure the horses; that delivered by the Rajah is new, and is better for them. But this is not the only loss which the Company will sustain by this arrangement: it is probable that the gram at Chittledroog would sell for something, and the Company lose by using it at Santa Bednore and Sera not only the excess of the expense of carrying it to those stations, but also all that it would bring by disposing of it by sale at Chittledroog. I beg, therefore, to

recommend that the gram furnished by the Rajah's government
for the regiments at Sera and Santa Bednore may be used by
the regiments at those stations, and that the gram in store at
Chittledroog may be disposed of by sale.

I have, &c.,

ARTHUR WELLESLEY.

[1177.]

To Lieutenant-Colonel Boles.

SIR,   Seringapatam, 10th June, 1802.

Captain Barclay has communicated to me your letter of the
7th instant with its enclosures.

I am of opinion that, under the order of the 10th April, an
officer commanding a battalion of Native infantry is bound to
provide cover for that battalion in peace or war from the 1st
of May; consequently, that the officer commanding the 2nd
battalion 2nd regiment ought to provide huts for the sepoys if
in cantonments, or tents if in the field, from that period. It is
also his duty to provide a sufficient building for a battalion
hospital. Accordingly, I have to desire that the officer commanding the cantonment or garrison in which the 2nd battalion
2nd regiment may be situated, may be directed to see that that
corps has sufficient covering to protect the sepoys from the effects
of the weather, and that orders to the same purport may be
published in Malabar and Canara requiring the same duties
from officers commanding all stations.

` In regard to the other points referred to in your letter, and
in that which you wrote to the officer commanding the 2nd battalion 5th regiment, a copy of which you have enclosed, I have
to observe that the general order of the 10th April does not
absolutely require that the tents should be mustered on the
1st August. It appears to me that it is in the power of officers
in command of divisions of the army a d stations to delay
ordering a muster of the camp equipage till they shall think it
proper. In the exercise of this power they will of course be
guided by circumstances; and those which you mention would
certainly induce me to postpone a muster of the tents for corps
in Malabar and Canara to a later period in the year. I
shall, however, consider it to be my duty to order a muster of
tents at the earliest period at which I may think it possible for

officers commanding corps to procure them ; and, in the mean time, I must insist upon the troops being properly covered from the effects of the weather.   I shall also, if circumstances permit, inspect all the corps in Malabar and Canara in the course of the next season, and I shall certainly then require to see the camp equipage provided for each corps ; and I must request that you will see it on the tour of inspection which you will make.

The other points referred to in your letter of the 22nd May to the commanding officer of the 2nd battalion 5th regiment belong to regimental detail, and I should wish to give no opinion upon them.   I conceive that, in case any of the corps are called into the field previous to the 1st of August, the commanding officer will be obliged to pay the expense of all the followers required for the attendance upon camp-equipage and stores, and that it is the intention of government that he should procure them as soon as possible after the 1st of May.   Government, however, have not ordered that they should be mustered till on or after the 1st of August: till that day, therefore, there is no check upon commanding officers, and they alone must be considered responsible.

I have also received your letter addressed to me of the 7th instant.   You will be so kind as to order a detachment to Panamburcottah under the command of Captain Dickenson, and you will state in your orders that it is sent there in consequence of a requisition from the collector.

I have, &c.,

ARTHUR WELLESLEY.

To Lieutenant-General Stuart.   [1178.]

SIR,   Seringapatam, 11th June, 1802.

I take the liberty of once more drawing your attention to the orders of government regarding the provincial paymasters drawing bills upon the Paymaster-General at Madras.   A detachment is now about to march from hence as an escort to part of the family of Tippoo Sultaun, and I know that 10,000 pagodas in gold are going down to Madras with it.   I have also reason to believe that other large sums of money are going with it. The distress which these large drains of specie will occasion in this country, where there is so little of it, and the means of procuring it so few, cannot easily be described; but the subject is well deserving the attention of government.

I have, &c.,

· ARTHUR WELLESLEY.

To Major Elliott.

MY DEAR ELLIOTT,   Seringapatam, 15th June, 1802.

I received your letter of the 12th last night, and I lose no time in replying to it. The first warrant which notices the charge of 2s. 6d. per man to be made for the alteration of clothing is that of the 7th of September, 1795; but I observe that that warrant applies only to regiments serving in Great Britain, Jersey, Guernsey, &c.; and I observe that it is particularly stated in the 15th Article that that article and the 14th apply only to the troops entitled to consolidated allowance. The troops in this country were not entitled to consolidated allowance, and therefore do not come within the terms of the warrant of the 7th September, 1795.

I have not by me the warrant which gave the increase of pay to the whole army, and which was dated I believe in 1797; and I cannot say whether that warrant makes any alteration regarding this allowance of 2s. 6d. for the alteration of clothing, or extends it to the troops of this country. You will be able to judge of this upon a perusal of it.

I am very certain, however, that if that warrant does not alter that part of the warrant of September, 1795, the men of the 33rd regiment have no right to the allowance of 2s. 6d., and therefore that they must themselves pay for the alteration of their clothing in the usual manner, as the warrant of April 9th, 1800, grants nothing on that head which was not granted by former warrants.

It appears that, by the new mode of cutting the coats of the soldiers, a saving is made in the expense incurred by the colonel for clothing of 1s. 10d. each man: this saving is applied in some countries towards making up a fund for providing great coats, which it is supposed are not necessary in India. The warrant, accordingly, directs that the saving shall be given to the men in useful necessaries, such as cumleys, &c. &c.* There is no doubt but that they have a right to credit for this amount in their accounts, and that the sum of 1s. 10d. each man ought to be charged to the Colonel, supported by the usual documents.

In my opinion, the 130 recruits whom you mention as having received clothing in September, 1801, although they had before received clothing for that year at Chatham, ought not to be charged more for the articles they received than they or the other soldiers would have been paid for the same articles by the Colonel, supposing that they had not been delivered to them, even if you should be of opinion that they ought to be charged something for them. Lord Cornwallis has always been, and wishes to be, generous towards his regiment; and in a case of necessity, such as must have existed when Colonel Shee directed that a second suit of clothing should be issued to these men, I am convinced that his Lordship would be much better pleased that they should not pay for it. I therefore recommend that this matter should pass unnoticed, and that no charge should be made against any of these 130 recruits for the surplus articles of clothing which they have received.

Believe me, &c.,
ARTHUR WELLESLEY.

To Lieutenant-Colonel Maxwell. [1180.]

SIR, Seringapatam, 16th June, 1802.

In consequence of directions which I have received from the Commander-in-Chief, I have this day given orders that the 19th dragoons under your command are to march to Arcot in the Carnatic. You will, therefore, commence your march as soon as it may be convenient to you, and proceed by Bangalore and the Pednaigdurgum pass.

As there are still a considerable number of sick in the 19th dragoons, and as you have been joined by the remount horses, I am aware that it will be impossible for you to march as expeditiously as you would otherwise. You will make short marches,

---

* *Cumley*—a coarse blanket, made of undyed wool.

and move only when you find that you can bring on your sick and your horses. You will be so kind as to take with you from Sera every man who is capable of moving. Such as it may be necessary to leave behind must remain in the hospital, and you will make such arrangements as you may think proper for the medical charge of them.

I have the honour to enclose the copy of a letter which I received last night from the Secretary of the Commander-in-Chief upon the subject of tent-allowance for the quarter-masters of dragoons, and of the horsekeepers for the care of the number of remount horses intended for the recruits not yet arrived from England. You will be so kind as to take measures to enlist the horsekeepers without loss of time.

I have, &c.,

ARTHUR WELLESLEY.

[1181.]   *To Lieutenant-Colonel Maxwell.*

MY DEAR COLONEL,   Seringapatam, 16th June, 1802.

The General Orders and my public letter of this date will apprise you of a circumstance which I acknowledge that I have expected, since I received your letter desiring to move the whole regiment to Cheyloor. This movement is the cause of these last orders.

I assure you that I part with you with great regret, and that I have done everything in my power to prevent your quitting this country. The 7th regiment of cavalry are to come to Sera.

We can get your horsekeepers here immediately, but it will be necessary that they should receive an advance of 400 rupees. If you want the horsekeepers, you must write to Mr. Crooks to desire him to make the advance.

I have apprised the Sircar of your march and of your want of gram.

Believe me, &c.,

ARTHUR WELLESLEY.

Mr. Bell must continue the works at Sera till they are finished.

To the Chief Secretary of Government.   [1182.]

SIR,   16th June, 1802.

In consequence of the orders of government, dated the 28th March, I have made arrangements for filling up the inner ditch of Seringapatam. The work was commenced under the superintendence of Captain Heitland, on the 20th of April, by 100 pioneers, who had been brought in from Bullum for that purpose, and by the commatties and coolies who were hired, and has continued ever since. I cannot exactly describe the progress which has been made. It is, however, so great, that on the 1st I was able to authorise the discharge of 500 commatties, and on this day the whole number of commatties employed is reduced to 800. There is still, however, some work for basket coolies; but from what I shall state hereafter, it will be observed that the expense of their hire is comparatively small.

The people who were employed last year on this work were absolutely necessary, their expense appeared to be moderate, and the Right Hon. the Governor in Council was pleased to approve of them. I have therefore authorised the employment of the same description of persons in the work this year, excepting the commatties and coolies furnished by the Rajah's government, the employment of whom I did not find to be quite so advantageous, although the rate of their hire was apparently cheaper than that of the other commatties and coolies. I have therefore authorised the employment only of the latter in the work this year.

The establishment of persons employed last year, and their expense, are detailed in a letter which I had the honour of addressing to the Chief Secretary of Government on the 30th of June, 1801; but as it will tend to elucidate this subject, I shall now proceed to state what persons have been employed this year, and the expense of each description.

The persons employed upon the work have been the pioneers, the hired commatties, and basket coolies.

The paper No. 1 contains an account of the expense of the daily pay of the commatties and of each description of basket coolies.

Before the inner ditch was dug, there were drains in the fort which went through the outer rampart, and carried the water from the fort, &c., into the outer ditch. It was necessary to reconstruct these drains, and to employ stone-cutters, masons, and bricklayers on this work; and as it was difficult to trace the drains, it was necessary to authorise the employment of a native who had had the superintendence of them formerly, and who was thoroughly acquainted with their course, utility, &c. &c. This man receives twenty pagodas *per mensem.* The enclosed paper No. 2 contains an account of his daily pay and that of the stone-cutters, &c.

In order to keep the tools in repair, I have authorised the employment of artificers, as stated in the enclosed paper No. 3; and to keep the accounts of all the different people employed, of writers as stated in the enclosed paper No. 4.

Captain Heitland, of the corps of pioneers, has superintended the work; he has done it much to my satisfaction and the public advantage, and it is as forward as could have been expected. I have given him orders to furnish the paymaster at the end of every month with a detailed account of the expense incurred on this work, which account is to be supported by a copy of the daily report of the number of workmen employed.

I have furnished Mr. Gordon with statements of the prices of hire of the different people employed, and with the establishments of artificers and writers which I have found it necessary to authorise Captain Heitland to entertain.

I have the honour to enclose an account, No. 5, of the number of people employed from the 20th of April to the 15th instant.

In the course of the performance of this work, a large quantity of cut stones have been found, which will be very useful hereafter in the reform of the fortifications. It has been necessary to pull down two houses, the materials of which have been sold by public auction, and produced, one 245 p. 26 f. 70 c., the other 444 p. 5 f. 47 c., and the materials of other houses are still to be sold and to be carried to the account of the Company.

The particulars of the sales of the first have been transmitted to be laid before the Military Board; as will those of the materials of the other houses as soon as they will be sold.

I have, &c.,

ARTHUR WELLESLEY.

To the Secretary of the Military Board.   [1183.]

SIR,   Seringapatam, 17th June, 1802.

I have the honour to enclose a list of unserviceable stores sold
at Seringapatam by public auction.   I likewise enclose a list of
unserviceable timber sold by public auction at the same time.
I have desired that the sum produced by these sales might be
lodged in the hands of the paymaster, excepting ten pagodas
which I have directed to be given to the person who sold the
articles.

The timber above reported to have been sold was taken down
from an unfinished part of the Palace of Tippoo Sultaun, being
a part of that building which could never be applied to any
public purpose without incurring a great expense.   The timber
which was sold was nearly rotten, and I enclose the proceedings
of a committee which examined the whole of it, in which are
stated the dimensions of that part of it which was found serviceable.   That upon which a report is made in these proceedings
is under charge of the commissary of stores, and is marked
with a P, in order to distinguish it from other timber, and
numbered.

I likewise enclose the particulars of the account of sales of
two old buildings taken down in the course of the performance
of the work lately ordered at Seringapatam by government.   I
have desired that the amount may be paid into the hands of the
paymaster on account of the Company, excepting 5 per cent.,
which I have desired may be paid to the person who arranged
the different lots and superintended the sale and collected the
money.

I have, &c.,

ARTHUR WELLESLEY.

To Major Kirkpatrick.   [1184.] .

SIR,   Seringapatam, 19th June, 1802.

I have had the honour of receiving your letter of the 7th
instant, and I shall lose no time in procuring and sending to
Hyderabad the bark which you require, if the tree can be found.*

* The bark of the tree referred to was recommended by the physicians of
the Nizam as a sovereign remedy for the palsy, with which his Highness had
long been afflicted.

I wish that it may be beneficial to the health of his Highness the Nizam, but I acknowledge that I fear the only benefit he will derive from the prescription will be that which a person who has long been afflicted with sickness derives from the hope of a cure.

I have, &c.,

ARTHUR WELLESLEY.

[1185.]

To W. H. Gordon, Esq.

SIR,   Seringapatam, 21st June, 1802.

In answer to your letter of this day's date, I have to inform you that I have consulted Major Symons regarding the rate at which the Bombay gold mohurs will pass at Seringapatam, and I find it to be as follows : viz., the old gold mohurs 13r. 11f. 20c. ; the new, 13r. 4f. 65½c. The loss to the troops and the general inconvenience by the issue of them will be so great that I should wish you to delay it till I can receive the orders of government upon the subject, consequent to a letter which I propose to address them. In regard to the Surat rupees, the number of them is so small that I don't think there will be any very great inconvenience in making a proportion of your payments in that coin, and I recommend that you should pay away half of them on the 1st of July and half on the 1st of August.

I have, &c.,

ARTHUR WELLESLEY.

[1186.]

To Lieutenant-Colonel Boles.

SIR,   Seringapatam, 21st June, 1802.

I have had the honour of receiving your letter of the 18th and its enclosures. There is no doubt but that Captain Fitzgerald's conduct in communicating officially with the commanding-officer in Malabar, upon a regimental subject, in any manner excepting through the commanding-officer of his regiment, is irregular and contrary to orders. When that communication, however, was received and listened to by the commanding-officer in Malabar, it would have been respectful in Captain Gibson to have waited, and to have refrained from writing a reprimand to Captain Fitzgerald ; that reprimand is, in fact, a reflection upon the conduct of the commanding-officer in Malabar, and Captain Gibson ought to have shown his sense of the impropriety of Captain Fitzgerald's conduct by making it a subject of complaint.

The subsequent letter of Captain Fitzgerald to Captain Gibson is entirely unjustifiable. The apology for it is, however, ample, and such as every gentleman ought to make when he is convinced of his error. From the candid manner in which Captain Fitzgerald has acknowledged his error and has apologized for his conduct, I am induced to believe that the following words in the last paragraph, viz. "while I am in the service," are not intended to convey any reservation, and that Captain Fitzgerald does not intend, notwithstanding the insertion of those words, to renew the dispute whenever his convenience may induce him to quit the service. In this belief, I am of opinion that Captain Gibson ought to accept the apology, and there to allow the matter to drop, because I observe that he has severely reprimanded Captain Fitzgerald for the crime stated in his first charge against him, and because Captain Fitzgerald has made him a full, ample, and gentlemanlike apology for that stated in the second. I think it probable that any general court-martial which may try Captain Fitzgerald on these charges will agree in the opinion which I have above delivered upon the subject; and that although Captain Fitzgerald may be found guilty, he will not be thought deserving of farther punishment. I therefore recommend that the charges may be withdrawn.

If, however, Captain Gibson should think proper to persist in bringing them forward, a general court-martial shall be assembled to take them into consideration.

I cannot conclude my observations upon this subject without remarking upon the conduct of Lieutenant and Adjutant Ogilvie. As for my part, I cannot admire that readiness in officers to submit their conduct to the trial of that awful tribunal a general court-martial, rather than to do what is their duty, viz., explain what is required from them as long as explanation can be asked for.

It was Lieutenant Ogilvie's duty to explain to Captain Fitzgerald, particularly when that explanation was called for by the commanding-officer of his regiment, all the circumstances regarding the payment of any sums of money to the men of his company; and he ought to be informed that the officers of the army have too much to do to be employed in the investigation of a matter so trifling as the sufficiency or insufficiency of his explanations upon that occasion.

I have also to observe that nothing tends so much to these trifling disputes as the habit of writing upon all occasions. I don't see any reason for which a line should have been written upon any part of this subject. Captain Gibson should have acquainted Captain Fitzgerald with Lieutenant Ogilvie's answer by word of mouth. He should have communicated his censure in the same manner, if he thought proper to make it; and then, in all probability, what followed would have been avoided.

I have, &c.,

ARTHUR WELLESLEY.

[1187.]   *To the Chief Secretary of Government.*

SIR,   22nd June, 1802.

I have the honour to enclose the copy of a letter which I have received from Mr. Gordon upon the subject of certain Bombay gold mohurs which he had received from Mr. Ravenshaw, in which he desires to have my opinion whether these gold mohurs shall be given to the troops upon the next issue of pay.

In answer to this letter, I have desired Mr. Gordon, in a letter of which I enclose a copy, to delay issuing these gold mohurs till I should receive the orders of government consequent on a representation which I proposed to address them upon the subject; because I recollected that, upon a former occasion, when the troops returning from the expedition into Malabar had brought some of these gold mohurs into circulation, great inconvenience was felt from the high rate at which they were valued, and having consulted Major Symons upon the subject, I received from him the enclosed paper, by which it appears that the Bombay gold mohurs are valued in the nerrick of Seringapatam at a rate much higher than they are really worth.

The nerrick of money at Seringapatam was established while

the Commissioners were sitting here, after a mature consideration of the relative value of the different coins in circulation, and taking the star pagoda at the Company's rate of exchange as the standard. This nerrick has been invariably adhered to ever since: the troops have enjoyed the benefit of an uniform rate in the exchange of money. The only inducement to a shroff to exercise his trade is the fluctuation in the value of the different coins in circulation. As long as he is obliged to give a certain number of rupees or fanams in exchange for a pagoda, and afterwards to exchange that pagoda again for the same number of rupees or fanams, or a settled equivalent to them, it is obvious that he can gain nothing; and therefore I conclude that the shroffs have gained nothing by the exercise of their trade of exchanging money at Seringapatam. The inducement to this useful class of people to reside here has been the security of property which they enjoy by living under the Company's government, and the advantage which they have at Seringapatam of the regular monthly expenditure of a large sum of money by the garrison, by means of which they are enabled to trade in money in the other large towns in Mysore, and in the provinces of Malabar and Canara. Accordingly, in those towns and on the coast of Malabar the fluctuation in the exchange of money is great.

It is obvious, however, that if any coin be issued from the pay-office at Seringapatam at a rate far above its intrinsic value, and that at which it will pass in other parts of Mysore and in Malabar and Canara, even though that value is assigned to it in the nerrick, the persons on whom all the traffic in the place depends must be losers, even in that part of their trade by which they are enabled to live at all. The loss would be trifling, and would probably not be noticed, if the sum to be issued and to be in circulation in this coin were small; but as it is so large as this sum is, they will be unwilling to submit to it, and it would probably be unreasonable to expect that they should. Indeed, the attempt to force them to it might have the effect of obliging them to quit the place and country for a time, and the distress which would be felt by the troops and all classes of the inhabitants for want of them would be extreme. I have, therefore, to request that the Right Honourable the Governor in Council will give permission either that these Bombay gold mohurs may be issued to the troops at the rate of exchange which they are really worth, or that they may be recoined.

I have, &c.,

ARTHUR WELLESLEY.

[ENCLOSURE.]

Statement of the Bombay Gold Mohurs.

Description.	Touch.	Intrinsic Value.			Weight.	Bazaar Exchange.			Government Exchange.			Loss to the Shroff.		
		C.Rs.	fa.	c.	Grains.	C.Rs.	fa.	c.	Rs.	fa.	c.	Rs.	fa.	c.
Old	11	13	7	18½	133½	13	11	20	15	0	0	1	1	48½
New	10½	13	0	64½	133½	13	4	65½	15	0	0	1	8	3

A True Copy.   (Signed)   J. H. SYMONS.

[1188.]   *To the Secretary of the Military Board.*

SIR,   Seringapatam, 22nd June, 1802.

In consequence of the orders of the Military Board, dated the 25th of May, regarding the buildings at Mangalore, I gave orders that a committee should be assembled at that station to ascertain the dimensions of the buildings which had been repaired and the quantity of materials which had been expended in the repair of them, and I desired the commanding-officer to request the collector to furnish him with a statement of the prices of materials and workmen at Mangalore. I have the honour to enclose a letter which I have received from Lieutenant-Colonel Spry, with the report of the committee which has surveyed the buildings, and a memorandum of the prices of materials and workmen at Mangalore, furnished by Mr. Ravenshaw the collector.

I also enclose an account of the expense of the repair of the buildings at Mangalore, made out at this place from the report of the committee above mentioned, and the statement of prices received from the collector, the number of workmen to be employed being taken from the engineer's estimate. I beg to draw the attention of the Military Board to Captain Atkins's letter to Lieutenant-Colonel Spry, enclosed with that from Lieutenant-Colonel Spry to myself.

By that the grounds appear upon which the estimate was framed of which the Military Board disapproved, and I cannot conceive that it is intended to incur the expense of employing an European officer in works of this kind whose judgment in framing his estimate of the quantity of materials required, or of the expense of them, is to be in any degree guided by a Native.

Captain Atkins declares in that letter that more work has been performed and less labour has been employed than he estimated. Upon this I have to observe that, in proportion as he has performed a greater work than that of which he estimated the expense, and as the labour employed upon that work has been less than he estimated it would be, his estimate has been erroneous, and has merited the disapprobation of the Military Board.

As after the buildings required for the troops at Mangalore will have been completed there will be no farther occasion for the services of an engineer at that station, I beg leave to recommend that Captain Atkins may be ordered to join the head-quarters of the corps at Bombay.

I have, &c.,

ARTHUR WELLESLEY.

To Lieutenant-General Stuart.   [1189.]

SIR,   Seringapatam, 26th June, 1802.

I am very happy to find that what I have written to you upon the subject of the orders of government, prohibiting the paymasters from drawing bills, has given you satisfaction.

After I had written to you on the 11th instant on that subject, I found that the sum sent away with the escort to Vellore was nearly 20,000 pagodas, and I know that another sum of 5000 pagodas in gold was sent to Madras yesterday.

I have, &c.,

ARTHUR WELLESLEY.

To Josiah Webbe, Esq.   [1190.]

MY DEAR WEBBE,   Seringapatam, 26th June, 1802.

I have delayed to thank you for your letters containing the news, till I could send you the estimate of the expense of building a house for the Resident at Mysore according to the plan given you by Mr. Goldingham, and another of a house according to a plan drawn by Piele, which we here think will answer better than the other. The objection to Mr. Goldingham's plan is that it gives you only one entertaining room, and that the accommodations for the gentlemen of the Resident's family are crowded together and inconvenient. Those allotted to the Resident himself are at a distance from the room in which he is to live, at the same time that they will not be private, as the Cutchery is to be in the same building.

The Resident ought to have two entertaining rooms; and, if his house were to be built at Seringapatam, one of them ought to be large enough to entertain the whole garrison. As, however, it is to be built at Mysore, rooms of the size of those in Piele's plan will be sufficiently large, and they are conveniently situated in respect to each other.

When people are to reside for a length of time in a place, nothing can be more inconvenient to them, particularly in this country, than to live in the same building. It is, therefore, far preferable that the gentlemen of the family should have each a separate bungalow. This arrangement will be more convenient to them, and, I imagine, to every body else. Upon the whole, I think that the house according to Piele's plan would be the most convenient of the two. Indeed the want of a second entertaining room in Mr. Goldingham's must condemn it entirely. The expense, however, of the former is far greater than that of the latter, but I imagine that it may be much reduced. In the first place, there is no necessity for verandahs of the breadth of eighteen feet to the principal building. The expense would be much diminished by their being reduced to fifteen feet the largest, and fourteen the smallest. The cross walls need not be two feet thick: this will again reduce the expense. The bungalows for the gentlemen are larger than it is necessary that they should be. They might easily be reduced in size so as to cost only 1000 instead of 1500 pagodas each. Upon the whole, I think that the expense of a house on Piele's plan may be brought to about 10,000 pagodas.

I send it to you as it is, in order that you may judge for yourself. Probably, from the two plans, some of your friends at Madras will be able to make out one which will answer better than either. They will be able also to estimate the expense of any building of which they may give you a plan, from the prices stated in the enclosed estimates.

Believe me, &c.,

ARTHUR WELLESLEY.

To the Secretary of the Military Board.   [1191.]

SIR,   Seringapatam, 27th June, 1802.

I should before now have reported to the Military Board the state of the barracks occupied by the Native corps at Seringapatam, and the arrangements which I proposed to make of them, consequent on the orders of government upon the subject of tent allowance, only that I waited till the work going on in the fort by order of government should be so far completed as that those arrangements might be forthwith carried into execution if the Military Board should approve of them.

There are in Seringapatam barracks for two Native corps, and there is a choultry at the Bangalore gateway which gives cover to five companies of another corps.

There is besides a building which has been completed for the artillery; but as it is not so well situated as the other building allotted to the Europeans, which affords sufficient space for the detachment of artillery, this building is at present unoccupied, and will answer for five companies of a battalion of Native infantry, and it is conveniently situated in respect to the choultry above mentioned.

Of these buildings occupied and which may be occupied by the Native troops, the barracks now occupied by the 1st of the 2nd, and the building which has been completed for the artillery, alone are serviceable, and fit for the purpose. The building occupied by the 1st of the 8th is nearly in ruins; it is inconvenient, and the floor of it, and the level of the yard, are much lower than the level of the adjacent street. The choultry belongs to the mosque; it is open to the street, and is unfit for the purpose of a barrack.

My wish is that the barrack occupied by the 1st of the 2nd should be allotted as a place of arms and store-room, &c., for that battalion and for the 1st of the 8th.

I have accordingly arranged for a piece of ground in the fort on which this battalion may hut. I should propose that the barrack occupied by the 1st of the 8th should be pulled down, and the materials disposed of on account of the Company, and that the 1st of the 8th should be hutted on the ground on which the barrack now stands.

The building intended for the artillery will answer as a place of arms, &c., for the 2nd of the 3rd, which corps may be hutted in a vacant space in its neighbourhood, and the choultry near the mosque may be given up to the convenience of the inhabitants and travellers for which it was intended.

It is very improbable that the building above alluded to will ever be required for the artillery, as by the departure of the family of Tippoo Sultaun there is another extensive and commodious building vacant, applicable to giving cover to European troops, which requires but small improvements and repairs ; but in case that building should ever be required for the artillery, the barrack of the 1st of the 2nd will afford space for places of arms and the stores, &c., of three corps.

Thus, then, according to this mode, the Native troops will be arranged at Seringapatam in the best manner without further expense to the Company.

I have preferred to pull down the barrack occupied by the 1st of the 8th, to recommending that it should be given over to the commanding officer of that battalion : first, because I observe that it is in a ruinous condition, and a very bad one ; secondly, because I deem huts a preferable mode to barracks for lodging Native troops.

Whether they have barracks or not, they will live in huts, which, when provided by themselves, are bad, and afford them no shelter ; and if not hutted by authority, they scatter themselves in all quarters of the place, and if their services should be suddenly wanted, it would not be possible to find them.

This inconvenience alone in a populous place might be very detrimental, and in my opinion affords a reason for hutting the Native troops at Seringapatam in spaces allotted to them for that purpose, even if that measure were not recommended by other circumstances.

I have, &c.,

ARTHUR WELLESLEY.

To Major Macleod.

[1192.]

MY DEAR MACLEOD,   Seringapatam, 27th June, 1802.

It gave me great pleasure to hear of your success against Goorkul, and I have strong hopes that we shall now have tranquillity in Malabar.

I don't know of any intention to deprive Major Howden of his command, and I don't believe that such an intention exists. I make it a rule to interfere as little as possible in the details conducted by Lieutenant-Colonel Boles, but I will certainly give him a hint that I wish that in his arrangements for the next relief of the troops Major Howden may not be removed, or if he should be removed, that he may be placed in a situation which will be as agreeable to him as Angarypur is.

If circumstances permit, I will visit Malabar in the next season, when I hope to see you.

Believe me, &c.,
ARTHUR WELLESLEY.

To the Secretary of the Military Board.

[1193.]

SIR,   28th June, 1802.

In answer to your letter of the 23rd instant, I have to inform you that I did not know of the orders contained in the letter of the 4th October, 1798, or I should not have ordered the payment of a sum of money to persons employed in the sale of the Company's property by auction of which the Military Board disapproved, nor should I have made arrangements for conducting those auctions which were likely to be the occasion of such expense, whatever might be otherwise their probable advantage. Although I had no reason nor a wish to cast an imputation upon any man, I conceived it to be preposterous to employ, in the sale of the Company's timber by auction, a person whose duty in his capacity of commissary of supply obliged him to purchase every piece of timber which could be at all useful in the construction of the various articles which he might be called upon to supply; and, accordingly, I employed in the sale of the timber of the houses pulled down, the garrison serjeant-major, who had before superintended the sale of the property of individuals by auction.

The Board have disapproved of the allowance made for auctioneers; but I beg to observe, that this timber was sorted and lotted at the expense of the serjeant by the work of many days, although the actual sale took up but one day for the timber of each building; and I shall be obliged to you if you will let me know whether he will be permitted to charge for the days on which he was employed in sorting and lotting the timber as well as for the days of sale.

I have, &c.,

ARTHUR WELLESLEY.

[1194.] *To the Adjutant-General.*

SIR,   Seringapatam, 29th June, 1802.

I have the honour to enclose the copy of a letter, with its enclosures, which I have received from Captain Johnson, of the Bombay engineers, stationed at Hullihall in Soonda, in which he requests leave of absence for fifty days to go to Cannanore.

This officer was some time ago appointed by the government of Bombay to the command of the Bombay pioneers, and he has frequently requested my leave to quit his station at Hullihall in order to join the pioneers in Malabar. I have always opposed this proposition, because I thought it proper that he should finish the works which he had undertaken, and the expense of which he had estimated, at Hullihall, particularly as the Military Board had not entirely approved of his conduct in regard to those works; and because, however important the works may be which are carrying on by the pioneers in Malabar, I conceived that those works could not be superintended by an officer more zealous or more capable of doing justice to them than Lieutenant Williams, who has had charge of the pioneers for nearly two years, since Captain Moncrieff quitted Malabar for his health. It appears, however, by the enclosed papers that the works at Hullihall are completed to as great a degree as they can be completed till the return of the fair season in October, before which period Captain Johnson's leave of absence will have expired, and the government of Bombay will have decided the question of the relative capability of Captain Johnson and Lieutenant Williams to superintend the works carrying on by the Bombay pioneers. I can, therefore, make no objection to Captain Johnson's quitting

Hullihall, and I beg leave to recommend that he may have the leave of absence which he requires, provided that it be clearly understood by him that he is to return to Hullihall, and that he is not afterwards to quit that station on any account till the works shall be completed.

I have the honour to enclose the copy of a letter and enclosures received from Lieutenant-Colonel Brown, on the subject of the employment of the Native troops at that station on working parties.

I have, &c.,
ARTHUR WELLESLEY.

To Major Kirkpatrick.   [1195.]

SIR,   Seringapatam, 1st July, 1802.

I have this day sent off two camel hircarrahs with the bark of the only tree remaining at Kope of the kind described in your letter to me, and some more of the bark of the tree at Chinroypatam : leaves, &c., accompany both parcels. I hope that they will be beneficial to the Nizam. They will, at least, prove the desire which I have, and which, I am convinced, every British officer has, to do what can be gratifying to his Highness.

I have, &c.,
ARTHUR WELLESLEY.

To W. H. Gordon, Esq.   [1196.]

SIR,   ·   Seringapatam, 2nd July, 1802.

I have received your letter of this day's date and its enclosure, and I agree entirely in opinion with Mr. Collector Read that the monsoon is so violent in the provinces of Bednore and Soonda that it is very inexpedient that troops should march in them in those seasons, and therefore it is desirable that provision should be made for the payment of the troops at Nuggur and Hullihall from the commencement of the rainy season till the end of October.

It appears that Mr. Read has left in the hands of the aumildar a sum amounting to 15,000 pagodas, which will be paid into your office as it will be required for the troops; but as that sum is placed there only for military purposes, it is my opinion that it might as well be kept in the paymaster's treasury as by the aumildar; and accordingly I recommend you to refer this matter, with my opinion, to the Paymaster-General.

The same circumstance which renders it advisable that provision should be made at Hullihall for the payment of the troops till the month of October renders it advisable that provision should be made at Nuggur till the same period. I recommend that you should refer this matter also to the Paymaster-General.

I have, &c.,

ARTHUR WELLESLEY.

[1197.]   *To the Adjutant-General.*

SIR,   Seringapatam, 4th July, 1802.

I have the honour to enclose the copy of a letter which I have received from Lieutenant-Colonel Boles, in which he reports the arrest and death of Elanbellan Cunnian, a notorious murderer in Malabar, and a supporter of the rebellion in Cotiote.

It appears to me, from a perusal of Lieutenant-Colonel Boles's letter, that the prisoner could not have made his escape in the manner reported excepting by the connivance of the sentry, and probably of others of the guard, and I have desired Lieutenant-Colonel Boles to inquire into this matter. At all events the sentry did not do his duty; and so far from being entitled to a reward, it is my opinion that if the head of the prisoner had not been brought in, the commanding officer, the havildar, and some of the guard would have been punished for a neglect of their duty.

I know from experience that the Rajah of Koorg is very averse to allowing his people to accept rewards, such as Lieutenant-Colonel Boles proposes should be given to them, and I have declined to offer them. I have consequently desired Lieutenant-Colonel Boles to lodge the property found on Elanbellan Cunnian with the paymaster, at the disposal of government, if he should agree in opinion with me regarding the claim of the guard to a reward.

I have, &c.,

ARTHUR WELLESLEY.

To Lieutenant-Colonel Boles.   [1198.]

SIR,   Seringapatam, 4th July, 1802.

I have had the honour of receiving your letter of the 30th June.

From the account of the manner in which Elanbellan Cunnian is said to have made his escape, I suspect that the sentry who had charge of him at the time, and probably others of the guard, were privy to it. I therefore request that you will have this matter strictly inquired into. At all events, the sentry cannot have done his duty ; if he had, the prisoner could not have drawn his hands from the irons and have broken the rope by which he was tied without his perceiving it. Under these circumstances, I cannot consider any of the guard entitled to a reward. Their commanding officer and the havildar, and some of the guard, would have been punished if they had not brought in the head of the prisoner.

I know that the Rajah of Koorg will be much disinclined to allow any of his people to accept the present which you propose should be given to them, and I prefer not to offer it to them.

If, therefore, you agree in opinion with me that the guard are not deserving of reward, the whole of the property found on the person of Elanbellan Cunnian must be lodged in the hands of the paymaster, at the disposal of government.

I have, &c.,

ARTHUR WELLESLEY.

To Lieutenant-Colonel Brown.   [1199.]

SIR,   Seringapatam, 4th July, 1802.

I have had the honour of receiving your letter of the 29th June, and I am much obliged to you for the intelligence it contains.

I beg that you will attend to the objects and motions of the different Mahratta chiefs on the frontier, and that you will communicate to me your observations on them from time to time.

Government, by their letter of the 6th November, 1799, having authorized me to make arrangements for procuring intelligence of the motions of the Mahratta chiefs on the frontier, I beg you to employ the same number of hircarrahs at the same rates of pay as were employed by your predecessors at Hullihall.

I have, &c.,

ARTHUR WELLESLEY.

[1200.]   *To Captain Wilks.*

MY DEAR SIR,   Seringapatam, 8th July, 1802.

I have received your letter of the 5th instant. The private property of Mr. ————, detained here, consists in a house, a bill due to him by government for the repairs of the arsenal, and bills for working money, the payment of which has been ordered.

I reported to the Commander-in-Chief and to government that this property was detained here to answer the demands which might be made against Mr. ————, in consequence of the sentence of the general court-martial, and I received the approbation and orders of the former still to detain it, subject to the orders of government, in a letter from the Deputy Adjutant-General, dated the 26th October, 1801, and of the latter to the same purport, in a letter from the Secretary of Government in the Military Department, dated the 23rd November, 1801.

It appears by your letters that government have determined to drop all farther proceedings against Mr. ———— on account of claims they may have against him consequent on the sentence of the general court-martial; and as they have determined that the claims of individuals against him must be brought forward in the usual manner in the Supreme Court at Madras, they will, doubtless, have no objection to giving him possession of his property. But as the property is now detained by the orders and under the authority of government, I cannot allow it to be restored to Mr. ———— till I shall have received the orders of government so to do.

I should imagine that all that is required to procure this order is an application from Mr. ————; and if there should be any difficulty in making it at Madras, I have no objection to forwarding it, with a recommendation that it may be complied with, if he will send it to me.

Believe me, &c.,

ARTHUR WELLESLEY.

To Lieutenant-General Stuart.   [1201.]

SIR,   Seringapatam, 9th July, 1802.

I have the pleasure to inform you that I have such good accounts of the progress made in the jungles in cutting the timber, that I have ordered out the conductor, lascars, &c., to perform the duties detailed in the instructions, of which I heretofore sent you the draft. The contractor tells me that he now cuts eighty trees every day, and he has many ready of very large dimensions.

I have received a letter from Major Macleod, in which he proposes to reduce half the corps of Bombay pioneers. I believe that corps was raised when you were in Malabar, and you will recollect the inconvenience which was felt for want of them. In fact, people for common work are not to be procured in Malabar, as in other parts of the country, and when wanted, they are sent for at great expense to Bombay and Paulghautcherry.

But there are in Malabar works of the greatest importance, which require the constant employment of such a body of men. The communications with this country through the Ghauts and the roads leading to them require repair annually after the rains, and it is necessary that the roads in Cotiote and those leading from the northern to the southern parts of the province, which were made with a view to the subjection of the Pyche Rajah, should be kept open. This can be done only by the labour of men at the conclusion of the rains annually. It may be said that men may be hired for these services when they are required, and that this mode will be cheaper than to keep in constant pay a corps of pioneers; but I doubt whether men can be hired for these or any other services at all in Malabar, and even if they can and are cheaper, it is worth while to pay the difference of expense in order to have always at command for all services a body of men so useful as this is.

I have received a letter from Major Robertson, in which he informs me that Lieutenant-Colonel Poole has applied for leave to go to Europe, and in case he should obtain it, he urges me again to request you would allow him to retain the command of the corps he belongs to, which, in consequence of the change which has taken place in the service, may now be consistent with your other arrangements. If this should be the case, I beg leave again to recommend Major Robertson to your favour as an active and zealous officer, to whom I am under many obligations.

I have to return you many thanks for your favour to Captain Freese, and

I have, &c.,

ARTHUR WELLESLEY.

[1202.]   *To Major Macleod.*

MY DEAR MACLEOD,   Seringapatam, 9th July, 1802.

I have received your letter of the 5th, and I shall certainly let you know before I commence my tour in Malabar.

I shall be glad to hear the result of your consultation with Macauley. The subject of it is very interesting, and has had much consideration from me.

Your account of the state of the finances in Malabar is delightful, and by far the best commentary upon the late arrangements for that province. You have forgotten, however, to insert in your saving that of the difference between full and half batta for nearly the whole Bombay army, as heretofore nearly the whole of it was in the field.

To this ought to be added all the enormous expenses attending a body of troops in the field in Malabar.

These two items were to be attributed to the system of the late government, and the saving ought to be attributed to the measures of this.

I don't agree with you respecting the reduction of the corps of pioneers, although it may be true that some of the work which they are called upon to perform might be performed at a cheaper rate by the inhabitants of the country. We have always found in Malabar a great want of persons to be employed on works of that kind; and, by the bye, that was the reason why the Bombay pioneers were raised, and we have been obliged to send for them to Bombay and Paulghautcherry. It is true that the province may be improved in that respect; but still where there is constant public work, it may as well be performed by persons constantly in the service, who may be turned to any purpose as they may be required.

There is constant work for the Bombay pioneers of the greatest importance; the repair of the passes leading to this country and of the roads communicating with them, and to keep open the principal roads which were made with a view to the subjection of the Pyche Rajah, are works of the greatest consequence which will constantly occur. It may be true that they might be performed at a cheaper rate than by keeping 400 pioneers always in pay; but I would give the difference for the convenience and advantage of having 400 men ready at all times for any service that may be required from them.

Some people are of opinion that we ought to discharge the Bombay and add to the Madras pioneers. But I hate prejudices which are to operate in favour of one and against another set of men; and I know that if I were to discharge the Bombay pioneers, unless the same men would enlist into the other corps, years would elapse before I should have 400 men of the Madras pioneers whose constitutions would stand the climate of Malabar, and whose habits would conform to the extraordinary customs of the natives of that province.

I am for economy, but it must be well understood; and in order to save money, we must take care to avoid depriving ourselves of the service of people who in war are absolutely necessary to us.

Believe me, &c.,

ARTHUR WELLESLEY.

To Lieutenant-Colonel Whitelocke.   [1203.]

SIR,   Seringapatam, 10th July, 1802.

I have the honour to enclose the translation of a letter which the Dewan has received from the peishcar at Chittledroog, and which has been communicated to me by the Residency.

If you had made inquiries at the pay-office at Chittledroog previous to your holding the communication which it is reported you did hold with the peishcar, you would have found that there was in the treasury at that place a sum considerably exceeding 30,000 pagodas in Bahaudry pagodas, which coins having been received from the collector in Soonda at the Mysore rates of exchange, must necessarily have been issued to the troops at the same. The result of these inquiries would probably have been, that you would have desired the paymaster's servant to pay the troops in Bahaudry pagodas, and the consequences would have been that the troops would have received their pay at an early period in the month, and much trouble would have been saved at Chittledroog, and in references to this place. I beg, therefore, to recommend inquiry upon all future occasions of this kind.

I have also to observe that if upon hearing of the difficulties likely to occur from the payment of the troops in the coins the rate of which was disputed, of which difficulties at Chittledroog I heard from Santa Bednore many days ago, you had stated them to me instead of urging the aumildar to alter the rate of exchange of the district, I should have informed you that I had power to apply a remedy which would be effectual. I beg, therefore, to recommend that upon a future occasion of this kind you will refer the matter to me at the earliest period.

I have, &c.,

ARTHUR WELLESLEY.

[1204.]   *To Captain Macalley.*

SIR,   Seringapatam, 10th July, 1802.

I have received your letter of the 8th instant. I beg that you will ascertain, as nearly as you can, the length of time which has elapsed since Madar Saheb has been at Bangalore, and that which has elapsed since he has had this money in his possession, which you say that he plundered at Seringapatam.

It is also desirable that you should ascertain from what person, or from what house, he took this property.

I have, &c.,

ARTHUR WELLESLEY.

To Lieutenant-Colonel Agnew. [1205.]

MY DEAR COLONEL, Seringapatam, 11th July, 1802.

When I gave over the command of the troops to General Baird, I gave him also my orderly book and my public letters. I have, therefore, no document to prove the appointment of Fitzpatrick, excepting the enclosed extract of a letter which I wrote upon the occasion of the appointment to the Governor-General.

In answer I received an approbation of the appointment in a letter which I handed over to General Baird.

I think it probable that this extract will remove all objections on the part of the Auditor-General; but if it should not, I recommend that Fitzpatrick should apply to government, as Lieutenant de Haviland, of the engineers, did. Government referred his application to me, and I reported that I had appointed him to the situation which he held on the expedition, and that the Governor-General had approved of the appointment; and I imagine that he gets his allowances. I have also to observe that there had been a decision against his claim in Egypt, which cannot have been the case with Fitzpatrick.

I am much obliged to you for the news you have sent me.

I have found a copy of the orders which I sent to the Governor-General with my letter of the 31st January, an extract from which I likewise enclose.

Believe me, &c.,

ARTHUR WELLESLEY.

To Lieutenant-Colonel Montresor. [1206.]

MY DEAR COLONEL, Seringapatam, 12th July, 1802.

I had last night the pleasure of receiving your letter of the 23rd June, and I am very happy to find that the contents of my letter of the 17th of April have given you satisfaction.

I sent a duplicate of that letter to Bombay to Captain Moore, because I heard that Mr. Rickards, to whom I had sent the original, was come to Malabar with the duplicate. I wrote you another letter in which I enclosed an extract of one which

I had received from General Stuart in answer to my proposition. Lest you should have received the original, and not the duplicate, I now enclose the same extract, by which you will be made acquainted with the General's sentiments.

Matters remain in Malabar exactly as they were when I first wrote to you. Lieutenant-Colonel Boles is the temporary commanding officer, and I don't propose that any officer shall be appointed permanently to that command till it is settled whether you can accept it. You will observe by the General's letter that the whole depends upon the station of the 80th regiment; I think that the Bombay government would be gratified, and that it would be a convenience to them to have the European regiment at Bombay, and if that removal is made it will be nearly as convenient to bring the 80th regiment from Bengal to Malabar as to bring there a regiment from any other part of India.

You are in the place in which you can best make this arrangement, and I hope to hear from you.

Believe me, &c.,

ARTHUR WELLESLEY.

[1207.]

To Major Malcolm.

MY DEAR MALCOLM,   12th July, 1802.

I am very much obliged to you for your letter of the 20th June,* which, with its enclosure, fully explains the College ques-

---

* *Major Malcolm to the Hon. Colonel Wellesley.*

MY DEAR COLONEL,   Calcutta, 20th June, 1802.

The late despatches from England have brought little new. All the ministers appear favourable to Lord Wellesley. The Court of Directors are, I believe, more in a flame than ever. I enclose the copy of a letter which I wrote yesterday to your brother Henry; it will explain the whole of the College question and some others. I think your brother will go home in January: nothing but supplications should prevent him. It would, no doubt, be of consequence to his reputation to remain one year after all his arrangements have been made; but it is of more consequence to his reputation to save the Indian empire, which he can only do by his presence in England: and unless ministers act upon Indian questions in a very different style from what they have done, a moment's delay is pregnant with danger. The rains are set in,

tion and the conduct of the Governor-General in regard to the orders which he has received.   It appears that he has taken the only ground that it was possible for him to take, and he is fully

the weather has become cool, and I never saw your brother in better health or better spirits.

I send this letter open to Webbe, who will forward it.

Yours ever most sincerely,

JOHN MALCOLM.

[ENCLOSURES.]

Josiah Webbe, Esq., to the Hon. Colonel Wellesley.

MY DEAR COLONEL,   Fort St. George, 8th July, 1802.

The enclosed letter came from Malcolm open under my cover.   I think that the mode adopted by Lord Wellesley is the only one by which the College can be saved; and the only means of giving it effect is by going home before the time expires.   I consider the question stated in Malcolm's letter to your brother to be decided.   His Lordship has received many assurances from the ministers, and at the same time such letters from the Directors as must destroy all confidence.   The same thing must continue to occur as long as the ministers for India are weak; and I do not see what hope of improvement remains, except that of an entire change of administration.

Baird brings no news, but confirms very strongly the impression of the expected change of ministry.   You will see by the paper of to-day that there are letters from England so late as 31st March; but I cannot ascertain that Lord Clive's resignation had been received in England, nor that the *Thurlow*, which carried the long letter to the Chairman, had arrived.   We know that she left St. Helena the 19th of January.

Ever most sincerely yours,

J. WEBBE.

Major Malcolm to the Hon. Henry Wellesley.

MY DEAR WELLESLEY,   Calcutta, 19th June, 1802.

The Directors have ordered the College to be abolished.   They praise its institution, and give Lord Wellesley's ability and genius credit for the conception; but their circumstances do not admit of such an appropriation of cash, which they describe as more terrible from having been made at a period when their investment was not complete.

This order offered difficulties to Lord Wellesley's choice which at first appeared insurmountable; but the plan he has resolved upon will, I think, reconcile his duty to the Court of Directors with the dignity of his own character, while it interferes with no other subject in reference, and gives, what is of most consequence, the best possible chance to the institution of surviving the mortal blow aimed at its existence.   Lord Wellesley means to pass a resolution abolishing, in obedience to the orders of the Court, the institution; but in consideration of a variety of circumstances, arising out of the nature of the establishment, which involves the interests of so many individuals, the date of its final abolition is to be fixed for December twelvemonth.   In the mean time, orders have been sent to Madras and Bombay to

Q 2

justified in delaying to abolish the institution by the approbation which the Court of Directors have given to it, which would
have induced them to continue it if the Company had not laboured

direct that no more civil servants may be sent to the College. Those whose time
is expired will quit it of course, and others who have qualified themselves for
employ will leave it even before the period prescribed by the regulations.
All grounds, house, &c., will be sold, and everything that gives an indication
of expected permanency will be done away. The arrangement will reduce
the expense greatly, and tend to remove any ground of complaint at its existence being protracted for such a period after orders were received for its
execution.

Lord Wellesley will write to the Court of Directors what he has done, and
tell them that though the state of finance and other considerations might
have justified his making a reference on this subject, he judged the necessity
of yielding a respectful obedience to their orders above all others; but that he
was happy they were afforded an opportunity, by the delay which unavoidably
attended the dissolution of an institution of such magnitude and which em-
braced such extensive objects, of reconsidering (with the very altered state of
their affairs before them) the propriety of abolishing altogether such an institution. He will then state such additional arguments as occur to recommend its preservation, dwell upon the full manner in which every hope entertained respecting it has been gratified, and conclude with assuring them that
if their orders disapproving of his having fixed its duration to so long a period
arrive in India before that period expires, he will carry them into the most
prompt execution. This line of conduct, while it involves no sacrifice of either
spirit or principle on his part, clears the question of all irritation, and, by
doing so, gives the institution the only chance it could have of standing. Had
he abolished it, it would never have been restored; and had he made a reference, his conduct would have been termed contumacious, and the necessity of
establishing the principle of implicit obedience to the orders of legitimate
authority (unless in cases where the indispensable necessity of suspending
those orders was more capable of demonstration than the present) would have
been made the plea, not only for the destruction of the College, but for a
censure on the person who had so boldly defended that institution.

Had his Lordship abolished the College and gone home, he would upon that
one point have abandoned the whole of the question respecting his government now in reference to his Majesty's ministers; and had he abolished it and
remained, his character would have suffered in public estimation; he would
have been thought adhesive to office, and would have lost a portion of that
character which he now possesses for high spirit and independent principle.
By the line he has followed he will gain as much reputation as the Directors
will lose. The world will see a proper principle of obedience in the resolution
he has taken, and that respect he owes his own character, combined with the
best means that could be adopted to preserve an establishment the great
importance of which is now, I believe, very generally acknowledged.

The Court of Directors are so irritated at Lord Wellesley on the question
of the private trade, that they act on all occasions where he is concerned in
prejudice and in passion. Lord Dartmouth is in violent opposition to them
on that and, indeed, on all matters, and Lord Wellesley may rely upon his
support as far as his power and his ability go. He may perhaps do the same
upon Mr. Addington; but the whole ministry appear to me unsteady, and I

under financial embarrassments (as they imagined), by the fact that those embarrassments no longer exist, and by the circumstances of the persons belonging to the institution, who, if it were suddenly abolished, would be deprived of bread.

I think that the question whether Lord Wellesley should go home or not, now stands precisely where it did before he received these orders. He had no reason to expect anything but injury from the Court of Directors till his appeal to the King's ministers should have been received, and till they could have acted in consequence. If the grounds were good on which he determined to remain in India another year, if the Court of Directors should desire it, should recall their offensive orders, and should promise support in future, and if the ministers should engage for that support, they are equally good at present. He expected injury when he was induced to come to this determination, and now that it has been received, he ought not to alter it. In fact, if the Court of Directors and the ministers should act as Lord Wellesley has required, the College question, as well as all others, will be given up to him. The government at home will approve of the delay in the execution of the orders recently received, and finally of that institution.

cannot persuade myself there is anything in their late treaty calculated to fix them in their seats or to secure the confidence of the nation.

Lord Wellesley's situation is, in my opinion, very delicate; and nothing should make him dream of protracting his stay beyond January but the most *unequivocal* assurance of support on the part of the ministers, and the most *complete* confidence on his, of their ability as well as inclination to give him that support.

There has been no approbation received of the Treaty of Hyderabad, nor am I at all clear (as far as relates to the Directors) that they will approve of your arrangements in Oude. These are *interests* of importance in India, but what are they when considered with the shipping *interests?* Nothing, less than nothing, in Leadenhall-street.

Your brother is in good spirits. He is satisfied with his resolution about the College; he is satisfied with the despatches he has sent to England; and, above all, he is satisfied with the unexampled prosperity of the finance, which must carry him triumphantly over the heads of all these cent. per cent. rascals.

I am fixed in my opinion that you should, if the settlement be made upon the principles I stated, return to Calcutta. You need not leave Bareilly until November or December, but you should declare your resolution publicly as early as possible. On this, however, you will, of course, communicate with your brother.

I am yours ever most sincerely,

(Signed)   JOHN MALCOLM.

In what I have above written I have not considered whether the Indian ministers have the power, the ability, or the inclination to force the Court of Directors to act as Lord Wellesley requires, or whether, if they have, the Court of Directors will be sincere and cordial in the support which they may engage to give. These questions I conclude were maturely considered when Lord Wellesley determined to remain in India another year on certain conditions; and they are not affected by the orders to abolish the College, and ought not now to be taken into consideration.

Believe me, &c.,

ARTHUR WELLESLEY.

[1208.]

To W. H. Gordon, Esq.

SIR,   14th July, 1802.

Having taken into consideration the rate of exchange at which you have lately received certain coins from the collectors in Canara and Soonda, and that at which those coins are current in this country, I am induced to desire that they may be issued to the troops at the rates stated in the enclosed Paper, and the balance carried to the Company's account of profit and loss on batta. This order is founded on an authority which I have received from government, in answer to a letter which I wrote upon this subject, extracts of both which are enclosed.

You will observe that authority is given to me by the fourth paragraph of the enclosed letter to order the issue of coins, the currency of Mysore, which may be received from the collectors in Canara and Soonda at the Mysore rates of exchange. Accordingly I have desired that the Ahmedy mohurs and the Sheddeeky mohurs, being the currency of Mysore, may be issued at the Mysore rates.

Authority is given to me by the 5th and 6th paragraphs of the enclosed letter to order the issue of coins not the currency of Mysore, which may be received from the collectors, at the rate of exchange which is their real value in the Mysore country. In fixing the rate at which I have desired you to issue the Surat and Pondicherry rupees, the Porto Novo pagodas, I have been guided as well by the rate at which those coins are current

in the country as by that at which you have received them from
the Resident, and by the value which is placed on them in the
nerrick of money of Seringapatam, which was settled under the
authority of the Commissioners of Mysore.

I have, &c.,

ARTHUR WELLESLEY.

[ENCLOSURE.]

RATE OF EXCHANGE OF THE UNDERMENTIONED COINS IN THE MYSORE
COUNTRY.

Coins the Currency of Mysore.

Ahmedy mohurs .. .. 4 Bahaudry pagodas at 100 to 108 Stars, equal to
1 Ahmedy mohur.

Sheddeeky mohurs .. 2 Bahaudry pagodas at 100 to 108 Stars, equal to
1 Sheddeeky mohur.

Coins not the Currency of Mysore.

Porto Novo pagodas .. 1 equal to 10 Canterai fanams or 2¾ rupees, and
31 cash or 37½ silver fanams.

Surat rupees .. .. 1 equal to 3 Canterai fanams 2 annas, or 11 silver
fanams 3½ annas.

Pondicherry rupees .. 345 equal to 100 star pagodas.

To Captain Macally.   [1209.]

SIR,   Seringapatam, 14th July, 1802.

I observe that by the declaration which you have enclosed,
Madar Saheb does not say whether he knows the person or the
house from which he plundered the property in question, and I
beg that you will press him again upon that point, and that you
will inquire from the Native magistrates at Bangalore whether
he has really resided at that place during the time that he declares he has.

If his declaration in this respect be true, and if he cannot
point out the house or the person from whom he plundered the
property, I shall desire you to restore it to him, as I acknowledge that I am of opinion that he has as good a right to the
property which he plundered upon that occasion as any other
man has to that which such person may have plundered, that is
to say no right at all; but at all events, it is as good as that

which may now be set up for the public or the captors of Seringapatam. To enter into the question now regarding the
disposal of property plundered at Seringapatam, if the real and
former owners of it cannot be discovered, would, I am afraid,
be attended with inconveniences and difficulties, the extent of
which cannot be foreseen, and probably the result of the discussion would be a determination to restore the property to the
actual owner.

If, however, it should be discovered that Madar Saheb does
know the person or the house from which he took the property,
I shall desire that it might be returned to the real and former
owner ; and if it should be discovered that he has not told the
truth regarding the length of time which he has resided at Bangalore, I shall be under the necessity of desiring that the property may be detained some time longer in order that further
inquiries may be made.

I have, &c.,

ARTHUR WELLESLEY.

[1210.]   *To Lieutenant-General Stuart.*

SIR,   Seringapatam, 15th July, 1802.

I have had the honour of receiving your letter of the 11th
instant, and I have lost no time in making inquiries regarding
the expenses which have attracted your notice. I find that when
garrisons were first fixed in those stations, the officers commanding them made out lists of the supplies which they would
each require from the barrack-master, and those lists have not
since been reviewed : I have therefore ordered that they may be
now reviewed, and that, considering the nature and situation of
the places, and the strength of the garrison in each, officers in
command or in charge of them shall make out a fresh list of
the supplies which they think it absolutely necessary the barrackmaster should furnish. I shall afterwards examine these lists,
and will submit them to you with a statement of the expense to
be incurred at each station ; and I have reason to believe that
the barrack expenses in this country will be much reduced.

I am afraid that there will be no reduction at Hullihall, as the
garrison there is very large.

There has never been any expense on account of officers' quarters in the barrack department, and of course there will be none hereafter.

The officers who have been in barracks at Seringapatam have occupied houses which were taken on the account of government when the place fell, and these houses were the property either of Tippoo's family, of Sirdars who had been killed, or of others who fled and joined the army of Dhoondiah Waugh. No repair has ever been given to them by the Company; and excepting those which have been repaired by the officers who occupied them, they are, in general, in ruins.

At present of course the Company will not repair them because the officers have tent allowance, and, on the other hand, the officers will not be so imprudent as to repair houses which belong to the Company, and of which they may be at any time deprived. To sell them, therefore, would be the best arrangement for the public as well as for the convenience of the officers of the garrison. But many of these houses have been repaired at the expense of the individuals who now occupy them, and without such repair they would now in fact be worth nothing. It would not be fair to such individuals to make them pay the full value of a property, the only value of which has been created by themselves at their own expense, particularly as none of these houses have cost the Company one farthing. I should therefore propose that a fair valuation might be put upon these houses, and that from this valuation should be subtracted the sum which each occupant at the present moment could prove that he had laid out upon the house which he occupies, and that the houses should be sold to the present occupants for the remainder.

In cases in which no money has been laid out in the repair of a house, or if improved it has not been so by the present occupant, the whole sum fixed as the value to be paid for it to the public; and if the occupant who has repaired a house does not choose to purchase it at the reduced price, it ought to be sold at the full price to any other person who would purchase it.

If you should approve of selling these houses and of this mode of doing it, I will make a proposition upon the subject to the Military Board.

I have, &c.,

ARTHUR WELLESLEY.

[1211.]   *To Josiah Webbe, Esy.*

My dear Webbe,   Seringapatam, 15th July, 1802.

I had no idea that Lord Wellesley would be able to find out a mode of preserving the College for some time longer. That which he has adopted appears to be the only one which could give the institution a chance of standing hereafter, which is justifiable from the imputation of disobedience of orders, saves him from the necessity of resigning his government immediately, and still leaves him the option of staying another year, or of going, as he may think advisable, at the close of this year.

In my opinion, the question whether Lord Wellesley ought to go home at the end of this year or not depends now nearly upon the same circumstances as would have guided his decision upon it if the orders recently received had never been given. If the Court of Directors recall some of their offensive orders and promise confidence and support, and the ministers engage for it, the question with Lord Wellesley must still be the degree of sincerity of the former, and the probability that the latter are either able or willing to see that they don't break their engagements. If he should have reason to confide in the sincerity of the one, or the activity and ability of the other, he may be very certain not only that his conduct regarding the College at present will be approved of, but that the institution will be established hereafter; but if he cannot confide in either, he ought certainly to go.

The appeal to the ministers was intended to rouse them, and to draw their attention more particularly to the state into which Indian affairs were likely to verge by the improper interference of the Court of Directors in the foreign government. It will be proper to wait to see the effects of that appeal before it can be decided whether confidence can be placed in their exertions, supposing them to be inclined to make them.

Lord Wellesley appears to have been inclined to trust the ministers; but I acknowledge that I have had very little confidence in them. However, the fair trial of them will be after they will have received information of the evils which are likely to be the result of their lazy system. Their effort, it is true, may be but momentary, even if it be made; but if it produce the recall of some of the late orders, it will have lasting effects in this country, and before matters can relapse again, Lord

Wellesley will have returned to England, having effected such an improvement in the state of the Company's affairs as must add greatly to his character, and, of course, to his power.

Upon the whole, therefore, as the necessity of obeying the last orders has been got over, I am rather inclined to think that that mark of want of confidence and injury done by the Court of Directors ought to be passed over for the present, and that Lord Wellesley ought to refrain from coming to any determination regarding his return to Europe till he sees the result of his last appeal.

Believe me, &c.,

ARTHUR WELLESLEY.

To Lieutenant-General Stuart. [1212.]

SIR, Seringapatam, 17th July, 1802.

I have had the honour to receive your letter of the 13th July. I have not yet commenced pulling down the palace at the Laal Baug, as the pioneers, who I intend shall perform that work, are now employed upon another, and the materials of the building are not immediately wanted, and they receive no injury by remaining for a little time longer in their present shape. Whenever buildings are pulled down, I take care to reserve for public uses such timbers as will answer for them; and I will take care to reserve for the gun-carriage manufactory such as will answer for the construction of gun-carriages.

I have, &c.,

ARTHUR WELLESLEY.

To Lieutenant-Colonel Whitelocke. [1213.]

DEAR SIR, Seringapatam, 17th July, 1802.

I return your letter of the 15th and its enclosure, because an application from you that an officer's guard-room might be built ought to be grounded upon your own knowledge of the necessity of it, and not upon a representation of the subalterns of the garrison to me, however respectful that representation may be in terms, and although your attention may have been drawn to the want of a guard-room by a similar representation.

I also recommend that you should omit to mention Colonel Stevenson's mistake in pulling down the guard-room, as well as that you perceive that there is no hope of the work being begun upon unless my approbation be first obtained. All these topics would draw the notice and animadversion of government, before whom I should be obliged to lay your letter. The building of the guard-room would be delayed till an inquiry should be made by what authority Colonel Stevenson pulled down the old guard-room; and probably if in the end you obtained a guard-room, he would be obliged to pay for it.

You will excuse me for suggesting these alterations in your application; when they are made I have no doubt but that I shall be authorized to order that the officers' guard-room may be built.

Believe me, &c.,

ARTHUR WELLESLEY.

[1214.] G. O.   Seringapatam, 17th July, 1802.

Colonel Wellesley was concerned to learn that any officer under his command had been put in arrest for "coming to the parade of his regiment in a state of intoxication;" and although it appears, by the evidence which has been brought before the general court martial of which Lieutenant-Colonel Mackay was president, that Major Bell, the commanding officer of ——— ———, may have been mistaken on this occasion, Colonel Wellesley is concerned to be under the necessity of observing that, if there had not been good reason to believe that ——— ——— was in the habit of drinking intoxicating liquors at undue hours, Major Bell would not have attributed his staggering upon the parade to intoxication, but would have supposed that it was occasioned by other causes. It is not to be imagined that any officer would cast such an imputation upon another upon the first symptom of his deserving it; and the observations made by ——— ——— in his defence, that his staggering ought to be imputed to indisposition, would be correct, if circumstances had not given too strong reason to believe that intoxication alone was the cause of it.

Colonel Wellesley therefore, in reprimanding ——— ——— for the crimes of which he has been found guilty, cannot avoid calling his attention, and that of the troops under his command in general, to the other crime of which he has been acquitted. It is one of the most degrading to the character of an officer, which renders him unfit for any part of his duty; and by the practice of it he fails in that most essential point, the setting an example to the soldiers under his command. Colonel Wellesley, however, has the pleasure of reflecting that this failing is rare among the officers under his command, in proportion as it is great; but he warns all against even the suspicion of it.

—— —— is hereby publicly reprimanded. He is released from arrest and directed to return to his duty.

ARTHUR WELLESLEY.

To Captain Scott.   [1215.]

MY DEAR SIR,   Seringapatam, 18th July, 1802.

I have received your letter of the 14th, and have perused the list of tools you will require. You must be the best judge of the number which will be necessary for the number of workmen whom you will employ; but I think that what you have required is a small proportion for the extended scale of the manufactory.

I think it probable that although you may not be able to procure many workmen at Madras at present, you will find no difficulty in getting them hereafter, when the contract will be at an end; and accordingly, if you should leave Madras, I recommend that you should employ an agent there to hire as many as can be procured.

I believe there are more good artificers at Trichinopoly than at any other place, and I recommend you to employ a person to hire some there for you.

Believe me, &c.,

ARTHUR WELLESLEY.

To Lieutenant-Colonel Whitelocke.   [1216.]

DEAR SIR,   Seringapatam, 18th July, 1802.

When Mr. Franks was here, I had some conversation with him upon the state of Chittledroog, and I took a memorandum of some of the wants at that place, to which, however, I omitted to refer till yesterday after I had written to you.

The 1st of these wants is a barrack for the artillery. I don't believe it to be the intention of the Commander-in-Chief to post at Chittledroog a detachment of artillery of greater strength than that which is at that station at present. It is probable that you can accommodate the detachment without any additional building; if you cannot, I recommend that you should apply for a building for them.

The next point is the guardhouse, respecting which I wrote to you yesterday.

The 3rd is the saltpetre godown. I recommend that you should report its state, and apply to have the roof repaired.

The 4th is the camp-equipage godown. Under the new system, I imagine that camp-equipage will not be kept in store at Chittledroog, and it is very probable that orders will be given to remove from thence all the camp-equipage which may not be sold there. To recommend that the godown may be repaired, therefore (which, if granted, will be useless), may prevent the repair of other buildings which are absolutely necessary to the garrison.

5th. The number of ordnance at Chittledroog. It will be best to defer the consideration of that subject to a future period.

6th. The number of garrison lascars is, in my opinion, sufficient; and I know they are reckoned so by the Military Board.

7th. The serviceable captured powder. I beg that you will indent upon Seringapatam for boxes, with copper nails, to contain this powder. Send the indent to me, and you shall have the boxes without delay.

Believe me, &c.,

ARTHUR WELLESLEY.

[1217.]   *To Major Macleod.*

MY DEAR MACLEOD,   Seringapatam, 18th July, 1802.

Within this short time I find that orders have been given to your aumildars on the borders of Coimbatoor to stop all persons going into that province from this country, and, in consequence, many merchants, sepoys, and others going thither on their lawful business have been stopped, and sent back to procure a passport from me. Either the person who gave these orders to the aumildars has mistaken the meaning of the passport regulations, or the aumildars have misunderstood his orders. It was never intended that natives should be prevented from going from one part of the country to the other, or that passports should be required from them. The passport regulations are intended only to apply to Europeans. It will give me some trouble if I am to give a passport to every native going out of this country, but that is of immaterial consequence in comparison with the evil which will result from it. Every native who gets a paper signed by the name of a person having any power makes a bad use of it, and generally contrives by its means to extort something to which he has no right. I have, therefore, always had a strong objection to giving papers of any kind to persons of this description.

It is a great object to this country that the communication with Coimbatoor and all the neighbouring provinces should be free and uninterrupted, and I shall be obliged to you if you will take measures to have it restored with the former province, upon the old footing, as soon as you can.

Believe me, &c.,

ARTHUR WELLESLEY.

To Lieutenant-General Stuart.　　　　　　　　　[1218.]

SIR,　　　　　　　　　　　Seringapatam, 22nd July, 1802.

The Dewan of the Rajah of Mysore has made a proposition to me that he may be permitted to build a bridge across the north branch of the Cauvery to the island of Seringapatam, at the Rajah's sole expense.

I have referred the subject, as it is likely to affect the Rajah, to the Resident, in a letter which I have written to him this day ; and I shall be obliged to you if you will be so kind as to favour me with your wishes upon it, as it will affect the Company.

It is very desirable that the communication between Seringapatam and the countries north of the Cauvery should be rendered as easy as possible consistently with the preservation of the strength of the place. It does not appear to me that, provided the bridge is built in a situation exposed to the fire of the fort, it will at all diminish its strength, or that it will do so even if built in a situation in which it will not be exposed to its fire. The reason of this is, that it will be built as the present bridge over the south branch of the river is, upon stone uprights fixed in the bed, which can at any time be taken down with astonishing ease and celerity, and thus the bridge can be destroyed.

Although it would certainly be preferable for the Rajah to build this bridge in a situation above or below the island of Scringapatam, because he would have his communication between his countries on both sides of the Cauvery free, and without the necessity of crossing the island of Seringapatam, the Rajah's servants prefer to build it at this place; and although I suggested to them that it would be more convenient to them to build it at a short distance, I acknowledge that I shall think the fort safer for having the bridge upon the island, than I should think it if it were placed at a short distance above or below the island.

We know that during the driest season there is no ford which can be depended upon as practicable for an army, or which is used, indeed, by individuals, nearer than Caniambaddy; but if we were to build a bridge across the river, we should enable but a weak army, in proportion to what is now required, to attack the two river faces of the fort by giving such an excellent communication. It is true that the bridge outside, as well as the bridge upon the island, may be destroyed; but I observe that wherever one of these stone bridges is made, the bed which is laid for it leaves a ford which cannot be removed but with great trouble and difficulty. This would be almost as advantageous outside during the dry season as the bridge would; but as there are many fords and passages over to the island, another made by the removal of the bridge would be of little consequence.

Upon the whole, therefore, I am of opinion that it will be highly advantageous to the Company to have a bridge over the Cauvery; that it will be better to have it upon the island of Seringapatam than above or below it, and that the nearer it is brought to the fort the better. If you should be of this opinion, I shall be obliged to you if you will make me acquainted with your wishes as soon as may be convenient, as it is desirable that, if the Resident sees no objection on the score of expense, the

Dewan should commence collecting materials without delay, and thus that the bridge may be fit for use when the river fills in the next year.

If you should see no objection to the measure, and the Resident should approve of it, I will have the honour of submitting the Dewan's proposition to government, and in the mean time he can make his preparations.

I have, &c.,

ARTHUR WELLESLEY.

To Josiah Webbe, Esq.   [1219.]

MY DEAR WEBBE,   Seringapatam, 22nd July, 1802.

Purneah sent to me yesterday to propose to build a bridge over the north branch of the Cauvery at Seringapatam, entirely at the expense of the Rajah of Mysore, *in the name of Lord Wellesley.* There is no doubt but that a communication across both branches of the Cauvery would be highly advantageous to the country, and worth the expense which it would cost; and although the Company ought to pay their share of the expense of a bridge across the Cauvery to Seringapatam, there is no reason why the Rajah should not construct one for the convenience and advantage of the people of his country immediately at his own expense, if the Company, on account of the expense of the work, are inclined to delay it for any considerable length of time. If, however, the Rajah is to pay the whole expense of the bridge, it would be more conveniently situated for him either above or below the island of Seringapatam, as the communication between the different parts of his country would then be complete without the necessity of passing through part of the Company's territory. In the course of my conversation with Bajee Rao upon the subject, I suggested this to him; but whether they expect to derive a positive advantage from having a more direct and easy communication with Seringapatam than they have at present, or than they would have supposing the bridge to be placed either above or below the island, or whether, the channel being so much more narrow at Seringapatam than elsewhere, they expect that the work will be completed at a smaller expense, they prefer to build it at this place.

SUP.—VOL. III.   R

As far therefore as the question whether the bridge shall be built or not is referable to the Rajah, I see no objection to it which has not been considered and got the better of.

There is no doubt but that it would be highly advantageous to the Company to have a bridge over the north branch of the Cauvery at Seringapatam. It ought to be placed, however, under the fire of the fort, to which the Rajah's servants have consented.

As we have a bridge over the south branch of the river, it may be supposed that, in a military point of view, it would be nearly as convenient to us that the bridge should be placed above or below the island as that it should be placed at Seringa-patam, and it would be so as far as regarded our communica-tion with the countries north of the Cauvery; but with a view to the defence of the fort, there is a great objection to placing a bridge over the Cauvery in its neighbourhood either above or below the island.

The bed of the river, for a great distance both above and below the island, is so rocky as to be impassable almost by single men during even the driest season. The ford by which the Bombay army crossed the river and communicated during the siege of Seringapatam with that under the command of General Harris was exceedingly bad, scarcely practicable, and it has never been used, I believe, even by individuals since that time. The Rajah's troops always go to Caniambaddy, about 12 miles above Seringapatam. The consequence, therefore, of building a bridge in the neighbourhood of Seringapatam, above or below the island, would be that there would be a free and easy communication for an army between the north and south sides of the river.

The principal point of the strength of Seringapatam is the impossibility of investing it with such a body of men as it can be reasonably expected can be brought against the place. There are three distinct points of attack, one of which the enemy must determine upon before he approaches the place; and if he should determine to attack on two sides, owing to the difficulty of crossing the river, he runs the risk of having part of his army cut off before he can give it assistance, and thus being beat in detail. But if there should be a good com-munication across the river, a comparatively small force will be sufficient to invest the fort on the two river-faces without risk.

It is better for the Company, therefore, that the bridge should be at Seringapatam, and immediately under the guns of the fort.

General Stuart having turned his attention lately to the state of the strength of Seringapatam, which the construction of a bridge over the Cauvery may be supposed to affect, I write to him upon the subject this day. It is desirable, however, that the matter should be decided soon, as Purneah will have time in that case to collect the materials before the river falls, and the bridge will be completed before it fills again in the next season. I shall be glad, therefore, if you will let me have your sentiments upon this subject as soon as convenient. If General Stuart should see no objection to it in a military point of view, and if you should see no objection to the Rajah's building the bridge on the score of expense, I shall recommend to government that he may be allowed to do so, and Purneah may commence immediately to collect his materials.

Believe me, &c.,

ARTHUR WELLESLEY.

To Captain Macally. [1220.]

SIR, . Seringapatam, 25th July, 1802.

I have to request that you will be so kind as to send for Madar Saheb, and, in presence of the aumildar of Bangalore, return him the money which was taken from him by your orders.

I have already apprised you of my opinion that this man has as good a right to the money which he plundered at Seringapatam as any other man can have to property acquired in a similar manner, and a better right to it than any man excepting the person from whom it was taken. I should accordingly have desired you to return the property immediately, only that I was desirous of ascertaining first whether the property was really plundered at Seringapatam, and next from whom it was taken; and I had determined, if the owner resided at Seringapatam, to put the case in the way of being tried in the Court of Cutchery, by the decision of which the question which has arisen would have been finally decided and closed. Under present circumstances, however, that cannot be done; and it is better to replace things as they stood before you gave orders that this property should be taken.

I cannot close this subject without remarking upon the irregularity of your proceeding in seizing this property at all. A moment's reflection would have convinced you that neither the Company nor those belonging to them had or could have the smallest right to it; and even if it were possible to suppose they had, the mode you adopted to secure the property was very irregular. You ought to have stated the case to the aumildar, and to have required him to secure the person and property of a man on whom you might imagine that the Company might have claims; but in no case ought you to seize or interfere in the property of any of the subjects of the Rajah of Mysore, and I beg that you will attend to this in future.

I have, &c.,

ARTHUR WELLESLEY.

[1221.]

To Lieutenant-Colonel Macalister.

SIR,   Seringapatam, 27th July, 1802.

In a letter which I received yesterday from the Secretary of the Military Board, the Board desire that the tents lately in use with the 5th regiment may be surveyed and valued by a committee, and that they may be disposed of by sale at the price which that committee may fix as their value.

It appears by your former letters that those tents have already been surveyed and valued; and you will, therefore, be so kind as to allow them to be disposed of at the price which has been fixed as their value to such persons as may choose to purchase them, who under the tent regulations may be entitled to use them. The purchasers of these tents must pay for them at the time they will receive them.

I request that you will be so kind as to desire the quarter-master of the 5th regiment of cavalry to send me a list of the names of the officers who may purchase any of these tents in consequence of these orders. This list is to contain the description and marks of each tent which each officer will purchase, and the price which has been fixed as its value by the committee which has surveyed the tents. He will likewise send me a return of the tents at Santa Bednore which may not be sold, in which are to be included the description and marks of them ; and I beg to have from you with this return a copy of the proceedings of the committee which surveyed and valued the tents.

The Military Board will hereafter give orders respecting the tent lascars who are at Santa Bednore, and who are to remain there till those orders are received.

I have, &c.,

ARTHUR WELLESLEY.

To Lieutenant-Colonel Brown. [1222.]

SIR, Seringapatam, 27th July, 1802.

I have received your letter of the 22nd instant, and approve of the conduct in regard to the quarrels between Goklah and the Rajah of Kittoor which you report that you have adopted.

I have to inform you, however, that by treaty with the Mahratta nation, the Company is bound to give up any of its subjects who may take refuge within our territories when called for. Although, therefore, it is consistent with humanity, and I approve of your suffering the inhabitants of the Kittoor country to take refuge within the Company's province of Soonda, it is not necessary to hold out protection or places of refuge to them publicly, or to give public assurances of such advantages, either to the Rajah of Kittoor or any other person.

I have, &c.,

ARTHUR WELLESLEY.

To Major Elliott. [1223.]

MY DEAR ELLIOTT, Seringapatam, 31st July, 1802.

I can scarcely credit the report that 400 volunteers from the army in Egypt are coming to India, because I know that the reason for which the 10th and 88th regiments were left in that country and are to go to England was because there was not tonnage to bring them to this country. The 88th did not consist of 400 men.

However, it may be true ; and, if it be so, it is more than probable that those men fit for horsemen will be drafted into the 19th, as the greatest part of the expense of a complete regiment of dragoons is incurred on account of that corps already, and it is probable that the General will be desirous to have the advantage of the service of that number of dragoons for which the Company have already provided horses and have incurred other expenses.

But, if this were not the case, I don't expect much advantage from any application from me.   The General will certainly divide the men among those regiments which are likely to remain in India which want them most, let the applications for them be ever so strong, or be made by those whom he may be inclined to oblige.

However, if you wish it, I'll mention the subject to him ; but I should wish to have from you a state of the actual strength of the regiment, excluding invalids in Europe and in India, who still appear upon the returns, as the ground upon which I should draw his attention to it.

In my opinion, you ought to write to the Deputy-Adjutant-General, to know what ought to be done with the purchase-money of Lieutenant-Colonel Shee's commission, and it ought to be lodged in the hands of a respectable house in Madras (Messrs. Harington and Co.) for Colonel Shee's use till the answer can be received.

I know of no regimental claims against Lieutenant-Colonel Shee excepting that of Lieutenant Fitzgerald, and you must proceed in regard to that according to the Articles of War. Tew's family have a claim upon him, but it is in his capacity of friend and administrator to the deceased, with which the commanding-officer of the regiment has nothing to do.

Quin is not well now, but I'll desire him to write you, when he recovers, upon the subject of the claims against Lieutenant-Colonel Shee.

> Believe me, &c.,
>
> ARTHUR WELLESLEY.

[1224.]   *To the Adjutant-General.*

SIR,   Seringapatam, 31st July, 1802.

I have the honour to enclose the copy of a letter which I have received from Lieutenant-Colonel Spry upon the subject of houses in the cantonment at Mangalore, the property of officers of the

75th regiment. I had already given my opinion to Lieutenant-Colonel Spry upon this subject ; * but as it is one in which every corps in the army may be interested eventually, I wished to receive a communication from him upon it in a form in which I should be enabled to obtain the decision of the Commander-in-Chief.

It appears that Colonel Hart, who commanded in the province of Canara, fixed upon a spot at Mangalore as a cantonment for a regiment of Europeans, on which particular lines were allotted to subaltern officers, captains, and staff. The officers of the 75th regiment, which corps first occupied this cantonment, built houses and other temporary buildings on this spot of ground, and it does not appear that they had any grant of the ground on which they built, or any property in it excepting that which they obtained by being officers belonging to the regiment which occupied the cantonment.

Notwithstanding this, they either retain possession of or have sold the houses to Native merchants and others at Mangalore ; and the officers of the 77th regiment, which corps now occupies the cantonment at Mangalore, are obliged either to submit to the imposition of these natives, and to pay large sums for purchase of the houses, or to move out of the cantonment entirely.

My opinion upon this subject is, that an officer who builds a house on a spot of ground allotted as a cantonment for a corps has no right to dispose of more of that house than its materials. Indeed the purchaser of more, unless he should be an officer belonging to the corps which should succeed to the supposed owner of the house, would be in an awkward situation, as the commanding officer of the corps occupying the cantonment might order him to quit the ground allotted by authority to the officers and men under his command. But although an officer belonging to a corps quitting a cantonment has no right to sell more than the materials of his house, it is my opinion that the officer who should wish to purchase it ought not to insist upon having it at the price of the materials.

It would be convenient to him that those materials should be allowed to stand in the shape of a house, for which convenience he ought to pay a sum in addition to the price of them.

According to this statement, the subject would become a matter of private agreement among the parties, and it would be

* See p. 193.

for their mutual benefit that they should agree; but as long as it is erroneously supposed that an officer who builds a house on ground allotted to a corps as a cantonment has a right to sell it to whoever he pleases, it is obvious that they never will agree, and that in the end the officers' lines in all these cantonments, instead of being occupied by officers, will be filled by merchants and strangers.

I beg that you will do me the favour to draw the attention of the Commander-in-Chief to this subject, and these observations upon it, and I shall be obliged to you if you will favour me with his sentiments.

I have, &c.,

ARTHUR WELLESLEY.

[1225.]   *To Major Elliott.*

MY DEAR ELLIOTT,   Seringapatam, 1st Aug., 1802.

I imagine that you must have been misinformed respecting the volunteers who you say are arrived. I have heard of no men excepting some belonging to the 8th dragoons, and to another regiment supposed to be coming from the Cape. However, I will still apply if you wish it, and will send me the state for which I asked in my letter of yesterday.

I have learned that Basil Cochrane has a power of attorney from Colonel Shee. It will still be necessary that you should apply at the Adjutant-General's office on behalf of the officers who have purchased in succession to him, to know what is to be done with the purchase-money. If the answer be that it is to be paid, it ought to be paid to Basil Cochrane (excepting the sums for which there may be regimental demands), provided he can produce the power of attorney.

If the answer from the Deputy Adjutant-General should not be decisive, or if the Commander-in-Chief should be of opinion that the money ought to be retained till His Majesty's pleasure on the promotions reaches India, it will be proper to consult with Mr. Cochrane regarding the disposal of it during the interval, and to do nothing in it without his concurrence.

Believe me, &c.,

ARTHUR WELLESLEY.

Upon considering Tew's case, I find that his claim as well as Lieutenant Fitzgerald's is regimental, as he also died in the regiment; and Lieutenant-Colonel Shee, as Major, proved the amount of his property before a regimental court martial, according to the Articles of War: his demand, therefore, ought to be discharged out of the purchase-money.

To the Chief Secretary of Government.   [1226.]

SIR,   Seringapatam, 2nd Aug., 1802.

I have the honour to enclose a letter which I have received from Captain Heitland, in which he requests to have the usual per centage on the expense of the works carried on at Seringapatam under his superintendence.

In the last year I had the pleasure of reporting to the Right Honourable the Governor in Council my sense of Captain Heitland's exertions, and his Lordship was pleased to order that he should receive the usual per centage on the work then performed in a letter from the Chief Secretary of Government, dated the 7th of August. Captain Heitland has conducted the work intrusted to his superintendence with the same zeal and ability in this year which obtained for him that mark of the approbation of the Right Honourable the Governor in Council in the last, and I therefore beg leave to recommend that his request may be complied with.

In the course of a short time the whole of the inner ditch of Seringapatam on the river faces will be filled; but I shall forbear to report the work complete till the end of the rainy season, lest the heavy rains at their breaking up should affect any part of it.

I have, &c.,

ARTHUR WELLESLEY.

To Lieutenant-General Stuart.   [1227.]

SIR,   Seringapatam, 3rd Aug., 1802.

I have this day transmitted to Madras a certificate on oath of the bad state of health of Major Ogg, which I imagine he intends as the ground of an application to be permitted to go to Europe for his recovery. If he should receive permission to go,

I should wish to recommend Lieutenant Knox of the 33rd regiment to succeed him as Persian interpreter.   He is a young man who has paid unremitted attention to the Native languages and to all the accomplishments which could render him useful as an officer in this country, and he has succeeded so far in his endeavours as to have induced me to recommend him for the office of Fort-Adjutant of Seringapatam, which he now fills, to have employed him upon various occasions in which knowledge of the country languages and customs was required, and now to think him the fittest person to succeed to Major Ogg's office of Persian interpreter, if that officer should obtain leave to go to Europe.

It is rare that officers in the King's service turn their attention to qualify themselves in this manner for the situations which the service in this country offers; and I have the greatest satisfaction in being able to recommend one upon the present occasion.

If, therefore, you have no objection to the measure, I shall take the liberty of forwarding an official recommendation of Lieutenant Knox for Major Ogg's situation as soon as I hear that the latter has obtained permission to go to Europe for the recovery of his health.

I have, &c.,

ARTHUR WELLESLEY.

[1228.]   *To Lieutenant-Colonel Boles.*

SIR,   Seringapatam, 4th Aug., 1802.

I have had the honour to receive your letter of the 29th of July, and I have taken into consideration the subject to which it relates.*

* *Lieutenant-Colonel Boles to the Hon. Colonel Wellesley, Commanding the Troops in Mysore, &c.*

SIR,   Cannanore, 29th July, 1802.

The bad weather prevented Lieutenant Williams of the Pioneer corps visiting Seringapatam early in this month agreeably to the permission you had granted him, whereby I was disappointed of the information he could have given you relative to the territory and boundary of the French settlement of Mahé; since which this officer has been employed in going round every part of their ground, as also that of the Coringot Nair, seeking information from the most intelligent and oldest of the inhabitants on the right of sovereignty which they always wished to assume over the Nair, who still resides (in what they

It appears that, at some period between the peace of 1783 and the war between the English and Tippoo Sultaun which ended by the peace in 1792, the French had possession of the

term their territory) on his estate southward and close to the redoubt of Kooreeohy, a place about two miles south of Tellicherry Fort, at present unoccupied by us, and covered with rubbish and weeds. The French possessed it and kept a small guard in it after the peace of 1783, after which they were deprived of it by Tippoo, and we made a military post of it on the breaking out of the war in 1790.

I therefore now submit to you the propriety of again making use of it previous to the arrival of the French on this coast. A barrack of temporary materials for the men and an officer will be the only expense, as the pioneers can do all the rest.

I beg leave to enclose for your perusal a copy of a correspondence taken from the old records of Tellicherry, which, if unknown to you before, throws a considerable light on the subject ; and should you think this matter of importance, I will with your permission send up Lieutenant Williams further to explain (he being still anxious to see Seringapatam), as soon as he has finished a sketch of the French and Coringot lands, which I desired him to make as being necessary, and which shall be forwarded to you.

I have, &c.,

B. Boles, Lieutenant-Colonel Commanding.

Copy of a Letter from the Governor of Mahé to R. Taylor, Esq., Chief of Tellicherry.

Sir,   Mahé, 5th April, 1792.

The Coringot Nair came yesterday to impart to me the order you gave him to come to Tellicherry. You cannot be ignorant, Sir, that this Nair and his country are under the protection of France since eighty years, during which they have always been comprised as such in our different treaties of peace ; and that besides the ancestors of this Nair have mortgaged this country for a considerable sum, of which still the greatest part remains due to the nation. You cannot but know, Sir, that an English commissary, sent two years ago by the government of Tellicherry on the subject of some representations made by that of Mahé, has ascertained the French boundaries such as they now are : your orders, therefore, to the Coringot Nair must have astonished me, and I have forbid him to obey. I have the honour to repeat to you, Sir, what I had mentioned to you in my preceding letter. If the English government has any dispute to raise against the rights we enjoy on this coast, I beg you would make it known to me, in order that I may acquaint the French Government General thereof, which alone can do justice in it.

I have the honour to be, &c.,

Larcher.

Answer to the foregoing Letter.

Sir,   Tellicherry, 7th April, 1792.

I have the honour to acknowledge the receipt of your letter of the 5th.

You astonish me by mentioning that you had forbid the Coringot Nair to obey my order to come to Tellicherry. It is necessary you should be undeceived : I gave him no order, and it is a matter of indifference whether he

country of the Coringot Nair, in the neighbourhood of Mahé;
that Tippoo drove them out of that country and took possession
of it; and that in the course of the war in Malabar it fell into

'comes or not. I do not pretend to examine into your rights or privileges, and
have to acquaint you that my actions shall be regulated by the orders of the
Bombay government, to whom I shall transmit a copy of your letter.

> I have the honour, &c.,
>
> ROBERT TAYLOR.

The Governor of Mahé to R. Taylor, Esq., Chief of Tellicherry.

SIR,   Mahé, 14th June, 1792.

After the complaints which have been made me by the Prince Coringot Nair,
that the peons of your establishment of Moondaal came to arrest the Native
cultivators of his country to conduct them to that establishment, I have the
honour to address my complaint to you, and beg you will give orders that this
does not happen a second time.

> I have the honour to be, &c.,
>
> LARCHER.

To the Governor of Mahé.

SIR,   Tellicherry, 15th June, 1792.

I do myself the honour to reply to your letter of yesterday.

Having in a former letter announced to you that, by the late treaty of peace
with the Nabob Tippoo Sultaun, the Malabar country has been ceded to the
English nation, I cannot avoid testifying my surprise at an application which,
if complied with, would be virtually to relinquish those rights which my nation
have acquired, and are determined to exercise, over the Coringot country,
now become the property of my employers.

I shall be happy at all times to promote the good understanding which
subsists with the settlement of Mahé, but in the present instance I should
violate my duty did I admit of any interference in the government of the
Coringot district.

> I have the honour to be, &c.,
>
> (Signed)   ROBERT TAYLOR.

Copy of a Letter from the Governor of Mahé to Robert Taylor, Esq., Chief of Tellicherry.

SIR,   Mahé, 16th June, 1792.

The letter which you did me the honour of writing me yesterday in answer
to mine of the 14th has very much surprised me, as you had never before im-
parted to me the terms of the treaty of peace between the English nation and
Tippoo Sultaun, of which I am totally ignorant. What connexion has this
treaty with the French possessions? Could Tippoo Sultaun cede to you what
did not belong to him? When his father Hyder Ali made himself master of
the Malabar coast, he looked upon the country of the Coringot Nair as a
possession belonging to France, and never molested it. Besides, Sir, can you
pretend to be ignorant that your nation has always considered it and re-
spected it as such; and in the two last wars between England and France has
not the principality of the Coringot Nair always met with the same fate as
Mahé? Did it not pay a tribute to the English nation till peace was concluded,

the hands of the English, in whose possession it has remained ever since. It has not so remained, however, without remonstrances on the part of the French government in that part of India. The Governor of Mahé claimed the country in the year

as a French territory? Besides, was not the Prince Coringot Nair kept as a French prisoner at Tellicherry during the last war, and was not he set at liberty at the request of Monsieur Marin, Commissioner for France, when he came to take back again the French possessions? These are circumstances which prove our rights of sovereignty incontrovertible to the territory of the Coringot Nair, rights which the appointment which has been intrusted to me by the Governor-General in the King's name obliges me to support by every means in my power. For which reason I protest against any infraction of the ancient treaties subsisting between England and France, and must look upon you as responsible for everything which may happen, till both of us have received instructions from our Governors-General in India concerning this discussion.

Be assured that, in spite of the jealousy which the colony of Tellicherry appears to show against that of Mahé, I am determined, upon all occasions, to do everything in my power to establish a good intelligence and harmony between the subjects of our respective nations in general, and particularly between those of Mahé and Tellicherry.

I have the honour to be, &c.,

(Signed)   LARCHER.

Answer to the foregoing Letter.

SIR,   Tellicherry, 17th June, 1792.

I have the honour to acknowledge receipt of your letter of the 16th instant.

I find it incumbent upon me to reply to such parts of your letter as require an explanation to set the matter respecting the Coringot district in its true light. Whatever might have happened in the time of Hyder Ali, which you state in order to prove the Coringot district a French possession, is now completely done away. Whether Hyder Ali did or did not take possession of the Coringot district, it is notorious that the Nabob Tippoo Sultaun took possession of it, and from this very district did the English forces dislodge those of Tippoo. It is a known fact that the Nabob was in possession of the Coringot district when the war broke out, and that the Nair had long before fled to the Travancore country for protection: how then can it be said that this district is a French possession, when they did neither keep it nor protect the Nair? On reference to my letter of the 2nd April last, I find it was the Calicut districts which I signified to you as being ceded to the English; but it is now made known to you that by the treaty of peace with the Nabob Tippoo Sultaun he has ceded and confirmed the Malabar country to the English nation.

I shall enter into no more argument, Sir, on the subject; and should any impediments be thrown in the way of the just rights of my nation by the settlement of Mahé, I hereby protest against you and all such as may have occasioned them, holding you answerable for the consequences.

I have the honour to be, &c.,

(Signed)   ROBERT TAYLOR.

Copy

1792 from Mr. Taylor of Tellicherry; and, upon the whole, the question regarding the right to this territory now stands on the same ground that it did at that time.

Copy of a Letter from the Governor of Mahé to Robert Taylor, Esq., Chief of Tellicherry.

Sir,   Mahé, 18th June, 1792.

Although you have been pleased to tell me that you will not enter into any further explanation with me on the protestation which I have made you on the subject of the possession of France over the territory of the Coringot Nair, I shall nevertheless make you another, and the last, which I beg you will consider well.

In supposing that Tippoo Sultaun had come to this coast with 60,000 robbers with an intention of ravaging the Nair countries, what could the commandant of Mahé do with a garrison of 80 men against this army, which had even posted itself within the district of Mahé? This conduct, even if Tippoo himself had been guilty of it, could only be considered as an usurpation on his part over the French nation, with which he was not at war.

I have the protest made to Tippoo by Monsieur Canap and by the Count de Conway on the irregular conduct of the officers of Tippoo who had possession of the principality of the Coringot Nair, and committed troubles at Mahé. I have also copies of Tippoo's letter addressed to the Count de Conway, and dated at Seringapatam, the 20th April, 1789, in which he says that he will give orders to his Sircar to prevent his troops from committing troubles on the French territories; and he proposes moreover in the same letter an exchange of three places, of Palur, Chambara, and Pandaquel, on account of these three places being occupied by robbers, supported, as he says, by the commandant of Tellicherry, and who constrained greatly the operations of his Sircar.

You see then, Sir, that if the English have found the troops of Tippoo posted within the French territories, it was contrary to the consent of the French, and after reiterated protestations on the part of the commandant of Mahé and the Governor-General of Pondicherry to Tippoo Sultaun.

I have every reason to believe that the government of Tippoo may have wished to profit by our present state of weakness to usurp upon the French; yet that it has never been the intention of your Court to limit us, I would answer for, from the opinion that I have of its greatness.

I repeat to you then, Sir, that it is you alone whom I render responsible for all the events that may happen after the information I have given you on this subject.

I have the honour, &c.,
(Signed)   LARCHER.

Answer to the foregoing Letter.

Sir,   Tellicherry, 20th June, 1792.

I have the honour to acknowledge the receipt of your letter of the 18th instant, a copy of which I shall transmit to my superiors, that they may be informed of the reason you urge in behalf of the claim you make to the Coringot district. Copies of your other letters with my replies will also be sent to them, that if any discussion takes place between superior powers, they may have the necessary information.

I have the honour to be, &c.,
(Signed)   ROBERT TAYLOR.

The Governor of Mahé asserted in 1792 that Tippoo had deprived the French of this territory unjustly and by force, and that remonstrances had been made to him upon that subject

Extract of a Letter from Robert Taylor, Esq., Chief of Tellicherry, to the Governor of Bombay, dated 21st June, 1792.

"From every information, it appears clearly that Tippoo conquered and possessed himself of the Malabar country.

"That the French were restricted to the settlement of Mahé and a small district about it, where even their flag could not protect fugitives.

"That the troops of Tippoo were stationed in the Malabar country when the war broke out, and particularly in the Coringot district.

"That they were expelled thence or fled when the war broke out, and the English troops marched against them.

"The treaty of peace cedes to the Honourable Company the Malabar country, and Kullaye is mentioned by name, whatever pretensions the French might have had formerly; and it does not appear that anything beyond receiving a mortgage for money lent to the Coringot Nair, and being on terms of friendship with him, can be produced in favour of the former claims of the French: but let them have been ever so strong, Tippoo made a conquest of the Malabar country without any respect to the French claims. The English have since taken the Malabar country by force of arms: it is confirmed to them by the treaty of peace.

"Having related what has appeared to me from information to be real fact, I hope I shall be considered as doing my duty in resisting the claims of the French to possess themselves of the Coringot district as an unjust and ill-founded pretension, and equally groundless as their claim to hoist their flag at Calicut."

Copy of a Letter from Robert Taylor, Esq., Chief of Tellicherry, to the Commissioners.

GENTLEMEN,   Tellicherry, 12th December, 1792.

I have the honour to reply to your letter of the 8th instant, which I received yesterday.

There is no fact more publicly known and admitted than that at the commencement of the late war Tippoo Sultaun possessed the whole Malabar coast as far to the southward as the Travancore dominions; that all the Malabar princes had fled, some to the jungle and others to the Travancore country, among which latter was the Coringot Nair, whose country lies in the neighbourhood of Mahé; and that the French at that time possessed no more than the fort and districts of Mahé, which extend a small distance beyond the fort, but do not comprehend, as far as I have been informed or can learn from inquiry, any part of the Coringot district.

When, in consequence of the breaking out of the war, a detachment from the garrison of Tellicherry, under the command of Major Alexander Dow, in the month of April, 1790, dislodged the troops of Tippoo Sultaun from our neighbourhood, Kooreechy redoubt, the principal military post in the Coringot district, was then garrisoned by Tippoo's troops; it was stormed and carried by our troops, who have remained in possession of it ever since. Several prisoners were taken, who were disarmed, and dismissed with others on certain conditions. No claim was then made by the French to the Coringot district, nor any by Count Conway. It is probable that this assertion is well founded; at all events it is possible that the copies of these remonstrances can still be produced.

protest against our proceedings; and it was not until the end of June following that I received a letter from Monsieur Larcher Le Tellier, the then Governor of Mahé, wherein he informed me that the sovereignty of the Coringot country had belonged to France from a date as ancient as the establishment of Mahé itself; that the Coringot Nair was a vassal of the King of France; and that this right had never been disputed by the English government nor by Hyder Ali Khan, who in taking the Malabar coast never made himself master of that sovereignty. That if Tippoo Sultaun or his people had usurped any possessions belonging to France, such usurpation could not in any degree weaken her rights; and that if we acted on those principles, we could not send troops on pretence that Tippoo's people were there. Such were the arguments used by Monsieur Le Tellier, who gave this notification in consequence of our finding it necessary to advance our troops a little nearer to Mahé, unwilling to hazard any dispute which might involve us with the French, and at the same time desirous of avoiding the slightest encroachment on the French districts of Mahé. I sent a deputation of three gentlemen to Monsieur Le Tellier, that he might point out to them what were their boundaries; and with respect to their claim of sovereignty as above stated, I left it to be canvassed by my superiors, not conceiving myself competent to decide on a matter of such importance. I have the honour to enclose a copy of the report made to me by the gentlemen who went to Mahé, which I recommend to your particular attention in your investigation of this business, because it clearly points out that the French Governor has produced no proof of his assertions, and equally demonstrates the importance the Coringot district must be of to us, as well as the reasons which induce the French to dispute the matter; and I beg leave to add that no proof has been produced to me of the right they wish to exercise. It is very certain that if the Coringot district becomes ours, Mahé will be so completely surrounded that their trade will be comparatively of little value, which may induce the French to the strongest exertions to maintain possession of what at present they have not proved their claim to.

I beg leave to state what appears to me to be the French claim on the Coringot Nair. Enclosed is copy of an ola delivered by the Coringot Nair to Monsieur Marin, who now resides at Mahé, which clearly evinces the claim they have upon that chief to be no more than a simple debt incurred to the French for money advanced by them, and which has been in part discharged. Monsieur Marin, to whom a part of this money was due, left an order with our linguist to recover what he could of his share at the time when the last surrender of Mahé to the English obliged him to go up to Bombay, and at the same time left with our linguist a copy of this ola in the Malabar language, of which the enclosed is a true transcript in that language. I send also a note at the same time from Monsieur Marin's clerk to our linguist in the Portuguese language, with a translation thereof. You will perceive by the translation of the ola that the Coringot Nair expressly calls the country his country, which would appear inconsistent with vassalage. This, from everything I can procure, is the full amount of the French claim, unless they shall prove the contrary, which they have not yet done; and if this claim be liquidated, I conceive they can have no more demands upon the Coringot district.

With respect to the Nair himself, you will judge of his claim to the country.

If this assertion be well founded, Tippoo can be considered only in the light of an usurper of the territory of the Coringot Nair.

The question upon this part of the subject is, whether, when a territory has been seized unjustly by one power, a perfect right to such territory is vested in the power which may conquer the usurping power in war.   The common principles of natural justice would induce me to decide that the right of the conquering power can be considered only in the same light with that of the usurper; but I am aware that expediency has great weight in the decision on all political questions, particularly in this country.   In fact, if the right of the Company to the territories

He was a fugitive at Travancore, and did not return until long after we had expelled Tippoo's troops.   He gave us no assistance whatever during the war, and although offered the Company's protection, which he at first accepted, yet he soon after changed and took that of the French.   He never has been formally restored to his country by the English; although, from a wish to avoid all disputes with the French until their claim could be investigated and decided upon, we have interfered no further than in keeping possession of Kooreechy redoubt as a mark of our having expelled the enemy from the country, and to keep up our claim thereto until a formal decision shall take place.

If I might offer my opinion, as far as appears to me, the present arguments may be reduced to these grounds: if the French fail to produce proofs of the Coringot Nair being their vassal, then ends the matter on their part, and the country becomes ours both by right of conquest, and the cession made of it to us by Tippoo; if the French establish their claims to the sovereignty, it is then to be considered whether Tippoo's being in possession of the country and its falling into our hands by conquest, and being confirmed to us by treaty, give us a right to the country, or whether it should be restored to the Nair independently by us, because he was formerly their vassal; for as to the Nair himself, if he does not choose our protection, I apprehend we shall give ourselves no trouble about him.   I may add that the French suffering this vassal, as they term him, to be dispossessed of and to fly his country without any interference or protection on their part is a bad proof of their being so intimately connected.

I have only to add that the present Governor of Mahé, Monsieur Larcher, lately called upon me to withdraw our troops from Kooreechy redoubt, which I did not think myself authorized to do, and declined accordingly.

                    I have the honour, &c.,
                 (Signed)   ROBERT TAYLOR.

Translation of an Ola from the Coringot Nair to Monsieur Marin, of which a copy was given to Monsieur Lafrenais, Tellicherry Linguist.

The difference which happened betwixt me and the Rajah of Cherical in the Malabar year 951 would not have taken place if Monsieur Repentignie had not refused the advice of Monsieur Marin afterwards to settle the same, or to bring about a peace.   I was constrained to pass a bond to the said Rajah for rupees 80,000, which sum all the French gentlemen of Mahé agreed to lend me.   The share of Monsieur Marin being rupees 6660 2 12, he received from the revenues which they have gained by conquest or negotiation from Tippoo and others depended upon the justice of the right of those from whom they have gained them, it is probable that their share of territory in India would be but small indeed. This question, therefore, resolves itself into one of expediency. When the French take possession of Mahé, it is certain that they will urge immediately the cession of the territory of the Coringot Nair, to which the Governor of Mahé heretofore laid claim. The question whether it is expedient or not to cede this territory to them, or to enter into the discussion at all, must of course be decided by government; but there are some points upon which information will be required, and upon which I request you to procure all that can be got.

The first point is, the utility of this territory to the Company's government in their hands either in a military or a commercial point of view.

Secondly, the facility which the French would derive from their possession of it to injure the Company in either.

Thirdly, the real origin of the claim of the French to this district.

Fourthly, the manner in which they got possession of it; the time; the nature of their possession; whether the revenues of the country were only mortgaged to them for the payment of a certain sum, or whether the country was made over to them; and if the latter, whether in perpetuity or only till a certain sum should have been collected from it; the nature of the instrument by which the country was made over.

of my country in two additions rupees 1645 3 5¼; and the balance, being rupees 5014 4 6¼, he is to receive from the same revenues.

Note from Monsieur Marin's Clerk to Monsieur Lafrenais.

Monsieur Marin advanced to the Coringot Nair to be delivered to the province of Cherical, to fulfil the sum of rupees 80,000 which is to be paid by the Nair to the said Rajah for negotiating the peace			Rs. 6,660 2 12
Monsieur Picot collecting the territories of the said Nair and Poyapurrutu Nair, paid in part to Monsieur Marin under 31st March, 1778 .. .. Rs. 1,068 0 0			
Ditto ditto 30th March, 1779 579 3 5¼			
			1,645 3 5¼
Balance upon the territory of the Nair			5,014 4 6¼

Fifthly, the length of time during which the French had possession of the district; the real history regarding the manner in which they were dispossessed of it by Tippoo.

Sixthly, the nature of the tenure of the Coringot Nair previous to the period at which he mortgaged or made over his country to the French; whether he was tributary to Tippoo, or to any of the Malabar rajahs whose countries had been conquered by Hyder or Tippoo.

In answer to your question, whether you are to occupy the redoubt of Kooreechy, I have to observe that your occupying it or not is of but little importance in the consideration of the question of right to the territory, or in the decision to whom it shall finally belong. If government should decide that the French are not to have it, it will always be easy to deprive them of it without the assistance of the redoubt; on the other hand, your occupying the redoubt makes no alteration in the claim of the French to the territory.

It is possible, however, that immediately upon their arrival at Mahé, and before government can have time to decide regarding their claim to the territory, the French may be induced to seize and occupy it with their troops. If the result of your inquiries on the first and second points above stated should be that their possession of the territory, even for a time, would be prejudicial to the Company, and if you should be of opinion that a body of our troops in the Kooreechy redoubt would either prevent them from occupying the territory or would preclude a part of the apprehended mischief if they should occupy it, you will be so kind as to give orders that the Kooreechy redoubt may be repaired, and you will post a body of troops in it without delay.

I have, &c.,

ARTHUR WELLESLEY.

To Lieutenant-General Stuart. [1229.]

SIR, Seringapatam, 5th Aug., 1802.

Since I had the honour of receiving your letter of the 29th July upon the subject of the bridge at Seringapatam, I have had a further conversation with the Dewan, from the tenor of which I find that the bridge cannot be built in the manner proposed, upon stone uprights, in the place which I prefer for it, and which I believe is the same with that marked as the best situation for a bridge in General Ross's plan. It is that between the north-east angle of the fort and the Dowlut Baug, and exposed immediately to the fire of the works at the north-east angle. The river in this part has a sandy bottom, and it is certain that it would not bear the foundation for the stone uprights without incurring a vast expense, and it is doubted whether even the largest expense laid out upon the foundation would make it a good one. The Native architects also doubt whether the bottom of the river in that part would bear the foundation of the piers of an arched bridge; they don't perfectly understand, however, the manner in which these bridges are constructed by European architects, and they don't give a decided opinion upon this point; but the opinion which they have given regarding the possibility of laying the foundation of the stone uprights makes it very clear that if the Rajah's government are to bear the expense of building the bridge, we must give up the notion of placing it in that situation which it is agreed by all would be the most convenient and advantageous.

There remain then two situations for a bridge over the north branch of the Cauvery: one near the western angle of the fort, where the bridge was placed heretofore; and the other below the Dowlut Baug, between that garden and the Caryghaut ford, and apparently beyond the common reach of shot from the fort.

The passage from the bridge, supposing it to be built near the western angle, would be not through the fort, as I imagined, but as it was heretofore, to the eastward, along the northern glacis; and notwithstanding that the bridge should be built there, it would still be in our power to open the old gate, called the Delhi Gate, or not, as we might think proper.

I will state the advantages and disadvantages which, in my opinion, are peculiar to the construction of a bridge in each situation and those common to both, and shall then draw a comparison between the two. If the bridge be constructed in the situation near the western angle, as the foundations are already laid and still complete, it will cost less money, and will be finished by the next year. The works for the defence of it are still apparent, and might be rendered complete at a small expense if wanted; but it will be effectually under the fire and control of the fort.

On the other hand, from its situation at the western angle, it will be absolutely necessary to destroy this bridge whenever there would be the appearance of an attack upon the place. We know by experience that all the works on the north face are exposed to the enfilade from the south side of the river, and the defence of the bridge therefore would be very precarious. It is possible, however, to destroy effectually bridges built as this would be in a very short space of time ; and from its situation in the neighbourhood of the fort this bridge could be destroyed with great facility. If the bridge is to be constructed in the situation between the Dowlut Baug and the Caryghaut ford, as the foundations must all be laid, three years will elapse before it is completed, and it will cost about half as much more than a bridge in the situation near the western angle. It will be so far from the fort that it will be necessary to construct a work for its ordinary defence. Those who will be desirous of using it as a passage from one part of the country to the other must pass under the guns of the fort to go to the bridge over the south branch of the river ; but not those whose object might be to remain on the island. In case of the apprehension of a regular attack upon the fort, the bridge, if built near the Caryghaut ford, must be destroyed : its destruction will not take much time ; but on account of the greater distance it will not be completed with the facility to the garrison with which, under such circumstances, the bridge if built near the western angle would be destroyed.

Upon the whole, it appears that the bridge near the western angle would be sooner built, would cost less money, and would be better situated for all common purposes than one near the Caryghaut ford ; either must be destroyed in case of the apprehension of a serious attack upon the fort, and that at the western angle would be destroyed with greater facility ; and in case of the apprehension of danger of less magnitude, such as the irruption of a body of horse into the Mysore country, &c., &c., it would be necessary to secure the bridge near the Caryghaut ford by works, whereas that near the western angle would be secured by the fort. I prefer to place the bridge near the western angle.

Before I make any proposition upon this subject to be laid before government, I should wish to be favoured with your sentiments upon the point above considered.

The Dewan has applied to me for some of the large flat stones from the Mysore Palace to be employed in the construction of this bridge. I have saved and collected from the rampart which has been pulled down, and from the yard of the Mysore Palace, which is clearing for the gun-carriage manufactory, a quantity of materials, the value of which will be a great set-off against the expense of filling the ditch. Some of the materials, however, found in the Mysore Palace, such as long flat stones and stones used as the bottoms of wooden pillars in the houses of natives, will never be of the smallest use to the Company; and as I find the Dewan so well inclined upon all occasions to serve the Company, I should be glad to be permitted to assist him in these works with such of these materials as he will want, as will never be of any service to us. I shall be glad to have your orders upon this point.

Since I addressed you last upon the subject of the Bombay pioneers I have made further inquiries regarding their expense. I find that the expense of the corps is, in round numbers, about 1600 pagodas *per mensem*, supposing them to be in the field. Besides this, they have attached to them 428 Bombay bigarries, whose expense is also about 1600 pagodas *per mensem*, supposing them to be in the field. I have to observe that the latter have never appeared in any return, and I did not know that they were in the service till I called for the Bombay pioneer abstracts; at all events, I conceive their service is very useless. If additional numbers are wanted for the Bombay pioneers, they can be either hired at Palghaut, or sent from this country when required, at a cheaper rate of monthly expense than is now incurred on account of these Bombay bigarries. I therefore take the liberty of suggesting to you that I may be permitted to order that these bigarries may be mustered and discharged, and sent to Bombay as soon as the season will permit.

I have, &c.,

ARTHUR WELLESLEY.

[1230.]   *To Josiah Webbe, Esq.*

MY DEAR WEBBE,   Seringapatam, 5th Aug., 1802.

You must be the best judge of Purneah's intentions regarding the disposal of the Rajah's ready money; but I should imagine that he could have intended nothing by his offer to dispose of it in any manner the government should think proper but a general assurance that it should be laid out for the benefit of the country under the general superintendence of the Resident, as all other money is. However, whatever may have been his intention, there is no doubt but he will be happy to advance it for the purpose of reforming the fort of Seringapatam, a work which may eventually be of the greatest importance to the Rajah; but I hope it will be only an advance, and will be faithfully repaid.

There is no doubt but that the two works can go on together; the demands for both will be gradual, and probably will not exceed 5000 pagodas for the fort and 2000 or 3000 for the bridge monthly.

It is possible that if Purncah should be called upon to make an advance for the repair of the fort, he will be inclined to execute the reform and repair by means of his own people. I should like this much; provided the work were superintended by one of our engineers, not with a commission upon the expenditure, but with a salary given for this special purpose.

I mention this subject now, that you may turn it over in your mind.

Believe me, &c.,

ARTHUR WELLESLEY.

To Lieutenant-General Stuart. [1231.]

SIR,   6th Aug., 1802.

When I heard in the month of January last that the preliminaries of peace between His Majesty and the French Republic had been signed, and that the French were again to have possession of their settlements in India, I gave directions to the commanding officer in Malabar to make a road round the French settlement at Mahé, in order that when they should come to take possession of it we might not be deprived of all means of communication between the northern and southern parts of that province.

In the course of the inquiries regarding the French boundary preparatory to making the new road which I had ordered, it appeared that the French had claims to the territories of the

Coringot Nair, which are situated part between Tellicherry and Mahé, and part to the southward of Mahé, which did not appear to be very well founded. The best line for the new road lay directly across that part of this territory between Tellicherry and Mahé, and there was another line rather longer, which went along its borders.

As I was desirous to do nothing which could appear like an intention to give up this territory to the French, I desired that the best line for the new road might be adopted ; and as I wished to keep the question open for the decision of government, and to be prepared for it whatever it might be, I desired that another road might be made along the borders of the territory the possession of which was likely to be disputed, which road, as it joins another road from Moondaal to Cotaparamba, has the appearance of a new line into the disturbed countries, rather than one made with a view to the cession of the Coringot Nair's territory to the French. These orders were given in March.

Within these few days, however, I have received from Lieutenant-Colonel Boles some papers which throw farther light upon this subject, copies of which I now enclose.* From these it appears that between the peace of 1783 and the breaking out of the war with Tippoo in 1790, the French had possession of the territory of the Coringot Nair ; that Tippoo deprived them of it ; that we drove Tippoo from it in the war of 1790, which ended at Seringapatam in 1792 ; that the French claimed the territory from us between the peace of 1792 with Tippoo and the breaking out of the war with them in 1793 ; but possession was never delivered to them.

The question whether the territory belongs to them or not stands precisely upon the ground on which it stood in 1792, and we have seen enough of the French to be certain that there is no claim, however remote, which they will not bring forward. As, however, it is desirable that a discussion with them should be avoided, that at all events, if necessary, it should be short, I lay these papers before you now, that you may draw the attention of government to the subject at an early period.

I likewise enclose an extract of a letter which I have written to Colonel Boles, which contains orders to inquire into certain points regarding this subject, and I shall be glad to receive

* See pp. 250-258.

your orders if you wish for any further information which is not likely to be brought out by the answers to these queries. This extract also contains an answer to a question from Lieutenant-Colonel Boles regarding the propriety of occupying the redoubt at Kooreechy, in a letter from Lieutenant-Colonel Boles, a copy of which is likewise enclosed.

I have, &c.,

ARTHUR WELLESLEY.

To Lieutenant-Colonel Brown.   [1232.]

SIR,   Seringapatam, 7th Aug., 1802.

In answer to your letter of the 1st instant, I have to request that you will not discourage the protection afforded to the inhabitants of Kittoor, who will fly for it to the Company's territories; only you must avoid encouraging it openly.

I have, &c.,

ARTHUR WELLESLEY.

To Captain Fraser.   [1233.]

SIR,   Seringapatam, 10th Aug., 1802.

As your party is placed at Bonawassi only for the protection of the collector's treasury, I conceive that, according to the regulations of government, the revenue ought to pay all the extra expenses attending it. These are full batta to yourself, and, whenever the troops move out, to them also. But I don't conceive that either the Native officer or havildar in command of the detachments at Sercey and Budnaghur has any claim to full batta.

I have, &c.,

ARTHUR WELLESLEY.

To Lieutenant-General Stuart.   [1234.]

SIR,   Seringapatam, 11th Aug., 1802.

I have the honour to enclose a letter which I have received from Mr. Gilmour. This gentleman has been doing duty at Seringapatam for nearly three years, and upon some occasions has had charge of the general hospital and of many corps, on account of the absence of the other medical gentlemen on field and other services. On all occasions I have found him very attentive to his duty and able in his profession, a character in which Mr. Anderson agrees; and I beg leave, therefore, to recommend him to your favour and protection.

I have lately made a trial of the carriage of which Mr. Bishop gave you a plan. I find that it will require a vast quantity of timber to make the body of it, that it will be very heavy, and after all, as it will be impossible to use it in this country in the form of a sled, the quantity of timber employed in its construction will be needlessly thrown away.

We have at Seringapatam a great number of unserviceable limbers which were brought here with the heavy guns for the siege. Of these I propose to make carriages to bring in the heavy timber, according to a form of which I have made one already, which upon trial answers perfectly. Two of these limbers are fastened together by a perch: the distance between each can be made greater or smaller, in proportion to the length of the timber which they are to carry, as the perch is fastened in the hinder limber by a pin, and it is moveable. On each limber is laid a bed to receive the timber, of such a height as that the wheels of the front limber will turn under the timber. The bed of the front limber traverses so that the carriage can turn.

The timber is fastened on this carriage, as it must be on every other, by ropes, and it has been tried on the worst roads here and has been found to answer. Its expense is nothing excepting the timber for the beds and for the perch, and a small quantity of iron.

I hope to-morrow to be able to send you a drawing of this carriage.

I have, &c.,

ARTHUR WELLESLEY.

[1235.]   *To Josiah Webbe, Esq.*

MY DEAR WEBBE,   Seringapatam, 14th Aug., 1802.

Some time in the month of May last I recommended Purneah, in concert with Piele, to attack a gang of thieves whose place of refuge was on the frontier of Mysore and Coimbatoor, and who had been in the habit of plundering both countries. I was aware that in the execution of this service it was probable that the Rajah's troops would enter the Company's territory, and I wrote to Mr. Read a letter upon the subject, a copy of which is enclosed. I believe Piele wrote to him upon the same subject, and I believe he received no answer.

Shortly afterwards I was informed that all communication between Mysore and Coimbatoor was stopped. Sepoys going to the southward on leave of absence, others discharged from the service and returning to their houses, and merchants going into Coimbatoor on their lawful concerns, were obliged to return here for want of a passport, which was required from them at the Gudjelhatty pass. I then wrote to Macleod upon the subject to represent the general inconvenience of this arrangement, and I enclose the copy of a letter from Mr. Read, which will show the ground of it.

It is needless to point out to you the inconvenience of discouraging the intercourse between Mysore and the neighbouring countries; instead of discouraging it, everything ought to be done which can have a contrary effect. But the intercourse with Coimbatoor in particular is very convenient and advantageous. Seringapatam is supplied with many articles by Coimbatoor only; and the number of people who go there is so great, that since this regulation of Mr. Read's has been established, a great part of the business of the country has been to draw out passports.

It may be said that as people can go into Coimbatoor if they have a passport, the intercourse is not discouraged to any degree that is inconvenient. But, in the first place, I deny that, as, even if the persons who would have the power of granting the passports were numerous, the trouble of obtaining them must operate as a discouragement.

But in this regulation of Mr. Read's he does not point out whose passport will be valid. He estimates that sepoys and others must have passports from their commanding officers, and I conclude that such are valid in all parts of the Company's territories; but he does not say one word respecting the dealers at Seringapatam and in Mysore, whose concerns may take them into Coimbatoor, for whose convenience it is as necessary to provide as it is for that of the sepoys.

If they must have passports, they must get them either from the Resident, or every aumildar in the country must have the power of granting them to the people of his own district.   If the former, the difficulty of procuring the passports must operate as a discouragement to the intercourse between the two countries. If the latter, the regulation can have no very beneficial effect in preventing bad people from entering Coimbatoor, as it is scarcely possible to suppose a man so bad that he could not procure a passport from some aumildar in Mysore, or if so bad, that he could not forge one.

The question here occurs, what end is the regulation to answer ? and I am sure I am unable to solve it.   Besides this, I have a great objection to trusting the generality of people in this country with passports or writings of any kind, signed by a person in authority.   They always use them in a manner in which they were not intended to be used when granted ; and for this reason, in all the arrangements which at different times I have made with Close for supplying the troops in the field, we have preferred to allow all persons who said they were going to the army to pass duty free, at the risk of some loss of revenue to the Sircar, to the granting of passports to our dealers. I wish that you would take this subject into consideration, and if you perceive the inconvenience of Mr. Read's regulation, as I do, you will take measures that it may be altered ; at all events, that you will require him to explain whose passports are to have the power of passing persons not military into the Coimbatoor country.

Believe me, &c.,

ARTHUR WELLESLEY.

To Lieutenant-General Stuart.

[1236.] SIR,   15th Aug., 1802.

If you have no objection, I propose in the next month to inspect the corps stationed at Santa Bednore, Chittledroog, Sera, and Nundydroog, and besides to visit the fort at Paughur. I likewise propose in the month of November to inspect the corps and visit the stations in Malabar and Wynaad, and afterwards, if circumstances permit, to go into Canara, and Soonda, and Bednore, for the same purposes.

It is probable that before long the arrangements will be made for commencing the reform and repair of the works of Seringapatam; and while those works are going on, particularly at their commencement and upon the first establishment of the gun-carriage manufactory, I should wish not to be absent from this place for any great length of time. Accordingly, I have arranged my plan so as to visit all the stations in Mysore, Malabar, Canara, and Soonda in the course of the next fair season, and I hope not to be absent from Seringapatam more than a month at a time.

It is very desirable that the repair of Seringapatam should be commenced at the earliest period in the next season; particularly that the breach made by the river in the southern stone glacis last year should be closed. If that be done, the other works can be carried on at any time.

I have, &c.,

ARTHUR WELLESLEY.

To Captain Scott.   [1237.]

MY DEAR SIR,   Seringapatam, 16th Aug., 1802.

The establishment which you inform me in your letter of the 12th is fixed for you is very small indeed, which, however, I consider of very immaterial consequence, provided it is to be much (*very much*) increased hereafter. It stands to reason that just at first you will have many arrangements to make and many difficulties to contend with, which will, of course, impede the progress of your work, and for that reason it is perhaps as well that you should begin with only a small establishment; but hereafter it is essentially necessary that it should be large, otherwise the manufactory will not stand its ground against the attacks which will be made upon it from various quarters. In the first memorandum which I gave General Stuart upon this subject, I recommended that an establishment should be fixed for the manufactory, and that the superintendent should be obliged to furnish the number of carriages monthly which it may be supposed the number of workmen in his service can make up. By this mode the exact expense of each carriage at the end of the year or of two years can be ascertained, and the cheapness of the work performed at the manufactory will be its best defence against all attacks, particularly if the number of workmen be so great as that they will do a large quantity, and the superintendent's salary bear but a small proportion of the expense incurred. But if only a small quantity of work be performed, the superintendent's salary will bear a great proportion to the expense of each carriage, and there will be a strong argument against the manufactory.

For instance, you have a salary of 500 pagodas *per mensem*, and an establishment has been fixed for you which I apprehend will not make three large carriages in a month. Your salary, therefore, will add to the expense of each carriage above 130 pagodas. We will suppose that you had an establishment which would make twenty carriages in a month (and, by the bye, if carriages are wanted, I don't see why you should not), the expense to be added to each carriage on account of your salary would be only 25 pagodas. Thus you see that the greater the number of artificers you have, the greater will be the number of carriages you will make, the smaller will be the expense of each carriage to the Company, and the smaller the proportion of that expense will be your salary.

Not only, therefore, is there a positive advantage in your having a large establishment, but your having it will deprive the enemies of the new system of their strongest argument against it, and will enable its friends to combat them by the best of all possible arguments, viz., the fact that carriages are made cheaper at the manufactory than they could be elsewhere.

I have heard it said that all kinds of military stores are to be made at this manufactory, and, in my opinion, this system will answer well hereafter. The first object, however, is gun-carriages, and till that is accomplished, nothing else ought to be attempted. From what I have heard, I am convinced that the manufactory will be strongly attacked at different periods, and the quantity of work done in a given period will be compared with the expense. The enemies of the system will take nothing into the account excepting gun-carriages: it will be in vain that its friends will show that other articles have been supplied for the service; the answer is obvious, that the dearness of the gun-carriages, and not of other articles of military supply, was the cause of the establishment of the manufactory, and that it was ridiculous to give a man 500 pagodas *per mensem* to make articles which were made by others for nothing. Although, therefore, hereafter the manufactory may be turned to these articles, I should wish it to prove the power of making gun-carriages, and of course those articles with cheapness, before anything else should be undertaken.   I have another objection to throwing indiscriminately all articles of military supply upon the manufactory, and it is that, in my opinion, by so doing the greatest check upon the superintendent is taken off.   A quantity of work ought to be required from him in proportion to the number of people he would have employed under him : this can be done only by adhering to one species of work.   It is obvious that if all kinds of articles are required from him, the workmen must be shifted from one kind to another, and nobody can know what quantity the manufactory ought to supply.   You see that I urge all these matters to you as if you were in no way concerned excepting to forward the object in view, which I am convinced is the case.

Upon the whole, I beg you to urge the Commander-in-Chief to increase your establishment, and that very shortly, and not to allow anything but gun-carriages to be thrown upon the manufactory until it has proved its benefit by its cheap operation.

I have excellent accounts of dry timber.   I shall have more than enough to keep you at work till the green timber cut in May last will be fit for use.

The number of sawyers you have is not sufficient; you should have European sawyers.   There are some excellent drunken fellows in my regiment who are capital workmen in that line.

The yard is not yet ready for you.   To clear it has been a work of more labour than I imagined; indeed, one of the most laborious that I have seen.   However, we will pitch some old flies on the parade for you to begin under.

I'll send for Roebuck's carriages when I receive the order to do so.   At all events, I have made some carriages that will transport with ease the largest timber, but I don't send out for any till the month of December, and there is plenty here to keep you at work.

Believe me, &c.,

ARTHUR WELLESLEY.

To Captain Wilks.   [1238.]

MY DEAR SIR,   Seringapatam, 16th Aug., 1802.

I am very glad that you communicated my sentiments upon the subject treated of in your letter of the 11th to General

Stuart. I am still of opinion that it cannot be intended to deprive the officers of the army of the pensions upon retirement. The inconveniences attending them are obvious; but every man who considers at all must see that they must be continued, or the old abuses abolished by the regulations of 1796 must be revived, or there can be no longer a local army in India. I believe the Court of Directors prefer keeping their army, even with this expense, to giving it up or to rendering it worse than useless by a revival of the old abuses.

Since the establishment of the pensions, the Court of Directors have been uncommonly liberal upon this subject. They have taken off many restrictions upon retirement, and they have given pensions to officers retiring at different periods of service on account of bad health. By these regulations they have undoubtedly added to the expense of the pension establishment. If they were a body capable of acting upon any systematic plan, either with a good or bad object in view, I should agree that the increase of the expense of the pension establishment has been made in order to render it more odious to the King's ministers and the public, and in order to render it more certain that it would be abolished; but we all know, both from the constitution of the Court of Directors and from the mode in which they do business, that they are not capable of forming a systematic plan of that kind, and of waiting quietly its result. If they wanted to destroy the pension establishment, they would have dashed at it at once rather than have increased its expense as the most certain mode of increasing the number of its enemies, and of finally obtaining its abolition. I am induced, therefore, to attribute the liberal arrangements above alluded to to a spirit friendly to the institution, founded upon a sense of its benefits to the military service, and, of course, to the power of the Company.

In all great bodies there are many who see only the inconveniences of an institution, particularly if it be attended with expense; but I can hardly believe that the Court of Directors in general are blind to the benefits of this institution, or that the King's ministers would allow them to abolish it as long as it is the policy of Great Britain to govern India through the Company, to have there a local army, and to keep the patronage out of the hands of the Crown.

Supposing, however, the institution to be abolished, I see that you and I will not readily agree as to the mode of finding a substitute for it. Close is a great authority, and I would submit to his decision upon most occasions; but let him hear the other side, and see how he'll decide then.

As to my plan, I prefer that the stoppage to be made from the allowances in order to carry it into execution should be by order, provided it is the general opinion that that mode will be the most agreeable to the officers of the army in general.

Believe me, &c.,

ARTHUR WELLESLEY.

To Lieutenant-General Stuart. [1239.]

SIR,   19th Aug., 1802.

I have had the honour to receive your letter of the 15th instant, and its enclosures, and I shall pay particular attention to the subjects to which they relate.

There are in this country fortresses not occupied by the Company's troops, and which it does not appear probable that they will ever occupy. They are all, however, useful to the Rajah in keeping up a respect for his government in the country, and in enabling him to collect the revenues with ease. They are maintained by him at little or no expense.

I should wish to know whether the 15th paragraph of the Instructions No. 1 is intended to apply to these forts, and whether it is wished that I should visit and report upon every fort in the Mysore country.

Much time would be saved to the committee, and they would be enabled to make a report which would be more satisfactory to the Military Board, would be better understood, and would be more useful hereafter, if an officer of engineers were ordered in the first instance to take a plan of all these forts. A description of a fortress, particularly of a hill fort, however accurately drawn, can never be well understood by any excepting those who draw it; but when that description is to be accompanied by proposals for reforms and improvements, which are to be carried into execution hereafter by persons who may not form part of the committee, plans and technical descriptions by engineers become more necessary. Your experience of hill forts in general, and particularly of the forts in this country, will make this proposition clear to you; but there is one fort,

Chittledroog, which is an object of great consequence, of which no man could give the Military Board an idea without the assistance of a plan. If you approve of this notion, I should wish that an engineer officer were ordered in the first instance to take a plan of every fort on which the Military Board are desirous of receiving a report. This, it is true, will delay the final report on the forts in this country; but I know from experience in Canara and Soonda that it will not delay it materially, and eventually the report will be really useful to the service.

There is an officer of engineers, either at Nundydroog or in the Ceded Districts, Lieutenant Tottingham, at present unemployed, who might be employed on this service with great advantage.

The other points referred to the committee in Instructions No. 1 are comparatively easy, and depend much upon those which I have already expressed a wish to refer in the first instance to an officer of engineers. I will take care that such details respecting them are given in the reports as will be satisfactory and useful to the Military Board.

If you should approve of this notion, the final report on No. 1, in the Mysore country, will be delayed for some time; but I will immediately take the Instructions No. 2 into consideration, and I will have a personal conference with Lieutenant-Colonel Agnew on that subject in the Ceded Districts in the month of December.

I have to observe that I can do this consistently with the plans which I had in contemplation for reviewing the troops and visiting the stations in Mysore, Malabar, and Canara in the course of the next fair season, which I had the honour of laying before you in my letter of the 15th instant.

I have, &c.,

ARTHUR WELLESLEY.

[1240.]   *To W. H. Gordon, Esq.*

SIR,   Seringapatam, 21st Aug., 1802.

Having taken into consideration the rate of exchange at which you have received certain Bengal gold mohurs, half and quarter mohurs, and koorzat from Mr. Read, the collector in

Soonda, and that at which they are current in the Mysore country, I have to request that, under the authority from government which I heretofore communicated to you, you will issue these coins to the troops at the rates hereafter mentioned, and carry the difference to the account of the Company as profit and loss on exchange, viz. :—

Bengal gold mohurs . . 16½ Company's rupees each.
Half mohurs . . . . Half.
Quarter mohurs . . . Quarter.
Koorzat . . . . . 16 Company's rupees and 12 cash.

I have, &c.,

ARTHUR WELLESLEY.

To Major Elliott.   [1241.]

MY DEAR ELLIOTT,   Seringapatam, 21st Aug., 1802.

I have received your letter of the 18th instant, and I recommend you to dispose of the purchase money as you propose, viz., to lodge the money in the hands of Messrs. Harington and Co., for which you will take their bond at 10 per cent. in triplicate, payable in one year to Captain Gaff, for the use of Lieutenant-Colonel Shee or his attorneys, or Major Crawford, according to the decision of His Majesty regarding the sale of Lieutenant-Colonel Shee's Majority.

One copy of this bond ought to be lodged in the hands of Captain Gaff, one in the hands of Major Crawford, and one in the hands of Mr. Cochrane as Lieutenant - Colonel Shee's attorney.

Quin has sent to Captain Gaff a statement of the claim of Lieutenant Tew against Lieutenant-Colonel Shee. The Articles of War do not give interest on sums belonging to deceased officers lodged in the hands of the Major of the regiment, and therefore interest cannot be demanded by the friends of these officers on the sums due to them.

It will be necessary that these sums should be lodged in the hands of Harington in a manner different from that in which the other part of the purchase money will.

The bond for these sums ought to be made payable to Captain Gaff for the use either of Major Crawford if His Majesty should not approve of his promotion, or for the use of

T 2

the friends of Lieutenant Fitzgerald and of Lieutenant Tew respectively if His Majesty should approve of the promotion; and it should be particularly specified in the bond that Lieutenant-Colonel Shee, as Major of the 33rd regiment, had taken possession of the property of those officers deceased, of which property these sums were the repayment.

Believe me, &c.,

ARTHUR WELLESLEY.

[1242.] *To the Officers commanding Chittledroog, Paughur, Nundydroog; to be communicated to those commanding Mudgherry, Mergasie, and Goorybunda.*

SIR,   21st Aug., 1802.

The Deputy-Adjutant-General will already have acquainted you with my intention to visit the station under your command in a short time, and he will hereafter make you acquainted with the exact period of my arrival.   In the mean time there are certain points which I am about to detail regarding the situation of the fortress under your command, into which I propose to inspect minutely, and I have to request you to be prepared with all the information in your power.

First. Regarding the works of the fort, you will be prepared—

1st. With a report upon the exact state of the works of the fort under your command; distinguishing those of the upper from those of the lower fort, with a statement of the materials of which those works are constructed.   To this report you will add your remarks upon the advantage or the disadvantage of the present works for the defence of the fort.

2nd. I should wish to have your opinion regarding the most practicable mode of improving the defences of the fort under your command.   In giving this opinion you will attend as much as may be practicable to the following points:—1st. To reduce the works as much as possible without weakening the defences of the fort; 2ndly. To the improvement of the communication for troops, the transportation of ordnance and stores and provisions not only from one part of each line to another, but from one line to the others; 3rdly. To the remedying of such glaring defects in the fortifications, the existence of which may be dangerous to the fort; to supply the deficiencies of the means of giving flanking fire, and to obtain the necessary degree of strength and security. 4thly. I wish you to examine particularly those parts of the upper fort which are deemed inaccessible, and therefore but slenderly or not at all fortified. You will report your opinion regarding the fact whether the fort is or is not accessible at such points.

Secondly. Regarding the ordnance on the works in the fort under your command, you will be prepared—

1st. With a return stating the number, description, and state of such ordnance, and a detail stating in what places it is situated.

2ndly. I should wish to have your opinion regarding the sufficiency of that ordnance for the defence of the fort, and of its deficiency. In giving this opinion I request you to consider whether light guns may not be preferable to heavy in many situations; and you will be so kind as to report particularly in what situations, on account of the abrupt steepness of the rock, the aid of depressing carriages would be desirable.

Thirdly. Regarding the possibility of using the fort under your command as a depôt of military stores and provisions, I request you to be prepared—

1st. With a report stating the number, size, description, and state of repair of the buildings in the fort under your command applicable to containing ordnance, military stores, powder, grain, and provisions respectively. In this report you will specify whether such buildings are in the upper or the lower fort; and if in the upper, you will state your opinion regarding the mode of communicating with them; whether it would be practicable to make a road to them for the use of bullocks or coolies, without injuring the strength of the work; and if that should not be practicable, whether it would be so to construct a simple machinery by means of which it would be possible to lodge and draw from such buildings the grain or stores as might be necessary. 2ndly. You will report the repairs necessary to these buildings, applicable to containing ordnance and military stores, grain, and provisions.

Fourthly. Regarding the garrison, you will be prepared with a report, stating, 1st. Your opinion regarding the number of troops necessary for the defence of the fort in case it should be attacked; 2ndly. You will report the description, state of repair, size, and number of the buildings in the fort applicable to the convenience of the troops, whether as barracks or hospital for Europeans ; barracks, hospital, or place of arms for natives, garrison guard rooms, &c. &c. In this report you will specify where each building is situated. 3rdly. You will report your opinion of the repairs necessary to the buildings detailed in the second article of this fourth head.

Fifthly. Regarding the stores at present in the fort, you will be prepared—

1st. With an accurate return of the description, number, state of the ordnance, and military stores in the fort under your command on the 1st of the month in which you will give in these reports.

2ndly. With an accurate return of the grain and provisions, dry and wet, on the same day.

Sixthly. Regarding the materials for building, and those for the construction of ordnance and military stores, you will be prepared with a report—

1st. Stating the quantities of store materials in store in the fort under your command applicable to store purposes respectively.

2ndly. The nature and quantities of materials for buildings found in the neighbourhood of the fort, in old or useless buildings.

3rdly. The price of materials for the construction of buildings, ordnance and military stores at the place under your command.

4thly. The distance from the fort under your command of the place or places at which such materials are found. The mode in which they are brought from such place, and the expense attending their transportation.

Seventhly. Regarding the workmen to be procured at the place under your command. You will be so kind as to report whether workmen can be procured there in any large numbers, the prices of their labour, distinguishing them as artificers and coolies.

Eighthly. You will be prepared with a report of the mode in which the fort is supplied with water, the number of reservoirs, where situated, and in what manner constructed, and if they contain water at all seasons.

You will be so kind as to ascertain whether all the different works in the fort under your command, such as bastions, redoubts, batteries, cavaliers, &c. &c., have names or numbers; and if they have, you will announce such names in the garrison orderly book as being the invariable names or numbers of such works. You will be so kind as to number such works as have not at present any name or number, and you will announce such number in the garrison orderly book, and you will have it marked in conspicuous figures on the work to which it will be assigned.

The magazines, the grain and provision and ordnance store-rooms, if not already named or numbered, should be numbered in like manner.

In the examination of the works, buildings, ordnance and stores, &c. &c., upon which I have above informed you that I shall require reports, I leave it to your discretion either to assemble committees to make this examination and to frame the reports, or to do it alone.

I have, &c.,

ARTHUR WELLESLEY.

To W. H. Gordon, Esq.   [1243.]

SIR,   Seringapatam, 22nd Aug., 1802.

I have received your letter of the 21st, and am concerned that I do not understand the nature of the return called for by the Paymaster-General, as far as it concerns Native officers invalided or pensioned.

I should wish to know whether it means a list of the names only of Native officers invalided and pensioned residing at Seringapatam, or whether to this list is to be added a specification whether they hold commissions from government, or whether it means a list of the names of the Native officers who have been invalided and pensioned from corps in this garrison, with such specification.

If the last return should be what is wished for, it will be necessary that you should inform me to what number of years past the return is to refer. I have ordered the return required from the corps now in this garrison.

I have, &c.,

ARTHUR WELLESLEY.

[1244.]   *To Mr. —— ——.*

DEAR SIR,   Seringapatam, 23rd Aug., 1802.

Since I had the pleasure of hearing from you, I have made inquiries respecting you with a view to obtaining your appointment to a corps; and I am concerned to find that the commanding officer of Chingleput has thought it necessary again to report that you are unfit for the service, although he has very lately reported a number of gentlemen to be fit for it who have not been so long at Chingleput as you have.

I have not the pleasure of being acquainted with Captain Bosc, but he is well spoken of in the army; and it is not to be supposed, and will never be believed, that a person who could be capable of doing a gentleman the injustice to keep him at Chingleput under instruction, and from the service, for no reason whatever, would have been appointed by the Commander-in-Chief to the situation which he fills. It is much more consistent with probability that he detains you at that place, and does not make a report in your favour, because you don't deserve it; and under these circumstances I shall take the liberty of writing you a few lines by way of advice. You will impute it to my respect for your father and your relations, and for the recommendation of my brother, and my sincere desire to render you service.

By coming to India as a cadet you have entered into a profession in which obedience to your superiors is essentially necessary. I am not acquainted with the system of education for the military profession adopted at Chingleput, but as I observe that gentlemen are reported to be qualified for the service in a very short time after their arrival in India, it must be confined to learning the common duties of a soldier, and the principles of subordination and obedience: these are not very difficult, and every gentleman who goes to Chingleput soon learns them, excepting yourself. Surely there must be some cause for your backwardness besides your inexperience, which I observe must operate nearly in an equal proportion against every gentleman who goes there.

I most earnestly entreat you to be obedient to the officer placed over you, attentive to the instructions which he will give you, and to conciliate him by the regularity of your conduct. Consider the impression which will be made of your character and capacity on those who are not acquainted with you, and of your want of diligence and attention on your father and those who know you, when they hear that you alone of so many have been twice reported unfit for military service in this country, from having been incapable of learning even its rudiments at Chingleput, of which all others have easily attained a competent knowledge.

I have taken measures to have you recommended to Captain Bosc, and I hope soon to hear an account of you far different from any that have yet reached me.

Believe me, &c.,

ARTHUR WELLESLEY.

To the Secretary of the Military Board.   [1245.]

SIR,   Seringapatam, 24th Aug., 1802.

I have the honour to enclose a letter which I have received from Mr. Gordon, which having induced me to order that the granaries might be surveyed, I found that the tiles have been broken in many places, and many have been blown away. There is besides a defect in the construction of the roofs on these granaries, viz., that the bamboos under the tiles are at too great a distance from each other.

Before I recommend that these roofs should be repaired, it is necessary that I should be made acquainted with the sentiments of the Military Board regarding the grain which the buildings contain. In consequence of the orders of the Military Board of the 6th of April, I consulted with persons at this place most likely to have a knowledge of the subject regarding the best mode of disposing of this grain, and the result of my inquiries was an opinion, first, that as the grain had been kept so long in store after the 4th of May, 1799, it was much injured in quality, and its real value diminished; secondly, that the price of grain in April last was nearly half what it was in the year 1799; and thirdly, that the greatest part of this grain would not sell at all, and that which would sell would bring but a small price.

In April, however, there was an appearance of irregularity in the monsoon, and it was imagined that the price of all kinds of grain, and of course of this, would rise. But there is now every appearance of an abundant harvest, and I am convinced that the price of grain in the next season will be lower than it is in this.

There is certainly a great part of this grain which will never be purchased; I doubt whether it would be carried away if given to the people, and it is not worth the expense of new roofing the buildings in which it is contained. A part of it is better, and may be worth something. As to the first, as it will sell for nothing, I should recommend that it may be given away or destroyed; that the best of the granaries should be applied to the preservation of the best of the grain, and that these should be put in a state of complete repair. Such a number of them only ought to be kept as granaries as would be necessary to contain the grain which the Military Board might think proper to keep in store at Seringapatam, and the remainder ought either to be pulled down or to be applied to other purposes.

As the state of the season at present promises an abundant harvest, I have desired that the sale of that grain which will bring a price may be recommenced; and if I should find an opportunity of disposing of any large quantity of it, I propose to do so under the orders of the Military Board of the 6th April.

I have, &c.,

ARTHUR WELLESLEY.

[1246.]   *To Captain Greenly.*

SIR,   Seringapatam, 25th Aug., 1802.

I have had the honour to receive your letter of the 25th, enclosing bills to which you have desired my counter-signature. I perfectly recollect that you sent a number of bullocks loaded with arrack from Hullihall to the camp at Hoobly, in the month of October, 1800, by my order; I do not recollect the number of bullocks, nor the number of days they were employed on this service; but the distance was not more than thirty miles.

Under the regulations of the government of Fort St. George you ought to have indented upon the Paymaster's office for these bullocks, and the Paymaster, as garrison store-keeper, ought to have incurred all the charges stated in the bill, with the hire of these bullocks. But as government are always willing to listen to a just demand when it appears clearly that the charge was incurred, I make no doubt but that these charges will be admitted, if supported by the proper vouchers, such as receipts of the people employed, certificates that the bullocks were employed the length of time charged, &c. &c., and that the irregularity of not indenting upon the Paymaster may be passed over.

You had nothing to do with a charge of bullocks for the 1st of the 4th. If you thought it necessary to order that the bullocks should be retained in the service, the person in charge of the corps, or the person who furnished the cattle, ought to send in the bill for their hire, supported by your order as a voucher, for the necessity of which you would be responsible.

The bill for the removal of stores from Soopah ought to be settled in the same manner as that for the carriage of arrack to the army. The pay office ought to have furnished the coolies or cattle upon your indent if the stores were military, or upon that of the garrison store-keeper if they were provision.

I know nothing about the Canarese interpreter; I never authorised one, and never knew that you had one.

I have, &c.,

ARTHUR WELLESLEY.

To Lieutenant-Colonel Montresor.   [1247.]

MY DEAR COLONEL,   Seringapatam, 26th Aug., 1802.

I have had the pleasure of receiving your letter of the 5th, and I am glad to find that I have a chance of succeeding in my object to get you in Malabar. I write to General Stuart upon the subject this day. You will be disappointed in your expectations of finding the division of the 80th under Lieutenant-Colonel Ford at Madras, as I hear that he sailed for Bengal some time ago. That, however, I should imagine, will make no difference in the final destination of the regiment.

I have no hopes of being able to go to Calcutta. My hands are full of business, and from this time till March my time is allotted to the inspection of corps and stations in all parts of my extensive division.

I will write to you as soon as I hear from General Stuart in answer to my letter of this day.

Believe me, &c.,

ARTHUR WELLESLEY.

[1248.]   *To Lieutenant-General Stuart.*   .

SIR,   Seringapatam, 28th Aug., 1802.

I have received a letter from the Secretary of Government, dated the 20th, in which orders are conveyed to me to commence the survey of the forts in Mysore in October, to nominate the members of the committee for this purpose, and to report their names to government. I propose delaying to answer this letter till I shall have received your sentiments upon the proposition which I had the honour to make to you in my letter of the 19th.

In the mean time, I have to mention that the more I consider the nature and extent of the objects proposed for this committee, the more convinced I am that without the previous assistance for which I have asked, I shall not be able to make a report which will even satisfy myself, much less the government. If, however, you should be of opinion that there is no occasion for such assistance, I should wish to begin the work in September, and to lie by in October, in which month and part of November, being those of the monsoon in the Carnatic, we have violent rains in this country.

I have heretofore been in the provinces of Harponelly and Anagoondy, bordering on Mysore, and have many papers and memorandums regarding those countries; I understand also that Captain Mackenzie surveyed a great part of them and the forts in the neighbourhood of the boundary, and I write to him this day for copies of the papers and plans which he has, which may be of use to me in carrying into execution the second part of your instruction.

Since the arrival of Lieutenant-Colonel Montresor in India I have taken an opportunity of informing him of your favourable intentions towards him, if the 80th regiment should be upon this establishment. I have heard from him from Bengal, and he informs me that his regiment is to be here, and I again take the liberty of requesting that he may be placed in the command of Malabar and Canara.   I know no officer more fit for that situation; he is acquainted with the country and the Bombay army, and he has good abilities, activity, and discretion.

I have, &c.,

ARTHUR WELLESLEY.

To Captain Mackenzie.

[1249.]

MY DEAR SIR,   Seringapatam, 28th Aug., 1802.

General Stuart has referred some points to my consideration regarding the frontiers of Mysore, and their connexion with the Ceded Districts, upon which a copy of your survey of the Toombuddra, from Hoonelly to Hurryhur, and to its junction with the Werdah, and of that which you made of the frontier districts of Mysore and of the Ceded Districts, would throw great light. I should also be obliged to you if you would favour me with a copy of your plan of Chittledroog as far as it is complete, and with copies of the plans of other forts which you may have taken either in the Mysore country or in the Ceded Districts, also with copies of any memorandums or papers of remarks which you may have on that part of Mysore and the Ceded Districts.

As the plans and papers are wanted for a public purpose, I have no doubt but that the General will give orders that you may have the assistance of persons from the engineers' office to copy them, if you will be so kind as to apply to him.

Believe me, &c.,

ARTHUR WELLESLEY.

To the Chief Secretary of Government.

[1250.]

SIR,   Seringapatam, 30th Aug., 1802.

I have had the honour of receiving your letter of the 20th instant. I had already requested the consent of the Commander-in-Chief to my taking advantage of the next fair season to visit all the corps and stations under my command in this country and on the coast, and I will certainly pay particular attention to the objects respecting which the Right Hon. the Governor in Council is desirous of receiving a special report.

In the month of October and in the beginning of November, being the time at which the monsoon in general commences on the coast of Coromandel, we have bad weather in this country: I am desirous therefore of lying by at that time; and in order that I may make an early progress in the survey, as well as that I may have time to accomplish the objects I have in view in the course of the fair season, I should wish to be permitted to commence it early in the next month: I shall therefore be obliged to you for an early communication of his Lordship's instructions.

The bad weather does not entirely cease, and it is inconvenient to travel in the Bednore country and on the north-west frontier of Mysore, till towards the end of the year. I should accordingly wish to delay surveying the forts, &c., in those parts till that period, which I must observe will be very convenient to the execution of my other plans.

I beg that Captain Cunningham and Captain Barclay may be the members of the Committee with myself.

I have, &c.,

ARTHUR WELLESLEY.

[1251.]   *To Lieutenant-General Stuart.*

SIR,   Seringapatam, 30th Aug., 1802.

In consequence of the receipt of your letter of the 26th, I have this day written to the Chief Secretary of Government to propose to commence the survey of the forts in Mysore in September, to lie by in that part of October in which we may expect the rains, and to conclude the survey towards the end of the year, when I may expect fine weather on the north-west frontier.

By your letter of the 26th, I perceive that you are aware of the difficulties under which we shall labour in giving a description of the forts which will prove useful: however, no pains shall be spared on my part to render the work as useful as it can be made.

I have proposed to the Chief Secretary of Government that Captain Cunningham and Captain Barclay should be the members of the committee with myself: any addition to the knowledge of these gentlemen on this subject will be very useful not only to me, but may be so to the service.

I have, &c.,

ARTHUR WELLESLEY.

To Lieutenant-Colonel Boles. [1252.]

SIR, Seringapatam, 1st Sept., 1802.

I have perused with great attention the papers which you have given me regarding Lieutenant ——.

It appears that this gentleman, in January last, went into Mr. Torin's house at Mahé, from which, on account of something that passed, of which Lieutenant —— himself gives an account in his letter to you of the 17th of June, he departed, Mr. Torin having desired one of his peons " to show him to the door," and to deliver him his sword, &c., &c. As the transactions upon that occasion became public and the subject of conversation, Lieutenant —— is desirous of being tried by a general court-martial, in order, as he says, to clear his character.

It ought to be understood by the officers of the army that a general court-martial is a tribunal to be assembled for the purpose of trying officers and soldiers for breaches of military discipline and order, and the former for behaviour unbecoming the character of officers and gentlemen. They should also understand that, before this tribunal can proceed to the trial of either officer or soldier, it is necessary that a charge or charges specifying his crimes should be given in against the person to be tried.

It is certainly very desirable that there should be no imputation against the character of any officer; but I conceive that such an imputation, particularly if of guilt of a crime not of a military nature, is not a sufficient reason to assemble a general court-martial in order that it may be removed.

In this particular instance, I observe that the officers of the battalion to which Lieutenant —— belongs, after a consideration of the circumstances of his case, to which they were called by you, do not think that charges against him ought to be preferred. I should think it unnecessary, at all events, to assemble a general court-martial to ascertain what passed at Mr. Torin's, as charges are not given in against Lieutenant ——, even if what passed there were not already sufficiently clear by the letters of Lieutenant —— to you, and of Mr. Torin to Lieutenant ——.   But as Lieutenant —— has acknowledged in his letter to you that he made use of terms which were not unlikely to occasion what afterwards happened, and as Mr. Torin has very explicitly acknowledged that he did order his servant "to show him to the door," &c., &c., I don't see any occasion to assemble a court-martial to give them the trouble of ascertaining facts already so clear; and as for Lieutenant ——'s character, supposing that I was inclined, or that it was possible for me, to assemble a general court-martial in order to remove the imputation under which he says he labours, I cannot see in what manner it could be remedied by anything which could appear before that court-martial.

I have, &c.,

ARTHUR WELLESLEY.

[1253.]   *To the Officer commanding at Sera.*

SIR,   Seringapatam, 1st Sept., 1802.

I shall have occasion to make a report regarding certain matters at Sera, into which I shall examine upon my arrival at that station, and I beg you to be prepared with reports to the following purport :

1st. A report of the exact state of the works of the fort, specifying the materials of which they are constructed.

2ndly. A report of the number, description, and state of the ordnance on the works, and a detail, stating the situations in which it is placed.

3rdly. A report, stating the number, size, description, and state of repair of the buildings at the station under your command applicable to containing ordnance, military stores, grain, and provisions respectively. In this report you will specify whether such buildings are within or without the fort.

4thly. A report stating the number, description, state of repair, and size of the buildings at Sera applicable to the convenience of the troops, such as barracks and hospital for

Europeans or Natives, place of arms or hospital for Natives, guard-rooms, &c., &c. You will specify where such buildings are situated.

5thly. A report, stating the repairs which, in your opinion, are necessary to the buildings alluded to in the 3rd and 4th articles.

6thly. Reports of the ordnance and military stores, grain, and provisions, wet and dry respectively, in store at Sera, exclusive of those articles intended for the use of the regiment under your command.

7thly. A report of the mode in which the fort of Sera is supplied with water, the number of reservoirs, where situated, in what manner constructed, and if they contain water at all seasons. You will be so kind as to ascertain whether all the different works at Sera, such as bastions, redoubts, batteries, cavaliers, &c., &c., have names or numbers, and, if they have, you will announce such names in the garrison orderly-books as being the invariable appellation of such works; if they have not, you will be so kind as to number the works, and you will announce such numbers in the garrison orderly-book, and you will have them marked in conspicuous figures on the works to which they will be assigned.

I have, &c.,

ARTHUR WELLESLEY.

To Lieutenant-Colonel de Meuron Bulôt.   [1254.]

SIR,   Seringapatam, 1st Sept., 1802.

I have had the honour to receive your letter of the 31st of August and its enclosures.

Only two days ago you transmitted a certificate of the bad state of the health of Lieutenant Baron de Müller, which I desired might accompany the general return to headquarters of the regiment under your command. You have now thought proper, notwithstanding the certificate that Lieutenant Baron de Müller is unfit for his duty on account of bad health, to desire that he may have an unlimited leave to remain at Madras in charge of the regimental stores of the regiment de Meuron. I have to observe—1st. That it is not usual to employ officers to take charge of stores at Madras, that duty being always performed by non-commissioned officers; 2ndly. That it is not usual to give officers unlimited leave of absence; 3rdly. That it is not usual to employ upon any duty an officer whose health is certified to be in such a state that he is unable to do duty. For all these reasons I decline to forward your application; and I beg that, if you should think proper to send it yourself, you will transmit with it a copy of this letter.

I have, &c.,

ARTHUR WELLESLEY.

[1255.]   *To Lieutenant-General Stuart.*

SIR,   Seringapatam, 3rd Sept., 1802.

I have the honour to enclose certain papers which Lieutenant-Colonel Boles has delivered to me regarding the Coringot Nair. I likewise send by this post a map of Mahé and its neighbourhood, which will point out exactly the situation of the districts which it is probable the French will claim.

Colonel Boles says the Nair is desirous to become dependent on the French. Indeed this inclination is apparent in the answers which he has given to the questions put to him.

Lieutenant-Colonel Boles is of opinion that the possession of those districts by either party is of no importance in a military point of view, excepting that it will oblige us to use a more circuitous route from Tellicherry to the southward, if given to the French. The new road now goes from Moilan Fort, Odeotecoonah, and *   to Moondaal, and passes through the districts the possession of which is likely to be disputed. The other road will strike off from the high road to Cota-paramba and will run through the Invernaad district, as marked by the dotted line in the plan, and will join the new road at Karie-coonah. The difference of distance will be about three miles, which, if there are bridges over the rivers, will be of immaterial consequence.

If the Company lay open the pepper trade in Malabar, and allow the French to purchase as large a quantity of that article as they wish to have, which will be their interest as sovereigns, the possession of these districts by the French will not be de-

* Blank in manuscript.

trimental to the Company in a commercial point of view; but if they propose to restrict the sale of pepper to the quantity which they can purchase and export, every enlargement of the territory of the French will interfere with this object, and the addition of these districts will do so particularly, as they produce pepper.

I conclude that when Mahé is delivered to the French, a commissioner will come round to give them that which will belong to them, and that he will decide regarding this territory. It does not appear that the possession of the Kooreechy redoubt is of much importance, excepting in this point of view. If the Commissioner should determine that they have no right to the territory of the Coringot Nair, and if they should not acquiesce in this determination, they might throw troops into the redoubt. We should then be reduced to the awkward alternative either to commence hostilities to drive them out, or to submit to their retaining possession of a post thus seized till the two governments in Europe should have decided the question.

Our possession of the redoubt at the time the Commissioner will arrive, if only by a small force, will preclude the possibility of our being reduced to this alternative. If they want it, they must drive out our troops, and this they will not choose to attempt. Although, therefore, it does not appear that the possession of the redoubt will at all influence the question, or will prevent them from collecting the revenues or pepper of the district, I should wish to occupy it, if you should have no objection, by a small force before the orders for the cession of the districts at Mahé can arrive.

I have, &c.,

ARTHUR WELLESLEY.

To Major Macleod.   [1256.]

MY DEAR MACLEOD,   Seringapatam, 3rd Sept., 1802.

It is intended by government to establish at Seringapatam a manufactory for gun-carriages upon a very extended scale, and by their order I have lately contracted with a man, by name Shamiah, to cut teak timber in the forests bordering upon Wynaad. The forests in which he now cuts timber belong to

the Rajah of Mysore; but I understand that in the neighbouring districts belonging to the Company there are some
very fine trees, conveniently situated with respect to the
roads.

It is probable that you do not rent these forests in Wynaad,
as there can be no sale for the timber.   At all events, whether
you do or not, I shall be obliged to you if you will desire the
aumildars, farmers, &c., to give no interruption to Naik Shamiah, who has a contract for cutting timber for the Company's
use.   If you will be so kind as to send me a paper to that
purport, I shall be very much obliged to you.

In consequence of what you mentioned heretofore regarding
the expense of the Bombay pioneers, I made inquiries on the
subject, and I found that besides the pioneers there were about
450 Bombay bigaries, who more than doubled the expense of
the corps.   I have settled with Lieutenant-Colonel Boles, who
is here, that the latter are to be discharged as soon as the
season will allow of their returning to Bombay; and in the
mean time they and the pioneers are to be employed in the
repair of the road from Malabar by the Cootioor pass.

I wish you would take into consideration some mode of
keeping open the principal of the roads which have been made
in Malabar, particularly in Cotiote, with a view to its tranquillity.   These roads were the principal cause of our successful operations; and I acknowledge that I am very anxious that
they should be kept open by cutting the young jungle upon
them annually.   The new system for Malabar and Canara is
to make the troops in those provinces entirely dependent for
their stores on this place, and to keep no more at Cannanore
than is absolutely necessary for their constant and daily consumption.   In order that this system may operate at all with
convenience, it will be necessary that the principal passes should
be practicable if possible for wheel carriages; but we know
that this cannot be unless the roads are repaired annually, and
the labour of the pioneers will be required on those which lead
through the mountains.

We must depend, therefore, on your civil arrangements for
the repair of those roads, which were originally made with a
view to the conquest and settlement of the country, and which
in my opinion are essentially necessary to its peace.

Take this subject into consideration, and let me know the result.

Believe me, &c.,

ARTHUR WELLESLEY.

To the Secretary of the Military Board.   [1257.]

SIR,   Seringapatam, 5th Sept., 1802.

I have the honour to enclose the bill of the contractor for cutting teak timber, for the quantity received in the month of August, for which the receipt is annexed. This receipt corresponds with the register, by which it appears that the greater number of these trees are dry and fit for immediate use.

I was in hopes that the register for the month of August would have contained a larger number of trees than now appear upon it, but I am informed by the conductor that although there are many trees collected in piles and ready for his inspection and measurement, and to be delivered over to him, the weather in the jungles has been so bad that he has not been able to measure, mark, and register them. He gives, however, most favourable accounts of the quantity of timber that is cut, as well as of the general appearance of the timber in the forests.

I have, &c.,

ARTHUR WELLESLEY.

To Lieutenant-General Stuart.   [1258.]

SIR,   Seringapatam, 6th Sept., 1802.

I have the pleasure to inform you that Captain Scott arrived here on the day before yesterday, and I have requested him to begin to build sheds for his working people on two sides of the square which is allotted to the manufactory.

He thinks that they will be completed in a short time, and I expect at a small expense, as I assist him with timber taken from an old building pulled down, and with other advantages in procuring materials. I have desired him to estimate the expense. This will be a cheaper mode by more than half, and a more expeditious one, than to employ the engineer to construct these sheds.

The clearing of this yard has been a very heavy work, and that part of it which is completed has been carried on by the people who were employed to fill the inner ditch of the fort. This work is so nearly finished that I gave orders on the 1st to discharge all the people employed upon it, excepting those absolutely necessary as basket people for the pioneers. The clearing of the remainder of the yard for the manufactory must therefore go on but very slowly, unless you will give permission that some people should be hired to be employed upon it. All the means that I can give to this work cannot complete it in less than six months, but by incurring a small expense it could be done immediately.

That which is to be cleared away is the foundation of large heavy buildings, and the earth and rubbish of buildings which have fallen, and have been pulled down, of the height of from twenty to thirty feet, and of vast extent. In some cases the rubbish has been found to cover heavy and extensive foundations, which has been the cause of my being disappointed in my expectations that the yard would be cleared before now, and is the reason for which no estimate can be framed upon any reasonable grounds of the expense which it will take to clear it.

If you should consent to the incurring this expense, all I can say is, that I will be answerable that every farthing laid out shall have a corresponding quantity of work done; and as I expect a large quantity of good materials for the fort from these foundations, they will be a set off against the expense.

The advantage in clearing the yard immediately will be, that the manufactory will be set agoing at once in proper style, and that time which might be spent in forwarding the objects for which it is established will not be lost in clearing the yard and constructing the necessary buildings.

I enclose a memorandum which I have received from Captain Heitland, which will show the quantity of materials for the fort which have been collected from the works pulled down; these may be valued at one rupee each at least, and would have been entirely lost if that work had not been performed.

I have received your letter of the 2nd instant, and am infinitely obliged to you for your attention to my recommendation of Lieutenant-Colonel Montresor.

I have desired the commissary of stores to give over to Captain Scott one complete company of lascars for the service of the manufactory, as I understand that that establishment has been fixed by the Military Board. These are supernumerary to the establishment for the garrison as lately fixed, and I will report this arrangement to the Military Board.

I have, &c.,

ARTHUR WELLESLEY.

To the Secretary of the Military Board.   [1259.]

SIR,   Seringapatam, 6th Sept., 1802.

I have the honour to enclose an estimate which has been corrected by order of the Military Board. The calculation of. the timber required made by order of the Military Board is upon an erroneous principle, which is caused, I fear, from my having omitted to explain to the Board the general price of timber at Seringapatam.

The common price of timber at Seringapatam is about 10 rupees for a beam of 11 feet in length by 1. This price is made up as follows :—The expense of cutting and paring the tree at the jungles is about 1 rupee, that of the carriage from the jungles to Seringapatam 2½ star pagodas, or about 8½ rupees, and about ½ rupee profit to the merchant. This beam will be green, and cannot be used in that state in the Company's work; dry beams, excepting occasionally, are not to be procured in the bazaar; and it stands to reason that the commissary of supply must have a store of timber, which must add something to the expense of that used in the Company's works.

It is true that the contractor who supplies the Company with timber does so at the rate of 1 fanam and 60 cash per foot; but for this sum he not only cuts and pares it in the jungles, the only operations which would be performed by the Native merchants, but he makes and collects it in piles, in situations accessible to the Company's wheel carriages, which last work alone costs about 60 cash per foot. It is to be observed that this timber is to be brought in upon the Company's carriages, drawn by the Company's cattle; but if it were to be brought in by means for which the Company would be obliged to pay, as the commissary of supply and every Native merchant are, an addition ought to be made to the price of cutting every beam of

11 feet in length of a sum of 2½ pagodas, being the hire of a buffalo bandy to the jungles and back again.

It is also true that the contractor offered to cut and pare timber in the jungles at the rate of about 68 cash per foot. But he had the advantage of a large contract to cut 5000 trees, which would have enabled him to afford to cut the timber at 12 cash per foot cheaper than the common merchant does.

It appears to me that the corrected calculation in the estimate which is enclosed is founded upon a notion that the commissary of supply could procure the timber at the rate at which it could be cut in the jungles, which is erroneous, as it is obvious that he must pay for the carriage from the jungles, and the profit to the Native merchant whom he may employ to procure it for him; and that he must besides incur expense in order that the timber which he will use in the Company's works may be seasoned. I trust, therefore, that the Military Board will see the propriety of directing that the corrected calculation in the estimate may be altered.

I have, &c.,

ARTHUR WELLESLEY.

[1260.] G. O.   Seringapatam, 6th Sept., 1802.

Colonel Wellesley has heard with much concern that, in some instances, the officers of the army in the provinces below the Ghauts, particularly officers of the junior ranks, and who have been but a short time in the country, have beaten the Natives of the country, whether in their service or employed by them, or generally followers of the troops, or residents of the place at which such officers are stationed. The practice is very irregular and illegal, and, if not speedily put a stop to, will tend to the material inconvenience and injury of the troops. In this country, any more than in England, no man has a right to take the law into his own hand, or to punish another for an offence or injury done to himself. There are magistrates, who have full authority to decide in every case which can occur, and to whom, if necessary, complaint ought to be made. Colonel Wellesley therefore prohibits this practice entirely, and desires that the officers commanding in Malabar and Canara, and those commanding stations and corps, will report to him any instances of the kind that may occur in future.

ARTHUR WELLESLEY.

To W. Richardson, Esq.   [1261.]

SIR,   Seringapatam, 7th Sept., 1802.

I have had the honour of receiving your letter of the 1st instant on the subject of a complaint which you imagine that Captain Bentley will have made to me regarding the payment of money by you to him. Captain Bentley has written to me upon the subject to which you allude, and I have written my sentiments regarding it to Lieutenant-Colonel Boles, who has returned to Malabar.

I beg to inform you that Captain Bentley never hinted in the most distant manner that you had received coins at one rate and issued them to him at another. The subject of his complaint was, that you had issued him a sum of money in coins not current at Cannanore, the place at which the expenditure is made in the department of which he is the head. Upon this complaint I have to observe, that it is the duty of the paymaster to allot the coins which he may receive in such a manner as that each body of troops or department may be paid in the coins which are current at the place at which it may be stationed, and that you ought to have paid Captain Bentley in the coins avowedly current at Cannanore, which you had lately received from Mr. Harvey. When Captain Bentley found that he could not pass the coins which he had received from you at all in some instances, or in any excepting at a great loss, he applied to you to exchange them for others, in the expenditure of which he would not experience such inconvenience. In answer to this application, you informed him that you could not be responsible for coins that had been taken away from your office; that they might or might not be the same you had paid, and that you had no great confidence in the honour of a cooly. Upon this reply I have to observe, that under the regulations it was your duty to have noted at the back of the bill, or abstract, the coins in which you discharged it and the rate at which you issued them. But even if you had omitted it, the sum you paid Captain Bentley was 1500 rupees, of which only 45 rupees had been in the hands of coolies; and I think that it would not have been inconsistent with the forms of business to trust Captain Bentley so far as to believe that the remaining coins of which he complained were the same that he received at your office. I have accordingly desired Lieutenant-Colonel Boles to call upon you for a return of the sums of money in your possession, specifying in what coins; and if he should find you have a sufficient sum in coins current at Cannanore to defray the demand of Captain Bentley, to request that you will issue them to him and receive back those the value of which is disputed. In future I beg that you will take care to pay each corps, department, and individual in the coins which are current at the place at which they are stationed.

Upon this point a question arises, upon which I have no difficulty in giving you my opinion; it is, what is to be done with the coins which you will receive back from Captain Bentley, or with others of the same kind which you may receive from time to time from the collectors of the revenue? Let them be issued to the troops stationed at those places in which they are current. It is probable that the collectors pay them to you at the rate of exchange at which they receive them from the ryots, and the troops can suffer no hardship if they receive their pay, and the ryots and people of the country none if they are paid by the troops for the provisions and other articles of their consumption, in the coins and at the rate of exchange at which the revenue is received by the collectors. The object is, that you should ascertain at what place each coin is current, which cannot be a matter of much difficulty. But it may happen that you will receive coins from the collectors or from other quarters which are not current in Malabar, or at rates of exchange at which they will not pass. In either of these cases it will be necessary that you should apply to the collector (in the police department) to remedy this inconvenience, or to receive back the coins, as you have already done, I observe, in this instance of Captain Bentley's; and if the inconvenience cannot be remedied in that manner, it will be necessary that you should apply to government.

I observe that you reside at Tellicherry; the largest body of troops in Malabar, and the head quarters, will always be at Cannanore; and your residence, even at a small distance from thence, must be highly inconvenient to yourself and the commanding officer, and to the army in general.   I have, therefore, desired Lieutenant-Colonel Boles to recommend you to remove to Cannanore as soon as you can without inconvenience.

I have, &c.,

Arthur Wellesley.

To Lieutenant-Colonel Boles.   [1262.]

Sir,   Seringapatam,   Sept., 1802.

I have the honour to enclose copies of papers which I have received from Captain Bentley upon the subject of certain coins which he has received from the paymaster in Malabar.

The subject of complaint is, that Mr. Richardson had paid him in coins not current at Cannanore, of some of which indeed it is doubtful whether they are current in any part of Malabar.   It is the duty of the paymaster to allot the coins which he may receive for the payment of the troops in such manner as that the troops at each station may be paid in those coins which are current at it; and accordingly Mr. Richardson ought to have paid Captain Bentley in the coins which he received from Mr. Harvey, the collector at Cannanore.   You will be so kind as to see that Mr. Richardson performs this part of his duty in future.

In the course of the discussion between Mr. Richardson and Captain Bentley upon this first subject of complaint, other matters have come out which call for my animadversion.   It appears by Mr. Richardson's letter, No. 2, that he is doubtful whether the coins in question were or were not taken from his office.   In the first place, I beg that he may be reminded that when he pays a bill or abstract, he is obliged to see that an endorsement is made at the back of it, stating the coins in which it is paid, and their rate of exchange.   If he had performed this duty, he could have had no doubt whether or not the coins in question were issued from his office.

In the next place, I observe that he paid Captain Bentley 1500 rupees, of which sum Captain Bentley paid to the coolies 45 rupees.   The honour of the coolies, therefore, could apply only to the latter, and I conceive that, without calling upon Mr. Richardson for any extraordinary stretch of confidence in Captain Bentley, it might have been believed that he had not exchanged the coins which he had received at the pay-office. You will be so kind as to require from Mr. Richardson a return of the sums of money he has in his hands, specifying in what coins. If he should have at present in his hands a sufficient sum in coins current at Cannanore to discharge Captain Bentley's demand, you will give orders that it may be discharged in such coins, those already paid being received back into the Treasury; and in future care must be taken that the troops are paid in those coins which are current in the place at which each body of them is stationed.

I observe that Mr. Richardson resides at Tellicherry. In the constant intercourse which ought to take place between the commanding officer in Malabar and the paymaster, his residence at such a distance from head-quarters, and at a place where there are no troops nor any garrison stores, must be very inconvenient to you, to him, and to the army in general. You will therefore recommend him to move to Cannanore, where the largest body of the troops' and the head-quarters are stationed, and you will request him to make his arrangements for that purpose without loss of time.

I have, &c.,

ARTHUR WELLESLEY.

[1263.]   *To Lieutenant-Colonel Boles.*

SIR,   Seringapatam, 9th Sept., 1802.

I have the honour to enclose an extract of the proceedings of a general court-martial on the trial of Captain ————, of the Bombay European regiment, by which it appears that certain irregularities have existed in the detachment of that corps stationed at Cannanore. This extract is taken from the written defence of the prisoner, and of course its contents want confirmation; but I am not desirous that any farther inquiry should be made into the subject. All I wish is, that you should pay particular attention to that detachment of the Bombay European regiment, and whatever abuses have or have not occurred, you should take measures to prevent their occurrence in future.

I have, &c.,

ARTHUR WELLESLEY.

G. O. Seringapatam, 10th Sept., 1802. [1264.]

Colonel Wellesley has received a report from Lieutenant-Colonel Brown, commanding at Hullihall, dated the 5th instant, upon the subject of the conduct of certain officers of the 1st battalion —— Bombay regiment, regarding a baker at Hullihall, which appears to him so extraordinary as to require this public mode of expressing his sentiments upon it.

It appears that Ensign ———, of the 1st battalion —— regiment, beat the baker of the place, in consequence of which Lieutenant-Colonel Brown issued an order to prohibit all officers and soldiers under his command from molesting the inhabitants of Hullihall in any manner. Colonel Wellesley entirely approves of that order issued by Lieutenant-Colonel Brown, and desires that he will see it carried into execution, and put in arrest and report to him the name of any officer who disobeys it.

In consequence of the beating given to this baker, or for some other reason, it appears that he does not choose to bake any longer at Hullihall, and that he quits the place and proceeds to Goa. Some of the officers of the 1st battalion —— regiment then write letters to Lieutenant-Colonel Brown to complain that they have not bread for their breakfasts, and others wait upon him to make similar complaints, having omitted to put on their side arms.

The officers of the 1st battalion —— regiment must be informed, 1st, that Lieutenant-Colonel Brown is by no means obliged to find a baker to bake bread for them; 2ndly, that, living in the same fort with their commanding officer, it is their duty to wait upon him, to make their complaints known to him, and not to write to him upon all these trifling occasions; and 3rdly, that, if they should find it necessary to wait upon him, or even to quit their quarters at all, the standing orders of this army, and the customs of every military service, require that they should wear their side arms.

Colonel Wellesley likewise calls the attention of Lieutenant-Colonel Brown to these orders; and he is astonished that Lieutenant-Colonel Brown should have passed unnoticed so extraordinary an instance of the disobedience of them as that which he reports in his letter of the 5th instant.

By the papers transmitted with Lieutenant-Colonel Brown's

letter of the 5th instant, Colonel Wellesley observes that Lieutenant ——— and Ensign ———, being officers of the day, reported that the " garrison is distressed," and " in great distress," for want of bread.   Colonel Wellesley desires that Lieutenant-Colonel Brown will make him acquainted with the orders for the duty of the officer of the day at Hullihall, particularly mentioning whether the state of the provisions in the bazaar of Hullihall comes under the cognizance of that officer.

ARTHUR WELLESLEY.

[1265.]   *To Lieutenant-Colonel de Meuron.*

SIR,   Seringapatam, 11th Sept., 1802.

Being about to depart from Seringapatam on a tour of inspection, the command of the garrison will devolve upon you.   Upon this occasion I have nothing to instruct you with excepting to draw your attention to those letters which I wrote to you on the 13th November and 5th of January last, when I left the garrison, of which I enclose copies.

I have, however, to apprise you that Lieutenant Knox at present conducts the department heretofore intrusted to Major Symons, during the absence of the latter, and I request for him the same countenance and assistance that I before asked for Major Symons.

The officers in charge of works, &c., have my directions how to proceed in the conduct of them.

I have, &c.,

ARTHUR WELLESLEY.

[1266.]   *To Captain Scott.*

MY DEAR SIR,   Gundessy, 13th Sept., 1802.

I have desired Captain Barclay to write orders to Mr. Adams and Shamiah to cut all the trees which may be felled hereafter, of the length of 24 feet and upwards, into two pieces.

This order will not apply to those trees felled at present, in number 2000.   They must be received in the state in which they are, as we could not force Shamiah to cut them again without putting him to an expense not provided for by the contract, and not in contemplation when it was entered into, and we could not cut them ourselves without incurring an expense and taking trouble of the extent of which we are not aware.

I have also desired Mr. Adams and Shamiah to consider themselves under your orders, and to obey all they may receive from you, without any reference to me. I shall be obliged to you if you will let me know what orders you may think it necessary to give to either, and if you will take care that they are not inconsistent with my instructions to the former and the contract with the latter.

Believe me, &c.,

ARTHUR WELLESLEY.

To Lieutenant-Colonel Boles.   [1267.]

SIR,   Banawoor, 14th Sept., 1802.

By desire of the Commander-in-Chief, I have to request that you will give directions that all the bigaries attached to the corps of Bombay pioneers in Malabar may be discharged from the service as soon as the state of the season will permit them to return to Bombay.

In the first instance, however, the corps of pioneers must be inspected, and such men must be discharged from it as are unfit for the service. The vacancies which this arrangement will occasion in the corps of Bombay pioneers are to be filled up by such of the bigaries as choose to enlist, and thus the corps is to be completed to its regulated establishment.

The remainder of the bigaries are then to be mustered, as well as the discharged pioneers, and each man, bigary and pioneer, who may be returning to Bombay, is to receive the sum which it has been usual to give to this description of persons in Malabar, when they have been dismissed from the service, in order to enable them to return to their homes. Care must be taken, however, that this indulgence is not extended to those bigaries or pioneers who belong to the province of Malabar, or who intend to reside there hereafter.

I have, &c.,

ARTHUR WELLESLEY.

To Captain Heitland.

MY DEAR SIR,   Adjampoor, 16th Sept., 1802.

I have received a letter from General Stuart upon the subject of clearing the yard of the gun-carriage manufactory, which renders it necessary that I should ask for your assistance in procuring the information which he requires upon that subject. I wish that you would be so kind as to examine the yard minutely, and have some of the large mounds of earth probed in order to endeavour to find out of what they are composed, whether of earth only, or of earth and stone, and of what proportions of each. My opinion is, that some of those foundations are not so heavy as they appear. The common way of building among the natives is to have a foundation and buildings on each of the four sides of a square, which is itself not raised higher than the general level of the ground; and if these foundations are those of such buildings, all the centre part will be earth only.

Having ascertained, as nearly as you can, the nature of the work to be performed, I wish you to consider whether you could use carts in removing any part of the earth and rubbish in the yard, and if you could, to what extent? whether to the extent of eighty carts?

I wish you then to endeavour to form an estimate of the number of men who would be able to clear the yard in a month, or if you think you could perform the work to greater advantage by allotting more time to it, and by the employment of fewer people, in six weeks or in two months, with the assistance of carts if you think you can use them, or without them if you think you cannot.

In this estimate I wish you to distinguish the number of commatties you will require, and the number of basket coolies of the different descriptions; and when I come to make the statement of the expense to be incurred to the General, I will subtract from the number of commatties demanded by you the number of pioneers who can be spared from other work for this purpose at the time it will be undertaken. In the mean time I beg you to go on with the work as you were when I quitted Seringapatam.

I wish you would call upon the engineer in my name to point out to you such stones in the yard as he thinks will never be of any use to the Company in the repair or reform of the fort, or in the repairs of buildings occupied by the troops, &c., such as square bottoms of pillars, long flat stones, &c., &c. If he should declare that they will be of no use, I beg you to inform Bajee Rao that you have my direction to deliver them over to him for the use of the Rajah's government, and that I request they will send people forthwith to carry them away from the yard, which I am desirous of clearing without loss of time. If Bajee Rao should consent to carry away the stones in question, I beg you to make all the arrangements for delivering them to his people when he will send them to take them away.

I beg you to communicate this letter to Captain Scott, and request his assistance in framing the estimate which I have required from you.

Believe me, &c.,

ARTHUR WELLESLEY.

To the Adjutant-General. [1269.]

SIR,   Malwajee, 17th Sept., 1802.

I have the honour to enclose the copy of a letter which I have received from Captain Mackay upon the subject of the Honourable Company's cattle, which I request you to lay before the Commander-in-Chief.

The carriage-cattle at present in the service are certainly, with very few exceptions, entirely useless, and ought to be disposed of, as proposed by Captain Mackay.

If an establishment of carriage-cattle be required, as soon as the numbers of it are fixed, it would be proper to transfer to the karkhanas of carriage-bullocks those draught-cattle mentioned by Captain Mackay as being too small for the draught, as soon as they will have been inspected by a committee of artillery officers and rejected for the draught. Those karkhanas of carriage-cattle might be kept complete by adding to them those calves received from the Dewan which may not grow to the proper size for draught-bullocks.

If an establishment of carriage-cattle should not be thought necessary, the sooner those now in the service are disposed of and their attendants discharged the better.

I do not agree in opinion with Captain Mackay that every bullock not thought fit for field service by a committee of artillery officers ought to be disposed of, particularly as Captain Mackay is of opinion that the attendants of all the karkhanas ought to be kept, as in case they should be wanted they cannot be collected again.

Bullocks are wanted for many departments in the field besides for drawing the train; and those of an inferior size, age, and strength, which would be rejected by the officers of artillery, would answer well for these departments. Those bullocks which will not answer for field service at all, will perform many other services for which draught-cattle are required, in the performance of which they are not likely to meet the hardships which they would in the field with the troops.

The question upon this point is, whether it is proper to keep up the attendants of forty-three karkhanas of draught-bullocks. I agree entirely in opinion with Captain Mackay that if they are once discharged, they are lost to the service; and that as the whole of them are useful people, who cannot be replaced and whose expense is trifling, they ought to be kept. The expense, however, of the bullocks in the Mysore country consists almost entirely in their attendants; their feed does not cost a rupee a month: and therefore I am of opinion that, as long as the number of servants is complete, and the number of bullocks incomplete, every bullock ought to be kept which can do work of any kind.

I agree in opinion with Captain Mackay that the calves received from the Sircar are too young; they ought not to be received before they are three years old; and if the Commander-in-Chief should wish it, I will make arrangements accordingly with the Resident.

In the last year the number of calves received from the Sircar was nearly 550. They were all produced to me at Seringapatam, and they were very fine cattle, and of the true breed; and I have no doubt but that hereafter the supply will be equal to the demand stated by Captain Mackay in the enclosed letter.

I have, &c.,

ARTHUR WELLESLEY.

[1270.]   *To Lieutenant-General Stuart.*

SIR,   Malwajee, 17th Sept., 1802.

I have the honour to enclose the copy of a letter from Captain Johnson, which I have received from Lieutenant-Colonel Boles, relative to some guns at Goa.   If you should approve of it, I will order not only that the guns and the stores mentioned by Captain Johnson may be moved from Goa to Hullihall when Goa will be evacuated by the British troops, but also that all the stores at Goa may be moved there, particularly those which I think will be useful at Hullihall.   As, however, the evacuation of Goa at the peace is not a matter of course, and a body of our troops may still be left there, I imagine that it will not be proper to do more at present, or till the evacuation, than to take all the preparatory steps to remove the stores, and to make the arrangements for receiving them at Hullihall.

There are bullocks at Goa which can move these guns whenever you please; and I write this day to Captain Johnson to desire that he will examine and report upon the road by which he proposes that they should come to Hullihall, and that he will send me a plan and estimate of the expense of the platform on which he thinks of moving them.

I send this day to the Adjutant-General a letter from Captain Mackay upon the subject of the gun-bullocks, &c.   In drawing your attention to this subject, I take the liberty of mentioning one connected therewith, for which I have to apologize, as the elephants to which it relates are no longer under my superintendence.   By the tent regulations, I observe that they are attached to the European regiments, and the Military Board have lately ordered that they should be detached to the places in which the regiments are stationed.

I know the people who have charge of them perfectly well, and I assure you that they are not to be trusted in the care of these valuable animals without European superintendence.   I have worked them more probably than any officer in the army, and I never saw them out of condition when they were under the eye of the agent; but whenever they have been detached they have fallen off in condition, and some have died, and frequent instances of frauds and thefts in feeding them have been discovered.

I therefore take the liberty of recommending to you that they should be placed under the immediate care of the quartermasters of the regiments, and that the attention of the commanding-officers should be called to the state of their condition.   It will in some cases perhaps be impossible that they should be kept in the place with the regiment to which they are attached; but it

x 2

will scarcely be necessary that they should be detached to a greater distance than twenty miles, and the quartermaster ought to see them constantly.

I have had the honour of receiving your letter of the 11th instant. I have proposed to Captain Heitland a mode of clearing the gun-carriage yard which I trust will effect that object at a small expense, and one of estimating the expense which I hope will be correct, and I will have the honour of addressing you again upon this subject as soon as I shall have heard from him.

I have, &c.,

ARTHUR WELLESLEY.

[1271.]   *To Captain Johnson.*

SIR,   Malwajee, 17th Sept., 1802.

Lieutenant-Colonel Boles has sent me a letter which you have written to him, in which you propose that certain guns and stores now at Goa should be removed to Hullihall. I shall be obliged to you if you will be so kind as to send me a report, stating in what manner you propose to move these guns and stores, whether they can be moved any part of the way by water, how far, and where they will be landed, and the nature of the road from the landing-place, whether it will require repair, &c. &c. The guns, however, are not to be moved, nor the stores, till I send farther orders upon the subject, after receiving this report.

I observe that you propose to Lieutenant-Colonel Boles to construct a travelling platform for the purpose of transporting these guns. I beg to hear from you whether these guns have limbers, and whether limbers could be used in moving them. I also wish that you would send me a plan and estimate of the expense of constructing the platform by means of which you propose to move these guns.

I have, &c.,

ARTHUR WELLESLEY.

[1272.]   *To the Secretary of the Military Board.*

SIR,   Santa Bednore, 19th Sept., 1802.

I have to inform you that I gave orders that the choultry at this place, which I reported to be capable of being converted into a storehouse for a regiment of cavalry, should have the additions made to it stated to be necessary by the committee whose proceedings I heretofore transmitted to you, according to the estimate of the expense of those additions given in by the aumildar. These additions are now nearly completed, and as soon as they will be complete the building will be surveyed by a committee, according to the regulations, and I will have the honour of transmitting their report, to be laid before the Military Board.

The commanding officer of the 5th regiment of cavalry at this station has represented the want of stabling for sick horses; and as there is reason to expect some very severe weather in the course of the next two months, I have requested the aumildar to prepare an estimate of the expense of constructing, of temporary materials, stabling for thirty horses, which is deemed sufficient, and to commence immediately to collect the materials for this building. I will transmit the estimate when I receive it, and I trust this order will be approved in consideration of the pressing want of a stable immediately, and of the loss of horses which the Company would sustain if it were not built.

I have to inform the Military Board that, excepting stabling, I have found at this station complete accommodation for a regiment of cavalry, built by Lieutenant-Colonel Macalister. But I conclude that he will address the Board upon this subject.

I have, &c.,

Arthur Wellesley.

---

*To His Highness the Nizam.**

[1273.]

21st Sept., 1802.

After the assurance of devoted submission, the representative of the sincere well wisher, Colonel Wellesley, has the honour to state to the attendants on the Presence, the treasury of bounty, of the unsullied Nabob of exalted titles, whose turrets are the heavens, and whose origin is celestial, (be his dignified shade extended!) that two purses, containing the illustrious enayetnamahs, replete with kindness, the one vouchsafing the acknowledgment of the bark of the Maumyah trees, and the

---

* Translated from a letter in Persian, on the records of the Residency at Hyderabad.

other communicating the extensive benefit which had been effected by it, with an order for the transmission of some bark from the trunks of both the trees, sealed, and under the charge of the camel hircarrah of the prosperous Sircar, honoured and elevated me by the grandeur of their approach and the dignity of their arrival.

On learning the circumstance of the benefit which had been experienced by the brilliant constitution, from the attendants on the Presence, from the application of the aforesaid bark, I derived the utmost happiness.

In compliance with the exalted order, two bundles of the desired bark, the one from the trunk of the tree at Chinroypatam, and the other from the trunk of that at the village of Kope, have been delivered, sealed, to the camel hircarrahs of the Sircar, abounding in kindness, and are despatched to the exalted Presence. They will pass, no doubt, under the noble inspection.

In consequence of the length of the journey from Seringapatam to the village of Kope, which is situated at the distance of 400 miles, and of the incessant rain in the vicinity of Nuggur, the passing and repassing on the road is very dilatory and difficult, and the procrastination and delay of some days have, therefore, occurred in obeying the orders of the unsullied Presence. I hope that the medicine which is transmitted, having attained the honour of application, may be beneficial in its effects on the constitution, replete with purity.

The desire of my heart, the seat of constancy, is that the exalted attendant will confidently regard and esteem the aforesaid bark as a memorable instance of the loyalty of the well wisher, and as a testimony of the anxiety of British officers to effect all arrangements which may be desired by, or beneficial to, the noble Presence.

May the God of his slaves grant that the orb of your Prosperity may shine and glitter from the eternal horizon, like the sun in the zenith !

ARTHUR WELLESLEY.

[1274.]   *To R. Rickards, Esq.*

MY DEAR SIR,   Woodanelly, 24th Sept., 1802.

I have received your letter of the 4th instant.

The office of brigade-major in Malabar is peculiarly situated.

When the command of the two provinces on the Coast was consolidated, and the staff in one province abolished, the senior brigade-major, Lieutenant Brutton, was the person who lost his appointment, and in the prospect of a vacancy in Malabar he has lately applied to me to be appointed brigade-major in that province : his claim is undoubted, and I have told him that I would mention it to the officer who should be appointed to command below the Ghauts.

I have made it a rule never to interfere in the appointment of any staff, excepting to those situations immediately about myself. I conceive that officers in command are responsible for their staff; and it is unfair to require that any officer should be responsible for the conduct of another whose appointment to office he has not recommended, and to whom he may have an objection. For this reason I can do no more than mention the claim of Lieutenant Brutton to the officer who will be appointed to command in Malabar ; and I will also mention to him your wishes in favour of Lieutenant George Browne ; but I can do no more. I must recommend for the appointment the person who he will think will be best able to give him assistance in carrying on the duties of his situation.

I have, however, in addition to this objection to recommending Lieutenant George Browne immediately, to inform you that I rather believe General Stuart intends that Captain Watson should be brigade-major in Malabar, which must of course supersede all recommendations from me or the commanding officer in that province.

I cannot conceive how General Nicholls can dispute the right of General Nicholson to command at Bombay. He has no particular commission as commanding in chief ; and in that case the question is, who is the senior officer ? General Nicholson has no commission from the King ; but I think I recollect that it has been decided that the want of a King's commission to an officer in the service of the Company shall not be prejudicial to such officer. This is reasonable enough, considering that it has been expressly stipulated by the King's ministers that every officer in the Company's service shall have a commission by brevet from the King of the same date with that which he holds from the Company.

I am now upon a tour of Mysore, but I shall soon return to Seringapatam ; and, even if circumstances should prevent you from visiting that place, I think it probable that I shall meet you this year in Malabar.

Believe me, &c.,

ARTHUR WELLESLEY.

[1275.]   *To Captain Scott.*

MY DEAR SIR,   Woodanelly, 24th Sept., 1802.

I had so much to do at Chittledroog that I had not time to answer your last letters. I'll write to Colonel de Meuron this day regarding the quartermaster of his regiment, if I have time, of which, however, I am rather doubtful. I think he won't refuse me.

I have received a letter from Captain Heitland, by which I find that he thinks it probable that clearing the yard to the extent which we first proposed will cost above 7000 pags.; and as the General thinks it will cost only 1500, it becomes absolutely necessary that we should curtail the extent. If you think that a yard of the size of that which you have stated will answer your purpose, I have no objection to it; and I beg that you and Heitland will consult upon the subject, and let me have from him an estimate of the expense of clearing that ground, and you must make out an indent upon Freese for the carts you will require for that work, and a requisition upon Mackay for bullocks. Send both to me to be countersigned.

I approve of the plan of your sheds; but I think it would answer better, and would save expense, if the back of the sheds were the walls of the yard. The roofs might still be the pent roofs, and might cover the tops of the walls. Indeed by this mode you would save one row of pillars, besides the building of the mud wall in the centre of each shed, and you would have an equal quantity of space.

Do me the favour to communicate this letter to Captain Heitland, to whose letter of the 20th it is an answer.

Believe me, &c.,

ARTHUR WELLESLEY.

To Captain Scott.   [1276.]

MY DEAR SIR,   Sera, 26th Sept., 1802.

My letter of the 24th will have conveyed to you my sentiments regarding your proposal to lessen your yard, and my
reasons for having delayed till this to answer your letters of the
18th and 20th.

I entirely approve of your commencing the shed along the
parade wall.

I conclude that you have communicated to Captain Heitland
my letter of the 24th, in which I request that he will estimate
the expense of clearing the yard to the extent that you have
now fixed for it, and that I shall soon have that estimate. If
it come within the sum fixed by General Stuart as that which
he can allow to be spent upon this work, I will send orders
forthwith that the commatties, &c., may be hired, and that the
work may be commenced ; if it exceed that sum, we must wait
for the answer and the reference which I must make to the
General.

In the mean time, however, at all events the pioneers may be
employed upon the work. I request you to be so kind as to fix
upon that work which you think it most advantageous to commence and finish first, and to point it out to Captain Heitland ;
and I beg that he will allot the largest number of pioneers that
can be afforded from other works to carry on that which you
will point out to him, with their proper complement of Native
officers and serjeants, as overseers, to make them work as they
ought.

I rather believe that the reason for which Purneah has
ceased to carry away the stores is, that the engineer says that
all that remain will be useful in the repair of the fort. If he has
not carried away all that are decided upon as useless, I beg
that Captain Heitland will remind Bajee Rao of the necessity
of carrying them away without loss of time.

As I don't rely implicitly on the judgment of Lieutenant
————, I shall be obliged to you if you and Captain Heitland will examine the stores still remaining in the yard, and
give over to Purneah all those that you may think will not be
useful in the reform and repair of the fort, or generally in the
Company's works.

In my last I desired you to indent for such carts as you might want. Captain Freese will give them to you without further trouble upon your application.

Be so kind as to communicate this letter to Captain Heitland, as I have not time to write to him.

Believe me, &c.,

ARTHUR WELLESLEY.

[1277.]   *To J. H. Piele, Esq.*

MY DEAR PIELE,   Sera, 26th Sept., 1802.

Before I quitted Seringapatam Mr. Knox mentioned to me that one of the persons belonging to you had ill treated one of the police peons in the garden at the Laal Baug, and that he did not know in what manner to proceed against him, as you objected to allowing any person attached to you to go into the Cutchery, and wished that all complaints against persons of that description might be referred to yourself. I desired Mr. Knox to act as Major Symons had desired him; and I intended to have spoken to you upon the subject before I quitted Seringapatam, but forgot it. I am sorry that I omitted to talk to you upon it, as I am convinced that in two minutes we should have understood each other, and that the question would have been settled for ever. I refer you to the regulation of government for the system of civil jurisdiction for the island of Seringapatam; under this you will observe that the police is placed under the direction of the commanding officer in Mysore, and for reasons of public convenience I have placed it in the hands of Major Symons, for whom Mr. Knox acts at present, and I have never interfered in its management excepting on those occasions when reference has been made to me. All the Native inhabitants of the island of Seringapatam are subject to the jurisdiction of the courts established by the regulation, and of course to the police. I am aware that even under the best institutions for the administration of justice political considerations must have their weight, and must at times operate to prevent the natural course of justice. This is particularly the case in this country, and is so at Seringapatam probably more than at any other place; and accordingly you will perceive in my correspondence with Colonel Close that I have restricted the jurisdiction of the courts as far as lay in my power in respect to

the servants of the government of the Rajah of Mysore residing
upon the island, and I have desired that certain complaints of,
and questions regarding, them might be referred in the first
instance to the Resident. This restriction was adopted because
Purneah and many of the principal servants of the government
resided at Seringapatam, and had property there, and it appeared probable that persons who might have complaints and
claims against them for acts done in the common transactions
of the government might lodge their complaints in the Cutchery,
and thus that the ordinary transactions of this government might
come under the review of the judge. In a place situated as
Seringapatam is, it is scarcely possible that questions should not
arise between the Rajah's subjects and those of the Company on
the island, many of which it is exceedingly proper, and others very
improper, that the judge should decide on; but you will perceive that the line is clearly drawn in my letter to Colonel Close;
and I have the pleasure to add that in this, as upon most other
occasions, he and I agreed in opinion. The question is, whether
the people attached to you are at all of the description of those
belonging to the Rajah's government in respect to whom the
jurisdiction of the court is restricted; some of them are certainly
people of a better description; others, against whom the majority of these complaints are made, are peons, gardeners,
shepherds, horsekeepers, &c. &c. This description of people
are liable to the jurisdiction, even if in the Rajah's service, and
are certain of punishment if they misbehave or break the peace.
The reason for which the jurisdiction was restricted in respect
to the higher rank of the Rajah's servants was, that they might
not be brought before the court for acts purely of government,
and that Purneah and his principal people might not be
frightened out of the place by the danger of being brought
before the Foujdarry by every drunken sepoy, dubash, or maty
boy who might choose to complain of them. But I beg to know
whether the same reasons apply to the principal people in your
service? They are not concerned in the government in any
manner, and as long as they are in your service they are
obliged to remain at Seringapatam if you do. The only reason
then for which they should not be brought before these courts
appointed by government to have jurisdiction over them is, the
prejudice they have themselves to it, and the desire they have
in common with every man to live under no control, and to be

the judges of their own actions.   But this reason, in my opinion, has no weight against the principle that the law is common to all, particularly in a case in which it is evident that no political consideration can have any influence.   In this view of the subject, I think that your servants, particularly the lower classes of them, ought to be made to attend the Cutchery when called, in the same manner as other Natives, and even Europeans are, and ought to be punished there for their public offences.

It may happen, however, that you or Mr. Webbe may think that the character of the Resident is lessened in the opinion of the Natives in general by the obligation that his servants should attend these courts, and you may therefore be desirous that all complaints against them should be referred to you.   I acknowledge that I am not of this opinion; I should imagine that Webbe is not, and I know Colonel Close was not; and when you consider the question on a broad principle, I think you will not.   But if you should be desirous for any reason that these complaints should be made to you, I can have no objection to it excepting upon the general principle, and when we meet we can talk over the subject, and I am convinced that we shall easily understand one another.

I observe by the papers which Knox has sent me that one of the persons who were sent by you to attend the Cutchery was, as he says, ill treated.   I beg that in the consideration of the general question this circumstance may be entirely laid aside. The judge of the Cutchery, or the person conducting the police, has no right to ill treat anybody.   I'll take care that such a thing, if it has happened, shall not happen again, and I shall be obliged to you if you will let me know when anything of the kind comes to your knowledge.

I have received two letters from Purneah since my departure from Seringapatam, and have written him answers, which you will have seen.   I am a Major-General.   I hope your brother is arrived.

You will have heard from other quarters of our transactions at Chittledroog.   We left plenty of water in the place, but not a drop of claret or beer.

Believe me, &c.,

ARTHUR WELLESLEY.

To Mr. ————. [1278.]

SIR, Goom Gootee, 30th Sept., 1802.

I have just received your letter of the 25th.

Part of it, I conceive, requires no reply. I proceed to reply to those parts which in my opinion require answers; and if you should have occasion to address me in future, and are desirous that I should take any notice of your letters, I request you to refrain from the abuse of other persons, and from all allusions to my conduct either public or private, excepting on the subject upon which you may have to write to me.

I sent the bills for the working money to Madras about a year ago, and recommended that they should be passed; they were passed accordingly, and remained in the hands of the Deputy Adjutant-General, in order to answer the demands of the public against you if ever they should be made. These bills shall be sent to you as soon as they can be got from Seringapatam.

I have also to remind you that there is in the hands of the paymaster a bill due to you passed by the Military Board for the repairs of the arsenal, which was detained for the same reasons by order of government, and which I doubt not will be paid upon your application to them.

I perfectly recollect to have given you orders to make up carriages for two three-pounders attached to the 4th regiment of cavalry, but I did not conceive that those carriages were to cost the public anything, otherwise I should not have ordered them without authority from the Military Board. It appears now that they did cost you something, and I have no objection to stating, in any manner that you please, that I did give you those orders under the circumstances that I have above mentioned. The Military Board then will judge of the propriety of paying your demand for the carriages.

I have, &c.,

ARTHUR WELLESLEY.

To Captain Scott. [1279.]

MY DEAR SIR, Lapatchy, 1st Oct., 1802.

I approve of the orders you have given to your overseer regarding additional artificers. They are in conformity with the orders which you have received from the Commander-in-Chief, and are in my opinion absolutely necessary.

In consequence of what you and Captain Heitland say upon the subject of the yard, I have determined to defer authorizing any expense on account of clearing it till I arrive at Seringapatam. In the mean time the work can be carried on by the pioneers; but as the filling up the low grounds round the fort before the northerly rains set in is a work of great importance not only to the comfort but to the health of every inhabitant within it, I should wish that no larger proportion of pioneers should be employed in the manufactory yard than is absolutely necessary to clear what you want for your buildings and the commencement of your work, and that the remainder should be employed in the drains and low grounds, so as to have them prepared for the deluge which may soon be expected.

Be so kind as to communicate this letter to Captain Heitland, to whom I have not time to write at present.

Take down the engineer's house whenever you may want the timber in it.

Believe me, &c.,

ARTHUR WELLESLEY.

[1280.]   *To Captain Scott.*

MY DEAR SIR,   Nundydroog, 3rd Oct., 1802.

I know nothing about the carriages at Ryacotta, excepting that I ordered the bullocks there to bring them away; and I understood from you that you had written to the Military Board to desire that the commanding officer at Ryacotta might have orders to send them as soon as the bullocks should arrive. In regard to the other bullocks, I imagine that there must have been some mistake between the drivers and the officer in charge of the detachment, for I know they went to meet the carriages.

There is a carriage road, and a very good one, to Mangalore, but it will be necessary to allow the monsoon to cease entirely before we begin to use it. There will be no difficulty in getting up the anvils on carriages in about a month.

As soon as I arrive at Seringapatam I intend ordering bullocks to Paughur to bring away the carts that are there; and in the mean time I think two or three more of the

transporting carriages might as well be made, and I write to
Freese upon that subject this day.

Believe me, &c.,

ARTHUR WELLESLEY.

To Lieutenant Brutton. [1281.]

SIR, Nundydroog, 3rd Oct., 1802.

As Brigade-Major Spens has applied for leave to remain at
Bombay to act as Deputy-Quartermaster-General, and that an
officer might be appointed to act for him during his absence
on this duty, an application which I think it probable the Commander-in-Chief will comply with, and that the present acting
Brigade-Major will continue to do the duty in Malabar, it is
almost unnecessary to write anything further upon the subject
of your claim to that office, the consideration of which must be
postponed for the present.

I am induced, however, to reply to your letter of the 26th
September, which I received yesterday, because I perceive that
you have founded hopes upon my letter to Lieut.-Colonel Spry
upon the subject of your claims which that letter was never
intended to inspire. As well as I recollect, I informed him
that I thought your case a hard one, and that I should be
glad to be able to do anything for your advantage. I then
pointed out to him the rule by which I had always been, and
should always be, guided in the recommendations I should
make of persons to fill staff situations, viz., to consult the wishes
of those who are most interested in their being properly filled;
and in the case of the Brigade-Majorship of Malabar, I should
think it proper to be certain that you were not disagreeable to the officer who should command there. I told him that
I should certainly recommend you to the commanding officer
in Malabar in case there should be a vacancy, and should state
to him my opinion of your claims to the office.

Upon this letter it appears now that you have founded hopes
that I should recommend you to head-quarters, whether you
should be approved of or recommended, or otherwise, by the
commanding officer in Malabar, and that you have in consequence refused another situation. But I am convinced that the

words of this letter do not justify any such hopes, and I cannot consider myself as the cause of your disappointment; and I have further to inform you that it is my opinion that if I were to recommend you for the office against the inclination of the commanding officer in Malabar, the Commander-in-Chief would not attend to me.

I have, &c.,

ARTHUR WELLESLEY.

[1282.]   *To Lieutenant-Colonel Cuppage.*

DEAR SIR,   Seringapatam, 10th Oct., 1802.

Captain Barclay has communicated to me your letter of the 6th and its enclosure. When I desired the Deputy-Adjutant-General to write you orders upon the subject of certain irregularities reported to exist in the hospital of the battalion under your command, I did not wish that any inquiry should be made regarding them, or that the conduct of any officer should be the subject of investigation before a general court martial, but that such evils should be prevented in future by your issuing the orders which were suggested to you, and by your seeing that they were strictly carried into execution. A line entirely different from that which I proposed has been adopted; a regimental court of inquiry has been assembled to ascertain the truth of a report made officially to me by the superintending surgeon of this division of the army, and as such communicated officially to you; and the result is that the gentleman acting as surgeon with the battalion under your command has been put in arrest upon a charge grounded either upon his own letter to you, in which he states that he did make certain reports to Mr. Anderson, or upon your conjecture of the facts on which Mr. Anderson founded his report.

I take this mode of acquainting you that I disapprove of this proceeding entirely. A gentleman ought not to be put in arrest on acknowledgments drawn from him in his own letter, which letter you will never be allowed to produce as evidence before a general court martial, that he did make the reports to Mr. Anderson of which you complain; and I disapprove still more of your putting him in arrest in consequence of an inquiry which could not be conclusive, and could not have all the merits of the case before it, because he did not choose to give any reply to what appeared to contradict his statement.

It is not necessary that I should now notice the irregularity of referring to a regimental court of inquiry a report made to me by the superintending surgeon, in order to ascertain its truth ; but I have to recommend caution in all your proceedings upon this subject, because, whatever may be the extent of the irregularity and impropriety which may appear before the general court martial, of the conduct of Mr. ——, in the same proportion will the commanding officer of the battalion be blameable, whose particular duty it was to superintend his conduct, and to bring him to punishment if it were not what it ought to be ; but not to bring him to punishment for any report he might make to the superintending surgeon.

Upon the whole, I recommend that Mr. —— should be released from his arrest, and that you should take care to prevent in future the irregularities complained of according to my original intention, rather than that you should bring him forward for having made an improper report to the superintending surgeon, which may occasion censure for the existence of those irregularities at all in the battalion.

You will excuse my writing you this letter, and I beg you to attribute it to my desire to stop an investigation which can tend to no good purpose, and will certainly go farther than is at present imagined.

Believe me, &c.,

ARTHUR WELLESLEY.

To Josiah Webbe, Esq. [1253.]

MY DEAR WEBBE,   Seringapatam, 11th Oct., 1802.

Before I had received your letter of the 6th I had received Piele's answer to mine, a copy of which I enclosed you, in which he agreed entirely in the principles which I stated to him. He seemed to think, however, that as you had particularly recommended to his care your servants and followers, as well as for the sake of the respectability of the Resident's character among the Natives, it was desirable that all cases arising on the island of Seringapatam, in which those persons should be con-

cerned, should be referable to him.   I had a conversation with
him this morning, in which I acquainted him with your sentiments generally upon this subject, on which I told him that I
had written to you ; and I am happy to say that I found him
as reasonable upon this occasion as I have upon others when
the question upon which a difference of opinion has been entertained has been placed in its true light.   There is no occasion
for your writing to him.

I returned here yesterday from a long tour in Mysore, and
I am happy to inform you that every thing appears to me to go
on well in the country, excepting in the districts of Chittledroog,
Mudgherry, Mergasie, and Paughur, which were heretofore
plundered by the Mahrattas, and in which a want of water has
been experienced for these last three or four seasons.   Indeed
this want is general in all parts of the country this year ; but
still it is covered with cultivation, and the people apparently
prosperous and happy.   I am glad to hear of your intention to
make a tour ; I intended to have recommended this measure to
you as soon as you should arrive in Mysore.   I am convinced
that the tours made by Colonel Close have been a great cause
of the prosperity of the country, and it stands to reason that
the expectation of a visit from Purneah and the Resident must
induce the aumildars to exert themselves, at the same time that
the tour must tend to check any extraordinary exactions from
the country by the government.   I heard of no complaints in
my tour excepting at Chilgut and near Bangalore, where I
understand from Piele that the ryots have in a manner rebelled
against the aumildar.

You cannot conceive how much rejoiced I am at the order of
government upon the subject of bazaars.   The situation of a
commanding officer is now placed where it ought to be, and is
respectable.   I observe, however, that no provision is made
by the General Orders for the commanding officers of forts, &c.,
in the Mysore country, excepting Seringapatam ; the order is
positive regarding their levying duties themselves, but it makes
no provision in lieu of that practice.

It is very desirable that the situation of a commanding officer
of a station in the Mysore country should not be worse than
that of a commanding officer in the Company's territories,
because if it be, we shall have here the dregs of the service
instead of the best, which we ought to have ; and I have there-

fore turned the subject over in my mind with a view to giving them an advantage equal to that which will be enjoyed by officers in similar situations within the Company's territories.

The Rajah pays the commanding officer at Chittledroog 500 Behaudry pagodas a month, and some small matter I believe to the commanding officer at Nundydroog; and at the other stations the arrack concerns have been entirely under the directions of the commanding officer, but nothing else. What I should propose would be to stop the allowance to the commanding officer at Chittledroog, which was given, as far as I could understand Colonel Close, in lieu of the arrack, and under circumstances at that station entirely different from those at present existing; to stop it likewise at Nundydroog; and that the arrack, &c. &c., should be managed by the Rajah's aumildars in the same manner as every other part of their revenue. I should then propose that at the periods at which payments on this account should be made by the government to the officers commanding stations in the Company's territories, payment should be made by the Rajah's government to officers commanding stations in the Mysore country of a sum equal in amount to that which the officers commanding stations of a similar description in the Company's territories will receive. The expense to the Rajah's government under this arrangement will not amount altogether to that now incurred by the payment to the commanding officer at Chittledroog only; and the advantage of it will be, that at the same time that the officers commanding stations in Mysore will have the same advantages with those of a similar description in the Company's territories, no person will have any right to interfere or to inquire into the administration of the revenues in this country.

I wish that you would turn this subject over in your mind; let me know if you approve of this proposed arrangement, and if you do, in what manner you think it ought to be carried into execution.

By your letter of the 6th I judge that a new Governor has been appointed to Madras, although I have heard none of the particulars. Surely Petrie will not go home if Lord Clive does, unless a Governor be appointed; and, excepting in the same case, Chamier will not go home, if either Lord Clive or Petrie go. From all I hear, I think it better that Lord Clive should go; I am told that he is treated ill at Madras, that he was so particularly at a concert lately at Mr. Chamier's, and that he felt it and quitted the room.

Nothing can be so fatal to the respectability of government as the prevailing habit of treating the Governor with incivility, and the sooner it is stopped by the arrival of a man whose manners and character will command respect the better.

Believe me, &c.,

ARTHUR WELLESLEY.

[1284.]   *To Colonel Montresor.*

MY DEAR COLONEL,   Seringapatam, 15th Oct., 1802.

I have just received your letter of the 11th, and I am glad to find that you are arrived. The 80th regiment must certainly have many wants, which the neighbourhood of Madras will be best able to supply, and this will delay their march to so late a period of the season, that it will not be possible for them to be clear of the Carnatic before the monsoon sets in with violence. It is, therefore, best that they should not move at all till after it is over.

You will regulate your motions according to your convenience. The detachment of your regiment under Captain White is arrived at Cannanore, and I have desired that preparations may be made for the reception of the whole corps at that station.

My plans at present are as follows :—I propose to go to Malabar as soon as the weather will permit, and I shall be back here by the end of November. I think it possible that I shall then meet you here; but if not, I shall again set out on a fresh tour to the provinces to the north-west, and probably into Canara, where it may be convenient to you to meet me.

Before you quit Madras it will be as well that you should make some arrangement respecting the person who is to be your Brigade-Major. Captain Spens will soon resign the office, which will then come to be filled up. I have long determined that I never would interfere in the appointment of any staff, as I think that those who are to depend upon the officers of the staff for assistance are the fittest persons to select those who are to afford it. It is proper, however, that I should make you acquainted with the claim of an officer upon the office of Brigade-Major in Malabar, in order that you may take it into consideration when you come to recommend for that appointment.

There were formerly two Brigade-Majors upon the Coast, one in Malabar, the other in Canara; one of which offices was lately abolished. Lieutenant Brutton, of the 75th regiment, was then the senior Brigade-Major; but, being in Canara, his office was discontinued. He thinks, with some ground, that he has a claim upon the Brigade-Major's office in Malabar if it should become vacant; and having applied to me, I have told him that I would make known the ground of his claim to the officer who should be appointed to command in the provinces. This I now do to you, but I beg you will remember that I don't wish to guide your decision; on the contrary, I wish you to appoint a person, whoever he may be, who you will think will give you the greatest assistance in carrying on your duties.

Believe me, &c.,

ARTHUR WELLESLEY.

To Lieutenant-Colonel Boles.   [1285.]

SIR,   Seringapatam, 18th Oct., 1802.

I have had the honour of receiving your letters of the 11th and 15th of October relative to the renewal of the disturbances in Wýnaad. As far as the information which you have transmitted to me goes, it does not appear that there has been any act of insurrection anywhere excepting at Pancoorta Cottah.*

---

* The particulars of the transaction referred to are contained in the following extract of a letter sent to Colonel Wellesley from Cannanore, by Captain Lewis, on 16th October, 1802 :—

"Ere this reaches you, you doubtless are acquainted with the melancholy occurrence at Pancoorta Cottah. The perpetrators of this accursed act were supposed to amount to between four and five hundred, divided into three parties, one of which secured the barrack of arms, another surrounded the officers' houses, and the third attacked the sepoys. The cantonments were set fire to in several places at the same time, and the men cut down as they came out of their huts. Captain Dickenson and Lieutenant Maxwell were mangled in a dreadful manner, twenty sepoys were killed and thirty wounded, few of whom are expected to survive; only one servant of Captain Dickenson's escaped; all his property (except his mare) was destroyed, and his horse-

I shall, however, proceed to take this subject into consideration in two points of view, supposing the insurrection to be general in the northern districts of Malabar and in Wynaad, and supposing it to be partial, and confined only to the attack of Pancoorta Cottah.

If the insurrection should be general, it will be absolutely necessary to collect a body of troops without loss of time, and to place them as forward as possible. In order to enable you to do this, you must occupy only the posts which are on the communication between the Coast and the Ghauts, and those only with the number of troops which are really requisite for their defence. The remainder of the troops must be in the field, equipped in such a manner as to be able to move with celerity to any point.

As soon as I shall hear from you that you find it necessary to collect the troops in the field in consequence of this supposed general insurrection, I shall forthwith send down from this country, through Koorg, supplies of cattle, &c. &c., which you will require, and which I can collect at Seringapatam without difficulty. It will be necessary that you should facilitate their march to join you by keeping possession of Ercoor, and by such other measures as you may think proper, and in the mean time that you should make the departments in Malabar exert themselves to supply all the cattle and other means of equipment which the province can afford.

Besides these measures to enable you to take the field in Malabar, the troops on this side shall not be idle, if their activity should be necessary. I have it in my power to put in the field in a short time a body which I hope will give effectual assistance on the eastern side of Wynaad.

If this supposed general insurrection should exist, it will be necessary that you should immediately bring the whole 77th regiment from Mangalore into Malabar.

keeper and his wife were found burnt to death. Major Macleod's Brahmins (of the Cutchery) are missing. It is said that the Rajah himself, with Coongan and Yeman Nair, were present; but this can be only mere conjecture, as every inhabitant in the vicinity of Pancoorta Cottah had deserted their houses. The arms of the detachment were secured by the rebels, but the ammunition being in Captain Dickenson's house, was fortunately blown up. After this business was over, they were seen on the same morning at the Cootioor Pass, where they robbed and severely mauled every traveller who was unfortunate enough to fall in with them. To what point they directed their course afterwards is not yet ascertained."

If the insurrection should be only partial, and confined to the surprise of the post at Pancoorta Cottah, it appears that you have adopted the measures most likely to check it.   In addition to these measures, however, I should wish you to send into Wynaad a company of Europeans, and to order Major ————— forthwith to encamp his battalion, and to prepare to fall upon the insurgents wherever he may hear that they are collecting.

I beg you also to call upon him for an account of his conduct in having omitted this obvious measure the moment he heard that the post at Pancoorta Cottah was attacked.

An officer within nine miles of him suffers himself to be surprised, and with his whole detachment is cut off; and Major —————, instead of putting the battalion under his command into camp, and moving quickly upon the rebels, sits quietly in his cantonment and takes no one step to oppose or stop the insurrection, or for the security of the troops or district under his command.   I declare that after such supine conduct, to say no worse of it, I should not be astonished if I were to hear that Major ————— and the remainder of the battalion had been cut off likewise.

This is not the mode in which the former rebellion in Wynaad and Cotiote was suppressed; it is not that in which this insurrection is to be stopped; but it is the certain mode of continuing it as long as a British soldier remains in that part of India.

Tell Major ————— that the troops lately sent to his assistance are not to be kept in a fort or cantonment; they are to be in the field in one or more bodies, according to his information of the strength of the enemy; and let him know that whatever may be the enemy's strength at present, I expect that when he will be joined by these reinforcements he will move out and attack him, and that by his future activity he will remove from my mind the impression which has been made upon it of the certain evil which the public interests will sustain from his late supineness.   The unarmed Nairs must not be suffered to pass our posts in Cotiote towards the Ghauts.   At all events, whether this insurrection is only partial or likely to become general, it must be a warning to every officer in Malabar of the danger which must always attend the want of precaution in military men; and I shall take an early opportunity of drawing their attention to it in this point of view.

In the mean time I request that you will take into your immediate consideration the state of the posts mentioned in the margin ;* that you will fix in your own mind the number of troops that are absolutely necessary for their defence in case of a general insurrection, and that you will see that each has in it six months' provisions for that number. I beg you to bear in mind that the great difficulty under which we laboured at the commencement of the last rebellion was to be attributed to our having shut up in Montana, by mistake or accident, a larger number of troops than we had provisions there to feed, or than were necessary for the defence of the post. In case, therefore, of this supposed general insurrection, I beg you to have no more troops in each of these small posts than are absolutely necessary, and to keep every man you can for active and offensive operations.

I have, &c.,

ARTHUR WELLESLEY.

[1286.]   *To Lieutenant-General Stuart.*

SIR,   Seringapatam, 18th Oct., 1802.

I have to inform you that I have received an account from Lieutenant-Colonel Boles, stating that the post of Pancoorta Cottah, in Wynaad, which was commanded by Captain Dickenson, was attacked by the Nairs on the morning of the 11th instant; that the cantonment of the troops was burnt, Captain Dickenson and Lieutenant Maxwell of the 1st of the 4th Bombay regiment and many sepoys killed, and a large number wounded. I have not received the particulars of this disastrous affair, but I imagine the detachment was surprised. The Nairs afterwards dispersed, and I have not heard of any farther act of outrage either in Wynaad or Cotiote, although, as is usual upon these occasions, a general insurrection is expected, and some unarmed Nairs have been seen passing our post at Canote on their way towards the Ghauts.

Lieutenant-Colonel Boles has reinforced the troops in Wynaad, and has taken preparatory measures for collecting a detachment in case the insurrection should be at all general,

---

* Cotaparamba.	:	Canote.
Pyche.	:	Eroor.
Montana.	:	Lakorycotta in the Tambercherry
Periwoil.		Ghaut.
Peria Ghaut.		Cotiangurry.

of which there is at present no appearance. I have the honour to enclose the copy of a letter which I have written to Colonel Boles, which will make you acquainted with the orders I have given him, and my opinion of the affair which is the occasion of this letter.

I have been for some days occupied in the inquiries on different subjects on which you have required information, and I hope to be able to despatch to-morrow or the next day answers on every thing referred to me.

I have, &c.,
ARTHUR WELLESLEY.

To Lieutenant-General Stuart.   [1287.]

SIR,   Seringapatam, 19th Oct., 1802.

Since I had the honour of addressing you yesterday I have received farther accounts of the affair at Pancoorta Cottah, which appears to have occurred nearly in the manner I related to you. The loss was Captain Dickenson and Lieutenant Maxwell killed, and 24 Native troops; and 21 Native troops wounded. The whole detachment, supposing all to have been at Pancoorta Cottah, was only 70 men.

I have received accounts from Wynaad as far as the 14th, and from Malabar to the 17th. No farther act of insurrection had taken place in either excepting an attack upon the stockade at the Cootioor pass, which I believe was occupied only by revenue peons; and I imagine that the report of this attack is to be attributed to the fact that travellers into Wynaad have been robbed and murdered near that Ghaut by the Nairs since the affair of the 11th.

In a letter written on the 14th, in the evening also, Major ———— expresses an apprehension that his post at Poollingal will be attacked. This I think not improbable from his own supine conduct, notwithstanding that the number of Nairs was altogether not more than 300 or 400 men, and armed only with bows and arrows (excepting the arms which they took from the detachment at Pancoorta Cottah, for which they had no ammunition, as that was blown up). He had determined to sit in his cantonment and act on the defensive.

Major Macleod arrived here this morning from Coimbatoor, and as it was necessary to give him an escort into Wynaad, or that he should go into Malabar through Koorg, I determined to send the 1st battalion 8th regiment with him. They march from hence on the day after to-morrow; they will be at Cancancotta on the 25th, and I have no doubt will bring the insurrection to a close. It depends entirely upon the activity of the officers, and I have urged active and quick movements as strongly as I can in the instructions which I have given to those who are to operate from this side as well as from below.

I will have the honour of reporting upon this subject through the Adjutant-General.

I have, &c.,
ARTHUR WELLESLEY.

[1288.]   *To Lieutenant-Colonel Boles.*

DEAR SIR,   Seringapatam, 20th Oct., 1802.

I have received your communications upon the subject of Wynaad and Cotiote, sent to me and Captain Barclay, and I approve of all the measures you have taken to be prepared with your force. I wish I could say as much of the conduct of the officers under you; but that is impossible. I declare that I cannot bring myself to send their reports to be laid before the Commander-in-Chief; they are so different from those which I have always been accustomed to send, and they show so little animation or activity in the officers in a cause in which success depends almost upon those qualities alone.

In the report you have lately sent me from Captain ——, he informs you that the communication between Cotaparamba and Montana is cut off; he does not tell you how he comes by that intelligence, in what manner, or by whom this communication is cut off; and above all I observe that he omits to tell you that he proposes to move out to ascertain these points, or to endeavour to re-establish this communication. The other reports are nearly in the same style; every thing that is bad is taken for granted, and every body appears determined to remain in his post on the defensive.

Consider, my dear Sir, how different the situation of our affairs is now from what it was in the years 1800 and 1801. Then the insurgents were in force, and had long been prepared for us; they had all the strong posts and holds, and every thing above the Ghauts; they were all well armed and were accustomed to success, and we were obliged to confine our feeble efforts to completing the roads to our posts, and to keeping them supplied with provisions, and we had no knowledge of the country. They were beaten, however, upon that occasion, and their chief became a wanderer; and the efforts which he has since made to re-establish his cause in a manner similar to his late attack upon Pancoorta Cottah have uniformly been defeated by the activity of the officers and troops. The consequence was, that till a week ago we were in quiet possession of Cotiote and Wynaad; we had posts established in both those districts, well supplied with provisions and every thing they wanted; we had good communications between these posts and the sea, between each other, and through the hills into the upper country; we had a knowledge of the country: on the other hand the rebels have no strong hold, they are not armed (I understand that those who attacked Pancoorta Cottah had only bows and arrows), they cannot be organised, and they have experienced more than one defeat. Under these circumstances for what reason are we to remain even for a moment upon the defensive?

· During the former rebellion I saw many accounts of the Pyche Rajah's strength, and I declare that not one of them ever made it amount to 2000 men. It is said that he is now collected in great force in Wynaad. I should like to know who has seen that force, and who knows that it consists of a larger number than the few assassins who surprised Captain Dickenson? Has he got his old 2000 men or not? If he has, how does he feed them, how are they armed, and have they any ammunition?

But if he has this large force in Wynaad, he cannot have it also in Cotiote, and it would be surely worth while for somebody to try the strength of the party below.

I beg that you will urge the officers to active measures. Let them put their troops in camp forthwith, excepting the number of men that may be absolutely necessary for the defence of the small posts against surprise. If the rebels are really in force, let a junction be formed, and then not a moment lost in dashing at them, whatever may be their force. If the rebels are not in strength, let the troops be kept in constant motion in different directions, and let the alarm be kept up, and they will never be in strength. At all events let them make long and frequent marches, and let them move, not in the column style, but with the flanks covered, particularly where danger is apprehended; and when an attack is to be made in paddy grounds or other places where the enemy may be posted, let a party get round upon their flank.

If something is not soon done, the rebellion will become regularly organised, and will get ahead, and then the system of warfare must be changed, and will become more tedious.

Captain Barclay will have informed you yesterday that I had ordered the 1st of the 8th into Wynaad with Major Macleod. I desire him to send you a copy of the instructions I have given their commanding officer.   This corps, with the reinforcements you have sent into that district, will make our numbers there 1500, I think; and if that number is not sufficient to beat the Pyche Rajah and his 2000, I wonder at it.   However, the success of this expedition depends upon Major ————'s holding his ground and his operations.   If he allows himself to be beat, or is obliged to go down the Ghauts, the whole of Wynaad must join the Pyche Rajah, and then this battalion will not be sufficiently strong.

They will be at Cancancotta on the 25th, and I have told them that I expected that they would move into the centre of the district on the next day, if the state of affairs would at all permit it.

Believe me, &c.,

ARTHUR WELLESLEY.

[1289.]   *To Lieutenant-General Stuart.*

SIR,   20th Oct., 1802.

I have been prevented from answering your several letters since my return to this place by the necessary attention to the objects on which you have required information, and by my wish to make that which I should give you as complete and satisfactory as I could.

The result of various plans for clearing out the gun-carriage yard, and estimates of expense attending the execution of each, is to leave it to be cleared by the pioneers, and to incur no expense on the work excepting for a few basket coolies.   Before Captain Scott arrived we had cleared as much of the yard as gave him space on which to erect half the buildings he requires, and a large space besides in the centre; and much ground has been cleared since. As I find that we cannot bring the estimate of the expense attending the remainder of the work within the sum which you mentioned in your letter of the 11th September, I think it best upon the whole to depend entirely upon the means already in the Company's pay, although we should thereby lose some time.

With the assistance of carts, &c., which I have given the pioneers, I think it probable that the work will require six months to finish it at least; but as there is already as much ground cleared as will answer for the first operations of the manufactory, I think this delay of no very great importance.

Captain Scott is now ready to commence his operations, and waits only for the instructions of the Military Board. The European artificers are expected, and I hope that he will be permitted to retain every one of them that can work at all. I know that in this country in particular one European artificer will do six times as much work as a Native, especially in the sawyers' work. I am, therefore, anxious that he should have many people of this description.

As a great part of the bullock establishment, viz., the breeding establishment, is entirely in the hands of the Rajah's government, I have been much delayed by the necessity of having papers translated in procuring for you the information which you have required upon the subject. However, I trust that that which I am about to detail will be satisfactory to you.

The bullocks originally came into the hands of the Company upon the fall of Seringapatam. At that time there were 35 karkhanas of draught bullocks, each containing 100 for the draught and 12 for forage, and 4 karkhanas of carriage bullocks and 2 of calves. The establishment of servants and attendants for these cattle is the same as in the time of the Sultan, and is for each karkhana of draught bullocks 1 daroga, 2 chowdries, 4 duffadars, and 37 drivers, and 1 head muttaseddee, 2 second, 2 third, 1 conicopoly, and 2 peons for the whole establishment. The establishment of servants for the karkhanas of carriage cattle and calves was the same as that for the draught cattle; but the number of carriage cattle and calves in each karkhana was not limited. There were at one time 150 carriage bullocks and 350 calves in each karkhana respectively, and now their numbers are reduced below those in the karkhanas of draught bullocks. To this number of 35 karkhanas of draught bullocks 8 karkhanas were added when the establishments on the coast of Malabar and at Goa were placed under the government of Fort St. George; and although the bullocks in those parts were not then on the same establishments, that in use with the Mysore bullocks was found so convenient and cheap that the bullocks on the Malabar coast and at Goa were formed into karkhanas in the same manner.

The total number, therefore, now is 43 karkhanas.

The expense of the servants of each karkhana, if complete, would be 86 pagodas 7 fanams *per mensem;* and the total expense of servants for the whole establishment is 70 pagodas *per mensem.†*

But the karkhanas are none of them complete in bullocks or in servants, as will appear by a reference to the returns; and accordingly the total expense of the servants of the draught bullocks is 3576 pagodas 18 fanams; of the servants of the carriage bullocks, 322 pagodas 21 fanams; and of the servants of the calves, 141 pagodas 20 fanams.

Besides this expense, the draught bullocks in Mysore cost each about ½ a rupee per month for gram. Each bullock gets one seer of gram, and of course this expense must vary according to the price of gram in the country in which the animals may be stationed. Accordingly the detachment of bullocks stationed in Malabar cost each for gram about 4 rupees, and those in Canara each about 3 rupees.

The straw which the bullocks eat in Mysore is not paid for. In this part of India a proportion of the straw belongs to the Sircar; and as it is not used, and there is no sale for it, the

			Pags.	Fms.		Pags.	Fms.
* 1 daroga	.. ..	..each	..		....	5	35
2 chowdries	.. ..	..	4	0	....	8	0
4 duffadars	.. ..	..	2	12	....	9	6
37 drivers	.. ..	..	1	30	....	63	18
						86	7

				Pagodas.
† Head muttasoddee	.. ..	15	....	15
2 second ditto ..	.. .. ..	12	....	24
2 third ditto	.. .. ..	10	....	20
1 conicopoly	.. ..	5	....	5
2 peons	.. ..	3	....	6
				70

Sircar's share is given to the Company's bullocks. This will last as long as the Sircar do not oblige the ryots to take their share of the straw, and to give money or other produce in lieu thereof, as is the custom in the Company's territories. In these all the straw used by the Company's bullocks is paid for, and this is an additional expense attending the bullock establishments. I understand that the collectors make the ryots take the straw, and receive other produce or money in lieu thereof; and if this be the case, it is but fair that the ryots should receive money for that for which they pay.

I have the honour to enclose the copy of a letter written by Lieutenant-Colonel Close to Lord Clive upon the subject of an agreement made by him with the Dewan for the care of the breeding part of this establishment. Before this agreement was made, the Colonel and I had made many inquiries and had had frequent conversations upon the subject. It appeared that there was no mode which could be adopted so likely to give the Company a constant supply of this fine breed of cattle at so small expense. That of taking the stud into our own hands would have been enormous, if the servants of the working bullock establishment were not attached likewise to the stud; and if they had been so attached, the Company would have lost the advantage of the services of these people at the time when they would most want them. Besides, I think it doubtful whether the breeding establishment under this arrangement would have produced a larger number of calves than under that adopted; and at all events we have in favour of our system the precedent of the benefits derived in all parts of Europe from the establishment of a similar system for the supply of horses, rather than from taking the stud into the hands and the immediate management of the officers of government. The price allowed for each animal is a fair compensation for the trouble and expense of rearing him, and at the same time it is so liberal that there is no temptation to sell these cattle to other purchasers.

Upon the whole, therefore, I am of opinion that this is the best mode of managing this breeding establishment.

In regard to the supply of cattle from it, that has not yet been so ample as might be expected; but there are various causes which have interrupted it, which will not occur again most probably. One of these is the confusion which existed in the

country immediately after the fall of Seringapatam; in consequence of which a large number of the cows, and nearly all
the calves, were made away with.   But by the enclosed paper,
which is made up from a variety of accounts received from a
muttaseddee belonging to the Residency, who has particularly
examined into this establishment, you will perceive that the
number of breeding cows as well as of calves is increasing; and
there is every probability that the stud will answer the demands
which will be made upon it.

The Dewan has readily consented to the proposal which I
have made to him to deliver the calves at three years old instead of at one year and a half.   But he and the Rajah's servants
are of opinion that a bullock at three years old cannot be broke
in to the draught, and he proposes that we should take them at
two years old, at which age he says that Tippoo was accustomed
to work the cattle.   In this the Natives differ with Captain
Mackay; but in order to ascertain the truth, I have desired
that twelve bullocks of three years old and twelve of two years
old may be brought here, and I will see which will answer best
for the service.

I have ordered a committee upon the bullocks, and I will
forward to you their proceedings as soon as they will have
examined them.   You will then be able to determine what
number shall be sold and what number transferred to the
carriage karkhanas.

Captain Mackay is instructed to prepare for the examination by selecting such as are now fit for the draught; the calves
that will be so; those unfit for draught, but fit for carriage;
the calves that will be fit for carriage; the bullocks and calves
that never will be fit for any service, and ought to be disposed of.

Each karkhana will be arranged in this manner, and the
report of the committee will specify the numbers in each under
these separate heads.

I shall be perfectly satisfied with your determination respecting an engineer for Seringapatam, and you are aware of our
want of one.

I returned to Seringapatam on the 10th, having surveyed the
following forts:—Chinroypatam, Cadoor, and Banawoor, not occupied by our troops, but on the road to the Mahratta frontier;
Chittledroog, Sera, Mudgherry, Mergasie, Paughur, Goorybunda,
Nundydroog, occupied by the Company's troops; Deonelly,

Severndroog, and Hooliadroog, not occupied by the Company's troops. I proposed to go to Malabar in a short time, and to return to the frontier to see Colonel Agnew, when he should be prepared to meet me, and to survey the remaining forts on the Mahratta frontier, and in the Bednore country; but the disturbances in Wynaad, which, by my separate letter on this subject of this day's date, you will observe may become more serious than they at first appeared, may oblige me to alter this plan.

It may happen that you are desirous that the reports on those forts now surveyed should be sent to Madras immediately; and if that should be your wish, they shall be copied and sent forthwith: if not, they shall all go together when the forts on the frontier will be surveyed.

I have, &c.,

ARTHUR WELLESLEY.

INSTRUCTIONS FOR CAPTAIN GURNELL.　　　[1290.]

Seringapatam, 20th Oct., 1802.

The post at Pancoorta Cottah, in Wynaad, has been lately surprised and cut off by the Nairs, and there is an appearance of insurrection in Wynaad. The collector, Major Macleod, is at present at Seringapatam, and it is necessary that a force should be employed not only to quell this insurrection, but to enable Major Macleod to pass through and settle the district.

You are accordingly to march with your battalion on the 21st instant towards Cancancotta, where you will be joined by Major Macleod, and you will proceed in concert with him to quell this insurrection in Wynaad.

There are at present in Wynaad the 1st battalion 4th Bombay regiment, consisting of about 500 firelocks, having a post at Manundwaddy, one at Pancoorta Cottah, each of eighty men, and the remainder of the corps collected in one body at Poollingal. There are besides posts in the redoubts at the head of the Peria and Tambercherry Ghauts. Since the post at Pancoorta Cottah has been cut off, the troops in Wynaad have been reinforced by five companies of Natives, and one of European infantry ordered to be sent there yesterday, and Major Drummond has directions to act offensively against the insurgents without loss of time.

In concert with Major Macleod you will communicate with Major Drummond immediately upon your arrival at Cancancotta, and as far as may be practicable you will combine your operations against the insurgents with his. But if that should not be practicable, I desire that you will lose no time in moving upon them with the utmost celerity, wherever you may hear that they are either collecting or collected, and that you will on no account keep your force stationary.

Major Macleod will assist you with every information that the country can afford; and I particularly desire that you will attend to his requisitions and to his advice upon all occasions.

I have called upon the Dewan to send 200 of the Rajah's horse with you, who will be placed under your orders.

I have given directions to the people belonging to the camp bazaar to prepare to accompany your battalion; and I have called upon the Dewan to turn towards Cancancotta all the supplies which the Mysore country can afford.

You will report to me your operations, and to the commanding officer in Malabar as soon as you can communicate with the troops to the westward, and I shall withdraw you from Wynaad as soon as I find that tranquillity is re-established.

You will do well to leave a guard at Cancancotta with everything that is heavy and likely to detain you in the active operations which I expect from you against these insurgents.

ARTHUR WELLESLEY.

[1291.]   *To Lieutenant-General Stuart.*

SIR,   Seringapatam, 20th Oct., 1802.

Since yesterday accounts have been received from Malabar, by which it appears that the insurrection is imagined to be more general than there was at first reason to suppose. The communication between Cotaparamba and Montana in Cotiote had been interrupted, but it does not appear by whom or in what manner, and the officers in command of those posts had made no effort either to re-establish it, or even to ascertain in what manner it was stopped; and no accounts had been received from Wynaad of a later date than the 14th. By a letter received by Major Macleod from Major Macaulay, it appears that the

Pyche Rajah, who had been traced into Travancore, and whose
person had been recognised and pointed out to the officers of
the government of the Rajah of Travancore, had been suffered
to escape from thence, and there is reason to believe that he is
in Wynaad.   However, when the 1st battalion 8th regiment
will arrive there, there will be in that district at least 1500
men, besides the force in Cotiote. We are in possession of
the principal posts in the district, the roads of communication
are all good, and we know that the insurgents have no post of
any consequence, and that they cannot yet have organised any
regular plan.   There is every reason to hope, therefore, that
this force will re-establish tranquillity and the authority of
government; and it certainly will succeed if the officers are
active.   Major Macleod, and the officers going from hence,
appear fully convinced that success depends upon their exertions.
But if, in consequence of the inactivity of the troops, as well in
Wynaad as Cotiote, any accident should happen in the former
before Major Macleod can get in with this battalion, it will be
necessary that we should be prepared to make arrangements to
attack that district with a respectable force.

In that case Major Macleod will leave the battalion near
Cancancotta, and will proceed into Malabar through Koorg,
and I must immediately collect all I can for this service.

I shall have no difficulty in collecting as many Native troops
as will be necessary, and I understand from Major Macleod
that there is a complete battalion at Erroad, which, in case of
the necessity of this service, you might think it proper to allow
me to draw up the Ghauts.   But we have no Europeans. Lieutenant-Colonel Boles has already called the 77th regiment into
Malabar; and however much I may respect the regiment de
Meuron, I conceive from what I have seen of them that they
are but little calculated for this species of service, and that it is
as necessary to have British soldiers to give them countenance
as it is with the Native troops. I mention these circumstances
at present only that we may be prepared for the worst. But I
acknowledge that if the officers sent in from this place behave
with their usual activity, I have no fears; and I attribute the
length to which this insurrection is supposed to have gone
entirely to the inactivity of the officers in Wynaad and Malabar,
and to their fears of the very name of this Rajah. A few days
will decide the matter. If I find that the insurrection is not got

the better of, I propose immediately to make arrangements to collect a force that will get the better of it; if we do get the better of it now, I propose to go into Malabar as soon as I can, according to the plan of which you formerly approved.

I have, &c.,

ARTHUR WELLESLEY.

[1292.] *To the Secretary of the Military Board.*

SIR,   Seringapatam, 20th Oct., 1802.

I was absent from Seringapatam when I had the honour of receiving your letter of the 13th September, and I was obliged to delay replying to it till my return to this place, when I could have an opportunity of ascertaining the points which the Military Board have been pleased to refer to me.

As all timber is sold at Seringapatam by weight, and there is in fact none to be bought sufficiently dry for the Company's use, it has been difficult to fix a value upon dry timber. However, it may be stated generally that green timber can be bought for one rupee per foot cube; and to this sum, in my opinion, ought to be added one fanam and a half as a fair compensation to the commissary of supply for the length of time he must have had the timber in his possession, and must have disbursed the money for it before it could be fit for use. This sum will be as nearly the value which the commissary of supply will really have disbursed for each foot of dry timber as it can be made.

I have, &c.,

ARTHUR WELLESLEY.

[1293.] *To the Adjutant-General.*

SIR,   Seringapatam, 21st Oct., 1802.

I have to report to you that the Nairs made an attack upon the post at Pancoorta Cottah, in Wynaad, on the 11th instant, which was occupied by seventy men of the 1st of the 4th Bombay regiment, under the command of Captain Dickenson and Lieutenant Maxwell. They succeeded in surprising the troops, killed Captain Dickenson, Lieutenant Maxwell, and twenty-four Native troops, and wounded twenty-one Native troops, of which I herewith enclose a return.

Accounts have been received from Major ————, who commands in Wynaad, of as late a date as the 16th, from which it does not appear that any other act of hostility has been committed since the 11th, excepting a firing upon the post at Manundwaddy, and that the communication throughout Wynaad is interrupted. No act of hostility has been committed by the Nairs below the Ghauts, or upon the troops belonging to the posts in Cotiote, excepting a firing upon a havildar's party in a stockade in the Cootioor pass, which was erected for the protection of the pioneers who were at work in that pass. It appears that the number of people who attacked this stockade are said to have amounted to 300 men, the majority of whom were armed with bows and arrows. The communication between the different posts in Cotiote had likewise been interrupted, but it has not been reported in what manner, by whom, or by what number of men.

I have the honour to enclose copies of the orders issued by Lieutenant-Colonel Boles, which will point out the measures which he has taken to reinforce the troops in Cotiote and Wynaad. I have besides desired him to send a company of Europeans into Wynaad.

I have ordered the 1st battalion 8th Madras regiment to march into Wynaad from Seringapatam with the collector, Major Macleod, who happened to be here on his way from Coimbatoor, and I have great hopes that this reinforcement will make our troops so superior in Wynaad as to crush the insurrection in that district immediately. It does not appear that matters have gone any length in Cotiote, and I think that when the detachment of the Bombay regiment and of the 80th will enter that district all symptoms of insurrection will disappear.

I beg to draw the attention of the Commander-in-Chief to the appointment of a Malabar translator made by Colonel Boles. The Colonel has frequently mentioned to me the necessity of such a person, and I am well convinced of it; but I have been unwilling to recommend any appointment which would create additional expense without at the same time pointing out where a saving might be made. Accordingly I proposed to inquire into this subject when I should visit Malabar. At all events, however, whether other expenses can be curtailed in order to provide for this or not hereafter, it appears absolutely necessary at present that the commanding officer in Malabar should have this assistance; and I beg, therefore, to request that this order may be confirmed.

Lieutenant-Colonel Boles has informed me that there are no tents in Malabar for the use of the European troops, and he can procure no cattle.

I have ordered to Cannanore all the Company's carriage bullocks, and 100 hired bullocks; and I propose to increase this number should circumstances render that measure necessary, and to send into Malabar the tents at present in store at Seringapatam for the use of the regiment de Meuron.

I have no intelligence whatever which can enable me to form an opinion of the extent of this insurrection, or of the strength of the body of rebels already assembled in Wynaad. It is said that the body which surprised Pancoorta Cottah consisted of 300 men, and I don't believe they had a firelock or matchlock among them, but were armed with Nairs' knives, and bows and arrows. They took the arms from that detachment, however, but not the ammunition, as that was blown up in the officer's house. It is said that the Pyche Rajah is in Wynaad, which may be true, as he has certainly come away from the Travancore country, and it is also said that he has been joined by all the inhabitants of the country. This may also be true, as no step has yet been taken for their protection by our troops. But I doubt much his having a large body of armed men with him.

There is no doubt but that since the 11th the rebels have been uncommonly inactive; and as this is so very unusual with the Nairs, particularly after success, I am rather induced to believe that the number of fighting men has not increased much beyond the number that struck the blow at Pancoorta Cottah. The Pyche Rajah has always been a formidable enemy in Malabar, and his force has been much magnified at all times. I have not yet seen any rational account of the number of people in rebellion, nor does it appear that any person in the Company's service has seen one of them, or has ascertained the nature of the impediments to the communication between our posts. But even supposing that the number of people in rebellion should be as large as it was ever supposed to be heretofore, and that we should consequently be obliged to make more solid arrangements to suppress it, we shall enter into the contest with great advantages derived from the situation of our posts, from the excellent communications between them, and in all parts of Malabar from our knowledge of the country and its resources, and from the want of the rebels of arms, ammunition, money, and provisions, and any thing like a post or stronghold in which they can take shelter. A few days will show what is to be the nature of the contest, and I shall lose no time in preparing the arrangements for collecting a force, if that should be necessary.

I have, &c.,

ARTHUR WELLESLEY.

To Major Macleod.   [1294.]

MY DEAR MACLEOD,   Seringapatam, 21st Oct., 1802.

Accounts have been received this morning from Malabar, by which it appears that matters are in a much better state in Wynaad than that in which they have been represented to be. Major ——— writes on the 16th to the officer commanding Calicut, that he had not been attacked, but he had drawn in the post from Pancoorta Cottah. The post at Manundwaddy had been attacked for two days, but nothing had happened. The Major also says that he had detached sections to Manundwaddy, and that he had reinforced the posts upon Tambercherry and Peria Ghauts. Now I should be glad to know how all this is possible, if it be true that the enemy are in such force in Wynaad as he states; and if they are not in such force, if he be really able to send small detachments to all parts of the country, ought he not to be ashamed of himself for not moving out to the attack at once?

However, the intelligence of this morning convinces me that if nothing serious happens to the troops now in Wynaad before you reach the borders, the object of your expedition is easily attainable, and I have no doubt but that in a few days I shall hear of your success. If any accident does happen in Wynaad before you reach the borders, the reputation, and of course the power of the enemy, will be so much increased thereby, that we must make farther and more solid arrangements; but I think it not probable that any thing will happen.

The "Ducks" are feeding upon damaged rice in all these

posts, and I hope they never will feed upon any thing else, if they choose to shut themselves up in them, and there remain till their throats are cut, or they are starved.

Believe me, &c.,

ARTHUR WELLESLEY.

Do every thing in your power to apprise Major ———— or any of the posts in Wynaad of your approach.

[1295.]   *To Lieutenant-Colonel Boles.*

DEAR SIR,   Seringapatam, 21st Oct., 1802.

The accounts received this morning are very satisfactory. It appears by Major ————'s letter of the 16th, first, that he had not been attacked; secondly, that he had been able to draw in the troops from Pancoorta Cottah (which by the bye he had no business to do without orders: however, that is of no consequence at present); thirdly, that he had been able to detach sections to Manundwaddy, and detachments to Peria and Tamberchery Ghauts. My conclusion from all this is, that matters are not quite so bad as he has represented them to be. In fact, if the enemy were in such force in Wynaad, how would it be possible to send these small parties about the country in all directions? And if they are not in the very great force stated, I should like to know why they are not attacked by the Major and driven out of the country? At all events, why he does not move out of Poollingal, and not wait there to be starved?

The intelligence of this morning makes me certain that the object of the expedition from hence is attainable, if no accident happens before the corps reaches the borders.

I will recommend to the Commander-in-Chief a confirmation of all your orders, and I am making arrangements for sending you tents and bullocks; of the latter 300 immediately, and as many more as you can require. I will also try to send dooly boys.

Believe me, &c.,

ARTHUR WELLESLEY.

To Lieutenant-General Stuart.   [1296.]

SIR,   Seringapatam, 21st Oct., 1802.

Since yesterday the accounts from Malabar have been more favourable.

Major ———— writes on the 16th to the commanding officer at Calicut that he had not been attacked, that he had drawn in the post from Pancoorta Cottah to his head-quarters at Poollingal, that he had reinforced with two sections the post at Manundwaddy, and had sent reinforcements to the posts at the Peria and Tambercherry Ghauts. My conclusion from this is, that matters are not quite so bad in Wynaad as they have been reported to be, that the enemy are not in such very great force, or if they were, it would not be possible for Major ———— to move his sections as he has to all parts of the country; and that the object of the expedition from hence will be attained with ease, if no very great accident happens in Wynaad before the troops reach the borders. If any such accident does happen, the reputation and of course the numbers and power of the rebels will be so far increased as to render more solid arrangements necessary.

I have, &c.,

ARTHUR WELLESLEY.

To the Secretary of the Commander-in-Chief.   [1297.]

SIR,   Seringapatam, 22nd Oct., 1802.

I have had the honour of receiving your letter of the 18th instant, and, in conformity to the orders of the Commander-in-Chief, I have given directions that the cots at Cochin and other stations in Malabar where they may not be required may be moved to Cannanore.

In regard to Goa, I have to observe that that station is within the range of the barrackmaster in Canara; a circumstance to which I imagine his Excellency did not advert. I understand that a barrackmaster is obliged, under the barrack regulations, to move the cots under his charge from one part of his range to another, when they may be required, for a certain sum allowed him by government monthly to defray that and other charges. But I understand that it is not expected that he should move the cots without that range.   I shall be obliged to you if you will lay this circumstance before the Commander-in-Chief, and request his orders regarding the removal of the cots from Goa: whether they shall be moved to Cannanore at the public expense, at that of the barrackmaster in Canara, or at that of the barrackmaster in Malabar?

I have, &c.,

ARTHUR WELLESLEY.

[1298.]   *To Lieutenant-General Stuart.*

SIR,   Seringapatam, 23rd Oct., 1802.

Since my last letter I have received accounts from Malabar, stating that the reinforcement from Calicut had joined Major Drummond in Wynaad without opposition.   Nothing had happened there as far as the 17th.

In Cotiote all was quiet as far down as the 20th, and the Nairs had made no opposition to the provisioning of Montana. There is, therefore, every reason to believe that matters will soon be in complete tranquillity again.

I have, &c.,

ARTHUR WELLESLEY.

[1299.]   *To Major Macleod.*

SIR,   Seringapatam, 24th Oct., 1802, 9 A.M.

I have just received your letter of the 22nd.   The experience which I have had of insurrections, similar to that now in Wynaad, makes it clear to me that the presence of yourself, or of some person possessing the supreme civil authority in that district, is essentially necessary to settle it.   The first operations must depend upon the troops.   Either the rebels must be beaten, or they must be dispersed; and at the moment at which either of those events takes place the presence of the civil magistrate is necessary in order to reap the good consequences of the success of the troops.   If the civil magistrate be present, he will immediately re-establish the civil organisation of the district, will recall the tahsildars and aumildars of districts and villages to perform their functions, the inhabitants will return to their homes, the whole will regain confidence, and the troops will enjoy the benefits of the resources of the country; but if the civil magistrate be absent, whatever may be the success of the troops, the country will not settle, there will be no communication between the inhabitants and the commanding officer, the villages will remain deserted, and the troops, instead of enjoying the benefits of the resources of the country, and being thereby enabled to continue their active operations against, and pursuit of, the rebels, must forthwith turn their attention to procuring subsistence, which must be drawn from a distance.

The consequence therefore of the absence of yourself, or of some person possessing the supreme civil authority in Wynaad at present, may be that, even if the troops should be successful, of which from the latest accounts I have not the smallest doubt, the rebellion may still exist, the contest will be lengthened, and will be concluded at last only by the arrival in the district of a person having civil authority, whom I now urge you to send there.

In opposition to this request you state the inconvenience which will be the result of your communication with the other districts being cut off. Upon this subject I have to observe, firstly, that it is not likely that it will be even precarious, as soon as the troops commence their operations in Wynaad, particularly if the country be settled as they get on; secondly, that even if it should be so, the inconvenience, loss, and expense to the public will not be so great as they will be by the lengthened contest in consequence of your absence.

Upon the whole, therefore, I most earnestly urge you to reconsider this subject, and, if you should not think it proper to enter Wynaad with the troops yourself, at least to send there Mr. Wilson and Mr. Warden, with full authority and instructions from you to settle the country.

I have, &c.,

ARTHUR WELLESLEY.

To Captain G. Gurnell. [1800.]

SIR, Seringapatam, 24th Oct., 1802.

I am concerned to inform you that I have received a letter from Major Macleod, in which he tells me that he does not

propose to enter Wynaad with the troops under your command.
I still hope, however, that he will alter this intention in consequence of the letter which I have written to him this day; or
that, if he should not accompany you, he will send to join you
either Mr. Warden or Mr. Wilson, or some of the gentlemen
having civil authority in Wynaad.

But whether Major Macleod or either of the gentlemen
above-mentioned join you, it is absolutely necessary that you
should enter that district without delay, according to my
instructions of the 20th instant. Unless you should hear that
the enemy are in force on this side of Manundwaddy, in which
case you are to proceed immediately to attack them, you will
march, in the first instance, to the neighbourhood of Manundwaddy, and communicate with the officer in command of that
station, and proceed afterwards according to the information
which you will receive from him. Recollect, however, that not
only your success, but even your safety, depends upon the
rapidity and length of your movements, and I strongly recommend you not to remain more than one day in any place.

On your marches you must always cover your flanks by
parties; and in your attacks of the enemy, which will probably
always be in a jungle, you must push parties through the
jungle upon the flanks of the enemy, at the same time that you
make your great attack; and in passing paddy-valleys, in particular, great attention must be paid to occupying the sides of
the valley with your parties before the main body enters it.

You will experience some inconvenience from the absence of
the civil authority, because your success will not settle the
country, and till that is settled again you cannot expect to
enjoy the benefit of its resources. It is, therefore, necessary
that we should make arrangements for supplying you from this
country. You have already received orders to occupy Cancancotta with a small party; that must now be increased to 50
men, commanded by a European officer.

You will take with you, on the men's backs or on bullocks, as
you may think proper, the 50 loads of rice which you have
already, and leave directions at Cancancotta that the bullocks
which you will not take may be returned to Seringapatam.

I shall forward rice and other articles of provision from
hence to Cancancotta, and you will either order forward what
you may require, or you will return to that neighbourhood to

procure fresh supplies, according to the success of your operations and the information you may have of the state of the communication between you and Cancancotta. Besides these supplies, which will be in the grain department, the Dewan will forward upon Cancancotta all kinds of supplies for the bazaar.

The officer who will be left at this post must be accurately instructed regarding the mode of forwarding these supplies, and must send to me all the information which he will receive from you.

Although Major Macleod may yet determine to accompany you himself, or may send with you Mr. Warden or Mr. Wilson, it is not probable that either of those gentlemen will arrive at Cancancotta on the day appointed, viz. the 25th instant. You will, therefore, leave at Cancancotta a letter addressed to these gentlemen, apprising them of the information you may have received and of your intended movements, and request them to follow you without delay.

I have, &c.,

ARTHUR WELLESLEY.

To Colonel Carlisle.   [1301.]

SIR,   Seringapatam, 24th Oct., 1802.

I have received the directions of the Commander-in-Chief to order a survey upon the Honourable Company's draught-cattle by a committee of officers of the artillery, and I have to request that you will give directions that a committee may assemble accordingly at Bellagode, a village about five miles from Seringapatam, on the road to Hussainpoor, on the morning of the 27th instant. The Company's draught-cattle are divided into 43 karkhanas, each consisting, when complete, of 100 draught and 12 forage bullocks. Some of the bullocks were received into the service about three years and a half ago, and were old cattle at that time, and many of them are supposed to be unfit for any service at present on account of their age; others were received from the Bombay government when the establishments on the coast of Malabar and at Goa passed under the government of Fort St. George, and some of these are so small as to be unfit for draught, although they may be fit for carriage, and some of them are supposed to be unfit for any service, and others have been received from the breeding establishment in the hands of the Rajah's government. Of these last it is supposed that a few will never be of sufficient size for the draught, although they may answer for carriage, and that some will never answer for either draught or carriage.

It will be necessary that the committee which you will appoint should direct their examination to ascertain the number of cattle of each description in each karkhana.

In order to facilitate their survey, I have directed Captain Mackay to arrange the bullocks in each karkhana separately, according to his notion of their capacity for service, and the committee will find them arranged in this manner on the ground at Bellagode on the morning of the 27th. I have the honour to enclose a form according to which I wish that the report of the committee should be made out. The bullocks will be found classed in the manner stated in this form.

I have, &c.,

ARTHUR WELLESLEY.

[1302.]   *To the Chief Secretary of Government.*

SIR,   24th Oct., 1802.

I have the honour to enclose the report of a committee which I ordered to survey the buildings used as ordnance and military store-rooms at Cannanore, and estimates of the expense of carrying into execution the repairs and improvements which this committee have thought necessary. As orders were sent at a very late period of the last season for the repairs required to these buildings, nothing could be done to them, and in consequence the ordnance and stores have been much exposed to the weather during the whole of the monsoon. Cannanore is now the only place at which there are stores upon the Coast; those heretofore at Cochin and Mangalore have been removed thither, and the Company is likely to sustain a great loss in this important article if the repairs required to these store-rooms are not commenced at an early period in the approaching fair season.

It appears to me, however, that all the store-rooms examined and reported upon by this committee may not be necessary to contain the stores which it is intended to lodge at Cannanore; and by repairing those only which are absolutely necessary, a great part of the estimated expense may be saved.

According to a plan approved of by the Commander-in-Chief, it is my intention, should circumstances permit, to visit the corps and stations in the province of Malabar as soon as the season is sufficiently advanced; and I propose particularly to inspect the state of these store-rooms at Cannanore.   As it is essentially necessary that some of them should be put in repair without loss of time, I beg to have the permission of the Right Hon. the Governor in Council to order the repairs and improvement of such as may be requisite to contain the stores according to the estimates of the expense enclosed, provided those estimates meet with the approbation of the Military Board.

I have, &c.,

ARTHUR WELLESLEY.

To Lieutenant-Colonel Cuppage.   [1303.]

DEAR SIR,   Seringapatam, 27th Oct., 1802.

I have just received your letter of the 23rd instant.   It was never my wish to cast an imputation or reflection on any person in regard to the matters respecting the regimental hospital. All I desired was to remedy a defect which was reported officially to me, and to make no farther inquiry.   I have still this wish, and am very desirous that no further investigation should be made in this matter, and accordingly that Mr. —— should be released from his arrest.

Believe me, &c.,

ARTHUR WELLESLEY.

To Lieutenant-General Stuart.   [1304.]

SIR,   Seringapatam, 27th Oct., 1802.

I have had no accounts from Malabar since I wrote you. Captain Gurnell arrived within one mile of Cancancotta on the 25th, but he was there stopped by a nullah which he had made arrangements to cross. The rains have been very heavy for these last few days, but the weather now begins to clear again. The impediments of this kind which the 1st of the 8th will meet on their road into the centre of Wynaad are well known here, and it is imagined that they will no longer exist when the rains will cease.

Captain Scott has desired that I would lay before you his intentions to place one non-commissioned officer in charge of all the Europeans attached to his department, in order to preserve regularity in their barracks and to insure that of their food. The man to whom he wishes to give charge of them is a corporal of the 19th regiment, and he is desirous that he should have the pay of a serjeant for this duty. In my opinion, the best mode of arranging this matter is that he should be appointed in orders to act as serjeant in charge of the Europeans attached to the gun-carriage manufactory, and his pay may be drawn in Captain Scott's abstracts; and if you approve of it, I will send an official recommendation of this arrangement.

Captain Scott has also desired that I should make myself acquainted with your wishes respecting the pay of the European artificers while on trial. He appears to think that 5 pagodas *per mensem* would be sufficient for each of them.

He is of opinion that very shortly he will be able to discharge all the establishment of artificers, and to depend upon the place for the number of men to perform the work ordered from time to time by the Military Board. I know that artificers can be got here; but as it is probable that the quantity of work which will be ordered by the Military Board will be limited only by the deficiency of materials, I imagine that Captain Scott will require not only his establishment, but every other artificer he can procure, at least for some time. It is, therefore, best to defer the consideration of this subject till it is seen how the whole machine works as now established.

My opinion of a great undertaking of this kind by government is, that the number of work-people and the quantity of work they should perform every month should be fixed, and then the exact expense of every piece of work is known, and there is a decided check upon the person at the head of the manufactory. It is true that this check is not required upon Captain Scott, but it may be upon his successor, and it is not worth while to give up a good principle in a great establishment of this kind to save the pay of a small number of artificers for a few days.

I have, &c.,

ARTHUR WELLESLEY.

To Lieutenant-General Stuart.   [1305.]

SIR,   Seringapatam, 28th Oct., 1802.

I have received a letter from Captain Gurnell this morning, in which he informs me that he had been able to march from Cancancotta to Sangaloo in Wynaad yesterday. At Sangaloo there is a nullah, about three feet deep, where the Nairs opposed the advance of Colonel Stevenson in 1801. Upon this occasion they occupied an old stockade which Colonel Stevenson had constructed for the security of his communication, and fired briskly upon Captain Gurnell as he advanced. However, he passed the nullah on the two flanks of the stockade, under cover of the fire of another party, and carried the stockade with the loss of only one man wounded. The Nairs sustained some loss.

Captain Gurnell intended to advance to Manundwaddy this day.

We know of no impediment between Sangaloo and Manundwaddy, excepting the river immediately under the fire of that place.

The road from Sangaloo is tolerably open, and is well known to a party of our pioneers with the 1st of the 8th, who made it, and indeed to the greater number of the 1st of the 8th themselves, who served in the campaign in that country. The distance is 17 miles. Although this affair with the Nairs was of no great magnitude, the consequence of it is that they have been driven from the only place in which they could hope to make any successful stand, and it must give confidence to our officers and troops in the mode of attack recommended to them.

Major Macleod does not go through Wynaad with the troops, as was arranged between him and me; but he is gone to Calicut through Coimbatoor by Paulgautcherry.*

* See letters to Major Macleod of 3rd Sept. and 21st Oct., 1802, pp. 291, 343.

I have written him my opinion of the necessity that either he or some gentleman having civil authority should go into Wynaad directly, as I know that in the present state of affairs nothing effectual towards the settlement of the district can be done in their absence; and I have done this in such strong terms that I think it possible that he will still return and join Captain Gurnell, or, at all events, send one of the gentlemen to him with full authority, and instructions in what manner to act.

In case he should not return, I will have the honour of submitting to you my correspondence with Major Macleod upon this subject for your information.* However, as I know Major

---

* The following letters from Major Macleod show the business on which he was occupied:—

Major Macleod to Colonel the Hon. A. Wellesley.

My DEAR COLONEL,   Coimbatoor, 18th Sept., 1802.

I ought long ago to have answered your letter of the 3rd instant, but it had been following me over the country, and till I reached this place on the 8th I have scarcely had a halting for the preceding fortnight.

There is no doubt but you can make up gun-carriages at Seringapatam for probably half the price they cost the Company at Madras. I enclose an order on Wynaad for teak, though I have always understood that the Mysore bounds were more celebrated for teak forests than Wynaad.

I have advertised the Malabar forests to be rented, but no favourable offers have yet been made for them. The parts of Wynaad bordering on Mysore need not be included, at all events, in the arrangements I may make, as being too far from water carriage.

I got the loan from Colonel Boles of six of the Company's elephants* attached to the military department in Malabar, and had them for a very short time employed in dragging to the sides of rivers some of the full-grown teak, which I principally intended to send to Madras on the public account as a trial for ascertaining if I can or cannot sell Malabar teak at our Presidency at lower rates than Pegu teak is sold there. I am sanguine enough to believe I can furnish the Bombay marine with teak timber at half the price the Company usually paid.

Among many other speculations I have in contemplation for improving Malabar, I shall try with what advantages ships may be built in that province.

I think your arrangement for discharging the supernumerary pioneers very judicious, as we can with confidence dispense with their services, by which means there will be a saving annually of perhaps 25,000 pagodas, and still we shall have enough of them to answer our purpose.

I have already anticipated in a great degree the hint you notice about the roads being kept in constant repair, for I am making up a complete set of pioneers' tools to be attached to each district; and after the whole of the public roads shall have been completed I shall distribute the tools among the Parbutties (Gours or Patels in Mysore), and hold them severally responsible for all public roads and bridges within their respective circles being kept in

---

* They were ordered away suddenly by Colonel Boles since I left Calicut.

Macleod to be a zealous, active, and able servant of the public, I am not desirous that it should go farther unless you should think it necessary.

I have, &c.,

ARTHUR WELLESLEY.

To Major Budden. [1306.]

SIR, Seringapatam, 29th Oct., 1802.

I have just received your letter of the 20th.

It is probable that you will have received mine of the 13th on the 22nd, and that you will have determined in consequence repair conformably to a separate regulation which shall be framed for their guidance.

The old roads in Cotiote you'll think very inferior to most of the roads made lately by the inhabitants of all the districts south of the Cottah river. The roads of Cotiote are mere pathways in comparison to them, for all our new roads have very substantial bridges on them, and much more of a civilised appearance than those which the pioneers made in Cotiote. But you will judge better by seeing them than from my account; and I need not say that I shall be happy in accompanying you through the Malabar province whenever it may be most convenient to you. I shall commence my *zig-zag* circuit through Coimbatoor on the 23rd; and about the 5th or 6th of October I expect to go through the Cauverypooram Pass. I'll remain two or three days at Colligall, from whence I mean to revisit the famous fall in the Cauvery, *Gunga-Chookee.* If you have not seen it, let me recommend that you take the trouble of visiting so grand a natural curiosity.

I return from Colligall by Wynaad to Malabar, through the Cootecoor Pass.

I send this letter by a peon to the Ardenhully aumildar, and if you favour me with an answer I'll thank you to send it to the tasseeldar of Colligall, who will forward it through the Cauverypooram Pass. I wish much to have the pleasure of seeing you; and even in the event of your not seeing the island of Sheevuna Samooder while I am at Colligall, it is more than probable I will go to see you at Seringapatam.

Yours ever faithfully,

WILLIAM MACLEOD.

I wish you could order the same six elephants to be spared for me.

Major Macleod to Major-General the Hon. A. Wellesley.

MY DEAR GENERAL, Talwarry, 22nd Oct., 1802.

From the aspect of affairs in Wynaad I have resolved not to encumber the battalion under Captain Gurnell, as I would be separated from the other districts; for to ask the troops for an escort to pass me through would be probably detrimental to their plans of operations, and as no offensive movement, so far as I can learn, has been made yet, the greatest activity will be wanted from the corps under Captain Gurnell. I send you a Hindonese copy of the last accounts I had from the man who was tasseeldar of Wynaad. He thinks all the Nairs have joined the Pyche.

I still think that Captain Gurnell's battalion should march to Manundwaddy and concert measures with the least possible delay with the main body of the not to allow the 1st battalion 3rd regiment to embark. If that should be the case, you are still to remain at Goa until you receive orders from the officers of the government of Fort St. George to quit it, or until you receive intimation from the government of Bombay that the intention of withdrawing the British troops from Goa is connected with instructions from the Supreme government.

In either of those cases the troops are to embark for Bombay without loss of time, and in the meantime the vessels are to be detained and all preparatory arrangements made, so that the embarkation and departure of the troops may take place with due celerity. I write to Lieutenant-Colonel Brown to desire that a company may be sent from Hulliball to Goa to take charge of the stores, so that the 1st battalion 3rd regiment may embark complete in numbers. But if that company should

troops, so as to attack the rebels from two quarters, and to be as much as possible in motion : the longer the marches the better. It is absolutely necessary to prepare a store of rice at Cancancotta, as no dependence can be placed on getting any in the district in its present state.

My baggage was on its way towards Cancancotta. I'll halt here to-morrow till it comes up.

The part of Wynaad called Niamkull Cottah is still undisturbed ; but with regard to supplies, it is scarcely nearer Manundwaddy or Poollingal than Serin-gapatam.

Yours very faithfully,

WILLIAM MACLEOD.

Major Macleod to Major-General the Hon. A. Wellesley.

MY DEAR GENERAL. Talwarry, 23rd Oct., 1802.

I was this morning favoured with your letter of the 21st. I had written you last night that I had determined to go from hence to Calicut by Coimbatoor.

By a letter from Tellicherry of the 19th everything is quiet in Cotiote, so I hope Captain Gurnell's corps will soon keep down the threats of the party of rebels. I am induced to believe that he may, with great safety, subdivide his corps in pursuit of them, having of course a place of rendezvous fixed on to rejoin. I hope you will cause provisions to be collected for them at Cancan-cotta, and sent after them under an escort, either to Manundwaddy or Poollingal ; and I hope Major D. has ere now begun in consequence of your orders to make offensive movements.

I have no account from Malabar that leads me to suppose that there is any thing like a general effort of interest against us, and I am only astonished that greater numbers are not assembled, when we consider the success of the gang at the onset, and our inactivity afterwards : but one thing is certain, that a continuation of the same inactivity will naturally cause all the thieves in the country to assemble.

I set out at three in the morning without my baggage.

Ever yours faithfully,

WILLIAM MACLEOD, .

not have arrived at Goa previously to the arrival of the information which will enable you to allow the 1st battalion 3rd regiment to embark, one company of that corps must remain at Goa in charge of the stores, &c., according to the instructions which you report to have received from Major-General Nicholson, and to the desire of the acting Resident, and of his Excellency the Governor-General of Goa. I beg to have from you, as soon as possible, returns of the ordnance, military stores, grain, provisions, garrison stores, &c., &c., in store at Goa, and generally of all the Company's property that you will leave behind you.

I have, &c.,

ARTHUR WELLESLEY.

I beg that you will apprise the acting Resident of my intention to order to Goa a company from Hulliball for the care of the stores, in order that he may take measures to procure from the Portuguese government the necessary facilities for the march through the Portuguese territories.

To Lieutenant-General Stuart.   [1307.]

SIR,   Seringapatam, 29th Oct., 1802.

I have the honour to enclose the report of the committee which surveyed the gun-bullocks in consequence of your order.

You will observe that 379 are reported as unfit for any service, and I should wish to have your orders respecting the disposal of them. If they are kept, they will cost each about half a rupee *per mensem* (I was mistaken when in a former letter I told you they would cost a rupee), and, bad as they are, they will do the work of the gun-carriage karkhana. At this moment we have nearly 200 bullocks employed on this service, and when the season for bringing in the timber will come round we shall have many more. Besides, cattle will constantly be wanted to move the finished work from the manufactory to the stations at which it will be required. On the other hand, it is probable that if you should determine that these bullocks should be sold, they will not bring a great price; and as their drivers and attendants are to be kept at all events, and their food costs only half a rupee a month, cattle for work can never be procured at so cheap a rate.

Upon the whole, therefore, I recommend that until the karkhanas can be completed from the breeding establishment, these bullocks should be kept.

The detached bullocks are in the Ceded Districts, Malabar, Canara, and at Goa, and Hullihall in Soonda.

I have, &c.,

ARTHUR WELLESLEY.

[1308.]   *To Lieutenant-General Stuart.*

SIR,   Seringapatam, 31st Oct., 1802.

I have the honour to inform you that I have received a letter from Captain Gurnell this day, from which I judge that it will be necessary to make arrangements to enter Wynaad in force. He had advanced to Manundwaddy from Sangaloo, on the 28th, seventeen miles; but he had been strongly opposed on the whole road, with trifling loss, only one sepoy wounded of the Company's troops; but of the 200 of the Rajah's horse, whom the Dewan sent with him, five were killed and some wounded, with seventeen horses. The communication between Manundwaddy and Sangaloo, the boundary, is entirely cut off, and the consequence is, that Captain Gurnell will be obliged to return to Cancancotta for fresh supplies.

Captain Gurnell was about to move on the 29th to attack a party supposed to be at a pagoda in the neighbourhood of Manundwaddy, and if he should fall in with this party the communication may be opened and matters may still go right; but if he should not, it is very obvious, from what has passed already, that although our troops can march through the country without loss, one battalion is not sufficiently strong to protect its baggage and supplies; that as long as the country remains in its present state, no supplies can be drawn from it; and that we must make more solid arrangements and enter the country in such force as not only to be able to march through it, but also to live in it by keeping up our communication with Mysore.

I am, however, still of opinion that if Major Macleod had entered Wynaad with this battalion, according to the arrangement agreed on between him and me before he quitted Seringapatam, his presence would have had such an effect in settling the country, that this battalion would have been sufficient.

I now enclose copies of the letters which have passed between Major Macleod and me upon this subject, which will point out the grounds on which I have formed this opinion. In addition to this, I must inform you that I wrote Major Macleod a private one, in which I offered to go into Wynaad with him myself with the battalion if he would return, and if he had no confidence in Captain Gurnell, its commanding officer.

I now propose to make arrangements to collect forthwith and to enter Wynaad in strength from this side at the earliest possible period.

With this view I have written to the commanding officer at Trichinopoly to send here the battalion which you have ordered to be in readiness to join me. We have, however, no Europeans. You will observe that 300 men of the 77th are ordered into Malabar. The remainder of the corps are about 150 men; and as Lieutenant-Colonel Boles has likewise drawn into Malabar the flank companies of the Native corps in Canara, I almost doubt the propriety of drawing the remainder of the 77th to this place. At all events, we ought to have more British troops than 150 men, and I hope that you will have it in your power to send some. If we could get only four or five companies of the 33rd for a short time, they would be sufficient.

The plan for the expedition will be for the Bombay troops to keep Cotiote and the lower country in tranquillity, and if possible, to enter Wynaad from the westward, while we enter from the eastward. We must establish ourselves as we get on, and at least make our communications with Mysore certain, and I have no doubt but that in a short time the whole party will disperse.

What has happened lately points out the necessity of our obtaining possession of the person of the Pyche Rajah. This can be done only by settling the country and dispersing the troops, as soon as the rebels will have dispersed; but the country cannot be settled without the assistance of the civil authority, and I beg leave to suggest that the collector may be desired to come round to join me as soon as I shall be prepared to enter the district.

I have, &c.,

ARTHUR WELLESLEY.

I have had no letters from Malabar for many days, and

cannot tell what Lieutenant-Colonel Boles is doing; but the communication is uninterrupted.

[1309.]   *To Captain Gurnell.*

SIR,   31st Oct., 1802.

I have received your letter of the 29th instant, from which I judge that you will be under the necessity of returning to Cancancotta for supplies, according to my instructions of the 24th instant. At all events it will be necessary that you should make a movement towards Sangaloo, in order that the Rajah's horse may return in safety; and as it appears that the country is so wet that their operations can be of little advantage to you, they must return to Cancancotta and remain there.

If you should return to Cancancotta, or so far as to cross the nullah at Sangaloo, it will be necessary that you should leave a post in the stockade at that place; and unless you should have settled a plan of operations with the officers of the Bombay army, which plan would be defeated by your omitting to return towards Manundwaddy immediately, or unless you should have reason to believe that your presence in the neighbourhood of Manundwaddy is essentially necessary to the safety of the troops in Wynaad, you are to remain on this side of the nullah at Sangaloo, between that place and Cancancotta, until you will hear farther from me. But if you should have settled a plan of operations with the officers of the Bombay army, or if you should have reason to believe that your presence in Wynaad is necessary to their safety, you must return towards Manundwaddy, and act again upon my instructions of the 20th and 24th.

At all events I expect to have from you an accurate detail of all that has passed since you quitted Sangaloo on the 28th instant, as soon as you will approach so near as that the communication will be secure; and I beg you to be very particular in your statements of the number of insurgents you saw, the mode in which they were armed, the present state of the country for military operations, and the natural obstacles which you met on the road to Manundwaddy, in order to enable me to form a correct judgment of the nature of the measures to be adopted to get the better of this insurrection.

I have, &c.,

ARTHUR WELLESLEY.

To the Officer Commanding at Trichinopoly.   [1810.]

SIR,   Seringapatam, 31st Oct., 1802.

The Commander-in-Chief has informed me that you have
received directions to hold in readiness a battalion of Native
infantry, belonging to the garrison under your command, to
proceed to this country, if I should find it necessary to call for
its services. I have reason to believe that the services of this
battalion will be required in this country, and I shall be obliged
to you if you will give orders that it may march to Seringapatam
by the Gudjelhatty Pass with all convenient expedition.

I have, &c.,-

ARTHUR WELLESLEY.

To Josiah Webbe, Esq.   [1311.]

MY DEAR WEBBE,   Seringapatam, 2nd Nov., 1802.

I have had the pleasure of receiving your letter of the 29th October, and I am happy to find that I agree in opinion with you
regarding the arrack concerns in this country.

My opinion of the mode in which the matter ought to be
settled is as follows: I ought to write to you a public letter,
stating nearly what I did in mine of the 11th October, pointing
out more particularly the reasons for which the government order
does not apply to the situation of the troops in this country, and
requesting you to urge the Dewan to give the officers in command
in this country a sum equal to that which those in similar
situations in the Company's territories will receive annually.
Upon this letter you can ground your communications with
Purneah ; and when matters will have been arranged with him,
I will issue a general order forbidding positively all interference
on the part of commanding officers in bazaars, &c., in obedience
to the government order.

At the same time I will say that I have received intimation
from you that it is intended by the Dewan to give annually to
officers in command of stations a sum at least equal in amount
to that which officers in similar situations receive in the Company's territories.   In this manner the whole transaction will be
public, at the same time that it will be felt that the payment
depends upon the good-will of the Rajah's government, and is

not a matter of right. But another circumstance will make this more clear, and that is, that upon the first occasion that a complaint of an officer in command is made, I shall recommend that this allowance from the government may not be given to him in future. I approve entirely of the intention to give more than in the Company's territories. We ought to have the best officers in this country, and there is no mode of getting them to remain here so certain as to reward their services handsomely; and we know that this arrangement will be a saving rather than an expense to the Rajah's government. It is impossible to state in the general order the exact sum which each commanding officer will receive, and it is best to leave it at large, as I have done, by saying a sum at least equal to that received by officers in command of stations in the Company's territories.

Let me hear from you upon this subject, and if you approve of this mode of arranging it, I will write you a public letter.

The General will have informed you of the progress of affairs in Wynaad. I think still that if I could get Macleod to go into the country, the business would be settled without any further assembly of troops, which is a great object as well on the score of expense as of reputation. The people are still in their villages; but they run away from and will hold no communication with our troops; and I am convinced that if Macleod would go in with his Cutchery and commence his communications with them, they would regain confidence in us, would give us intelligence, and supply us. If they continue to hold off, we must go in in force, as we see that one battalion can do no more than march through the country, and we should require at least two more to keep up its communication with Mysore in order to feed it, and Europeans in case of anything serious.

I sent Piele a memorandum yesterday respecting a disputed boundary between the Rajah of Koorg and the Rajah of Mysore, which I have desired him to send to you.

I thank you for what you propose to do for Murray.

> Believe me, &c.,
>
> ARTHUR WELLESLEY.

To Major Macleod.

MY DEAR MACLEOD,   Seringapatam, 3rd Nov., 1802.

I imagine that you will by this time have arrived at Calicut, and I therefore write to inform you of the state of affairs in Wynaad.

Captain Gurnell was opposed in crossing the nullah at San-galoo, on the borders, by some Nairs in a stockade ; but he suc-ceeded in carrying it with the loss of only one man wounded by crossing the nullah on both flanks, and thus entering it. The Nairs sustained some loss. He marched on the following day, the 28th, from Sangaloo to Manundwaddy, seventeen miles. He was opposed in many places, and the opposition appears to have been brisk, but we lost only one sepoy wounded. The Rajah's horse sustained some loss in killed and wounded, and some fol-lowers were killed ; but I attribute this to the badness of the road and its narrowness, which obliged them to extend their line, and prevented them from effectually covering their flanks. This they were prevented from doing also by the nullahs, which were full, and across which the Nairs fired at them.

A party went on the 29th to attack a pagoda, about three miles from Manundwaddy, but the Nairs had left it. On the 30th five companies of the 1st of the 8th marched back from Manundwaddy to Sangaloo to escort the Rajah's horse, which were found to be useless, as the country was so wet, and to procure supplies of provisions. They were not opposed on their march, and they were to return to Manundwaddy yesterday.

I have not yet had from Captain Gurnell any accurate account of the numbers of the enemy, which can enable me to form an opinion of the extent of the insurrection, or of the measures which must be ulteriorly taken to suppress it. I have, how-ever, called for the troops which will be necessary in case we must proceed in force, and I shall be ready for operations before the season will be sufficiently advanced. I am clearly of opinion that before any farther expense is incurred, it will be worth while that you should take a trip to Wynaad. All accounts, public and private, agree that although the inhabitants are still in their villages, they fly from them upon the approach of our officers and troops : they hold no communication with us, we have no intelligence, and they afford us no supplies.

The reason is that which I before gave you in my public

letter, the civil organization is destroyed; but your arrival in the country with your Cutchery would set all that matter to rights directly. It is obvious from what has passed already that a battalion can march anywhere without loss; but till the country is resettled the communication will be interrupted, that force will be put to shifts for its subsistence, and in the end the insurrection will get so far, so many people will be embarked in it, that we must proceed regularly to work with a large force.

I have information from Wynaad by means of the woodcutters. I hear that the insurrection is by no means pleasing to the majority of the inhabitants, and that the common cry is for you to return. Indeed our government must be strangely odious to the people if it were otherwise, as I understand from you that they have paid their revenue, which cannot, therefore, be very burthensome on them, and it is not possible that they can already look to the permanence of the power of the Pyche Rajah, considering that the insurrection is only a fortnight old.

Allow me to entreat you, then, to go into Wynaad. But if you cannot go yourself, send there a sensible, discreet man, with full powers and instructions, and, above all, the Cutchery. By means of that alone will you communicate with the inhabitants.

When I hear next from Gurnell, I shall probably be able to decide what is to be done further in a military way. If I send more troops, I shall go with them. But I am so sensible that nothing can be done by any military men unless the country is settled as they go on, that I have determined not to go in till your people are prepared to accompany me. I arranged the settlement of Wynaad upon this principle before, and I have always acted upon it in Soonda, in the Mahratta country, and in Bullum, and I may say in the Ceded Districts, which were taken possession of by troops sent in by me, and by my plans.

Believe me, &c.,

ARTHUR WELLESLEY.

By the bye, I hear that since Major Drummond has been released from Kyde, he says that the insurrection is nothing at all.

To Major Macleod.   [1818.]

My dear Macleod,   Seringapatam, 4th Nov., 1802.

Lieutenant-Colonel Boles has sent me a letter from Captain Watson, which proves more clearly than ever that your presence alone in Wynaad is wanted to settle the country again. Allow me, therefore, to urge you again to go there with your Cutchery. The inhabitants appear ready to come in, and only wait to be called ; but they will not go to the officers, who, by the bye, have neither the right nor the means of communicating with them.

Believe me, &c.,

ARTHUR WELLESLEY.

———————————

To Captain Fraser, or Officer commanding at Bonawassi.   • [1814.]

Sir,   Seringapatam, 4th Nov., 1802.

I have the honour to enclose you a letter, which I beg you to forward without delay to the Nabob of Savanore, who, I imagine, is residing at Polliam under the Company's protection. I have lately heard that this person is collecting troops within the Company's boundary, or in its neighbourhood, with a view to attacking the Mahrattas ; nay, that he has even attacked them at Haungul, in the neighbourhood of Polliam, of which place he has got possession. This letter is written to warn him against such proceedings, and to apprise him that I shall give orders that the people he will collect, if within the Company's boundaries, may be attacked, and that if he collects troops at all he must quit the asylum which he has hitherto had in the Company's territories.

I beg that you will be so kind as to gain information of the conduct of the Nabob of Savanore. If you should find that he is collecting troops within the Company's territories, you will take an opportunity of moving out from Bonawassi and attack them by surprise in one of the moonlight nights.

You will take care previously to ascertain precisely their situation, so as not to miss them or to involve your own troops in a scrape, and you will afterwards be upon your guard lest an endeavour should be made to surprise you. At the same time you might endeavour to seize the person of the Nabob of Savanore.

If you should find that he is collecting troops, but not within the territories of the Company or of the Rajah of Mysore, you will be so kind as to communicate to him my desire that he will, with his family, quit the Company's territories forthwith, and not return to them again till he is determined to conduct himself in the same peaceable manner that originally acquired for him an asylum within the British territory.

I have, &c.,

ARTHUR WELLESLEY.

[1315.]   *To Alexander Read, Esq.*

SIR,   Seringapatam, 4th Nov., 1802.

I have received your letter upon the subject of the Cazis proceeding from the districts under your management towards Madras, and I will take care that they shall be well treated on their route.

The Rajah of Mysore's servants have given me intelligence that the Nabob of Savanore, who has been for some time living under the Company's protection at Polliam, for which favour he was recommended to you by me, has lately been collecting troops in the Mysore country, as well as in Soonda and the Mahratta territories, with a view to committing depredations on the Mahrattas, which he has actually commenced by an attack upon and taking possession of Haungul. I imagine that he has been urged to this conduct by a man by name Imaum u Deen, who left Seringapatam lately with a letter of introduction from me to you. I hope, however, that I have secured his person at Shikarpoor.

I need not point out to you the evil consequences which may be the result of this conduct of the Nabob of Savanore, particularly if it be not made clear to the whole world that he acts not only without the sanction but in disobedience to the direct orders of the Company's servants. There is nothing which the Mahrattas desire so much, or the news of which they would receive with so much pleasure, as that of the commencement of a system of robbery and plunder from our territories into theirs, as they would thereby have a fair pretext to retaliate, and they would do so to the utmost of their power.

I have, therefore, thought it proper to give the Nabob of

Savanore an early intimation of my sentiments upon this subject, and of my intentions, if he should persevere in this conduct, which I have done in very explicit terms, as you will perceive by the enclosed translation of the letter which I have written him. I also enclose a copy of the letter which I have written to Captain Fraser at Bonawassi, which will explain to you the measures which I propose should be adopted in case the Nabob should have collected any people in arms within the Company's territories, or should have collected them within the Mahratta territories, still using for himself the asylum at Polliam.

As these measures are solely of precaution, and directed to preserve the tranquillity of the territories of the Company and of the Rajah of Mysore, I am convinced that you will approve of them, and that they will have the advantage of your co-operation to carry them into effect.

I have, &c.,

ARTHUR WELLESLEY.

To W. H. Gordon, Esq.   [1316.]

SIR,   Seringapatam, 4th Nov., 1802.

I have received intimation from the Rajah's government that certain rupees of a base kind, called Sicca rupees, have been issued to the troops from the pay-office at Chittledroog, in such numbers that the country is likely to suffer inconvenience from their currency, and that orders had consequently been given to cry them down in the bazaars, and not to allow them to be current in the Mysore country hereafter. As there remained 2000 rupees in this debased coin in the hands of the troops at the time these orders were given, the commanding officer at Chittledroog found it necessary to call them in, and to direct the servants of the pay-office to issue other coins in lieu thereof. My attention was drawn to this subject by Lieutenant-Colonel Whitelocke some time ago, and having referred to the lists of coins received by you at Chittledroog from the collector in Soonda, and the Resident, I do not find any rupees of this denomination among the number; and the Rajah's servants declare positively that they never gave those coins in payment of the Rajah's kist to the Company.

I therefore request you to let me know where these coins were received, from whom, and in what manner, and at what rate of exchange; and I beg that no more of them may be issued to the troops till further orders.

I have written to the commanding officer at Chittledroog to desire that he will ascertain what coins are now in the pay-office at Chittledroog.

I have, &c.,

ARTHUR WELLESLEY.

[1317.]   *To Lieutenant-Colonel Lawrence.*

SIR,   Seringapatam, 5th Nov., 1802.

I have had the honour to receive your letters of the 1st and 3rd instant, which were brought to Cancancotta by Captain Gurnell. By all accounts I judge that our first object in Wynaad must be to secure the subsistence of the troops. I have no doubt whatever of being able to effect that object most amply from this country, provided we can bring forward to the troops the cattle and people in safety. The communication appears to be safe on the side of Malabar, but interrupted on this. However, you will observe, by the enclosed instructions to Captain Gurnell, that I have taken measures to cover and secure the communication. In the mean time it is possible that the covering party at Sangaloo, and the advanced position of the battalion, together with movements which you may make to communicate with it, may secure the communication without the assistance of the posts. If you should find that to be the case, you will be so kind as to order forward the supplies from the Mysore country without loss of time, and as they come in to Cancancotta and Sangaloo.

You will observe by the enclosed letter that I have taken measures to fix upon a spot for one post between Manundwaddy and Sangaloo, in the neighbourhood of the latter. I request you to fix upon the spot for the other post near Manundwaddy, and that you will commence constructing it. As soon as these will be finished, there will be no doubt of your subsistence.

I enclose proclamations, which I request you to have copied and circulated.

I have pressed Major Macleod strongly to enter Wynaad,

and I hope that he will comply with my request.   Nothing but his presence will settle the country, and I am convinced his presence will have that effect immediately.

Notwithstanding that you may be employed in constructing the post at Poollingal, and that which I have above requested you to construct between Manundwaddy and Sangaloo, you must keep the troops in motion constantly, and do not fail to attack the enemy wherever you may hear he may be, and whatever may be his force and position.

If you should find that your provisions are running short, you will do well to order some of the troops to approach the magazines in Malabar, and to retain no more in Wynaad, till you have plenty of provisions, than are necessary to keep up the terror of the insurgents.   But the troops which, under this suggestion, may thus approach the magazines, are not to remain below the Ghauts, or even on the borders, for any length of time, but they are to return to the scene of action as soon as they will have received the provisions which they will require.

I have, &c.,

ARTHUR WELLESLEY.

Be so kind as to send a copy of this letter to Lieutenant-Colonel Boles.

To Captain Gurnell.   [1318.]

SIR,   Seringapatam, 5th Nov., 1802.

I have received your letter of the 4th.   You have my permission to return to Seringapatam, and you will hand over the command, with all my instructions, papers, &c. &c., to Lieutenant Harris.

Immediately upon receipt of this letter arrangements must be made to construct a post at Sangaloo for musketry only, and it must be commenced without loss of time.

I have ordered Captain Davies, with a party of pioneers, to join the 1st battalion 8th regiment, carrying with him entrenching tools for a working party.   This must be furnished him daily from that battalion in such numbers as may be practicable.   It does not appear to me that it will be necessary to place a larger number of men at Sangaloo than one company.

After the post will have been constructed at Sangaloo, two

more of the same description are to be constructed between that place and Manundwaddy. You will be so kind as to fix upon that situation which you may think will answer best for the post in the neighbourhood of Sangaloo, and I write to Lieutenant-Colonel Lawrence to request that he will fix upon the situation which he thinks will answer best for the post near Manundwaddy.

In the meantime, however, although a part of the troops under your command may be thus employed in constructing these posts and in covering those employed on the work, there does not appear to me any reason why the main body of the battalion should be in the rear of Sangaloo; they will accordingly cross the nullah and keep in motion in front of that place, between that and Manundwaddy, and proceed to the attack of the enemy according to my former instructions, wherever it may be reported that they are.

It has been reported to me that large quantities of supplies for the bazaar (the particulars of which I will enclose if I should receive the account before this letter will be sent off) have gone to Cancancotta; and besides, I have already sent from hence from the stores to the grain department 200 loads, which, at half a seer for each man, the usual allowance in the field, ought to last the 1st battalion 8th regiment, &c., for forty days from that on which the corps entered Wynaad at Sangaloo, supposing that since that day there have been no supplies in the bazaar. Besides this quantity, and that sent and to be sent for the bazaar, I propose immediately to forward a large supply of grain from hence for the general service of the troops.

It does not appear that the communication has been at all interrupted between Cancancotta and Sangaloo; and as a covering party will be left at the latter place, everything may be forwarded thither with great safety. When the remainder of the battalion will be forward, it may be a question whether it will be practicable to communicate with it from Sangaloo, which you will be best able to decide. However, if it should not be so, it does not appear that there is any difficulty in moving to all parts of Wynaad, and the battalion must only return to the neighbourhood of Sangaloo for fresh supplies when they may be wanted.

I enclose proclamations, which you will endeavour to distribute among the inhabitants, and a translation of them. You will be so kind as to have them copied and circulated as much as possible.

I beg that every encouragement may be given to the inhabitants to return to and remain in their villages by all kinds of protection to their properties and persons, and every other means in your power.

I have desired that my assent may be given to a proposition made by Govind Rao to seize the families of some of the principal rebels, and to give encouragement to certain inhabitants to return to and remain in their villages. You will be so kind as to facilitate his operations to gain these objects.

Although I have addressed this letter personally to you, it is to be considered as equally addressed to the officer who will succeed to the command in your absence.

I have, &c.,

ARTHUR WELLESLEY.

I beg that the letter which accompanies this may be sent to Lieutenant-Colonel Lawrence. If there should be no other safe mode of conveyance, a detachment must be sent with it.

[ENCLOSURE.]

PROCLAMATION.

Major-General Wellesley, commanding the troops in Mysore, Malabar, and Canara, &c., has heard with concern of the renewal of the disturbances in Wynaad, which have been the cause heretofore of such loss to the inhabitants of the country, and the occasion of the dreadful but well-merited punishments which they have witnessed. In the force now collected for the purpose of reestablishing tranquillity, the peaceable inhabitants of Wynaad must see the means of their own safety and the determination of the government to subdue the insurgents with celerity, and to bring them to the punishment they deserve.

Major-General Wellesley, therefore, calls upon them to return to and remain in their villages; to communicate with and give intelligence of the haunts of the insurgents to the commanding officers of the troops; to supply them for payment with the produce of the country; and to wait in security under the protection of the Company's arms till they receive the orders of Major Macleod, the principal collector.

[1319.]   *To Major Macleod, Principal Collector in Malabar.*

SIR,   Seringapatam, 5th Nov., 1802.

I have the honour to inform you that the 1st battalion 8th regiment, commanded by Captain Gurnell, entered Wynaad on the 27th of last month, having been opposed by the Nairs in crossing the nullah at Sangaloo, and marched the next day to Manundwaddy, on the road to which place they were strongly opposed. The loss, however, upon both these occasions was only two sepoys wounded, a few of the horse of the Rajah of Mysore and some followers.

Since that time Captain Gurnell has made some excursions with the troops under his command, but he has never been so fortunate as to fall in with any of the insurgents; one of his detachments returned to Cancancotta with the Rajah's horse, and marched back to Manundwaddy, and the whole battalion have since marched to Sangaloo, on the borders, and have seen or heard of no enemy.

On the other hand Lieutenant-Colonel Lawrence has entered Wynaad from Malabar, and has in that district a large body of troops. I understand that the communication is open between Manundwaddy and the Peria Pass, the cantonment at Poollingal and the Cotiady Pass. The troops move about the country in all directions, and don't hear of an enemy.

Still, however, the inhabitants will hold no communication with the officers commanding the troops; they fly from them whenever they see them, give them no intelligence of the enemy, and omit to supply their wants. Under these circumstances I have taken upon me to issue a proclamation, of which the enclosed is a translation; but I again take the liberty of suggesting to you the propriety of your entering the district with your Cutchery, or of sending there one of the gentlemen having civil authority, in order to communicate with the inhabitants and settle the country. Till that is done the troops can do no more than keep up the communication with Mysore on the one hand and the sea coast on the other, in order to provide for their subsistence, and run at the enemy wherever they may by chance hear that they are collected. But it is obvious that till the inhabitants are brought to remain in their villages no effectual steps can be taken towards quelling the insurrection.

In this opinion I am not singular; all the officers in Wynaad with whom I have corresponded, call for the presence of the civil authority; and my experience of former insurrections points out to me the absolute necessity for it.

The following are the objects for the troops in Wynaad at present. It appears that the roads between Manundwaddy and Poollingal and the Ghauts are so intersected by rivers and nullahs, all full at the present moment, that the supplies cannot be brought from Malabar, although the communication is open: the troops in Wynaad must therefore be supplied from Mysore.

As the rebels are in strength, if they are so anywhere, on the road between Cancancotta and Manundwaddy, it is necessary to provide for the safety of the convoys of provisions by establishing posts on that road. Accordingly I have given directions that a post may be established at Sangaloo, and two more between that place and Manundwaddy.

Besides this, in order to have a larger proportion of disposable troops for the field, it is necessary to construct a post at Poollingal. The troops under Lieutenant-Colonel Lawrence and the 1st battalion 8th Madras regiment are employed on these works; but they have my orders, notwithstanding this employment for a part of them, to keep the majority in motion in all directions, and above all, to move to the attack of the enemy wherever he may be, or whatever may be his force, when they shall receive intelligence of him.

Thus you'll perceive that the matter is settled as far as it can be by the troops; that they can move in all directions; that they can find no enemy to oppose them, and that their only operation now is to provide for the security of their own subsistence. Till the measures for this purpose, however, are in some degree advanced, and if the country, notwithstanding our superiority, still remains in this unsettled state, I greatly fear that Lieutenant-Colonel Lawrence will be obliged to send a part of the troops out of Wynaad to the borders, in order that

they may subsist, and to retain in the district only those necessary to keep up the terror of our arms.

I have, &c.,

ARTHUR WELLESLEY.

[1320.]　　　　　　*To Lieutenant-General Stuart.*

SIR,　　　　　　　　　　　　　Seringapatam, 9th Nov., 1802.

Since I wrote to you on the 31st October I have commenced
the operations in Wynaad, by means of which I propose to throw
into that country the supplies of Mysore, without stopping the
pursuit of the rebels by the troops in order to form escorts, &c.
&c.　If Major Macleod will enter the district, I think it possible that everything may still be settled without employing more
troops ; and if I should find that to be the case, I will order the
companies of the 33rd and the 1st battalion 14th regiment to halt
for your farther orders.

The great object is now to supply the troops who are already
in Wynaad, and I hope that may be effected, and I am certain
will be so without employing a larger force if Major Macleod
will come up ; and although I am clearly of opinion that in this
species of warfare it is better to have too many than too small a
number of troops, yet as soon as we find that the insurgents are
so far subdued or terrified as that small parties of our troops can
march through the country, and that all that is required is to
secure their baggage and provisions and their communication
with their rear, which the settlement of the country with the
other measures adopted will effect, it is better to pause a little
and to omit to collect more troops for this service.　There are
two considerations which have much effect on my mind on this
occasion : one is that of expense, which will certainly be much
increased by every increase of our force ; the other is that of our
credit.　Although we must take care to have a body of troops
fully sufficient to crush this rebellion at once, it will not be very
creditable to us, particularly in the eyes of foreign nations, who
will be witnesses, that it should be necessary that we should have
a large army to cope with a few Nairs.

I have made preparations to throw a large quantity of rice
from this country into Wynaad at a small expense, viz., half a
pagoda a bullock load ; at the same time I have arranged the

business in such a manner with the bullock-owners as that, if they are wanted, I shall have all their bullocks in the service. Thus I have provided for the present exigency at a small expense; and if events should oblige me to go into the country in force, I have at command the cattle by means of which I shall be enabled to move from hence on the day after the troops sent by you will arrive.

I wrote to the Secretary of Government, on the 29th October, on the subject of the battalion at Goa, in answer to his letters of the 23rd October ; and I judge, by your letters of the 2nd and 5th, that you cannot have seen that letter.   However, in consequence of the orders contained in your letter of the 2nd, I have directed the battalion at Goa to embark, of which I have apprised the government of Bombay ; and I shall report upon the subject to this government as soon as I shall have received your official orders.

Part of the 2nd battalion 18th regiment having arrived in the garrison of Seringapatam, Captain Grant, the town major and barrackmaster in Mysore, has taken the command of this corps, as being the senior officer in India attached to it.   He does this under the general orders of the 22nd December, 1801.   I am well aware of the effect which a precedent has in a case of this kind, particularly when it occurs under the eye of an officer who, it is to be supposed, would not suffer an irregularity in the service : I am, therefore, desirous of being favoured with your sentiments upon this subject, whether it is considered that an officer holding the situations held by Captain Grant is one whose staff duty admits his retaining the immediate command of a corps. . Captain Grant is an officer to whom I wish well; but as I have doubts upon my mind regarding his construction of this order, it is proper that this matter should be ascertained.

I have, &c.,

ARTHUR WELLESLEY.

To Captain Mackay.   [1321.]

SIR,   Seringapatam, 10th Nov., 1802.

I have received your letter of this day's date, and as I observe that the matter which you have referred to me is already before the Military Paymaster-General, with whom both you and Mr.

Gordon are in direct correspondence, I must beg leave to decline to give any decision upon it. However, as the bullock concerns of the time in which this matter of difference arose were conducted under my orders, it may be desirable that I should give my opinion upon the subject, which I now proceed to do.

The difference appears to me to arise from a mistake of Mr. Gordon's. He says that he made the advances on account of your department, and through you only they can be recovered. Mr. Gordon is paymaster in the Mysore country, and one of the duties attached to that office is to entertain bullocks for the public service, when ordered so to do. These bullocks ought to be mustered and registered, and then handed over to the public agent, or otherwise disposed of, as the commanding officer of the troops may think proper; but it is very obvious, from a perusal of the regulations, that till the cattle are handed over to the public agent, with all these formalities, he has nothing to do with them, and that the responsibility and charge of the cattle must rest with the officer whose duty it is to entertain them, viz., the paymaster. It appears that the cattle in question not only were not handed over to your charge, but although advances for them were made to persons calling themselves owners of cattle, they were never produced at muster; and I cannot conceive on what grounds Mr. Gordon claims the advances from you, excepting on his notion that they were made on account of your department, which I have above shown to be erroneous, or on the claim that one public officer has upon another for assistance in recovering the public money, which I shall now consider.

Mr. Gordon was ordered to entertain cattle for the public service, and was authorized to make advances of cash; and to facilitate this service, under this authority, he made advances for 429 bullocks, which were never produced at muster. Of the men calling themselves owners, some had other bullocks in the service, others had none. These advances were public money, and the persons who received them must be considered as debtors to the public; and when they came to receive from the public balances due to them on account of other bullocks which they really had in the service, it was but fair that the debts which they owed to the public should be subtracted from the amount of such balances. This principle, however, is restricted in some degree, even in respect to those who had bullocks in the service. Under the bullock regulations, in my opinion, the first sums which the hire of a bullock ought to pay are the debts contracted on account of itsèlf.   A bullock entertained, mustered, and registered at Seringapatam might die in the Mahratta country, of which there were numerous instances at the time in which this subject of difference arose.   Fresh advances must be made to his owner to replace him, and it is but fair that such sums, and others which might occasionally be given to purchase food, and all charges for grain or stores embezzled, should be set against the hire of bullocks really in the service, before sums advanced to the same owner for bullocks which he never produced.   Therefore I conclude that although Mr. Gordon had a right to expect that you would recover for the public the advances which he made for bullocks which were never produced, to owners who besides had bullocks in the service, when you should be paying them their balances, he had no right to expect that you would recover these sums before you should have recovered those for which the bullocks themselves were really responsible.   After providing for these demands, then Mr. Gordon's might with propriety be enforced, if there should be any balance, and it gives me great satisfaction to observe that you have recovered so large a proportion of his demand.   But Mr. Gordon made advances for bullocks which were never produced at muster, not only to persons styling themselves owners, who had already bullocks in the service, but to others who had none.   You had no accounts to settle with these persons, no sums of money to pay them on account of balances due to them by the public; and I cannot conceive upon what grounds he places upon you the responsibility for the sums advanced them, excepting on the notion that he made the advances on account of your department, which I have above shown is erroneous.

Upon the whole, I conceive that Mr. Gordon was doing the duty of his own office when he made advances to bullock owners for bullocks to be produced in the service; that he had a right to expect from you that you would endeavour to recover the debts due to the public on account of these advances from the persons to whom you might be paying sums of money as balances due by the public to them, an expectation which I observe you have not disappointed, as you have recovered 647 pagodas; but he had no right to expect that you would recover sums of money from other persons, with whom you had no accounts to settle, although advanced on account of bullock hire.   Under these circumstances, I consider that the sum still remaining due by the persons to whom advances were made on account of bullock hire ought to be carried to the debit of Mr. Gordon, instead of to yours, in the books of the Paymaster-General; and I conclude that that officer will so transfer it when he will have considered this subject.

I have, &c.,

ARTHUR WELLESLEY.

[1322.]   *To Lieutenant-Colonel Boles.*

SIR,   Seringapatam, 10th Nov., 1802.

I have received a letter from the Governor of Bombay, enclosing one to the Governor in Council of Fort St. George, in which he requires that the Bombay European regiment and a battalion of Native infantry should be sent to Bombay from Malabar, in the *St. Vincent, Marquess Cornwallis,* or *Sir Edward Hughes,* now on the coast. It is my opinion that a battalion of Native infantry cannot be spared under present circumstances, but the Bombay European regiment may, as the greater part of the 77th is in Malabar, and that province is still in tranquillity. If you should be of opinion that the services of the Bombay European regiment can be spared from Malabar, I beg that you will be so kind as to concert measures with Mr. Torin, under whose orders the ships above mentioned are placed, for their embarkation. If you should be of opinion that this corps cannot be spared, you will detain them in Malabar till further orders.

I have had the honour of receiving your letter of the 8th. Your recommendation to the collector is in exact conformity with all those I have sent him, and I have received information from government that he is ordered to go into Wynaad. I am doing everything in my power to forward supplies into Wynaad; but before they can enter that country we must secure the road from Sangaloo to Manundwaddy, upon which the troops on this side, as well as Lieutenant-Colonel Lawrence, are now employed. The supplies of Mysore, in great abundance, have been turned towards Cancancotta, and are already in that neighbourhood; and I have besides sent a supply of grain in the grainkeeper's department for the use of the 1st of the 8th, and a large quantity of the same description will leave this on the day after to-morrow, and will arrive at Sangaloo before the second post on the road will be finished.

I cannot promise you money, as under the late arrangements of the pay department there can be no more cash in any division of the army than is absolutely necessary for the payment of the troops.

I have, &c.,

ARTHUR WELLESLEY.

To Josiah Webbe, Esq.   [1323.]

MY DEAR WEBBE,   Seringapatam, 11th Nov., 1802.

I enclose herewith my letter upon the subject of the arrack concerns ; I likewise send the draft of the order which I propose to publish.   It includes all the stations to which officers are appointed by government, and I have added to them the Rajah's guard at Mysore, as I think that situation ought to be an object, and to be held by a respectable man.

It has occurred to me that it would be best to fix the amount of the allowance in orders ; for instance, to give all but the commanding officer of Paughur, &c., and of the Rajah's guard, either the allowance of the second class, or one-half more than the allowance of the third class, and to the commanding officers of Paughur and of the Rajah's guard the allowance of the third class.   If you should be of that opinion, let me know it, and I'll alter the order ; or if you like it best as it is, it shall so remain.

Let me know if you approve of the mode in which I propose to fill up the blank in the last page.

Believe me, &c.,

ARTHUR WELLESLEY.

To Josiah Webbe, Esq.   [1324.]

SIR,   11th Nov., 1802.

I have lately adverted to the effect of the government order of the 22nd September on the situations of officers commanding stations within the territories of the Rajah of Mysore, to which subject I beg leave to draw your attention.

The officers in command of forts and military stations within the territories of His Highness the Rajah of Mysore have hitherto had some of them certain advantages and emoluments of the same nature with those enjoyed by officers in command of similar stations within the Company's territories; and others, viz., the commanding officers of Chittledroog, Nundydroog, and Paughur, &c., allowances from the Rajah's government in lieu of those advantages.   Under the order of the 22nd September, the officers in command of this country are, like others, prohibited from receiving any emolument of command after the 1st of January, 1803, and of course those advantages must cease.   It is reasonable to expect also that as the allowances given by the Rajah's government to the officers commanding the stations of Chittledroog, Nundydroog, and Paughur were made in lieu of certain advantages which officers commanding other stations enjoyed, they will be discontinued at the time that those advantages can be no longer enjoyed under the orders of government.

The orders of the 22nd September do not provide for the situation of officers in command of stations in the Mysore country. The reason appears to be that government was unwilling to interfere in the management of a concern belonging exclusively to the Rajah's government.   But the consequence is, that officers in command of stations within the Mysore country will find their situations less advantageous than those in command in the Company's territories, and it is reasonable to expect that those entitled to the rewards of the service will always be desirous to quit it.   Under these circumstances I beg leave to suggest to you the propriety of urging the Rajah's servants to pay to the officers in command of stations in Mysore such an allowance as they may think proper as an equivalent to that which the officers in command in the Company's territories will receive under the orders of the 22nd September.

In case the Rajah's servants should consent to an arrangement such as I have above proposed, I should wish to announce it to the troops in Mysore in the general order, in which I shall enforce obedience to the government order of the 22nd September.

I have, &c.,

ARTHUR WELLESLEY.

To Josiah Webbe, Esq.   [1325.]

MY DEAR WEBBE,   Seringapatam, 12th Nov., 1802.

I received your letter of the 9th this morning.* I have made arrangements for filling Hullihall in Soonda with ordnance, military and provision stores (rice and arrack and shot, in particular, from Goa), which had been approved of before by the Commander-in-Chief. I have also desired Piele to give Purneah a hint to put the fort of Hurryhur in some kind of order as well as Hoonelly, both on the Toombuddra. I have the brinjarries in hand already, and will answer for the supplies they can afford for our armies. I have plenty of bullocks, and the ordnance and military stores are now ready at this place. We only want the troops, therefore, and some few articles of store, for which I shall write to Madras as soon as I shall receive the General's letter, which I expect this night.

You have not told me what part I am to act in this business. I think I can be more useful in it than anybody else. Independent of the experience I have of the country, the principal Sirdars are acquainted with me, and I have kept up a communication with them ever since I was there before. This will be of great consequence in our operations. It will not be inconvenient that I should quit Mysore, as I have been so long

---

* *Josiah Webbe, Esq., to the Hon. Major-General Wellesley.*

MY DEAR GENERAL,   Fort St. George, 9th Nov., 1802.

The Peshwah's and Scindiah's troops have been again defeated by Holkar, with great slaughter, in the immediate neighbourhood of Poonah, and the Peshwah will in consequence have fled. Colonel Close has therefore apprised this government of his despatches to the Governor-General, by which we shall be required immediately to send a force from the Toombuddra. The Commander-in-Chief will accordingly send the orders necessary for assembling such a force as can be collected; and in communication with his Excellency and Lord Clive, I send to you the earliest intimation of this event, in order to prevent your detaching any troops for the service in Wynaad. The force required by Close ought probably to be sufficiently large to meet Holkar's army; and therefore the necessity of this case supersedes all other considerations.

General Stuart will write to you by the ordinary post as soon as he shall have made his disposition of the corps about to be immediately ordered for field service. In the meanwhile measures must, according to Close's request, be conducted with as much concealment as possible. I have therefore suggested to Lord Clive that it is proper to keep the subject from his dissenting council, and to transmit all orders either from himself or through the Commander-in-Chief.

Believe me ever yours most sincerely,

J. WEBBE.

accustomed to the business and have so perfect a knowledge of the country that I could conduct the details of the service even though at a great distance from it ; and, in fact, no inconvenience was experienced when I was in the Mahratta country before.

I wish you would do me the favour to mention this subject to the General and Lord Clive, and offer my services : at all events, however, they may depend upon my doing everything in my power to forward the object in view.

Believe me, &c.,

ARTHUR WELLESLEY.

[1326.]   *To Alexander Read, Esq.*

SIR,   Seringapatam, 12th Nov., 1802.

I have to inform you that I have given directions to Mr. Gordon, the paymaster of Seringapatam and in the Mysore country, to lay in at Hullihall in Soonda 30 garce of rice. I shall be obliged to you if you will give directions to your servants in Soonda to give Mr. Gordon every assistance in performing this service.

It is probable that I shall find it necessary to desire Mr. Gordon to lay in at Hullihall a farther quantity of rice, and I shall be obliged to you if you will let me know whether you think that the province of Soonda can furnish it.

I have given directions and made arrangements for moving from Goa to Hullihall certain ordnance, military and provision stores at the former place, and they will come to Hullihall by the Tenin Ghaut. It is probable that that Ghaut will require repairs, and I shall be obliged to you if you will desire your servants to attend to the requisitions which the officers in Soonda will make for assistance to repair it.

I take the liberty of mentioning to you that, in my opinion, your presence in Soonda at the present moment would be very advantageous to the public interests, and of urging you to go there, if you can quit the other districts under your management without inconvenience to the public.

I have, &c.,

ARTHUR WELLESLEY.

[1327.]

To the Officer commanding the Troops at Goa.

SIR,   Seringapatam, 12th Nov., 1802.

I am desirous of moving to Hullihall in Soonda, from Goa, the ordnance, military provisions, and garrison stores at present at the latter place.

I received some time ago, from Captain Johnson of the Engineers, a proposal to move to Hullihall six 12-pounders at Goa. I have this day accepted of this proposal, and have desired Captain Johnson to carry it into execution, and I beg that you will give him every assistance in bullocks, lascars, &c., which the place under your command can afford. I have besides written to Lieutenant Dillon, the acting resident at Goa, to request that he will undertake to have removed to Hullihall the ordnance and military stores and provision stores at Goa, and have pointed out 12 and 6-pounder shot and arrack as the articles which I was desirous should be first moved. You will be so kind as to communicate with Lieutenant Dillon upon this subject, and facilitate, as far as may be in your power, the performance of the service which I have requested Lieutenant Dillon to undertake.

The commissary of stores at Goa is to assist in every way in his power to forward this service.

I have, &c.,

ARTHUR WELLESLEY.

[1828.]

To Lieutenant Dillon, Acting Resident at Goa.

SIR,   Seringapatam, 12th Nov., 1802.

I have the honour to inform you that I am very desirous that the Company's stores now at Goa should be removed to Hullihall in Soonda.

Captain Johnson of the Bombay Engineers made me a proposal some time ago to remove thither the Company's ordnance at Goa, with which I have this day acquiesced, and have desired him to take measures for their removal. I shall be obliged to you if you will be so kind as to urge the Portuguese government to give him every assistance he may require in performing this service.

In regard to the stores, I am desirous that the 12 and 6-

pounder shot, if there be any, and the arrack may be first removed. The latter must, of course, be put into kegs.

The common mode, under the government of Fort St. George, of defraying the expense of the removal of all articles of store, is for the person charged with their removal to indent for carriage upon the paymaster in his department of commissary of supply. It is furnished by him, and he charges the expense of it in his bills. In case you should think it proper to adopt this mode of procuring carriage for the removal of these stores, I have written to Mr. Reeves, the paymaster in Canara and at Goa, to apprise him that you may indent upon him, and to desire that he will comply with your demands, and, of course, he will require your assistance in procuring at Goa the carriage wanted. Persons, however, in your situation have the power of incurring expenses and sending bills for the performance of services of this kind, and you may think it proper to procure the carriage yourself for the removal of the stores, and to charge for it in your accounts. I have no opinion to give upon this point; I have only to request that the stores which I have above mentioned may be sent to Hullihall without delay, and that you will use your discretion in adopting the most economical and most expeditious mode of transporting them.

You must have the same option in regard to the mode to be adopted of procuring kegs for the removal of the arrack, and I have apprised the paymaster of the probability that you may call upon him for this article.

I have informed Major Doolan, the commanding officer at Hullihall, that I have made these requests, and have desired him to afford you every assistance which the troops under his command can give as escorts, working-parties, &c. &c., which you may require.

I have, &c.,

ARTHUR WELLESLEY.

I observe that the commissary of stores is still at Goa, and orders are sent to him to remain there till all the stores are removed from thence to Hullihall, and you will be so kind as to make such use of his services as you may think necessary upon this occasion.

To Josiah Webbe, Esq.   [1329.]

My dear Webbe,   Seringapatam, 13th Nov., 1802.

My letter to General Stuart of this date will show you that I have given attention to all the points that can tend to forward the equipment of the army to be formed upon the Toombuddra. There has been a smaller quantity of rain in Mysore this year than usual, but I have no doubt that there is plenty of grain ; and I have settled with Purneah to stop the exportation of rice from the western countries, and of gram from the eastern, at least till the new gram comes in.

There is no necessity for your moving. You may depend upon it that everything will be arranged to your satisfaction in this country, which will not be the case at Madras, if you should leave that place.

You will see by my letter to the General that I have adverted to the Rajah's army, and to the troops of the Mahratta Sirdars on the frontier.

I enclose you a letter just received from Malcolm. I send him from Veerajundrapett in Koorg to Batmunglum in Mysore. You must arrange for him afterwards. I write, however, to Dallas upon the subject.

Believe me, &c.,

Arthur Wellesley.

I enclose you a letter from Sydenham, with one from Lord Dartmouth, which is very satisfactory.

To Lieutenant-General Stuart.   [1330.]

Sir,   Seringapatam, 13th Nov., 1802.

I have had the honour of receiving your letter of the 9th instant,* and I proceed to give my opinion on the points upon

---

* *Lieut.-Gen. Stuart to Major-General the Hon. Arthur Wellesley.*

Dear Sir,   Choultry Plain, 9th Nov., 1802.

Mr. Webbe's letter by express will have informed you of the state of affairs at Poonah, and the necessity there is, in consequence thereof, of our assembling, with as little delay as possible, a respectable disposable force upon the banks of the Toombuddra. I should think, from looking at the map, that the neighbourhood of Harponelly would be a convenient place ; but of this you, from your local knowledge of the country, roads, &c., must be a better judge than I which you have been pleased to desire it. The first question is, at what place the force shall be assembled which you propose to have upon the Toombuddra.

It ought to be as near as the circumstances of forage, grain, and water will permit to the great roads into the Mahratta territory. There are two of these: one which leads along the right of the Toombuddra, and crosses that river below its junc-

am. I shall therefore leave the fixing of the place for assembling that part of the forces under your command to be employed upon the intended service to yourself, and which you will be so good as to inform me of as soon as possible.

The number of troops, European and Native, that can be spared for the intended service you will be pleased to order to assemble wherever you think most eligible; and those I leave to your discretion. The two regiments of cavalry, five companies of the 33rd, and a sufficient detail of European artillery and gun lascars to man completely the ordnance that is to accompany the Mysore troops, must form a part of your force; the other corps you will draw from above and below the Ghauts, where you may be of opinion they can be best spared; keeping in mind that all inferior considerations must give way to the present intended great equipment, so as to form with the least possible delay on the banks of the Toombuddra as respectable a force as possible. To enable you to form your arrangements for this purpose, I have ordered the 2nd regiment of cavalry and three battalions of Sepoys from the southern division, in addition to the one now on its march, to join you at Seringapatam as soon as possible; likewise a battalion of Sepoys from Vellore to Bangalore to wait your orders. The Sepoys from the southern division march without guns, as you will be able to furnish them with six-pounders in Mysore. These troops will be followed by the ordnance and military stores intended to be sent from this to join you at the place of rendezvous, escorted by the 19th light dragoons, the 74th regiment, Scotch brigade, and one battalion of Sepoys. Major-General Campbell is ordered to encamp, and hold in readiness to join the force to be assembled at the general rendezvous, the 25th light dragoons, with two Native regiments of cavalry, the 73rd regiment, and three battalions of Sepoys. Thus far I have detailed to you the intended force, as far as I at present know; and you will oblige me by giving me as early information as possible of the force that you will be able to assemble in Mysore, and from below the Ghauts, in addition to that above stated; likewise whether you will be able, from the stores in Mysore, to complete the corps with their field pieces, stores, gun and musket ammunition, &c. &c., and what will be necessary for me to send from this (in addition to that required for the other troops sent from hence, &c.) to equip completely the different corps who are to march from Mysore under your immediate command for field service.

I wish likewise to have your opinion as to the most convenient station in the Mysore country for a depôt of stores and provisions for the army while employed in the Mahratta country. Bellary, I should suppose, will be the most convenient place for that purpose in the Ceded Districts.

You will, of course, inform me of all your probable wants; and I shall trust to your favouring me with your sentiments without reserve upon all subjects.

I have the honour to remain, with the greatest esteem,

Dear Sir, your most faithful, humble servant,

J. STUART.

tion with the Werdah; the other, which crosses the Toombuddra at Hurryhur, and afterwards the Werdah between Deogherry and Savanore.

Harponelly is at no great distance from the former road, nor is it at any great distance from Hurryhur; but the neighbourhood of Hurryhur is the best situation for an army, from which it might be expedient to use either.

In case the entry of the troops into the Mahratta territory should be delayed for any length of time, the enemy may advance towards the frontier and threaten an attack on Mysore or the Ceded Districts.   He must advance by one of two lines: either into Bednore on the left of the Toombuddra, or cross that river below its junction with the Werdah into the Harponelly or Anagoondy districts.

A force in the neighbourhood of Hurryhur is well situated to impede the execution of either of these plans.

Supposing that in respect to the situation or designs of the enemy it should be a matter of indifference by which route the British army should enter the Mahratta territory, I should prefer that which crosses the Toombuddra at Hurryhur and the Werdah at Savanore, because it is the nearest to the rice countries of Mysore, with which it is connected; because it goes at no great distance from the frontier of Soonda, from which rice can be procured; and because, by means of the advance through the country lying between the Werdah and Toombuddra, it will be possible to settle it, which is absolutely necessary for the future security of the supplies from Mysore.   Another reason for preferring the assembly near Hurryhur is, that I propose that that place should be made a depôt; and another is, that I think the arrangements of the Mysore country are more favourable to the easy subsistence of the troops than those of the Company's territories, in case the army should remain any time at the place of rendezvous.

I have turned over in my mind the number of troops that I can move forward to the rendezvous from this country.   They will be 3 battalions of Native infantry (2 from this garrison and the 1st of the 8th from Wynaad), besides the 2 regiments of cavalry, the artillery, and the 5 companies of the 33rd mentioned in your letter, and 400 pioneers.

I might draw troops from Malabar and Canara, viz. the 77th regiment and two battalions of Native infantry; but I am induced to omit giving any orders upon the subject till I receive your sentiments on the considerations which I am about to detail, which induce me to think that they ought not to be employed on the proposed service.

If you should be of opinion that they ought, they will still be at the rendezvous in good time.

In the last campaign in the Mahratta territory, notwithstanding all the exertions I could make, I found it very difficult to feed the Europeans, particularly to give them arrack. The consumption of those you have already set down in your letter will be above 15,000 sheep a month, besides commatties, nearly all of which must come from Mysore. Their arrack must come from Madras, excepting such as I may procure from Goa by Hullihall. With a view to this difficulty, I yesterday wrote orders to have all the arrack at Goa moved up to Hullihall immediately; but even with this supply, and giving only one dram, it is much to be apprehended there will be a scarcity of this article.

I therefore think that the number of European troops ought not to be increased, unless you should have intelligence of the force of the enemy which should induce you to be of opinion that the largest possible number of this description of troops ought to be employed.

The Bombay corps of Native infantry are, in general, incomplete. They are not very healthy, have many men at drill, and, excepting the 1st of the 2nd, and 2nd of the 5th, part of each of which is in Wynaad, they are not in very good order. I enclose returns which show the state of their drills; the returns to the Adjutant-General's office will show the state of their sick.

Besides the 8 corps in Malabar and Canara, there is one at Hullihall in Soonda, which is more profitably employed, with a view to this expedition, than it could be elsewhere.

All this force is absolutely necessary to prevent the present insurrection from spreading into other parts of Malabar, into Canara, Mysore, and along the Ghauts.

In respect to this object, I have to observe that the Mahratta territory produces no rice, nor any other grain excepting jowarry, and that the troops operating within it must depend for their supplies of rice upon the province of Canara and upon the rice countries of Mysore, which are principally those running along the Western Ghauts from Koorg to Soonda, and for their supplies of gram, sheep, and bullocks upon Mysore. Therefore, I conclude that, considering the difficulty of feeding European troops in the Mahratta territory, and the weakness of the Bombay corps in general, and the consequences to be feared from drawing the 77th regiment from Malabar, they cannot be employed to greater advantage to the cause than by preventing the present insurrection in Malabar from spreading and disturbing the tranquillity of those countries from which the supplies for the troops in the Mahratta territory must be drawn.

However, I deliver this opinion with due deference to your superior judgment and your better knowledge of the strength of the enemy with whom we shall have to contend.

There will remain in Mysore the regiment de Meuron, which, for some of the reasons which operate respecting the 77th, as well as for others peculiar to itself, it is proper to leave in this garrison; 1 battalion in Seringapatam, 1 in Chittledroog, 5 companies in Nuggur, and 5 companies in Nundydroog and its dependencies.

It will be necessary to keep the garrisons of Chittledroog and Seringapatam of this strength in order that they may be able to afford the escorts to the stores, &c., which may be required from them.

Nuggur is an essential point, which must be secured; and the consequence of withdrawing the garrison from Nundydroog would be that the Polygars in that country would rise, and the communication with Madras would be impeded.

The whole force which will be collected, as appears from your letter and what I have above detailed, will be as follows:

> 2 regiments of dragoons.
> 5 of Native cavalry.
>
> Artillery.
>
> 3 regiments of Europeans.
> 5 companies of the 33rd.
>
> 12 battalions of Native infantry: viz.
>
>> 4 from Southern division.
>> 3 from Mysore.
>> 1 from Vellore.
>> 1 with 19th dragoons.
>> 3 from Ceded Districts.

I have made an estimate of everything that would be required for a force with twenty field-pieces, and I enclose you an account of articles which Mysore cannot furnish. These twenty field-pieces, with all the equipments for the troops in proportion, are what the stores of Mysore ought to furnish under your arrangement; besides, they can furnish 9 more field-pieces.

I should wish to take four iron 12-pounders and their equipments out of Chittledroog. I have already ordered shot for them from Goa to Hullihall.

I shall be obliged to you if you will do me the favour to order that the list of stores to be forwarded from the Carnatic may be sent to me.

The troops which will be employed upon this occasion in the Mahratta territory must, as is usual, have with them a park or moving arsenal; but they ought at first to depend for the additional supplies of stores, &c., which they will require upon Chittledroog.

There ought to be a depôt of grain at Hurryhur, on the Toombuddra; and I have already urged the Dewan to have that post put in decent repair.

Their first operation must be to get possession of Darwar, either by force or persuasion; and to that place ought to be moved all the stores, grain, arrack, &c., which I have made arrangements to collect at Hullihall in Soonda, as well with a view to taking possession of Darwar by force as to supplying it with celerity as soon as it will be ours. After Darwar will be in our possession, that place ought to be our depôt, and it might be supplied either from Bombay by Goa or Seedasheeghur, or from the Mysore country. It is probable that this last mode will be the most convenient, as we must have constant supplies of bullocks from Mysore, which may as well bring grain and stores as come empty.

Bellary, in the Ceded Districts, is entirely out of the line, and would not answer for a depôt for operations in the Mahratta territory.

Having now answered in detail all the queries which you have put to me, I shall proceed to consider certain other points to which you have not adverted, and state what steps I have already taken regarding them.

1st. The brinjarries:—

I had already had some communication with this useful class

of people residing in Mysore preparatory to my proposed expedition into Wynaad, and they are loading. We cannot have too large a number of them, and I know that there are some tandahs in the Barahmahal and the Ceded Districts. It would be desirable that the gentlemen in charge of those districts should be desired to attend to my letters and requisitions upon the subject of these people.

2ndly. Grain department :—

I have always found it useful to have some rice in a grain department, as well to keep down the price of that necessary article as to provide against any casual discontent among the dealers which might occasion a temporary scarcity.

I would, therefore, propose to have 2000 loads of rice in a grain department, which would give the proposed army 20 days' rice at half allowance. I have desired that arrangements may be made for hiring 2000 bullocks for this purpose, and they will be procured.

3rdly. Provision department :—

The movements of this army must occasionally be very rapid, and it is not possible that at all times the sheep can keep pace with the troops. I therefore propose that upon some occasions of this kind they should have salt provisions, and I have desired that 30,000 pounds should be prepared.

This will require about 100 bullocks.

Arrack ought to be sent up to Chittledroog from Madras, and I shall order thither all that there is in the arrack-stores at Bangalore and Seringapatam.

It would be advisable also to desire the government of Bombay to keep Goa supplied with arrack, and to send there some kegs, as the large casks cannot be moved up the Ghauts to Hullihall. I will take care that the arrack at Goa, and that which the government of Bombay will send there, shall be moved to Hullihall.

4thly. Pay department :—

I cannot estimate exactly what the expense of this body of troops in the field will be ; I should imagine, however, nearly two lacs of pagodas *per mensem.* I conclude that the troops coming from each division will bring with them the funds provided in that division for paying them as far as they may be available at present.

Hereafter it will be advisable that the collectors of the Ceded Districts, the Barahmahal, and the districts of the Carnatic from which the troops will have been drawn, should transmit to Chittledroog the sums which they will have at their disposal.

This, with the permission to draw bills and the other supplies of cash which government may find it convenient to send, may enable us to get on. But it is very certain that, without the regular disbursement of the pay of the army, the supply of grain, &c., will soon cease.

4thly. The mode of managing those departments :—

When I was in the field before, those three departments and that of the hired bullocks were managed by one person. They were, however, each in a separate department of which he was the head. This person was considered also as the deputy of the paymaster in Mysore, and he transmitted regularly to Seringapatam all his papers and vouchers, where Mr. Gordon made out all the accounts. The consequence was, that the usual excuse for delay in settling them, viz. the frequent and long marches of the army, was avoided, and when the army broke up not an account remained unsettled.

I don't see any reason why these departments attached to the body of troops at present to be assembled should not be managed in the same manner, and I should be obliged to you if you will let me know whether you approve of this plan, and whether I shall make arrangements accordingly.

5thly. The Store department :—

A commissary of stores and an establishment of conductors, &c., will be necessary.

Captain Scott is, of course, out of the question ; but either Sir John Sinclair or Lieutenant Francke, the present commissary of Chittledroog, would fill this office well.

I beg to know your wishes upon this subject. I have desired that bullocks may be hired to carry the stores in this department.

6thly. Gram department :—

The Gram Agent-General ought to be sent to the Mysore country as soon as possible. If he should want bullocks, and will correspond with me upon the subject of them, as well as of his gram, I will take measures that there may be no delay in his being supplied.

The new gram will not come in for three months, but I imagine that we shall have enough of the old for the cavalry, and I have begged that the exportation may be stopped.

7th. Dooly boys :—

These people must be sent from Madras for the troops coming from the Carnatic and the Ceded Districts.

8thly. The troops of the Rajah of Mysore and of the Mahratta Sirdars upon the frontier :—

A body of this species of troops is essentially necessary to our army for a variety of purposes which it is not necessary at present to point out. The Rajah of Mysore can give 2000 good horse and a large body of infantry and peons, all of whom would be useful. The Mahratta Sirdars upon the frontier have likewise large bodies of this description of troops. I have been in constant communication with them since the last campaign in the Mahratta country, and I have no doubt that I shall be able to prevail upon them to join and co-operate with the British army upon this occasion, particularly if we interfere as the allies of one of the contending parties. I should wish to have your sentiments upon this subject.

9thly. The time at which you wish that I should order the troops to assemble :—

Those from Mysore, with their stores and everything belonging to them, will be ready to march from hence in a few days; before the 33rd will arrive. I also wish to know whether it is your desire that I should write to Major-General Campbell for the troops from the Ceded Districts to join when those from Mysore will be ready.

Since writing the above, I have received your letter of the 10th, to which I have given answers in this, excepting as to the bullocks. I will answer you upon that subject to-morrow, and will order the bullocks which can be sent to you to commence their march to the Carnatic. There will be no carriage bullocks among them.

I have in this letter given you my sentiments respecting taking any part of the regiment de Meuron to the field; but I should feel myself infinitely obliged to you if you could send the whole of the 33rd regiment to Mysore, or at least the head-quarters of the corps.

I have ordered the repairs required to be given to all the carriages, and I write to the Military Board upon that subject.

I have, &c.,

ARTHUR WELLESLEY.

[1331.]   *To Lieutenant-General Stuart.*

SIR,   Seringapatam, 14th Nov., 1802.

I have the honour to enclose a letter which I have received from Mr. Anderson upon the subject on which you wrote to me on the 6th instant.

Since I wrote to you on the 9th instant a detachment of the 1st battalion 8th regiment has had a smart action with the Nairs in Wynaad, in which they sustained a considerable loss. They had marched to Manundwaddy with a despatch to Lieutenant-Colonel Lawrence, and on their return were attacked near a swamp at which the battalion had been hard pressed heretofore. The Nairs took the advantage of a nullah which was impassable, across which they fired at them, and killed nine and wounded eighteen. The officer in command of the battalion, however, at Sangaloo, sent out three companies to the support of the other detachment, and the Nairs were driven off with considerable loss. Many of those on this side of the nullah were put to death in the road. By all accounts the troops behaved remarkably well upon this occasion.

We are continuing the plan of operations which I mentioned in my letter of the 9th. All that is wanting in Wynaad is provisions, and the presence of the collector. I believe they have troops enough, if not to check, at least to prevent the insurrection from spreading.

I mentioned to Colonel Montresor your wishes, as stated in your letter of the 10th, and he departs for Malabar forthwith. It was impossible for me to talk to him with sincerity upon the subject of affairs in Malabar and Wynaad without apprising him of the circumstances which were likely to prevent his receiving any assistance from this country towards settling those provinces. I have therefore taken the liberty of doing so, under the strongest injunctions of secrecy. He has desired me to request that you would allow him to join the troops to the northward as soon as he will have settled the affairs in Wynaad.

I was in hopes that I should have been able to send you this day the account of the bullocks which will not be wanted for the equipments in this country, but I am obliged to defer it till to-morrow.

I have, &c.,

ARTHUR WELLESLEY.

———————

To Major Macleod. [1332.]

MY DEAR MACLEOD, Seringapatam, 14th Nov., 1802.

I cannot express to you how much annoyed I am to observe not only that you have omitted to answer the private letters which I have written to you upon the subject of Wynaad, but that your public letter is written in a style of coldness to which I am but little accustomed, particularly from you. We have been long acquainted, and have long and frequently communicated upon public subjects; and however we may differ in opinion upon certain topics, I know that I have always done you the justice to believe you to be zealous, active, able, and honest in the public cause, and I don't see any reason which has occurred lately for an alteration in the style of our correspondence. If I have done anything which has made you feel uncomfortable, I beg that you will let me know it, and you will find me disposed to make you amends. I declare that I never should have written a line publicly upon this subject, or one which any body else would have seen, if it had not been in answer to your first letter.

I now proceed to the consideration of affairs in Wynaad. You will have heard of the terrible defeats sustained by the Peshwah and Scindiah in their contest with Holkar; in consequence thereof we are preparing to interfere in force, and every disposable soldier in Mysore will be marched to the Mahratta frontier. This is between ourselves. The contest in Wynaad therefore must be carried on by the Bombay troops only; and Colonel Montresor leaves this place in a day or two to take the command of them. The operations which are going on at present are with a view to introducing the supplies of Mysore into Wynaad with safety; and accordingly posts are constructing on the road between Sangaloo and Manundwaddy.

In case, however, the war is to be carried on in the Mahratta territory, the supplies of Mysore must be turned towards the north, and our exertions must be made to feed the troops in Wynaad from below the Ghauts. But I don't stop the operations now carrying on; they will certainly be of use in enabling us to feed the troops in Wynaad, if only for a time, and at all events will keep that part of the country in awe.

It appears by the accounts I have received from Lieutenant-Colonel Boles that the posts on the tops of all the passes are filled with grain; but Lieutenant-Colonel Lawrence writes that for want of means of moving that grain towards Manundwaddy or Poollingal, the troops will be in distress, and will be obliged to go to the tops of the Ghauts and there receive their provisions, and then come back into the country. This is but a poor system of carrying on the war, and will never bring it to a conclusion unless it can be altered, either by the introduction of the supplies of Mysore, or by enabling the troops to move forward their supplies from the posts on the Ghauts.

The former cannot be depended on for any great length of time; but as for the latter, I have already sent the bullocks into Malabar, and I send more to-morrow morning; and the best thing you can do to assist them is to hire as many Palghaut and other coolies for their use as you can procure.

Colonel Montresor intends to go into Wynaad himself, and I strongly recommend you to meet him. He is to have full powers from government to try rebels by summary process, and punish them with death; and between you, you will have every power which can be necessary to enable you to settle the country again. You will find him to be a good soldier and a gentleman, both in his manners and understanding. I think him the fittest man in the army to command in that province, otherwise I would not have recommended him as I have done for the situation.

I cannot conclude this letter without adverting to your letter of the 9th to Lieutenant-Colonel Boles. You will permit me as a friend to tell you that I don't think it was called for by his letter to you, to which it is a reply; and I hope that when you consider of it you will do something to soften it.

My wish is to see all matters go on quietly, and that persons in authority should refrain from writing these violent epistles to one another; but if in a moment of warmth they should do so, it is best that they should settle matters amicably.

.Believe me, &c.,

ARTHUR WELLESLEY.

To Lieutenant-Colonel Lawrence.   [1333.]

SIR,   Seringapatam, 15th Nov., 1802.

Three hundred and fifty bullocks loaded with rice left this place for Sangaloo on the 12th instant, with Mr. Assistant-Surgeon Dickson, who went with doolies to bring to Seringapatam the sick and wounded men of the 1st battalion 8th regiment; the bullocks are likely to arrive at Sangaloo on the 17th or 18th instant.

They are contract cattle, taken to lodge grain at Manundwaddy, and to return to Seringapatam as soon as they will have performed that service.

As soon as they will arrive at Sangaloo, I beg that the following arrangement may be made to get these cattle forward to Manundwaddy :—

You will be so kind as to move forward with that part of the troops which you brought with you to Sangaloo to the swamp between that place and Manundwaddy, at which the 1st battalion 8th regiment have been so frequently attacked, of which ground you will take possession, and remain encamped in its neighbourhood on the night you will arrive there; the 1st of the 8th is to march on the following morning to the place at which you will be encamped, as an escort to the loaded cattle, leaving at Sangaloo the working party, and a covering party for it, and the pioneers.

The whole will move on together from the swamp to Manundwaddy, if it should be found that the cattle are able to get on; but if they should not be so, they must move to Manundwaddy on the next day.

The rice must be received into store at Manundwaddy, and the cattle must be sent back to Seringapatam immediately; and care must be taken to escort them back to Sangaloo in safety, either by a movement such as I have above directed, in order to get them forward with their loads, or such other as you may think proper.

This grain belongs to the Company, and is to be received on the books of the garrison storekeeper in Wynaad.

While encamped in the neighbourhood of this swamp, I wish that you would reconnoitre and ascertain whether there is not some mode of turning and avoiding it ; or if not, whether it would not be possible, by taking possession of some of the hills in the neighbourhood, to command the ground from which the Nairs fire on the parties who may be passing the swamp.

I trust that you have taken measures to construct the post which I recommended between Manundwaddy and Sangaloo.

Colonel Montresor is at Seringapatam, and is proceeding into Malabar forthwith.

Mr. Dickson, with the doolies he took with him, and the sick and wounded, is to return to Seringapatam immediately.

I have, &c.,

ARTHUR WELLESLEY.

[1334.]   *To Lieutenant-Colonel Lawrence.*

SIR,   Seringapatam, 16th Nov., 1802.

I have received your letter of the 15th. I conclude that Captain Barclay's letter of yesterday will have prevented you from marching, and that you will have received mine of yesterday in the course of this day.

I leave it to you to fix on the spot which you think will answer best for the post between Manundwaddy and Sangaloo; but it appears to me that it would be desirable to fix one post in the neighbourhood of the swamp in question.

I have taken into consideration your proposal to destroy the villages which you may find deserted, to which I cannot consent for the following reasons : It is probable that the inhabitants of the villages in question have been forced by the rebels to join them, and their own safety requires that they should remain with them till our superiority is so decided as that they may remain in their villages in safety under our protection. The fact you mention, that Chuttoo is with Captain Watson, at the same time that the inhabitants of the villages on his estate fly upon the approach of our troops, is a strong proof that this is the case ; even his influence cannot prevent them from adopting that line of conduct, which it appears their safety absolutely requires.

Before the villages are destroyed, when the inhabitants are found to have quitted them, it will be necessary that the superiority of our arms should be established, and that the civil authority should make an effort to settle the country again. If the inhabitants then remain away, their spirit of disaffection will be manifest, and that will be the time to lay waste the country, and destroy the property within it.

The case of Coongan Nair's property, however, is entirely different; he is a proscribed rebel, and ought not to have been allowed to hold any property after he had been proscribed. The proper measure to be adopted with his property would be to confiscate it; but as it is probable that you would not find any person to take charge of it, the best thing to do would be to destroy it entirely; and I authorise you to destroy the houses and property you mention belonging to this man lying between Poollingal and Manundwaddy.

It will be necessary, however, that before you destroy those houses you should ascertain from Mr. Riddle that the owner of them is really the proscribed Coongan Nair.

I have, &c.,

ARTHUR WELLESLEY.

To Lieutenant-Colonel Boles.   [1335,]

MY DEAR SIR,   Seringapatam, 16th Nov., 1802.

Colonel Montresor leaves this place to-morrow morning for Malabar, and I expect that he will arrive at Cannanore on the 23rd.

I have recommended to the Colonel to make certain arrangements of the cattle and coolies attached to the troops below the Ghauts, which I think will answer, and will enable the troops to move with more facility than they do at present.

My idea is that there should be three departments, one of stores, one of provisions, and one of grain. A conductor ought to be at the head of the former of these, and the paymaster, in his capacity of commissary of provisions and of grain, at the head of each of the others. Each of the two first departments ought to have allotted to it the number of bullocks necessary to transport the number of loads of stores or of provisions which the body of troops in the field can require for the operation which may be proposed; and the remainder of the bullocks ought to be allotted to the grain department.

In order to enable Colonel Montresor to make his arrangements on this subject with celerity, it is desirable that you should meet him at Cannanore, with states of the troops in the field; states of those allotted to the defence of each post, which are not to be considered as in the field, and of course are not to live upon the field magazines; states of the stores required to be carried with the troops in the field; states of the numbers of bullocks and coolies at present in pay, where situated, how employed, &c.

Captain Dufty and Mr. Richardson ought likewise to meet him at Cannanore, and I beg that you will inform the latter gentleman that I have recommended to Colonel Montresor to call for his services in the field, in order that he may personally superintend the departments under his management as paymaster.

Mr. Richardson will be so kind as to be prepared with a return of the quantities of provision stores in his charge, as garrison storekeeper, at the different stations in Malabar, specifying at what stations.

Lieutenant-Colonel Lawrence has come on to Sangaloo, and I have desired him to wait there till to-morrow, in order that he may be joined by some grain sent from hence, and that he may take measures to insure its arrival in safety at Manundwaddy.

Believe me, &c.,

ARTHUR WELLESLEY.

[1336.]   *To Lieutenant-General Stuart.*

SIR,   Seringapatam, 16th Nov., 1802.

I have the honour to enclose an account of the bullock establishment, which will show the numbers available for the proposed service, and the demands for them arising in this country. According to this account there will be about 400 to send to the Carnatic, exclusive of 388 stationed in the Ceded Districts, which I conclude are available.

The great advantage of these cattle is their condition, which they always lose when detached from under the eye of the agent, particularly when to the Carnatic, where they get no forage. I therefore beg leave to recommend that all the equipments to be sent to this country may be sent by means of hired draught cattle, to be discharged as soon as the troops will arrive in Mysore, and that the distribution of the Company's cattle may be made here under the eye of the agent. · By this mode the cattle will enter on the service in good condition.

I have the honour to enclose a translation of a letter which I received last night.

As soon as I learn from you the nature of the contest in which we are likely to be engaged, I will have the honour of submitting to you my notions of the plan of operations to be adopted. The subject is familiar to me, as I had occasion to turn my mind to it very particularly in the year 1800.

I shall be very much obliged to you if you will do me the favour to urge government to allow Major Symons to return to Seringapatam. It will be the greatest advantage to the cause to have him here as soon as possible.

I have, &c.,

ARTHUR WELLESLEY.

P.S. I enclose copies of papers which I have received from Lieutenant-Colonel Boles for your information. I don't wish to have any public notice taken of these papers at present, as I have endeavoured to make Major Macleod sensible of the impropriety of the language he has used; and if I should succeed in that, I hope the matter may be settled without further reference. If it should not be so, I must report it through the Adjutant-General.

[ENCLOSURE.]

Reported by the Committee fit for heavy draught present ..	1362
Absent at Seringapatam, not seen	116
„ in the Ceded Districts, ditto	322
„ at Mangalore on service	45
Total available for this service of heavy draught ..	1845
Add reported fit for light draught	470
Grand Total	2315

Bullocks which may besides be called for if required :—

At Mangalore, stationed	143
At Hullihall* in Soonda, ditto	47
At Goa,* stationed	151
At Cannanore, ditto	196
At Angarypur, ditto	36
	573

Estimated number of bullocks for heavy draught required for the equipment at Seringapatam	692
Add four 12-pounders and their equipments	300
Add treasure tumbrils	50
Add bullock agent's tumbril	12
	1054

Estimated number of bullocks for light draught required for the equipment at Seringapatam	360
Add arrack carts	200
Add medical stores	16
Add pioneers' stores	8
	584

* The bullocks stationed at Hullihall and at Goa are now employed in moving the ordnance and stores from Goa to Hullihall, from which service they ought not to be taken. Those stationed at Cannanore and Angarypur ought likewise to be left where they are. Those at Mangalore might be withdrawn.

[1337.]

To Lieutenant-General Stuart.

SIR,   Seringapatam, 17th Nov., 1802.

I have had the honour of receiving your letter of the 13th, and I hope that by this time you will have received mine in answer to your letters of the 9th and 10th. The ordnance attached to the 5th regiment of cavalry have had new wheels, and they as well as the carriages attached to the 7th regiment are fit for service, excepting the defects in the construction of the carriages which I reported in my review report of February last, and which exist equally in the carriages attached to both regiments.

I don't exactly know the nature of the gunny bags at Tellicherry and Cannanore, but I rather imagine that they are Bengal ship bags. If that be the case, they will not answer for anything excepting to hold rice in store; but they will be useful for that purpose in the depôt which I propose to form at Hurryhur.

As I do not think of carrying more than 2000 bags of rice, many gunny bags fit for the carriage of this article will not be required. The brinjarries and dealers always have their own bags.

I have written to Cannanore to have some of these bags sent up. I do not send down cattle for them, as I fear that they would not return before it would be necessary for the troops to march. If, however, I should find that you are not desirous that the troops should assemble very early, I will send down cattle to bring up all these bags.

The returns I have of the brinjarry cattle make them amount to 40,000: however, I do not expect that they will bring more than 25,000 loads. There are tandahs in the Ceded Districts not included in this account, which may make the number 10,000 more. Besides brinjarries, there are other descriptions of dealers who have always attended the armies in Mysore, who will add considerably to this number. They are called Wirdywas. Some of them are now employed in Canara in the betel-nut trade, and others in the Carnatic; and six weeks or two months will elapse before they will be able to attend the troops. But they have all been called for, and I have no doubt that all will come. If we should have a good Native army, I have no fears for our supplies.

In the last campaign in the Mahratta territory the bazaar people from all parts of Mysore brought supplies to the camp; but this was attended with much inconvenience to them, and it is not possible to expect that they will follow the troops the greater distance which it may be probable that they will go. I have in contemplation, therefore, a plan for receiving at Hurryhur in the first part of the campaign, and afterwards at Darwar, all that these people will bring, and to send the brinjarries to those places to fill their bags. There are several points, however, to be considered, and referred to the Dewan, before I decide upon this plan so far as to be able to lay it in detail before you.

I have, &c.,

ARTHUR WELLESLEY.

2 D 2

[1338.]   *To Lieutenant-Colonel Boles.*

MY DEAR SIR,   Seringapatam, 17th Nov., 1802.

I have not by me a return of the garrison stores in Malabar, but I learn from General Stuart that there are at Cannanore 14,631 rice bags, and at Tellicherry 12,241. These articles may be exceedingly useful in this country, and I shall be obliged to you if you will be so kind as to take measures to have some of them sent up to Seringapatam. I am not desirous that in order to perform this service you should employ the cattle intended for the service of the troops in the field respecting the future arrangement of which I wrote to you yesterday ; but I wish that you would desire Mr. Richardson to endeavour to hire cattle to take up to Seringapatam as many of these bags as he can send.

It happens sometimes that there are cattle in Malabar, the owners of which may not choose to hire them for service in that country, but who may be willing to hire them to cárry loads to this country. In that case, or in case cattle should be procurable which are not wanted for the service in Wynaad, which I think very probable, I beg that they may be hired for this purpose.

In the mean time I wish to have from you a particular account of the state of these gunny bags, their nature, from whence they come, whether they have been used, and how long they have been in store.

Believe me, &c.,

ARTHUR WELLESLEY.

[1339.]   *To Jonathan Duncan, Esq.*

MY DEAR SIR,   Seringapatam, 17th Nov., 1802.

Some time has elapsed since I have addressed you, but I have really had no intelligence to communicate deserving of your attention. In consequence of the disasters which have lately befallen the Peshwah, it is intended to collect a large army on the Toombuddra, and I have received directions to make all the preparations and arrangements for feeding and supplying it. One of our great difficulties in such a campaign as we may expect is to provide the Europeans with arrack ; in the last campaign in the Mahratta territory I supplied them in a great measure by means of Hullihall in Soonda and Goa, and I have made arrangements for supplying them in the same manner in this campaign ; but the quantity of arrack at Goa is but small, and I must beg for some assistance from Bombay. I shall, therefore, be obliged to you if you will be so kind as to give orders that arrack in large quantities may be sent to Goa, consigned to the care of the Resident, Lieutenant Dillon, at that station.

This arrack is to be moved up a Ghaut to Hullihall which is not practicable for wheel carriages ; and even if it were so, there are no wheel carriages in that part of the country which can be applied to this purpose. It is, therefore, necessary that the liquor should be carried by cattle or men, and in order to facilitate this operation it must be put in kegs. I shall therefore be obliged to you if you will be so kind as to send to Goa at the same time with the arrack 400 kegs of about four gallons each. These ought to have iron hoops, and to be so strong as to bear all kinds of bad usage.

If you could also send to Goa about 30,000 pounds of salt provisions packed in small kegs, each containing fifty pounds, with the liquor and pickle, it would be a most desirable acquisition.

I shall hereafter have to trouble you upon other subjects of this nature ; and as our preparations will then be made public, I shall address you in a public form : in the mean time, however, no time is to be lost, and I adopt this mode of making known our wants. In case the war should go on, I have in contemplation a plan of operations in which your Presidency will act a conspicuous part, and which I will have the honour of communicating to you as soon as I shall learn from government the extent to which they intend to go.

Believe me, &c.,

ARTHUR WELLESLEY.

To Lieutenant Dillon.   [1340.]

SIR,   Seringapatam, 17th Nov., 1802.

Since I wrote to you on the 12th instant I have received more particular returns than I had before of the state of the stores at Goa, and I observe that there are no kegs among them. It is possible also that you may not be able to procure any at Goa.

I have therefore to inform you that there are a large number of kegs at Hullihall in Soonda. I understand that they are in want of some repairs, but it may probably be in your power either to have them repaired at Goa when they will arrive there, if you should find it necessary to send for them, or to send coopers to Hullihall to repair them.

I write by this post to the commanding officer at Hullihall to request that he will attend to your requisitions regarding these kegs, and I beg that you will make him acquainted with your wishes in case you should not be able to procure any at Goa.

By a letter transmitted to me by Major Budden, I observe that the Governor-General has ordered that the troops may be withdrawn from Goa. I hope, however, that you are to remain there; and at all events I beg that you will remain there till you receive the farther orders of government. In the present situation of affairs in this part of India it is essentially necessary that a person should reside at Goa on the part of the British government who possesses the confidence of, and has an influence over, the persons at the head of that settlement.

As I apprehend that I shall require supplies of arrack for the European troops in greater quantities than are at present at Goa, I have written to Mr. Duncan to request that he will send them there, together with 400 kegs, and 30,000 pounds of salt provisions packed in kegs. I beg that you will do me the favour to forward these supplies to Hullihall as soon as they will arrive at Goa.

I have, &c.,

ARTHUR WELLESLEY.

[1341.]   *To Lieutenant-General Stuart.*

SIR,   Seringapatam, 18th Nov., 1802.

I omitted to inform you that in consequence of your letter of the 9th I desired Lieutenant-Colonel Boles not to allow the Bombay European regiment to embark.

I have had some conversation with Mr. Anderson respecting

the medical arrangements to be adopted in consequence of the proposed armament, and to-morrow I shall have the honour of submitting to you what he proposes. As I imagine that the direct communication between Madras and Bombay is stopped, and as I find that the quantity of arrack at present at Goa is not large, I have taken upon me to write to Mr. Duncan to request that he will send there a large quantity, as well as 400 kegs of four gallons each. I have likewise requested him to send to Goa 30,000 pounds of salt provisions, packed in kegs of fifty pounds each. I have written to him privately, as I observe that none of the orders for this armament are yet made public.

I observe by a letter which I have received from Goa, that the Governor-General has informed the Governor of Goa that he has given orders that the troops may be withdrawn from thence. They are already gone in consequence of your directions, as I heretofore informed you. I think it very necessary, however, that the resident or acting resident, Lieutenant Dillon, should remain there for some time longer; as Goa is a most important source of supply for an army in the Mahratta territory, and we have no chance of using that place in that manner unless we have a person residing there on the part of government in whom the Portuguese have confidence, and who has some influence over the persons at the head of their government. Lieutenant Dillon is of this description, and I have taken upon me to desire that he will remain at Goa till he receives farther orders from government, notwithstanding any orders he may already have received to withdraw.

I have, &c.,

ARTHUR WELLESLEY.

To the Adjutant-General, Bombay. [1342.]

SIR, Seringapatam, 18th Nov., 1802.

I have the honour to enclose letters which I have received from Major Doolan, which I beg you to lay before the Commander-in-Chief, with my request that they may be transmitted to be laid before the Hon. the Governor in Council.

They contain an application from Captain-Lieutenant Wood for permission to resign the appointment of Adjutant to the 1st battalion 5th Bombay regiment, and a recommendation by that officer and Major Doolan that Lieutenant Martin may obtain it. It is probable that he is qualified for the situation, as his commanding officer, Major Doolan, has recommended him; but in general I do not approve of the practice of officers naming their successors on resigning their situations; for which reason, and because I have no knowledge of Lieutenant Martin, I do not request that Major Doolan's recommendation may be attended to.

I have, &c.,

ARTHUR WELLESLEY.

[1343.]   *To Lieutenant-General Stuart.*

SIR,   Seringapatam, 19th Nov., 1802.

I have the honour to enclose a letter and certain other papers which I have received from Mr. Anderson, written in consequence of a conversation which I had with him relative to the medical arrangements for the body of troops proposed to be assembled in the field.

There are two objects to be provided; one is the field hospitals, and the other the supplies of medicines for regimental hospitals, during the time which it may be expected that the troops will be out of this country. With a view to the establishment of the former upon a good system at such places as it may be either necessary or convenient to the army to have them, the Doctor proposes, 1st, that there shall be a medical staff, consisting of two surgeons and four assistant-surgeons, attached to this body of troops, in order to preclude the necessity of attaching to the field hospitals those medical gentlemen in charge of or attached to corps; 2ndly, to carry a certain quantity of clothing, and country medicines and servants, at the public expense, which articles and persons are to be allotted to the field hospitals in the proportions which may be required, and to be paid for by the gentlemen in charge of them. By these means it is certain that the sick in each field hospital will have the articles which are known to be necessary to them, at the same time that in order to supply them it will not be necessary, as it has been heretofore, to take from the regimental surgeons those articles which they may have provided for the use of the men of whom they may be in charge.

The expense to the public of these arrangements, which will tend so materially to the comfort of the sick, will be the hire of about 100 bullocks, and the monthly pay of the servants from the time they will be hired to that at which they will be handed over to the gentlemen who will have charge of the field hospitals.

In regard to the second object, the Doctor proposes that the regimental surgeons of European corps should have with them a supply of European medicines for three months, and that he should carry and have charge of a supply for three months more. The expense of this will be six carts; and you will observe that I have adverted to the probability of a demand for four in my estimate of bullocks. Besides this the Doctor will require two medical compounders.

The next consideration is the future supply of country medicines, &c. Upon this point I have to recommend the stores at Bombay as the most certain source from whence they can be drawn.

Besides these arrangements the Doctor adverts to certain others in the enclosed letter which are of the greatest consequence to the comfort of the sick. The first is the carriage of the Native sick. I imagine that it will be impossible to alter the existing mode of carrying them at present, although I know that that is probably the greatest abuse now in the service. However, I enclose the copy of an order which I issued on my return from the service in Bullum in the last year, and I have sent copies of it to all the officers commanding corps who have received orders to prepare for the field in this country, and I propose to send copies of it to all those who will come to this country, as soon as I hear that they have entered Mysore. Besides, I propose to give them every assistance in my power in procuring proper carriage.

The proposal, however, of the Doctor that all the dooly carriage attached to the European corps should be placed under his charge, as it was heretofore, is an excellent arrangement for the reasons he states, and ought to be adopted. It is well worth the expense which he proposes should be incurred on this account, viz., a writer and two head dooly maistries.

I have made arrangements for collecting materials to

build an hospital at the place at which the troops will be assembled.

In this letter I have adverted generally to the points on which Dr. Anderson has gone into detail, and I beg leave to refer you to his letter and the enclosed papers.

I have, &c.,

ARTHUR WELLESLEY.

[1344.]   *To Lieutenant-General Stuart.*

SIR,   Seringapatam, 19th Nov., 1802.

I have to inform you that there is no camp equipage in store here for the 1st battalion of artillery, nor at Cannanore for the detachment of Bombay artillery which I have called from thence. However, I have desired that the latter may have the use of some of the camp equipage belonging to de Meuron's regiment, which I lately sent into Malabar for the service of the troops in that province.

If your answer to my letter of the 13th should contain a wish that I should put the troops in the field immediately, I will procure camp equipage for these detachments of artillery either from the commissary of supply or from the commanding officers of corps of Native infantry; but if it be not your wish that they should take the field immediately, there will be time to send camp equipage for them from Madras, or to receive your orders regarding the mode of providing it.

I have, &c.,

ARTHUR WELLESLEY.

[1345.]   *To Alexander Read, Esq.*

SIR,   Seringapatam, 20th Nov., 1802.

I have had the honour to receive your letter of the 12th.

The Nabob of Savanore has been arrested by Lieutenant Stuart, who succeeded Captain Fraser in the command at Bonawassi, the latter being sick; and I have given directions that he might be conducted to the borders with his family and attendants, and allowed to go where he pleases, excepting into the territories of the Company or of the Rajah of Mysore. It is fortunate that he has been arrested, although contrary to my instructions to Captain Fraser, as it will prove to the people of the country that the raising of the men not only was not authorised by, but was directly contrary to the wishes of the Company's servants.

I recommend you to prosecute Soma, Abdul Cauder, and Cooper But before the Court of Circuit; or if it be supposed that the jurisdiction of that court ought not to extend to crimes committed previously to its establishment, that you should punish them yourself, and that in the most public manner, within the province of Soonda.

I have this day sent directions to Lieutenant Stuart to communicate with the aumildar of Bonawassi regarding the removal of the treasury to Onore, and to send with it a jemidar's party as an escort as soon as it will be prepared to move. I have likewise desired Lieutenant Stuart to march to Nuggur from Bonawassi with his party as soon as the treasury will have been sent to Onore; as in fact its being at Bonawassi was the only reason for having a body of troops at that station. Orders are sent to Cundapoor to furnish a subahdar's guard for your treasury, &c., at Onore.

I have, &c.,

ARTHUR WELLESLEY.

To Lieutenant Stuart.   [1346.]

SIR,   Seringapatam, 20th Nov., 1802.

I have had the honour of receiving your letters of the 15th and 16th instant, and I beg to refer you to my letter to Captain Fraser of the 4th instant, by which you will observe that the case did not exist under which he, and consequently you, was authorised to seize the person of the Nabob of Savanore. It is absolutely necessary that officers should pay the strictest attention to their instructions, and not take any step not authorised by them.

I trust, however, that although you have seized the person of the Nabob of Savanore, you have treated him with the humanity and attention which his situation requires.

Upon the receipt of this letter I beg you to wait upon him, and inform him that I am much concerned that his conduct within the Company's territories has been such as to render it necessary for me to desire that he will withdraw from thence: you will at the same time have in readiness an escort to attend him to the frontiers, of which you will inform him, and you will see that he is conducted to the borders in safety, where he is to be allowed to go wherever he pleases, excepting in the territories of the Company or of the Rajah of Mysore; all his attendants, family, &c., are to be allowed to accompany him.

I have received a letter from Mr. Read, in which he has desired that an escort should be furnished for his treasury, which it is his wish to remove from Bonawassi to Onore in Canara. I beg that you will communicate with the aumildar of Bonawassi upon this subject, and learn from him at what time he proposes to remove the treasury, and you will furnish a jemidar's guard from the troops under your command to proceed to Onore as an escort to it. As soon as the treasury will be removed from Bonawassi, there is no occasion for your remaining there any longer; and you will march with the troops under your command to join the detachment of the corps stationed at Nuggur. The detachment going to Onore must likewise receive instructions to join its corps at Nuggur after the treasure will have been lodged at the former place.

I have, &c.,

ARTHUR WELLESLEY.

[1347.]   *To Lieutenant-Colonel Lawrence.*

SIR,   Seringapatam, 20th Nov., 1802.

Upon a perusal of your letter of the 18th I judge that the place which you have fixed on for the second post from Sangaloo is different from that fixed on by Captain Gurnell. It is necessary that the two posts between Sangaloo and Manundwaddy should divide the road nearly equally, if it be true that all parts of it are equally liable to attack; but besides this object in these posts there is another, viz., that one should be constructed at that point at which the enemy have appeared most frequently, and have most strongly opposed our troops.

If the spot which you have fixed on should answer equally well with that fixed on by Captain Gurnell to cover and secure the road generally, and at the same time a post there would secure a point at which the enemy have frequently attacked our troops, that situation will be the best for our post; but if it should not secure the road so well as the other, it will be best to have three posts instead of two between Sangaloo and Manundwaddy, viz., one at the place fixed on by Captain Gurnell; one at that fixed on by you, at which the troops have been so frequently attacked; and the other in the neighbourhood of Manundwaddy, at the place which I originally desired you to fix upon.

I understand that the post at Sangaloo is finished, and I have given orders that provisions may be thrown into it for seventy men for six months.

It will take a few days before arrangements can be made for this purpose by the officers here, and therefore I wish that it should be provisioned for a fortnight at first, and that the troops allotted for its defence should be placed in it.

No time ought to be lost in commencing to construct the other post; the 1st of the 8th and pioneers ought to move forward for this purpose without loss of time.

If the rice mentioned in my letter of the 15th should have arrived, I conclude that you will have moved forward with it; and that you will have left the Coast pioneers, the working party of the 1st of the 8th, and the covering party at the place at which you propose that the post should be constructed according to the tenor of the orders which that letter contains. If, however, the rice should not yet have arrived, which, on account of the badness of the weather, is possible, I beg that you will order forward the pioneers and 1st of the 8th (leaving a company at Sangaloo for the care of the post), with directions to construct the post at such place as you may think proper, according to the tenor of the instructions upon this subject already given and contained in this letter. You will wait yourself with the Bombay detachment at Sangaloo till the rice arrives there, and you will then proceed with it first to the place at which the 1st of the 8th will be constructing the post, where you will leave the rice and bullocks. You will then march on with the Bombay detachment to take possession of the swamp according to my instructions of the 15th, and the rice is to follow on the next day with that part of the 1st of the 8th which will not be employed in the construction of the post, or in covering the working party and pioneers.

It is not necessary that these posts should be made very large : the largest number of men which it can be necessary to have in one of them is a company ; and they should be so constructed as that it might be practicable to hold them with a smaller detachment.

I beg to know from you the names of the places at which the different posts will be constructed.

I have, &c.,

ARTHUR WELLESLEY.

[1848.]   *To Lieutenant-General Stuart.*

SIR,   Seringapatam, 21st Nov., 1802.

I have had the honour of receiving your letter of the 16th. Directions have been given to prepare for the brass 12-pounders, and everything will be ready by the time they arrive. I am not certain whether the construction of the carriage for the brass 12-pounders has been improved lately ; but I recollect that those I had with the Nizam's detachment in the last war with Tippoo were so bad that the carriages could not bear the firing of the gun. I rather believe that this is an old complaint of the 12-pounder carriages on this establishment.

You will observe by my letter of the 13th that I have proposed to have four iron 12-pounders. These battering guns are necessary, and they will not delay the march of the troops if a few more than the regulated number of bullocks are yoked to them. In the last campaign in the Mahratta territory I had two of these same guns : they were attended by an elephant, and kept up with the line on every march.

I have desired that the lead should be sent to Chittledroog from Mudgherry, Mergasie, and Paughur. You will observe by my letter of the 16th that I recommend that the equipments from the Carnatic should be sent up by means of hired cattle, and that the Company's draught cattle should be kept here and given out as soon as the equipments will join. My opinion upon this subject is strengthened by the accounts I have received of the state of the weather and roads in the Carnatic, from which I fear that the cattle for service will suffer much, as well as from the want of forage.   However, in consequence of your letter of the 16th, I have ordered off 400, being the number in this country surplus to what will be required for the equipments provided here.   If I observe by your answer to my letter of the 16th that you are of the same opinion with me regarding the risk of sending these bullocks to the Carnatic, I will send orders to stop them.

By your letter of the 16th, I observe that you have provided an equipment at Fort St. George larger than that which you originally intended.   Supposing the number of corps to be employed on the service to be as I enumerated them in my letter of the 13th, there will be from Fort St. George two 12-pounders for each of the European corps, and two field-pieces for each of the Native corps; besides a reserve of four 18-pounders, one 12-pounder, two 6-pounders, two 8-inch and two $5\frac{1}{2}$-inch howitzers. The equipment preparing here (exclusive of the preparations for the six 12-pounders) will consist of eighteen 6-pounders, seven lacs of musket ammunition and one lac of carbine, and 500 sets of intrenching tools.   The other articles are merely to complete this equipment.

From Chittledroog I should have ordered two 6-pounders only, as their tumbrils and ammunition are prepared here, and the four iron 12-pounders with their equipments. I could, besides, take from Chittledroog nine more 6-pounders and as many tumbrils as I can want.

Considering the state of the weather and of the roads in the Carnatic at present, and that they will not mend till the end of next month, I take the liberty of suggesting to you that the four 18-pounders and the four howitzers may be the first completed and sent up to this country, and that our dependence should at first be upon the stores in Mysore for all the other articles required.   A small effort will bring up these pieces of ordnance, and when they and the troops arrive we shall be prepared for the service.   But it will take a great length of time to prepare and remove hither the large equipment which you have mentioned in your letter.

Your answer to my letter of the 13th will make me more clearly acquainted with your intentions on these points; but I know that I can prepare here all that you want, excepting the four 18-pounders and the four howitzers, supposing that the pieces of ordnance mentioned in your letter of the 16th are the extent of the equipment which you propose to have in the field.

Since writing the above I have received your letter of the 17th. I shall see Captain Scott this evening, but not before the post goes out. I saw this morning in his yard everything in a state of preparation for the galloper carriages, and as the timber for the naves and fellies is on the road, I think they will be ready as soon as that arrives. However, I shall have the honour of writing to you again to-morrow upon this subject, and will let you know what Captain Scott says regarding the platform carts.

I am anxious to receive your orders respecting Captain Grant's commanding his corps.

I have, &c.,

ARTHUR WELLESLEY.

[1349.] G O. Seringapatam, 21st Nov., 1802.

Captain Scott having reported that —— ——, of the 77th regiment, employed at work in the yard of the gun carriage manufactory, has been repeatedly drunk and absent from his duty, his pay as an artificer is to be discontinued from the 20th instant, and he is to be sent to join his corps by the first opportunity. Further orders respecting this man will be given in the garrison of Seringapatam.

It is necessary that the European artificers should understand that they are not brought to Seringapatam to receive a large allowance and to get drunk. It is essentially necessary that they should perform with regularity the work allotted to them; and if they fail in doing so, their pay as artificers must be stopped.

Accordingly, Captain Scott is requested to keep an account of the number of days in each month in which any man may be absent from work on account of drunkenness, and a deduction is to be made from the pay of the men thus absent for a proportionable number of days, and credit for this sum is to be given to the Company in the abstracts. Besides, any man who perseveres in these irregular habits will be sent back to his corps, and be otherwise punished.

ARTHUR WELLESLEY.

To Lieutenant-Colonel Whitelocke.   [1850.]

SIR,   Seringapatam, 22nd Nov., 1802.

I have this day ordered bullocks from Seringapatam to Chittledroog to bring hither nineteen ammunition tumbrils; you will be so kind as to give orders that they may be sent off as soon as the bullocks will arrive.

I have also to request that six 6-pounder field pieces may be prepared for service at Chittledroog as soon as possible. I enclose a statement of articles required for this equipment, with articles of the kind which are in the stores at Chittledroog and those wanting to complete.

The following articles, wanting to complete, will hereafter be furnished from hence, viz. 188 bottoms for 6-pounder shot (unless I should hear from you that these articles can be turned at Chittledroog) ;

1233 serge cartridge bags ;
2 sets of drag ropes ;
9 tar and grease kegs ;
7 tumbril tarpaulins ;
4 tumbril chain traces ;
4 tumbrils.

The limbers wanting are in store at Chittledroog, and must be filled. Besides these field-pieces, I shall require two more; but the equipments of these will be sent from Seringapatam.

I beg that you will have the musket ammunition in the stores at Chittledroog examined very particularly, and let me know whether it is at this moment fit for service. A small guard must accompany these tumbrils to Seringapatam.

I have, &c.,

ARTHUR WELLESLEY.

To Lieutenant-General Stuart.   [1851.]

SIR,   Seringapatam, 22nd Nov., 1802.

I have had a conversation with Captain Scott upon the subject of making platform carts. The result appears to me to be as follows :

He expects here the Bengal wood for the naves and fellies

of the wheels of the cavalry carriages on the 7th of next month, and by that time the other parts of twenty 6-pounder carriages and ten tumbrils for that service will be ready, and the whole will be put together in a very few days afterwards. If the artificers are taken from this work and employed upon the platform carts, not only will this work be at a stand, but that upon the platform carts will not advance much, as, in the first instance, all the wood must be sawed up for them, which will take much time. Besides, it appears that, although you are desirous to have platform carts, you are most anxious about the cavalry carriages; that you ordered the former to be made only because you imagined the latter would not be completed, which is not the case. Upon the whole, therefore, I have thought it best not to interrupt the work on the cavalry carriages.

I have to inform you that Mr. Gordon has platform carts ready in his yard, which were overplus to the number last indented for at this place; he has likewise ready the component parts of more, and I have indented upon him. If you should approve of this mode of procuring these carriages, by the time I can receive your answer the artificers in his yard will nearly have completed our equipment here, and I will indent for more.

I have likewise to inform you that there are ten serviceable platform carts at Chitteldroog.

I have, &c.,

ARTHUR WELLESLEY.

[1352.] MEMORANDUM FOR MR. PIELE.

22nd Nov., 1802.

There is one regiment of cavalry coming from the southern division of the army by the Gudjelhatty Pass and Seringapatam, one of dragoons from Arcot by Bangalore and Sera, and one of dragoons and two of Native cavalry from the army in the Ceded Districts towards Hurryhur.

It will be necessary to provide gram for these different corps, as well as for those at present in Mysore, and the following mode is proposed :—

1st. That as much gram as can be conveniently got together should be laid into store at Santa Bednore, as well for the consumption of the regiment at that station as to give it a bullock load for each horse when it will march, and to provide for the demands of the other regiments of cavalry when they will arrive upon the frontier.

2nd. Instead of having the whole of the gram procurable to the northward stored at Santa Bednore, it might be convenient that the store for the regiments coming from the Ceded Districts, amounting to 1200 horses, and requiring that number of bullock loads of gram, should be lodged in Chittledroog: if that should be the case, or if any other arrangement should be more convenient to Purneah, it will be the same thing to me, only care being taken to apprise me exactly of the situation of each quantity of gram in due time.

Santa Bednore, however, will be the best place, as well because there is a good and capacious store-room there as because it is the nearest to the scene of the proposed operations.

3rd. The regiment coming from the southward ought to be provided with a load for each horse (about 400) at Seringapatam, and be provided besides on the road to this place and forward to the frontier.

4th. The regiment coming from Arcot ought to be provided with a load for each horse (about 500) at Bangalore, and be provided besides with gram on the road by Sera and Chittledroog.

5th. The regiment at Sera ought to be provided with a load for each horse when it will march (about 400), and, besides, on the road to Chittledroog and the frontier.

By these arrangements we shall carry up to the frontier, by regimental means, one fortnight's gram for the whole of the cavalry, besides what Purneah may be able to lay in store at Santa Bednore for the use of the regiment at that station while it remains there and when it will march, and for the general consumption.

No communication has yet been received from the gram-agent general, either stating his wants of cattle and gram from this country or his means already provided in the Carnatic.

It is probable, however, that he will provide some cattle in the Carnatic, will require others from hence, and loads from Mysore for them all: I should therefore recommend—

6th. That Purneah should be prepared with a statement of

2 E 2

the places to which he would propose that these cattle should go to receive their loads of gram.

I should wish to have this 6th article attended to as soon as possible, in order that I may be able to have an early communication with the gram-agent general upon the subject, and direct the cattle, immediately upon their arrival in Mysore, to the places at which they are to receive their loads.

ARTHUR WELLESLEY.

[1353.]   *To Major Macleod.*

MY DEAR MACLEOD,   Seringapatam, 23rd Nov., 1802.

Your letter of the 20th is very satisfactory to me, and I beg that the whole subject may drop. In regard to Lieutenant-Colonel Boles, the expression he uses in his letter of the 8th November is as follows:—"The people throughout Malabar complain of their distresses, and declare that their grievances have never been heard." He does not say one word respecting the truth or falsehood of this complaint or declaration; but he states, as a fact, only that the complaint and declaration have been made. I think therefore that your reply to him was harsh, and was not called for by what he had written you.

In your letter of the 20th you tell me that you will render him any satisfaction that I may judge suitable. I can only tell you what I should do under similar circumstances. I should write Lieutenant-Colonel Boles a letter, in which I should tell him that I had misconceived his expression in his letter of the 8th November, and that under that misconception I had written the letter of the 9th; and I should assure him that under no other circumstances would I have written him in such terms; and I should request that they might be considered as having never been written. This, with assurances of respect for his character, which he really deserves, would conciliate him and settle the matter: and this is what I recommend to you. I can only say that it is what I should do were I in your situation.

I have no news for you: matters remain to the northward and in Wynaad nearly as they were. I have sent to Manundwaddy from Cancancotta a supply of rice.

Believe me, &c.,

ARTHUR WELLESLEY.

To Captain Fitzpatrick.   [1354.]

MY DEAR SIR,   Seringapatam, 23rd Nov., 1802.

I have just received your letter of the 18th November.
When I was about to depart from Fort St. George in December,
1800, to take the command of the troops at Trincomalee, I
applied to the government for the services of a detachment of
the corps of pioneers stationed at Vellore, and government
granted my request. At the same time, a gentleman high in
the confidence of government, who is now dead, represented to
me the probability that I should not derive much benefit from
the services of this body of pioneers unless an officer commanded
them, and he recommended me to apply that you might be
sent with them, although at that time you had been removed
from the corps of pioneers and were employed in another situation in the Mysore country. He, at the same time, pointed out
that you would suffer by this arrangement unless something was
done for you in the body of troops assembled at Trincomalee;
and it was settled either that you should be appointed Mustermaster to the Coast troops, and establishments employed upon
the expedition, or that Major Ogg, the other Mustermaster in
Mysore, should; and that in that case the person to be appointed Acting Mustermaster in Mysore should be in his room,
and that you should retain your office in Mysore. On my
arrival at Trincomalee I made the former arrangement, finding
it the most convenient for the service, and I submitted it to
the Governor-General, who approved of it.

General Baird afterwards thought proper to deprive you of
this situation because you commanded a corps of pioneers in
the army. He was the best judge of the propriety of any
appointment in the body of troops under his command; but
I have to observe upon this objection to you, that it was perfectly well known at Fort St. George, when you left that place
to proceed upon the expedition, and equally so to the Governor-
General at the time, that his Excellency thought proper to
approve of your appointment.

This is the state of the case as far as regards your appointment being considered as a remuneration for the loss you would
sustain on going upon the service. It was certainly so considered in fact; but it was not, and could not be, so publicly
stated.

Whether government will consider it so or not at present is what I cannot decide; but I enclose you extracts from letters from the Governor-General to General Baird upon the subject of the officers belonging to the Coast establishment who did me the honour to volunteer their services when I was appointed to command the expedition, which will show what his Excellency's sentiments were regarding the situation of those gentlemen when he altered the arrangement. It is possible that, in conformity with these sentiments, the government of Fort St. George may think it proper to give you a remuneration, and I sincerely wish they may.

I have long determined that I never would write a line publicly upon the subject of that expedition to Egypt, and I never have, excepting in cases which have been referred to me arising from a construction put upon my own orders. I, therefore, can do nothing to forward your wishes. But if you think that a communication of this letter and its enclosures to the gentlemen in the confidence of the Commander-in-Chief can be of any service to you, you have my permission to show them to them.

Believe me, &c.,

ARTHUR WELLESLEY.

[1355.]

To Lieutenant-General Stuart.

SIR,   Seringapatam, 24th Nov., 1802.

I have had the honour to receive your letter of the 19th instant, and it gives me the greatest satisfaction to find that all that I have done has met with your approbation.

In regard to the depôt at Hurryhur my plan was as follows:—
1st. To carry to that place as much of the rice as should be beaten out at Chittledroog, and to lodge it in bags. 2ndly. If we should find that the Mysore dealers in general would be unwilling to advance to the army when it should be in the Mahratta territory, to purchase from them at Hurryhur all that they would bring there, and afterwards to forward it on to the army either by the Company's means or those of the brinjarries.

In regard to the first, orders have been given to beat out the paddy in store at Chittledroog; but that work goes on slowly, and it is probable that some time will elapse before any very useful progress will be made in it. I intend therefore, as soon as the bullocks for the intended grain department will be hired, to send them off to Hurryhur with their loads of rice, and after they will have lodged these at that place to employ them in carrying forward from Chittledroog all that will be beaten out, and in carrying to Hurryhur all the rice which may be collected at different stations in that neighbourhood by the Dewan. By this mode the depôt at Hurryhur may have in it by the time the troops will be collected upon the Toombuddra about 4000 bags, besides the quantity in the field grain department.

In regard to the second, the propriety of adopting it will depend upon the inclination of the Mysore dealers in general to follow the army any distance in the Mahratta territory. If they should be willing to follow, it would be most convenient that they should do so; if they should not be willing to follow it, this is the only plan by which we can avail ourselves of the resources which they will bring forward.

There are no buildings at Hurryhur; and, as well for the purpose of holding the grain which will be lodged there as for an hospital, I have requested the Dewan to collect materials to construct the necessary buildings. In the meantime the rice will be lodged in some small pagodas not used at present for the purposes of religion.

Some of the arrack which you have ordered from the Carnatic ought certainly to be forwarded to Hurryhur, and I will give directions accordingly.

In regard to the gram I have made the following arrangement with the Dewan, respecting the detail of which I will correspond with the gram-agent general as soon as I shall hear from him :—

1st. That the largest quantity he can collect is to be lodged at Santa Bednore, in the large gram-store lately provided there. Santa Bednore is about thirty miles from Hurryhur. This gram is to provide for the consumption of the corps stationed there, to give this corps a bullock load for each horse when it will march from thence, and for the general consumption when the troops will be assembled upon the Toombuddra. The Dewan will not be able to collect a very large quantity at Santa Bednore; but he will have sufficient for the two first objects, and will, besides, have 2500 loads at Hurryhur, or in other places equally near to that place with Santa Bednore, of which he will give me an account. Besides these 2500 loads applicable to the general consumption, there are in Chittledroog about 30 garces. All this is of old gram; but when the new gram comes in, about the latter end of January, the quantity to be supplied by the Dewan may be quadrupled.

2ndly. For the particular consumption of corps I have arranged that each corps, on coming into the Mysore country, shall receive a bullock load for each horse at the first convenient station at which it will arrive; and that besides that, measures are to be taken to provide each with gram daily on its march from its entrance on the frontier to the Toombuddra; so that every corps will arrive there with one bullock load for each horse.

3rdly. For the provision of gram for the gram-agent general's department I have arranged that his bullocks are to be loaded at six stations immediately on their entrance into the Mysore country from the Carnatic. I will send him the orders on each station for the gram as soon as I shall hear from him. The stations are either on, or immediately in, the neighbourhood of the high road.

So that, by these arrangements, each regiment will arrive on the frontier with one fortnight's gram; the gram-agent general will have all his bags full; and there will be for the general consumption, while the troops remain upon the Toombuddra, about 5000 bags, either at Hurryhur or within thirty miles of that place, and at Chittledroog.

All this is independent of the brinjarries, many of whom will be loaded with gram. I have directed that the paddy at Hullihall may be beaten out; and besides that, that thirty garces of rice may be laid in at that station. Soonda produces no gram.

The four iron 12-pounders will be prepared at Chittledroog: they will have one tumbril for each gun of fixed ammunition; and I propose that they should have 500 rounds of shot, &c., carried on bullocks. Notwithstanding this arrangement, I still go on with the preparations of the equipments for the brass 12-pounders, the carriages for which are coming from Madras. I am afraid that you will be disappointed in the gunny bags in Malabar: they are sand-bags, as Lieutenant-Colonel Boles informs me.   I have, however, desired that gunny bags may be prepared at all the stations in Mysore.

No expense has been incurred here that will not at all times be of service, excepting for the hire of bullocks.   But I know no mode in which any preparation can be made without preparing the cattle; and in case of war the difference of the state of preparation, if they are entertained, is so great that I consider that money well laid out.

I have, &c.,

ARTHUR WELLESLEY.

To Alexander Read, Esq.   [1356.]

DEAR SIR,   Seringapatam, 24th Nov., 1802.

I have had the pleasure of receiving your letter of the 20th, and I assure you that I do you the justice of believing that no private motive would induce you to absent yourself from any part of the countries under your management in which the public interests might require your presence.   Of course you must have business in different parts of the country, of the nature of which I cannot be aware; and you must be the best judge in what part it is most pressing and it is most necessary that you should be present.   You will have heard of the late disasters which have befallen the Peshwah in the neighbourhood of Poonah: the consequence is, that preparations are making to assemble a large body of troops on the frontier, and it is possible that the British government may interfere with force in the affairs of the Mahratta state.

My object in wishing you to be in Soonda at the present time was, that I wished you to give every assistance to the officers of supply which might lie in your power, in order that, in the present crisis, the army might reap the full advantage of the resources of that province.   I know also that it is not uncommon for the evil-disposed in all parts of India to take advantage of a moment of difficulty such as may be expected, and of the employment of the troops against a public enemy, to breed discontent, to disseminate disaffection towards the Company's government, to collect men in arms, and, finally, to be guilty of acts of insurrection and rebellion against the Company's authority.   It is an object of the greatest consequence to prevent these evils in Soonda at the present moment; because this province is so contiguous to the road which the army must eventually use for its communication with Mysore, and it is one of those places which must be reckoned as a source of supply of rice.

There is no mode of preventing them so certain as the presence of the gentleman who has the management of the district, to whom all will look up. Your presence may be more necessary elsewhere; but it is certain that that of Mr. Wilson is necessary in Soonda, and I hope that you will send him there with full powers to act in every possible case.

The Ghaut which I wish to have cleared at present is the Tenin Ghaut, on the road to Goa.

Believe me, &c.,

ARTHUR WELLESLEY.

[1357.]   *To Lieutenant-Colonel Whitelocks.*

SIR,   Seringapatam, 25th Nov., 1802.

In my letter of the 22nd I requested that certain preparations might be made at Chittledroog for the equipment of six 6-pounders. Since that time I have had reason to believe that those pieces of ordnance will not be required from that garrison, but that four iron 12-pounders will be required. Accordingly I have to request that four iron 12-pounders may be prepared, together with the articles of equipment detailed in the enclosed list. An indent must be made upon the commissary of supply for the articles which the stores cannot furnish, and which cannot be made up therein.

The six concave sponges wanted will be sent from hence.

Besides this equipment for those four 12-pounders, all of which will go upon bullocks, or upon the carriages of the guns, four tumbrils with fixed ammunition will be prepared at this place. The nineteen tumbrils must still come to Seringapatam as soon as the bullocks will arrive for them.

I have, &c.,

ARTHUR WELLESLEY.

To Major-General Campbell.   [1358.]

SIR,   Seringapatam, 26th Nov., 1802.

I have the honour to inform you that the aumildars in the Mysore country have been directed to see and examine the passports of all Europeans passing through the districts under their management; in consequence of which I have issued an order to the troops under my command, a copy of which is enclosed. I beg that you will do me the favour to apprise the troops in the Ceded Districts of this arrangement, in order that all Europeans passing through Mysore may pay attention thereto.

I have, &c.,

ARTHUR WELLESLEY.

To Colonel Leighton, commanding Ryacottah.   [1359.]

SIR,   Seringapatam, 26th Nov., 1802.

I have the honour to inform you that the aumildars in the Mysore country have been directed to see and examine the passports of all Europeans passing through the districts under their management, in consequence of which I have issued an order to the troops under my command, a copy of which is enclosed. I beg that you will do me the favour to apprise all Europeans who may pass the station under your command, with intention to enter the Mysore country, of the above arrangement, in order that they may pay attention to it.

I have, &c.,

ARTHUR WELLESLEY.

To Captain Walker.   [1360.]

DEAR SIR,   Seringapatam, 26th Nov., 1802.

I received your letter of the 23rd last night, and I proceed to give you answers upon the subjects on which you have desired my sentiments.

There are two : first, the mode of paying for the gram which the regiments of cavalry may procure in the Mysore country ;

secondly, the mode of supplying it, supposing that a body of cavalry should be collected in the field.

Upon the first subject I have to observe, that it is one of official detail, respecting which it is immaterial to the public interest in what manner it is settled. The gram must be paid for; but whether it is paid for by the regiments as they will receive it, or whether they will pass the receipts for it and you will pay the Sircar for the whole, is a matter of but little consequence.

It is necessary, however, that if it should be determined that the quartermasters of regiments should pay for the gram they will receive, notice of this arrangement should be given to the aumildars in the country; and that the regiments should be immediately, and at all times hereafter, sufficiently supplied with money, so as not to be obliged to take gram upon receipt in future. The aumildars will not understand that sometimes they are to be paid for gram and at others not; and they will create more difficulty in producing the article, and you will experience still more afterwards in settling the accounts. Upon the whole, therefore, although these difficulties are but of trifling importance, it is best that they should not exist; and unless you are certain that the regiments stationed in and passing through Mysore will always have a command of money, it is better that they should continue to take what they want, as they have hitherto, upon their receipts.

Upon the second subject I have to observe that there are three objects to be provided for: one is, that the gram-agent-general should have a supply of gram to be carried with the army; I will suppose 1000 bullock loads for each regiment (7000 bullock loads): the next is, that the regiments should have each of them on the frontier a bullock load for each horse; and the third is, that there should be on the frontier such a quantity of gram as that neither the gram-agent-general's stock nor that with the regiments will be consumed, or either touched, during the time that it may be necessary that the troops should remain within the Mysore territory. I shall proceed to state to you the arrangements which I have made, with a view to ensuring these three objects. I must observe to you that, although Mysore is a plentiful gram country, and there is enough now within it for all these objects, the produce last year was not so great as it has been heretofore; that there has been a great exportation throughout the year to the Ceded Districts and the Carnatic; and that we are now nearly at the end of the last crop, as the new gram will come in at the end of January: we must therefore arrange so as to bring forward to the frontier the gram of the distant countries towards the Eastern Ghauts and the southward.

With a view to the first object, viz., the supply for the gram-agent-general, I have arranged that he is to receive 1000 bullock loads at each of the following places, all of them either on or immediately in the neighbourhood of the high road to the frontier, viz.: Batmunglum, Colar, Ooscotta, Ambajee Droog, Yarculwa, near Ambajee Droog, Bangalore, Sera. Hereafter I will send you orders on each of the places for this quantity of gram, and you will have nothing to do but to send your servants and cattle and bags for it, and either pay or pass your receipt for it, as you may think proper.

With a view to the second object, viz., the regimental supply of one bullock for each horse, I have arranged that the regiment at Santa Bednore and that at Sera shall be supplied as long as they remain at those stations, that they shall have ready one bullock load for each horse when they march, and that their consumption shall be supplied daily on the road. The regiment coming from the southward will be supplied daily on its march to the frontier from Gudjelhatty, and will receive one bullock for each horse at this place. The 19th dragoons will be supplied daily on its march from Batmunglum to the frontier, and will receive a bullock load for each horse at Bangalore. The regiments coming from the Ceded Districts will be supplied daily on their march, and will receive a bullock load for each horse at Chittledroog. I will send you the order for all this gram hereafter. Thus you will observe, the whole will arrive upon the frontier with full bags.

With a view to the third object, viz., the supply for the consumption while the troops may remain assembled within the Mysore territory, I have arranged that the Sircar shall have at different stations, within thirty miles of the frontier, 2500 bags, of which I will hereafter send you a list; and, besides that quantity, there are in store at Chittledroog 30 garces.

All this is independent of the brinjarries and bazaar people, who you know always bring a large proportion of gram to our

camps, and of the new crops to the northward, which there
is every reason to believe will be plentiful, and may be available
at the time at which the troops will be assembled upon the
frontier. I hope that this arrangement will suit you; at least
you will agree that I have not been inattentive to my friends of
the cavalry.

If you should want assistance in hiring bullocks, I believe
I can afford you some; at all events, if you require any, I will
try what I can do for you.

Believe me, &c.,

ARTHUR WELLESLEY.

[1361.]   *To W. H. Gordon, Esq.*

SIR,   Seringapatam, 26th Nov., 1802.

I have the honour to inform you that it is my intention to
have a store of rice at Hurryhur, on the Toombuddra, which will
consist of about 70 garces: you will therefore make your
arrangements immediately for placing there the proper number
of servants for the care of this grain, and measuring it upon its
receipt or issue.

There are no buildings at Hurryhur applicable to the purpose
of containing this rice, and it must therefore be stowed in bags
for the present in such places as may be most convenient. The
Dewan has promised that he would have some pagodas put in
repair for the purpose of containing this grain, and I propose to
erect a temporary building for the same purpose; but some time
will elapse before the latter will be ready.

I propose to send from hence 2000 loads of grain, which will
form part of this depôt. I, besides, propose to lodge there as
much of the rice as may be beaten out of the paddy at Chittledroog; and I request you to purchase in the neighbourhood of
Hurryhur as much more as you can procure. In the course of
a few days I hope to be able to communicate to you the names
of the places in the Mysore country, in the neighbourhood of
Hurryhur, at which you will be able to procure rice.

I have, &c.,

ARTHUR WELLESLEY.

G. O.   Seringapatam, 26th Nov., 1802.   [1362.]

With a view to render the orders of the Right Honourable the Governor in Council regarding passports to Europeans travelling through the territories of Fort St. George more efficient in the Mysore country than they have hitherto been, the aumildars have been directed to require a sight of his passport from every European, of whatever rank or nation, who may propose to pass through the districts under their respective management ; and they have been required in the most positive manner to detain every such European who does not produce a passport corresponding with the printed form transmitted to them by the Resident.

The aumildars have been particularly informed that the above orders do not extend to officers commanding bodies of troops, to those troops, or to the public officers of government who may have a passport authorizing them to travel post on the public service.

Colonel Wellesley publishes the foregoing regulations to all concerned, and he requires all European officers, non-commissioned officers, and private soldiers of His Majesty's or of the Honourable Company's service, and also all other Europeans proposing to pass through any part of the territories of the Rajah of Mysore, to produce their passports to the servants of His Highness' government whenever they are required to do so ; and he directs that, in every case wherein the aumildars, thinking that the passport does not correspond with the form transmitted to them, require the person producing it to remain at the place where his passport has been demanded until reference can be made to the Resident, or to the nearest military station, such person shall remain there quietly, without giving any molestation to the aumildar or to the inhabitants, until such reference has been made.

ARTHUR WELLESLEY.

To Lieutenant-General Stuart.   [1363.]

SIR,   Seringapatam, 27th Nov., 1802.

I have had the honour of receiving your letters of the 22nd and 23rd.

Major Macleod has shown a disposition to make an apology

to Lieutenant-Colonel Boles, and I hope that I shall not have occasion to trouble you again upon that subject. He is going into Wynaad, where he will meet Lieutenant-Colonel Montresor.

I have ordered the 1st of the 2nd, 2nd of the 3rd, 2nd of the 18th, and 2nd of the 10th, and 1st of the 8th, for service from the garrisons in this country, and I shall put in Seringapatam one, and in Chittledroog another of the corps coming from the southward. I shall see them all on their march up, and will put the worst in garrison.

I believe that I shall use as escorts to everything going to the northward one of the corps of this garrison whose officers understand the nature of the arrangements of the government of this country, which is desirable. The strangers know nothing about the matter.

I have ordered back the cattle which I had ordered away on the 24th, and I have called up the cattle from Mangalore.

It is impossible to give a decided opinion upon the particular operations before the decided object of the Governor-General is known; but whatever may be that object, as the means of attaining it must be the defeat of the formidable body of troops collected by Holkar, time is not thrown away in considering certain subjects connected with the operations against that chieftain.

It is obvious that the intentions of the British government regarding the affairs of the Mahratta empire cannot be carried into execution unless Holkar's army is either defeated or dissipated. The object of the campaign must therefore be to bring him to a general action at as early a period as possible. This object, I have to observe, is not one of which, like the siege of Seringapatam, or the operations of a former war against Tippoo, the time it will take to attain it can be calculated. If it be our interest to bring Holkar to a general action, it is his to avoid it; and it may be depended upon that he will avoid it as long as he can.

His army is light, and chiefly composed of cavalry. The whole composition of our armies is heavy; even our cavalry, from the nature of their constitution and their equipments, and owing to the food eaten by the horses, are not able to march with greater celerity for any length of time than our infantry. His troops and his horses subsist on the grain the produce of the country. Our troops come from countries the general produce of which is rice; they, and even their followers, must have a certain quantity of that grain; and the horses of the cavalry must likewise have a grain not the general produce of the Mahratta territory, which, in addition to the inconvenience of the necessity of boiling it, must be brought from a distance.

Holkar, therefore, will have not only the inclination but the means of avoiding the result which, I take it for granted, can alone bring the war to a conclusion; and it is obvious that no man possesses a datum on which he can calculate the length of time which will elapse before he can bring the contest to that state.

Putting the European troops out of the question, the mode of equipping our Native armies, the food which they and their followers and horses are in the habit of using, will render it necessary that a large stock of provisions should be carried for their consumption. But however large that stock may be, no man can pretend to say that it will last till the general action will take place, which will alone bring the contest to a conclusion, because I have already shown that the enemy will be inclined, and will have the means of avoiding it. Therefore I conclude that, after a certain period for which our stock of provisions will have been provided, we shall be obliged to return to our own country for a fresh supply.

There are but two modes of carrying on this war by which we may avoid this disagreeable result: one is to place the seat of it in a country so near our own resources as that we shall be able with ease to command our supplies, or in one which is capable of affording us the supplies we require; the other is to keep up our communication with our own country, whatever may be the distance from it of the seat of the war. In regard to the first, viz., to command the seat of the war, I have to observe that we shall no more be able to do that than we shall to command its operations. The result is to be a general action with the enemy, and I have already shown that we must fight that action where he pleases, and therefore we cannot fix upon the seat of the war.

The second mode then is that alone by which we can succeed. By this mode we shall always supply ourselves; the enemy may protract his defeat, but sooner or later it must happen. The question is, in what manner is this desirable object to be attained?

The long operations of conquering and establishing ourselves in the countries on this side of the Kistna I put out of the question, as suitable neither to the state of our force at the present moment nor to our finances. Besides, it is probable that before we should have brought matters to that state thet we should be able to commence the operations against the enemy which are to bring the war to a conclusion, other revolutions would happen in India which would entirely alter the situation of affairs.

The manner then by which I would propose to keep up the communication with our rear would be to take into our alliance and call for the co-operation of all the Mahratta chiefs on this side of India.

Upon this subject I observe that my opinion is different from yours, and I am aware that the question is political, upon which I am not called to give an opinion at all; but it is so intimately connected with the military operations that it is not possible to consider the one without considering the other.

In all cases of war, particularly with such a nation as the Mahrattas, there can be no doubt but that generally it is desirable that a part of them should be on our side; and I proceed to consider whether there is any reason which ought to induce us to reject the alliance of those Mahrattas whose services I believe we can now command. The great objection to our adopting it is the engagements by which we or the Peshwah may be fettered hereafter. I do not think it probable that we shall be under the necessity of entering into such engagements; but even if we should, the object of the contest is not territory for ourselves, but the defeat of a power from which we or our ally apprehend danger; and the question regarding the engagements must be decided by that of the value or the necessity of the assistance of those with whom they are to be entered into.

The Mahratta territory is divided among jaghiredars, all of whom have troops in the service of the state, or it belongs to Polygars, who pay a peshcush, or it is managed by the aumildars of the Sircar. But the peshcush of these Polygars, and everything collected by the aumildars, is applied to the payment of the Peshwah's troops, whose chiefs have tuncaws upon the

revenues, or in payment of the debts of the state, also upon
tuncaws.   The Mahratta government was formerly as regularly
organised as any in India, and these jaghiredars completely
under the control of the Peshwah as head of the empire; but
during the late troubles they have become in some degree independent of his authority, and they look to other sources besides
his favour for their security.   There is no doubt, however, but
that all that they could claim from us in return for their assistance would be protection in the enjoyment of their jaghires,
which, in case of our interference in the affairs of the empire
hereafter, it is more than probable that we should afford them
at all events.   The promise of this protection would not prevent
us from availing ourselves of any advantages to be derived hereafter from any subsidiary engagements which might be entered
into with the Peshwah.   The countries which it is probable we
should wish to have under such an arrangement are Savanore
and Darwar, on which there are no jaghires.   Their revenues
are applied in part to the payment of Goklah's army, being the
army of the state, and in part of a debt due by the state to the
family of Pursheram Bhow; and all that would be necessary
would be to urge the Peshwah to make some other arrangement for the payment of this debt.   Upon the whole, therefore,
considering the nature of the tenures of the chiefs who command the troops in this part of the Mahratta territory, and their
probable objects and ours, I cannot conceive that we can be
fettered hereafter by any engagements we may enter into with
them.

I now come to consider what assistance they can give us.

In the first place, the government of the countries through
which the British army must pass to fight this battle is in their
hands.   By having them in our camps the inhabitants of these
countries will be friendly to us; we shall enjoy the supplies
which they can afford, and our own supplies will pass through
them with comparatively small escorts.   In short, we shall
enjoy advantages nearly as extensive as we should supposing
that the countries were in our own hands, without spending time,
money, and lives to conquer them.

In the second place, we shall have the assistance of a body
of cavalry amounting to not less than 20,000 men.   I don't
mean to hint that we shall require this assistance in the day of
battle, but we shall to escort our supplies, to guard our baggage

and provisions on our marches, to keep our camps quiet, to cover our forage, and save our own cavalry.

In the third place, we shall have the advantage of the best intelligence, particularly of any designs upon our rear. With such a body of cavalry in your camp, the enemy would not dare to detach small parties to your rear to distress your communications; and if he did, those parties would not remain there, as you would have the earliest intelligence of their movements, and might detach superior bodies immediately; and the fear of weakening himself too much in front of such a body of cavalry as you would have would equally prevent him from detaching a large body.

There is no doubt but that the advantages to be derived from this body of men are very great, and probably will more than counterbalance the perils to be expected from an alliance with them; and when it is recollected that by their assistance a prospect is afforded of keeping open our rear, and thus of bringing the contest to the only possible conclusion, I think that the necessity of encouraging them is obvious.

I have previously stated that these troops belong to the Mahratta state, for whose subsistence payment is already provided by the arrangements of that government; therefore the employment of them will occasion no expense. They likewise and their horses, like all other Mahrattas, live upon jowarry, the grain of the country, and their consumption will not fall upon our supplies.

I have, &c.,

ARTHUR WELLESLEY.

[1364.]   *To Lieutenant-General Stuart.*

SIR,   Seringapatam, 30th Nov., 1802.

I have to return you my best thanks for your recommendation of me to the Honourable the Governor in Council, to be appointed a General officer on the staff of this establishment. This favour in itself, as well as in the manner in which it is conferred, is most gratifying to my feelings, and I hope to merit a continuance of the good opinion of me which you have manifested upon this occasion.

I have for some time had au aide-de-camp, Captain West,

and have been assisted in the duties I have to conduct by the Deputy-Adjutant-General in Mysore, the Persian interpreter, &c. I imagine that this circumstance did not occur to you when you wrote to me on the 26th, and desired that I should send you the name of the officer to be appointed my Brigade-Major; but if it did, and you think that notwithstanding my having this assistance, I ought as a Major-General on a staff to have a Brigade-Major, I will hereafter have the honour of recommending to you an officer for that situation.

In writing upon this subject I advert to that part of your other letter of the 26th, in which you desire to have my sentiments upon the subject of the necessity of a Town-Major at Seringapatam. It is frequently necessary for me to be absent from Seringapatam, and the command does not devolve on every occasion upon the same officer : it is therefore desirable that the staff officer of the station should be a man of some observation and experience, who can upon all occasions state to the temporary commanding officer in what manner the duty has been conducted. It is not possible to expect that an officer of that description will accept the office of Fort-Adjutant : the garrison of Seringapatam is at all times very numerous, and there are many details of sick, artificers, &c. &c., who are under charge of the Fort-Adjutant, and respecting whose accounts this officer holds a very troublesome correspondence with nearly every corps in the service. I don't think that one officer would be equal to the duties of both situations, and one of experience and respectability would not accept that of Fort-Adjutant with all its present duties in addition to those of the Town-Major.

I have, &c.,

ARTHUR WELLESLEY.

To Colonel Montresor.   [1365.]

MY DEAR COLONEL,   Seringapatam, 30th Nov., 1802.

Malcolm's arrival here, and the many subjects I had to talk over with him, have prevented me from answering your letters of the 24th and 26th till this day.

I refer you to the regulations for the grain department for the rule of your conduct in the issue of provisions to public and private followers. It would certainly be desirable that you should have a bazaar in Wynaad, and I have tried to persuade some of my people here to go into that district; but although they may promise, they will not move that way as long as they have hopes of a more plentiful harvest to the northward. If you can't get a bazaar, you must feed the people who are absolutely necessary, and the troops, from the public stores; but with that necessity another exists equally disagreeable and obvious, and that is, to have as few followers as you possibly can. The troops in Cotiote cannot be considered on full batta; field allowances were given to them at the end of the campaign of 1801, for particular reasons stated by Colonel Stevenson, and enforced by me at that time; but government granted what we then asked with the greatest difficulty. When an officer goes out with an escort, of course he and the troops composing it get batta, and the troops may receive the rice and provisions laid in at the station when none can be procured in the bazaar, but they must pay for it at the rate of * .

I have perused with attention all the papers enclosed in your letter of the 26th. Captain Watson's affair is not very creditable to the troops: however, I trust no blame can attach to him, and I beg that you will take an opportunity of informing him that I think he has done all he could do, and has shown an example of activity, which, if it had been shown at first, or had been followed since, would have stopped the rebellion at once. Either our Madras troops had a better story to tell, or they told it better, when a small body of them was lately attacked; but I trust that we shall hear no more of these disastrous affairs.

There may be much truth in the ' Observations, &c., upon Wynaad :' when a man goes into a strange country, as Macleod has, and the first operations of his administration are to put down a civil list amounting to near a lac of pagodas annually, it is not possible to expect that he will be very popular, and he must have many natural enemies of his system. On the other hand it is equally reasonable to expect that, however wrong they may be, Macleod is equally prejudiced in favour of all his own measures. One of the particular objects of a man in your situation should be to hold the balance between these two parties. You must, in the first instance, form your own opinion of the real state of affairs, not from the interested reports of

* Blank in manuscript.

either of these parties, but from your own observation of facts. You will find Macleod a good, an able, and a zealous servant of the public; candour and firmness on your part will beget the same on his, in all his communications with you; and you will find him not disinclined to your opinions upon all subjects relating to his duties, provided he finds them to be formed on your own observations, and not on the reports of others, who he must know to be his enemies. When I write this to you, I beg that you will not imagine that I think you have formed any opinion on these subjects, grounded in the manner that I deprecate; for you have positively told me in your letter of the 26th that you have not. But you must attribute it to the real motive, my sincere desire that you should succeed in all your objects, and my knowledge of the great use which you can be to the public by the adoption of the line which I recommend.

I have no news for you. General Stuart has recommended me to be appointed to the staff, and I was appointed on Friday last. Your promotion is in orders. I return Captain Watson's letters. I wrote you publicly on the subject of store-rooms at Cannanore.

Believe me, &c.,

ARTHUR WELLESLEY.

To Lieutenant-General Stuart. [1366.]

SIR, Seringapatam, 30th Nov., 1802.

I have had the honour to receive your letter of the 26th, and I now perfectly understand everything that will be required from this country.

According to your former orders I have directed 50 shells to be prepared for each of the brass 12-pounders, making in the whole 300, to be carried in six tumbrils.

By a letter of the 26th November, received last night, the Military Board have ordered from 2000 to 2500 $4\frac{1}{2}$-inch shells to be prepared, 600 of which to be filled, fuzed, and fixed to bottoms. If these are in addition to the other 300, we shall require twelve tumbrils to carry them, and we have only one now in the Mysore country undisposed of. If the 300 ordered by you are part of this order, we shall require six tumbrils to carry the remainder, which must be sent from the Carnatic.

I enclose copies of some letters received from Colonel Montresor, which give a melancholy account of affairs in Wynaad. However, the Colonel left Cannanore on the 26th with an intention of entering that district. The collector was to meet him. I have recommended him not to separate his detachments too much till he will have gained some decided success against the rebels.

Captain Watson gives a melancholy account of the behaviour of the troops.

A convoy of grain from this country had reached Manundwaddy in safety, and the people and bullocks have come out again.

The inhabitants on this side have begun to hold some communication with our troops.

I have, &c.,

ARTHUR WELLESLEY.

[1367.]   *To Captain Baynes, President of a Committee.*

SIR,   Seringapatam,   Nov., 1802.

I have to inform you that certain rupees of a base kind, called Sicca rupees, have found their way into the pay office at Chittledroog, and the object of the committee of which you are president is to inquire in what manner they came there, by whom paid in, at what rates of exchange, and at what times.

The first information which I received upon this subject was a letter from Lieutenant-Colonel Whitelocke, dated 11th October, a copy of which is enclosed (No. 1), in which he reports that out of 10,000 pagodas paid into the treasury on the 22nd September by the aumildar, 11,000 rupees had been Sicca rupees. In answer to this letter I wrote to him on the 13th October a letter a copy of which is enclosed (No. 2), and sent him a copy of the receipt of the pay office at Chittledroog for the sums paid by the aumildar on the 22nd September, by which it appeared that Sicca rupees had not been paid.

In the mean time, however, the aumildar of Chittledroog thought proper to allow the Sicca rupees to be current at Chittledroog at the rate of exchange of Company's rupees; and I received from Lieutenant-Colonel Whitelocke the letters of which copies are enclosed (Nos. 3 and 4), dated the 12th and 15th October.

On the 29th October, in consequence of farther instructions from the Dewan, the aumildar again cried down the Sicca rupees, and I received a letter from Lieutenant-Colonel White-locke, dated the 1st of November, of which a copy (No. 5) is enclosed.   In answer I wrote Lieutenant-Colonel Whitelocke a letter of the 4th November (No. 6), and I received the papers required in a letter from Lieutenant-Colonel Whitelocke, dated the 7th November (No. 7).

You will observe that he reports in that letter not only that the writers of the pay office declare that they received 11,000 Sicca rupees as Company's rupees from the aumildar, but that the acting aumildar acknowledged that 5000 rupees had been paid in that coin.

You will make this matter a particular subject of your inquiry.

I wrote a letter to Mr. Gordon upon this same subject on the 4th November, and received his answer of the 11th, copies of both of which are enclosed (Nos. 8 and 9).

On the 17th November Lieutenant-Colonel Whitelocke wrote me a letter, a copy of which is enclosed (No. 10), in which he informs me that the aumildar had told him that he was very well acquainted with the people who brought the Sicca rupees into that part of Mysore, who were willing to receive them back without loss to the Sircar.   I beg to call your attention par-ticularly to this part of the subject, and to urge you to sift it to the bottom.   The question is not in what manner the rupees came into Mysore, but how they came into the treasury; and from this statement of the aumildar it is obvious either that they were placed there improperly by the paymaster's servants, and that he has now a knowledge of the transaction, and wishes to screen them, or that they were paid to them by him, having been procured by improper means, and without the knowledge of his own government.

I have written to Lieutenant-Colonel Whitelocke to desire that all persons belonging to the garrison of Chittledroog upon whom you may call may attend you, and answer such questions as you may put to them; and directions to a similar purport are sent to the aumildar of Chittledroog.   You will, therefore, call upon whoever you may think proper.

I beg to have a detailed report of the proceedings of the committee.

I enclose an account (No. 11) of the sums of money which have been paid into the pay office at Chittledroog since the month of May, specifying in what coins.

I likewise send five of the Sicca rupees which have been given to me by the officers of this government.

I have, &c.,

ARTHUR WELLESLEY.

[1368.]   *To Lieutenant-General Stuart.*

SIR,   Seringapatam, 1st Dec., 1802.

I have had the honour of receiving your letter of the 27th November, and I shall pay every attention to its contents.

Before I take any steps to induce Captain Barclay to undertake the duties of Major Symons's office, or inform him that he is not to take the field, I should wish to have your sentiments upon a subject connected therewith in which I am personally interested. It is, whether it is your wish that I should retain the command in Mysore, while in advance with you, as I did heretofore, or whether you are desirous that it should be in other hands.

It is impossible for an officer to have been in a situation of this kind so long as I have without having a considerable degree of influence in the country, all of which, of course, depends upon his holding his situation. The exercise of this influence is certainly useful to you at present, and may be more so hereafter, when the army will be in advance.

If you should be of opinion that it will be expedient that I should still hold the command in Mysore, it will be necessary that Captain Barclay in particular, of all the other staff, should accompany me. If you should think it proper that another officer should be appointed to the command in Mysore, of course Captain Barclay must attend that officer. In either case arrangements can be made for doing the duties of Major Symons's office, independent of Captain Barclay, who I don't think would like to undertake them.

I acknowledge that I am not indifferent upon this subject; but, at all events, I should wish to have your sentiments upon it as soon as may be convenient to you, as I have many public as well as private arrangements to make preparatory to my quitting Mysore.

In my opinion, 12-pounders are sufficiently heavy for any place which it may be necessary for you to attack that I have seen in the Mahratta territory. I have not seen those to the northward of the Kistna, but I don't believe they are so strong as those I have seen, as the latter were in general either built or repaired by Hyder or Tippoo, who built better forts than the Mahrattas ever have. If 12-pounders will answer as well as 18-pounders, the difference in equipment is so great as to give the former the preference decidedly; but another reason for preferring them is that we shall have 12-pounder shot at Hullihall, whereas the full complement of 18-pounder shot for the four guns must be taken from the Mysore country, and these will add very much to the weight of your store department. My notion of an equipment for this service is that it should be as light as it can possibly be consistently with efficiency; that as much should go upon carriage-cattle, and as little upon carts, as possible; and that nothing should be taken that is not absolutely necessary. It must be expected that the army will have to make very long marches occasionally, accompanied by all its equipments, and the greater the number of carriages, the greater will be the difficulty of all these operations.

Impressed with this idea, I have forbidden all wheel carriages for private baggage, as I have always done heretofore.

Captain Scott has desired me to make known to you his wishes to go upon the proposed service in the field. In case you should comply with his request, Lieutenant Francke could do his duty at this place.

In consequence of your letter of the 26th November, Captain Grant relinquishes the command of the 2nd battalion 18th regiment. In justice, however, to Captain Grant, I have to inform you that I received a letter from him some days ago, in which he desired leave to accompany it to the field, and to resign his situation as Town-Major in case it was deemed improper that he should hold it and go to the field at the same time. I delayed to forward this letter till I had received your sentiments regarding his taking the command of the corps at all; and as they are conclusive upon the subject, even in his situation of barrackmaster, I have returned it to him.

I have, &c.,

ARTHUR WELLESLEY.

[1369.]   *To Colonel Montresor.*

MY DEAR COLONEL,   Seringapatam, 1st Dec., 1802.

In my letter of yesterday I omitted to mention to you that I had reason to believe that Lieutenant-Colonel Boles had made a mistake respecting the gunny-bags about which I wrote to him.   He informed me that they were sand-bags, and were in charge of Captain Dufty ; but the gunny rice-bags, if there are any, must be in charge of Mr. Richardson, the garrison store-keeper.

I shall be obliged to you to be so kind as to inquire about them, and let me know if there are any ; of what nature ; whether they are intended to carry rice upon bullocks' backs or are ship-bags ; and if they are now fit for service.   If there are any bags, I wish you could have some sent up, according to the orders I heretofore gave to Lieutenant-Colonel Boles.

Believe me, &c.,

ARTHUR WELLESLEY.

[1370.]   *To Josiah Webbe, Esq.*

MY DEAR WEBBE,   Seringapatam, 1st Dec., 1802.

I have received your letter of the 27th.   I agree entirely in opinion with you regarding the silladar horse, and I have requested Piele to lose no time in delivering your letter to Purneah.   I think that he will not be able to procure so many of this cavalry as he expects.

I have received a letter from the General, by which I judge that in case I should go into the Mahratta territory with the army, it is his intention that I should relinquish the command in Mysore.   This is not a matter of indifference to me ; but, of course, if it be necessary or proper on public grounds, I must put private considerations out of the question.

I cannot have been so long in the command of the troops in this country without acquiring a good deal of influence in it, the exercise of which is now making preparations for the arrival of the army and their subsequent operations, and must be useful to the General hereafter.   The moment it is known that I am to be removed, and that consequently I break up my house and establishments at this place, that influence will cease, and I can be of no more service to the General than the man who will succeed me.

Purneah has sent me word that several people lately have endeavoured to pass with matchlocks and other arms from Mysore by Batmunglum to the Carnatic, and, when questioned regarding their object, they have answered that they were going down to take service with the Company. They have been stopped, and some of them disarmed. I mention this only to put you on your guard. These people have certainly either been called down or are going down in expectation of a breeze in the Carnatic.

I think that Lord Wellesley will come to Madras, if this expedition goes on upon the great scale.

Believe me, &c.,
ARTHUR WELLESLEY.

To Lieutenant-General Stuart.   [1371.]

SIR,   Seringapatam, 2nd Dec., 1802.

I have had the honour to receive your letter of the 28th of November, and I will do everything in my power to complete the number of doolies that you will require. I know that I can get some, but the people are not properly palanquin or dooly-bearers, and go six or eight under a dooly, which they carry in the same manner that they do a stone. However, this conveyance is equally, if not more, easy to the sick men than that commonly used, and is not more expensive; as, although there may be 12 people attached to a dooly, they do not receive more pay than six of those hired at Madras and to the northward. But they are the working people of the country, which of course suffers from their absence, and the greater the number required the greater the inconvenience. However, in a case of necessity, such as this is, it must be borne.

I have always had these people with me, and they appear to be much attached to Mr. Anderson, who takes care that they are not ill-treated. They have never deserted.

In regard to the bazaars, my opinion is that the arrangement made by Lord Cornwallis for their conduct is the best that can be adopted, viz. that no duties should be collected on any articles; that every Native corps should have its bazaar, and the whole be uuder the grand bazaar and the superintendence of an

European officer. The only deviation from Lord Cornwallis's plan which I could recommend is, that every European as well as Native corps should have a bazaar. My reason for this is, first, it is a great convenience to the soldiers and their followers; secondly, it ensures a greater number of bazaar people in camp, as it may be expected that if it be known that the European corps are to have bazaars, some bazaar people will follow each from its station, otherwise not; and thirdly, there is no public inconvenience in the measure, as, even supposing that the number of bazaar people is not increased, the supplies of provisions which they will bring in and sell will be equal, whether they encamp in the rear of one corps, or in that of another, or in the grand bazaar.

It will be necessary that the brinjarries should be under some regulation, viz. that all their grain should be brought to a golah, and that they should be under the superintendence of one person. The advantage of this arrangement is that you will always know the exact quantity of grain in your camp, and can regulate the quantity of it sold daily. I was frequently obliged to stop the sale of rice entirely, to purchase from the brinjarries at the golah, and issue it to the fighting men only, and to oblige the followers to live upon the grain of the country, or the small quantities of rice which the bazaar people themselves could bring in.

I will inquire for a proper person to superintend the bazaars, and will have the honour of addressing you upon that subject hereafter.

I have the honour to enclose a letter from Mr. Anderson, in which he recommends that Mr. Fleming and Mr. Gilmour may be appointed surgeons on the staff. I have the pleasure of being acquainted with both these gentlemen, and I think that you will be pleased with them. In case you should appoint Mr. Gilmour to this situation, I beg leave to request that it may not prejudice his situation at this place, but that a gentleman may be appointed to act for him during his absence.

I find that I shall be able to furnish from the stores here 62 doolies, besides 20 for the 33rd and 12 for the artillery, for all of which I will endeavour to procure bearers, and I think I shall succeed.

I have, &c.,

ARTHUR WELLESLEY.

To the Chief Secretary of Government.   [1372.]

SIR,   Seringapatam, 2nd Dec., 1802.

I have the honour to report for the information of the Right
Hon. the Governor in Council that the proposed work upon
the inner ditch of Seringapatam is completed.   I heretofore
reported the measures which I had taken to enable Captain
Heitland to complete this work, and I now enclose an abstract
of the whole expense incurred upon it, against which is set off
the value of the materials gained, and of others sold for the
Honourable Company, which if this work had not been performed would never have turned to any account.   In this
account certain other materials have not been included which
have been used in the construction of the Honourable Company's buildings, the value, and consequently the expense, of
which has been saved by the performance of this work.

I cannot say too much in favour of Captain Heitland for his
attention, his zeal, and his ability throughout the whole of it.
Besides the mere act of filling the ditch, large drains were to
be constructed to carry the surplus water of the fort across it,
of many of which it was necessary to lay the foundation in its
bottom.   The rains of the season 1801 had entirely destroyed
the work which had been begun previous to their commencement; the earth was carried away, and it was necessary to
go to a distance to procure much of that which at present
fills the ditch.   In the performance of this, ground has been
cleared and levelled on which three Native corps are hutted in
the fort, and a great part of the yard has been cleared which is
now applied to the purposes of the gun-carriage manufactory;
and other buildings, which were nuisances, have been removed.

For all these works expense must otherwise have been incurred,
and some of the conveniences have been constructed that Mr. Anderson heretofore recommended as a measure absolutely necessary for the preservation of the health of the inhabitants of this
fort and island.   The result of the work is that the fort is now
a dry, clean, and wholesome place of residence, and is in such
a state as that the reform of the works can be commenced
with advantage whenever the Right Hon. the Governor in
Council may think proper.   The accounts, of which the enclosed is an abstract, have been given in monthly, supported

by the vouchers ordered, the nature of which I heretofore reported.

I have, &c.,

ARTHUR WELLESLEY.

    To Lieutenant-General Stuart.

SIR,   Seringapatam, 3rd Dec., 1802.

Since I wrote to you yesterday, I find that the deficiency of dooly-bearers with the 33rd is very great; those they have desert daily; and the whole, as well as all their public followers, declare that they were promised by the public office at Vellore that they should not go farther than Seringapatam. In a conversation I had with the Dewan this morning also, I find that I cannot get so many bearers from the country as I imagined I should. I cannot, therefore, engage to have as many doolies as I said I should have yesterday; but you may depend upon it that I will have as many as I possibly can, and I will spare no pains to complete the number that I stated yesterday that I should have.

I have, &c.,

ARTHUR WELLESLEY.

    To Lieutenant-Colonel Whitelocke.

SIR,   Seringapatam, 3rd Dec., 1802.

I have the honour to enclose the report of a committee which I lately ordered to assemble at Chittledroog to inquire into the mode by which certain rupees, called Sicca rupees, came into the pay-office at that station. I have taken measures with the Resident that the sum in this coin placed there by the aumildar, and with the paymaster that the remaining sum placed there by the paymaster's cash-keeper, may be replaced by those persons respectively by other coins the currency of Mysore. I have also directed that the cash-keeper may be dismissed from the Honourable Company's service as a person entirely unworthy of any public trust. It appears, however, that, besides purchasing base coins with the Company's cash, and lodging those base coins in the treasury, which is a fraud, he has likewise been guilty of trading with or lending out the Company's money in his charge at interest.   This is a breach of trust.   You will, therefore, be so kind as to seize the person of the paymaster's cashkeeper ; you will take measures to ascertain the amount of all his property at Chittledroog, upon which you will put your seal ; and you will order a garrison court-martial to try him for the two crimes abovementioned.   You will send the proceedings of this court-martial to me.   I beg to caution you particularly against the chance of his making away with any part of his property before you will have got possession of it, will have ascertained its amount, and will have taken measures for its security during the time that his person may be in confinement.   The transactions which have come out before the committee of which Captain Baynes was President, point out clearly the necessity that the regulations regarding the care of the Company's cash should be put in force at Chittledroog.   You will, therefore, be so kind as to call for one of the keys of the cash chest, and never suffer it to be opened excepting you are acquainted with the cause, nor any money to be put in or taken out without knowing how much and for what purpose.

I have, &c.,

ARTHUR WELLESLEY.

To Josiah Webbe, Esq.   [1375.]

MY DEAR WEBBE,   Seringapatam, 3rd Dec., 1802.

I had a conversation with Purneah this morning respecting the silladar horse. He has in his service at present of this description of troops 1200 horsemen and 300 stable horse. He lately discharged 500 silladar horse. He says that, including those 500, there are now in Mysore 2000 silladar horse, of which number 1000 are good, and 1000 such as he would not entertain. He has made arrangements for entertaining the 1000 good horse, and he wishes to have farther directions respecting the bad.

As they will be wanted chiefly for the purposes of foraging, &c., and very little for fighting, I am of opinion that it would be best in the first instance to take them all, and afterwards to discharge such as we may find to be of no use.

Besides these 2000 horse in Mysore, Purneah says that about 4000 of the 8000 silladar horse who were in Tippoo's service are now in the countries to the southward of the Kistna belonging to the Mahrattas, chiefly about Darwar, Hoobly, Savanore, Gujundergur, &c., and that he thinks they could be got. However, he is not certain upon this point. I know that nearly all these troops were in the service of Dhoondiah Waugh, and were destroyed in that campaign. Besides the bodies of troops usually on foot in those countries, two others have lately appeared: one commanded by Bappojee Scindiah, the killadar of Darwar, and the other by the Rajah of Kittoor. It is probable that these chiefs will have entertained all the horse of this description whose services could be hired.

However, whether they are to be hired now or not, Purneah does not imagine that it is intended that he should take measures to hire those not in Mysore.

Let me have your opinion upon the points contained in this letter which require decision: whether he shall hire the bad as well as the good in Mysore, and whether he shall hire all that can be got, though not residing in Mysore.

Purneah says that he proposes to pay all the horse whom he will entertain in Mysore himself, but I have discouraged this notion. He may make an advance of the money to the Company, but he ought not to incur an expense of this kind which he is not required to incur by the treaty, and it is better that we should owe him money for the services he will render upon this occasion than gratitude. The expenses incurred by him, which probably ought to be incurred by the Company, on account of useful works for the country, stand upon grounds entirely different.

When our army will move out of Mysore, I think that the Rajah's army ought to be assembled at some convenient place to the northward. Purneah will be in that quarter, of course, as he was in the campaign of 1800, with a view to forwarding our supplies, &c., &c. I spoke to him upon this subject also this morning, and he agrees in opinion with me. He has already three of our 6-pounders; he wishes to have another and a 12-pounder, which can be given to him, and 2000 stand of new arms for his infantry: the last alone I cannot furnish,

and I wish that you would mention the subject to General
Stuart, and ask him to send that number of arms to this country
for this purpose.

Believe me, &c.,

ARTHUR WELLESLEY.

To W. H. Gordon, Esq.   [1376.]

SIR,   .   Seringapatam, 3rd Dec., 1802.

I have the honour to enclose the report of a committee which
I ordered to assemble at Chittledroog, in order to inquire into
the mode by which certain rupees, called Sicca rupees, came
into the pay-office at that station.

Although it is not denied that 2313 rupees were paid in
that coin by the aumildar in the course of the month of September, it is equally clear that by far the largest part of the
sum in those coins was lodged in the pay-office by your cash-
keeper, and that he purchased them in the neighbourhood
of Chittledroog. There is also reason to believe that he has
been in the habit of trading with or lending upon monthly
interest the Company's cash in his charge. I have written to
the Acting Resident to request that the sum of money which
was really paid by the aumildar in Sicca rupees, amounting to
2313 rupees, may be replaced by a similar sum in other coins
the currency of Mysore. It is my opinion that the remainder
of the sum of money in Sicca rupees which may now be in the
pay-office at Chittledroog ought to be replaced by your cash-
keeper by other coins which are the currency of Mysore, and I
request you to take measures accordingly. You will also be
pleased to dismiss from all service in the pay-office in Mysore a
man who appears to be so entirely unworthy of any public
trust as this cashkeeper. It is my opinion that the transactions
which have been investigated by the committee at Chittledroog
could not have been carried on without the knowledge and consequent connivance of Soobayrayloo, the head-writer. He also,
and, indeed, all the servants of that office, ought to be dismissed from the Company's service. As large sums of money
may hereafter be lodged in the cash-chest at Chittledroog, and
it is of the utmost importance to prevent in future the abuses
which it appears have existed there, I write orders to the com-

2 G 2

manding officer of that station to keep one key of the chest, and not to allow any cash to be taken from it without knowing how much and for what purpose.

I have, &c.,

ARTHUR WELLESLEY.

[1377.]

To J. H. Piele, Esq.

SIR,   Seringapatam, 3rd Dec., 1802.

I have the honour to enclose the copy of the report of a committee which I appointed to meet at Chittledroog, to inquire into the mode by which certain Sicca rupees came into the pay office of that station. You will observe that it is very clear that the greater number of them were placed there by the cash-keeper of the paymaster, to whom I write upon this subject; but it is not denied that a sum amounting to 2313 rupees was paid in Sicca rupees to the pay office at Chittledroog by the aumildar. As the circulation of this coin has been stopped with great propriety by the Rajah's government, I beg to suggest to you the propriety of paying back to the Sircar the sum of 2313 Sicca rupees, and receiving in lieu thereof a similar sum in other coins which are the currency of Mysore. I wish to draw your attention to a circumstance which has appeared before this committee, viz., that one of the farmers of the revenue has paid sums of money direct into the pay office without their passing through the hands of the aumildar. This appears irregular, and may be the source of much abuse; I therefore beg to suggest the propriety of forbidding this practice in future.

I have, &c.,

ARTHUR WELLESLEY.

[1378.]

To Colonel Montresor.

MY DEAR COLONEL,   Seringapatam, 4th Dec., 1802.

I enclose a letter from Lieutenant Harris, by which you will observe that matters are not going on badly in the eastern part of Wynaad. I beg that you will communicate this letter to Macleod, with whom I conclude that you are in communication.

Matters are getting so forward for the army to take the field to the northward that it is absolutely necessary that the 1st of the 8th should be here by the 15th. I shall, therefore, be obliged to you if, upon receipt of this letter, you will take measures for relieving this corps, and give them and the pioneers with them orders to march here with all convenient expedition. They are to leave in Wynaad all the grain they have with them, but are to bring away everything else.

I'll endeavour to prevail upon Purneah to send one of his battalions to Cancancotta; but I am afraid I shall not succeed, s he also is about to form an army to the northward. I have no news for you.

Believe me, &c.,

ARTHUR WELLESLEY.

I send a duplicate of this by Sangaloo.

To Captain Walker, Gram-Agent General.   [1379.]

DEAR SIR,   Seringapatam, 6th Dec., 1802.

I have now the pleasure to enclose you orders upon the aumildars in Mysore for 7000 loads of gram. You will receive this gram on two lines of road leading from the Carnatic towards Sera: one to the northward, which does not go by Bangalore, the other which passes Bangalore. The first place on the northern line where you will receive gram is, Yarculwa, 1400 bags; Ambajee Droog or Chintomeny Pett, 700; Chuta Balapoor, 300; Burrah Balapoor, 700; from thence the road passes by Mudgherry, 12 coss, to Sera, 7 coss.

The first place on the southern line is, Batmunglum, 1500 bags; Tiacul, 500 bags; Colar, 1400 bags; Ooscotta, 500; thence to Bangalore and by the high road to Sera. You will do well to make that place the rendezvous for all your bullocks. It will be necessary that you should send a conicopoly and measuring-men to each place with the enclosed orders. Directions have been given that there may be no delay in the delivery of this gram; but, of course, in a great concern of this kind there may be some, and I beg you to warn the conicopolies and others against any improper behaviour in the country, for which the delays of the servants of the Sircar in the delivery of the gram will be no excuse. The mode in which it is to be measured is stated in each order. Your servants are to give a receipt for the gram which will be delivered to them at each place, and the account will be settled with the Resident.

Believe me, &c.,

ARTHUR WELLESLEY.

[1380.] *To Captain Campbell, Deputy-Adjutant-General.*

DEAR SIR, Seringapatam, 6th Dec., 1802.

I have received yours of the 2nd. As I did not imagine there would be any objection to Mr. Clarke's going to marry Mr. Read to Miss Bond, and as I was strongly urged to allow him to depart as soon as possible, I permitted him to commence his journey. In consequence of your letter, however, I have stopped him.

I have to inform you that Mr. Clarke is aware that he must not marry any persons without the permission of the Right Hon. the Governor in Council, and I shall be obliged to you if you will let me know whether I may permit him to go into Canara, if I should hear from Mr. Read that he has obtained that permission to marry Miss Bond.

Believe me, &c.,

ARTHUR WELLESLEY.

[1381.] *To Lieutenant-Colonel Orrock.*

DEAR SIR, Seringapatam, 6th Dec., 1802.

I have received your letter of the 5th. I have written to Colonel Montresor to request that he will take measures to relieve the 1st battalion 8th regiment under your command, and that he would allow them and the pioneers to march from Wynaad so as that they may reach Seringapatam, if possible, by the 15th. You will be prepared to execute the orders which you will receive from Colonel Montresor upon this subject.

You are to bring away with you everything in Wynaad excepting the rice, which is to remain. As soon as the post at

Wylout is finished, it will be proper to lodge therein half the rice laid in at Sangaloo until the garrison storekeeper in Wynaad can take measures for lodging in each post the proper quantity for the number of troops that will occupy them. I beg that, until you receive the orders from Colonel Montresor to withdraw from Wynaad, you will not mention to anybody the intention to withdraw you. The post at Cancancotta will be relieved by a battalion of the Rajah's troops, who marched this morning from Mysore.

Believe me, &c.,

ARTHUR WELLESLEY.

To Major Doolan.   [1382.]

SIR,   Seringapatam, 7th Dec., 1802.

I have just received your letter, with an enclosure from Lieutenant Martin which I return. Under the orders of the Commander-in-Chief it is the duty of the Adjutant of a corps, at a station at which there is no Fort Adjutant, to perform the functions usually performed by the latter, when such an appointment exists; and accordingly if Lieutenant Martin be Adjutant of the 1st battalion 5th Bombay regiment, stationed at Hullihall, he must do the duties of Fort Adjutant of that station without any additional allowance. I return Lieutenant Martin's letter because I conclude that he was not aware of this regulation.

In regard to the stores expected at Hullihall from Goa, they are of two kinds, garrison and provision stores, and ordnance and military stores. The former, under the regulations of the government of Fort St. George, to which I refer you for more detailed information upon this subject, are to be placed under the charge of the garrison storekeeper, Mr. Gordon, who, I conclude, has servants at Hullihall to take charge of them; the latter, the ordnance and military stores, are under the charge of the commanding officer of the place, under the same regulations. He has usually the assistance of certain ordnance officers to take charge of them, and I propose that there should be such an establishment at Hullihall. But until this establishment can be formed, I conclude that neither Lieutenant Martin nor any other officer can, with propriety, refuse to give you the assistance which you may require, either in arranging the stores or in taking care of them, particularly when they will learn that the establishment of this depôt of stores at Hullihall is an object of the utmost importance.

If, contrary to my expectations on this subject, either Lieutenant Martin, whose duty it is to assist you, or any of the other officers under your command, should refuse to give you the assistance you may require, I request to have from you the names of such officers in order that I may lay them before the Commander-in-Chief.

I have, &c.,

ARTHUR WELLESLEY.

[1388.]   *To Lieutenant-General Stuart.*

SIR,   Seringapatam, 9th Dec., 1802.

I have had the honour to receive your letter of the 5th.

There will be six tumbrils, with 50 4½-inch shells in each. Besides which there will be 300 4½-inch shells, fixed to bottoms, carried on bullocks' backs. Fuzes for these last will be carried likewise.

The 2500 shells are examined, and will be sent if you should think proper to call for them.

All the platform-carts shall be repaired, and ready to go. At present 50 of them are gone to the jungles to bring in timber, but they will be here in less than ten days. I thought it as well to make use of the time which was likely to elapse before the troops could take the field to bring in some timber for the use of the gun-carriage manufactory.

I am afraid that you will be disappointed in your expectations of musket ammunition from Mysore. The order which I first gave was for seven lacs, which, indeed, is a large proportion for the number of troops for whom you desired me to prepare equipments.

I caused an indent to be made for boxes to carry and paper to make this ammunition, from which the Military Board struck the number and quantity which would carry and make two lacs. I therefore concluded that five lacs only would be required from Mysore. However, as I informed you that I should prepare seven lacs, I am going on making up musket cartridges, and as many as can be made shall be prepared both here and at Chittledroog. With all the assistance, however, that this place can afford, only 30,000 are made on each day, and we cannot expect a sixth of that number to be made at Chittledroog.

I will make inquiry respecting the cattle of the size of the Company's gun-cattle, and I should be glad to know whether you wish that any should be purchased, if I can find any.

I propose to carry 500 rounds for each of the iron 12-pounders. Besides this, there will be a quantity of powder and about 4000 12-pound shot at Hullihall. The stores are getting up there from Goa in a better style than I expected they would.

The grain goes off this day to Hurryhur. I have delayed to send it till now on account of the want of gunny-bags, and, according to the tenor of your instructions, I did not think it proper, by sending this quantity of grain and an escort, &c., to Hurryhur, to make public so far the object of your preparations.

I have the pleasure to inform you that a vakeel from Chintomeny Rao, one of the Putwurdun (or Pursheram Bhow's) family, is on the road from Hurryhur to this place; and I am informed that the object of his mission is to know what orders I have to give him in the present crisis of the Mahratta affairs.

I have, &c.,

ARTHUR WELLESLEY.

To the Secretary of the Military Board.   [1384.]

SIR,   Seringapatam, 10th Dec., 1802.

I have the honour to enclose the report of a committee which has surveyed and valued the Company's quarters at Seringapatam.

Of the buildings surveyed there are three, Nos. 7, 8, 9, which are at present occupied by sick, of which it will not be proper to dispose till the sick can be removed into the building which is preparing for an hospital. No. 3, also, is used as the pay-office, and I imagine that it will not be proper to dispose of that building. No. 14 is the Town-Major's quarter. This building joins to and is part of Hyder's palace, which has been converted into an hospital. In my opinion, it will not be proper to dispose of it by sale, as the owner might either pull it down, which would endanger, or might make alterations in it, which would render exceedingly inconvenient, the hospital.

There are two other buildings belonging to the Company and occupied by officers at Seringapatam, which have not been surveyed and valued because, I conclude, that the government is not desirous that they should be disposed of: one, the Dowlut Baug, in which I live; the other, a part of the palace immediately over the main-guard, and joining to, and forming part of, Tippoo's zenana, of which I conclude that government will avail themselves hereafter for quarters for European troops. An owner of this building might do material injury to that which I suppose will be allotted hereafter to the troops. It is now occupied by Colonel Carlisle.

If the Military Board are desirous that those buildings should be valued, they shall be so without loss of time.

I have to observe upon all the buildings which have been surveyed and valued, that, according to the orders of the Military Board, the ground on which they stand, and which belongs to them, has been valued also. When the Commissioners in Mysore were assembled at Seringapatam, the tenure of the ground in the fort attracted their attention from observing its crowded state, which would render it necessary to clear a great part of it, and a knowledge that they had that some of the officers of the garrison had procured grants of ground from the Sirdars about to depart at that time with the Nizam's troops. They therefore gave me the order of which the enclosed is a copy.

This order has been in force ever since, and although ground has been allotted from time to time to many officers to build upon, none of it is considered as private property, and it is liable to be resumed whenever it may be required by the Company for public purposes. The sale of the ground on which the Company's quarters stand will materially alter this state of the tenure of the ground in the fort. The purchasers of the quarters will, of course, be proprietors of the ground. But as it may be convenient at some time or other that the Company should have it in their power to resume the ground, and as the value assigned to the ground is very small, I beg leave to recommend that it may not be sold; and that it should be understood that the purchasers of these quarters are to stand in respect to the tenure of their ground exactly in the same manner as other officers do, under the order of the Commissioners, who have had ground allotted to them to build upon.

In case the Military Board should think proper to order that the quarters should be disposed of, it is desirable that I should receive their directions upon this subject at an early period, in order that I may have an opportunity of arranging the business before it may be necessary for me to quit Seringapatam.

I have, &c.,

ARTHUR WELLESLEY.

To Lieutenant-General Stuart.   [1385.]

SIR,   Seringapatam, 11th Dec., 1802.

I have been much gratified by your letter of the 7th instant, for which I beg to return you my best thanks. I never had any reason to doubt your wish to do whatever was consistent with propriety in order to gratify my wishes; but when you proposed that in case of the advance of the army into the Mahratta territory I should leave in Mysore the principal officer of the staff, and as I knew that you intended that I should have the honour of accompanying you, I concluded that you proposed that another officer should hold the command in Mysore during my absence, with whom Captain Barclay was to remain. As I was desirous to make certain arrangements before I should quit the command, I wished to know your sentiments particularly upon that point as soon as might be convenient; and I now perfectly understand the reasons for which you desire that Captain Barclay should remain in Mysore, and the mode according to which you propose that the business should be conducted.

The force in Mysore, although distributed in garrisons which, under the treaty with the Rajah, are under the orders of the government of Fort St. George, is properly subsidiary; and on this ground it was that the staff now existing was attached to the command of it, according to the model of the staff attached to the subsidiary force with the Nizam. I am perfectly aware of the necessity of preventing jealousies in the army, which certainly might be occasioned by the staff in question ; and although I shall regret the loss of the assistance of Captain Barclay, I do not wish to take him if you think his accompanying me will have that effect.

Goklah's vakeel waits here till I shall hear from Madras.

I have, &c.,

ARTHUR WELLESLEY.

I have omitted to mention to you that there is a corps in Mysore destined for field service, to which there is no field officer, viz., the 2nd of the 18th.

[1386.]   *To Major Malcolm.*

MY DEAR MALCOLM,   Seringapatam, 11th Dec., 1802.

Since you wrote to me on the 7th, General Stuart has written to me a very satisfactory letter upon the subject of the command in Mysore. I imagined that he intended I should relinquish it when the army should take the field, because he desired me to make arrangements for leaving the staff in this country, and I concluded that the staff ought to be with the commanding officer ; and, as I was certainly to accompany him, another officer was to be appointed to command in Mysore during my absence. It appears, however, by his last letter, that his wish that I should leave the staff behind is founded upon his fear of creating a jealousy in his army in the minds of other officers. This fear is rather vague, as they ought to recollect that the staff is attached to me as commanding a subsidiary force, and jealousy may as well be expected from any other advantage I may have, which they have not. However, the General's wishes must be complied with, and I shall say no more respecting the staff. I assure you that, if he had removed me from Mysore, or in any case that can occur, I shall do everything that I think can forward his objects.

If the war is to go on, on the great scale for which preparations are making, the Governor General must come round to Madras. All the reasons which operated to induce him to come to Madras at the commencement of the war with Tippoo exist at present, and there are others which did not exist at that time. You are well acquainted with the existing state of the government of Madras : General Stuart I consider as the heart and soul of it ; and, as soon as he shall depart to take the command of this army, the whole will fall to pieces, and a scene of confusion will follow, which must be disastrous to the army in the field.

I don't know enough of Mahratta politics to be able to give an opinion as to the necessity of the great preparations which are making. I understand that the object is to support the Peshwah in his government ; and the operation, supposing that hereafter it should be deemed advisable to undertake it, may or may not require a very large army, according to the real strength of the power in rebellion against the Peshwah. It appears to be imagined now that there is a chance that Holkar and Scindiah will unite against us and the Peshwah, if we should interfere in his affairs. It is possible that the disunion of those chiefs may be more advantageous to us than any arrangement we could make with the Peshwah, and that we ought not to interfere in such a manner as to induce them to unite. If that should be the case, it will be proper to pause for a time ; and the great preparations at present making will not be necessary.

It is possible that the Peshwah's authority at Poonah may be restored by the natural course of the contest between these two chiefs, and that that will be the time for us to conclude our arrangements with His Highness to lodge our subsidiary force at Poonah. The Governor General alone can decide upon these questions, and many others connected with this subject. But it is possible that the nature of them will change every day, and that he will have much earlier intelligence of every event at Madras than he can at Calcutta. Besides, if the General takes the field, nothing but Lord Wellesley's presence can keep the government of Madras in the direct line. I wish that you would urge him upon this subject.

> Believe me, &c.,
>
> ARTHUR WELLESLEY.

[1387.]

To Captain Mahony.

SIR,   Seringapatam, 12th Dec., 1802.

I have received your letter of the 8th instant and its enclosure, of the latter of which I had already received a copy sent to me from Fort William, by order of the Governor-General. You will observe that the decision upon one of the principal points which are to form the subject of your communication with the Rajah of Koorg is referred to the Right Hon. the Governor of Fort St. George, and it is advisable that you should not quit Madras till you receive his Lordship's sentiments upon it.

The Governor-General has been pleased to desire that I should lay before the Governor of Fort St. George my sentiments upon one of these points, and I shall take the earliest opportunity of obeying his Excellency's orders.

Although it is scarcely necessary to advise you to have no communication with the Rajah of Koorg or with any other person whatever regarding the purport of your mission to him till you will have been made acquainted with the sentiments of Lord Clive, and will have received his orders upon the whole subject, I look upon it to be so important, that I take the liberty of recommending to you the greatest reserve upon all these points.

I have, &c.,

ARTHUR WELLESLEY.

[1388.]

To Lieutenant-General Stuart.

SIR,   Seringapatam, 12th Dec., 1802.

I have received the orders of the Right Hon. the Governor in Council, of the 8th instant, written in consequence of my letter to you of the 2nd. In my letter of the 4th, however, I communicated to you two propositions from Goklah's vakeel, to which I did not refer in my letter of the 2nd: one, that in case Goklah should be obliged to retreat, he should be permitted to retreat within the territories of the Company or of the Rajah of Mysore; the other, that an asylum within these territories should be given to the families of Goklah himself and of some of his principal adherents. His Lordship has given me no orders upon these propositions; and in case he should not have done so before you receive this letter, I shall be much obliged to you if you will draw his attention to them, and request him to give me his orders upon them.

The vakeel has not expressed any impatience to depart, and I dare say that he will stay till I can receive an answer to this letter.

I have made all the arrangements for sending into the Mahratta territory a person who will ascertain the sentiments of the Mahratta chiefs in general upon the present state of their affairs. He is one of the officers of the Rajah's government, by name Govind Rao, who was with me in the Mahratta territory in the year 1800, and is well acquainted with the affairs of that country. I have acted upon this occasion in concert with the Dewan, and I should be obliged to you if you will let me know what allowance you think it proper I should give this officer while he is employed, or whether you wish that I should leave that question to the decision of the Dewan, through whose hands, at all events, whatever he will receive ought to pass.

I propose to send to Goklah the presents mentioned in Lingo Punt's letter.

I have, &c.,

ARTHUR WELLESLEY.

To Captain Walker.   [1389.]

DEAR SIR,   Seringapatam, 12th Dec., 1802.

In my last letter I omitted to say anything to you respecting the gram for the regiments of cavalry, to be carried by themselves.

The 19th dragoons from Arcot is the only corps coming from your part of the Carnatic that I hear of, and they will receive their gram at Bangalore. I shall see the 2nd regiment, and will take care of them myself, as well as of the 5th and 7th.

In regard to the corps coming from the Ceded Districts, viz., the 25th, 4th, and 6th regiments, the question is, will they bring gram with them, and if they do not, by what route will they enter Mysore? I have provided for them at Chittledroog, and

I hope they will march by that place; but if they do not, I must endeavour to have their gram at some other place, if they do not come supplied.

Shall I send you the order for the gram for the 19th at Bangalore, or to the commanding officer when he will enter this country?

The supplies of this article which I am preparing for your department will entirely drain this country till the end of January, when the new gram will come in. I wish, therefore, that you would inform officers, &c., coming up, that they will do well to bring with them as much gram as they can procure.

Believe me, &c.,

ARTHUR WELLESLEY.

[1390.]   *To Lieutenant-General Stuart.*

SIR,   Seringapatam, 13th Dec., 1802.

I have had the honour of receiving your letter of the 9th.

In consequence of your wishes, expressed therein, I have communicated to Captain Barclay your intentions regarding the Mysore staff, and your desire that he should superintend the bazaars, &c. He told me that he had wished to have nothing more to do with the bazaars of the army, but that he would undertake the duties of any situation in which you might think proper to employ his services, to which he might think himself equal, rather than not serve in the expedition for which preparation is making.

What I meant by the brinjarries being under one person was, that one of themselves should be at their head. They will, of course, be under the general superintendence of the European officer at the head of the bazaars. There is a man here who has always been at the head of the brinjarries in this country, to whom government lately gave a jaghire near Conjeveram, at my request. I will send you a report which he is preparing regarding these people, which will give you an accurate account of what you may expect from them, and a memorandum detailing the mode in which the brinjarry golah has been managed.

I shall have dooly boys in this country in sufficient numbers to carry sixty doolies: the demands for the 33rd and the artillery supposing all the bearers whom the former brought with them should desert, will amount to about thirty-seven doolies. If the European troops should not want the remainder, they will be useful to the Native corps. I should have had more, only that I sent twenty-five sets into Malabar and twelve into Wynaad at the commencement of the disturbances in that district before I knew of the demands for troops in other quarters.

I calculated upon four bullocks to each arrack cart, of which there are thirty in store. I intended to use twenty of the platform carts to carry arrack, making in all fifty from this place. The four bullocks to each cart are necessary.

It is possible that in consequence of the communication from the Governor-General, which has induced you to delay the movement of the troops and stores, you may wish that I should delay commencing to form the proposed depôt at Hurryhur. This will not be difficult. I have sent off the grain and ordered a company from Paughur, under Captain Baynes, to march to Hurryhur, where I intended that he should superintend the arrangements to be made. The grain can go to Santa Bednore, and the escort, of one company of the 2nd of the 18th and the company under Captain Baynes, may wait there likewise, or at Chittledroog. If you should make me acquainted with your wishes upon this subject by return of post, there will be time to make these alterations.

The 5000 bullocks ordered here are ready. I enclose a statement of the manner in which they will be employed. If you intend to draw bullocks in future from this country, it is desirable that I should give notice of this intention to Mr. Gordon as soon as possible. I know that you will get as many good bullocks in this country as you can possibly want; but a few preparatory arrangements are necessary.

From what I observe of the want of arms of the troops coming from the southern division, and of those in this country, I think that 2000 stand of arms ought to be sent from the Presidency.

I have, &c.,

ARTHUR WELLESLEY.

[ENCLOSURE.]

Statement of Carriage Bullocks wanted for the Equipment in Mysore.

		Bullocks.
Gram	2000 loads.	
Spare	333	
		2333
Stores, including spare	1600	
Deduct for 1600 4½ shells included ; as 1900 were calculated for, and only 300 will be carried	160	
Add spare for that number	27	
Deduct	187	
Remain	1413	
Add for 12-pounder shot not provided for, 450 for each of 4 guns ..	180	
Powder for those guns	120	
Spare	50	
Total stores	1763	1763
Provisions, being salted beef, biscuit, &c.	700	
Spare	116	
		816
Total		4912

N.B. Carriage will besides be required for the tents of the artillery, and of Mr. Anderson; tarpaulins for the grain and provisions; three or four tents for the bazaars, &c., which will make up the 5000 bullocks.

[1391.]   *To Josiah Webbe, Esq.*

MY DEAR WEBBE,   Seringapatam, 13th Dec., 1802.

I received a letter from General Stuart last night, in answer to one which I wrote to him on the 4th, in which I reported to him that Goklah wished to have an asylum for his family in Mysore, and the General tells me not only that he sees no objection to granting protection to the families of these chiefs, but he thinks that having them within our territory will give us a strong hold over them. I wrote to General Stuart yesterday, and told him that I should detain Goklah's vakeel till I should receive Lord Clive's orders upon this and another particular proposition; and although I conclude that his Lordship's sentiments are the same as those expressed by the General, I shall still detain the vakeel if I can. In the meantime I have spoken to Purneah upon the subject, and have requested that he would point out the place in which it would be most convenient to him to lodge Goklah's family, supposing that Lord Clive should be of opinion that they ought to be received, and he has pitched upon Sacrapatam. This place is some distance from the frontier, and lies towards Oostara and the Bullum country, and is no great distance from the Western Ghauts. They will have complete security in it, and at the same time we can secure their persons, if we should think proper.

Let me know if you have any objection to this plan.

I wish to have your answer upon the subject of the commands in this country, that the order which I propose to issue may be circulated before the 1st of January.

Believe me, &c.,

ARTHUR WELLESLEY.

To Colonel Montresor.   [1392.]

MY DEAR COLONEL,   Seringapatam, 14th Dec., 1802.

I have received your letters of the 6th, 7th, 9th, and 12th, to which I now proceed to give answers, as I find that you are within reach.

I shall send the estimate for building the barrack at Cannanore for the 80th regiment to be laid before government, with my recommendation that it may be built forthwith: the concern is too large to be undertaken without their previous sanction.

You must write me a public letter recommending Lieutenant Hardy's appointment as one absolutely necessary at present, and I will recommend it to the Commander-in-Chief.

I shall do nothing respecting the office of Brigade-Major. It appears that General Stuart has offered it to Captain Watson, and in that case the recommendation of any other person will be disagreeable to him. You will do well, therefore, to keep this appointment in its present state, only if you find it necessary to have another officer instead of Captain Osborne, who I understand is Malabar translator, you will do well to appoint one to act, and send me the order for confirmation.

2 H 2

Appoint the private to be serjeant of pioneers in general orders, and send me the order for confirmation.

I'll send you a copy of my letter to General Stuart on the subject of the distribution in Malabar and Canara, which is the paper to which you allude.

Colonel Boles has written me respecting the gunny rice bags, and is sending some.

I write to General Stuart upon the subject of your powers in Malabar, &c.; in the meantime, till you can receive such as I have, it is desirable that you should appoint a court of inquiry to ascertain the circumstances of the guilt of any prisoners you may have, and what they have to urge in their defence. Send the proceedings to me, and I'll send orders for their execution if I should hear from you that that measure is advisable. I cannot depute to you the powers which I have: the exercise of them by you would be illegal, and might be dangerous in these times.

Take care that the act of rebellion of each prisoner is made very clear before the court of inquiry.

I wish that it were in my power to leave the Madras corps with you any longer; but at the time I wrote I expected that we should march from hence about Christmas. Since that time a small change has occurred. Between ourselves, it appears that the Governor-General does not wish to interfere in Mahratta affairs in the great style for which preparations have been made. He seems to fear that our interference will occasion a peace between Scindiah and Holkar, and to think that the continuance of hostility between those chiefs towards each other is the best state of Mahratta affairs for our interest. It is his wish, therefore, that although a force should be prepared in this country, we should delay to interfere for some time.

Nothing has happened which can alter this wish, excepting the supposed detention by Holkar of Lieutenant-Colonel Close at Poonah. If that be true, and if Holkar does not allow him to depart and provide for his safety on his road to Bombay, we must go to war as a nation, on account of that barbarous act of hostility; but otherwise I still think that the Governor-General will adhere to the line of policy which he has already thought the best.

The result at present is, that the troops are not to march from the Carnatic till further orders are received from Calcutta, and, of course, the troops in this country likewise stand fast ; but the great preparations are still continued.

The 1st battalion 8th regiment are become so weak from sickness that they could not be of much service to you, and although not wanted here directly, as I at first imagined they would be, the only chance they have of recovery and of being of any service is to have some rest here ; I therefore still wish them to come.

I'll give orders for the supply of the post at Wylout, as well as at Sangaloo.

Believe me, &c.,

ARTHUR WELLESLEY.

Upon referring to the estimate of the expense of the barracks for the 80th, I find that it will not answer to send to government, as it is only an abstract. I wish, therefore, that you would desire Bentley to send me a detailed estimate direct as soon as he can.

To Lieutenant-General Stuart.   [1393.]

SIR,   Seringapatam, 14th Dec., 1802.

I have the honour to enclose an extract of a letter from Colonel Montresor, giving an account of an action with the Nairs. It will be necessary that the Colonel should have powers to try rebels by summary process, and to punish with death. I have given him directions to inquire into the circumstances of the guilt of the prisoners taken, and I will give orders for their punishment, should it be necessary.

I am desirous of obtaining your sentiments on the subject of the gun-carriage manufactory-yard. As the pioneers are to take the field, it will be impossible for them to finish it, and I wish to know whether you will allow the sum of 1500 pagodas still to be laid out on that work. I think it could be done for that sum.

I have, &c.,

ARTHUR WELLESLEY.

[1394.]   *To Colonel Montresor.*

MY DEAR COLONEL,   Seringapatam, 15th Dec., 1802.

I have this instant received your letter of the 14th. Purneah sent his sepoys to Cancancotta at my request, but I promised him that they should not go into Wynaad excepting on a particular emergency, with supplies to the nearest posts. He will not consent to their occupying our posts at Sangaloo and Wylout; and even if he would do so on my proposing the matter to him, I should doubt the propriety of placing them there. As they are a very inferior species of troops to ours, they would certainly be attacked, and the result would probably be very disagreeable, and at all events would oblige you to move to their relief. If I were to choose between not occupying the posts at all and having those troops in them, I should prefer the former.

I know that you have a disagreeable service on hand, and I am convinced that you will do everything in your power to bring it to a speedy conclusion. Your most certain mode, I think, at present is to collect all your disposable troops in one body, and persevere in moving in strength upon the rebels wherever you may hear that they are. This must succeed at last.

I wrote you all the news I had yesterday; nothing has occurred since. I have not heard a syllable of the advanced detachment, excepting by report.

Believe me, &c.,

ARTHUR WELLESLEY.

[1395.]   *To Lieutenant-General Stuart.*

SIR,   Seringapatam, 15th Dec., 1802.

I have just heard that the collector in the Barahmahal is making advances to certain brinjarries in that district, and that he has called to his Cutchery at Darampoory not only those actually within his jurisdiction, but four naiks of tandahs stationed in Dankerycottah, within Mysore, viz., Nalah, Lieka, Bogwan, and Chimmana. I am also informed that the brinjarries at present in the Barahmahal belong to Mysore, and are only gone into that country to trade in grain, and have been called by their heads to attend the army in this country. However, whether they belong to the Barahmahal or Mysore, Mr. Cockburn ought not to make them advances. We have long discontinued that practice. I have never advanced any money excepting 6000 rupees in the campaign of 1800 to certain brinjarries who were taken by our troops and whose grain was plundered; and the consequence of the advances made in the Barahmahal will be not only that advances will be required by the great number of brinjarries in this country, but as they will imagine that they are trading on the Company's money, and that everything will be done by its officers to enable them to repay it, they will come forward with many other troublesome and vexatious demands.

I therefore recommend that the advances should not be made, or if they are made anywhere, I may be permitted also to make them to those brinjarries who will demand them in Mysore.

I have, &c.,

ARTHUR WELLESLEY.

To Josiah Webbe, Esq.   [1396.]

MY DEAR WEBBE,   Seringapatam, 15th Dec., 1802.

I have published the order upon the arrack concerns exactly in the form in which you saw it. If Purneah thinks it proper to give officers in command of stations in Mysore the allowance of commands of the second class, it will be very well, and will occasion no demands from officers in command in the Carnatic, which would be occasioned by announcing such an intention in general orders at present.

I have already written to you respecting the remuneration for the Rajah of Koorg.

I have many reasons to doubt that the Rajah of Koorg now requires the remuneration which it is proposed by Captain Mahony to give him, or indeed any remuneration at all, for his services during the war against Tippoo. I have had frequent conversations with him, in which he did not conceal his grievances or his claims upon the Company; but he never mentioned or even hinted a wish to receive any addition to his territory. Marriott went to him last year to be present at the marriage of his daughter with the Rajah of Soonda, and he was then silent upon the subject; and, in fact, I have never heard of the wishes

mentioned by Captain Mahony from any persons excepting himself and Mr. Uhtoffe.

It is very probable that the Rajah of Koorg, like others with
territories, may wish to enlarge them; but I think that he will
not feel dissatisfied with the Company, nor will imagine that his
services are not duly estimated, if he does not receive the remuneration proposed to be given to him, and that, in fact, he does
not expect it.

Supposing, however, that he did expect it, and would be dissatisfied if he did not receive it, the question is, whether those
countries proposed to be taken from the Rajah of Mysore ought
to be given to him? If there were no ancient enmity between
the two families, it is certain that this appearance of partiality
towards one at the expense of the other would create it, and
would be by no means agreeable to the party at whose expense
the remuneration would be made; but when it is considered that
there is an ancient enmity between the families, that nothing
but the authority of the Company prevents them from coming to
hostilities, it must be expected that by this arrangement we shall
vastly increase that enmity, and that the injury we shall do to
the Rajah of Mysore will be felt in a much greater degree than
the benefit will by the Rajah of Koorg.

But there is another objection to the arrangement, which
applies particularly to the territory proposed to be given to the
Rajah of Koorg. The villages in the neighbourhood of Periapatam are the ancient jaghire of Purneah himself. This I
imagine was the cause of their being so roughly handled by the
Rajah of Koorg during the war, and is the cause of Purneah's
extreme anxiety to have him forced to give back the inhabitants
whom he carried off. It will be very hurtful to his feelings if,
after all, this territory is to be given to the man who, above all
others, he detests.

I am, therefore, decidedly of opinion on every ground, not
only that this arrangement, as far as it respects the territory of
the Rajah of Mysore, should not be made, but that it should not
even be hinted to either of the parties.

I have always thought it advisable to conciliate the Rajah of
Koorg by every kind of indulgent and liberal policy. We owe
him much : the position of his country is highly important to us,
and it is more so to our character in this country to keep him
in the situation in which he is, and in good humour with our

government. For this reason I would give him the territory in
Canara proposed to be given to him, and I would arrange his
boundary on the Mysore side permanently, by means of a
European gentleman, in a manner that would be satisfactory to
him.

I observe in your letter to Piele that Malcolm has started a
proposition to give Wynaad to the Rajah of Koorg. I think that
it would be convenient to us to get rid of that district, and it is
probable that the Rajah of Koorg would be glad to have it; but
we must recollect that the Rajah of Mysore has an interest in it
as well as ourselves, for which we must make provision in case
of such arrangement. We ought also to recollect that when we
give Wynaad to the Rajah of Koorg, he will have in his possession all the passes from Mysore to Malabar, between Soobramany and Paulghautcherry. I am convinced that as long as the
Rajah lives, and we continue towards him the liberal policy by
which we have been guided in our transactions with him hitherto,
they could not be in better hands; but we don't know what
kind of man his successor may be, and if we adopt this arrangement, and indeed in any case if we give him territory, we ought
to urge him to point out his successor. In fact, a dispute for
the succession to the government in those territories would be
almost as inconvenient and prejudicial to us as to have in it a
man who should be inimical to our interests.

I have delivered these sentiments to Piele; let me know
whether they agree with yours. If they should, I will write to
Lord Clive to the same purport, omitting, however, my opinion
that the Rajah of Koorg does not now look for remuneration, as that would be a ground for giving him nothing, and
might be used as one for a disapprobation of the measure at
home.

Matters appear to have gone very far in the Mahratta territory; I am afraid so far, that we must take up a ruined cause
if we interfere at all in favour of Bajee Rao. Close's departure
from Poonah, if it be true, materially alters the question. If
Holkar had continued to detain him, we must have gone to war,
even if we had had no other reason for interfering in force; but
now, whether we shall interfere at all, in what manner and at
what time, are questions which the Governor-General alone can
decide. In my opinion he ought to come to Madras, if only to

have a nearer view of them and earlier and more authentic intelligence of events as they will occur, and so I have told him.

If the plan is to be defensive, we ought, in my opinion, to prevail on the Nizam to allow us to occupy Copaul and Moodgul with tolerably large detachments, by which means and by having a corps in the field on this frontier we shall effectually prevent the plunder of the Dooab, of the Kistna and Toombuddra, and the Ceded Districts.

In respect to Malabar and Wynaad, I have heard many reports respecting the mode in which the revenue has been raised, particularly in the latter district; but I have no facts by which I can be enabled to form an opinion upon the subject. Malabar is still in tranquillity. I don't believe that the disturbances in Wynaad are to be attributed to extortion on the part of the revenue officers. They appear to have commenced by an accidental murder and riot, after which the party proceeded to surprise the post at Pancoorta Cottah and murder the officers, and then finding that the troops did nothing to defend themselves or to revenge the murder of their comrades, Coongan Nair, who was at the head of the former acts of insurrection, issued a proclamation, calling upon the inhabitants to meet him on a certain day at a pagoda not far from Manundwaddy, another of our posts. They met there to the number of 5000, and have been in rebellion ever since.

An extraordinary circumstance is that Macleod was here a very few days after the rebellion commenced, and he assured me that there was not a farthing of revenue due for the revenue year which had just then closed.

If they can pay their revenue so regularly, I conclude that it does not press very heavily upon them; and if it did, and that was the cause of the last rebellion, they would have broken out at an earlier period of the rainy season, when it would have been more difficult for our troops to carry on operations against them, and before they would have paid in the revenue of the last year.

Believe me, &c.,

ARTHUR WELLESLEY.

To Major Symons.

My dear Symons, Seringapatam, 17th Dec., 1802.

I have received your letters, and Knox has this day given me the papers from the Board of Revenue, upon the subject of the mode of conducting the military bazaars.

These papers, as far as they respect Seringapatam, are to be viewed in two lights: first, the mode of managing the revenue to be collected from country arrack, &c.; secondly, the mode of arranging the police and of providing for its expenses. In regard to the first object I have nothing to say to it more than I have to any other of revenue upon this island, excepting with a view to prevent the sale of spirits to the European troops.

The mode in which the arrack concerns upon this island have been managed by you hitherto has been perfectly satisfactory to me in this respect, and I think is the only one by which that object can be secured. If there are to be a large number of licensed dealers at Seringapatam, as at Madras, we may depend upon it that some of them will sell to the soldiers; and we shall not be able to fix upon and punish the seller as we can now, when there is only one. I am, therefore, clearly of opinion that the arrack business at Seringapatam ought to be kept up on its present footing. In respect to the police within the fort and on the island of Seringapatam, the Board of Revenue appear not to be aware of, or have not adverted to, the fact that under the regulation for the due administration of justice at Seringapatam, " the care and management of the police, and all the powers and authorities incident thereto," are " vested " in me as " officer commanding the forces in Mysore." The powers thus vested in me are not military, but purely civil; they are not affected by the General Orders of the 22nd September, 1802, nor can they be so by any orders which the Board of Revenue may think proper to issue. I am, therefore, still, and till the Governor in Council thinks proper to make an alteration I shall continue to be, at the head of the police within the fort and island of Seringapatam. There are certain expenses attending the management of this police, which, on account of local circumstances, are perhaps greater at Seringapatam than they would be elsewhere. These expenses may properly be classed under two heads, viz., those attending the management of the police within the fort, and those attending the management of the police without.

The first have been paid out of sums which have been hitherto deemed the emoluments of the commanding officer; the last have been paid out of a revenue raised by you on the inhabitants of Sheher Ganjam by authority of the Board of Revenue.

Although the orders of the 22nd September do not deprive me of the jurisdiction given me by the regulation of government, they certainly prevent me from enjoying any emoluments: .t is therefore necessary that some provision should be made for the expenses attending the police of the fort.

In respect to the expenses of the police of Sheher Ganjam, they are already provided for, and I conclude will remain as they are.

The question is, in what mode shall provision be made for the expenses of the police in the fort? Although they have hitherto been defrayed out of sums which are hereafter to be carried to the account of the bazaar fund, it is probable that government will not wish that they should be paid out of those sums hereafter. I think, therefore, the best mode of proceeding would be, to state generally what the establishment of the police of the fort is, what its expense, that this expense has been paid hitherto by the commanding officer, and to desire to know in what manner it is to be paid hereafter. I think that this may be done with great propriety, either by me, who am at the head of the police, or by you who have conducted its details, and who are to pay the expense hereafter ; and I leave it to you to decide upon this point. At all events the present police establishments are necessary, and must be kept up. If you prefer that I should make the application to government upon this subject, you must make me acquainted with the exact police establishment of the fort, its expense, &c. &c.

In regard to the other point in your letter, I agree entirely with you that matters at Seringapatam ought to remain as they are. They cannot be better, and they might be worse, under any new arrangement; and I am sure that we now experience fully the benefits of our present system.

I wish that you would communicate with Webbe upon this subject, and if you choose it you may show him this letter.

I will arrange who is to act for you as soon as I shall be

certain that you are to take the field, but I still think that the Foujdarry, Cutchery, and magistrates' courts ought to be adjourned till you can return.

Believe me, &c.,

ARTHUR WELLESLEY.

To Lieutenant-Colonel Whitelocke. [1398.]

SIR, Seringapatam, 17th Dec., 1802.

I have the honour to enclose the proceedings of a garrison court martial of the garrison of Chittledroog, of which Captain Ridge was president, which I request you to confirm.

The sentence is to be carried into execution in the following manner :—The prisoner, Ramapah Chitty, is to replace with an equal number of Company's rupees 5846 Sicca rupees which were lodged in the Company's cash chest by his means. In respect to the fine of 100 star pagodas, so much of it is to be immediately levied on the prisoner as will pay the expense of exchanging for Company's rupees the Sicca rupees which may still remain in the treasury after 5846 Sicca rupees above mentioned will have been exchanged, and 2313 Sicca rupees will have been exchanged by the aumildar, according to directions which he will have received from the Dewan. I remit the remainder of the fine to Ramapah on condition that he never again attempts to obtain a situation in the Company's service. After the sentence will have been carried into execution in this manner, Ramapah is to be released, and his property to be restored to him. I request you to send me back an authenticated copy of the proceedings of the court martial.

I beg that you will request the aumildar to turn Yankatapah out of Chittledroog, and not allow him to return there.

I have, &c.,

ARTHUR WELLESLEY.

To Captain Baynes. [1399.]

SIR, Seringapatam, 17th Dec., 1802.

The object in ordering you to Hurryhur is, that you may superintend the formation of a depôt of provisions which I have given directions to the garrison storekeeper in Mysore, Mr. Gordon, to make at that station.

Two thousand loads of rice, with a certain quantity of salted beef and biscuit, left this place on the 11th, under charge of an escort, commanded by Lieutenant Lee, on their way to Hurryhur; and Mr. Gordon has orders from me to lay in at Hurryhur as much rice as he can procure in that neighbourhood, besides all that will be beaten out from paddy at Chittledroog.

On the arrival at Hurryhur of the escort with Lieutenant Lee, the first object will be to send off to Chittledroog such a number of the bullocks as will be necessary to carry to Hurryhur the rice which will be ready, and for which there will be bags at Chittledroog.

You will be so kind as to communicate with Lieutenant-Colonel Whitelocke upon this point, and send off the bullocks accordingly.

The Dewan informs me that he has given directions, and that the pagodas at Hurryhur will have been prepared for the purpose of receiving our grain and provision stores; and those which will arrive are to be lodged in them. It will be necessary that Mr. Gordon should use the gunny bags which will carry the rice from Seringapatam, and afterwards those which will be received from Chittledroog, and the bullocks, in bringing in the grain which he may be enabled to purchase in the country. The rice must therefore be lodged in store in bulk, and I request you to be very particular in pitching upon a proper place for it; and you will allow Mr. Gordon's servants to have the care of the bullocks and rice bags which they will require.

I request to hear from you from time to time regarding the progress making in collecting this depôt.

I have, &c.,

ARTHUR WELLESLEY.

[1400.]   *To Lieutenant-General Stuart.*

SIR,   Seringapatam, 18th Dec., 1802.

It is necessary that I should make you acquainted with a circumstance which has come to my knowledge regarding the collection of the depôt of grain at Bellary, which I imagine may be of material consequence to you hereafter. It is that the grain is collected by means of the brinjarries; of whom there is no doubt whatever but that they will be able to lay in the quantity required in the time proposed; but after they will have laid in this grain they must go to the rice countries to load again, before they will commence their march towards your army. I am not so well acquainted with the seats of the resources of the Ceded Districts as I am with those of Mysore; but I imagine that the rice countries are those on the banks of the Pennar, below Pennaconda, and as far down as Gurrum-conda; and I have reason to believe that the brinjarries would not be upon the banks of the Toombuddra, in the neighbourhood of Hurryhur, till the middle of March.

It may be a question, therefore, whether it would not be proper to make these brinjarries load at Bellary with the rice which they will have brought there.

I have, &c.,

ARTHUR WELLESLEY.

To Sir William Clarke.   [1401.]

MY DEAR SIR,   Seringapatam, 19th Dec., 1802.

I have had the pleasure of receiving your letters of the 9th. I had heard of your successful operations with much satisfaction, and I beg you to accept my congratulations upon them.

It is a difficult matter to decide upon the motives which induced Mr. Duncan to appoint Lieutenant-Colonel Woodington to command the subsidiary force stationed at Brodera, especially when it is considered that he might have obviated all the difficulties to which this appointment has since exposed him by the appointment of yourself to command that force, either directly or in addition to any other to which he might have appointed you. It is an arrangement which cannot last. It is said that an European regiment is to be attached to the subsidiary force; and although it may be possible for a time to keep an officer of superior rank to Lieutenant-Colonel Woodington away from his corps, he must at length join it. The only remedy is to send the Bombay European regiment to Brodera, which, however, until relieved, cannot be spared from Malabar.

I should be glad to employ you as you propose, but I can tell you that you cannot, under present circumstances, do any thing which will eventually prove so advantageous to us as to preserve such an influence over the minds of the members of the Portuguese government as that they will aid and assist in forwarding our stores and provisions which we may have or land at Goa, to Hullihall in Soonda. I will, however, mention to General Stuart your wishes. It is probable that he will take the field in person, if the war should go on on the grand scale for which preparations have been made.

I am obliged to you for your good intelligence respecting the transport of our ordnance stores and provisions hitherto, contained in your public letter of the 9th; and I approve of your having called upon the military paymaster for cash.

Since writing the above I have received your public letter of the 13th. I don't want the platforms, but I have called for the sand bags to hold our rice in store at Hullihall, and I propose to apply the sand bags to that purpose till the rice bags can be procured.

Believe me, &c.,

ARTHUR WELLESLEY.

[1402.]   *To W. H. Gordon, Esq.*

SIR,   Seringapatam, 20th Dec., 1802.

I have the honour to enclose a Mahratta letter for the head aumildar of the districts of Nuggur, &c., and letters for the aumildars of different villages hereafter named, who are to deliver for the Company's use the quantities of rice opposite the name of each village, viz. :—

Simoga	1300 bags.
Shikarpoor	400 „
Beder Hoonelly	250 „
Luckodly Danwas	2200 „
Oodagunny	850 „
Total	5000 „

You will be so kind as to transmit these orders to your servants at Hurryhur, and give them directions to apply to the officer commanding at Hurryhur for bullocks and gunny bags, to be sent to each place to bring the rice which it is to furnish under these orders.   There are not at Hurryhur at present a sufficient number, either of bullocks or of gunny bags, to bring in the whole of the rice at once ; and it will therefore be necessary that your servants should arrange with Ram Rao, the head aumildar, who is at present at Hurryhur, to what place the bullocks should be first sent.   If it should be equally convenient in other respects, I should prefer to have the rice brought from the most distant places first ; and I know that, of those above-mentioned, Simoga is the most distant from Hurryhur.   This rice is to be received according to the Company's measurement.   Your servants are to pass their receipts for it to the aumildars of the villages above-mentioned, and the amount will be settled hereafter.   When received it is to be laid in store at Hurryhur.   Besides this rice, I have requested the Dewan to order that a depôt of gram might be formed at Hurryhur, and I have to request that you will give directions to your servants at that station to receive and lodge in store all the gram which may be offered to them by the servants of the Sircar.   This also is to be received at the Company's measurement.   Your servants are to pass their receipts for it, and the account is to be settled hereafter.

I transmit a copy of this letter to Captain Baynes, the officer who will command at Hurryhur, and I desire him to give your servants every assistance they can require in the collection of this grain.

I have, &c.,

ARTHUR WELLESLEY.

To Captain Gifford.   [1403.]

SIR,   Seringapatam, 20th Dec., 1802.

Your letter of the 17th instant has been communicated to me, and I have to request that you will desire the heads of villages in the neighbourhood of your post, to whom you have given cowle, to proceed immediately to Major Macleod, the principal collector, who has his Cutchery either at Manundwaddy, or Poollingal, or Pancoorfa Cottah, and to obey all orders they will receive from him.   Inform them that otherwise the cowle you have given them will be of no avail.

I have, &c.,

ARTHUR WELLESLEY.

To Lieutenant Francke.

SIR,   Seringapatam, 20th Dec., 1802.

By the orders of this day you have been directed to proceed to Hurryhur, to perform a service respecting which you would receive instructions.

The service alluded to is to construct certain buildings at Hurryhur for the purposes of an European and Native field hospital, if such buildings should be required at that place, and for the purpose of containing grain.

It is intended to have five buildings, each of which is to be 80 feet long and about 20 broad, having in the centre a row of wooden uprights to support the junction of the beams, which you will observe by the enclosed list of materials provided for the purpose of those buildings are only 10½ feet long.

The walls are to be of unburnt bricks ; roof Malabar fashion, and tiled ; each building is to have four doors and eight windows, for which you will observe that plank has been prepared.

I enclose a list of materials which have been laid in at Hurryhur for the purpose of these buildings.   You will be so kind as to take with you to Hurryhur the carpenters, &c., whom you will require for this service, belonging to your department. The aumildar at Chittledroog will receive directions to assist you with other workmen as far as may be in his power ; and I have ordered to Hurryhur and Santa Bednore certain lascars, of whose service you will have the use.

You will estimate the expense of the buildings as soon as you can, including in the estimate the price of the materials collected by Ram Rao, the aumildar of Hurryhur, the list of which is enclosed.

In respect to your department at Chittledroog, you will be so kind as to give directions to the conductor under your orders, in what manner its duties are to be carried on during your absence ; and as Hurryhur is at no very great distance from

Chittledroog, and as your business at the former may not at all times require your immediate personal superintendence, I request you to go over to Chittledroog occasionally to see that the preparations ordered in the store department may not be stopped by your absence.

I have, &c.,

ARTHUR WELLESLEY.

You will be so kind as, in communication with Captain Baynes, to fix upon a convenient spot for these buildings. As well as I can recollect, the best place would be an open space within the pettah, and close to the ditch of the fort.

[ENCLOSURE.]

List of Materials laid in at Hurryhur for building Barracks, dated the 16th December, 1802.

- 140 beams, each three and a half guz long.
- 210 uprights, each two and a half guz in length.
- 210 planks, two and a quarter guz in length.
- 210 bodkeys (cross sticks for laying on the uprights).
- 605 planks, each two and a half guz in length.
- 20 door cases and doors.
- 195 small uprights, laid on the beams for supporting the roof.
- 195 seers or sticks, for laying tho bamboos on, each two and a quarter guz in length.
- 19,500 bamboos.

21,285 Total.

151,000 tiles wanting.

Large tiles	1,000
Small ditto	150,000
Total	151,000

There are 15,000 tiles now ready; for tying the bamboos 500 bundles of small rope; for building the walls 75,000 raw bricks (or small pieces of mud dried in the sun and used in building walls in that country).

Seringapatam.   Translated 17th Dec., 1802.

To Lieutenant-General Stuart.   [1405.]

SIR,   Seringapatam, 20th Dec., 1802.

You will observe by my letter to the Adjutant-General of this day's date, that Captain Grant has resigned his office of

Town Major of Seringapatam. I have not an idea of his motive for resigning at the present moment, which is certainly for many reasons the most inconvenient that he could have fixed upon; but I have forwarded the resignation to be laid before you, and have recommended that Captain Baynes should be appointed his successor.

This officer has strong claims upon the service; he was Adjutant, and had a principal share in the formation, of the corps to which he belongs; and he has lately commanded at Paughur, Mudgherry, and Mergasie, where he had every thing in such order upon my late inspection of these posts that I pitched upon him to superintend the formation of our depôt at Hurryhur, to which place he is now gone. I do not mean to take him away from this duty, but I propose that an officer should be appointed to do his duty here, if you should think proper to recommend that he should be appointed Town Major.

I have the pleasure to inform you that we have got in above fifty large beams from the jungle exactly in the manner I proposed in the first memorandum I had the honour of submitting to you upon this subject. This timber, lodged in the yard at Seringapatam, costs the Company only one silver fanam and sixty cash per cubic foot. Some of the carts go off again to-morrow, and I hope will be back before the bullocks will be required for the army equipments.

Although the weather and roads were very unfavourable, they were only one fortnight away the last time, which is less time than I ever estimated.

I have, &c.,

ARTHUR WELLESLEY.

[1406.]   *To Lieutenant-General Stuart.*

SIR,   Seringapatam, 21st Dec., 1802.

I have had the honour of receiving your letter of the 17th instant. My letter to Lord Clive of the 19th will have made known to you the result of the conferences with Goklah's vakeel. I have arranged the allowance for the Sirdar gone into the Mahratta territory in the manner you propose. I expect to have at least seven lacs of musket ammunition in the store department besides that for corps; certainly more if the march of the troops be delayed for any time. We are making 30,000 *per diem* here, and about 5000 at Chittledroog, and will continue as long as there is paper.

Upon receiving your second letter of the 17th, I reconsidered the proposition which I had laid before you to delay to form the depôt at Hurryhur. Some gram was already lodged and some rice collected at that place, and all the materials for constructing the hospital and granaries prepared; and I found that it was probable that the convoy of grain, &c., sent from this place would be close to Hurryhur before my orders to turn off to Santa Bednore could reach them. It was therefore very clear that wherever that grain might be lodged, it would be well known that it was our intention to form a depôt at Hurryhur. Secrecy was the object proposed in lodging our grain at first at Santa Bednore, but as that object was clearly not to be attained, I thought it best to complete our preparations at Hurryhur in order that you may enjoy the full advantage of the depôt at that place. This can only be done by sending on all the rice bullocks and gunny bags there without loss of time, and the troops and the officer at Chittledroog, &c., to superintend the formation of the depôt, and I have therefore thought it best not to stop them, or alter their destination.

I have, &c.,

ARTHUR WELLESLEY.

There will be at least seven lacs of musket ammunition in readiness here, besides that ready and preparing at Chittledroog.

To Colonel Montresor. [1407.]

MY DEAR COLONEL, Seringapatam, 23rd Dec., 1802.

I have this morning received your letter of the 16th.

I last night received one from General Stuart, in which he tells me that you will receive powers to try the rebels by summary process, and to punish capitally; and you have, therefore, two modes of arranging the question respecting the punishments which have been already inflicted by your orders: one is to delay to make any report upon them till you receive your authority from government, and then to report those instances as the first on which you have executed it; and the other is to report publicly to me the names of the persons who have suffered, stating particularly the crimes of which they have been guilty, such as opposing the Company's troops with arms, &c. &c., and I will send you official orders for their execution. In either case you will be fully indemnified, as you ought to be, for you did only what was necessary and proper.

I have sent off Bentley's estimate, and the recommendation of Hardy's appointment, and your letter to the Military Board.

Not only an officer commanding a division or district, but every officer commanding a garrison, corresponds directly with the Military Board, and you ought to do so likewise. In cases, however, which may be doubtful, and in which you may either have suspended the orders of the Board or have given orders yourself, you may as well send your letter to me, as I may have it in my power to assist your views by my recommendation of them, as I have in this instance.

Let Major Drummond indent for arms for the corps under his command on the stores at Cannanore, and on those at Seringapatam for accoutrements. The latter shall be sent as far as Sangaloo or Wylout the moment that the indent is received here.

I approve of your notion of the police in Cotiote, and I wish that you would apprise Macleod of my sentiments on this subject. Why does he not move towards this part of the country into which the inhabitants have returned? By means of them he might probably be able to communicate with those belonging to other parts, and at all events settle permanently this eastern part.

I have no public news for you. No orders have yet been received from Bengal upon the subject of the equipments, and matters remain exactly as they were when I wrote you last.

You will have heard that West is married.

Believe me, &c.,

ARTHUR WELLESLEY.

I send a duplicate of this letter through Malabar. General

Nicholls is Commander-in-Chief at Bombay.   The question has been decided in his favour.

To Lieutenant-General Stuart.   [1408.]

Sir,   Seringapatam, 23rd Dec., 1802.

I have had the honour of receiving your letter of the 19th. Captain Barclay will, with pleasure, undertake to superintend the bazaar.   The country carts will answer for arrack, for which there may not be Company's carts drawn by Company's bullocks, but the latter are alone what must be depended upon for long marches, &c.   The former will also answer well to bring arrack from the depôt at Chittledroog or Hurryhur. Major Robertson's observations upon the Mysore salted beef are perfectly correct, viz., that it will last longer and keep better in large casks than in small kegs; but I know that it will last for a year in the latter, and I don't think there will be any occasion to make provision for its lasting longer.   It would be very convenient for the gentlemen at the head of each of the store and provision departments if a large quantity of the articles under their charge respectively were carried upon carts, because they would thereby save the trouble of loading and unloading every day, piling, &c. &c.; but such an arrangement would be highly inconvenient, if not entirely destructive of the army.   The ordnance carriages, tumbrils, store carts and arrack carts, which are absolutely necessary for the equipment or the subsistence of the body of troops under orders for field service, will amount to such a number to be moved on one road as will render it very difficult to make such long and rapid marches as will inspire either our friends or our enemies with respect for our operations; but if any addition is to be made to them, either of private carts or of carriages to carry any articles in the store or provision departments which can be carried on the backs of bullocks, we must expect that this difficulty will become an impossibility.   On this ground, therefore, I should prefer to use bullocks for the carriage of the salted beef. This article is not to be used on common occasions, but only when the length or rapidity of a movement, or the difficulty of a country through which it is made, may have rendered it impossible to bring forward the ordinary provision for the Euro-

pean troops.   But if it is to be carried upon carts, it is certain
that if other articles of provision are behind, this will be so also;
and therefore to place it upon carts will defeat one of the principal
objects in carrying it at all.   Major Robertson's observations
upon sheep are also very correct: large flocks are difficult to be
moved ; the sheep are very slow, and by marching they lose their
condition, and it is difficult to protect them.   But I don't think
that your army ought to take with it from the Toombuddra more
than 20,000, or one month's supply ; and Major Robertson will
recollect that he has conducted a provision department on very
long marches, having as many sheep in it as that number.
The further supplies must follow; and as it is probable that they
will not march with such rapidity as the army, they will arrive
in better condition.   Fresh beef is a good substitute for mutton,
and ought certainly to be given to the soldiers whenever it can
be procured; but nearly all the objections which apply to the
movement of sheep apply to that of bullocks, with this one
in addition, that those which are really worth having lose their
condition, and become bad food, sooner than sheep, and this Major
Robertson will also recollect: besides, there is a political objection to feeding the European troops in the Mahratta territory
always upon beef, which, if there were no other, would be
sufficient to prevent its being made their ordinary food.
Bullocks can be got in nearly all parts of the Mahratta territory that I have seen, and I would recommend a dependence
upon that country for this article of supply in preference to
bringing it from Mysore.   There will be ten days' salted beef
and biscuit for 3000 Europeans from Seringapatam, ten days' (I
understand) for the same number from Madras, and ten days'
from Bombay by Goa and Hulliball.   Thus, on entering the
Mahratta territory, you will have sixty days' provision, including
20,000 sheep for your European army, together with what you
may reasonably expect to draw from the country itself: this,
if your rear be likewise kept open, is a supply which I believe
no European army ever had with it before.

The pioneers are going on with the yard as fast as possible,
but I fear they will not be able to finish it before they will
march from hence.

I think it will be desirable that the Barahmahal brinjarries
should be allowed to do as they please, as the others are. If Mr.
Cockburn will give them every facility in loading their bullocks

within his district, and will allow them to pass through it duty free, they will join your army without any further interference on his part. I have not yet got a particular account of the number of brinjarries, but I expect it daily; and as soon as I receive it, I will have the honour of transmitting it to you.

I have, &c.,

ARTHUR WELLESLEY.

To Captain Walker.   [1409.]

DEAR SIR,   Seringapatam, 25th Dec., 1802.

Your bullocks, 2000 in number, left this, I believe, the day before yesterday for Batmunglum, at which place they will be delivered to a person whom you may send to receive them, by a servant of Mr. Gordon, with all their accounts, &c. &c. The advance made has been two pagodas for each bullock.

The 19th will have their bags (300) filled with gram at Bangalore, and they will be supplied daily on their march.

I have heard nothing of the march of the 1st regiment of cavalry, and have consequently made no provision for that corps; but if I should receive timely notice of its march, I doubt not that I shall be able to make provision for it as well as for others. It would be improper to take any steps upon the subject till its destination is certain, as to provide gram upon the high road is expensive to the Sircar, and is the cause of loss if it should not afterwards be taken by the corps for which it was provided.

Believe me, &c.,

ARTHUR WELLESLEY.

To Lieutenant-General Stuart.   [1410.]

SIR,   Seringapatam, 25th Dec., 1802.

Upon the subject of the yard for the gun-carriage manufactory, I have to inform you that the pioneers have been employed upon it for some time past, and that they will be so exclusively till they will take the field. But I conclude that the troops coming from the Carnatic will have advanced so far

upon their march as that those now encamped in this neighbourhood, in this garrison, and expected in a few days from
the southern division of the army, ought to march some time
between the 10th and 15th of January, in order to form the
junction according to your former arrangement communicated
to me. The pioneers at Seringapatam are part of these troops;
and when they will go away, either the yard must remain in an
unfinished state or some people must be hired to finish it, as
there are no public servants in this garrison who can be so
employed. Its present state is very inconvenient; it has not
been possible to enclose it, and there are, of course, many
articles lying in different parts of the yard which are of some
value, and liable to be stolen either by the artificers or other
workmen who must have access to it, and who have so many
different ways to get out of it.

I have forwarded, to be laid before you, a letter from Captain
Mackay, upon the subject of straw purchased by him for the
public cattle employed at Seringapatam, in the service of the gun-
carriage manufactory, in clearing the yard, drawing in bricks,
tiles, &c., for the buildings, and bringing charcoal from the jungle.
When I arranged with the late resident, Lieutenant-Colonel
Close, that the Company's bullocks were to have the Sircar share
of the straw gratis, it was settled that they should never be kept
for any great length of time near any large town or cantonment
of the troops. The ground upon which I asked for, and they
granted the straw, was that they could not make use of it, that
there was no sale for it, and that it was allowed to rot, and
that it could be no loss to them to give it to the Company's
cattle. This is not the case in the neighbourhood of a large
town, and therefore it was agreed that the cattle should never
be detained in such a situation for any length of time. In fact,
the Sircar have no straw at this moment at Seringapatam or
in the neighbourhood; the whole has either been sold or consumed by the Company's cattle; and if a demand were made
upon them for it, they must purchase it themselves. In respect
to the straw at a distance, they have furnished Captain Mackay
with all that belonged to them in the neighbourhood of the
grazing ground, and he has supplied the cattle at work in the
gun-carriage yard till within these few days; but that straw is
all consumed, and some time will elapse before the straw of
this year's crop will come into use. It is therefore absolutely

necessary that he should have permission to purchase straw for the cattle at work at Seringapatam for a short time.

You will have observed, by my letter of the 21st, that the arrangements for the formation of the depôt at Hurryhur are in progress, and I trust that you will have there a valuable store by the time that the troops will be assembled on the Toombuddra.

I have, &c.,

ARTHUR WELLESLEY.

To the Adjutant-General.   [1411.]

SIR,   Seringapatam, 25th Dec., 1802.

I have the honour to enclose extracts of the orders issued by me to the 22nd instant, which require the confirmation of the Commander-in-Chief.

The order of the 26th September, relative to cots and quilts for the regiment of Native cavalry stationed at Santa Bednore and Sera, was issued in consequence of an application to that purport from Mr. Anderson, the superintending surgeon in Mysore.

The orders of the 20th October, relative to the payment of the public followers and bullocks attached to the 5th regiment of cavalry, were occasioned by the following circumstances :— Mr. Sturt went to the Carnatic on a sick certificate on the 15th of December, 1801, and took with him his tent; the lascars and bullocks, &c., &c., attached thereto accompanied it; but Mr. Sturt omitted to procure a certificate from the paymaster, stating the last pay which had been given to these people : consequently he could draw no pay for them, and they actually received none from that time till the month of May, when the orders respecting tent allowance were issued, and they were paid by Mr. Sturt himself as long as they were in his service. When I inspected the 5th regiment of cavalry at Santa Bednore these people complained to me upon this subject, and, having inquired into all these circumstances, I issued the order of the 20th of October.

The company ordered from Hullihall to Goa on the 30th of October was intended to take charge of the Honourable Company's stores at the latter station from the 1st battalion 3rd Bombay regiment, about to proceed to Bombay.

The committee ordered to be assembled at Chittledroog on the 21st November was for the purpose of inquiring into certain improprieties committed by the cashkeeper in the paymaster's office at that station.

Although the corps intended for field service were not ordered by general orders to prepare to take the field till the 5th December, I gave orders by letter to the 5th and 7th regiments of cavalry on the 14th of November, and to the battalions of Native infantry on the 17th of November, to make the necessary preparations for field service. My reasons for giving these corps this early notice were, as well in compliance with the orders of the Commander-in-Chief as that the former might be prepared with bullocks for their gram and doolies and bearers, and the latter with doolies and bearers.

The two companies of the 3rd battalion 18th regiment, ordered from Paughur and Seringapatam on the 8th of December, the latter being in charge of gram, &c., are to proceed to Hurryhur, where they are to be under the orders of Captain Baynes, for a purpose respecting which I will enter into details hereafter.

The order of the 20th December to Lieutenant Francke was given in order that he might superintend the construction of certain buildings eventually wanted at Hurryhur.

I now proceed to detail the preparations which have been made, and are making, for the service of the army in the field, which will require the confirmation of the Commander-in-Chief.

I have ordered that stores may be prepared in the arsenal of Seringapatam for a force requiring 20 field-pieces, in which are included seven lacs of musket ammunition and 500 sets of cutting and intrenching tools.

Of the field-pieces above mentioned, four with their tumbrils are ordered to be prepared at Chittledroog.

Besides this equipment, preparations have been ordered at Seringapatam for six brass 12-pounders, including fifty $4\frac{1}{2}$-inch shells filled, and fifty $4\frac{1}{2}$-inch shells fixed to bottoms, not filled, for each gun; and at Chittledroog for four iron 12-pounders, with 500 rounds of powder and shot for each gun, fifty of which for each gun, to be fixed and carried in tumbrils, are preparing at Seringapatam. Returns of the particulars of this equipment will be forwarded to be laid before the Military Board.

I have ordered 2000 loads of rice to be prepared, to be carried in the grain department. Also 30,000 pounds of salted beef, and 30,000 pounds of biscuit, to be prepared for the provision department.

In order to carry the stores, grain, and provisions above mentioned, I have ordered the paymaster, acting in his capacity of garrison storekeeper, to hire 5000 carriage bullocks, and have authorised him to make an advance to the owners of two pagodas for each bullock.

Besides these supplies to be carried with the troops in the field, I have made other arrangements for establishing depôts of grain, &c., upon the frontier, which will require the confirmation of the Commander-in-Chief.

I have ordered the paymaster to lay in at Hurryhur, on the Toombuddra, as much rice as could be procured in that neighbourhood.

In order to enable him to perform this service at a small expense to the public, and with expedition, I have sent off from hence the 2000 bullocks loaded with the rice intended for the grain department of the army in the field, with their spare cattle, and *   bullocks loaded with salted provision and biscuit, with their spare *   , making in the whole *   carriage bullocks collected at Hurryhur.

I have directed the paymaster to beat out the paddy at Chittledroog, and, in the first instance, to employ the bullocks above mentioned in moving to Hurryhur that rice.

I have given him orders upon stations in the neighbourhood for 5000 bullock loads of rice, which are next to be brought in by these bullocks; and, upon the whole, I expect that in a short time there will be a store of rice at Hurryhur consisting of 7000 bags, besides 2000 bags sent from hence, and belonging to the grain department in the field.

I have also directed the paymaster, acting as garrison storekeeper, to receive at Hurryhur as much grain as the servants of the Rajah of Mysore may offer him; and I have reason to believe that, before much time will have elapsed, they will have laid in there a quantity amounting to 7000 bags.

In order to hold all this field grain, and to provide for the

* Blank in manuscript.

establishment of an hospital, which it is probable may be at Hurryhur, I have directed materials to be prepared for constructing five temporary buildings, each 80 feet long by 20 broad ; and I have desired Mr. Francke to proceed to Hurryhur to construct them, of the expense of which he will send me an estimate.   These buildings, with the pagodas which have been already prepared at my request by the servants of this government, will hold all our stores.   But the rice will receive damage unless lodged in store in bags ; and I have therefore desired the paymaster to prepare the necessary number of gunny bags at different stations in Mysore, and to forward them to Hurryhur.   I have likewise called for gunny bags from the stores in Malabar, which, if they should be found to answer the purpose required, shall likewise be forwarded to Hurryhur.

For the care, receipt, and issue of this grain at Hurryhur I have desired the garrison storekeeper to employ at that station the necessary number of writers, conicopolies, measuring men, sewers, &c. &c.

With a view to collecting a depôt of ordnance, military stores, and provisions at Hullihall in Soonda, I have made the following arrangements, which require the confirmation of the Commander-in-Chief :—I have desired Captain Johnson, of the Bombay engineers, to carry into execution a plan which he proposed to me some months ago for moving from Goa to Hullihall the six 12-pounders at the former place ; and, to facilitate the execution of this service, I have requested the officers commanding at Hullihall and at Goa to afford him every assistance in their power respectively in bullocks, lascars, troops, &c., and the acting envoy at Goa to prevail upon the Portuguese government to assist him with coolies, &c., whom he might require. I have also requested Mr. Read, the collector in the northern division of Canara, to have the road repaired which leads from Goa to Hullihall.

I enclose copies of returns of the provision and military stores at Goa, all of which, excepting those mentioned in the enclosed paper, I have requested the acting envoy to have sent up to Hullihall in Soonda, beginning with the 12-pounder shot and the arrack ; and I have the satisfaction to report that, by the last accounts, great progress has been made in this service. I have requested the commanding officers at Hullihall and at Goa to give every assistance in their power to forward it.   As the only mode of transporting arrack up the Ghauts in that part of the peninsula is in small kegs, I have requested the acting envoy at Goa to have kegs made at Goa for this service, and to have those at present at Hullihall repaired.

I expect that a large supply of salted provisions and of arrack, both contained in small kegs, will shortly arrive at Goa from Bombay; and I have requested that these articles also may be sent to Hullihall in Soonda by the acting envoy.

I enclose a return of the quantity of grain already at Hullihall. I have given directions that the paddy may be beaten out into rice; and besides this quantity, I have directed the paymaster to lay in at Hullihall in Soonda 30 garces of rice, a store which I propose further to increase to the amount of 50 garces. I understand from Mr. Read, whose assistance I have requested for Mr. Gordon in the execution of this service, that the province of Soonda will afford to supply that quantity.

It will be necessary that this rice should be lodged in store in gunny bags, and I have desired the paymaster to prepare and lodge at Hullihall the requisite number.

Besides these arrangements, which require the confirmation of the Commander-in-Chief, I have made others for the supply of the troops in the field, which I hope will receive his approbation.

For the food of the European troops arrangements have been made with the servants of this government to supply 20,000 sheep every month, and 60,000 sheep on this account will be ready between Sera and Chittledroog.

For the food of the horses of the cavalry, arrangements have been made with the servants of this government to supply the gram-agent-general with 7000 loads of gram at eight stations on the eastern frontier, all either on or in the neighbourhood of the high road from the Carnatic, orders for which have been sent to him. The regiments of cavalry also, in this country and coming from different parts of the Carnatic, will receive each at a convenient station on the road one bullock load of gram for each horse, and their daily food on every day's march to the frontier, so that they will arrive there with full bags. Orders for this gram will be sent to the commanding officer of each regiment. Two thousand bullocks also have been hired at Seringapatam for the gram-agent-general, and despatched to him.

For the food of the Native troops, besides the quantity of rice provided for the grain department, that in store at Hurryhur on the Toombuddra, and that in store at Hullihall in Soonda, arrangements have been made to keep the brinjarries and other dealers loaded and ready to march to whatever part the Commander-in-Chief may think proper to direct. I have taken measures to prevent their being employed in the formation of any of these depôts, in order that there may be no excuse for their not appearing when they may be called for.

I cannot at present state with sufficient accuracy the number of loaded cattle belonging to this useful class of people which will be ready to attend the army, or the probable contents of their loads; but I hope to be able to forward to the Commander-in-Chief a report on this subject on which he may depend.

Having thus detailed all the measures taken with a view to the equipment and supply of the troops to be assembled in the field on the frontier of this country, it is but justice to the servants of the government of the Rajah of Mysore to make known to the Commander-in-Chief their readiness to co-operate in every plan which could tend to forward the service, and that they have done everything which I could wish them to do.

I enclose a report of working parties in Wynaad, of which I request the Commander-in-Chief's confirmation.

I have, &c.,

ARTHUR WELLESLEY.

[1412.] *To Captain Macally.*

DEAR SIR, Seringapatam, 25th Dec., 1802.

I have received your letter of the 23rd.

You are desirous that your present allowances, of which you do not state the amount, may be continued to you, under the head of table allowances, and you wish that I should interfere to procure them for you. I have to observe upon this application, that the body of troops under your command is the smallest that is placed under the command of any officer in the Mysore country; indeed so small that an European officer, particularly one of your rank, ought not to be placed in the command of them. The fort of Bangalore, also, however important it may have been heretofore, cannot be considered at present as a place of any consequence. Under these circumstances I cannot perceive any public grounds on which I can recommend that the allowance should be given to you which you require. It appears by your letter that the allowance which you have enjoyed hitherto, an equivalent to which you now desire to have continued to you, has not paid your expenses: your situation, therefore, however agreeable in other respects, cannot have been an advantage to you, and I observe that your request wants private as well as public grounds to recommend it.

Yours faithfully,

ARTHUR WELLESLEY.

To Lieutenant-General Stuart.   [1413.]

SIR,   Seringapatam, 27th Dec., 1802.

I have received a report of the number of brinjarry cattle which will be ready to attend your army, having been counted and muckelkas to that effect taken from their owners, which makes them amount to above 21,000. In this account are not included 4000 in the Colar district, and I believe not 3000 belonging to another tandah; and I delay forwarding you the report till the exact numbers of these will be ascertained. There will not be less upon the whole, however, than I originally stated.

You will be satisfied, I hope, when you see by my report to the Adjutant-General that the depôt at Hurryhur will contain double the quantity of rice and double that of gram that I originally proposed.

I have, &c.,

ARTHUR WELLESLEY.

To Colonel Montresor.   [1414.]

MY DEAR COLONEL,   Seringapatam, 27th Dec., 1802.

I have only the day before yesterday received your letter of the 19th December. I am sorry you did not send me the

letters which you say that you have written me : it will not be
easy to state the confidence which I have in your judgment and
discretion ; and I am convinced that if you should deliver any
opinion upon the subject on which you say that you have written
to me, it will be formed on facts. In respect to the present
disturbances in Wynaad, as far as I have it in my power to
form a judgment, it is my opinion they are to be attributed to
accident, and the circumstance of the Rajah and some of his
principal adherents being still at large. I have been informed
that the insurrection began by an accidental murder and riot,
subsequently to which the party concerned in them went to surprise the post and murder the officers at Pancoorta Cottah. The
troops did nothing to revenge this loss, and Coongan Nair, who
was at the head of those who performed these feats, issued a
proclamation, calling upon the inhabitants of Wynaad to meet
him at a pagoda in the neighbourhood of Manundwaddy, where
they did meet him to the number of 5000, and they have been ·
in rebellion ever since. At the time when this insurrection
broke out the revenue year was closing, and not one farthing
of the revenue remained unpaid. There had been no symptoms
of disaffection before ; and if there had, Captain Dickenson,
who was well acquainted with the affairs of the country and
the disposition of its inhabitants, would not have been surprised
in his post : and upon the whole, I am induced to believe that
accident alone was the original cause of an insurrection which
has grown to be a rebellion from the subsequent inactivity of
the troops.   Indeed, one strong proof to my mind that it
cannot be attributed to the officers of the revenue, is, that it
broke out after the revenue of the year had been realized, and
at so late a period of the monsoon that it was every day probable that the country would be in such a state as that our
troops would carry on operations against the insurgents. If the
oppression of the people had been the cause, it would have commenced before they had paid their money, and at an earlier
period of the monsoon. This being the case, candour would
induce me to pause before I formed a decision respecting the
system of management of any man who might have had in his
hands the civil and financial government of that district ; and I
should certainly not decide that the insurrection is to be attributed to him unless conviction was produced upon my mind
that it was so, not by any single detached fact, much less by

rumours and reports, but by a careful examination of the whole question, and every circumstance relating to it. This would be my mode of proceeding if any man were collector of Malabar and Wynaad, but I shall consider it particularly necessary to adopt this mode when called upon to form a decided opinion in a case where Major Macleod is concerned.

This gentleman was originally selected by Lord Cornwallis as one of the agents to introduce the British government into the Barahmahal when that district was conquered from Tippoo. If Lord Cornwallis has one quality as a man at the head of a great government more conspicuous than another, it is the talent of choosing proper instruments to be employed in the different departments under him ; and this is so well known, that to have been selected by Lord Cornwallis for any situation is strong presumptive evidence in a man's favour that he is fit for it.

Major Macleod was a collector of the Barahmahal till the commencement of the last war with Tippoo Sultaun; and it is a well-known fact that there is no part of the British territories in India in which the British authority has been so completely established, and in which the country itself, its people, the amount, and the sources of its revenue, are so well known as in the Barahmahal. All this could not have been done without much labour by those to whom the civil government was intrusted, and Major Macleod had under his charge a very large division of the Barahmahal.

After the last war with Tippoo, he was chosen by Lord Wellesley to introduce the British government into Coimbatoor ; and we know by experience, that when there have been disturbances in every province, nay, district, subject to the British government, from Ganjam on one side, and Goa on the other, as far as Cape Comorin, Coimbatoor alone has been undisturbed ; the revenue has been increased far beyond the amount of the schedule of 1792, its sources are perfectly known and ascertained, and this increased revenue has been realized to this day.

When it was thought proper to try a new system of government for Malabar, Major Macleod was the person fixed upon to carry it into execution, and he undertook the duty, to my certain knowledge, much against his inclination. The result of his administration in Malabar has been, first, that the revenue has been increased 1 lac and 20,000 pagodas, and has been realized; secondly, that a saving has been made of civil expenses to the amount of 70,000 pagodas *per annum*; thirdly, that a saving has been made of military expenses to the amount of 1 lac of pagodas *per annum*; making Malabar, upon the whole, a better concern to the Company than heretofore by nearly 3 lacs of pagodas *per annum*.   This saving of military expenses is not of those which ought properly to be called military: they are those on account of sebundies, peons, &c. &c., who attended the government of the Commissioners, who were actually useless in a military point of view, and with whom the military commanding officer had nothing to do, and which ought never to have been carried to the head of military charges.

I contend, therefore, that it is peculiarly due to Major Macleod to examine with minute care and attention all points relating to his management before any decided opinion is formed and delivered upon that subject.

I don't mean, my dear Colonel, to insinuate that you have formed any opinion upon this subject on light grounds; but I am perfectly aware of the strange and improper conduct of some in Malabar, and of the dangerous steps taken by them against Major Macleod and his system.   I know the advantage which such a party would derive from the sanction of the opinion of a person of your character in your situation, and the pains they would take to convince your mind of the truth of those statements and reports which they are putting in circulation.   I have therefore written thus much to warn you upon this subject, to urge you again to an unreserved communication with Major Macleod on all points, and to avoid forming any opinion either regarding his character or his system of management not founded upon your own observation, your complete knowledge of facts, and your own reasoning upon them.

In respect to Major Macleod's conduct in Wynaad, as alluded to by you in your letter of the 19th, I have to observe that it is natural he should have no knowledge of the interests of the inhabitants of that district, and no influence over them, because till now all of them have declined to have any communication with him.   The same cause must prevent his inquiries into their grievances and the sources of them.   But you have entirely mistaken the character of Major Macleod, or he must be strangely altered, if you suppose that he is not a candid man with the natives, is unwilling to enter into inquiries, or is a character to which the natives of any part of India will ever have an antipathy.

It is notorious that Major Macleod is the most elaborate inquirer in this part of India, and he is so happy as to enjoy a mildness of temper and of manners and a patience which are supposed to be the qualities which have never failed to conciliate the natives of India.   I have known him for many years, and I declare that in my opinion he possesses the qualities which I have above stated to be notorious; and if I were called upon to state what I thought the fault of Major Macleod's character as a public man, I should say that he had too good an opinion of the natives in general, and that he paid too much deference and attention to what they said to him.

Believe me, &c.,

ARTHUR WELLESLEY.

I wish that you would not forget the mats, respecting which I spoke to you before you left this place.

I shall also be much obliged to you if you will be so kind as to desire Mr. Gourlay to send here two children inoculated with the cowpox.   I want to have my godson inoculated.

The troops march from the Carnatic as soon as they can get their bullocks.   No other orders.

To Lieutenant-General Stuart.   [1415.]

SIR,   Seringapatam, 28th Dec., 1802.

I have the honour to enclose you the translation of a letter written by Major Munro to a man, by name Baboo Rao, in this country.   This Baboo Rao was formerly at the head of the brinjarries in Tippoo's territories, and served both Hyder Ali and him in that capacity; and he offered his services to me in the same manner in the campaign of 1800, which I declined to accept, because I found he was a very old man and infirm, and because I had already employed one in that capacity with whose services I had reason to be satisfied.   There is no doubt, however, but that Baboo Rao has considerable influence among the brinjarries, and that, having such a letter as that from Major

Munro in his possession, he may draw after him many of the heads of tandahs.

I believe that the man whom I have employed to bring them forward, who is the same that served General Harris and myself before, and who has received a reward from government for his services, will produce every man and bullock that the country can afford. But if Baboo Rao be employed, and has orders at this late period of the equipments to bring the heads of tandahs to Major Munro in the Ceded Districts, not only will Mickin Lalle (the man I have employed) fail in bringing forward the number for which he has engaged, but Baboo Rao also will fail in bringing them forward at the time at which they will be wanted.

You have approved of Captain Barclay's taking upon him the superintendence of supplies; and I take the liberty of suggesting, therefore, that all questions relating to the brinjarries should be referable to him, and that he should have authority to correspond with the collectors in the Barahmahal and the Ceded Districts upon this subject.

I have, &c.,

ARTHUR WELLESLEY.

[1416.]   *To Josiah Webbe, Esq.*

MY DEAR WEBBE,   Seringapatam, 28th Dec., 1802.

I perused your letter to Mr. Rickards, and forwarded it to Colonel Close. If I have not mistaken Rickards's character, it will do much good; and if it does not, he ought to be sent back to Bombay. It is impossible for any man in an arduous situation to carry on its duties if there be a party in the country ready to find fault with everything he does, instead of supporting him, according to the true principles of their duty.

I think that the proclamation which you propose should be issued will be useful. In the first place, it will show the judges the true line of their duty in a public manner, and will give them reason to apprehend punishment if they deviate from it; and secondly, it will prove to the officers of the army (which is, I assure you, a great object), and to the people in Malabar, that the judges have nothing to do with the executive civil government or the revenue, both of which departments remain still in the hands of Major Macleod.

Purneah has been spoken to respecting the silladar horse. If he cannot have new arms, he must be content with good repaired arms ; but I wish he could have the former.

I'll take care that Captain Mahony's mission shall be settled as you suggest. He is a kind of man, however, to whom it will be necessary to speak with firmness ; and I shall give him to understand that he is responsible that the object of his mission is not discovered till every circumstance relating to it is arranged.

I have not heard one word respecting what you say about Cochin, and I cannot believe it to be true. The report would have reached me from Mahé sooner than it could Macaulay.

Believe me, &c.,

ARTHUR WELLESLEY.

To Lieutenant-General Stuart.   [1417.]

SIR,   Seringapatam, 29th Dec., 1802.

I have had the honour of receiving your letter of the 25th. I beg that you would let me know whether it is your wish that spare carriages of the common construction should accompany the troops from hence, to be used when you will order the galloper carriages to be transferred to the cavalry. If that should be your design, it will probably be as well that the galloper carriages should be moved to the frontier without having guns on them. On the other hand, if it should be your intention that these carriages should be attached to the infantry during the campaign, it will be necessary to make some alteration in the construction of the pole, &c. &c.

I will endeavour to procure some horses for two brigades of guns ; and if I should procure any, I will hand them over to the 2nd regiment of cavalry to be trained to the draught. I should wish to have your directions in whose hands these horses are to be placed, and on what establishment.

The great convenience of the light guns attached to the cavalry is, that the regimental system for the care and food of the horses, and the superintendence of the officers, is introduced without difficulty.   If more ordnance of this description, drawn by horses, be required, the best mode of arranging it at present would be to give one additional piece to each regiment.   They might be allowed to entertain horse-keepers and grass-cutters to attend the horses, and drivers to drive the guns, which might move with the advance guard of the infantry, attended by European artillerymen to work them.   I see no other mode of insuring the care and food of the horses; and it will throw no additional trouble upon the regiments of cavalry, nor will it take any men from their other duties.

I beg leave to inform you that a man of the name of Beckwith, who was provost-marshal with the army under the command of General Harris, and who has since resided at Seringapatam, has desired me to lay before you his wish to obtain the same situation in the army under your command.   He is well known to officers of the General Staff.

I shall be obliged to you if you will let me know whether, in reference to the late decision of the Governor-General and the Commander-in-Chief in India upon the claims of General Nicholson and General Nicholls to command the Bombay army, you consider the order of Sir Alured Clarke, of the 15th January, 1801, published to this army on the 11th February, 1801, as still in force.   I ask this question because I believe it is not improbable that a question may arise upon the subject in this country.

I beg leave to remind you of the propriety of suggesting to Colonel Close to ask the Peshwah for an order to the killadar of Darwar to deliver that place up to you.   It is absolutely necessary that you should have it; and it will be better that you should obtain it in this manner than by open force.   I have mentioned this subject to Colonel Close in a letter which I have written to him.

I have, &c.,

ARTHUR WELLESLEY.

[1418.]   *To the Secretary of Government.*

SIR,   Seringapatam, 31st Dec., 1802.

I have the honour to enclose an extract of a letter which I have received from Mr. Read, the collector in the northern division of Canara, in which that gentleman complains of the inconvenience felt on that part of the coast from the appearance of the pirate boats. I shall be obliged to you if you will lay this letter before the Hon. the Governor in Council of Bombay, with my request that, if it should be otherwise convenient, he will be so kind as to give directions that an armed vessel may be stationed on the coast of Canara to cruise between Goa and Mangalore.

I have, &c.,

ARTHUR WELLESLEY.

To Lieutenant-General Stuart.   [1419.]

SIR,   Seringapatam, 31st Dec., 1802.

I have had the honour of receiving your letters of the 26th and 27th. After making his payments of this month, Mr. Gordon will have in his treasury about 20,000 pagodas, and he will receive from the Residency on the 1st of February about 55,000 pagodas, making in all 75,000 pagodas applicable to the payments for January. The demand for the troops now in this country will be about one lac of pagodas; the deficiency, therefore, 25,000 pagodas.

Mr. Anderson has frequently made inquiries from me regarding your determination upon the medical arrangements, particularly whether the articles of which I had heretofore the honour of sending you a list would be prepared at Madras, and whether means would be provided there for their carriage.

I also beg leave to recall to your recollection the want of tents for the 1st battalion of artillery, and for that part of the medical department not provided for by the tent regulations.

You mention in your letter of the 26th that you propose to keep a squadron of the 1st regiment of cavalry as an escort to yourself. Is it your intention that that corps, or any part of it, should march through this country? as if it be, it will be necessary to provide gram for it upon its march, which I have not done yet.

I have received your order respecting Captain Monteath, and I will give him such instructions as I may think will best answer to bring him to the army. In respect to Captain Cunningham for the charge of the remount lot, I will have the honour of writing you upon that subject to-morrow, when I shall have had more time to consider it. It will be necessary that you should look forward to the establishment of boats upon each of the rivers Toombuddra, Werdah, Malpoorba, Gutpurba, and Kistna, in the beginning of the month of June; and I had turned my mind to Captain Cunningham as the officer to superintend these establishments. He did this duty before for me, and understands it. It may be possible, however, for him to bring up the lot of remount horses before the month of June, and to take the superintendence of the boats on himself after that period.

I have, &c.,

ARTHUR WELLESLEY.

Upon referring to the instructions from the Adjutant-General to the officer commanding at Sera, I observe that Lieutenant Monteath is not ordered to purchase horses that may have been already brought down to the coast for sale; but he is to select, approve, and send off horses that may arrive there for the Honourable Company. Would you wish that I should explain this matter in the instructions which I shall give to Lieutenant Monteath?

[1420.]   *To Colonel Montresor.*

MY DEAR COLONEL,   1st Jan., 1803.

In answer to your letter of the 26th, I have to tell you that I will recommend that application should be made to Bombay for arms for you, and I will urge forward the measure so that you will have the arms soon. I am glad that your measures of severity are likely to have some success: they appear to me to be absolutely necessary. I approve of Captain East. I also approve of Major Howden's enlisting the nine men; but you must write me a public letter on the subject, as I must refer it to head-quarters. The prohibition to recruit was made by the Commander-in-Chief.

Preparations are going on for the campaign to the northward. The troops were to march on this day or to-morrow, and General Stuart to leave Madras on the 10th. I march between that day and the 20th. I don't understand the report of Harness having a brigade: the 80th don't take the field.

Purneah is to form an army in the northern parts of Mysore, and he wants the battalion at Cancancotta. He will replace it by peons.

Believe me, &c.,

ARTHUR WELLESLEY.

To Josiah Webbe, Esq.

[1421.]

MY DEAR WEBBE,   Seringapatam, 1st Jan., 1803.

Purneah was with me this morning, and I spoke to him on the subject of the muskets.   He wishes not to have the repaired arms ; he prefers those he has, and certain foreign arms, of which I believe we have still some good ones in the arsenal of Seringapatam.   He says that if he could get a good set complete for his infantry, he would take them ; but those which he has now, and which are repaired, will be as good as those which we may have repaired and will give him.

He will march from hence with his troops nearly at the same time that I shall.

My reason for wishing that you should be in Mysore if General Baird should come in the command of the troops is, that it will be very difficult to keep all matters as they are unless there is a person at the head of the government for whom he would have a respect.   However, it appears that if he should come before General Stuart, much time will not elapse before the latter will follow him and take the command of the troops ; and that is a situation of affairs which I have long contemplated, and respecting which I have no uneasiness, even if you should be absent.   If I have not mistaken General Stuart's character, his object will be to uphold this government, and that is everything.   In the meantime, while General Baird is in the command, I will do all in my power to conciliate him ; and I hope that all will go on well.

It is absolutely necessary that you should remain at Madras. I will assist Piele with my advice and opinion on every point on which I may think that I can be useful to him, and I dare say that you will find that he will continue to conduct himself as well as he has hitherto.

I should have written to General Stuart before now upon the subject of our operations, only that I did not see clearly what our object was to be. It appears now to be, to dislodge Holkar from Poonah, and to restore the authority of Bajee Rao. I know of no obstacle upon the road to that place, and I will immediately write to Close my opinion regarding the length of time which will elapse before we shall reach it from Hurryhur.

I cannot tell when the army will be at Hurryhur, or the length of time it will halt there. These events depend upon the present state of the equipments in the Carnatic, and upon General Stuart; but I think it probable that we shall not be able to march from Hurryhur till the end of February, and we shall not reach Poonah till the middle of April.

Goklah's vakeel went away when he received his answer; but I have written to him in consequence of Lord Clive's letter of the 26th. I have also apprised Govind Rao (whom I sent by General Stuart's desire to find out the intentions of the Put-wurdun, &c.) of the probable improvement in the state of our connexion with the Peshwah.

Piele and I had a conference with Captain Mahony on the day before yesterday, and we have made an arrangement for the Rajah of Koorg which I think will answer.

First, we have agreed that he shall not have any part of the territories of the Rajah of Mysore, and that this government shall not be informed that it was ever in contemplation to give him any part of them.

Secondly, that he shall have the districts of Panjah and Bellary, below the Ghauts in Canara, which appear to join to Murca and Soobroo, and which were claimed for him by name, by his friends Mr. Uhtoffe and Captain Mahony, at the time of the settlement of the treaties with the Nizam and the Rajah of Mysore by the Commissioners. These districts are small, and it is supposed will not be more than 6000 Canterai pagodas *per annum.*

Thirdly, that he shall have in Canara districts equal in value to those which were claimed for him in Mysore, and which circumstances prevent us from giving to him, viz., Periapatam, Belladpoor, and Arkelgoor, &c., being in value nearly 18,000 Canterai pagodas annually, according to the schedule.

Fourthly, that the districts to be given to him shall connect Murca and Soobroo, or Panjah and Bellary, with the Buntwell river.

Thus the Rajah will have about 24,000 Canterai pagodas annually.

It appears by Captain Mahony's accounts that the Rajah incurred an expense for the Company, on account of the late war with Tippoo Sultaun, amounting to nearly four lacs of rupees; for which, if he had consented to be reimbursed, he would have received in February, 1799, bonds of the government of Bombay bearing interest at 12 per cent. *per annum.* It may fairly be said, therefore, that the Company are indebted to him at this moment about six lacs of rupees.

Thus by this arrangement he will get an income which is equal to the interest of this sum, and possession of two districts below the Ghauts, to which he thinks he has a claim, and other districts equal in value to certain districts above the Ghauts which he wished to have; and he will be connected with the river Buntwell.

I don't think it possible to make a better arrangement. It is founded, first, upon the Rajah's just demand for money laid out, and the interest due upon it; next, upon his supposed claims to certain territories; and thirdly, upon a compensation for those claims which circumstances prevent us from gratifying.

Captain Mahony, who wishes to give the Rajah of Koorg a square kingdom about four times as large as Koorg, although he cannot point out the advantage of that figure, says that by this arrangement we shall have been just, but not generous. I think we might dispute that assertion; but it is sufficient for us to know that we have been just, and if the Rajah be not taught to think otherwise, to be certain that he will think that we have been generous.

While writing upon this subject I may as well allude to a report that is in circulation, that Captain Mahony is to be Resident in Koorg. In the first place I don't see any necessity for such a person; it is impossible for anything to go on better than all our communications and arrangements with the Rajah of Koorg. But if there should be a person employed in Koorg in that situation, he ought to be under the orders of the Resident in Mysore, and to be in fact one of his assistants. This ought to be the case, particularly if Captain Mahony should be the person, as it is well known that the Rajah of Koorg himself is not more prejudiced against and inimical towards this government than Captain Mahony.   Allow me to recommend you to write a line to Malcolm upon this subject.

A letter has been written to the collector in Canara, in order to procure the necessary information to enable us to decide what districts are to be ceded to the Rajah of Koorg.

Piele will have informed you of the result of his inquiries regarding the letters which you sent to him supposed to be from Purneah, viz., that they were written by a person belonging to Trimmul Rao.   Purneah is very anxious that the writer, who has calumniated the Company, and has been guilty of a fraud, should be punished; and my opinion is, that the best mode of punishing him would be to try him in the Foujdarry.   You will be the best judge what ought to be done with Trimmul Rao.

Believe me, &c.,

ARTHUR WELLESLEY.

[1422.]   *To Alexander Read, Esq.*

SIR,   •   1st Jan., 1803.

I have had the honour of receiving your letter of the 24th December, and I have applied to the Governor of Bombay that an armed vessel may be sent to cruise on the coast of Canara, between Goa and Mangalore.

In case, in consequence of this application, a vessel of this description should appear upon the coast, I shall be obliged to you if you will give the officer in command of her any information you may have respecting the pirates.   In respect to the other part of your letter regarding the evacuation by your peons of the island of Buswarajah Droog, I have to inform you that I have given orders that the stores of that place may be brought to Mangalore, and that you may receive notice as soon as they will have been brought away.   I think it proper, however, notwithstanding that the stores may be brought away, to recommend you not to withdraw the peons from Buswarajah Droog till you will have referred the subject again to the decision of the Board of Revenue.   In the present state of affairs in the west of the Peninsula, it must be expected that the depredations of the pirates will be vastly increased, and that they will readily seize such a hold as Buswarajah Droog in

order to carry them on with more facility and advantage on
the coast of Canara. That place ought, therefore, to be occupied ; and as regular troops to occupy it cannot be spared from
the services above the Ghauts or in Malabar, it must be held
by peons. On the other hand, as it is probable that the country
will be involved in a war of some extent, and as nearly all the
troops will be withdrawn from Canara, I conceive that it will
not be very politic to take this opportunity of throwing out of
employment so many idle persons, whose only profession is that
of arms. We have generally experienced in India that internal
commotion and insurrection are the consequences of external
war, and it does not appear to be politic at this moment to
increase the number of idle people of the profession of arms,
who are always the instruments of these partial rebellions.

Under these circumstances, therefore, I recommend, not only
that Buswarajah Droog should not be evacuated, but that
generally you should forbear to discharge the peons in your
service.

I have, &c.,

ARTHUR WELLESLEY.

To Sir William Clarke.   [1423.]

SIR,   Seringapatam, 1st Jan., 1803.

I have the honour to acknowledge the receipt of your letters
of the 18th, 20th, 21st, and 23rd December.

In respect to the store establishment at Goa, I have issued a
general order regarding it, which you will receive probably
with this letter. I accept the offer of the services of Captain
Fisher, and in the mean time, till he can join the troops in the
field, he is to take charge, as deputy commissary, of the stores
at Hullihall, which he will have properly arranged.

I am much obliged to you for the manner in which you
have disposed of the stores which I supposed not to be necessary
to me, and for the purchase of the twenty leaguers of arrack.

It gives me great satisfaction to observe that everything has
been brought up from Goa with so much speed, a service on
which the officers employed must have exerted themselves much
and zealously ; and I shall take an opportunity of reporting to
the Commander-in-Chief my sense of their conduct.

I do not think that it will be necessary that carriages should be made at Goa.

The amount of the sale of stores at Goa is to be paid to the paymaster, and carried to the account of the Company.

I have, &c.,

ARTHUR WELLESLEY.

[1424.]   *To Lieutenant-General Stuart.*

SIR,   Seringapatam, 2nd Jan., 1803.

I have had the honour of receiving your letter of the 29th December.

The time at which the troops ought to march from hence in order to form the proposed junction with you will depend upon the road which you wish they should take. If they are to join you at or in the neighbourhood of Sera, and the whole proceed together by Chittledroog to Hurryhur, they ought to march from hence two days before you will march from Bangalore. If they are to proceed by the lower road, by Chinroypatam, Benkypoor, and Hooly Honore, and join you at Hurryhur, they ought to leave Seringapatam on the day that you will leave Bangalore.

I recommend the latter road, because, the troops being divided, forage and grain will be procured with more ease for the whole; and, indeed, I doubt whether the road from Sera to Chittledroog, and thence to Hurryhur, in the country by far the most barren in Mysore, would afford subsistence for such a body of men and cattle as will be upon it if the two bodies are to join at Sera.

I observe that Colonel Montresor is appointed to command only in Malabar. I shall be much obliged to you if you will let me know whether this is a mistake, or an arrangement made in consequence of my former recommendation upon this subject. If the latter, I have to observe that I believe it would be more convenient under present circumstances if he were appointed to command in both provinces, as other officers have been.

There is a great want of arms in all the corps in Malabar, and I think the best mode of supplying them would be to request the Bombay government to send down 5000 stand of new arms to Cannanore. I imagine that the application upon this subject must go from the government of Fort St. George.

Everything in my power shall be done to close in the yard of the gun-carriage manufactory before we march from hence.

I think that Captain Cunningham will perform the service on which you have proposed to employ him at Mangalore with great advantage to the public, and that he will still be able to superintend your boat establishments. If you think it proper, I will give him instructions regarding the horses.

I will draw a memorandum upon the subject of the boats, which I will have the honour of sending to you, or of laying before you when I shall see you.

I have, &c.,
ARTHUR WELLESLEY.

I don't yet send you the detailed account of the brinjarries, as it is not yet complete, although more than 25,000 bullocks for loads have been mustered and are loading. I expect to have an account of many more; I believe 9000. I have this day ordered out guards to collect and put in motion the different tandahs towards Chittledroog, and by the end of this month they will be at the back of the Chittledroog hills.

To the Adjutant-General at Bombay.

[1425.]

SIR,   2nd Jan., 1803.

Since I had the honour of receiving your letter upon the subject of the recommendation of Lieutenant Martin to be Adjutant of the 1st battalion 5th Bombay regiment, I have inquired further respecting the grounds of the recommendation of that officer by the commanding officer of the battalion to which he belongs. I find these to be such as fully to justify it, and I therefore beg that you will lay my recommendation before the Commander-in-Chief that Lieutenant Martin may be appointed Adjutant of the 1st battalion 5th regiment.

I have lately judged it expedient to remove the stores at Goa to Hullihall, and I have hitherto detained Captain Fisher, the commissary of stores at Goa, in order that he might afford his assistance in the performance of this service. These stores are now removed to Hullihall, and at the request of Captain Fisher I have appointed him to do duty with a detachment of Bombay artillery ordered for service and now encamped at this place. In the meantime, and till it will be in his power to join this detachment, I have desired him to take charge of and arrange the stores at Hullihall. I hope the Commander-in-Chief will approve of this detention of Captain Fisher, occasioned first by the necessity of having his assistance to remove the stores from Goa, and next by that of employing him to arrange the stores at Hullihall, and by the want of an officer to the detachment of Bombay artillery ordered for field service.

I have, &c.,

ARTHUR WELLESLEY.

[1426.]   *To Lieutenant-General Stuart.*

SIR,   Seringapatam, 3rd Jan., 1803.

I have had the honour of receiving your letter of the 30th December. I have not heard from Colonel Montresor that he wants more troops, but he was very desirous to detain the 1st battalion 8th regiment; and since, that Purneah should occupy the posts of Sangaloo and Wylout: I therefore conclude that the battalion which you have it in contemplation to send into Wynaad will be very acceptable to him. No great progress has been made in the suppression of the rebellion in Wynaad, but the inhabitants have returned to their villages in the eastern districts; and Colonel Montresor hints in his last letter that the prospect of an end to the insurrection was more favourable than it had been before. I will write to him for a particular account of every circumstance that has occurred, and a statement of his wishes regarding troops, which I will have the honour of forwarding to you. I don't think he can be reinforced from Malabar or Canara.

The brass 12-pounder carriages are not yet arrived here. I have spoken to Captain Scott respecting your wishes to have some of the 12-pounders mounted on galloper carriages, and he will commence constructing them forthwith. It is doubtful, however, whether they will be finished before the troops will march from hence.

I have, &c.,

ARTHUR WELLESLEY.

SIR,   Seringapatam, 3rd Jan., 1803. .

It is necessary that I should have the honour of submitting to the Right Hon. the Governor in Council a report concerning the police establishments of the fort and island of Seringapatam, and that I should request his orders regarding the payment of them in future.

By the regulation of government for the better administration of justice within the fort and on the island of Seringapatam, the police is placed under my directions as commanding officer in Mysore. I have the honour to enclose lists of the servants employed in it within the fort and on the island respectively, and the wages of each denomination, and an account of the average expense of the whole establishment. When the local situation of Seringapatam and the nature of its population are considered, I hope that it will be found that the police could not be well conducted with a smaller establishment of servants, or at a smaller expense.

The island, which is of no great extent, is surrounded by the territories of the Rajah of Mysore, into which thieves can escape without difficulty after having committed their depredations upon the more respectable inhabitants of Seringapatam, and where they can remain in security, and dispose of the articles which they may have stolen. The objects of police therefore at Seringapatam are principally to watch property and to prevent robberies, to effect which a large number of servants are required.

The inhabitants of Seringapatam are generally the followers of camps, and the servants and families of officers and soldiers. They are people of the lowest class in the community, and probably the most addicted to thieving. They require to be particularly watched, and they can be so only by a large number of servants.

The establishment of Sheher Ganjam has hitherto been paid by a tax levied upon the inhabitants by authority from the Board of Revenue, an account of which I have the honour to enclose. I conclude that his Lordship will be desirous that this part of the expense should still be defrayed in the same manner.

The expense of the establishment of Seringapatam has hitherto been defrayed by the commanding officer; but as the commanding officer will no longer have the means of defraying this expense, I beg leave to submit to his Lordship that a tax similar to that levied in Sheher Ganjam may be levied in the fort of Seringapatam, adding thereto one-fourth, according to the enclosed estimate ; and that a daily tax should be levied on moveable shops in the fort, according to the enclosed estimate.

It is supposed that the former would produce 1070 star pagodas *per annum*, and the latter about 1000 star pagodas *per annum*, which, with the police tax in Sheher Ganjam, amounting to 1020 star pagodas *per annum*, would give 3090 star pagodas *per annum* for the whole.

The average expenses of the police, according to the enclosed account, are 218 star pagodas 42 fanams 65¼ cash *per mensem;* and the sum above proposed to be provided for the payment of them will leave a balance to be laid out in the repair of roads, bridges, &c., being works which are at times absolutely necessary, but the expense of which cannot be accurately estimated.

The camp cutwahl's establishment in the police charges of the fort is one belonging to a camp bazaar, which remains upon the island ready to move with any body of troops at a moment's warning.

The balance will be regularly accounted for in such manner as his Lordship may think proper to direct.

I have, &c.,

ARTHUR WELLESLEY.

[1428.]

The Deputy Adjutant-General to Major Burrows.

4th Jan., 1803.

Major-General the Honourable A. Wellesley, commanding in Mysore, directs me to transmit to you the accompanying statement of the circumstances which occasioned the complaint of the Dewan of Mysore, communicated to you in my letter of the 31st ult., the outline of which was sufficiently acknowledged by the soubahdar yesterday to induce the General to give credit to every part of the statement ; and he therefore directs me to inform you that he considers the soubahdar's conduct as improper in the highest degree ; that the aumildars in this country are not amenable for articles stolen in camps, although they are ready enough to cause search to be made for them, and the thieves; and the soubahdar's insisting upon the man giving a muckelka to produce the stolen goods was an assumption of authority, highly unwarrantable, and deserving of punishment. Neither has any one a right to compel any of the inhabitants, much less the particular servants of the government, and the principal servants in their villages, to attend him about the country, as the soubahdar obliged the parbutty and patel to do, running before his horse; and had the soubahdar carried his violence so far as to compel any of those people to conduct him to Mysore, and thereby to have alarmed the Rajah's family, consisting of an infant boy and some old women, no consideration would have induced the General to have overlooked his behaviour. As matters are, he only desires that you will cause the impropriety of the soubahdar's conduct to be explained to the regiment; and further, that no person, excepting the commanding officer in any camp or cantonment, has a right to send for, or have any communication with, the servants of government. Commanding officers may, in such cases, do what appears proper to them, upon their own responsibility; or they may refer any matter of complaint to the officer commanding the division. The General has observed with satisfaction the propriety of your conduct on this occasion, and also that the soubahdar was not countenanced by any of the European officers.

Some things stolen in your camp at Nunjengoor have been found upon people who appear to be from below the Ghauts, and to have come up along with the regiment, which circumstance shows that the aumildar in this country ought not to be held amenable for thefts committed in camps. The articles here alluded to will be delivered up to any person sent by you to receive them.

                                        ARTHUR WELLESLEY.

- - - - - - - -

                To David Cockburn, Esq.   [1429.]

SIR,   Seringapatam, 7th Jan., 1803.
    I have the honour to inform you that I have received information that a party of thieves of some strength have collected near Dankery Cottah, where they have committed considerable outrages, and a proposal has been made to me by the Dewan of the Rajah of Mysore to send a party of the Rajah's cavalry

within the Company's territories to endeavour to take them, or
at all events to disperse them. In concert with Mr. Piele, I
have taken this proposal into consideration, and strongly recommended its immediate execution, as I consider the service will be
of the greatest consequence to the territories of the Company
and of the Rajah of Mysore, and to the security of the communication between Madras and the army about to assemble on
the frontiers of Mysore. I have, therefore, given letters for
your aumildars on the frontier to the Rajah's officer who will
command this party of horse, and I shall be obliged to you if
you will give directions that they may be treated as friends
within the Company's territories.

I have, &c.,

ARTHUR WELLESLEY.

[1430.]   *To Lieutenant-General Stuart.*

SIR,   Seringapatam, 7th Jan., 1803.

I have had the honour of receiving your letters of the 2nd
and 3rd instant.

Captain Barclay has already opened his correspondence with
Major Munro and Mr. Cockburn. Exclusive of the brinjarries
which may be expected from the Ceded Districts and the Barahmahal, the musters of cattle and muckelkas of brinjarries in
Mysore amount to more than 32,000, which will be at the end
of this month at the back of the Chittledroog hills with loads.
Of these there are 3000 in the Carnatic, who may be stopped
by Mr. Cockburn, or included in his accounts; but, at all events,
you will have the services of them.

I shall take from this 100 platform carts and 30 arrack carts.
I propose to indent for ten at Chittledroog, which I understand
the commissary of supply can furnish there. Of this number,
only seventeen and the arrack carts will be loaded in this country;
the remainder will be at your disposal. If the march of the
troops be delayed at all, I shall have more, and I certainly will
take every one that I can get. My letter of the 31st December will have pointed out to you the state of our resources
in money: in addition thereto, I have to inform you that we may
reckon upon nearly 50,000 pagodas every month from the Resi-

dent.   If Mr. Cockburn sends his lac of pagodas here instead of to Vellore, I will take care that it shall go on to the frontier, and no more shall be left in this treasury than is absolutely necessary for the common disbursements.

Captain West has been for some time in the government orders as my aide-de-camp; but if it should be necessary that he should now be appointed again, I shall be obliged to you if you will recommend him.   I delay to recommend a brigade-major till the troops take the field.

I shall be very much obliged to you if you will make me acquainted with your wishes regarding a Town-Major for Seringapatam.

The troops marching from hence shall take as many galloper carriages as may be ready.   There will be no difficulty in altering the pole, or future inconvenience from the alteration.

I will endeavour to procure horses for two brigades of guns, but I am afraid I shall not succeed, as every man who has a horse can now procure means of subsistence, of which he would be deprived if he were to sell him.   If the two brigades are to be drawn by horses, it will be best that the tumbrils should be so likewise, and those of the new construction ought, in my opinion, to be used on this occasion.   I have given directions to Captain Heitland to complete his corps according to your desire, and he will be able to do so at this place without difficulty.

I think it probable that you will want a recruit of bullocks on your march through this country, or on your arrival at Hurry-hur.   If you should approve of it, I can easily have between 3000 and 4000 ready at Bangalore, and as many more at Hurry-hur, provided I have a few days' notice of the want.

I have, &c.,

ARTHUR WELLESLEY.

I have no account whatever of the 20,000 gallons of arrack which you informed me were sent to this country, although I have frequently inquired for them.

[1431.]   *To Sir William Clarke.*

Sir,   Seringapatam, 7th Jan., 1803.

I have had the honour of receiving your letters of the 30th December and 2nd instant.

I am much obliged to you for the trouble you have taken in the removal of our ordnance and stores, and for the arrack you have purchased. My wish is that the latter should be in such kegs as a bullock can carry, and that these should be made so strong as to stand all kinds of bad usage. A bullock can carry from 120 to 140 lbs., and from this you will be best able to judge whether two of the 8-gallon or two of the 9-gallon kegs will be the more proper load ; but the whole load, including keg, liquor, and gunny-bag, ought not to weigh more than 140 lbs.

I have given orders respecting the commissary of stores and his department at Goa, which will have reached that place before you will receive this letter.

I beg you to form your own opinion regarding Mr. Pereira's offer, as you must be the best judge whether the bargain will be reasonably fair for the Company, and I request you to close with him according to your own opinion upon that point. I don't know what the expense of arrack or kegs is at Goa, or that of the removal of the supposed quantity from thence to Hullihall, and am, therefore, entirely unable to form an opinion upon the subject; but I know that it is very desirable to have a large quantity of arrack so forward. In making your bargain with Mr. Pereira, I request you to advert to what I have above written regarding the size of the kegs.

I have, &c.,

ARTHUR WELLESLEY.

[1432.]   *To Lord Clive.*

My Lord,   Seringapatam, 9th Jan., 1803.

I have the honour to enclose a paper containing the purport of a conversation which I have had with a vakeel sent here by the Rajah of Kittoor. Under your Lordship's former orders I have given him every encouragement, and have told him that the officer in command of the British troops will hereafter communicate with the Rajah.

The accounts I have from the frontier are not very favourable. The country is in great confusion: the heads of small districts and villages have ceased to obey all the formerly constituted authorities, and have taken the supreme authority each in his own district, and they are carrying on against each other a destructive warfare.

I have, &c.,

ARTHUR WELLESLEY.

[ENCLOSURE.]

Purport of a Conversation held with Suba Rao, Vakeel from the Kittoor Rajah.

Seringapatam, 8th Jan., 1808.

My master, Mulsurjah Shumsheer Jung Behauder Surdeshie (commonly called the Kittoor Rajah), sent me to the Honourable Major-General Wellesley, to whom he was formerly under so many obligations when he protected him from Bappojee Goklah, Chintomeny Rao, and others,* who were at variance with him; and he has directed me to inform him that he is ready to obey any orders he may choose to give him, and that he will be particularly happy to serve in the same cause with him as he did on a former occasion against Dhoondiah; and as he gave him a cowle † on that occasion, he hopes he will give him a similar one now: and that he is ready to give every assistance in his power in the way of supplies, &c., to any army which may come near his country. The Rajah has about 1000 horse, 7000 or 8000 infantry, and four guns; and if the General thinks proper to order him, he will increase the number of his troops. Suba Rao requests the General to write a letter to the Rajah. As he knows that an assurance of his friendship will make him very happy, he has a pair of hircarrahs here ready; and if he will be kind enough to send the letter to him, he will have it conveyed to the Rajah as quickly as possible.

To Lieutenant-General Stuart. [1433.]

SIR, Seringapatam, 9th Jan., 1803.

I have had the honour of receiving your letters of the 5th. Lieutenant Williams, of the Bombay pioneers, has received

* These chiefs were desirous of plundering the Rajah of Kittoor, but were prevailed upon by Major-General Wellesley to refrain from doing so, at least as long as the Rajah's troops remained in the British camp.

† The cowle was only to extend to personal safety and to protection of his country during the time that he might be in the British camp, and his troops serving with the British troops, and to permission to depart whenever he wished to do so.

orders to go to Bombay, and I have requested Colonel Montresor to make arrangements for the command of that corps. Captain Johnson is now usefully employed in Soonda; and as he has been in the Mahratta territory heretofore, particularly at Darwar, and is well acquainted with it, I believe it will be best to detain him in that quarter, at least till you have an opportunity of judging whether he can be of use to you.

Mr. Gordon included in his credit the sum expected from the Resident on the 1st of February, and 22,000 pagodas of the lac which he has required from the collector in the Barahmahal, according to the orders of the Paymaster-General and Accountant-General, founded upon his last year's estimate. He has not included, however, any of the sums he may get for bills. You may depend upon it that I will bring forward to the frontier every farthing that can be spared from this treasury.

I did not know of the proposed march of the 1st regiment of cavalry till I received your letter of the 5th instant. Gram, however, will be provided for this corps, as well as for all the others, and I shall send this night to the commanding officer an order upon Bangalore for its gram, similar to that which I have already sent to the commanding officer of the 19th dragoons.

I will instruct Lieutenant Monteath as you desire, and I hope that he will be able to join at Hurryhur before the end of February. In respect to Captain Cunningham, I conclude that he will have to wait in the Mysore country with the great remount till an opportunity will offer for the horses to join the army forward.

Upon this point, however, there will be no occasion to come to any immediate decision. I shall, therefore, only instruct him to bring the horses by a certain route into Mysore as soon as he can, and I shall inform him that he will receive further orders respecting their ulterior destination.

I have the honour to be, &c.,

ARTHUR WELLESLEY.

[1434.]   *To Lieutenant Monteath.*

SIR,   Seringapatam, 9th Jan., 1803.

You will have received the instructions of the Commander-in-Chief, through the Adjutant-General, to proceed to Mangalore to examine and receive charge of such horses arriving there for the Honourable Company as may appear to you to be fit for the service, and to send off to Mysore such horses as you may select and approve, under further instructions from me.

By a letter from the Commander-in-Chief, I understand that the horses which you are to view are not those which have been commissioned by Captain Walker, acting as agent on the part of the Company, and which are not expected till the end of February, but certain other horses which certain dealers have brought to Mangalore for sale, of which the Commander-in-Chief is desirous to avail himself for the service at present. Upon this subject you will have received a communication and instructions, as I am informed, from Captain Walker.

There remains, then, only for me to desire you to commence your march from Mangalore on the 31st of January, with such horses as you may then have procured for the Honourable Company, and proceed by a route which is enclosed to Hurryhur, on the Toombuddra.

I will to-morrow procure from the Dewan orders to the aumildars to supply you with forage on the road, and I will arrange with him the stations at which you will be supplied with gram. If I can give you any further assistance, I beg that you will let me know it. You will be relieved by an officer before the 30th of January.

I have, &c.,

ARTHUR WELLESLEY.

[ENCLOSURE.]

Route from Mangalore to Hurryhur.

		Coss.	
Mangalore to Feringypet	.. ..	3	A river.
Buntwell	.. ..	2	A river.
Poojalcotta	.. ..	3	A nullah.
Kulbangarry	.. ..	5	A nullah.
Mailbungarry	.. ..	3	A nullah.
Koovay	.. ..	3	A nullah.
Karhulla	.. ..	3	A nullah.
Oostara	.. ..	3	Tanks.
Baswanhully	.. ..	3	A tank.
Sacrapatam	.. ..	3	
Bramsamoodrum	.. .. ..	8	
Beeroor	.. ..	8	

Turrikerra

					Cos.
Mangalore to Turrikerra	..	..	..	..	4½
Benkypoor	..	..	..	..	4½
Hooly Honore	..	..	..	..	4
Anagoondy	..	..	..	..	3
Davenhully	..	..	..	..	5
Nundevarah	..	..	..	..	3½
Hurryhur	..	..	..	..	3

[1435.]   *To the Hon. Basil Cochrane.*

SIR,   Seringapatam, 9th Jan., 1803.

I have the honour to inform you that I have received intelligence and frequent complaints from the troops that your conicopoly Ramalingum was in the habit of adulterating the Honourable Company's arrack in his charge, in consequence of which I brought him to trial before a garrison court martial, and I enclose an extract of the proceedings on his trial and the sentence of the court martial.

I besides ordered a committee to survey the arrack in the different arrack stores, and to compare the contents of the casks with those of the muster bottles. Almost all of the latter corresponding with the casks, the contents of which are bad liquor, had been opened, and were of the same kind of liquor as the contents of the casks of which they were respectively the muster. I have given directions that the troops may have the good arrack, and that the bad may be laid aside till you send directions respecting it, which I beg you to do as soon as may be convenient to you. I have likewise given orders which I hope will prevent the recurrence of this evil in future. It will be necessary that you should send here another conicopoly.

I have, &c.,

ARTHUR WELLESLEY.

[1436.]   *To Colonel Montresor.*

MY DEAR COLONEL,   Seringapatam, 10th Jan., 1803.

I am very much obliged to you for your letters of the 31st December and 2nd January.

I never had the smallest doubt that everything would be done by you that was active and useful to get the better of the insurrection in Wynaad, and I perceive by your journal that you have not been idle. I am glad also to perceive that your mode of proceeding is likely to be successful, and that some of the rebels have already come in.

You must send me the sick certificates, that they may go to government. No officer can leave the territories of the government under which he serves, excepting by their permission. Pray don't allow any of them to go to Bombay; they never come back.

Your letter of the 2nd gave me very great satisfaction. You may depend upon it that the longer you are acquainted with Macleod the better you will like him, and that what I told you respecting him in my letter was strictly true. God send that by your joint endeavours you may soon get the better of this insurrection.

Matters remain as they were in regard to Mahratta affairs. General Stuart cannot move from Madras for want of bullocks. I have been ready here for above a month, and have all my troops encamped in different situations in this neighbourhood. He has fixed upon different days for quitting Madras with his head quarters; but I hear that he has now deferred his departure till the 15th of this month, and this will defer mine till the 30th. In that case we shall none of us be at Hurryhur till the end of February. Everything is in readiness and in great style here.

I have no late news from Poonah. Holkar appears to have an intention to place on the musnud a son of Amrut Rao's, a measure which it is supposed would conciliate the Rajah of Berar and most of the Southern chiefs, whose power is yet unbroken, and would be pleasing to the Nizam. On the other hand, the Peshwah is at Bassein, and he has made every demonstration of an intention to conclude with us. I have had vakeels with offers of assistance from all the Sirdars on the frontier; but the country is in terrible confusion, and becoming more confused every day. The heads of villages and small districts have shaken off all the formerly constituted authorities, and have seized upon the supreme power each in his own district, and they are carrying on a destructive war against each other. Our first object, therefore, must be to settle the country through which we pass, and to take it for ourselves, or to give it to the rightful owners; otherwise these petty wars will be as prejudicial to us and our supplies as those carried on against us by the more formidable powers of the empire.

All my arrangements respecting Hullihall have succeeded, and that place is full of stores, and arrack from Goa.

Believe me, &c.,

ARTHUR WELLESLEY.

The mats are for two rooms, one 36 feet by 15, and one 15 feet square.

[1437.] *To Lieutenant-General Stuart.*

Sir, Seringapatam, 10th Jan., 1803.

I have the honour to enclose a copy of the instructions which I propose to give to Captain Cunningham, and I shall be obliged to you if you will let me know whether they meet with your approbation.

I beg to draw your attention to the following points: First, I have not told Captain Cunningham that he is to take horses from the dealers who may have brought some upon their private speculations, but he is to receive charge of those commissioned by Captain Walker expected at Mangalore in February and March, which he may select and approve. I should wish to know whether you approve of this, or whether Captain Cunningham is to take any horses from the dealers which have not been commissioned by Captain Walker, or whether he is to select and approve some of those which have been commissioned, or is to take the whole number of 700. I believe the mode proposed of procuring the food, followers, and equipments of these horses is that which is commonly adopted.

The second point to which I wish to draw your attention is the place to which I have directed him to bring the horses in Mysore. I have pointed out this place because it is the cavalry cantonment on the frontier, and is convenient to Hurryhur and to Chittledroog, if it should be necessary to take shelter at that place. It does not want forage or gram, and there are at that place the necessary store-rooms.

The third point on which I have to request your orders is the assistance for Captain Cunningham in Native officers and troopers from the Native cavalry. I conceive that he will want this assistance, and believe some of this kind has always been afforded to an officer employed on this duty.

The fourth is the necessary communication from Captain Walker to the dealers, in order that Captain Cunningham may procure from them the horses. I shall give him the instructions as now submitted to you, and he shall leave this place as soon as he will have procured a sufficient number of followers. It will not be difficult to alter or add to the instructions afterwards, according to the orders I shall receive from you.

I have, &c.,

ARTHUR WELLESLEY.

To Captain Cunningham.　　[1438.]

SIR,　　　　　　　　　　　　　　　　10th Jan., 1803.

Horses to the number of 700 have been commissioned by order of government by Captain Walker, of the 4th regiment of Native cavalry. They are expected to arrive at Mangalore in the months of February and March, and it is necessary that an officer should proceed to that place to take charge of them. The Commander-in-Chief has been pleased to desire that you might be employed on this duty, and that I should give you instructions for your guidance in the performance of it.

Before you will leave Seringapatam you will entertain the number of followers who will be necessary to attend upon the horses expected. These must be mustered when entertained. No persons of this description can be procured at Mangalore or in the Mysore country, excepting at Seringapatam. On the arrival at Mangalore of the horses commissioned by Captain Walker, you will examine them and receive charge of such as you may select and approve of as being fit for the service of the Honourable Company. You will provide for their food, their followers, and their equipments, according to the regulations of government for the conduct of the horse-agency. As soon as the whole number will have arrived at Mangalore, you will march them into the Mysore country to the cantonment at Santa Bednore, according to the enclosed route (A.), where they are to remain under your charge till you will receive further orders.

It may happen, however, that you may be able to procure forage and gram for the horses with greater ease by sending them into Mysore by detachments than by bringing them in one lot. If you should be of that opinion, you are at liberty to do so, adverting to the general inattention of the Natives to animals intrusted to their charge, and to their inclination to apply to their own use the gram intended for their food and the money to purchase their straw. If on your arrival in the Mysore country you should be of opinion that it will not be safe for you to remain at Santa Bednore, you will proceed to Chittledroog by a route which is enclosed (B.); and you will do the same from Santa Bednore, if at any time you should have reason to believe that it is not safe for the horses to remain at that station.

In case you should be ordered from Santa Bednore or Chittledroog, you will at the same time receive a route by which you will march.

I write to the collector in Canara, Mr. Ravenshaw, to request he will give you every assistance in bringing up the horses to the Mysore country, and I will arrange with the principal servants of this government to supply you with gram at certain stages on the road, of which I will hereafter send you a statement, and I will procure orders for you on the aumildars for straw, &c.

A store of gram will likewise be provided for you at Santa Bednore or at Chittledroog, according as circumstances may enable you to remain at the one, or may oblige you to remove to the other.

It is necessary that you should proceed immediately to Mangalore in order to relieve Lieutenant Monteath, of the 7th regiment of cavalry, who is at present employed on the service proposed for you. I enclose a copy of his instructions, by which you will observe that he is to leave Mangalore on the 31st instant, and I beg you to take measures to arrive there before that time.

I will hereafter let you know whether you can have any and what assistance in Native officers or troopers from the corps of Native cavalry. You will receive a communication from Captain Walker regarding the mode in which the horses are to be procured from the Native dealers.

I have, &c.,

ARTHUR WELLESLEY.

[ENCLOSURES.]

(A.)

Route from Mangalore to Santa Bednore.

	Coss.	
To Feringypet	3	A river.
Buntwell	2	A river.
Poogecottah	3	A nullah.
Kulbangarry	5	A nullah.
Mailbaugarry	3	A nullah.
Koovay	3	A nullah.
Karhulla	3	A nullah.
Oostara	3	Tanks.
Baswanhully	3	A tank.
Sacrapatam	3	A tank.
Bramsamoodrum	3	A tank.
Beeroor	3	
Adjampoor	4	
Marawinjee	4	
Santa Bednore	5	
	—	
	50	

(B.)

Route from Wostana to Chittledroog.

	Coss.		Coss.
To Baswanhully	3	To Hullul Kerah	4
Sacrapatam	3	Chittrehully	3
Bramsamoodrum	3	Chittledroog	4
Caroor	3		—
Adjampoor	4		31
Singinhully	4		

To the Officer commanding the 1st Regiment of Cavalry.   [1439.]

SIR,   Seringapatam, 10th Jan., 1803.

I have the honour to enclose an order upon the aumildar of Bangalore for 500 bags of gram for the 1st regiment of cavalry, likewise an order upon the villages on the road from Batmunglum to the frontier for the daily consumption of the horses of that regiment.

A store of gram for the cavalry has been provided at Sera, and it will be proper that it should be used by the regiments as they will pass that place. Accordingly I shall be obliged to you if you will be so kind as to give directions that the gram which the regiment will receive at Bangalore may be used on the road between that place and Sera, instead of taking the daily consumption from the villages through which you will pass; and I enclose an order upon Sera for 250 bags of gram, which I suppose may be the consumption between Bangalore and Sera.

You will be so kind as to give your receipt for all the gram that you will receive in the Mysore country.

I have, &c.,

ARTHUR WELLESLEY.

[1440.]   *To Lieutenant-General Stuart.*

SIR,   Seringapatam, 11th Jan., 1803.

I have had the honour of receiving your letter of the 7th.

I have shown Purneah's people the foreign arms which we have in store at this place, but he does not like them, and, indeed, they are not worth having. I have, therefore, given him some repaired captured arms and some of the unserviceable captured arms delivered into store by corps. He is still very desirous to have a complete set of new arms for his infantry, and, if he is to get them, they must be sent from Madras, as, after providing for the corps coming from the southward and those at this place, we shall not have one stand left.

I don't at present think that there will be any necessity for calling upon the collectors in Canara for any supplies, excepting of money. Mysore will furnish more rice than we have means of carrying away. If we are to draw any of that article from Canara, we must send cattle to bring it up the Ghauts, for which we have not time at present, and hereafter the rains in that country will prevent us from sending there. Mr. Ravenshaw, however, might do us some good by preventing a great exportation from Canara by sea in this year, and by keeping the markets in that province full. Although the growth of rice in Canara is far beyond its consumption, the exportation is so great that there is commonly a scarcity, and then the rice is sent into it from the rice countries in Mysore which lie along the Ghauts. By keeping the markets of Canara full, therefore, he will stop the exportation from Mysore, and it will be more easy to supply our army.

I will write to Mr. Ravenshaw upon this subject.

The object of your operations, it is probable, will now be to march to Poonah and re-establish there the old government. The country in the neighbourhood of Poonah is entirely exhausted, and it would be very convenient to you to have a depôt at Panwell, opposite Bombay, or at Bassein. This must be supplied from Bombay.

I rather imagine that the government of Bombay can have no command of rice excepting from Canara, and for this object, therefore, it would be desirable that Mr. Ravenshaw should take measures to stop the great exportation from Canara.

In respect to money, I will write to Mr. Ravenshaw this day, and request him to send all he can spare into Mysore as soon as possible. After a certain period it ought to be sent to Hullihall in Soonda, but not along the frontier, as the whole of the Mahratta territory is in confusion, and it is probable that this money would not reach its destination in safety.

I have the honour to enclose the copy of a letter received from Sir William Clarke, containing a proposal to supply the station of Hullihall with arrack. I don't know the price of kegs at Goa, or the expense of removing arrack from Goa to Hullihall; but I have desired Sir William Clarke to take these circumstances into consideration, and to agree to Mr. Pereira's proposal, if he should think it reasonable for the Company. I have also apprised him that the kegs which Mr. Pereira proposes to furnish are too large, and that a bullock can only carry from 120 to 140 pounds, including liquor-kegs, gunny bag, &c.

As I have drawn your attention to the depôt at Panwell, it may be proper that I should remind you also of the great essential, money, to be at that place, likewise salt beef and arrack. I have given Mr. Duncan a hint upon this subject, and, if you approve of the notion, I will write to him upon it in detail. It will be necessary that Colonel Close should obtain an order from the Peshwah for the possession of Panwell, or whatever place may be fixed upon, and that it should be made a post to be occupied by the Bombay troops.

By this arrangement your line will be shortened above three hundred miles, and you will have the advantage of carrying on the war at Poonah with Bombay resources, and an army equipped with cattle, &c., from the eastern side of the Peninsula. Our brinjarries will be well pleased to fill their bags again with so much ease.

> I have, &c.,
>
> ARTHUR WELLESLEY.

--- --- -- ----- - ---- - ------

[1441.]   *To the Secretary of the Military Board.*

SIR,   11th Jan., 1803.

Captain Scott has communicated to me a letter from you, in which you have conveyed to him the directions of the Military Board to complete the establishment for the gun-carriage manufactory from the European artificers at present on trial under his directions, and that the overplus should be still kept at work upon the allowance of five pagodas *per mensem*, till vacancies in the fixed establishment shall occur. I am of opinion that this allowance is fully sufficient, and an equivalent for the work performed by these Europeans. It is proper, however, that the Military Board should be informed that these artificers have expected large allowances; that they were much dissatisfied when this allowance was settled for them by me, and have continued to manifest this dissatisfaction ever since, particularly within these few days; that they have many of them desired to be sent back to join their corps, and have behaved with such impropriety as soldiers that some of them will be tried for their conduct before a garrison court-martial to-morrow.

Under these circumstances, I have to submit to the Military Board whether it would be proper to increase the allowances of any of the artificers at present by placing them on the establishment. There is no doubt whatever that this measure will increase the dissatisfaction of those who may not be chosen, and that the whole will desire to be sent back to join their corps. If they should make this demand, I beg to have the orders of the Military Board respecting a compliance with it. In my opinion, the best mode of settling this matter entirely would be to give each European artificer 9 fanams *per diem* for each day that he should work, including Sundays, and to allow Captain Scott to increase this allowance as far as a rupee to those men who by their diligence, their ability, or their good conduct should appear to him to deserve this indulgence. If they work every day in the month, which is not to be expected from men of their habits, they will receive each six pagodas instead of five, and the public will have the advantage of not paying any man for work which he does not perform.

This, it is probable, will satisfy them, particularly if they are informed that they have nothing further to look forward to; but to admit a few to a higher rate of pay will only increase the present dissatisfaction. They will all desire to return to their corps, and they must either be forced to work, which will be very inconvenient, or they must be allowed to depart, which, under present circumstances, would be very prejudicial to the service. In consequence of these considerations, I have requested Captain Scott to delay to fix the establishment of European artificers till he should have received further orders from the Military Board.

I have, &c.,

ARTHUR WELLESLEY.

To J. G. Ravenshaw, Esq.   [1442.]

SIR,   Seringapatam, 11th Jan., 1803.

I received a letter from General Stuart some days ago, in which he desired me to correspond with you upon the subject of the supplies of money and grain which you might have it in your power to afford for the service of the army about to be assembled in the field under his orders.

In respect to the supplies of money, if you should have any sums in your hands at present unappropriated, I recommend that you should send them into Mysore. If what you may be able to send should leave Mangalore by the end of this month, and should be sent towards Hurryhur by the Currut Kull Ghaut, Oostara, Turrikerra, Hooly Honore, and Hoonelly, I shall meet them on my march to the frontier with the troops now assembled at this place. I shall be obliged to you if you will write to me upon this subject, and let me know the sums which you will send, and the time at which they will leave Mangalore.

I beg that you will apply to the commanding officer at Mangalore for an escort for any money that you may send.

In respect to supplies of grain, I have to observe that if we are to draw them from Canara for the service of the army assembled in this country, I must send cattle for them ; and as Mysore can supply more grain than I can carry away, much valuable time would thus be lost. I don't therefore propose at present to send to Canara for any supplies of grain.

In a private letter from you, which General Stuart has sent me, you inquire whether it would be desirable that you should prevent the great exportation of grain from Canara in this season, in order that you may provide for the possible demands of the army. One of the consequences of the exportation of grain from Canara is that much grain is carried from the rice countries of Mysore, bordering on the Western Ghauts, into that province, particularly since the settlement of the disturbances in Bullum. This trade is highly beneficial to Mysore, and it is very desirable that in general it should be encouraged; but under present circumstances, as the army must depend in a great measure upon Mysore for its subsistence, and as every drain from this country will lessen the chance of procuring it with ease, it is better that this trade should cease for the present ; and as the best mode of putting a stop to it, that the markets in Canara should be kept full by a general discouragement of the exportation of grain for some time. I know that the trade can be prevented in some degree by other means, and I have urged the Dewan to prevent as much as possible the exportation of grain by the western passes. But the best mode of putting a stop to it will be to deprive those who carry it on of all prospect of advantage by keeping the markets in Canara tolerably well supplied by a general discouragement of exportation.

Another reason for which I am desirous that the exportation of rice from Canara should be discouraged is, that I have recommended to General Stuart the formation of a depôt of rice, by means of the Bombay government, at one of the Mahratta ports, opposite the island of Bombay or Salsette. In case he should adopt this plan, I apprehend that the government of Bombay must draw the supplies of rice which will be required from Canara, and they will not be available unless the exportation is discouraged immediately. It is obvious, however, that, until I know whether General Stuart will adopt this plan, or whether the government of Bombay have any other resource from which they can draw supplies of rice excepting Canara, I cannot write to you positively upon this subject. I have

therefore stated to you generally the inconveniences which may
be the result of the continuance of the exportation, and the
objects which will be answered by discouraging it, and I must
request of you to act as you may think best for the service.

I have, &c.,

ARTHUR WELLESLEY.

To Lieutenant-General Stuart.

[1443.]

SIR,

12th Jan., 1803.

The carriages for the brass 12-pounders arrived some days
ago, and I have forwarded to be laid before the Military Board
a report upon their state.   Captain Scott had commenced making
limbers for two of them, to which horses might be attached ;
but he is of opinion that the woodwork of the carriages is so
bad that they will not answer, and he therefore proposes to
make carriages as well as limbers.

They will not be in readiness to move from hence with me,
and must follow by any route you may think proper.   Four
6-pounder carriages and two tumbrils will be ready, however,
and two 8-inch howitzer and two 5½-inch howitzer carriages,
likewise constructed at the manufactory.   I shall bring all these
with me.   I have purchased some horses for the guns, and I
hope to be able to procure more ; they are good horses, and
will answer well for the purpose for which they are intended.
Their price will, upon the whole, be rather higher than that of
the Company for the remount lots, which, I believe, is 120
pagodas for each horse.   But it must be recollected that the
gun-horses of the cavalry are the best in each regiment, that
each would probably sell for 250 or 300 pagodas, and that the
Company lose many horses out of those brought for them to
Mangalore, and for which they pay ; and then it will be found
that the horses which I shall have bought are not dear.

I have, &c.,

ARTHUR WELLESLEY.

[1444.]   *To W. H. Gordon, Esq.*

SIR,   13th Jan., 1803.

I have the honour to inform you that the number of bullocks hired which will be required to carry stores from hence is 1791, including spare; the number for grain is 2000, besides spare; and the number for salt beef and biscuit is 700, including spare. It is desirable, therefore, that you should, as soon as possible, arrange the bullocks with these three departments, and have registers prepared to be handed over with the bullocks required for each department to its head. Besides the three departments above mentioned, the demands of which I observe amount to the whole number of 5000 bullocks hired, there are other departments not yet provided for, for which provision must be made. There are, first, the tarpaulins for the grain and provision departments not yet provided for; 2ndly, the medical storekeeper's department, 101 carriage bullocks; 3rdly, the Quartermaster-General's department; 4thly, the camp equipage of the Coast and Bombay artillery. The amount of these demands, and of others which may occur, and which I cannot foresee, may be about 400 bullocks; and I have to request that you will, as soon as convenient, hire that number in addition to those already entertained. These likewise must have a separate register for each department, and be handed over to its head.

I have, &c.,

ARTHUR WELLESLEY.

[1445.]   *To Lieutenant-General Stuart.*

SIR,   Seringapatam, 13th Jan., 1803.

I have inspected all the corps arrived from the southward, and I have fixed upon the 1st battalion 14th for the garrison of Seringapatam, and the 1st of the 13th for the garrison of Chittledroog, as being the two corps of all those now in this country the least fit for service in the field. It is necessary, however, that I should apprise you that the 1st of the 8th, one of the corps which I have pitched upon for field service, is remarkably sickly at present, having brought nearly 300 sick from Wynaad; and I don't believe they will leave less than 200 sick at this place at the time we shall march. I have preferred to take this corps to the field to either of the others above mentioned, first, because I know it is a good corps, which has seen much service, and, secondly, because it has been in the Mahratta territory before, which you may find an advantage. If, however, you should be of opinion that these advantages do not overbalance the disadvantage of being 100 men weaker than the others, I can easily, upon hearing from you, order it up to Chittledroog, and the 1st of the 13th into the field ; or one or two flank companies of the 1st of the 13th may take the field to make up the deficiency of numbers of the 1st of the 8th.

As the 1st of the 8th are recovering fast, it is hoped that they may be quite well before I shall march ; but I mention the subject in order that I may receive your directions upon it, in case they should not.

The 1st of the 4th will join you at Bangalore, and the 2nd of the 10th at Chittledroog.

I have, &c.,

ARTHUR WELLESLEY.

Seringapatam, 14th Jan., 1803.   [1446.]

Account of Sums of Money laid out by the Hon. Major-General Wellesley to make his Quarters at the Dowlut Baug habitable.

	Star Pagodas.
12 large Venetian folding doors with frames, at 10 pagodas each ..	120
18 large panelled ditto, at 9 pagodas each	162
4 large plain ditto, at 4½ pagodas each	18
12 large Venetian folding windows with frames, at 9 pagodas each..	108
6 ditto, at 8 pagodas each	48
4 ditto, at 6 pagodas each	24
22 Venetian folding windows with frames, for offices and godowns, at 4 pagodas each	88
A large wooden double staircase, with 16 steps each side	95
84 pair brass hinges, for 42 large folding doors and windows, at 1½ pagoda per pair	126
42 pair brass bolts for ditto, at 1 pagoda per pair	42
40 pair brass hinges for 10 Venetian folding windows, at 1 pagoda per pair	40
10 pair brass bolts for ditto, at 22 fa. 40 cash per pair	5
44 pair iron hinges for 22 Venetian windows, for offices and godowns, at 22 fa. 40 cash per pair	22
8 pair iron hinges for 4 large plain folding doors, at 1 pagoda per pair	8
36 door brass locks, at 4 pagodas each .. ..:	144
	1050

To Lieutenant-General Stuart.

Sir,   Seringapatam, 15th Jan., 1803.

I do not delay answering your letter of the 12th, just received.

The corps taking the field from this country are detachments of the Bombay and 1st battalion Coast artillery; 33rd regiment; 1st of the 2nd; 1st and 2nd of the 3rd regiment; 1st of the 4th; 1st of the 8th; 2nd of the 10th; 2nd of the 12th; 2nd of the 18th regiments; and the 2nd, 5th, and 7th regiments of cavalry. The corps remaining in Mysore will be the 1st battalion of the 5th regiment, the 1st of the 13th, and 1st of the 14th.

I am about to send off to Chittledroog the bullocks for the draught of the four 6-pounders from that place, and of the four iron 12-pounders: also the carriage bullocks for the powder and shot for those guns.

These carriage bullocks will take up to Chittledroog 3 lacs and 40,000 rounds of musket ammunition. I should be obliged to you if you would let me know whether I am to provide bullocks to carry that and the other ammunition which will be prepared at Chittledroog by the time the army will reach that place, or whether they will come from the Carnatic.

The whole quantity which will be at Chittledroog will probably be 7 lacs.

There will be besides about 10 lacs, which I shall carry with me from hence.

I wish to have your orders upon this subject as soon as possible, if you should determine that this country is to furnish these cattle.

I have, &c.,

ARTHUR WELLESLEY.

To Lieutenant-Colonel Whitelocke.

Sir,   Seringapatam, 15th Jan., 1803.

I have the honour to enclose the translation of a paper which I have received from the Dewan, from which it appears that the mode in which the Company's paddy at Chittledroog is beat into rice is an intolerable grievance to the people of that place.

First, it is necessary that the demand of people of this description to beat out the rice should be limited by the capability of the place to furnish them ; and upon this point I request you to have a communication with the aumildar, and not to require a greater number of people, or, in other words, a greater quantity of rice to be beat out, than he is of opinion can be afforded without material inconvenience.

In the next place, it is necessary to regulate the quantity of good rice without flour, or the quantity of rice and of flour, that the paddy in the Company's stores will yield when beat out.   In order to ascertain this point you will be pleased to appoint a committee, who are to see such a quantity of paddy beat out as will give you a general average, by which you will be enabled to frame a regulation which will apply with justice to the whole quantity of paddy in store.   You will inform the aumildar that you have appointed this committee, and with what view ; and you will invite him to send persons likewise to see the paddy beat out, and the quantity of rice and of flour which it will yield.

After this is ascertained I request you to settle with the aumildar accordingly the quantity of rice and of flour which the ricebeaters are to return to the stores, in proportion to the quantity of paddy which may have been given out to them ; and this settlement is to be permanent as long as this species of paddy is in store and is to be beat out.

If you should find that the produce of the paddy beat out in the presence of the committee is materially less than the quantity of rice which the ricebeaters have been compelled to give in proportion to the quantity of paddy delivered to them from the stores, as complained of by the aumildar in the enclosed paper, it will be necessary that the excess which has been received from them should be returned to the aumildar, in order that he may distribute it among those who have suffered.

I have, &c.,

ARTHUR WELLESLEY.

[ENCLOSURE.]

Translation of the Copy of an Arzee, written by the Soubahdar of Chittledroog, Vinkitaya, to the Presence, dated the 11th January, 1803.

You sent orders for beating out the paddy into rice which was in the Company's granary.   According to your orders I gave out the paddy to be beaten to the following descriptions of people:—to the cloth and grain merchants; the kompteys; the bulzewacers; the shepherds; potmakers; Mussulmans; jogey jungums, and dancing girls; and they have this day given in 1500 bags ready beaten. There are still 2000 to 3000 bags of paddy remaining, which they say must be also beaten out.

There are no ricebeaters in this place, and the rice which has been beaten out falls far short of the paddy, and the wages paid the ricebeaters amount to a considerable sum.

The rice is hard, and therefore moulders into flour. They say we must buy new rice in the bazaar, and give it to them in room of this flour; in consequence of which the people have been obliged to pay 10 and 20 fanams, and some even 30 fanams, to make up the deficiency sustained by this flour. If there be more of it given out to be beaten, there will be a great quantity of flour from it, and the rice itself will not be good.

From the above circumstances, many of the poorest of the ryots, dreading they should not be able to pay the sum which would make good the deficiency, left the rice in their houses, which they shut up and ran away.

The inhabitants of the pettah are very much distressed by the beating of this rice, and say they cannot possibly beat any more. The paymasters, gomastah, and the killadar say that the whole of the paddy must be beat into rice and given over to them. There are not any ricebeaters here, and, as I mentioned before, the inhabitants of the pettah are much distressed by it. There are several kinds of grain amongst that now in the granary, and in beating it out there will be a great quantity of flour. They require eight kowdoor* of rice to a kundy of paddy, which is the regulated quantity; but from the quantity of flour which arises from it in the beating it out, and the being obliged to supply the place of this flour by good rice, there is a great loss sustained by the ryots of the pettah. Although there were no ricebeaters in this place, yet, from the urgency of the occasion, I contrived, but with difficulty, to beat out 1500 bags, and give it to them. But the ryots openly declare that, if they are to have the rice put upon them continually in this way, they will not be able to stand it; I have, therefore, written to let you know these circumstances.

Received and translated at Seringapatam,
     the 14th January, 1803.

[1449.] G. O.   Camp near the French Rocks, 16th Jan., 1803.

Major-General Wellesley will see the 1st battalion 2nd regiment, the 2nd battalion 3rd regiment, and the 2nd battalion 12th regiment out in line to-morrow morning. He will be on the ground at about half past six; and he particularly requests the commanding officers of corps not to allow the men to come out of their tents before the sun rises.

* There are twenty kowdoor in a kundy.

The officers commanding corps will receive certain general memoranda upon the subject of the exercise of several corps in line, to which he particularly requests their attention.

                                    ARTHUR WELLESLEY.

To Lieutenant-General Stuart.   [1450.]

SIR,   Seringapatam, 17th Jan., 1803.

Having heard that some of the arrack was detained at Ryacotta on account of the robbers on the road between that place and Bangalore, I have sent off two companies of Major Hill's battalion to escort it to the latter place. I have likewise sent one company of the same battalion to the Pednaigdurgum Pass, to escort to Bangalore the arms coming up for Purneah. This company has orders not to wait for the arms after the treasure will have ascended the pass, but to proceed with the treasure to Bangalore to join its corps, otherwise it might be too late to join the army.

A detachment of Purneah's horse is now employed in pursuit of these robbers in the Dankery Cottah district, bordering upon Mysore; but I am afraid that, unless the Company's collectors entertain sebundy peons, the robberies will still continue all along the Ghauts, and the communication between this country and Madras will become very unsafe: in fact, the majority of these robbers are the discharged peons, who, now that they are discharged, have no other means of gaining a livelihood excepting to rob on the highway.

Captain West does draw pay as my aide-de-camp, and always has.

I have bought 18 good horses for the guns; their price is about 150 pagodas each upon an average.

When I wrote to you that I should be able to have a recruit of bullocks for the service at Hurryhur, I meant that I must hire them here. There are no maistries or people of the description of bullock-owners in any part of the country excepting at Seringapatam, and all the bullocks must be hired here. I have desired Mr. Gordon to hire 3000, to be taken into pay on the 1st of February. They would be about three weeks marching from hence to Hurryhur, so that they will be in the service only one week sooner than you would require them; but I think it possible that you may want them at Bangalore or at Sera, and if you should, by having them in pay on the 1st of February, you will have the command of their services at either of those places. If I should find that you do not want them at Bangalore or at Sera, I propose to make them carry to Hurryhur 3000 loads of rice to add to our depôt at that place.

I have, &c.,

ARTHUR WELLESLEY.

[1451.]

To Lieutenant-General Stuart.

SIR,   Seringapatam, 19th Jan., 1803.

I have had the honour of receiving your letter of the 15th.

As soon as I shall learn from you the exact number of horses required for the body-guard of the Governor of Fort St. George, I will give Captain Cunningham an additional instruction to send to Madras direct the horses intended for that remount, for that of the body-guard of the Governor-General, and all the mares for the stud.

I am happy to find that the instructions he has received meet with your approbation.

I have received letters from Colonel Montrésor, by which it appears that there is some prospect of tranquillity in Wynaad. He had continued the system of calling upon the inhabitants to return to their habitations, and to hold communication with and lay their complaints before the collector; and he had moved through the district in different directions, and had destroyed the houses and property which he had found abandoned. Many of the principal inhabitants had met him; and in his last letters he told me that he was about to march to a centrical position in the district, from which he would be better able to communicate with the inhabitants of all parts.

The rebellion, however, still exists, and the rebels plunder and destroy the property of those who communicate with the British officers as soon as the troops are removed to a short distance.

In answer to my letter, in which by your desire I required to know from Colonel Montresor whether more troops were absolutely necessary to him, he says that the 2nd of the 1st would certainly be useful; and as it would enable him to preserve the property of the well disposed of a great tract of country, its services would tend to settle the country at an earlier period. He does not, however, wish to intimate that its services are absolutely necessary, or to express a desire to have this corps at the expense of great inconvenience to any other part of the Company's territories.

I have the honour to enclose a return which I have received from Colonel Montresor of the number of troops at present employed in Wynaad. It does not appear of what corps they are, and I have called for another in a different form. I don't imagine that he can increase the number of troops in Wynaad, as some of the insurgents have appeared in Malabar, and there are reports of an intended insurrection of the Moplahs in the southern division of the province; and, at all events, the strength of the Bombay army is in Wynaad.

In consequence of a conversation which I have had with Mr. Piele, who is Postmaster in Mysore, as well as first assistant to the Resident, I wish to draw your attention to the arrangements for the carriage of letters with the army. When I was in the Mahratta territory in 1800 one of the servants of the Mysore post-office attended the army, and the business was conducted under the superintendence of my aide-de-camp, Captain West. There is an inconvenience, however, in this arrangement, which applies to the Residency, as well as that it is not of sufficient efficiency for an army of the size which will now be assembled in the field: it is that the expenses of the post-office in Mysore are part of those of the Residency; and if those of the post-office of the army in the field are added to them, they will be vastly increased on an account which does not properly belong to them.

The letters will be carried for the army by the Mysore tappall as far as Hurryhur; and I beg leave to recommend that they may be taken up at that place by runners employed by an army postmaster.

I have, &c.,

ARTHUR WELLESLEY.

[1452.]   *To Lieutenant Monteath.*

Sir,   Seringapatam, 19th Jan., 1803.

Since I wrote to you on the 9th instant I have received further information regarding the movement of the troops expected in Mysore from the Carnatic, from which I am led to believe that the army will not be assembled on the Toombuddra till the close of the month of February. In consequence of this information, and as I observe by your letter to the Deputy Adjutant-General that you will not arrive at Mangalore till this day, and as you would have but a short time to transact the business intrusted to you if you were to quit that place on the 30th instant as heretofore ordered, which moreover is not now necessary, you have my permission to delay commencing your march from Mangalore till the 7th of February, if you should be of opinion that this delay will be of any advantage to the attainment of the object for which you have been sent there.

I beg to impress upon you, however, the necessity of your commencing your march on that day, in order that you may join the army in time.

                       I have, &c.,

                       ARTHUR WELLESLEY.

[1453.] G. O.   Camp near the French Rocks, 19th Jan., 1803.

All beats of the drum to be taken up from the 33rd regiment till further orders.

The commanding officers of corps in camp are requested not to allow their men to sleep out of camp: neither are they to be allowed to absent themselves so far from camp as the fort and island of Seringapatam without a pass in writing, signed by the officer commanding their company, and the commanding officer of the corps to which they belong.

Major-General Wellesley has heard that exchanges of men have been made by some of the corps in the Mysore country without the permission of the Commander-in-Chief. No man can be exchanged without receiving a discharge from the corps which he quits, and no man can receive a discharge without orders from the Commander-in-Chief. Major-General Wellesley therefore recommends that all those exchanged sepoys should return to the corps to which they originally belonged; and he positively forbids such exchanges in future.

Commanding officers of battalions are requested to pay particular attention to the memoranda which have been sent to them regarding the exercise of several corps in line. They are taken either from the regulations, or are the necessary consequences of them, and are given, as they may not occur to officers who have not been in the habit of seeing large bodies of troops act together, however well acquainted they may be with other parts of their profession.

ARTHUR WELLESLEY.

To Colonel Montresor.   [1454.]

MY DEAR COLONEL,   Seringapatam, 20th Jan., 1803.

I have had the pleasure of receiving all your letters; the last, that of the 17th, last night.

You will observe by the enclosed duplicate of a letter which I have sent into Malabar, that the 80th regiment are to leave you. The whole of that corps are going to Hyderabad between ourselves, and those at Madras are to move from thence either by sea to Masulipatam, or by land as soon as they will be relieved by one of the regiments daily expected from the Cape. Under present circumstances, therefore, it is not very material whether the barracks to be built at Cannanore are or are not finished in this year; and I am not quite certain that it would not be better that a monsoon should pass before they are covered in.

Although you lose the 80th, you must have some Europeans at Cannanore during the next season; and I recommend you to keep half of the 77th and all the Bombay regiment.

I am glad to observe by your letter to Macleod that matters are going on so well in Wynaad. I think the insurrection is nearly at an end, and I hope that Macleod will make a liberal, and, therefore, a permanent settlement in that district. Revenue from it is no object to the Company; we must have it in our hands and in tranquillity, or we must spend more money than that district and Malabar are worth. I will write to Macleod upon this subject.

Do as you think proper regarding the posts in the neighbour-

hood of Sangaloo, only recollect that we have stores of grain,
&c., in each of them. I think, however, that they might be
immediately weakened with safety, particularly if a detachment
be kept in motion in that quarter of the district.

Whenever you issue an order to deliver half a seer of rice
gratis, you must send it for approbation, as there is no regulation on the subject. The necessity of doing it must be founded
on a statement of prices in the camp bazaar, and of the quantity
of rice belonging to government in your grain department.
Whenever rice sells in camp at six seers for a rupee, or under
it, the measure is obviously an economical one for government;
it may be so under other circumstances; and it may be expedient or necessary on account of the want in the grain
department in camp, although it may not be so as a measure of
economy.

I mention these circumstances in order that you may advert
to them in the report which you will send upon the subject, with
your orders for approval.

You may keep the 350 bullocks as long as you think proper.
I can raise at Seringapatam any number that I choose without
difficulty. I have already got 7000, and I ordered 3000 more
on the day before yesterday for General Stuart, which I shall
have on the 1st of February.

I send you the paper for which you asked. I believe it will
be necessary to alter the distribution proposed therein, so far as
to have a battalion upon the island of *   to watch
Cochin, particularly if the report be founded that the Dutch
have ceded that place to the French.

General Stuart arrives at Bangalore, as he now tells me, on
the 6th of next month, and I march from hence much about
that time. We shall join at Hurryhur at the end of
February.

You will have heard from Bombay that matters are con-
cluded between us and the Peshwah. His Highness is still at
Bassein, and I believe that a body of our troops are in that
place as a guard for his person. Holkar's looties are in
the neighbourhood. Our tappall still runs from Bombay to
Madras as regularly as formerly; and I hear that Holkar and
Amrut Rao, as well as Scindiah, have written to the Governor-
General to conciliate the friendship of the British government.

* Blank in manuscript.

The Sirdars to the southward have as yet taken no decided steps, excepting against each other. Rastia and the Bhow's family have driven Goklah down towards the Toombuddra, but all these will, I believe, join us when we shall enter the Mahratta territory. 10,000 men of Holkar's army had joined Appah Saheb upon the Kistna, for the purpose of punishing the Kolapoor man, as they call it; but they have returned to Poonah upon hearing that a large army of Scindiah's was marching south from Burhampoor with great expedition.

Believe me, &c.,

ARTHUR WELLESLEY.

You will have observed that Hardy's appointment is confirmed.

To —— ——.

[1455.]

Seringapatam, 20th Jan., 1803.

I have had the honour of receiving your letter of the 15th this day, and I lose no time in replying to that part of it in which you inform me that the Rajah, or Dessaye, of Kittoor has expressed a wish to be taken under the protection of the British government, and has offered to pay a tribute to the Company, and to give you a bribe of 4000 pagodas, and me one of 10,000 pagodas, provided this point is arranged according to his wishes. I cannot conceive what could have induced the Rajah of Kittoor to imagine that I was capable of receiving that, or any other sum of money, as an inducement to do that which he must think improper, or he would not have offered it. But I shall advert to that point more particularly presently.

The Rajah of Kittoor is a tributary of the Mahratta government, the head of which is an ally, by treaty, of the Honourable Company. It would be, therefore, to the full as proper that any officer in command of a post within the Company's territories should listen to, and enter into, a plan for seizing part of the Mahratta territories, as it is for you to listen to, and encourage, an offer from the Rajah of Kittoor to accept the protection of, and transfer his allegiance and tribute to, the Honourable Company's government. In case you should hear any thing further upon this subject from the Rajah of Kittoor, or in future from any of the chiefs of the Mahrattas on the

2 N 2

frontier, I desire that you will tell them, what is the fact, that you have no authority whatever to listen to such proposals; that you have orders only to keep up with them the usual intercourse of civility and friendship; and that, if they have any proposals of that kind to make, they must be made in a proper manner to our superiors. You may, at the same time, inform them that you have my authority to say that the British government is very little likely to take advantage of the misfortunes of its ally, to deprive him either of his territories, or of the allegiance or tribute due to him by his tributaries.

In respect to the bribe offered to you and myself, I am surprised that any man, in the character of a British officer, should not have given the Rajah to understand that the offer would be considered as an insult, and should not rather have forbidden its renewal than have encouraged it, and even have offered to receive a quarter of the sum proposed to be given to him for prompt payment. I can attribute your conduct upon this occasion to nothing excepting the most inconsiderate indiscretion, and to a wish to benefit yourself, which got the better of your prudence. I desire, however, that you will refrain from a renewal of the subject with the Rajah of Kittoor at all; and that, if he should renew it, you will inform him that I and all British officers consider such offers as insults on the part of those by whom they are made.

You shall hear from me to-morrow regarding the store establishment of Hullihall. The battalion under your command is not destined for field service at present.

ARTHUR WELLESLEY.

[1456.]

To J. G. Ravenshaw, Esq.

SIR,   21st Jan., 1803.

I have had the honour of receiving your letter of the 18th instant. I understood that the balances likely to be at different times in the hands of the several collectors of the revenue had been appropriated by order of government to the various purposes of the service; and when I requested that you would send the sum which you might have which should not be appropriated, I meant that which should not be allotted by government to any other service.

The sums of 80,000 star pagodas which you will have at your
disposal on the 1st of February, and 50,000 pagodas which you
will have at your disposal on the 1st of March, appear to be of this
description, not allotted by government to any other service,
and I shall therefore be much obliged to you if you will send
the former into Mysore by the route stated in my letter of the
15th.   As by late letters, however, received from the Commander-in-Chief, I have reason to believe that the army will not
be collected upon the Toombuddra till the end of February, I
think it will be more convenient if this sum of money does not
leave Mangalore till the 6th or 7th of February, rather than
on the 1st as I at first proposed to you.   In respect to the sum
which you will have at your disposal on the 1st of March, the
best mode of sending that to the army will be through the
northern division of Canara, and by the Yellapoor Ghaut to
Hullihall in Soonda.   I mention this road because it is probable that at the time that this sum of money will leave Mangalore the army will have entered the Mahratta territory, and
it may not be safe for the money to follow it, or proceed along
the frontier of Soonda to Hullihall.   There appears, however,
no risk in sending it up the Yellapoor Ghaut and in the rear
of Hullihall.   Mr. Read will be able to furnish you with the
particulars of the road.

From what I have above mentioned you will observe that
it will not be convenient that the sum which you will have
on the 1st of February should be detained till the 1st of March.
The coins in which you propose . to send these sums of money
are the most convenient in which we could possibly have them.

General Stuart has been pleased to approve of the plan which I
informed you in my letter of the 15th that I had proposed to
him, to form a depôt on the coast opposite to the islands of
Bombay or Salsette by means of the Bombay government, and
he has desired me to write in detail upon that subject to the
Governor of Bombay.   I have done so accordingly, and I have
requested Mr. Duncan to lay in at this depôt 600 Madras
garces of rice of 4800 pucka seers each.   I have informed Mr.
Duncan that I had requested you and Mr. Read to discourage
the exportation from Canara till he should let you know
whether he would require your assistance in procuring this
rice, and I shall be obliged to you if you will be so kind as to
adopt such measures as you may think necessary in order to

facilitate the purchase of the quantity of rice which the government of Bombay may require. In your private letter to which
I attended in my letter of the 15th, you recommend that
steps should be taken immediately to procure the rice which
might be required for the army; and you state your opinion
that no loss will be incurred by government even if it should
not be wanted. If you should still hold this opinion, I take the
liberty of suggesting to you the propriety of purchasing immediately, and having in readiness to be embarked, the quantity
of rice which I have above informed you that it is probable
the government of Bombay will require; a probability which is
strengthened by your accounts of the state of the markets
from which Bombay has usually drawn its supplies. In respect
to the proposal contained in the sixth paragraph of your letter
of the 18th, viz., to lay an additional duty on rice exported
to foreign parts, I am afraid that if the demand is likely to
be so great as you imagine in those parts, the rice will be
exported first to other parts of the Company's territories, and
thence to foreign countries, without paying the additional duty;
and in this manner the levy of the duty will be nugatory. As
I before observed to you, it will not be necessary for the army
to draw rice from Canara, excepting the government of Bombay
should require it to supply the depôt to be formed; and for
the reasons stated in my letter of the 15th, it will be highly
advantageous to the army that the markets in Canara should
be kept full. If, therefore, the proposed additional duty will
discourage the exportation, I recommend that it should be
levied on rice exported to the Company's territories (excepting
that exported to Bombay on account of government), as well
as that exported to foreign parts.

I have, &c.,

ARTHUR WELLESLEY.

[1457.]   *To Lieutenant-General Stuart.*

SIR,   22nd Jan., 1803.

I have the honour to enclose an extract of a letter which I
have written to Mr. Duncan upon the subject of the depôt to
be formed upon the coast. The principle upon which I have
gone is to give you two months' supply of every thing excepting

of gram, of which I have asked for only the quantity that the bullocks belonging to the cavalry and in the gram-agent-general's department can carry away. I have limited to this the demand for gram, because I believe Mr. Duncan will have great difficulty in procuring the quantity for which I have asked. I calculate your consumption of rice at ten garces *per diem*; and it will certainly be greater if it be not much restricted. The number of brinjarry cattle, and those in our grain department, will be able to carry off all the rice at one trip. The formation of this depôt will not be very expensive, and it is probable that, excepting the provisions for the Europeans, the gram for the horses, and that part of the rice which will go with the grain department, the remainder will cost the Company nothing.

I enclose the copy of a letter which I have received from Mr. Ravenshaw in answer to one which I wrote him on the 15th instant, and the copy of my answer, which will point out to you the state of his treasury, and the measures which I have recommended in order that Mr. Duncan may certainly be supplied with his rice. Before I had received your letter of the 15th instant Captain Cunningham had hired 570 horsekeepers according to my instructions, of which you had approved. I have given directions, however, to discharge the. 70, as I find that Captain Walker has already provided 200. It is absolutely necessary that the whole number of attendants required for the horses should go to Mangalore immediately, although it may happen that the services of some of them will not be required till the beginning of March. None of this description of people can be procured in Canara, or even in Mysore, excepting at Seringapatam; and if not entertained before the troops march from hence, they will follow them to gain a livelihood by bringing wood and grass for sale to camp, and then it will probably be impossible to procure any. I have therefore thought it best not to incur the risk of the want of the services of any of them, particularly as it is certain that a horse that will not have his proper attendants will lose his condition, and will be of no service. A salestry will be absolutely necessary to Captain Cunningham, and I have therefore desired that the person of that description gone to Mangalore with Lieutenant Monteath may be left there till I shall receive your further orders. Lieutenant Monteath did not arrive at Mangalore till the 19th, and as I find that the army will not arrive at the Toombuddra till the end of the month of February, I have permitted him to remain at Mangalore till the 7th February, which will give him more time to perform the duties intrusted to him.

I have, &c.,

ARTHUR WELLESLEY.

[1458.]   *To Josiah Webbe, Esq.*

MY DEAR WEBBE,   Seringapatam, 23rd Jan., 1803.

I received a letter from Malcolm last night of the 3rd, by which I learn that he is coming here as Resident, and that Lord Wellesley intends to send you on a mission to Berar as soon as you can be spared. I don't know whether this will be agreeable to you, but' I hope that this arrangement will be altered, and that you will return to your old office.

Piele told me some time ago that you had proposed to remove him to the office of Deputy Registrar of the Sudder Dewanny Adawlut, and of Deputy Persian translator to government. I have not apprised him of the probability of Malcolm's appointment to this Residency; but I imagine that he will be desirous of obtaining the situation which you proposed for him at the Presidency if this change should take place here; and I mention the subject now, as I hear that the principal judicial appointments will soon be filled.

I have spoken to Piele upon the subject of the repairs to the palace at Bangalore preparatory to Lord Wellesley's reception there, and we have agreed upon the mode in which it shall be repaired and improved. As you mention, however, only a possibility that Lord Wellesley will visit Mysore, and as Malcolm does not in his letter to me notice any such intention, and as the repairs and improvements intended will not take much time, we defer commencing them till we find that Lord Wellesley really has this intention. The reason is, that if Purneah be led to expect him, which he will be if these repairs are commenced, he will be much disappointed if he does not come; and to tell you the truth, if you leave Madras, I don't see how Lord Wellesley can quit that place likewise, particularly as, in respect to his correspondence with Close, there is so little difference between Bangalore and Fort St. George.

From Malcolm's letter to me, I judge that he will be at Madras by the time that you will receive this letter.

Believe me, &c.,

ARTHUR WELLESLEY.

Malcolm tells me that he is bringing one or two of Lord Wellesley's horses for me. I wish that you would desire him to send them off as soon as he will arrive.

I wish to have your sentiments upon the subject of the Courts here as soon as you can, in order that I may write to government regarding them before I march. My idea is that the Foujdarry, Cutchery, and magistrates' courts ought to be adjourned till Symons's return; and my reason for thinking so is, that I know that no time will be gained by keeping them sitting, because every cause decided during his absence will be brought forward again in the form of an appeal to government upon his return. The police and the revenue matters can be carried on as they have been hitherto by Mr. Knox; and I don't think that people in general will feel any great inconvenience from the adjournment of the other courts. Let me hear from you upon this subject.

To Lieutenant-General Stuart.   [1459.]

SIR,   24th Jan., 1803.

I have had the honour of receiving your letter of the 20th. You will be glad to find that I have already taken measures to remove from Bellary the grain which has been stored there. Captain Barclay has written to Major Munro to suggest that it may be delivered out to those brinjarries who will take it at the price at which they can purchase rice in any part of the Ceded Districts. This rice has cost the Company about a rupee for eighteen seers, and they will probably get for it a rupee for twenty-one or twenty-two seers; but it is better to sell it at this rate, or cheaper, or even to give it for nothing, rather than not have the use of it, or of the brinjarry bullocks in the Ceded Districts, by means of which the grain has been laid in at Bellary. While writing upon this subject I may as well advert to Major Munro's letter to you upon the subject of the brinjarries, an extract from which you enclosed me. I think that

Major Munro is mistaken regarding the necessity of giving advances to the brinjarries, and that to give these advances, excepting in the manner I shall point out, would be more prejudicial than beneficial to the service. The brinjarries are merchants who trade in grain and attend armies in time of war, and trade in salt between the sea coast and the inland countries of the peninsula and carry on a small trade in time of peace. The trade which they carry on in grain in time of peace is of no great extent, because there are few species of grain which will pay the expense of a long land carriage, loaded as all grain is with duties; and the trade which they carry on in salt does not give employment to the number of cattle which they can employ in time of war. They keep these cattle, however, in time of peace, although they have no employment for them, and the whole are ready to attend armies in the field when their services are called for. As merchants, it is obvious that the brinjarries must have at all times a sufficiency of capital to provide loads for the bullocks employed in carrying on their trade in peace; indeed they must have more, as the contents of their loads being salt, are more valuable than any load of grain. The necessity of giving them advances of cash to provide loads for the cattle, therefore, if it exist at all, exists only in respect to that proportion for which they have not employment in peace. Upon this statement the first object should be to ascertain what number of their cattle have usually been employed in peace, and in what manner, and then the number of cattle belonging to each tandah for which there has been no employment. An advance might be made for each head of these last (provided it should appear that the tandah had not capital) sufficient to purchase a load for each bullock, and an engagement ought to be taken from the owner of the cattle to whom the advance should be made, to produce at a certain period for the service of the army the whole number of bullocks loaded which it might have been ascertained he had in his possession. The consequence of adopting a different line of conduct, and of giving advances (either of cash or loads of grain, which is the same thing) generally without such previous inquiry, is that the brinjarries lay out the money given to them and purchase new cattle instead of loads for those they have long had; they then find more difficulty in procuring the number of loads they require; and as they are always unwilling to move till every bullock is loaded, there is an additional delay, and the service suffers greater inconvenience.

I informed you on the 17th that I had sent a detachment from Major Hill's corps to bring on the arrack from Rya-cotta. I have the honour to enclose a letter from Lieutenant-Colonel Boles, by which you will observe that there is little pro-bability that tonnage for the detachment of the 80th regiment will be procured in Malabar: would you wish me to write to Mr. Duncan upon the subject? I have the pleasure to inform you that I have very good accounts from Colonel Montresor of the state of Wynaad; he has every hope that he will be able to settle that district again in a short time. Coongan Nair was wandering with a few followers in the Western Ghauts, and the inhabitants had nearly all returned to their habitations.

I have, &c.,

ARTHUR WELLESLEY.

To Major Macleod.   [1460.]

MY DEAR MACLEOD,   25th Jan., 1803.

It is long since I have heard from you, but I think it proper to write to congratulate you upon the prospect of approach-ing tranquillity in Wynaad. Colonel Montresor informs me that excepting in the districts in which Yeman Nair's estates are situated, the inhabitants have returned to their villages, and have communication with him, and that they have manifested a disposition to submit themselves to government; he also says that Coongan Nair has retired to the Ghauts, with about 200 followers. You will now have an opportunity of effecting a set-tlement of Wynaad, which I hope will be lasting, and will insure its peace. Upon this occasion I wish to recall to your recollection that the district of Wynaad is no object to the Company as one from which revenue is to be drawn. It is essential to us to hold it as a military position, which awes the whole of the province of Malabar; but it will fail entirely of pro-ducing that effect, if, in order to hold it at all, we are obliged to keep in that district all the troops which can be spared from the general service for the defence of Malabar and Canara. I wish you to keep this in mind in making the settlement in Wynaad.

I hope that you will not conceive that I have travelled out of my line in writing you the above, or that I entertain the opinion which has been industriously circulated, and as firmly combated by me, that the late insurrection in Wynaad is to be attributed to your revenue arrangements, or to the faults of your revenue officers. I assure you, my dear Macleod, that I entertain no such opinions, and I believe that I have successfully exposed their fallacy to those who have entertained them; but feeling strongly the benefits of the possession of Wynaad, particularly if we can keep it in peace, and knowing that it is most likely that it will be kept in peace if the people residing in it have a practical knowledge of the benefits to be derived from living under the British government, such as they would have if they should find that they pay less to the Company than they would to their own Rajah, I take the liberty of an old friend to recall these principles to your recollection. At the same time I well know how difficult it is for a man in your situation, who must have based his former arrangements and settlements upon facts, which facts he must have reported together with the settlements founded upon them to his official superiors, to alter those settlements without adducing any material alteration of the facts originally brought forward in their support. I am also aware of the difficulties of this nature with which a man of your profession, in particular one holding a revenue employment, would have to contend. However, upon this point I have to tell you that if you should think it desirable to yourself in any point of view that I should put in a public form what I have herein written privately, as a ground for which you should depart from your former settlement in Wynaad, I will do it with pleasure; nay, more, I will send a copy of my proposed letter to you to the Commander-in-Chief, and obtain for it the sanction of government. Let me hear from you upon this subject as soon as you can, as I am very anxious about it.

We have been in readiness here since the end of December, when the troops arrived from the southern division of the army; and I believe I shall march about the 6th or 8th of February, to form a junction with General Stuart at Hurryhur by the end of that month. You will have heard that Lord Wellesley is coming to Madras; his object is peace, and from recent events at Bombay I am induced to believe that he will effect it.

Colonel Harcourt's news from England is very satisfactory to

Lord Wellesley, and he brings complete satisfaction on all the points on which there was reason to complain since the beginning of the year 1800.

Believe me, &c.,

ARTHUR WELLESLEY.

To Major-General Baird. [1461.]

SIR,   26th Jan., 1803.

I have the honour to enclose a state of the troops under my command, made up from the latest returns which I have received. Of the troops, those stated in the margin* are encamped in the neighbourhood of this place in readiness to march to the frontier when orders to that purport will be received.

The 7th regiment of cavalry at Sera, and the 5th regiment of cavalry at Santa Bednore, are likewise in readiness to join this force. The 1st battalion 13th regiment are on their march to Chittledroog, of which place that corps is to form part of the garrison; and the 2nd of the 10th, at present at Chittledroog, are to take the field when relieved. The 1st of the 4th are encamped at Bangalore, and the commanding officer of this corps will place himself under your orders. The 1st battalion Coast artillery, the regiment de Meuron, and the 1st of the 14th are the garrison of Seringapatam; five companies of the 2nd of the 5th are the garrison of Nundydroog, Goorybunda, Paughur and its dependencies, and five companies of the same corps the garrison of Nuggur. The 1st battalion 5th Bombay regiment are the garrison of Hullihall in Soonda, and there are two companies of the 2nd of the 18th in charge of the fort of Hurryhur upon the Toombuddra, in which collections of grain, &c., are making for the use of the army. Of the troops belonging to the provinces of Malabar and Canara, there is a detachment in the field in Wynaad, under Colonel Montresor, of the strength of which it is not at present in my power to transmit you a particular return. The

---

* 2nd regiment of cavalry.	1st of the 3rd.
Detachments of Coast and Bombay artillery.	2nd of the 3rd.
	1st of the 8th.
33rd regiment.	2nd of the 12th.
1st of the 2nd.	2nd of the 18th.

other corps in those provinces are stationed as stated in the enclosed return.

The equipments prepared in Mysore for the army are at Seringapatam two 8-inch howitzers, two 5½-inch howitzers (for these the shells, &c., &c., are coming from Madras), six brass 12-pounders, sixteen brass 6-pounders, ten lacs of musket ammunition, and equipments for a force in the field requiring twenty field pieces, and fifty rounds of fixed ammunition for each of four iron 12-pounders. At Chittledroog four iron 12-pounders with powder and shot, 450 rounds for each gun, four brass 6-pounders, and seven lacs of musket ammunition, of which three lacs and 40,000 rounds have been sent from Seringapatam. Draught and carriage cattle are in readiness at Seringapatam to move these equipments, as well as 100 spare platform carts prepared, and the medical stores and grain which have been ordered; and draught cattle are in readiness at Chittledroog to move from thence the ordnance which I have above mentioned to be prepared at that place. Carriage cattle are also there for the removal of the powder and shot for the iron guns, and I have in readiness the cattle for the removal of the musket ammunition from Chittledroog, and as soon as I receive intimation from the Commander-in-Chief that they will be required I propose to send them off. A depôt is forming at Hurryhur, upon the Toombuddra, which in a short time will admit of 7000 bullock loads of rice and 6000 of gram; and another is formed at Hullihall in Soonda, consisting of about 7000 loads of rice and a large quantity of arrack. To this last will be added in a few days 30,000 pounds of salted provision for the European troops, and a large quantity of arrack in 400 kegs, recently received at Goa from Bombay. 2000 loads of rice, 30,000 pounds of salted provision, and 30,000 pounds of biscuit are at present at Hurryhur, upon the Toombuddra, with bullocks to move these articles; and there are 60,000 sheep in different flocks between Sera and Chittledroog in readiness to be handed over to the commissary of provisions. A servant of this government will meet him at Sera with the accounts of them.

7000 loads of gram have been prepared at different stations on the eastern frontier for the gram-agent-general, and he has in his possession the orders for their delivery; and measures have been taken to deliver to each regiment of cavalry a bullock load of gram for each horse, either on its arrival in the Mysore country, or, if already stationed within it, on its march from its station, and to provide each regiment with the quantity required daily for its food on its march to the frontier. The officers commanding regiments of cavalry have the orders for the delivery of the gram above mentioned. 32,000 brinjarry bullocks loaded will be collected behind the Chittledroog hills at the end of this month. By desire of the Commander-in-Chief I have given notice to the Rajah's servants of your march through the Mysore country, and measures have been taken to provide the troops under your command with whatever they may require.

I have no intelligence from the frontier at all deserving your attention. In consequence of the late events at Poonah, the country is in general in great confusion; the heads of villages and districts no longer obey the chiefs who had governed them, each has assumed the supreme authority in his own district, and they are carrying on a petty but destructive warfare against each other. As far as I have been able hitherto to learn their sentiments, the chiefs of the Mahratta empire on the frontier are favourably inclined to the cause which the British government is likely to espouse.

I send this letter to the aumildar of Batmunglum, to be delivered to you on your arrival in Mysore. I should have had the honour of meeting you on your entrance into this country, only that my absence from hence at the present moment might be very inconvenient and prejudicial to the various arrangements carrying on in this country for the equipment and supply of the army in the field.

I have, &c.,

ARTHUR WELLESLEY.

P.S. I have omitted to mention in this letter that I have ordered two companies of the 1st of the 4th from Bangalore to escort thither arrack from Ryacotta, and one company to the Pednaigdurgum Pass to escort to Bangalore arms intended for this place: the former will have arrived at Bangalore before you reach that place; and I have instructed the officer commanding the latter to return with the escort coming up the Ghauts with the treasure, even if he should not have met the arms before he meets that escort. I have been induced to order out these

. detachments because the Company's territories bordering on the Ghauts have lately been much infested by large gangs of thieves.

[1462.]   *To Major-General Baird.*

My dear General,   26th Jan., 1803.

I have had the pleasure of receiving your letter of the 23rd, and I am glad to find that you are getting on so well. I wrote you a long letter this morning with a return, &c., which I sent to the aumildar at Batmunglum, to be delivered to you upon your arrival within the boundary of the Rajah of Mysore. It contains all the information which I have it in my power to give you.

I am sorry to hear that your bazaars are not so well supplied as you could wish. If you have a sufficient number of bazaar people attending the troops, you will have no want of supplies on your march through Mysore; but if you want bazaar people to bring into the camp for sale the articles which are prepared for the troops in the villages in the neighbourhood of the road, you may experience some difficulty, unless you encamp near the large villages in which there are bazaars. You will see by my public letter of this date that the brinjarries are collected on the frontier, and I can give you no assistance of bazaar people till I join you : but if you have these, you will have plenty in your camp; and if you have not, if you will encamp in the neighbourhood of the large villages you will experience no want. The aumildars have directions to keep their bazaars open and full, and to sell whatever you may require. I take this opportunity of recommending the people of the country to your protection ; you will find that they will deserve it, as they will do every thing in their power to supply your troops and to gratify your wishes.

I wrote to Major Robertson some time ago respecting his wants on his march to the frontier, but I have received no answer from him. I have, however, settled that the aumildar at Bangalore shall be prepared to give him a supply of sheep that will carry him on to Sera, if he should require it; and he will even get what he may want before he reaches Bangalore. I should wish to hear something positive from him upon this subject.

There appears a mistake regarding arrack at Bangalore, which it may be in Robertson's power to rectify. General Stuart desired, and I gave orders accordingly to Captain Macally, that all the arrack should be sent on to Chittledroog and the frontier. Captain Macally writes that Mr. Cochrane's man at Bangalore has orders to detain there seventy-five casks of arrack. I conclude that this supply is intended for the use of the troops on the march to the frontier. It appears to me, however, to be much more than they will require; and I know that as the arrack is on country carts, it will materially delay the progress of your troops. I therefore recommend that Major Robertson may be called upon to state what quantity of arrack he will require at Bangalore for the use of the troops till they will reach the frontier. After having ascertained this, if you will be so kind as to write to Captain Macally, who commands at Bangalore, to desire him to detain only what Major Robertson will require, and to send on the remainder to Chittledroog, I shall be much obliged to you.

Lord Wellesley is expected at Madras, but whether he stays there or goes to Bombay I cannot say. At the present moment it appears to me that his presence is most necessary at Madras; in two or three months hence it will be most necessary at Bombay.

Believe me, &c.,

ARTHUR WELLESLEY.

To Lieutenant-Colonel Whitelocke. [1463.]

SIR, Seringapatam, 27th Jan., 1803.

I have the honour to inform you that I have sent draught bullocks as follows hereafter to Chittledroog, viz. :—

For four 6-pounders	40
Six tumbrils with 6-pounder ammunition ..	72
Four iron 12-pounders	200
Ten platform carts	40
	352

These bullocks are to remain in the neighbourhood of Chittledroog till the ordnance for which they are intended shall be ordered out from thence; and you will be so kind as to desire one of the persons attached to the ordnance department at Chittledroog to see them occasionally, and that they are fed and taken care of by the persons attached to them.

I have likewise sent to Chittledroog 340 bullocks loaded with musket ammunition, with their complement of spare cattle. The musket ammunition is to be lodged in store at Chittledroog, and these bullocks are destined to carry 450 rounds of powder and shot for the iron 12-pounders; which articles are, I conclude, prepared at Chittledroog according to my former orders. As soon as these bullocks will have reached Chittledroog, you will be so kind as to fix upon a good grazing ground in its neighbourhood for them, to which place you will send them; and they are to remain there till the ordnance will be ordered out.

I imagine that the musket ammunition in store at Chittledroog will not be required for the army; if it should be so, I will inform you of it, and will send bullocks to carry it away.

You were heretofore informed by the general orders that the 1st of the 13th were to go into garrison at Chittledroog. By letters which I received last night from the Commander-in-Chief, I find that the 1st of the 17th are to be in the garrison of Chittledroog, and the 1st of the 13th are to take the field. The 1st of the 13th therefore are not to go into garrison at Chittledroog according to my former orders, but are to remain encamped in the neighbourhood of that place till further orders, and the 2nd of the 10th are to remain in the garrison (but in readiness to move out at a moment's notice) till the 1st of the 17th will have reached Chittledroog.

The carriage bullocks above mentioned are with the 1st of the 13th. The draught bullocks will probably arrive at Chittledroog at about the time that you will receive this letter.

I have, &c.,

ARTHUR WELLESLEY.

[1464.] *To Lieutenant-General Stuart.*

SIR, Seringapatam, 27th Jan., 1803.

In consequence of your orders I have desired the 1st of the 13th to prepare for field service instead of going into Chittledroog.

You will observe by my review reports that this corps is nearly in the same state of discipline with the 1st of the 14th, and it had marched for Chittledroog, and is by this time as far as Sera. If I had placed it in Seringapatam instead of the 1st of the 14th, it must have returned; and it is not so strong by nearly 100 men as the 1st of the 14th, which is an object, as the corps stationed here has to do not only the duties of this garrison, and to furnish the escorts required from it, but likewise to furnish the Rajah's guard at Mysore.

I doubt whether the 1st of the 13th would have been sufficiently strong for this duty. Another circumstance is that the 1st of the 14th are very badly commanded, by an officer who appears very unwilling to accept any assistance from those under his command able to give it to him. All these considerations induce me to prefer the 1st of the 13th for the field, although the 1st of the 14th may have some advantages in point of reputation. The 1st of the 13th will join you at Chittledroog.

I shall take from hence every farthing of money that can be spared. I cannot now say exactly what the sum will be; but I rather believe from 1 lac and 80,000 to 2 lacs of star pagodas, including 80,000 expected from Mr. Ravenshaw, which I shall meet upon the road from Mangalore.

I have the pleasure to inform you that I expect to finish the gun-carriage yard before I quit this place. I should wish to be acquainted with your sentiments regarding a proposition which Captain Scott has expressed a wish that I should make to the Military Board before I take any steps in it: it is that advantage should be taken of the dry season to bring in as much of the timber which has been cut down as possible; and that expense should be incurred for this purpose. You will recollect that in the statement which I heretofore transmitted to you upon this subject, I made out the expense of the carriage of the timber from the jungles to Seringapatam to be about seven or eight times that of cutting it, &c., in the jungle. It will in fact cost about eight or nine fanams a foot to bring it in.

The only advantage that I see in bringing the timber in now is that it will season sooner and better than it will in the jungle; but, on the other hand, to hire carts to bring it in is very expensive, and it is an expense not necessary upon the present occasion, as I believe that Captain Scott has, at this moment, as much timber in his stores as he can work up between this time and the return of the fair season in December next.

If this be the case, my opinion is that the additional expense ought not to be incurred; but if it be not the case, if he can work up more than he now has, he ought to receive permission to employ as many carts as would bring in the quantity of timber which he can work up. If these sentiments should agree with yours, I will write to the Military Board upon the subject. But I am very anxious to avoid incurring any additional expense for the gun-carriage manufactory during your absence from Madras.

I have written to General Baird, and have sent him a return of the troops, &c., in this country, an attention which I conceive to be due to his rank, and which I hope will be satisfactory to you.

I have, &c.,

ARTHUR WELLESLEY.

[1465.]   *To Lieutenant-General Stuart.*

SIR,   Seringapatam, 28th Jan., 1803.

By a letter which I have received from Lieutenant-Colonel Bell I observe that he has with him two 8-inch howitzers, and upon reference to your letter to me of the 26th November last I find that that is the whole number of that description of ordnance which you propose to have with you. Carriages for two of each have been made, however, at this place, and I propose to take them with me to the frontier according to your former directions, unless I should receive your orders to the contrary. But as no ammunition has been provided for the howitzers here, and as it is probable that provision has been made in the park for only two of each description, and as it will take as many of the gun bullocks to draw these howitzers as would be sufficient for two brigades of 6-pounders, I take the liberty of suggesting that I may be permitted to leave them behind. If, however, you should be desirous of having them upon the frontier, they can be brought there without any inconvenience.

I have, &c.,

ARTHUR WELLESLEY.

To Sir William Clarke. [1466.]

MY DEAR SIR, Seringapatam, 28th Jan., 1803.

I have received your letter of the 21st. In respect to the proposal made by the merchant to place in Hullihall a store of rice, I have to observe that his price is enormous. His bag will contain 82 seers, and the price of the rice at Goa will be about 1 rupee for 12 seers. The price of rice in Canara, from whence he will bring it, is about 1 rupee for 30 and 40 seers.

He will lodge this rice at Hullihall for 12 rupees a bag, which will make the rice there about 1 rupee for 7 seers; whereas I have there at this moment not much less than 7000 bags of rice, which have been purchased for the Company at the rate of 1 rupee for about 20 seers. I cannot accept of this proposal.

I have no news from Govind Rao. General Stuart was to leave Madras on Monday last, the 24th, Vellore on the 26th, and expected to be at Bangalore by the 6th of February, and upon the Toombuddra by the end of the month. I shall march from hence on some day between the 6th and 10th of February.

Believe me, &c.,

ARTHUR WELLESLEY.

To Lieutenant-General Stuart. [1467.]

SIR, Seringapatam, 30th Jan., 1803.

I have had the pleasure of receiving your letter of the 28th, and I am exceedingly happy to find that you are pleased with the arrangements which I have proposed to Mr. Duncan for the formation of the depôt at Panwell.

I write this day to Mr. Ravenshaw to urge him to purchase rice immediately.

You will observe that I request Mr. Duncan to send for the

rice if he should want it; and if not, that he will apprise the collectors in Canara thereof. I conclude that he will send vessels for it, as he must be well aware that Canara cannot afford the number of vessels which will be required to transport this large quantity of rice.

I have anticipated your wishes regarding the remount horses. When I found that it was not likely that you would arrive upon the Toombuddra till towards the end of the month of February, I desired Lieutenant Monteath to remain at Mangalore till the 7th of that month, instead of till the 31st of this, according to the instructions sent from the Adjutant-General's office.

He has hitherto been able to purchase only fourteen horses out of sixteen which were sent to Mangalore as a private speculation. Nine of the remount horses, however, had arrived on the 27th instant, and more were expected; and as he has orders to remain at Mangalore till the 7th, I have no doubt that he will be able to bring with him a handsome recruit of horses for the cavalry. I have written to him to bring as many as he will think fit for the service.

I will give the necessary directions to Mr. Gordon regarding a fresh supply of bullocks.

I have, &c.,

ARTHUR WELLESLEY.

[1468.] *To Captain Cunningham.*

DEAR CUNNINGHAM, Seringapatam, 30th Jan., 1803.

Upon referring to my papers regarding bringing the remount horses from Mangalore, I find that orders had been given by government to the collectors in Canara to supply Captain Walker with any money that he might require; and the Commander-in-Chief was of opinion, upon a question which I put to him on this subject referable to Lieutenant Monteath, that Captain Walker would take care that money should not be wanted by any of the officers sent to Mangalore upon this service. I conclude, therefore, that he will have settled with Mr. Ravenshaw upon this subject. If he should not have done so, if you will apply to Mr. Ravenshaw, I have no doubt but that he will supply your present wants, and I will take care that this matter is properly arranged as soon as I shall learn from you that it has not been settled by Captain Walker.

It is useless to do anything in the business till we know whether Captain Walker has really settled anything, according to the notions of the Commander-in-Chief. I enclose the copy of a letter which I have written to Lieutenant Monteath.

I likewise enclose with this instructions to send remount lots of horses and all the mares to Madras by a certain route, and rahdarries for this route, and that to Santa Bednore for the remount lots of the cavalry. When you have fixed the period at which you will send off these lots, it will be necessary to apprise the Resident or his assistant thereof, and the number of horses that will march. You ought also to write to the collectors of the Barahmahal and of the districts of the Carnatic through which the horses and mares will march to Fort St. George.

Believe me, &c.,

ARTHUR WELLESLEY.

To Alexander Read, Esq.   [1469.]

SIR,   Seringapatam, 31st Jan., 1803.

I have the pleasure to inform you that I have received a letter from the Secretary of the Government of Bombay of the 19th instant, by which I learn that the envoy at Goa has received directions to employ against the pirates on the coast of Canara the Hon. Company's cruiser *Piper* and two armed patamar boats, and I understand from Sir William Clarke that these vessels are already arrived at Goa.

I request you to send to Nuggur, and thence by Simoga to Hooly Honore, whatever sums of money you may be able to allot for the service of the army in the field.

Major Ker will furnish you with a small guard on your applying to him for it, which will accompany the treasure as far as Bednore, and I write to Captain Macfarlane, who commands there, to desire that he will relieve that guard by an officer's party.

It is desirable that you should send off the money as soon as possible, as I propose to march by the route of Hooly Honore, and shall take it up there; but if I should have passed that place before it will arrive there, I will leave directions for the officer commanding the escort from Bednore by what route to follow me.

I shall be much obliged to you if you will let me know at what time you expect that the treasure will leave Cundapoor.

I have, &c.,

ARTHUR WELLESLEY.

I delay answering your letter upon the subject of the dispute between the Mysore and Soonda Brahmins for some days.

[1470.]   *To Lieutenant-General Stuart.*

SIR,   Seringapatam, 31st Jan., 1803.

I have had the honour of receiving your letter of the 29th.

I have settled with Purneah that he is to receive the arms intended for him at Bangalore. The aumildar there will take charge of them if you will be so kind as to give orders that they may be delivered to him. Purneah is desirous that the carts should be allowed to come on with them.

Captain Scott will not have occasion to send to the jungles for any timber: therefore I don't propose to mention the subject to the Military Board. I have this day authorised him to hire fifty draught bullocks to bring in charcoal, in an order which I shall have the honour of transmitting to-morrow to be laid before you for your approbation. Besides these fifty I propose to leave here one hundred of the Company's draught cattle to be employed in this work. The consequence of bringing in the charcoal by means of the Company's draught cattle is that the quantity used at the manufactory in every month costs about eight or ten pagodas, and if it were brought in and sold in the bazaar, or were brought in upon hired carts with hired cattle, it would cost 300 pagodas. I have therefore allotted these one hundred bullocks to this work, and if I could spare them I would allot fifty more; but that, at the present moment, is impossible.

I have had my doubts whether you would approve of leaving here even these one hundred bullocks; but the galloper 12-pounders will be to be sent after us; and if you should not approve of this employment for the bullocks, they can be sent to the army with those pieces of ordnance ; or they can be brought away now, if you will let me know your wishes upon this subject.

I propose to order the regiment of cavalry at Sera off your road, and to join me by a road which goes by the back of the hills. This will give the remainder of the troops with you, and the cattle, a greater advantage of forage and water. The last season was very dry in Mysore and to the northward, and I have bad accounts of the water from all quarters. I will write to Colonel Orr regarding the water between Sera and Chittledroog.

I have desired Mr. Gordon to take into the service the bullocks which you wish should join you at Darwar on the 14th of February. I imagine that you will arrive at that place by the 14th March, and these bullocks ought to be in the neighbourhood of Hullihall nearly about that time.

We do not want any stores that I know of at Hullihall ; and as the bullocks will be wanted for work immediately after their arrival, and if they go through Soonda they will have to travel upon very bad roads, I rather think that it would be best to send them empty, or at least to load only half of them.

I have, &c.,

ARTHUR WELLESLEY.

To Colonel Montresor.   [1471.]

MY DEAR COLONEL,   Seringapatam, 1st Feb., 1803.

My own boys and Barclay's went out to meet you yesterday evening, as soon as I received your letter of the 30th, but I have called them back this day.

I have written to General Stuart to recommend that the 2nd of the 1st should be placed at your disposal immediately. You must be the best judge whether they will be most useful to you in Wynaad or in Malabar, and will let me know your opinion upon this point. I should wish to hear from you upon it soon, as I must turn them into Malabar by Paulghautcherry, if you should prefer to have them in that province.

Let me hear also whether you think it necessary that they should bring with them any provisions, supposing that you should prefer to have them in Wynaad, and what quantity.

Major Macleod's letter upon the subject of Captain Osborne taking charge of Wynaad is very vague indeed. His making any settlement, or taking charge only for a day, would be worse than useless, unless Major Macleod should engage to confirm all he should do. But it does not appear by the letter that he intends that Captain Osborne should make a settlement of the revenue, only one to induce the people to remain in their habitations. This will never answer; the people must have a permanent revenue settlement; and I have already written my opinion to Macleod regarding the necessity of its being moderate, and calculated to impress on their minds a notion of the practical benefits derived from living under the Company's government.

I regret exceedingly the disturbances in Corumnaad, and the check with which our troops have met; however, your presence will be highly useful there. I recommend you to talk publicly of the arrival of reinforcements from this country, and even to make arrangements for their reception both on the Goondilpet and Cancancotta roads, and on that into Malabar by Paulghautcherry. The people in Malabar certainly are induced to rise in some degree from their knowledge that there is employment to the northward for the troops in Mysore; and the expectation that reinforcements from hence will enter Wynaad may stop the insurrection of many whose rebellion would be certain otherwise, and may be prevented entirely hereafter by the arrival of the 2nd of the 1st.

I shall receive General Stuart's answer on the day after to-morrow, as he is to be at Colar this day; and you may depend upon it that you will not be disappointed in the arrival of the 2nd of the 1st. I have stated my opinion decidedly that this corps is necessary to you.

I have no news for you. I march on the 8th certainly.

Believe me, &c.,

ARTHUR WELLESLEY.

[1472.]   *To Lieutenant-General Stuart.*

SIR,   Seringapatam, 1st Feb., 1803.

I am sorry to have to inform you that the disturbances which have prevailed in Wynaad have spread into Malabar. The inhabitants of the district of Corumnaad are in rebellion, and I enclose the copy of a letter upon that subject, which Colonel Montresor has received from the collector.

It appears that Captain Leighton had been in Corumnaad with a detachment of the 2nd of the 4th; and upon first hearing of these disturbances, Colonel Montresor detached Major Drummond with a force from Wynaad to his assistance. Captain Leighton was, however, attacked on the day that Major Drummond joined him, and lost a considerable number of men, as by the enclosed copy of the return of killed, wounded, and missing upon this occasion. Colonel Montresor, therefore, informs me in a letter, of which I enclose a copy, that he proposes to proceed immediately into Corumnaad. He leaves the troops in Wynaad under the command of Lieutenant-Colonel Lawrence.

I don't give much credit to private accounts received from Malabar, because I know that the writers of them are much prejudiced, and have lost all recollection of the state of affairs in that province from the time that it first came under the government of the Company. They all agree, however, that it is probable that the insurrection will become more general; that the inhabitants look forward to the prospect of the troops on this side being engaged in the Mahratta territory, and that they will have to oppose those only which are usually placed in the country as the ordinary guards.

I cannot forget that, till within these few years, the province of Malabar has always been in a state of either partial or general rebellion; and the opinion which I have formed, that nothing but a force which will be formidable to its inhabitants can keep them in subjection.

Under these circumstances, I think it advisable that the 2nd of the 1st should be sent into Wynaad. There is no doubt whatever that the inhabitants of that district, as well as of Malabar, have talked of the war with the Mahrattas for a length of time; and Major Macleod, in his private letters, has more than once stated his fears of an increase of the rebellion as soon as the accounts should arrive in Malabar of the march of the troops from this place. The arrival of a corps from this side therefore will have the very best effects upon their minds, and will show them that the government is able to send troops to keep them in order notwithstanding its exertions against a foreign enemy, besides the great additional strength which it will give to Colonel Montresor.

I have written to Colonel Montresor to inform him that I had applied to you for this corps; and I had desired him to make it public that he expects it, and even to make . preparations for its reception.

I enclose an indent which has been received by the commissary of stores at this place from the commissary of the army in the field. We have ten lacs of musket ammunition ready, and no more in store, as the Military Board lately sent orders to stop the making of them. Is it your wish that the ammunition included in this indent shall be supplied from that now prepared, and ready to march with the troops? Allow me to suggest that the commissary in the field should take this ammunition from Chittledroog, at which place there are lacs of ammunition which will not be called for.

I wish also to draw your attention to another article of the indent, platform carts. Nearly 100 spare carts are prepared. Am I to bring no more than are included in this indent, or the whole number prepared?

I conclude that the spare howitzer carriage is that respecting which you wrote to me on the 30th of January.

I have, &c.,

ARTHUR WELLESLEY.

Only four galloper 6-pounders will be ready, and on these there will be guns according to your orders. There will also be two galloper tumbrils for them, and two common tumbrils in the park. The indent for the commissary cannot be complied with in this article.

[1473.]   *To the Adjutant-General.*

SIR,   Seringapatam, 1st Feb., 1803.

I have the honour to enclose copies of orders issued by me from the 28th December to the 31st January inclusive, which require the confirmation of the Commander-in-Chief.

The order of the 1st of January respecting the transport of stores from the island of Buswarajah Droog was issued in consequence of an intimation received from the collector that he was about to draw off the peons from that station, and I was desirous to prevent the stores (which are of no consequence or value to the Company) from falling into the hands of the pirates whose boats were then cruising on the coast.

The order of the 1st of January regarding the store establishments at Goa and Hullihall was issued in consequence of the transfer of the ordnance and stores from the former to the latter. The guards ordered on the same day from Seringapatam and Nundydroog were destined to see that the brinjarries, with whom engagements had been made, commenced and continued their march to the frontier in such a manner as to insure their attendance upon the army.

The order of the 5th January was issued, as the soldiers alluded to belonged to corps which were destined to take the field, and it was better that they should reach their corps under the care of the officers of the 33rd, than that they should be allowed to march through the country alone.

I will hereafter have the honour of transmitting to the Secretary of the Commander-in-Chief an account of the purchases of gun-horses made by his Excellency's orders.

The order of the 29th January, appointing Lieutenant Brown to take charge of the ordnance and stores proceeding from this place for the use of the army in the field, was issued because there is only one conductor belonging to this arsenal who could take such a charge, and he could not be conveniently spared from his situation at Seringapatam; and at all events I did not think it proper to place so large and important a charge under a non-commissioned officer.

It is intended that the 7th regiment of cavalry should march from Sera to Banawoor, and there join the body of troops which will march under my command to the frontier, in order that there may be as great a quantity as possible of forage for those troops and their cattle who must necessarily march upon the road from Sera to Chittledroog, and thence to the frontier.

Captain Scott has been authorized to entertain draught bullocks to draw in charcoal for the service of the gun-carriage manufactory, because he can no longer have the use of all the Company's draught cattle which he requires for that service, and because it has been found that it is much cheaper when bought in the jungles and brought in in this manner than when bought in the bazaar of Seringapatam.

I have, &c.,

ARTHUR WELLESLEY.

[1474.]   *To Captain Baynes.*

MY DEAR SIR,   Seringapatam, 2nd Feb., 1803.

I wish that you would let me know as soon as possible—

1st. What quantity of grain you have in store at Hurryhur?

2nd. What quantity has been received of the grain which you were heretofore informed was to be brought or sent into Hurryhur from the different villages in the neighbourhood?

3rd. What quantity of that grain still remains to be brought in, and whether the aumildar proposes to bring it in, specifying the villages?

4th. What quantity of grain has been brought from Chittledroog to Hurryhur?

5th. What quantity of grain has been laid in by Mr. Gordon?

6th. What quantity of grain there is in store at Hurryhur?

The answers to the 2nd, 4th, and 5th queries, with 2,000 bags sent from Seringapatam, will give the answer to the 1st.

I wish also that you would write a note either to Barclay or me, when any addition will be made to the stock of grain in store.

I imagine that much grain is arrived at Hurryhur which is not yet measured and received on the books; but I want to know what quantity there is at Hurryhur, and not what has been measured and is received officially on the books.

Believe me, &c.,

ARTHUR WELLESLEY.

You may as well let me know also what quantity of salt beef and biscuit you have received.

Sir,   Seringapatam, 2nd Feb., 1803.

I have the pleasure to inform you that I have arranged for the removal of the store of grain from Bellary in a manner which I hope will be satisfactory to you.

Sixteen thousand brinjarry bullocks take out a corresponding number of loads, at the rate of the country, viz. 30 seers of rice and 60 seers of gram for a rupee. They will pay for this grain in camp. I hope that they will be in the neighbourhood of Hurryhur at the end of the month.

Besides this number, Major Munro writes that there are 5000 loading in the Ceded Districts, who may also be expected at the rendezvous by the end of February, making the total number from the Ceded Districts 21,000.

Besides the brinjarry bullocks in the Ceded Districts employed in the removal of the store from Bellary, there is in those countries a class of people called Wirdywas, who have offered their bullocks for hire by the trip, which is the mode in which they trade with their cattle. I have requested Major Munro to agree with them for the removal of the remainder of the store to Hurryhur, and forward from thence 11 or 12 marches (meaning to Darwar) if you should think it proper to have the rice so far forward.

Captain Barclay has accounts of 10,000 brinjarry bullocks which have received orders for a corresponding number of loads in the Barahmahal, and they are now loading. You may have their services. If you should, the number of brinjarry cattle with your army will stand thus:—Mysore brinjarries, 32,000; Ceded Districts, 21,000; Barahmahal, 10,000: total, 63,000; besides the Wirdywas, who may be expected to bring forward the remainder of the grain from the store at Bellary.

I have, &c.,

ARTHUR WELLESLEY.

Sir,   Seringapatam, 2nd Feb., 1803.

I have to inform you that I expect that a certain quantity of treasure will be sent by Mr. Read, the collector of the northern division of Canara, for the use of the army to be assembled in the field. It is probable that it will leave Cundapoor on or before the 14th instant, and it will come as far as Bednore in charge of a guard belonging to the battalion in garrison at Cundapoor.

On the arrival of the treasure at Bednore you will be so kind as to relieve the guard of Bombay Native infantry by an officer's detachment of the troops under your command, and you will order the officer to march in charge of the treasure to Hooly Honore by the route of Anantpoor and Simoga.

I shall be at Hooly Honore with a detachment of the army about the 20th instant. If I should not arrive there, the officer is to halt till the troops under my command will reach it. If I should pass that place before he should arrive there, I will leave with the aumildar orders for his guidance.

You will do well to correspond with Major Ker regarding the time at which the treasure will leave Cundapoor; and I beg that it may not be delayed at Bednore or on the road.

Upon reference to Major Ker's return, I observe that he cannot well spare a guard for the treasure to be sent from Cundapoor. You will therefore, upon the receipt of this letter, send a jemidar's guard to Cundapoor to receive charge of the treasure in question, and write by the tappall to apprise Major Ker that you have done this by my direction.

The treasure, however, is to be sent on under charge of an European officer from Bednore, according to the directions in this letter.

I have, &c.,

ARTHUR WELLESLEY.

[1477.] *To Lieutenant-General Stuart.*

SIR, Seringapatam, 4th Feb., 1803.

I have had the honour of receiving your letters of the 1st and 2nd instant. As I have every reason to believe that there will be no enemy in the country, and as I know that you will be much distressed for forage on the road between Chittledroog and Sera, I have not countermanded the orders which I had given to the 7th regiment of cavalry to march and join me.

I have daily intelligence from the frontier, and shall have the earliest of the appearance of the hostile force even on this side of the Kistna. In case such a force should appear, I believe it would be proper, not only that you should be joined by the 7th regiment of cavalry, but that the whole force should join you. If the Quartermaster-General will be so kind as to let me know your proposed route and the days on which you will be at each place, I can easily reach you through the hills at any of the stages between Cheyloor (where you enter upon the high road from Seringapatam to Chittledroog) and Chittledroog.

In the mean time, as there is no reason to believe that a hostile force will appear, I think it best that the 7th regiment of cavalry should be out of your way.

I don't hope to be able to get any bullock-drivers for Major Symons: the rate of hire is too low. We can get grasscutters at about that rate; but we take whole families of them. None but men will answer as bullock-drivers, and they will not go for a pagoda and a-half *per mensem*. I will speak to Purneah upon the subject of providing carts to draw here his arms.

The name of the killadar of Darwar is Bappojee Scindiah, and it is not included in the list which you have sent me. At all events he could not give up his fort on the order, a translation of which you have enclosed. I conclude that Colonel Close will send a specific order to that purport: if he does not, as the fort is absolutely necessary to you, it must be taken.

I am glad that you find the aumildars attentive, and that your camp is well supplied. They have positive orders from Purneah upon the subject; and indeed, to do them justice, I have always found them disposed to assist as far as lay in their power in forwarding the objects of the British troops.

I have, &c.,

ARTHUR WELLESLEY.

To Major-General Nicholls. [1478.]

SIR, Seringapatam, 4th Feb., 1803.

I have just countersigned an indent upon the stores at Bombay for certain articles required for the use of the gun-carriage manufactory at this place, the principal of which is sea-coal. I take the liberty of adopting this method to solicit your support of this indent at the Military Board, as I assure you the articles it contains are much wanted, and cannot be procured at Fort St. George.

In case the Military Board should give the articles indented for, if they are sent by sea to Cannanore, means will be taken to transport them to this place.

I march from hence on the 8th with a detachment of artillery, five companies of the 33rd, and six battalions of Native infantry, and a regiment of Native cavalry, six brass 12-pounders, and ten 6-pounders, to join General Stuart upon the Toombuddra. I shall be joined by two more regiments of Native cavalry on my march. General Stuart will be at Bangalore on the 7th, and will march from thence on the 8th.

> I have, &c.,
>
> ARTHUR WELLESLEY.

[1479.] G. O.   Camp near the French Rocks, 4th Feb., 1803.

Major-General Wellesley is well satisfied with the attention which the commanding and other officers belonging to the corps in camp have paid to the exercises of the troops in line. He particularly requests their recollection of the different objects to which he has had occasion to draw their attention, in the course of the exercise, as the invariable principles upon which all great bodies of troops must act together, and those which will elucidate the system of discipline for individual corps, ordered by the Commander-in-Chief.

The operations of great bodies of troops may be more complicated : they may be formed of two or more lines, composed of cavalry, artillery, and infantry, according to their numbers and the nature of the country which may be the scene of their operations. But whatever may be the nature of those operations, the mode in which each individual corps is to act will be the same as that which has been practised for the last fortnight by the troops in line.

Major-General Wellesley also flatters himself that the objects proposed by each manœuvre laid down in the book of regulations, or those to be practised by individual corps, are more clear than they were when the exercise commenced.

> ARTHUR WELLESLEY.

To Lieutenant-General Stuart.   [1480.]

SIR,   Seringapatam, 5th Feb., 1803.

I have had the honour of receiving your letter of the 3rd.
I understand perfectly the commissary's indent. All the articles indented for, as well as 15 tumbril poles, will be supplied
here, excepting the spare 6-pounder carriages: these will be
supplied at Chittledroog.

Enclosed I have the honour to send a list of the articles prepared at Chittledroog, and a return of the draught and carriage
cattle there in readiness to move them.

There will not be quite 100 platform carts, as 6 have been
taken for medical stores, and there will be 2 for pioneers' tools
and stores; but there will be, I think, 96, and 30 arrack carts.

I have received a letter from Lieutenant-Colonel Maxwell, in
which he mentions that the gram which he has received from the
aumildars is not very good. It is not new gram, which is, undoubtedly, the best for the horses; but it must be recollected
that this gram has been collected and prepared for the cavalry
for a great length of time, and the new gram has not yet been
reaped. I hope, therefore, that they will not be allowed to
throw back upon the hands of the Rajah's government any gram
that may be found serviceable, although it may not be new.
I take the liberty of mentioning this subject to you at this time,
because I am aware of the possibility of complaint, and know
the gentlemen concerned well enough to be certain that, without
adverting to the difficulty of procuring for them this vast quantity of gram, or the convenience to themselves of the mode of
delivering it, or its cheapness to the Company, they will not fail
to complain if they can.

I write this day to Colonel Maxwell upon the subject. I intend to take from hence on the platform and arrack carts as
many arrack casks of the size of from 50 to 70 gallons as I can
get in the arrack stores, and as much arrack as can be spared
from this garrison. The casks of this size are the most convenient. I write to Major Robertson upon this subject.

I have, &c.,

ARTHUR WELLESLEY.

2 P 2

[ENCLOSURE.]

List of Ordnance and Military Stores prepared at Chittledroog for the Service of the Army, and Return of the Draught and Carriage Cattle provided to move them.

Ordnance and Stores.	Draught Cattle.	Carriage Cattle.
4 iron 12-pounders	200	
450 rounds of powder and shot for each 12-pounder ..		388*
4 brass 6-pounders	40	
6 tumbrils with 6-pounder ammunition	72	
10 platform carts	40	
5 spare 6-pounder carriages	30†	
	382	388

* Including spare.

† These cattle leave Seringapatam on the 6th February.

[1481.]

To Sir William Clarke.

MY DEAR SIR,   Seringapatam, 6th Feb., 1803.

I have received your letter of 31st January. I request you to keep open the negotiation for the purchase of the Batavia arrack in such a manner as not to allow its owner to raise the price. I have written to the Commander-in-Chief, who is this day at Bangalore, to recommend that it should be purchased, and I wish to wait for his answer.

I march on the 8th.

I have some thoughts hereafter of forming a depôt at Shawpoor Belgaum, between the rivers Malpoorba and Gutpurba. This place is about sixty miles from Goa, and the communication with it is by the Ram Ghaut. I wish that you would be so kind as to make inquiries respecting this road, of what kind it is, what the exact distance to Belgaum from Goa, what length of Ghaut, through whose territories the road leads, near what towns, &c., and any other circumstances which you may think will enable me to decide correctly upon the subject of forming this depôt.

My letter to Mr. Duncan, alluded to in that to Colonel Close, was upon the subject of forming a depôt at Panwell, opposite Bombay. It contained a detailed plan for that purpose.

My vakeel had not had an interview with Appah Saheb on the 27th of last month; but Appah Saheb had sent a karkoon to meet him, and a body of horse to escort him in safety to his presence.

Believe me, &c.,

ARTHUR WELLESLEY.

To Lieutenant-General Stuart.   [1482.]

SIR,   Seringapatam, 6th Feb., 1803.

I have had the honour of receiving your letter of the 4th, and I have ordered the 1st of the 13th into Chittledroog. ·

I have received a letter from Sir William Clarke, in which he has proposed to purchase at Goa a quantity of old Batavia arrack, amounting to 30 leaguers, at the rate of half a rupee a gallon more than the price contracted for with Mr. Pereira for the Colombo arrack. I have desired Sir William to treat for the purchase of this liquor in such a manner as not to allow the owner to raise the price, but not to conclude anything till he will hear further from me.

My opinion is that when all Mr. Pereira's arrack will have reached Hulliball, the stock there will be as large as can be required, and it will be useless to increase it.

I think, however, that it will be prudent to purchase this Batavia arrack with a view to the formation of another depôt which I have in contemplation, at a place called Belgaum, between the rivers Malpoorba and Gutpurba, at no great distance from the latter. I have not seen this place, but Colonel Stevenson saw it, and reported that it was of some strength. It lies on the road which I would recommend, from Darwar to Poonah; and has a communication with Goa by means of the Ram Ghaut, the distance about 60 miles, which I understand is not very difficult. Upon this point, however, I have written· to Sir William Clarke for further information. It is close to the country of the Rajah of Kittoor, whose vakeel is now with me, and upon whose assistance I can depend. His country produces rice, and he has already proposed to furnish whatever it can afford which the British army can want.

Supposing that you should not occupy this post, and should not form a depôt there, I would recommend the taking of this arrack, because it will always be of use; and I suspect that the merchants of Goa are not the only people concerned in these contracts for the supply of our troops, but that the members of the government have some share in them. If that be true, we shall be sure of having the use of that convenient station as a link in our communication with Bombay, as long as they have a beneficial contract in view.

I beg to be favoured with your sentiments upon this subject.

I have lately rejected an offer made through Sir William Clarke by some merchants at Goa to supply Hullihall with rice at a rate which would bring the rice at that place to about 8 seers for a rupee. I did this because rice is not wanted at Hullihall, because this price is exorbitant, and because I knew that in case you should adopt the notion of forming the depôt at Belgaum, and it should be necessary to use the Goa merchants in doing it, we should always be able to renew the negotiation with them at that or even a cheaper rate.

I have the honour to enclose a letter which I have received from Captain Lieutenant Smyth, of the 1st of the 14th. It is always meritorious in an officer to be desirous of going upon service, and I therefore forward you this letter. I understand that Captain Smyth has some claims upon the service, and that, in particular, when serving with the Nizam's troops, he was very ill treated in a mutiny at Gurrumconda. I beg to have your orders whether I shall allow him to accompany the troops to the frontier.

While writing upon this subject, it is but fair to other officers to make known to you the names of those who have applied to me to be recommended to be employed on the staff of the army in the field. There are Captain Gurnell and Lieutenant Harris of the 1st of the 8th, and Lieutenant Brice Lee of the 2nd of the 18th: the last was recommended to me by Lieutenant-Colonel Brunton.

With the concurrence of Colonel Carlisle I propose to appoint Captain Quin, of the 33rd regiment, to do Captain Baynes's duty here during his absence in the field. Captain Quin has been living in my family for some time since his appointment was discontinued, and he is well acquainted with all circumstances regarding this place; but his health is in such a state that he is not able to go to the field, otherwise I intended to have recommended him to you to be my Brigade-Major.

I have, &c.,

ARTHUR WELLESLEY.

G. O.   Camp near the French Rocks, Monday, 7th Feb., 1803.   [1483.]

Major-General Wellesley requests that every man not on public duty may march with his corps in the line. There is no occasion whatever for guards among the baggage, and the use of them is positively forbid.

The sick and convalescents who may be able to walk, but cannot march with their corps, are to move on the reverse flank of the column of march, and those of each corps are to be kept together as much as possible.

The *general* and assembly will beat off to-morrow morning by order of the senior officer present in camp, at the hours appointed.

The orderly hours are 12 o'clock on halting days, and 4 P. M. on marching days, when the adjutants of corps will attend at the Deputy Adjutant-General's tent.

ARTHUR WELLESLEY.

To Colonel Carlisle.   [1484.]

SIR,   Seringapatam, 8th Feb., 1803.

I have to inform you that I am about to march from hence with the troops destined for service in the field, and the command of the garrison of Seringapatam devolves upon you during my absence. I beg to refer you to the enclosed copies of letters which I wrote to Colonel de Meuron upon the occasion of my absence from the garrison heretofore; and I have nothing further to trouble you with, excepting to request, generally, that the duties may be carried on as they have been hitherto according to the standing orders of the army and of the garrison.

I have appointed Lieutenant Knox to conduct the police of the fort and island of Seringapatam during the absence of Captain Symons, and I request for him your support.

I have reason to believe that the communication with the army will always be open, and I beg to hear from you occasionally.

I have, &c.,

ARTHUR WELLESLEY.

The staff of the garrison will wait upon you with states, &c.

[1485.] *To the Officer Commanding the 2nd Battalion 1st Regiment.*

SIR,   Camp at Atticoopah, 9th Feb., 1803.

The corps under your command, which has been ordered into Mysore, is destined to serve in Wynaad under the orders of Colonel Montresor. You are accordingly to march from Gudjelhatty to *   , eleven miles, and thence by   * to Ardanelly, twenty-five miles. At Ardanelly you turn off the high road to Seringapatam, and proceed by a route which is enclosed to Edatera, on the borders of Wynaad. Either previous to or on your arrival at Edatera you will report to Colonel Montresor, or the officer commanding in Wynaad.

Colonel Montresor has expressed a wish that the corps under your command should enter Wynaad with thirty days' provisions.

According to this wish I have desired the paymaster in Mysore to send to Ardauelly to meet you 30,000 seers of rice, with servants to deliver it to the men. I have also requested the servants of the Rajah's government to provide at Ardanelly a large supply of ghee and curry stuff, which your men will have an opportunity of purchasing.

It is necessary, however, that I should apprise you that it is probable that you will find some inconvenience in marching in Wynaad with the large number of bullocks which must accompany you to carry 30,000 seers of rice, and I therefore recommend you to deliver seven days' provisions to each man on your arrival at Edatera, and to send back to Seringapatam, to be discharged with the empty gunny bags, the bullocks which will thus be deprived of their loads. It may happen that you will arrive at Ardanelly before the rice will: you will in that case wait at Ardanelly till you are joined by it, and apprise the officer commanding at Seringapatam of your arrival through the means of the aumildar.

I have, &c.,

ARTHUR WELLESLEY.

---

* Blank in manuscript.

To W. H. Gordon, Esq.   [1486.]

SIR,   Camp at Atticoopah, 9th Feb., 1803.

I have the honour to inform you that the 2nd battalion 1st regiment have been ordered from Erroad, in Coimbatoor, into Mysore, and that this corps is destined to serve in Wynaad under the orders of Colonel Montresor. By letters which I have received from Colonel Montresor, I learn that it is his wish that this corps should take into Wynaad with it one month's provisions. It consists of 1000 men, and it will therefore be necessary that you should provide for it 30,000 seers of rice. This quantity of rice is to be sent upon carriage bullocks to be hired for this service, to Goondilpet, in Mysore, on the road to Edatera, where the 2nd battalion 2nd regiment will meet it. The commanding officer of Seringapatam will, upon your requisition, furnish you with a naig's guard to escort it. Although I am desirous that this provision for the 2nd of the 1st should be sent off as soon as may be convenient, you are to consider the service in Wynaad and every other service as secondary objects to that of supplying the army in the field on the northern frontier, and therefore you are not to allow the supply of the bullocks to carry this rice to interfere with the supply of those which I have already ordered, and which are to be entertained on the 14th instant. In making your arrangements for hiring these bullocks to carry the provision of rice for the use of the 2nd of the 1st, you will also advert to the probability that they will be discharged, some before the corps will enter Wynaad, and others as soon as they will have arrived at Pancoorta Cottah : therefore the advances to be made to their owners must be moderate.

I have, &c.,

ARTHUR WELLESLEY.

Upon reconsidering this subject, I think it most advisable that the rice should meet the 2nd of the 1st at Ardanelly, at the top of the Gudjelhatty Pass.

You will accordingly send it thither by Nunjengoor, and you will send with it proper persons to deliver it to the sepoys.

[1487.]   *To D. Cockburn, Esq.*

SIR,   Camp at Atticoopah, 9th Feb., 1803.

I have the honour to enclose you an account of money which was taken from certain thieves whose names are contained therein, who have been seized in the Mysore country, amounting to rupees 664 6, together with a silver bangle and 7 pice.   As it does not appear that any persons have been robbed in the Mysore country, and as it is probable that this money is part of the property which was stolen at Dankery Cottah, the Dewan is desirous of giving it over to you, and will deliver it to whoever you may authorise to receive it.

The thieves are in confinement in the fort of Bangalore, and will be sent to you if you are desirous to have possession of them.

I have, &c.,

ARTHUR WELLESLEY.

[1488.]   *To Alexander Read, Esq.*

SIR,   Camp at Atticoopah, 9th Feb., 1803.

I have had the honour of receiving your letter of the 4th February.

The only Ghaut which I desired Major Doolan to urge the aumildar of Soonda to have cleared is the Tenin Ghaut, leading rom Hullihall to Goa; and I was desirous to have this Ghaut cleared in order to facilitate the transport of the ordnance and military stores from the latter to the former place.

It is possible that the three Ghauts mentioned to you by the aumildar. may be three passes on the same road to Goa ; however, I have written to Major Doolan for explanations upon this subject, and I will let you know the result.

He was desired by me to urge the aumildar to repair the Tenin Ghaut; and if he has executed the repairs himself, he has no right to call upon the aumildar to pay the expenses.   At all events I will take care that, in future, all works of this kind are executed exclusively by the civil magistrates.

I have, &c.,

ARTHUR WELLESLEY.

To Lieutenant-General Stuart.   [1489.]

SIR,   Camp at Atticoopah, 9th Feb., 1803.

I marched from Seringapatam yesterday, and arrived here this morning.

I sent off yesterday morning towards Sera seventy empty platform carts. These are intended to carry forward the arrack from Chittledroog to Hurryhur. They will arrive at Sera on the 14th or 15th. Lieutenant Kingdom of the 2nd of the 3rd, who is gone with a guard in charge of these carts, has an order upon the villages for straw and gram, and it will probably be as well that he should remain in charge of these cattle till he will reach Chittledroog.

I should have sent you the arrack carts, only that they are loaded with arrack casks full, and staves and hoops to make casks of the size of from 50 to 70 gallons; or more platform carts, only that they are loaded with the stores lately indented for by Sir John Sinclair.

I have written to Colonel Whitelocke to desire that he will order forward to Hurryhur the arrack which may arrive at Chittledroog after the receipt of my letter, upon the bandies which will have brought it to that place from Madras and Bangalore. Thus I hope that the greatest part of the arrack will be out of your way and at the most forward point of the frontier.

According to your orders upon the subject of family certificates, none will be issued till the army will advance from the frontier. The commanding officers of corps, however, with this division are apprehensive that this delay will be the cause of some inconvenience, and have represented the matter to me; and as I don't perceive that an immediate issue of the family certificates will have any bad consequences, I am induced to draw your attention to the subject. The commanding officers assert that the families of a great proportion of the sepoys have accompanied them hitherto, and that every march they make forward, the probability that they will remain with them during the campaign is increased, from which, as the number of useless people in camp, and number of mouths to be fed, will be increased, much inconvenience will be felt. On the other hand, those sepoys who have left their families behind them are exceedingly anxious respecting their fate, and become more so daily as they advance; and the commanding officers fear that the delay in issuing the family certificates will create much desertion among this class. Upon the whole, therefore, I take the liberty of mentioning this subject to you, and of requesting your orders upon it.

I have, &c.,

Arthur Wellesley.

[1490.] G. O.   Camp at Atticoopah, Wednesday, 9th Feb., 1803.

Lieutenant Brown, in charge of the stores, having complained that there were not a sufficient number of bullocks in readiness to carry off the loads in the store department this morning, and that he was under the necessity of procuring seven bullocks, the expense of procuring these bullocks is to be charged against Chinny Chitty, owner of bullocks, who had not at the ground of encampment of the store department this morning the number of bullocks which, it appears by the register, are hired by him for the service.

All the owners of bullocks attached to this department must have been blamable this morning, and must have employed their spare cattle in an improper manner. Major-General Wellesley therefore desires that it may be clearly explained to them all, that, the next time that bullocks are wanting to move off the ground the loads in any department, a deduction shall be made, from the monthly hire to be paid to each owner, of the sum which he ought to receive for the spare bullocks belonging to him, for one day ; and if this practice be continued, a muster will be ordered on every day after the march.

Major-General Wellesley requests that Captain Mackay will give orders to the drivers not to allow the draught bullocks to run. The commanding officer of artillery also is requested to give orders to the officers and non-commissioned officers of the artillery, detached with brigades, or attached to the park, not to suffer the drivers to allow the bullocks to get into a trot.

Whether, in consequence of this order, Major-General Wellesley shall be able to prevent the cattle from being driven in this manner or not, he positively forbids commanding officers of corps from following the guns beyond the rate at which the troops can march with ease to themselves. The commanding officer of each corps is to lead his battalion at a steady, even pace, and the commanding officer of each company his company at the same pace. When the badness of the road, or an obstacle, may occasion a halt, and a consequent break in the line, the corps or company which may have halted is not to run to regain its distance.

Commanding officers of corps and companies are responsible that this order is strictly attended to, as one most essential to their men. They will not be able to bear the fatigue of the marches which they will be required to perform, if they are to be forced to move at a pace at all quicker than that at which they can march with ease.

The Commander-in-Chief having declared his intention to appoint Mr. Beckwith to be provost marshal to the army in the field, and Mr. Beckwith being at present in camp, he is to act as provost marshal till the orders of the Commander-in-Chief shall be received.

The heads of all villages in the country have orders to sell straw, &c., to the troops and their followers; and the Major-General requests that, in case any officer should have occasion to complain that the inhabitants refuse to sell their forage, he will be so kind as to send with his complaint the person who can point out the village in which the person resides, and the person who refused to sell what may have been required. At the same time, as it is probable that this road will be much used by convoys, &c., coming to the army, officers will be aware of the necessity of requiring from the villages no more forage than is absolutely necessary to them.

ARTHUR WELLESLEY.

To Lieut.-Colonel Montresor.　　　　　　　　　　[1491.]

MY DEAR COLONEL,　　　　　Camp at Atticoopah, 9th Feb., 1803.

I have just time to answer your letter of the 5th. The corps will enter Wynaad by the route of Goondilpet and Edatera, or Edittacottah. It will carry with it thirty days' provisions, part on the men's backs, part on bullocks.

You will give your own orders respecting the disposal of this rice and the bullocks, which will amount to near 400.

I have desired the officer commanding the 2nd of the 1st to report to you or the officer commanding in Wynaad as soon as, or before, he will reach Edatera.

Believe me, &c.,
ARTHUR WELLESLEY.

To W. H. Gordon, Esq.

DEAR GORDON,   Camp at Kikerry, 10th Feb., 1803.

By a letter from General Stuart I learn that the treasure expected from the Barahmahal was to leave Bangalore upon 47 bullocks on the 8th instant.   It is possible Macally may not have finished the history of his captivity, and may have detained the officer in charge of it till the 9th, in which case he will have received my letter of the 7th in time to order him to follow the army by the road to Sera; or, having suffered him to depart on the 8th without hearing the end of the history, he may think it necessary to recall him, in order that he may join the army by the shortest route.

However, there is no trusting to either of those suppositions, and we must make arrangements for bringing forward this money in the most expeditious manner.   I calculate that the money will arrive at Seringapatam on the 13th; the moment it arrives you must have it packed in the manner most convenient for carrying it upon seven elephants, which leave this to-morrow morning to bring it away.   Four of these animals will carry each eight bullock-loads, and three will carry, one six, one five, and one four bullock-loads : you will make your arrangements accordingly.

The money should leave Seringapatam certainly on the 14th, if it should arrive there on the 13th; if possible on the same day if it should arrive there on the 14th; at all events at the earliest possible period of time.   An officer with a company of Sepoys will proceed with the elephants; he will arrive at Seringapatam on the 13th, and will receive and escort the money to the frontier according to instructions which he will have, as soon as you will deliver it to him; you ought likewise to send a person in charge of it.

Believe me, &c.,

ARTHUR WELLESLEY.

If the money should have proceeded from Bangalore by the route by which I wished to send it, you shall hear again from me to-morrow.

If you should think it necessary to open and count the money before you send it on in charge of a man of yours, and cannot perform this operation in the space of time above allowed you, you must send on in charge of it the collector's servant.

To Lieutenant-General Stuart.   [1493.]

SIR,   Camp at Kikerry, 10th Feb., 1803.

I have had the honour of receiving your letter of the 8th instant. Sir William Clarke has already been desired by me not to purchase the Batavia arrack, but to keep open the negotiation for it. I write to him this day to apprise him that you object to taking it on any account.

It will be impossible to take any steps for the formation of the depôt at Belgaum till we reach that place. I only mentioned the idea as a ground for the purchase of the arrack, in case you should approve of it. It will be time enough to decide upon the expediency of forming this depôt when you will move forward. I have already urged the Rajah of Kittoor to be prepared with all kinds of supplies for your army, which his vakeel has promised.

The treasure which you mention to have left Bangalore on the 8th has been expected at Seringapatam for some time; but as we had received many and contradictory accounts of its amount, I cannot now say what it is. It amounts to something between 40,000 and 70,000 pagodas, and is part of the treasure which I heretofore informed you that I should bring forward to the frontier.

When I found that it had not arrived and I received no accounts of it on the 7th, I wrote to Captain Macally at Bangalore to desire that it might be sent after the army by the route of Sera and Chittledroog. He will have received that letter on the 8th, and I hope that the money will have followed you. Lest it should not, however, I send off an escort and means of moving the treasure with celerity; and I am sure that we shall have it at Hurryhur at all events at the time that you will reach that place.

The state of our finances in Mysore is on this day as follows: I have in camp 1 lac of pagodas in gold. I shall be joined on the road to the frontier by 80,000 pagodas in gold from the collector of the southern division of Canara, and by 50,000 pagodas in gold from the collector of the northern division of Canara; making altogether 230,000 pagodas in gold, which I shall bring with me. Besides this sum there may be 70,000 pagodas from the collector of the Barahmahal: total 300,000.

There are at Seringapatam 10,000 pagodas to pay for any

sudden demand of advances of bullock-hire, purchases of rice, &c., &c. The expenses of Mysore when we leave it will be about 28,000 pagodas (not including the amount for family certificates), which the Rajah's kist of about 50,000 pagodas will more than repay. But as several corps have their families in Mysore, and there may be heavy demands for bullock hire, I believe it would be proper to leave the whole amount of the Rajah's kist at the disposal of the Mysore paymaster. The troops, &c. are paid in arrear for January and advance for February, and means are left in the hands of both the collectors in Canara to defray all the charges usually thrown upon them; such as the pay of the troops in that province, in Soonda, purchases of rice, &c., &c.

I write to Seringapatam about the bullock-drivers, but I cannot engage that you will have any.

I have, &c.,

ARTHUR WELLESLEY.

[1494.] *To the Secretary of the Military Board.*

SIR, Camp at Gundessy, 14th Feb., 1803.

I have the honour to enclose an indent which I have received from the deputy commissary of stores at Hullihall in Soonda.

In case the Military Board should think it proper to comply with this indent, I beg leave to recommend that it may be addressed to the commissary at the arsenal of Bombay, that the Governor in Council of Bombay may be requested to give orders that it may be complied with, and that the stores may be brought by sea to Goa and transported thence to Hullihall.

I have, &c.,

ARTHUR WELLESLEY.

END OF THE THIRD VOLUME.

LONDON: PRINTED BY W. CLOWES AND SONS, STAMFORD STREET, AND CHARING CROSS.